Georges Clemenceau

Portrait of Clemenceau by Manet, now in the Louvre

DAVID ROBIN WATSON

GEORGES CLEMENCEAU

A Political Biography

DAVID McKAY COMPANY, INC.
New York

First American Edition, 1976

DEC 19 '77

Library of Congress Catalog Card Number: 76-28607
ISBN 0-679-50703-5

9-12-79

10 9 8 7 6 5 4 3 2 1
MANUFACTURED IN THE UNITED STATES OF AMERICA

CONTENTS

Part three: Defeat and Resurgence, 1889-1906

Part four: The First Ministry, 1906-1909

Part five: Opposition, 1909-1917

Part six: Père-La-Victoire, 1917-1918

Part seven: The Peace Settlement and After, 1918-1929

Part eight: Conclusion

Appendices

ILLUSTRATIONS

ACKNOWLEDGEMENTS

I am very conscious of the large number of debts which I need to acknowledge here, and also conscious that too long a list might seem inappropriate to the work that follows; *Parturiunt montes: nascetur ridiculus mus.* So, I wish to state at once that I am extremely grateful for much assistance that I have no room to catalogue here. I must first thank those institutions whose financial assistance made possible the research for this book, the University of Dundee, and the French government, which, through the agency of the British Council, awarded me a C.N.R.S. fellowship during the years 1967–8. I must also thank the University court of St Andrews University for granting me a term's sabbatical leave to permit me to do research in France. I also wish to take this opportunity, on the occasion of the publication of my first full-length book on French history, to thank the French government for their generous financial assistance over a period of more than ten years, from the time when I began research into French history. I am very grateful for the facilities and assistance provided by the French government and its educational institutions, extended so freely to foreign students, and I wish to record here my appreciation of the assistance that I have received at various times from the Centre National de la Recherche Scientifique, from COPAR, and from the Ministry of Education. I also wish to thank all those who guided my first steps as a student of the Third Republic, and especially MM. F. Goguel, O. Wormser and J. Millerand. I hope that they will accept these belated thanks, although their assistance was not directly relevant to this study.

I am extremely grateful to the custodians of the Balfour papers, the Milner papers, the Chamberlain papers and the Lloyd George papers for their assistance, and to the three last-named for permission to quote from MSS in their care. Material quoted from Crown-copyright records in the Public Record Office appears by permission of the Controller of H.M. Stationery Office. I wish to thank the librarians and archivists of the Archives Nationales, of the Bibliothèque Nationale, of the Bibliothèque Victor Cousin, of the Institut de France, of the Bibliothèque de Documentation Internationale Contemporaine, of the Service Historique de l'Armée, and of the Senate, for their help, and for permission to use the documents in their care. I am especially grateful to the staff of the Archives Nationales for their guidance. I am very grateful to the late Mme Pierre Goujon, to Mme Antoinette Scheurer, and to M. Stanislas Mangin for their great kindness in receiving me, and for permission to quote from the Reinach, Scheurer-Kestner, and Mangin papers respectively. Professor James Joll sought to help me to gain access to the unpublished material at the Musée Clemenceau, and I am very grateful to him for his assistance. I am indebted to those who allowed me to consult the unpublished theses listed in the bibliography, and especially to Dr D. S. Newhall.

I wish to express my appreciation to Mme Boilot, once Clemenceau's secretary, and in recent years in charge of the collections of the Musée Clemenceau, who gave me all the help she could. I wish to thank General Sir E. L. Spears who was kind enough to meet me, and to give me his recollections of Clemenceau in 1918. M. Albert Krebs of the Bibliothèque Nationale generously placed his unrivalled knowledge of the early years of Clemenceau's life at my disposal. I am deeply indebted to him, and to the others who have read and commented on different parts of my text, in particular to Dr M. Anderson, Mr P. Morris, Dr M. Larkin, and Professor Douglas Johnson. I have a special debt to those who transformed my drafts into a typescript, Miss J. Milne, Miss I. Cairns, Mrs. B. L. Kennedy and Mrs. J. Young.

Finally, my deepest debt of gratitude is due to my wife, who has read the whole text, and in the intervals of a very busy life found time to remove many solecisms and infelicities of style. Her encouragement, criticism, and assistance in a thousand forms have been essential. It only remains to say that errors and imperfections are to be ascribed to me alone.

Because of the unavoidable delays of publication, it is necessary to point out that the research for this book was carried out between 1967 and 1970, with a final brief visit to the archives in July 1971, and that the major part of the text was completed by September 1971. In the course of revision since that time I have made use of relevant scholarly works appearing down to September 1972.

D.R.W.

Part one

CHILDHOOD, YOUTH AND THE COMMUNE

1841-1871

1

CHILDHOOD AND YOUTH

I. ANCESTRY AND CHILDHOOD

Georges Clemenceau was born on 28 September 1841 in a modest house in the main street of the village of Mouilleron-en-Pareds, in one of the most remote parts of the Vendée. He was the second child and eldest son of Dr Benjamin Clemenceau and his wife Emma, née Gautreau. The Vendée, the area along the Atlantic coast south of the mouth of the River Loire, was one of the poorest parts of France, economically backward and conservative in politics. Large towns, modern industry, modern methods in agriculture had still not reached the Vendée even at the end of Clemenceau's long lifetime. At the time of his childhood and youth the peasants who made up the great majority of the population followed a way of life burdened by grinding poverty, which had changed little over the centuries. The railways hardly penetrated the area, and roads were notoriously bad. When Clemenceau, the rising young politician of the early Third Republic, returned to the family home, the Château de l'Aubraie near the village of Féaule, it still involved a long journey by horse and carriage from the nearest railway station. It was a strange background for one who was to lead the Left wing in politics, and to speak, at least for a time, for the industrial working class.

The Vendée is indeed one of the most distinctive regions of France. There is no grandeur in its scenery, but great charm, and much diversity within a small area. It is divided into three quite distinct parts, the *bocage*, the *plaine*, and the *marais*. The *bocage* consists of small, abrupt hills and deep valleys, covered with thick woods, traversed by narrow roads. The *plaine*, the open countryside, is closer to the normal type of farmland in northern France. Finally there is the *marais*, the marshy regions by the coast, in part a wilderness visited only by fishermen and

huntsmen, in part drained and dyked to provide tiny polders of rich farmland, accessible only by boat. Clemenceau's birthplace, Mouilleron-en-
Pareds, and the family property of Le Colombier, were in the heart of the
bocage, in one of the most remote parts of the province. The Château de
l'Aubraie, however, was less remote : it was close to the frontier between
plaine and *bocage*, and on the main road from Nantes to La Rochelle.
Even so, it was still far from any large town. Clemenceau was always a
man of the Vendée. His deep love for his native province shines through
many of his speeches and articles, in spite of the fact that the majority
of the peasants of the Vendée were on the other side in politics. The
only parts of his imaginative writings which have any impact are those
dealing with the Vendée. Parts of his novel *Les Plus Forts* and several
short stories and semi-fictional pieces set in the Vendée have authenticity,
in contrast to the mechanical banalities to which he was reduced when
he attempted fictional portrayals of other milieus.

He returned frequently to the family home as long as his father
remained alive (until 1897), and after his retirement in 1920 spent much
of his time in a tiny cottage on the edge of the sea. But his political
career could not be based on his native province like that of many
politicians of the Third Republic, who operated from a strong local
fief. For Clemenceau was a 'blue', one of the minority of republicans
who stood out in opposition to prevailing local opinion – that of the
royalist 'whites' in this most Catholic and conservative part of France.[1]
The special characteristics of the area go back to 1793 when counter-
revolutionary forces challenged the authority of the Republic on a scale
without parallel elsewhere. Only in the Vendée did the Revolution bring
outright civil war, followed by the *chouannerie*, guerrilla warfare which
lasted nearly ten years. These years impressed on the Vendée the tradition of a clean-cut conflict between the Revolution and its enemies which
endured throughout the nineteenth century.

Clemenceau's ancestors belonged to the middle class of lawyers,
bailiffs, doctors and Huguenot pastors who gradually accumulated
enough wealth to set themselves up as landed gentry; they were lords of
the manor, but not nobles.[2] They can be traced in the Vendée from

---

[1] C. Pelletan, *Georges Clemenceau* (1883), p. 5. The names 'whites' and 'blues'
were adopted by the supporters of the counter-revolutionary and the revolutionary
parties respectively in the civil war of 1793–5. (Unless otherwise stated, place of
publication of French books is Paris, of English books London.)
[2] The most reliable account of Clemenceau's ancestry is to be found in the
Bulletin de la Société de l'Histoire du Protestantisme Français (1929), LXXVIII, pp.
440–4; this article corrects the mistakes of the genealogy given in *L'Illustration*,
30 November 1929, which has been frequently quoted. Cf. the articles of l'abbé
Gaillard, 'L'Aubraie des Clemenceau', and 'Le Catholicisme et les Clemenceau', in
Revue du bas Poitou (1930–2), and J. Martet, *M. Clemenceau Peint Par Lui-Même*
(1929), pp. 131–8. These conversations with his private secretary provide most of
the information about Clemenceau's childhood used in this section.

the sixteenth century. By the eighteenth century they were rich enough to live mainly from their property, with professional activity only as a sideline. They were not rich, but comfortably off. At this time they owned the manor of Le Colombier, together with a house in the nearby small town of Mouchamps. Shortly after the Revolution marriage brought into the family a larger estate at Féaule, in the commune of Ste Hermine, and the Château de l'Aubraie, virtually a small medieval castle with tower and battlements, surrounded by a moat. The family took a step up the social scale, Clemenceau's great-grandfather being a member of the Council of Five Hundred under the Directory and later a dignitary of the Napoleonic régime.

The most interesting points in the family history are the tradition of medical practice and the connection with Protestantism. Several of Clemenceau's ancestors in the seventeenth century were apothecaries or doctors, and his great-grandfather, grandfather and father all took degrees in medicine. This does not mean that they actively followed the profession. Clemenceau's father hardly ever treated a patient,[3] and this seems likely to have been true of earlier generations. The wealth and social status of the family, from the eighteenth century on, were not those of country doctors. The study of medicine was seen as an education in natural science rather than as training for a job.

Clemenceau's ancestors were Protestant, and only returned to the Catholic religion under duress during the reign of Louis XIV. Another branch of the family fled to England after the revocation of the edict of Nantes. The family never returned to the Protestant religion, but there is surely a connection between this forced imposition of Catholicism and the revolutionary and anti-clerical position which they took up in 1789. That the Vendée had been one of the areas where the Protestant religion had been most firmly established is certainly one element in an explanation of the bitter conflict between Revolution and Counter-Revolution in this area. The areas of the province where the Left was strongest in the nineteenth century, and where support for the Revolution had been strongest in 1793, were also those where Protestantism had been strongest in the sixteenth and seventeenth centuries.[4] Clemenceau's grandfather was formally a Catholic, paying pew rent in the parish church, and contributing generously to its funds, but he was not given a religious funeral. Clemenceau's father was openly an atheist, and insisted that his children be brought up without any religious education. His wife, however, was a devout Protestant. Clemenceau himself, although he never wavered in his adherence to his

[3] J. Martet, op. cit., p. 182: 'Fortunately my father only ever had one patient; he killed him outright!'
[4] L. Monnier, La Révolution de 1848 en Vendée (Fontenay, 1949), p. 44.

father's atheism, had a good knowledge of the Bible, and an understanding of the Protestant position, no doubt derived from his mother, for whom his affection was as deep as that for his father.

Although the family traditions were of the Left, Clemenceau's father was much more extreme than the others, and Clemenceau was contemptuous of his grandfather and his uncle as reactionaries.[5] As the eldest son, he was particularly close to his father. There were six children in all; the eldest was a girl, Emma, born just over a year before Georges in 1840. The two other sisters, Adrienne and Sophie, were born in 1850 and 1854 respectively and Clemenceau's two younger brothers, Paul and Albert, in 1857 and 1861. Georges's relationship with his brothers, particularly with Albert, was almost a paternal one. The family remained close-knit. Albert was associated with his elder brother's career on several occasions, notably during the Dreyfus Affair when he acted as Zola's lawyer.

Soon after the birth of his eldest son Dr Benjamin Clemenceau set up house in the town of Nantes, where he remained until the death of his father in 1860; this allowed him to move to the Château de l'Aubraie. His father had a great influence on the political and intellectual development of the young Clemenceau; he commented on it on many occasions, and everything we know about his early life confirms it.[6] One of his earliest memories was of seeing his father return home one morning in February 1848, looking extremely pleased. His elder sister told her brother that it must mean that the King had died. It turned out to be even better! the news of the revolution which swept away both Louis Philippe and the monarchy itself. On 25 February his father, who had already been given a medal for his part in the revolution of 1830 in Nantes, was one of those who signed a poster acclaiming the Republic and the Sovereignty of the People.[7] Although he does not seem to have played an active part in politics, he was important enough to find himself one of those arrested after Louis Napoleon's *coup d'état* of 2 December 1851, which swept away the short-lived Second Republic. He must have been released fairly soon, as Michelet's diary records a meeting with him on 31 July 1852.[8] The Romantic-republican historian, with his vision of the people rising up to throw off the chains of oppression by Church and King in the Revolution of 1789, had a great

---

[5] J. Martet, op. cit., p. 161.
[6] Ibid., p. 181: 'I think that the only influence which had any effect on me was that of my father.'
[7] Anon. (in fact L. Brunschwieg), *Souvenirs d'un Vieux Nantais* (Nantes, 1888), pp. 12 and 39.
[8] Archives Nationales, BB[22]140, for his imprisonment: he refused to ask for release. J. Michelet, *Journal* (1959 seq.), II, p. 203. Michelet had been dismissed from his professional chair for his republican opinions, and stayed at Nantes from June 1852 to October 1853, gathering material for his history of the Revolution.

influence on the ideas of Benjamin Clemenceau, and, through him, on those of his son.

Clemenceau's father was associated with a secret society, La Marianne, which plotted a republican rising in a very ineffectual way until it was suppressed in 1855.[9] He was not arrested then as his complicity could not be proved, but he was to be imprisoned again and sentenced to transportation to Algeria after the Orsini bomb attack on the Emperor in 1858. After this incident the government decided to carry out widespread arrests in order to intimidate the republican opposition. At Nantes five workers and Dr Benjamin Clemenceau were arrested. Four of the workers were transported to Algeria, but there was such a public outcry against the transportation of Dr Clemenceau that he was released after being taken as far as Marseilles.[10] This arrest led to a famous scene. Clemenceau, aged seventeen, went with his mother to say farewell to his father in the prison at Nantes the night before his departure. The son said, 'I will avenge you', to which his father replied – 'if you wish to revenge me, work.'[11]

Already Dr Clemenceau had instilled in his eldest son the ideas that were to remain throughout his life the basis of his intellectual and political creed. His devotion to the memory of the Revolution, and hatred of Catholicism would never change. He said: 'My father made a cult of the Revolution: there were portraits of St Just and Robespierre and others of their kind in every corner at L'Aubraie.' And again: 'My father was a romantic who had translated into politics the literary ideas of Victor Hugo and those people.'[12] Clemenceau's earliest education was given by his mother, after which he went to a small private school before entering the lycée at Nantes in 1853, when he was nearly twelve years old.[13] When he reached the top class of the lycée, where the pupils began to study philosophy, Clemenceau's father began to discuss with him in the evenings the ideas that he had heard in class that day. The next day the youth could go back and refute the teacher's arguments. Surprisingly, this recalcitrance improved his marks. After a mediocre career in the lower forms he carried off two prizes in his final year.[14]

Clemenceau never lived permanently at the Château de l'Aubraie. By the time that his father inherited it he was already nearly twenty years

---

[9] G. Frambourg, Le Dr Guépin, un Philanthrope et Démocrate Nantais (Nantes, 1964), pp. 277–8, F. Rémi, La Marianne dans les Campagnes (Auxerre, 1881), and F. Simon, La Marianne, Société Secrête au Pays d'Anjou (Angers, 1939).

[10] A. Dansette, L'Attentat D'Orsini (1964), pp. 90–1. E. Tenot and A. Dubost, Les Suspects en 1858 (1869), p. 199; G. Frambourg, op. cit., pp. 278–9. A friend of Dr Benjamin Clemenceau, a Dr Aubinois, who had contacts with the Imperial family, intervened on his behalf.

[11] J. Martet, op. cit., p. 183.

[12] Ibid., pp. 146–7.

[13] Ibid., p. 181.

[14] Ibid., pp. 181 and 187–8.

old, and enrolled in the medical faculty at Nantes. Soon afterwards he was to go to Paris to pursue his studies. But from his earliest childhood he seems to have spent most of his holidays there, and he always talked of it as the family home. The house was several centuries old, and consisted of extensive farm buildings in front of a fortified manor

1. France

house, surrounded by a moat.[15] Modern comfort of any sort was lacking. It had stone-flagged floors, bare stone walls, massive oak beams and vast rooms that were impossible to heat in winter. After he came to live at l'Aubraie, Clemenceau's father became almost a recluse.

Relations between landlord and peasant were still feudal in character

[15] G. Clemenceau, *Les Plus Forts* (1898), and M. Clemenceau-Jacquemaire, *Le Pot de Basilic* (1928). This description of the Château de l'Aubraie is based on their accounts, and on my own impression of the house as it is today. I wish to thank M. and Mme. G. Clemenceau for their great kindness in showing me the house.

in the Vendée, even when the landlord held firm republican and demo-cratic principles. Clemenceau's daughter wrote :

> The tenants, who called my grandfather 'not' maître', extended that appellation to all his family, young and old : whereas we used the familiar form 'tu' to all the village, everyone used the respectful 'vous' to us. Even my nurse called me 'Mamzelle'. In practice one could not have had a more aristocratic education, in spite of the most republican principles. I easily discovered the flagrant contradictions between the dogmas I heard proclaimed in the most categorical terms, and the real conditions of life in which I had my small share. How could I not see the difference between our habits and those of the peasants. We had nothing in common, not even language.[16]

But the traditional concern of the good manorial lord for his dependants was also preserved. Dr Benjamin Clemenceau and his wife devoted a large part of their income, and of their time, to charitable concern for the poor in the surrounding villages, and to vagabonds of all sorts who passed by. Their own household, on the traditional scale, with at least thirteen female and five male servants, all living at the château, was 'a sort of community, full of *bonhomie*, where it was not at all hard to be in service'.[17]

2 MEDICAL STUDENT

While his father was being harassed by Napoleon's police, Clemenceau passed the *baccalauréat* examination which ended his schooldays. It was an examination in classical languages, and in literature and philosophy, but it opened the way to any university faculty, including the faculty of medicine. There was no hesitation about his next step. Like his ancestors he would study medicine, and, like them, Clemenceau entered the medical school primarily for an education. He may have had ambitions for a career at a higher level in medical or scientific research, but, distracted by politics, he did not even win a place as an *interne* at one of the Paris hospitals. In any case he did not have the temperament for patient research and long-drawn-out intellectual enquiry, although he had the journalist's or lawyer's facility for rapid assimilation and clear, if superficial, exposition.

His father seems to have destined him for intellectual pursuits and Clemenceau was drawn that way himself. He even tried to pretend, after 1893, that they had always been his real love, and that politics had been a distraction. But he was first and foremost a political animal.

[16] M. Clemenceau-Jacquemaire, op. cit., pp. 136–7.
[17] Ibid., pp. 49, 138–142 and 230.

He could not take part in politics under the Second Empire, but its fall in 1870 opened the road. After the heady excitements of his political baptism of fire during the Commune, he settled on a career in politics.

On 1 November 1858 he entered his name at the preparatory school of Medicine and Pharmacy at Nantes. He was one of the better pupils, passing the examinations which allowed him to become first an *externe* and then an *interne* in the Nantes hospitals.[18] In October 1861, when he was just twenty years old, his father accompanied him to Paris. It was time for an ambitious young man to leave the restricted circle of life at home in a provincial city. His father took him to Henri Lefort, one of the republicans who had vainly tried to organize resistance in the streets of Paris after the *coup d'état* of December 1851. As Clemenceau later recalled:

> My father was more concerned that I spend my time with Lefort, than at the faculty; for, through Lefort, who had known Victor Hugo, all doors opened.[19]

This meant the doors that opened into the world of liberal and republican opposition to the Second Empire, and Clemenceau was soon well known, both in the middle-class drawing-rooms of the liberal opposition, and in the Bohemian society of the cafés and artists' studios of the Latin Quarter.[20] His life was a busy one, for, in addition to his social life and his political activity, he continued to work for his medical examinations. In December 1861 he took tenth place out of 330 in the *Concours* for the *Externat*, the last time he was to win such a high place.[21]

The early 1860s were a classical period of student revolt and intellectuals' engagement in politics. The régime, with its stuffy and hypocritical image, its association with Catholicism and its repression of political activity, was unpopular in the big cities, especially Paris, and with the younger generation. Liberalization had not yet gone far enough

[18] For his career as a medical student, *see* his *dossier* at the Paris faculty of medicine, published in *La Presse Médicale*, 73, 15 May and 4 December 1965, pp. 1435 and 3029.

[19] J. Martet, op. cit., p. 208. Lefort was one of the bourgeois republicans who sought most eagerly to associate the working class with the anti-Imperialist movement. He promoted workers' candidacies in the 1863 elections, and went to London to help found the First International. He was soon expelled from the International for being too much opposed to the Imperial government. *See* J. Maitron, *Dictionnaire Biographique du Mouvement Ouvrier Français, Première Partie 1789–1864*, II, I. Tchernoff, *Le Parti Républicain au Coup d'Etat et sous le Second Empire* (1906), pp. 45, 73, 146, 343, and 447, and MM. Drachkovitch (ed.), *The Revolutionary Internationals 1864-1943* (1966), p. 6.

[20] *See* J. Martet, op. cit., pp. 205–8, I. Tchernoff, *Le Parti Républicain*, pp. 216–8 and *Dans le Creuset des Civilisations* (1936–8), III, p. 148. Clemenceau recalled the passionate discussions they had at the café de Cluny, 'meeting point of the old and the young republicans', in an article in *La Justice*, 25 August 1894.

[21] *Gazette des Hôpitaux Civils et Militaires*, 151, 26–28 December 1861, p. 604.

for there to be many channels of political activity. The *Corps Législatif*, without proper debates, was a rubber stamp for the government, newspapers were censored, and political parties banned. But really strict repression had been relaxed, political prisoners released, and political exiles allowed to return. There was considerable opposition but few legal means for its expression. Hence the exaggerated importance of the activities of students, meeting in cafés and private rooms, organizing associations which escaped the law banning political associations, publishing ephemeral newspapers, reviews and pamphlets.

Clemenceau was soon involved in all these activities, and also in one of the few attempts to organize a protest demonstration in the streets. He was one of a group of students, including the novelist Zola, and Méline, thirty years later to be a conservative prime minister, who founded a weekly news-sheet entitled '*Le Travail, Journal Littéraire et Scientifique*'. Clemenceau contributed several articles, mainly reviews of plays and books. In order to avoid censorship the magazine had to be ostensibly non-political, and could only allude indirectly to political subjects. Clemenceau managed to do this, in his review of a volume of Michelet's *History of France* which dealt with Louis XIV's persecution of the Protestants, and, more daringly, in an article of 22 February 1862 entitled 'The Martyrs of History'. It began with Socrates and ended with an eulogy of the great revolutionary leaders of 1793, openly acclaiming the Terror. In an interesting anticipation of a position he was later to sum up in the phrase 'The Revolution is a *bloc*', he wrote:

> There are some people who think themselves progressives who say quite seriously—'We accept the principles of 1792, but we reject the violence of the Revolution'. Those who say this are either stupid or hypocrites. Can they not see that the violence was the inevitable result of the appearance of such principles.[22]

Moving rapidly from theory to practice, Clemenceau, with his friend Taule, a fellow medical student, organized a derisory demonstration in the Place de la Bastille on 24 February 1862, the anniversary of the 1848 revolutions. The people did not support them, and the would-be revolutionaries were soon rounded up by the police; Clemenceau escaped and was arrested in his lodgings two days later.[23] His father came to Paris but was unable to prevent his son's sentence of a fine and a month's imprisonment. Added to the time he had spent in prison before trial, this

---

[22] *Le Travail*, 22 February 1862.
[23] G. Wormser, *La République de Clemenceau* (1961), pp. 475–6. Clemenceau was condemned for seeking to provoke a riot; *see* the report of the public prosecutor to the minister of justice, Archives Nationales, BB¹⁸1649, dossier 6657, 9 April 1862. This affair led *Le Travail* to cease publication, as most of its contributors had been arrested.

meant he was imprisoned for over two months. He served his sentence at Mazas, the prison for common law offenders, and not at Ste-Pélagie, where political offenders were detained in much pleasanter conditions.

Ste-Pélagie was almost a centre of republican propaganda, so free were the rules about visiting. Going to visit his friend Taule, who remained in prison there for some months after his own release, Clemenceau got to know several leading republicans, of whom the most important were Blanqui and Scheurer-Kestner. There could hardly have been two more contrasting figures. Scheurer-Kestner, eight years older than Clemenceau, was the manager of his father-in-law's chemical works at Thann in Alsace, and already well on the way to acquiring a substantial fortune. He was in everything except political conviction a well-established member of respectable society. However, the ardent republicanism for which the whole Kestner family was famous had led him to help with the smuggling of clandestine opposition literature and of printing presses across the frontier, and hence to imprisonment.[24] Blanqui was a much older man, born in 1805, and had spent most of his adult life in prison for attempts to overthrow every régime since 1815, including the Second Republic. He was a social pariah and looked on with horror by all except the most extreme republicans. Personal relations with him were difficult, as his life of alternating conspiracy and imprisonment had given him a persecution mania.

Clemenceau admired Blanqui's revolutionary principles, personal courage and self-sacrifice, and established good relations with him which endured intermittently to the end of Blanqui's life. But he was never a Blanquist, or prepared to accept guidance about practical political action from the old revolutionary. He was for a time entrusted with the care of a secret printing press. Soon, however, Blanqui told Clemenceau to hand over the press to another disciple. The occasion of the quarrel was that Clemenceau had been seen associating with a rival leader, Charles Delescluze, the Jacobin who was to die on the barricades of the Commune, but Clemenceau never accepted the complete subordination that Blanqui demanded of his followers.[25] Blanqui's plan was to organize a secret society to overthrow the State and social order. In order to achieve surprise, absolute obedience was demanded of the members, who were

[24] A. Scheurer-Kestner, Souvenirs de Jeunesse (1905), p. 63. Cf. D. R. Watson, 'Pillar of the Third Republic', History Today, 18 May 1968, pp. 314–20.
[25] For the printing-press incident, see I. Tchernoff's Le Parti Républicain, pp. 143 and 338, and M. Dommanget, Blanqui et l'Opposition Révolutionnaire à la Fin du Second Empire (1960), p. 53. For Blanqui's political ideas see M. Dommanget, Les Idées Politiques et Sociales d'Auguste Blanqui (1957), and A. B. Spitzer, The Revolutionary Theories of Louis Auguste Blanqui (New York, 1957). On Delescluze, see M. Dessal, Un Révolutionnaire Jacobin, Charles Delescluze 1809–1871 (1952). Clemenceau remained in contact with Delescluze; during his visit to the United States he tried unsuccessfully to obtain subscriptions for Delescluze's newspaper: Clemenceau to Scheurer-Kestner, 27 December 1867, Bib. Nat., NAF, 12704, I, p. 443.

not supposed to maintain contacts among themselves, but simply await orders from the leader. The fiasco of February 1862 convinced Clemenceau of the futility of such attempts, and he was never again to take part in such schemes.

Meanwhile he pursued his medical studies, sitting the examination for *internes* in October 1862. He came next to bottom of thirty-four *internes provisoires*, and had to take up residence at the Bicêtre hospital for mental diseases[26] – not a popular appointment. Clemenceau, however, found this of interest, writing to his friend Scheurer-Kestner:

> This hidden world is not without interest for a materialist like me. I would dare the most ardent spiritualist to discover the immortal soul of an idiot or a cretin.[27]

He dispersed his energies over a wide field. His letters to Scheurer-Kestner reveal that he was reading philosophical works and books on the French Revolution. After reading a book by Chassin on the Revolution he commented:

> We are poor specimens by the side of those bourgeois scarcely separated from us by two generations. We are dwarfs by the side of our fathers.[28]

He kept up with current political pamphlets, and such works as Michelet's *La Femme*. He found this an odd production, 'not one which a mother would allow her daughter to read,' he said, and criticized the obscurity of Michelet's style.[29] The social position of women interested him, and a few years later he began to write a treatise on the subject, seeking to refute J. S. Mill's essay, *The Subjection of Women*, by the use of some of Michelet's ideas.[30] Clemenceau was firmly convinced of male superiority; at the same time he was strongly attracted by the fair sex, and usually a great success with them. There was, however, one exception.

[26] Some confusion has been caused by the fact that he sat this examination twice, in October 1862, and again in October 1863. He was at the Bicêtre hospital until July 1863, when he was suspended for being absent without permission. In August 1863 he was moved to La Pitié hospital, where he stayed for the rest of his training. He never achieved the position of a full *interne. Gazette des Hôpitaux Civils et Militaires*, 150, 25–27 December 1862, p. 600, and 151, 24 December 1863, p. 604. Clemenceau told his friend Scheurer-Kestner of his move to La Pitié, in a letter of 30 August 1863, Bibliothèque Nationale, Nouvelles Acquisitions Françaises, 24409, fol. 43.
[27] Clemenceau to Scheurer-Kestner, 2 February 1863, Bib. Nat., NAF, 24409, fol. 38.
[28] Clemenceau to Scheurer-Kestner, 16 September 1863, Bib. Nat., NAF, 24409, fol. 46.
[29] Clemenceau to Scheurer-Kestner, 12 October 1863, Bib. Nat., NAF, 24409, fol. 48.
[30] His notes for this work, and the opening pages, were published in J. Martet, op. cit., pp. 257–69. *See* D. R. Watson, 'Clemenceau and Mill', *The Mill News Letter*, VI, i, 1970, pp. 13–19.

In June 1863 he paid a brief visit to Geneva, and returned through Strasbourg and Alsace, calling to see Scheurer-Kestner, now home again in Thann. There he met and fell passionately in love with his friend's sister-in-law, Hortense Kestner. This affair was the theme of several long letters from Clemenceau to Scheurer-Kestner, and was commented on at length by the latter in his memoirs. Scheurer-Kestner regarded the failure of Clemenceau's suit as a decisive factor in the development of his character, and argued that his failure as a politician – for Clemenceau's career seemed to have ended in failure when he was writing – could be traced to it. Scheurer-Kestner wrote:

> Who knows but that if his destiny had been completely changed [by marriage to Hortense Kestner] he might have become one of our leading statesmen. Under the beneficent influence of an intelligent and ambitious woman, Clemenceau would have organized his life quite differently. He would, perhaps – I say, perhaps, for I am not certain of it – have overcome that instability of character of which the extent can only be measured by someone who had known him intimately over a long period.[31]

The affair and its consequences – his visits to the U.S.A. and a marriage on the rebound to a young American girl – certainly had an important influence on the development of his character. His failure to win Hortense only heightened the arrogance of his behaviour. Hortense Kestner, with her velvet-brown eyes, black hair and Roman nose, was a beautiful and accomplished young woman.[32] But she was one year older and there were several other suitors. Her parents were not favourably inclined towards the young man, finding him arrogant, extreme in his opinions, and unstable in temperament. Even among republicans the conventions of respectable society put severe limitations on contact between a girl and a young man who were not betrothed. Clemenceau's main concern, as shown in his letters to Scheurer-Kestner, seems to have been that she was at least informed of his feelings.[33] In January and February 1864 he paid two rapid visits to Alsace in the hope of breaking

---

[31] Scheurer-Kestner's unpublished *Journal*, Bib. Nat., NAF, 12704, p. 418.

[32] On this affair *see* A. Krebs, 'Le secret de Clemenceau', *Miroir de l'Histoire* (1958), pp. 426–34, and A. Krebs, 'Le secret de Clemenceau, révélé par les souvenirs d'Auguste Scheurer-Kestner', *Bulletin de la Société Industrielle de Mulhouse*, 735 (1969), pp. 67–86, which reprints most of Clemenceau's letters referring to the affair. The description of Hortense, and the unfavourable impression given by Clemenceau, are taken from Scheurer-Kestner's unpublished *Journal*, Bib. Nat., NAF, 12704, pp. 417 and 428.

[33] Clemenceau to Etienne Arago, 4 January 1864: 'It seems to me that I have a right to be refused only by Mlle Kestner herself, or, at least, by her father or her mother.' Arago was another friend whose advice Clemenceau sought on this affair. Bib. Nat., NAF, 24409, fol. 53, quoted in *Bulletin de la Société Industrielle de Mulhouse*, 735 (1969), p. 72.

down the resistance of her parents, but in vain. His letter to Scheurer-Kestner of 9 February 1864 reveals the depth of his feelings:

> And now, tell me, my friend, have you spoken with your brother-in-law? What did he say? And what do you both think? I put these questions to myself every day, and they are still unanswered. Do not be afraid to write to me and tell me the whole truth, whatever it is. I prefer it to uncertainty. I pass my time in recapitulating every one of your words, considering each in the light of my mood of the moment, and the invariable conclusion is that I am much afraid. Then I say to myself that I must be mad to hope, and the desire to know the truth is replaced by the anxiety of learning what I fear, and I shift ceaselessly between these two feelings. I await your letter, and yet I will probaby keep it on my table for an hour, turning it over without daring to open it. Why do I lack the words to make you understand what I feel? I told you the other day of all the fine speeches I make when you are not here. It is different now. Every day I plan feats of eloquence, and everything dries up when I come to put it on paper. If I am unable to transfer to your heart, my friend, what is in mine, it is the fault of my words, not of my feelings. But no, in such a case one or two really sincere words will suffice, and I think I have said them. . . .
>
> In any case I have just written to my father and told him at length about my situation. I needed to do that. My father is, and always has been, first and foremost a friend. Since I attained the age of reason, I have never heard him give me an order, and I have had neither joy nor grief that we have not shared together.[34]

Several other letters reveal the emotional disturbance into which he had been plunged by his passion for Hortense. The affair tells us much about the character of the young Clemenceau – his impetuosity, his obstinacy, and his refusal to admit the difficulties which lay in the way of his projects. Scheurer-Kestner, writing his memoirs around the year 1893, after copying long sections of his letters, commented thus:

> I will not attempt a psychological analysis of his character, so strong and yet so tender. The contrast between Clemenceau's head and his heart stands out in every line. When he became a man, he remained what he had been as a student. I have always found him with the same heart that he had then. But experience of life did not ripen him, and after having harmed himself by his lack of common sense, he finished by wreaking harm on all around him without realizing it.

[34] Clemenceau to Scheurer-Kestner, 9 February 1864, Bib. Nat., NAF, 24409, fol. 58–9; long sections of this letter are quoted in *Bulletin de la Société Industrielle de Mulhouse*, 735 (1969), pp. 73–4.

The Republic has had no more ardent defender than Clemenceau whenever She was in the sort of danger that was obvious and easy to see; but in other circumstances, as a journalist, a deputy and a public figure, he has harmed Her unconsciously, and if it had been possible to kill Her, it would have been Clemenceau who was the executioner.[35]

This was Scheurer-Kestner, the Opportunist, condemning Clemenceau, the Radical, but behind the party prejudice there is some truth in his unfavourable judgement on the first half of Clemenceau's political career, and in his view that the actions of Clemenceau the politician were foreshadowed in his behaviour at this time. Eventually in September 1864 his proposal was put before Hortense, indirectly and by letter. Her refusal plunged him into the deepest gloom, although Scheurer-Kestner had long been warning him that he could have little hope. This disappointment, added to disillusionment with politics and the mediocre success of his medical studies, led him to make the decision to depart for the United States of America.[36] Hortense Kestner later married Charles Floquet, Clemenceau's colleague in Radical politics for many years; this sentimental rivalry was not allowed to interfere with his later political association with Floquet, which continued until Floquet's career was ended by the Panama scandal in 1892.

Meanwhile Clemenceau was working at medicine, and also, to Scheurer-Kestner's surprise, enrolled at the faculty of law. In addition, he embarked on the translation into French of John Stuart Mill's *System of Logic*, only to abandon it when he found someone else was already engaged on it. Although he seems to have taken no further part in illegal political activity, he was active in setting up another student magazine, *Les Ecoles de France*, of which Charles Longuet, later to be the son-in-law of Karl Marx, was the editor. Another project was the *Bibliothèque Démocratique* – a series of books and pamphlets in defence of the republican cause. The relaxing of the censorship had made this sort of propaganda possible. On 8 May 1864 he was elected President of the Society of Medical Students. Intended by the authorities to be a non-political organization, the election of Clemenceau and his friends ensured that it would be primarily concerned with political protest.[37]

[35] Scheurer-Kestner, *Journal*, Bib. Nat., NAF, 12704, p. 440.
[36] Clemenceau to Scheurer-Kestner, 10 February 1865; 'You ask me what I will do. I don't know. I go, that is all. Chance will do the rest. Perhaps I will become a surgeon with the federal army: perhaps something else. I leave behind only one regret, my father. . . .' Bib. Nat., NAF, 24409, fol. 97–8, quoted in *Bulletin de la Société Industrielle de Mulhouse*, 735 (1969), p. 82.
[37] For all these activities *see* Clemenceau's letters to Scheurer-Kestner, Bib. Nat., NAF 24409, fol. 64 (1 March 1864), fol. 67 (20 April 1864), fol. 71–2 (9 May 1864). *Les Ecoles de France, Journal Littéraire et Scientifique*, 8 May 1864, reports Clemenceau's election as President of the medical students' society.

In view of all this extra-curricular activity, it is not surprising that his studies were no more than adequate. In the summer of 1864 he decided to abandon the attempt to become a full *interne*, the necessary step towards a career at the higher levels of medicine, and to submit his thesis and get his degree. He wrote to Scheurer-Kestner in February 1865 that, although he was going to submit his thesis the next month, he had not yet begun it, or even chosen the precise subject; his thesis did not embody much personal research.[38] Nor would this have been expected. It is, in fact, a résumé of the views of Professor Robin, the teacher Clemenceau chose as his supervisor and as president of the examining jury. Robin, known as the 'Gendarme of Materialism', was a prominent figure in intellectual and political activity at the time. He combined a latent republicanism with an ardent defence of Comte's Positivism and of a materialist approach to biology and medicine. Precisely at this time the crude materialist view of the nature and origins of life had been disproved by the work of Virchow, Pasteur and Schutze. Pasteur's work disproved the materialist claim that there was no radical distinction between living and non-living matter. He had really put an end to the spontaneous generation controversy, but the materialist school refused to be convinced. The question was much debated in 1863 and 1864, with Robin as a leading spokesman for the anti-Pasteur school.[39]

This was the question to which Clemenceau addressed himself in his thesis, '*De la génération des éléments anatomiques*', in which he expounds Robin's views. It is lively and well written, but comes down resoundingly on the wrong side of the question in view of Pasteur's definitive experiments.[40] There is little reference in it to recent work and none to the crucial discoveries of the previous six years. Nevertheless, with Robin as president of the jury, Clemenceau was awarded his degree.

3 VISITS TO THE UNITED STATES

On 25 July 1865 Clemenceau and his father crossed the Channel to England, where they met Herbert Spencer and John Stuart Mill, and

[38] Clemenceau to Scheurer-Kestner, 10 February 1865, Bib. Nat., NAF, 24409, fol. 98.
[39] See *Les Ecoles de France*, 17 April 1864, for reports of a lecture by Pasteur attacking the spontaneous generation theory, with a reply by Robin, and *Gazette des Hôpitaux Civils et Militaires*, 23 August 1864, where Robin outlined his own views on spontaneous generation of life in a review of Comte's *Cours de Philosophie Positive*.
[40] Clemenceau's account of his oral examination in which Robin rescued him from another examiner who wanted to question him on scarlet fever, instead of the origins of life, is in J. Martet, op. cit., p. 201. Clemenceau himself in later life called his thesis 'une surenchère de positivisme carabin', *Au Fil des Jours* (1900), p. 409.

arranged that Clemenceau should translate Mill's essay on 'Auguste Comte and Positivism' into French.[41] In return for this work the publishing firm of Baillière were prepared to publish a second edition of his thesis. His father returned to France, and Clemenceau embarked at Liverpool to cross the Atlantic. He was only to return permanently to France in the summer of 1869, but he did not spend all of the intervening four years in America. He crossed the Atlantic no fewer than eight times. His main source of income was an allowance from his father, supplemented by freelance journalism. The first of his articles on American politics appeared in the French newspaper *Le Temps* on 11 October 1865, dated from New York 28 September, and they continued to appear until 1870, some time after his return to France. Some of these articles have been collected and published in an English translation providing an interesting picture of American politics in the reconstruction era, and of his own political views at the time.[42]

Clemenceau was, of course, in sympathy with the most radical elements in America, the Emancipationists, who now felt that the fruits of victory in the Civil War were being allowed to slip away. He was most interested, not in the question of slavery, but in the American political system, which offered a great contrast to political life under the Second Empire. He was witness of one of the most dramatic and complex constitutional crises of American history – the impeachment of President Jackson. Clemenceau's comments on this affair, and on the elections of 1868, show his knowledge of American constitutional law and of the realities of political life in what was then the world's most democratic country. In later life he said that this experience of democracy cured him of his youthful illusions about the goodness of the people, but this seems to be an over-simplification. It is true that he came back from the United States more prepared for compromise with the Empire than he had been when he left.[43] But as the Empire became more liberal there was more room for republicans to operate within the legal framework. Clemenceau was not alone in this evolution, and it should not be

[41] J. Martet, op. cit., p. 208. W. M. Simon, *European Positivism in the Nineteenth Century* (Ithaca, 1963), p. 157n, has denied that Clemenceau can be regarded as influenced by Positivism. I have sought to refute this view in 'A note on Clemenceau, Comte and Positivism', *The Historical Journal*, XIV (1971), pp. 201–4.
[42] G. Clemenceau, *American Reconstruction, 1865–1870*, ed. F. Baldensperger (New York, 1928, and new edition by O. H. Olsen, New York, 1969). Cf. also, F. Baldensperger, 'L'Initiation Américaine de Clemenceau', *Revue de Littérature Comparée*, VIII (1928), pp. 127–54.
[43] Scheurer-Kestner, *Journal*, Bib. Nat., NAF, 12704, p. 458: 'When he set off for America he was more intransigent than I, when he returned he was more tolerant, or, at least, more "practical". He admitted, although regretting it, legal opposition to the Empire, because he realized that our "pure" policy had achieved nothing. I admit that on reading his letter I was not too satisfied with my friend: I thought that the utilitarian atmosphere of the United States had somewhat deformed the Clemenceau that I had known.'

attributed simply to his American experience. Knowledge of a different political system was valuable, and perhaps some elements of the programme he advocated in the 1880s can be attributed to his American experience; but in the main lines of his political ideas he did not depart from the traditions of French republicanism learned from his father.

His acceptance of social Darwinism also emerges at this time. Although Darwin's work was not then well known in France, Clemenceau's friends Lefort and Laurent-Pichat were the editors of *La Réforme Littéraire* which in 1862 published a synopsis of Darwin's *Origin of Species*. Social Darwinism owed more to the writings of Herbert Spencer than to Darwin himself, and Clemenceau's father had introduced him to Spencer's ideas. He studied both Spencer and Darwin while in New York, and his article for *Le Temps* of 23 November 1869, discussing the future of the negro race, fully espoused the doctrine of the struggle for life:

> Their task must be, as Darwin said, to struggle for existence, physical and moral. In this ruthless struggle for life [in English in the original] for which society is the stage, the weaker must yield to the stronger, be it physically, intellectually or morally.[44]

In the spring of 1866 Clemenceau returned to France, and spent some time with student friends in Paris. He joined the society *Agis Comme Tu Penses*, whose members promised not to take part in any religious ceremony, not even marriage, and signed an outspoken manifesto of belief in atheism and materialism.[45] He soon returned to the United States, and travelled through the southern states, witnessing the lynching of a negro by an hysterical mob and discussing the negro question with southerners who earnestly sought to convince him that slavery was justified in the Bible; being a convinced atheist, he was only too happy to agree.[46] He was still translating John Stuart Mill's book on Positivism, and writing an introduction which was never published. Then in September 1867 he tried to persuade his father to send him money to buy land in the Middle West. His father replied that it was time he returned to France, and, when he refused, cut off his allowance.[47]

Instead of returning home he became teacher of French and equitation at Miss Aitken's academy for young ladies in Stamford, Connecticut. Before long he was involved in a love affair with one of his pupils, Mary Plummer. Once again, things did not go smoothly for him, and his insistence on a purely civil marriage led to a definite refusal by Miss Plummer's guardian. This affair, as far as we can tell, did not disturb

[44] *American Reconstruction*, p. 297.
[45] I. Tchernoff, *Le Parti Républicain*, p. 316.
[46] Clemenceau referred to these incidents in an article in *L'Homme Enchaîné*.
[47] A. Krebs, 'Le mariage de Clemenceau', *Mercure de France* (1955), pp. 641–2.

Clemenceau as his passion for Hortense had done, and in June 1868 he set sail for France with no immediate thought of returning to the United States. He spent a few days in Paris and then returned to his family home. He wrote to Scheurer-Kestner on 27 July 1868, saying that he intended to spend the summer there and then go to Germany, to learn the language. He had already acquired a good idiomatic command of English even if sometimes incorrect. He had no other plans, though he thought vaguely that he might return to America after a year or two. This was still his intention when he wrote again to his friend on 13 October, arranging to meet him on his way to Germany. But the trip never took place. On 12 November he wrote he had to return to the U.S.A. Mary Plummer had persuaded her guardian to allow the marriage to take place, even without a religious ceremony. At the same time Hortense Kestner announced her engagement to Charles Floquet. On 21 November Clemenceau sailed from Brest to New York to make arrangements for the marriage. He did not stay long, however, and by 3 February 1869 was back home in the Vendée, still without his fiancée, who had stayed behind in New York. He wrote to Scheurer-Kestner describing her in jocular fashion:

> I am engaged to a young American 'miss' aged about 18. . . . Brunette, 29 teeth (3 to come), Medium height, etc., etc. Character: I cannot say as I have only known her for two years: ideas, still being formed.[48]

At the end of May he crossed the Atlantic again to marry. The ceremony took place on 23 June 1869 in New York, and five days later Dr Clemenceau and his bride sailed back to France.[49] The young couple went to live with his parents at the Château de l'Aubraie where the way of life of Clemenceau's family and the peasants around them, hardly changed over the centuries, must have come as a shock to the elegant young American lady.

At first Clemenceau stayed there too, riding and hunting and even practising medicine. This cannot have taken a great deal of his time, but was more serious than his father's practice of medicine had ever been. He treated patients regularly around Féaule between November 1869 and August 1870, and again between May and October 1871, after which he moved to Paris, and set up his consulting rooms in Montmartre, combining medicine and politics – a combination in which politics gradually ousted medicine.[50] On 2 June 1870 their first child was born,

---

[48] 11 February 1869, Bib. Nat., NAF, 12704, p. 456.
[49] Krebs, op. cit., p. 647.
[50] A notebook, recording his visits, treatments and fees has been preserved. Extracts printed by F. Jayle, 'Clemenceau, sa vie professionelle', *La Presse Médicale*, 73, (1934), pp. 1433–6.

a daughter, Madeleine, who was to be followed by another, Thérèse, and then a son, Michel. Throughout this time his wife continued to live with his parents and unmarried aunts, but after August 1870 Clemenceau only returned for short visits, except for the period between May and October 1871. One or two letters from Clemenceau to his wife remain from this period, notably one that never reached her, which was sent out from the besieged city of Paris by balloon in November 1870. This shows that he was still the tender and affectionate husband, but quite soon estrangement began. Around 1875 Madame Clemenceau moved to Paris, but seems to have played no part at all in her husband's political and social life. By the 1880s Clemenceau was a notorious man-about-town, frequenter of the *coulisses* of the Opéra, and elegant escort of the most fashionable actresses and demi-mondaines. Mary Plummer had faded out of his life long before the divorce of 1892. She returned to the United States for a while, but she had by then no family or friends there and some time later returned to Paris, where she lived completely forgotten until 1923. After the divorce Clemenceau never made any public reference to her and seems to have had no further contact with her.

2

THE COMMUNE

I THE SIEGE OF PARIS

Clemenceau's political prospects were to be transformed by the declaration of war on Prussia in July 1870. Within two months the shattering French defeats, culminating in the surrender of the Emperor himself at the head of one of his armies, led to the fall of the Empire and the proclamation of the Republic. Some of his father's friends were prominent actors in these dramatic events, and Clemenceau was at once thrust into political action. But at the outbreak of the war he did not envisage such an outcome and was plunged into despair. A French victory, which would restore the prestige of the Empire, was just as abhorrent to him as the thought of defeat. He wrote to Scheurer-Kestner on 23 July:

> I am more disheartened than I can say at everything I see, hear and read. Whatever happens, this war will be a terrible disaster. For my part, I never expected such a prostration of public opinion. Even Delescluze is trying to convince himself and others that the enemy of European liberty is to be found at Berlin, and that we will carry the revolution on our banners.[51]

Clemenceau never wavered from the position he had adopted in 1863 when the possibility of intervention on behalf of the Polish rebels was mooted. To him a victory for the Empire was a defeat for republicanism

[51] Clemenceau to Scheurer-Kestner, 23 July 1870, Bib. Nat., NAF, 14114, fol. 514. Clemenceau must have been reading Delescluze's article in *Le Réveil* of 18 July, in which this Jacobin republican began with many reservations about Imperial policy, but ended with a ringing call for support of the government, as his patriotism overcame his hatred of the Empire. M. Dessal, *Un Révolutionnaire Jacobin*, pp. 275–6.

and therefore against the true interests of France.[52] His anxiety about the safety of his friend's family, living in Alsace close to the German frontier, shows that he was not carried away by the facile optimism of the great majority who looked forward to a French invasion of German soil. His forebodings were soon to be confirmed by the first French defeats. We have no evidence of Clemenceau's reaction to these disasters, but it seems clear from the above letter that, in spite of his intense patriotism, such a result must have been welcome to him. Victory would have strengthened the Empire, but a complete defeat opened the way for a revolution. Then, it was thought, and by none more fervently than Clemenceau, popular enthusiasm would repeat the glorious reversal of fortune of 1792. The armies of the Republic, reinforced by a *levée en masse*, volunteers fighting for an ideal, would wipe out the defeats of the conscript regiments of Louis Napoleon. Some time in August Clemenceau went to Paris to be close to the centre of events, staying with his friend Lafont in Montmartre, leaving his wife and baby behind at the family home in the Vendée.

The first French defeats had already produced demonstrations and an abortive Blanquist rising in early August. The rapid expansion of the National Guard transformed it from a body of respectable citizens into a dangerous and undisciplined army, useless against the Prussians, but a key element in the political situation.[53] Further defeats would obviously produce another riot in Paris, which the Imperial authorities had neither the military force nor the self-confidence to suppress. The event was the most complete disaster imaginable. On 1 September 1870 the main French army was surrounded at Sedan and forced to surrender. The Emperor himself, who had thought it essential for a Bonaparte to command his troops in person, was made prisoner. The régime could not hope to survive this blow.

The question was not whether the Empire would fall, but what would succeed it. The liberal opposition, which included many of the republican members of the Corps Législatif, hoped that a formula could be found for a legal transmission of authority to some sort of Parliamentary cabinet, based on the last Imperial Parliament. But others further to the Left were determined on a revolution, according to the traditional *scenario*. The Corps Législatif arranged to debate the situation on the afternoon of 4 September. But during the night of 3 September plans were laid for a demonstration to coincide with the opening of the debate.[54] By midday on 4 September a huge crowd had gathered around

<hr>

[52] Clemenceau to Scheurer-Kestner, 14 March 1863, Bib. Nat., NAF, 24409, fol. 40.
[53] L. Girard, *La Garde Nationale, 1814-1871* (1964), pp. 348-51, and G. Duveau, *Le Siège de Paris* (1939), p. 78-9.
[54] R. Gossez, 'Le 4 Septembre 1870, initiative et spontanéité', *Actes du 77e Congrès des Sociétés Savantes, Section d'Histoire Moderne et Contemporaine* (1952),

the Parliament building. It was a beautiful sunny day and the crowd was in a good humour. There was little violence because there was virtually no opposition as the crowd forced its way into the debating chamber and stopped proceedings. Clemenceau, along with his friend Ranc, and many other young republicans, was among this crowd.[55]

Gambetta, a republican member of the Corps Législatif, soon to be a key figure in the provisional government, proclaimed the destitution of the Empire, and announced that the Republic should be proclaimed from the Hôtel de Ville, the town hall of the city of Paris. When the republican deputies arrived at the Hôtel de Ville they found that it had already been occupied by the Blanquists, who were engaged in drawing up lists of names for a Provisional Government. They had to find a formula that would exclude the extremists but still win the approval of the mob. Ferry, another republican member of the Corps Législatif, had the happy thought of declaring that all those who had been elected for Paris constituencies should form a Government of National Defence. The formula had the great advantage of including nearly all the leading republican deputies and excluding both the Right and the Extreme Left. The problem was that republicanism covered a wide range of opinion from the moderate bourgeois liberalism of Ernest Picard, Jules Simon and Jules Favre, through the more radical tendency of Gambetta and his associates, to the extreme democratic and socialist ideas of the Blanquists, the members of the First International and others. At first all tendencies united to resist the Prussian invader, but the continuing military disasters soon produced bitter criticism of the Government of National Defence, and two attempted *coups* in Paris which prepared the way for the final explosion of the Commune.[56]

On the evening of 4 September Clemenceau accompanied his friend Floquet to the Luxembourg palace, meeting-place of the Senate, where a few senators remained awaiting the assault of the mob which never arrived. The guard commander accepted the authority of the representatives of the new government, turned out the old gentlemen and locked up the empty building.[57]

Next day Clemenceau was appointed mayor of Montmartre. One of

---

pp. 506–31, provides the best account. It is more specific than that of E. Jéloubouskaia, *La Chute du Second Empire et La Naissance de la Troisième République en France* (Moscow, 1959).
   [55] Eye-witness accounts of the invasion of the Parliament building are given by E. Dréolle, *La Journée du 4 September* (1871), and by A. Ranc, *Souvenirs—Correspondence 1831–1908* (1913), pp. 155–64.
   [56] On the formation of the Government of National Defence, *see* P. de la Gorce, *Histoire du Second Empire* (1894–1905), VII, pp. 417–9, H. Guillemin, *Cette curieuse guerre de 70* (1956), pp. 112–76, J. Simon, *Souvenirs du Quatre Septembre* (1874), one vol. ed., pp. 237–47.
   [57] E. Arago, *L'Hôtel de Ville de Paris au 4 September, et Pendant le Siège* (1874), pp. 28–9.

the first tasks of the new government was to provide for the government of the capital. Here again it was a question of out-manœuvring the extremists, who were demanding the immediate election of a municipal council, the Commune of Paris, a name which evoked memories of the days of the great Revolution when the Commune had played a vital role in the dual task of pushing on the Revolution to ever more extreme courses, and of organizing the vigorous prosecution of the war. To many it seemed that an elected Commune would serve a similar purpose in 1870. The Government of National Defence shared some of these illusions about the military virtues of spontaneous popular effort, but was determined not to let control of events slip out of its own hands. Accordingly, Etienne Arago, friend of Clemenceau's father, and a member of the famous revolutionary family, was installed as Mayor of Paris at the same time as the Government of National Defence was set up, and given the task of appointing reliable republicans as mayors of the twenty districts.[58] Clemenceau, whom he had befriended eight years before, seemed a natural choice for Montmartre, one of the most working-class areas of the city. He was young, energetic, as ardent in his patriotism and belief in democracy as any of the extremists, and only separated from them by his unflinching adherence, now that the Empire had been overthrown, to the principle of Parliamentary legality. His friendship with Blanqui, for a short time commander of one of the 18th district's battalions of the National Guard, was a measure of the extent to which he found himself on the frontier between the supporters of the Government of National Defence and the Extreme Left.[59] This was a tenable position in September 1870, when all factions rallied round the *de facto* government in the face of the advancing Prussian armies, but it became steadily more difficult to adhere to it as military defeat led the Extreme Left to attack the supposed treachery of the government.

At that time the 18th district, consisting of the Montmartre hill and the northern-facing slopes behind it, was the second most populous of the districts, with 130,456 inhabitants at the last census; it was also one of the poorest. The famous landmark, the Church of the Sacred Heart, was not yet built: it was to be offered as an expiation of the sins of France by the Catholic majority of the National Assembly elected in 1871. Instead the top of the hill was an open space, where were to be parked the cannon whose attempted recapture sparked off the insurrection of March 1871. The slopes of the hill were covered with a network of narrow streets and close-packed buildings, many of them quite

[58] E. Arago, op. cit., pp. 40–1. Clemenceau's friend Floquet helped Arago draw up the list of mayors, *Enquête Parlementaire sur l'insurrection du 18 mars 1871* (1872), Deposition Floquet, p. 298.
[59] Clemenceau preserved copies of Blanqui's newspaper, *La Patrie en Danger*, from this period, all his life: they are still in the Musée Clemenceau.

recently erected, into which were crowded some of the poorest inhabitants of the city, expelled from the centre by the demolition and rebuilding of the previous decade, when Haussman planned most of the great boulevards of modern Paris. As well as dwelling houses, there were many small workshops. To the north, around the railway line, there was an area of heavy industry with some large factories of a more modern type. But their workers did not play much part in the revolutionary ferment of the siege and the Commune. The skilled artisans – cobblers, engravers, jewellers and metalworkers – who formed the rank and file of the political clubs, of the committees, and of the revolutionary battalions of the National Guard, made Montmartre, together with Belleville, the centre of the political agitation which culminated in the Commune.[60]

The latent conflict between the Extreme Left and the liberal republicans of the Government of National Defence was temporarily suppressed by the overwhelming need to organize the defence of the city. Blanqui and Delescluze, the two most prominent extremists, promised their support to the government. On 23 September the Prussian armies completed the encirclement of Paris, and the three months' siege of the city began. The government made a fatal mistake by remaining in Paris, thus forfeiting the possibility of diplomatic and political action, and placing itself at the mercy of the Extreme Left. A delegation, at first composed of minor figures, but soon galvanized into action by Gambetta after his escape from Paris by balloon, ran the rest of the country from Tours and sought to raise new volunteer armies. Meanwhile the government in Paris prepared for an assault that never came. The Prussian command realized that its best course was to wait until the prospect of starvation made the French accept their terms, which grew harsher as the weeks went by. The mayors had a key role to play in organizing recruitment of the National Guard, in making arrangements to provide for the physical well-being of the civilian population, and in maintaining political control, a mixture of political, administrative and military activity that suited Clemenceau very well. The text of a poster which he issued on 23 September shows the spirit in which he set to work:

> The enemy is at the gates of the city. The day is perhaps not far off when our breasts will be the last defence for our country. We are the children of the Revolution. Let us take inspiration from our fathers of 1792, and, like them, we will conquer.[61]

Besides helping to organize the National Guard, he allowed a group who were manufacturing bombs to use the cellars of the town hall. This

---

[60] For the social geography of Paris, see the map on p. 18 of J. Rougerie, *Paris Libre 1871* (1971).
[61] Printed in J. Martet, op. cit., pp. 165–6.

brought him trouble in the period of repression which followed the attempted insurrection of 31 October. The new prefect of police wanted to arrest him for encouraging a scheme which seemed more likely to produce munitions for a rising against the government than for use against the Prussians. Clemenceau was able to persuade the authorities that his intentions were honest and purely patriotic. Nevertheless, the manufacture was stopped and the bombs confiscated.[62] Another task of the mayor was to run municipal relief schemes to provide for the poor, particularly women and children, who were hardest hit by the rapidly rising prices and lack of employment in the besieged city. Bread was not rationed until January, but meat and other items were rationed from the beginning of the siege. Clemenceau set up a municipal scheme for the distribution of the rationed goods.[63] He also issued a circular forbidding religious education in the public schools of his district, a good example of the atmosphere of spontaneous initiative which reigned at the time, although he did not go as far as the mayor of the 11th district, who was dismissed by the government for his anti-clerical activities.[64]

The mayor also had a crucial political role to play. The government had little physical force with which to control the capital, now that most of the regular troops were in the field and the Imperial *gendarmerie* totally demoralized. Self-appointed, the government had little moral authority, and its first intention to organize elections for a Constituent Assembly had to be abandoned because of the Prussian advance. The mayors acted as a liaison between the government and the extremists who had organized committees of vigilance in each district in order to supervise the activities of the government and its nominees. From the first the extreme elements, who, although only a tiny minority in the total population of the city, formed an appreciable proportion of the total number of republican militants, were suspicious of the government, and fearful of rumours of an armistice which could only mean that a Prussian victory had been conceded. The mayors began to have regular meetings with Arago, mayor of the whole city, and Ferry, whose position was equivalent to that normally held by the prefect of the Seine department.[65]

The conflict between the government and the Extreme Left first erupted on 31 October when the news of Bazaine's surrender reached Paris, combined with the rumour that peace proposals were being put to Bismarck. Clemenceau issued a poster in which he stated that 'the

[62] E. Cresson, *Cent Jours du Siège à la Préfecture de Police* (1901), pp. 32–40, and Cresson's evidence to the enquiry, *Enquête sur l'insurrection du 18 mars 1871*, p. 237.
[63] G. de Molinari, *Les Clubs Rouges pendant le Siège de Paris* (1871), p. 163, and G. Duveau, op. cit., p. 129.
[64] Ulysse Parent to Arthur Ranc, 27 October 1870, Ranc, op. cit., p. 173.
[65] E. Arago, op. cit., pp. 127–65.

municipality of the 18th district protests with indignation against an armistice that the government cannot conclude without treachery'.[66] On the morning of 31 October the Government of National Defence was virtually without support in Paris. This was revealed when the National Guard – even those regiments recruited from middle-class areas of the city – refused to clear the crowds of demonstrators away from the town hall. The mayors were summoned to give their advice and re-iterated their demand for the immediate holding of municipal elections. Indeed, the mayors and Arago exceeded their authority, promising municipal elections for the next day.[67] About noon the mayors left to make arrangements for these elections, and Arago took the text of the poster advertising them to the government who were in session in an adjacent room of the town hall. While they were discussing what to do, the rioters broke in and held the government prisoner. For the next twelve hours the situation was extremely confused, but with more elements of farce than of tragedy. It soon became clear that the revolutionaries could think of nothing better to do than to stand on the table (until it collapsed under their weight) making speeches. Eventually some of the middle-class battalions of the National Guard rallied to the support of the government, while the mob, tired of standing around in the rain, began to go home. By the middle of the night some members of the govern-ment had been rescued, others still being held prisoner by a few hundred rioters, while a stronger force of loyal troops surrounded the building. The two sides eventually agreed on an ambiguous formula promising immediate elections and no reprisals, and everyone went home to bed.[68]

The formula was interpreted by the extremists as meaning the replace-ment of the Government of National Defence and the election of a Commune of Paris. For the government it meant the election of the mayors of the twenty districts who would remain limited in their authority, and a plebiscite to determine whether voters supported the Government of National Defence as at present constituted. Accordingly, on 1 November the government ordered the tearing down of the posters put up by the mayors on the previous afternoon announcing elections that day. Instead there was to be a plebiscite on 3 November and the election on 5 November, not of a Commune, but of the mayors of each district. On hearing this, most of the mayors went back to the town hall and declared that they would hold municipal elections as planned.

[66] Printed in J. Martet, op. cit., p. 166.
[67] E. Arago, op. cit., p. 309.
[68] Contemporary accounts of the events of 31 October are provided by E. Arago, op. cit., pp. 240–80, J. Simon, op. cit., pp. 115–72, A. Duquet, *La Guerre de 1870–1871* (1893), pp. 342–5. Modern commentaries are provided by H. Guillemin, op. cit., pp. 329–73, G. Duveau, op. cit., pp. 180–97, M. Howard, *The Franco-Prussian War* (1960, Fontana ed. 1967), pp. 337–9, and M. Kranzberg, *The Siege of Paris 1870–1871* (Ithaca, 1950), pp. 52–61.

They were told that they would be arrested. Thereupon several, including Clemenceau, resigned.[69] But the government's plan was put into effect.

The relative strength of the government and the extremists was revealed by the plebiscite which gave the Government of National Defence an overwhelming majority, and in the election of the mayors, where supporters of the government were returned in all except four of the most solidly working-class districts. One was the 18th district, where Clemenceau defeated a government supporter. Elected as his assistants (*adjoints*) were his friend Lafont, and two extremists, Dereure and Jaclard, who had played a leading role in the attack on the town hall. On 31 October Dereure and Jaclard were to be prominent Communards, and Clemenceau's electoral alliance with them shows how far to the left he had moved at this point. He was supported by the local Committee of Vigilance, one of the extremist bodies from which the Commune was to emerge. He was, however, soon to be involved in attempts to found a less extreme committee, the Association des Défendeurs de la République.[70] Clemenceau now clearly emerged as an opponent, in principle, of the Government of National Defence, although his feeling was still that it should be supported because of the exigencies of the military situation. He wrote to his wife (in English) on 20 December:

> We have the best reasons in the world to be full of hope, and we all feel sure that our efforts will be rewarded with success. In fact it is hardly possible otherwise, for since the beginning of the siege we have all been at work with great activity. . . . We have made cannon, guns, cartridges, powder, etc., etc. We have armed and equipped the *Garde Nationale*, organized a new army. We have fortified Paris in such a manner that the Prussians did not dare attack our walls, now the time has come when we may go and attack them. . . . I guess the Prussians will soon find that they have a hard nut to crack as a Yankee would say. The spirit of the people has never been so good as it is now. They are very patient since they know that the government means to fight to the very end, and will never treat with the enemy whatever may happen. There is not the slightest disturbance in the city, and there will be none.

He found time to end with long instructions about the weaning of his baby daughter.[71]

[69] Clemenceau's letter of resignation is printed in G. Wormser, op. cit., p. 105.
[70] G. de Molinari, op. cit., pp. 62–5. R. Wolfe, 'The Parisian Club de la Revolution of the 18th arrondissment 1870–1871', *Past and Present*, 39 (1968), pp. 81–119; for the Association des Défenseurs de la République, *see* handbill preserved at Musée Municipal de St Denis, displayed as exhibit 276 in *Exposition du Centenaire 1871–1971, La Commune de Paris*.
[71] This letter is preserved at the Musée Clemenceau, and, unlike all the other letters in their possession, is on view to the public.

Some of this optimism was perhaps designed to reassure his wife, but there seems little doubt that he still believed in the possibility of resistance. Even in February 1871 he voted against making peace, and to the end of his life argued that this was correct.[72] He greatly exaggerated the chances of the untrained and undisciplined National Guard in a sortie against the Prussians, and based his optimism on the fact that the total number of troops within the city was greater than the effective Prussian besieging force. The Army command and the government had not the least faith in the fighting quality of the National Guard and were desperately seeking a way of concluding an armistice. The premise for Clemenceau's statement that there would be no further disturbance was that the government would not try to make peace; if it did, by the same argument, the danger of an internecine conflict would be very great. To understand the politics of this period it is essential to realize that it was the Left that was most nationalistic, demanding the prolongation of resistance, while those who were more conservative accepted the need to come to terms with the Prussians. The moderate republicans of the Government of National Defence already represented a more anti-Prussian position than the former supporters of the Empire, while the most extreme revolutionaries, the Blanquists, were the most hysterical in their chauvinism. When the government was forced to accept the realities of the military defeat, they were regarded as traitors by the Extreme Left.[73]

By January 1871 food supplies in the city were almost exhausted; there was no longer any hope of relief from the armies raised by Gambetta south of the Loire. The only hope was the long-promised sortie of the troops in Paris. This had long been dismissed by the authorities as a serious military operation. Nevertheless, it had to be undertaken to justify five months' frenzied preparation. To conclude an armistice without attempting the famous sortie would be seen as treachery by the over-excited populace, still living in a dream-world where revolutionary fervour made up for lack of military training and discipline. The sortie took place and was beaten back ignominiously at Buzenval on 19 January 1871. When the government met to discuss the situation, the mayor began by declaring that 'Rather than capitulate they would die of starvation or be buried in the ruins of the city'.[74] In spite of this rhetoric, the government convinced the majority of the mayors of the futility of further resistance, and when the extremists

---

[72] At the meeting of the mayors with Jules Favre, the foreign minister, on 29 December 1870, Clemenceau and Delescluze led the attack on Trochu, and insisted on a sortie by the National Guard, A. P. Dréo, *Gouvernement de la Défense Nationale, Procès-verbaux des Séances* (1906), p. 457.
[73] The point of view of the Left governs the interpretation of H. Guillemin in his trilogy *Les Origines de la Commune* (1956–60).
[74] M. Howard, op. cit., p. 368.

attempted another rising on 22 January they won little support. This showdown encouraged the government to approach Bismarck. Measures were taken to suppress the Extreme Left, several arrests were made, two newspapers were stopped and the political clubs were closed down. The majority of the mayors supported these decisions, but Clemenceau announced his opposition in an open letter to the *Electeur Libre* of 24 January.[75] Clearly the great majority of the population had no stomach for the continuation of the war with all its privations. Hunger and cold were taking their toll and the death rate in the city, especially of children, was many times its normal level.

2 THE OUTBREAK OF THE COMMUNE

The terms of the armistice, signed on 28 January, were for a ceasefire of three weeks, during which a National Assembly would be elected with authority to conclude peace. Paris was to capitulate, and its garrison to lay down its arms, excepting 40,000 men to maintain order. The National Guard were to retain their arms. Bismarck was not worried about their capacity as a fighting force, and, in any case, no one could see any way of forcing them to disarm. So the problem of maintaining order in Paris was made even worse. Furthermore, as soon as the gates were opened, a large section of the richer citizens left the city. The poorer inhabitants, who had no country houses, remained, moving the political centre of gravity of the National Guard to the left. For a few days there was doubt as to whether Gambetta, who dominated the Delegation, now at Bordeaux, and thus controlled all unoccupied territory except Paris, would accept an armistice concluded without his agreement. He did accept it only as a pause during which to reorganize his armies, and was determined to ensure a republican Assembly. He decreed all those who had held office under the Empire ineligible, and showed signs of using other means to 'make' the election, but was eventually persuaded to resign. He offered Clemenceau the key post of Mayor of Lyons, but by the time the offer reached him Gambetta had resigned.[76]

Clemenceau remained in Paris for the brief campaign preceding the elections of 8 February. Each department formed one constituency and a simple majority sufficed for election. This produced an unusually clear-cut division between Left and Right which largely coincided with

---

[75] Printed in G. Wormser, op. cit., p. 108. 'The government has systematically kept us on one side, avoided asking our advice, and rejected it when we offered it. Now, for obvious reasons they seek to give the appearance of consulting us. . . . It is a manœuvre that we will not lend ourselves to. Those gentlemen have taken on the responsibility for the conduct of affairs, let them keep it to the end.'
[76] Gambetta's letter of 3 February 1871 is printed in J. Martet, op. cit., p. 153.

attitudes about the war. The Right had long advocated peace, while the republicans had organized the continuance of the war, a policy which had only added to the disaster. Revulsion against their failure played a large part in the massive victory of the Right, of 430 against 200, but in Paris the republicans triumphed. Clemenceau was included on the main radical republican list and came twenty-seventh.[77]

The election was everywhere confused, but especially so in Paris, where the Seine department made up a constituency with forty-three seats. The large number of candidates and seats, and the great variety of lists, many overlapping, produced a great dispersal of votes. Apart from symbolic figures like Louis Blanc, Victor Hugo, Gambetta, and Garibaldi, who headed the list, most of those elected in Paris were local figures like Clemenceau, whose role during the siege had brought them into the public eye. There was very little support for the Government of National Defence; on the other hand only four candidates of the Extreme Left were elected. The general tendency was that represented by Clemenceau – radical republicanism, not socialist or revolutionary, but opposed to the moderates of the Government of National Defence, mainly because of their disastrous record against the Prussians. The votes in Paris took so long to count that the results were only known on 13 February, when the National Assembly had already met at Bordeaux. The Paris deputies arrived in a body on 16 February, a considerable addition to the republican section of the predominantly monarchist Assembly. At Bordeaux Clemenceau met his old friend Scheurer-Kestner, elected for his native Alsace. In his memoirs Scheurer-Kestner describes the official meetings of the radical republican group, dominated by the long-winded oratory of Louis Blanc and Victor Hugo, and also more enjoyable informal meetings of a small circle of radical deputies and journalists in a café:

> There one met old relics of 1848, their successors who had been prepared to swear the oath of loyalty to the Empire, and younger men who a few weeks later became the leaders of the Commune. One could mingle with Blanqui, whose presence prevented Delescluze from coming. Floquet, Clemenceau, full of youth, and noble illusions, the good Benoit Malon, the gentle and scientific Socialist Raoult Rigault with his sinister but very witty cynicism. . . .[78]

---

[77] He was also endorsed by the extremists, being one of the candidates on a joint list sponsored by the Alliance Républicaine, the Union Républicaine Centrale, the Association des Defendeurs de la République, and the Association Internationale des Travailleurs, that is, the First International. This joint endorsement is a good example of the coalition of left-wing forces to be shattered by the Commune. See electoral poster preserved at the Musée Municipal de St Denis.

[78] Scheurer-Kestner, *Journal*, Bib. Nat., NAF 12706, p. 163. A shortened version of his impression was printed in *Souvenirs de Jeunesse*, p. 248.

De Marcère, seeing Clemenceau for the first time at the National Assembly, says he was

remarkable for the strangeness of his face, with its dead complexion, his deep-sunk black and gleaming eyes, his short hair and his moustache as black as if it were dyed, a face of rather Asiatic type, striking by its harsh and energetic expression.[79]

The first act of the Assembly was to appoint Thiers, the incarnation of bourgeois liberalism and advocate of constitutional monarchy under the Orleans branch of the royal house, as 'head of the executive of the French Republic', with the right to name a new government. By 19 February he had formed his government and set off for Paris to negotiate the peace terms with Bismarck. In his absence the Assembly adjourned, and Clemenceau also returned to Paris.[80] He was back in Bordeaux for the debate of 1 March, at which the Assembly ratified the terms of peace by which Alsace and Lorraine were handed over to Germany. Clemenceau did not speak in this debate but cast his vote, along with the great majority of the Paris deputies, against the peace. Scheurer-Kestner re-counts how he spent the next day with Clemenceau on the beach at Arcachon. Clemenceau tried to distract his friend's sombre thoughts by discussing how long the inhabitants of Alsace could be expected to retain their loyalty to France. At that time, says Scheurer-Kestner, no one thought it would be more than five or ten years before France re-established her military strength and recovered the lost provinces. But their mood was one of despair with regard to both internal and foreign politics.

Returning to Bordeaux after that excursion we were overcome by profound sadness. The tranquillity of Nature, the peace and silence around us, the stillness of the sea, had calmed our over-excited nerves: we returned completely deflated. The Republic seemed to be not merely in jeopardy but definitely lost.[81]

A few days later Clemenceau returned to Paris to concern himself with the affairs of his municipality, and in particular with the question of the cannon which had been taken from their unguarded parks on 26 February by the National Guard. About 250 of them had been placed on the top of the Montmartre hill, in his municipality. The government's attempt to recapture these cannon was to spark off the insurrection of 18 March 1871 which led to the proclamation of the revolutionary Commune.

[79] E. L. G. H. de Marcère, *L'Assemblée Nationale de 1871* (1904), I, p. 37.
[80] Scheurer-Kestner to his wife, 23 February 1871, Bib. Nat., NAF, 12706, p. 221.
[81] Scheurer-Kestner, *Journal*, Bib. Nat., NAF, 12706, pp. 200–3.

The danger of another revolution in Paris had been a major pre-occupation of the French government from September onwards, but the attempts of the Extreme Left to overthrow the Government of National Defence had not attracted much support, except for a few hours on 31 October. Although the great majority of the population did not support the extremists, they were not prepared to support the government. This was even more true after the election of the National Assembly. A whole series of decisions exacerbated public opinion in Paris against the National Assembly and Thiers – middle-class, respectable republican opinion as well as that of hostile extremists. The National Guardsmen were only to be paid if they could prove poverty, though this was not enforced; the unpopular Imperialist General d'Aurelle de Paladines was made commander of the National Guard; the law of 11 March ended the moratorium on debts, threatening thousands of small businessmen and shopkeepers with bankruptcy; and the decision of the Assembly to move not to Paris, but to Versailles, seemed the supreme insult to the city that regarded itself as the capital of Europe as well as of France.[82]

But more important than all these was the gulf between opinion in Paris and in the provinces during the siege, added to the older conflict between the republicanism of Paris and the conservative opinions represented by the majority of the National Assembly. On 10 March Thiers and the majority of the Assembly made the so-called Pact of Bordeaux, by which it was agreed that the nature of the régime should be held to be an open question. Among the conservative majority some wished to proclaim the restoration of the monarchy at once, but even this compromise was a bitter blow to republican opinion as it challenged the theory that the Republic had been established on 4 September 1870. Safeguarding the Republic, memories of December 1851 and the long years of the Empire all weighed on Parisian opinion.

Finally there was the problem of physical control of the city. There were many signs that the government had only nominal authority in Paris by the end of February. There were two alternatives: either the government had to act so as to retain the support of the National Guard, or it had to be crushed once and for all. In fact neither Thiers nor the majority of the National Assembly considered the first alternative. Thiers had long decided the appropriate strategy in case of revolt of the National Guard – to pull the regular army completely out of the city, only return-

---

[82] For the Commune, see A. Dansette, *Les Origines de la Commune de 1871* (1944); J. Rougerie, *Procès des Communards* (1964), and *Paris Libre 1871* (1971); H. Lefebvre, *La Proclamation de la Commune* (1965); J. Dautry and L. Scheler, *Le Comité Central Républicain des vingt arrondissements de Paris* (1960); R. L. Williams, *The French Revolution of 1870–1871* (New York, 1969). S. Edwards, *The Paris Commune 1871* (1971) (appeared too late to be utilized).

ing in force and in good order, methodically clearing out the rebels, quarter by quarter. His great fear was that the regular army would go over to the side of the rebels, and he thought that if Louis Philippe had followed this strategy, the revolution of 1848 would have been prevented.[83]

When Thiers arrived in Paris on 17 March he decided to bring matters to a head. The Assembly was adjourned, giving him a free hand; he wished, if possible, to have the matter settled before the Assembly met again at Versailles on 20 March. He decided to send troops to remove the cannon from Montmartre and Belleville. This cut across negotiations in which Clemenceau had been acting as intermediary between the government and the National Guard. He thought that he had that very day found a face-saving formula for the handing over of the cannon.[84] This was probably too optimistic, but explains his intense indignation when at 6 a.m. on 18 March he was awakened by Dereure with the news that the regular army had marched in, and were waiting to remove the cannon when they had the necessary equipment. It seemed to Dereure and the other extremists of the 18th district who had until then been prepared to accept Clemenceau's leadership, that his negotiations had been merely a blind. Clemenceau rushed up the hill to expostulate with the general in charge, who replied that he did not involve himself in politics, but simply obeyed orders.[85]

At first there seemed no doubt about the success of the operation. The few National Guardsmen in charge of the cannon had been easily overpowered, but the operation was badly planned. It would have been difficult to move 250 cannon down the steep and narrow streets, and the horses and other equipment did not arrive for several hours. The troops stood around, and were gradually surrounded by crowds of civilians and National Guardsmen. By 9 a.m. the situation had deteriorated to such an extent that General Lecomte ordered his men to fire on the crowd. They refused, and from there it was a short step to the complete disbanding of his regiment and the arrest of its officers. Clemenceau, who had returned to his town hall to continue with his normal administrative

---

[83] See his evidence before the Enquête Parlementaire sur l'Insurrection du 18 mars 1871, p. 177, quoted by J. Rougerie, Paris Libre 1871, p. 102.

[84] Enquête Parlementaire sur l'Insurrection du 18 mars 1871, Déposition Schoelcher, p. 317, and Déposition d'Aurelle de Paladines, pp. 367–8; F. Damé, La Résistance, les maires, les députés de Paris et le comité central du 18 au 26 mars (1871), pp. 28–33; J. Claretie, Histoire de la Révolution de 1870–1871 (1872), p. 590.

[85] J. Martet, Le Silence de M. Clemenceau (1929), pp. 271–3. Martet published (pp. 271–99) the account of his activities on 18 March 1871 that Clemenceau had written shortly afterwards. Martet states that this was only part of Clemenceau's account of his role during the Commune, amounting to two hundred pages, which he intended to publish one day. The publication never took place. In 1967 the documents which Martet had obtained from Clemenceau, presumably including the full account of his role during the Commune, were still in the possession of Madame Martet. I was not granted permission to consult them.

work, learnt about 10 a.m. that Lecomte and his officers were held prisoner by the National Guard. As yet no one believed that the lives of the prisoners were in danger, and the main question was how the government would recapture the cannon and restore its control. Clemenceau did not think that the government would simply withdraw all the troops and abandon the city.

About half past four, Simon Mayer, an officer in the National Guard, dashed into the town hall with the dramatic news that General Thomas had been seized, and that he, as well as General Lecomte, would be murdered unless Clemenceau came at once to save them.[86] He seized his mayor's scarf and ran as fast as he could up the steep hill to the little committee room from which the National Guard had organized the guard over the cannon. The prisoners had been brought here from the Château Rouge, a public dance hall, where they had been held since morning. They arrived too late, but intervention would probably have meant that Clemenceau shared the fate of the generals. No one in authority, either in the National Guard or in the revolutionary committee of vigilance, authorized the execution of the two generals. It was an act of mob violence, whose participants were never identified.

Clemenceau described the scene he found :

> Soldiers, National Guardsmen, women and children, all were shouting like savage beasts, without realizing what they were doing. I saw there the pathological phenomenon of blood-lust. . . . Children perched on top of a wall were waving indescribable trophies, dishevelled women were waving their naked arms in the air, and uttering harsh, inarticulate shouts. . . .

As it was obviously too late to save the generals, he did not enter the house, but returned through hostile crowds to where the other prisoners were still under guard, to verify their safety, and then on to his town hall. Only his resolute presence allowed him to dominate the crowd and withdraw from the scene. He describes his descent :

> When groups gesticulated at me, I turned round, went up to them, and asked them to explain their accusations. I told them several times that they had disgraced the Republic and that the murders upon which they were congratulating themselves would have the most disastrous consequences both for them and for the country. . . . If one man had dared to bring out to my face the precise charges that were in the minds of all, a thousand voices would have been raised against me, and my profound conviction is that I would have shared the fate of the generals.[87]

[86] J. Martet, *Le Silence*, pp. 292–3.
[87] Ibid., pp. 296–8.

Thiers had already decided to abandon the city. Seized with panic, he left at 3.30 p.m., and ordered all remaining regular troops, high officials and members of the government to leave. By evening the rebels realized that the city was in their hands. There was no question of defeating the government forces; they found a vacuum, and the Central Committee of the National Guard installed itself in the town hall. They decided to organize elections for that Commune of Paris which had been so much debated since September.

In the meantime the only other claimants to authority in the city were the twenty mayors, who during the siege, by their regular meetings and consultations with the government, had been recognized as the spokesmen of the people of Paris. On 19 March they sent a delegation to talk with the Central Committee. On behalf of the mayors Clemenceau said 'he accepted that the demands of the capital were legitimate, and deplored that the government's action had aroused anger, but he denied the right of Paris to rebel against France'.[88] The main issue was whether the mayors would give their authority to municipal elections. They said they could not, without the consent of the government; they offered to go to the National Assembly and ask for legislation permitting the elections, together with other proposals to satisfy the Parisians' grievances. Those mayors who were also deputies would put this conciliatory programme before the Assembly, Clemenceau proposing a bill for municipal elections, Lockroy one allowing the National Guard to elect its own commander, and Millière one restoring the moratorium on debts. This programme was agreed by both sides.

Next day Clemenceau made his maiden speech supporting municipal elections amid uproar in a violently hostile Assembly. His first clash with the majority came when he interjected into Thiers's speech that the cause of the insurrection was 'that the government had attempted a *coup de force* which failed'. This was not a tactful beginning, and his own speech met with roars of protest when he blamed the government for deserting Paris. Debate continued next day. Thiers agreed in principle, but said that it would take time to draw up a proper bill, and that there could be no compromise with revolutionaries. Clemenceau's proposals aimed at rapid action so that the elections would produce not a revolutionary Commune, but a legal municipal council. He spoke again amidst uproar, and was so upset that he had to explain that, confused by the interruptions, he had gone too far in his condemnation of the government's action. He ended by saying that he had no illusions about the possibility of compromise with the Central Committee of the

[88] P. O. Lissagaray, *Histoire de la Commune de 1871* (1876, ed. Maspero, 1969), p. 123; F. Damé, op. cit., pp. 82–6; C. Rihs, *La Commune de Paris, structure et doctrines* (Geneva, 1955), pp. 27–33.

National Guard, but that the legalizing of the elections would allow moderate opinion in Paris to express itself. In that event, a peaceful solution might be found. Jules Favre followed and produced a hysterical tirade against the revolutionaries. This brought the Assembly to such a pitch of excitement that all distinctions between moderate and extremist opinion in Paris, and between the Central Committee of the National Guard and the anonymous murderers of the two generals, were forgotten. Clemenceau rose again in fury to declare, 'After the provocative speech of the minister for foreign affairs, I declare in my own name, and in that of my colleagues of the Left, that I withdraw my bill'.[89] However, after Thiers had poured oil on the troubled waters, the Assembly agreed to reconstitute the municipal administration on the basis of elected councils in Paris and in the provinces as soon as possible.

That evening the mayors met again to discuss their line of action; they sent Clemenceau and Lockroy to ask the Central Committee to postpone the elections. They were received 'insolently', and their request refused. The mayors then issued a poster calling on the populace to boycott the elections, and the Central Committee of the National Guard responded by turning the mayors out of their town halls and suspending their authority. They were replaced by the revolutionary committees of vigilance which had existed in an ambivalent relationship with the authorities since September. Determined on a last attempt at conciliation, the mayors went again to the Assembly with compromise proposals. Further negotiations led to a division of opinion, and on 25 March one group, including Clemenceau, agreed to give their authority to the elections, which were held the next day. This action was repudiated by the Assembly.[90] The 'party of the mayors' had now split three ways: Delescluze and Millière joined the Commune and were to die on the barricades, Clemenceau and Lockroy resigned their seats in the Assembly and returned to Paris to continue attempts to mediate, while another group remained in the Assembly.

The mayors' authorization meant that many people thought the elections were legal. Half of all registered voters cast their ballots, not a low figure in view of the disorder of the lists and the large numbers who had left the city. About 150,000 votes were cast for representatives who continued to sit when the revolutionary nature of the Commune became apparent. This was about three times the normal revolutionary

[89] The debate of 20 March 1871 is to be found in *Annales de l'Assemblée Nationale* (1871), pp. 29–43. A detailed commentary is given in F. H. Brabant, *The Beginning of the Third Republic in France* (1940), pp. 169–74.
[90] F. Damé, op. cit., pp. 130–213; P. O. Lissagaray, op. cit., pp. 141–8. Texts of the various posters issued by the mayors during this week are given by Damé and by F. Maillard, *Affiches, professions de foi, documents officiels, clubs, et comités pendant la Commune* (1871).

vote in the elections of November 1870 and February 1871. The combination of the hostility of even moderate Parisian opinion to the National Assembly, and the mayors' attempts at compromise, had contrived the worst of both worlds. They had not been able to get out the moderate vote in its normal strength, but by casting a cloak of legality over the elections they persuaded many who otherwise would not have done so to vote; their votes were given to candidates of the revolutionary party. Only in middle-class districts were moderates elected. Elsewhere candidates supported by the revolutionary Committee of the Twenty Districts, bringing together the committees of vigilance in each district, triumphed. In Montmartre a revolutionary list including Blanqui, Ferré and Dereure, the *adjoint* who had been so suspicious of Clemenceau on the morning of 18 March, was elected, while Clemenceau and his friend Lafont received a derisory 752 votes. The attempt to prove that Paris as a whole supported the party of the mayors, and not the revolutionaries, had failed completely.[91] Paris was now in open rebellion, and the second siege had begun, although for the first month there was very little military activity. Thiers had very few troops at his disposal and the Commune did not take the offensive.

3 THE LIGUE D'UNION RÉPUBLICAINE

Even now the group of Radical mayors and deputies – Clemenceau, Floquet and Lockroy – did not give up their attempts to mediate between Versailles and the Commune. On 3 April they decided to set up the *Ligue d'Union Républicaine pour les Droits de Paris*, and published a manifesto demanding the right of Paris to govern herself by a freely elected council, 'sovereign within the limits of its attributions', and 'the defence of Paris, exclusively by the National Guard'.[92] The League's record, in spite of almost daily meetings throughout the six weeks of the Commune, was one of complete ineffectiveness. There was never any real willingness to compromise on either side. Thiers was determined to crush the rebellion by force and to disarm the National Guard. He listened to the proposals of the League simply in order to gain time to assemble a strong force of regular troops. On the other side, as Clemenceau despairingly pointed out, it was impossible to extract from the

[91] R. Wolfe, in his article previously cited, *Past and Present*, 39 (1968), p. 112, has a very just estimate of the significance of the elections: 'On 22 January the committee of vigilance had sought to make a revolution in its own name and failed. Its triumph on 26 March was a result of its defence of a radical programme, which the radicals themselves with very few exceptions were not prepared to uphold by revolutionary means. In this paradox lies the whole essence of the revolution of 18 March and the birth of the Paris Commune.'

[92] *See* A. Lefèvre, *Histoire de la Ligue d'Union Républicaine des Droits de Paris* (1881), and the minute book and other documents in the Floquet papers, Archives Nationales, 49 AP.

Commune any coherent set of realistic political demands: it was a 'body ruled more by instinctive than by political reactions, and which was sending men into battle without a defined aim or any hope of victory'.[93]

It would not be worthwhile to follow the League's fruitless proposals, but its minutes throw a good deal of light on Clemenceau's attitude towards the Commune. The basis of his position was that the majority of the Assembly wanted to overthrow the Republic. Although he never lost his contempt for the revolutionary programme, he wished to use the insurrection to bring about a new balance of forces, to safeguard the Republic. He put this position most clearly in a meeting of the League on 21 April. He reminded the meeting that the Assembly was hostile to the Republic, and that this had been at the root of the revolt of 18 March. They could not rely on Thiers's personal guarantee of republicanism. Thiers could not speak for the Assembly, which alone had sovereign power. We must find a way, he went on, to commit the government. 'That way is the principle of the exclusion of armed force' (i.e. the exclusion of the regular army from Paris). He had been told by Schoelcher that Thiers was willing to let the National Guard keep their arms. 'That is the point to insist on: that is the way to guarantee the safety of the Republic.'[94]

Clemenceau wanted a compromise which would leave the National Guard under the control of radical republicans; they would use it to safeguard the Republic against the monarchist Assembly, while abandoning Utopian schemes of social revolution and decentralization advocated by the Commune. It was a clever idea, but had no chance of being realized. Thiers regarded the complete disarmament of the National Guard as the first priority. And, as the League found whenever it approached the Commune, the revolutionaries had not the least intention of abdicating before the radicals. Swayed by his arguments, the League designated Clemenceau and Floquet as emissaries to the Commune. But the Commune refused to meet them.

Clemenceau also took part in another attempt to provide for the expression of moderate Parisian opinion, midway between the irreconcilable revolutionaries of the Commune and reactionaries of the Assembly. This was a group calling itself *La Conciliation par l'Action*, which put up candidates – some of them supporters of the Commune and others mainly members of the *Ligue d'Union Républicaine* – for the by-elections to the Commune held on 16 April to fill the seats not filled on 26 March. These candidates had no success. Moderate opinion now

[93] At the meeting of the *Ligue d'Union Républicaine* of 16 April 1871, p. 31 of the minute book, Arch. Nat., 49 AP.
[94] Minute book, pp. 78–9, Arch. Nat., 49 AP.

realized that the Commune was a revolutionary body, and one not likely to succeed: the poll was low and revolutionary. These elections showed the futility of attempts to mediate between the Commune and the Assembly. However true it was that this middle way represented the majority view in Paris, in the circumstances of April 1871 it was impossible to find support for it.[95]

The final attempt of the League to mediate came on 5 May when, forced to abandon the idea of direct negotiation, they took up the idea of using a proposed 'Municipal Congress', a meeting of delegates from the municipal councils of the large cities which had chosen republican representatives. Clemenceau hoped that this congress would start a vast republican movement which could be used to put pressure on the Assembly to make terms with the Commune, and guarantee the existence of the Republic. He argued that if the government refused to allow the congress to meet, they should hold it outside French territory, at Geneva. On 8 May Clemenceau was chosen as one of the League's delegates to the Congress scheduled to be held at Bordeaux.[96] Although the delegates were given safe conducts by the Commune, they did not find it easy to get away from Paris. Clemenceau managed it by borrowing an American passport and talking to the sentries in English. Two of the League's delegates got to Bordeaux, only to find that the government had indeed forbidden the Congress and that it had been abandoned. Two other delegates were arrested by the government. Clemenceau avoided arrest, but gave up the attempt to reach Bordeaux. He seems to have tried to get back through the lines to Paris, but, fortunately for his own safety, without success. Eventually he found his way back to his parents' house, and to the wife and baby he had not seen since August. If he had been in Paris the likelihood is that he would have found death at the hands of one party or the other during the Bloody Week of 21–28 May in which the city was recaptured and the insurrection crushed with merciless severity. He wrote to Scheurer-Kestner on 7 May 1871:

> We are a dozen or so of simple souls who have given ourselves the pleasant task of speaking the language of reason to the madmen of all parties who are so gaily taking the remnants of our country to disaster. I need not tell you what encouragement we have had. You will well believe that as soon as my departure does not appear to be a desertion, I shall jump out of this foul sewer where we are all futilely struggling.[97]

[95] F. Maillard, op. cit., pp. 186–8; E. Lockroy, *La Commune et l'Assemblée* (1871), pp. 27–37; C. Rihs, op. cit., p. 190.
[96] A. Lefèvre, op. cit., pp. 251–7; minute book of the League, pp. 194–209, Arch. Nat., 49 AP.
[97] Clemenceau to Scheurer-Kestner, 7 May 1871, Bib. Nat., NAF, 12706, p. 300.

Looking back at the end of his life on his role during the Commune, he remarked ironically,

> It was a good initiation into the stupidity of public life. I found my-self between two sets of people, both of which wanted my death; and even that didn't cure me.[98]

Clemenceau's experience during the Commune was very significant for his future career. He made a fundamental and difficult choice, which he never rescinded. As he wrote to Scheurer-Kestner:

> The greatest moral torment a man can suffer is to have to choose his line of conduct in some supreme crisis which demands an immediate decision, and not be able to see it clearly. In that respect, the torture of my last eight days in the National Assembly will never be sur-passed.[99]

But he did make his decision to break with the Extreme Left in spite of his personal sympathy with Blanqui, Delescluze, Louise Michel and others, who chose the side of the Commune. He made it in spite of his indig-nation against the Government of National Defence, whose incompe-tence, he thought, had lost the war, and his hatred for Thiers and the National Assembly which was seeking to destroy the Republic. Never-theless he did not join the Commune, but adhered to the principles of democratic legality. As he said on many subsequent occasions, revolu-tionary violence was only justified against a régime such as the Empire, which was itself based on illegality and violence. Once the Republic had been established, with free democratic elections, the verdict of the majority must be respected, even if it was repugnant. He would only seek to change it by legal means. His conduct during the Commune goes a long way towards mitigating the often-made charges of im-petuosity. He was passionate and intemperate, but he knew how to restrain his impetuosity: in the last resort his head, not his heart, governed his political actions. He could see what was politically possible, what was in accord with basic principles, and could reject what was not. This rational assessment of the situation is a striking contrast to those who joined the Commune and substituted rhetorical play-acting for sensible political analysis.

His role during the Commune had a decisive influence on Clemen-ceau's subsequent career for at least twenty years. On the one hand the extremely unfair account of his part on 18 March which circulated widely among conservatives, and also among middle-of-the-road repub-lican opinion, and the fact that he had remained in Paris and sought to

---

[98] J. Martet, *Le Silence de M. Clemenceau*, p. 210.
[99] Clemenceau to Scheurer-Kestner, 7 May 1871, Bib. Nat., NAF, 12706, p. 300.

mediate between the Commune and the government, gave the impression that he had been a supporter of the Commune.[100] This was one reason for the sort of tacit veto that excluded him from office. On the other hand the Extreme Left never forgave him for not supporting the Commune. This became the touchstone by which a true Leftist was judged, and on this rock foundered Clemenceau's attempts in the 1880s to build up a strong radical republican party, supported by the working-class voters of Paris.

[100] It was hinted that Clemenceau had done nothing to prevent the murder of Generals Lecomte and Clément Thomas. He fought a duel against an army officer who had made the accusation openly, but nothing could eradicate the suspicion. Clemenceau was particularly hurt as Clément Thomas, who was an old republican of 1848, had been, if not a friend, at least an acquaintance. Scheurer-Kestner recounts that Clemenceau asked him to persuade Madame Clément Thomas to see him, so that he could explain to her that he had done everything he could to prevent the murders. She refused, saying, 'I do not wish to meet my husband's murderer'. Scheurer-Kestner, *Journal*, Bib. Nat., NAF, 12706, pp. 301–3.

Part two

THE RADICAL ATTACK

1871-1889

3

CHALLENGER
FROM THE LEFT

I INTRODUCTION

Clemenceau had two political careers, divided by five years in which
he sought an alternative outlet for his energies in literature and journalism. His first political career was ended by defeat in the 1893 elections,
but had already run into the sands by 1889, by which time his overall
challenge to the ruling republican faction had failed. With the Dreyfus
Affair he made virtually a new beginning, coming into the cabinet for
the first time in 1906 at the age of sixty-four, and going on to become
the grand old man of French politics with his triumphant second ministry of 1917–18 when he became the living embodiment of France's will
to fight to the end for national survival.

This chapter begins by describing the political background of the first
period, in which he challenged the ruling republican groups, who rapidly
became the real conservatives of France.

The Third Republic had been proclaimed on 4 September 1870, but
the circumstances of the war meant that it remained only a provisional
régime, without the moral authority conferred by elections. When the
elections were held in February 1871 they produced a National Assembly
with a majority of monarchists. It was to take eight years before the
Republic was definitely established, during which the question of the
régime monopolized the political stage. In these years Clemenceau played
only a minor role. He acted as a loyal supporter of the republican cause
from the extreme left wing of the republican party. This meant that he
was on the extreme left of legal political life, outflanked only by the
revolutionary Socialists who sought to overthrow existing society, and
all its institutions, both social and political. They were, in any case,
absent from the scene until 1879. Clemenceau had made his choice at the

time of the Commune, and never changed his mind. He rejected revolution once democracy had been established. Representative institutions he thought should be used to provide political and social reform by the will of the majority. The republican movement, even when the extreme left of revolutionary Socialists is ignored, included many different shades of opinion. There were, of course, no political parties in the modern sense, no formal organizations. People talked of the 'republican party' but there was only a movement, an informal grouping of those who adhered to a loose ideology. There were Parliamentary groups, but both their composition and their names changed at frequent intervals. It is better to stick to general descriptive terms for this brief background analysis.

The essential factor in the situation was the rapid evolution of the great bulk of the republican movement from being a left-wing, reforming movement, to one which sought to preserve the *status quo*. As Thiers had said, 'the Republic must be conservative or it will not be at all'. It rapidly became so. Gambetta, the leading republican politician until his death at the end of 1882, who had seemed a dangerous left-wing demagogue in 1870, had evolved by the 1880s into a conservative-minded, middle-of-the-road politician. Ferry, whose position was always slightly to the right of Gambetta, emerged as an even more cautious and conservative political leader. Under the leadership of Gambetta and Ferry, and then of Ferry alone, the great bulk of the republican movement, christened 'Opportunists' because they wished to postpone far-reaching reform to an 'opportune' time, became the bulwark of the existing social and political order. This was only partly because the main planks in the old republican platform had been legislated: many others had been postponed or abandoned.

This evolution opened up the possibility of the creation of a new reforming republican party, the Radical or Radical-Socialist party, to challenge the Opportunist monopoly. As soon as the Republic was firmly established, in 1879, Clemenceau began to mount this challenge from the Left, with the aim of carrying through the full republican programme. His campaign, begun in 1879, and continued through the next decade, reached its high point in the sustained attack on the Opportunists in the election campaign of 1885. But although he was able to defeat his principal rival, Ferry, the situation produced by the 1885 elections proved unfortunate for Clemenceau and the Radicals. For instead of the old monarchist Right fading from the scene, as he had hoped, France's disenchantment with the ruling Opportunist republicans benefited the Right just as much as the Radicals. The evolution of the political forces in these years can best be studied in the accompanying diagrams, which show how the revival of the Right in 1885 produced a three-fold division in the Chamber of Deputies, ensuring that those in the centre held the balance of power.[1] The ruin of Clemenceau's schemes was completed between 1887 and 1889 by the remarkable phenomenon of Boulangism, which posed a serious threat to the continued existence of the Republic. General Boulanger had caught the popular eye while minister of war because of the erroneous idea that he had forced a diplomatic retreat on Bismarck. When he was forced out of office he began to encourage demagogic manifestations which eventually led to his removal from active military command. This allowed him to become the figurehead of an extraordinary political movement between the autumn of 1887 and February 1889. At that point energetic government action led to his flight to Belgium, and the bubble of Boulangism burst even more rapidly than it had blown up; the Boulangists had relatively little success in the 1889 elections, becoming only a small increment of strength to the traditional Right. But the Boulangist phenomenon left several permanent marks on French politics: one of them was the eclipse of the Radical Socialism of the 1880s of which Clemenceau had been a leading exponent. The Third Republic settled into a period of conservatism, from which it was only to be dragged by the Dreyfus Affair.

Boulangism was all the more damaging to Clemenceau in that General Boulanger had first entered politics, as minister of war, under his aegis. Many of Boulanger's lieutenants were ambitious young politicians who had been associated with Clemenceau, and the Boulangist movement which united the Left and the Right against the *immobilisme* of the Centre was in a way a continuation of Clemenceau's earlier campaign. The difference was that with Boulanger the likely beneficiary of a successful challenge to the existing rulers would be the old monarchist Right.

The first part of Clemenceau's career, then, is to be studied against this background of the establishment of the Third Republic in the hands of the conservative Opportunist republicans, and the failure of his attempt to create a viable left-wing Radical-Socialist party in opposition to the ruling group.

2 THE ESTABLISHMENT OF THE THIRD REPUBLIC, 1871–1879

In spite of his bitter experiences during the Commune, Clemenceau did not abandon politics. He was a candidate on the list sponsored by the *Ligue d'Union Républicaine* for the Seine constituency in the by-elections of July 1871. Those elected were predominantly republicans of a conservative variety; only 20,000 votes were cast for Clemenceau, while

[1] *See* diagrams at Appendix IV, p. 422.

90,000 were needed for election. It was a far cry from the radical triumph in Paris in February.[2]

Nevertheless the results overall were a tremendous encouragement for the republicans: nearly a hundred republicans were elected and only a dozen monarchists. Although the monarchists retained their majority in the Assembly the implication was clear: the February elections had been a vote not for the monarchy, but for peace, and the Commune had not produced a conservative backlash. The monarchist argument that it was the inevitable consequence of republicanism was rejected by the electors. As Clemenceau said to his friend Arthur Ranc: 'The Republic is saved: provincial opinion has not been frightened.'[3]

The next month Clemenceau was elected to the Paris municipal council, and to the Conseil-Général de la Seine for one of the Montmartre wards; for the next four years his political activity was confined to local government. He was a member of the poor relief committee, and convener of the children's sub-committee, in which post he attempted to reduce the appalling mortality figures among babies taken into public care. Those who could be breast-fed had a reasonable chance of survival, but the mortality rate among those entrusted to 'nourrices sèches' was forty-two per cent in 1873. The great majority of these babies were, of course, illegitimate. Clemenceau argued that the best solution was to allocate public funds to the mothers so that they could keep their own children.[4]

In the autumn of 1871 he established his family at 15 rue Montaigne, in a respectable residential quarter of Paris. He had a surgery in Montmartre where he combined medical and political consultations, becoming known as 'le médecin des pauvres'. But his medical practice only took a small part of his time, and seems to have been almost entirely charitable. Presumably his father provided his income.[5]

He moved in republican political circles, being a frequent guest of Scheurer-Kestner, who played host to both the supporters of Thiers and of Gambetta. Scheurer-Kestner claimed that these social gatherings did

[2] A. Lefèvre, op. cit., pp. 345–8. O. (really A.) Ranc, De Bordeaux à Versailles (1877), p. 37. W. de Fonvielle, La Foire aux candidats, Paris électoral en Juin 1871 (1871), p. 71. Clemenceau also tried to stand as a Radical republican at Nantes, but was not selected by the local militants. P. Sorlin, 'Gambetta et les républicains Nantais en 1871', Revue d'Histoire Moderne et Contemporaine (1963), pp. 121–6, and P. Eudel, Le Comité républicain de Nantes 1870–74 (Niort, 1903), pp. 213–21, for discussions of a possible candidacy there in the February elections.

[3] J. Jaurès, 'Le Socialisme et le radicalisme en 1885', printed as an introduction to Discours Parlementaires (1904), p. 65: 'Clemenceau said to me, "it was that which solaced Ranc and I the most, as, one evening, walking along the quays of the Seine shortly after the crushing of the Commune, we talked of the future. The first by-elections showed a movement to the Left."' For an analysis of the election results, see J. Gouault, Comment le France est devenue républicaine (1954), p. 116.

[4] Procès-Verbaux du Conseil-Général de la Seine (1871), pp. 703–14; (1874), pp. 761–80.

[5] Sénateurs et députés: silhouettes à la plume (1876), p. 130.

much to reconcile the different tendencies among the republicans, essential if they were to take advantage of the monarchist disunity to engineer the definite establishment of the Republic.[6] Clemenceau's friend Floquet was elected president of the municipal council in May 1875, marking its leftward drift, and Clemenceau succeeded him in November. His inaugural speech stressed the conflict between the Republican ideal and clericalism.[7]

Meanwhile the constitutional laws which were to provide the framework of the Third Republic were at last voted by the Assembly which had at first hoped to restore the monarchy. The trouble was that the majority was divided between Legitimists, Orleanists, and Bonapartists. The refusal of the Comte de Chambord, the Legitimist pretender, to accept the throne on terms acceptable to the Orleanists meant that they melted away to join the republicans. The Orleanists, exponents of constitutional monarchy, found that they had more in common with the conservative republicans than with the Legitimists who followed Chambord in his hankerings after the white flag of the Bourbons and all it symbolized. But a majority could only be attained for the Republic if all the republican deputies cast their votes for a constitution more like the Orleanist monarchy than the republican ideal. A republic traditionally involved a single Chamber legislature, and either no head of state or a democratically elected President, although the collapse of the Second Republic had discredited that idea. The constitution of 1875 provided, it is true, a democratically chosen Chamber of Deputies, but checked its power with an upper house, the Senate, and a President, neither of them directly elected by the people. It was not clear at the time that the President would be a weak figurehead, and that the landowning gentry would lose control of the Senate. It was an agonizing decision for the radicals, but in the end most of them agreed, with the openly declared intention of pressing for constitutional revision, once the principle of the Republic had been consecrated. Thus was prepared the conflict between the Opportunists who wanted to postpone these reforms to an opportune time, which according to the journalists Rochefort meant 'never',[8] and the radicals who demanded their immediate implementation.

When the constitutional laws had been voted, the National Assembly was dissolved, and elections for the first Chamber of Deputies of the new régime were held in February 1876. Clemenceau stood as a Radical, on the extreme left of the republican party. The leader of the extreme left was the old Socialist of 1848, Louis Blanc, in whose Parliamentary

---

[6] Scheurer-Kestner, *Journal*, Bib. Nat., NAF, 12707, IV, pp. 106–7.
[7] *Procès-Verbaux du Conseil Municipal de Paris*, 29 November 1875, p. 885.
[8] In the newspaper *Les Droits de l'Homme*, 11 February 1876. *See* Appendix II below.

group, the *Extrême Gauche*, Clemenceau enrolled when he re-entered the Chamber in 1876. Most of the members of Louis Blanc's group were also in Gambetta's *Union Républicaine*, a duplication which exactly represented their position as a small ginger-group on the extreme left, accepting Gambetta's general leadership.[9]

Clemenceau's electoral programme included the following points: amnesty (i.e. for those condemned for their part in the Commune); free, compulsory and secular primary education; freedom of the press, of meetings and associations; the expulsion of the Jesuits; compulsory military service for all, and 'intégrité du suffrage universel', a vague way of demanding reform of the constitution. In the open letter announcing his acceptance of the programme, Clemenceau devoted considerable space to the social question, albeit in general terms:

> The aim which we set ourselves is to complete the great renewal of 1789, which the bourgeoisie began, but abandoned before its accomplishment, that is the re-establishment of social peace through the development of justice and liberty.[10]

The National Assembly had altered the electoral law, abolishing multi-member constituencies, so Clemenceau was standing only for the 18th district of the city in which his position was very strong. It can have been no surprise when he was elected by 15,204 votes against 3,772, on 20 February 1876.[11]

Shortly after his election Clemenceau made a long speech demanding an amnesty for those condemned for their part in the Commune. He widened the issue into a discussion of the causes of the insurrection, not seeking to defend it, but to explain it in terms other than the naïve conservative view that it was a premeditated attack on society by a vast horde of bandits, led by dangerous agitators. He declared:

> You will not find an insurrection with less premeditation, or one where human wishes had less impact on events . . .

and ended with an appeal for social harmony:

> I tell you that it is only by the reconciliation of classes that you will achieve social pacification. Mere repression will not prevent the

---

[9] L. Blanc, *Questions d'Aujourd'hui et de demain, 5ᵉ serie* (1884), pp. 391–2: Clemenceau was one of those who spoke in favour of allowing members to join other groups simultaneously at the first meeting of Blanc's group. On Louis Blanc's group *see* L. Loubere, *Louis Blanc* (1961), pp. 212–6; on Gambetta's position at this time, P. Barral, *Les Fondateurs de la Troisième République* (1968), p. 117.

[10] Clemenceau's electoral manifesto is printed in J. Kayser, op. cit., pp. 324–5.

[11] Election results in *Biographie Complète des 534 Députés*, by three journalists (1876), pp. 169–73. *See* Appendix III on electoral systems.

recurrence of these crises which grow out of the conflict of capital and labour, out of the sufferings of the workers.[12]

This speech established him as one of the most effective orators in the Chamber, and marked him out as the potential leader of the Extreme Left in Parliament. But his discussion of the means for resolution of the social question was perfunctory. The burden of his proposals was the need for political reform to make the Republic genuinely democratic.

The amnesty was rejected and this question was soon overwhelmed by the renewed threat to the Republic posed by President MacMahon's dissolution of the Chamber on 16 May 1877. The royalists in the National Assembly had forced Thiers to resign in 1873 and replaced him as head of state with MacMahon, a Bonapartist general, who was supposed to prepare the way for a restoration of the monarchy by exercising sweeping personal powers for seven years. The dissolution was perfectly constitutional, but what followed was not. There was a long delay before elections were held, during which a monarchist cabinet sought to put every pressure on the electorate to vote against the republicans. When, in October, the elections produced a new Chamber with a republican majority, MacMahon still refused to appoint a ministry that could command a majority in the Chamber. Instead he made General Rochebouet prime minister, with a cabinet of officials most of whom were not in Parliament at all. The great question was whether the President was planning a *coup d'état*, now it had been proved conclusively that the republicans had a majority. This threat to the existence of the Republic temporarily healed the divisions among republicans. On 6 November 1877 they set up a committee (the *Délégués des Gauches*), of which Clemenceau was secretary, to watch over the situation. Gambetta contacted generals, so as to be able to offer more effective opposition if MacMahon attempted a *coup*. In the end the President gave way, and at the end of December appointed a republican ministry. Talking about these plots fifty years later, Clemenceau found them comical, and declared that it was fortunate that MacMahon had withdrawn: 'otherwise, we would all without doubt have been locked up.'[13] At the beginning of 1878 the crisis was over; only when the republicans won a majority in the Senate in January 1879 did MacMahon finally resign. His obstinate refusal to abandon an untenable position

[12] *Journal Officiel, Annales de la Chambre des Députés*, 16 May 1876, pp. 35–53, cf. J. T. Joughin, *The Paris Commune in French politics 1871–1880* (Baltimore, 1955), I, pp. 112–13, Scheurer-Kestner, *Journal*, Bib. Nat., NAF, 12707, IV, p. 510.
[13] J. Martet, *M. Clemenceau peint par lui-même*, pp. 210–11; Martet prints the minutes of the meeting of the *Délégués des Gauches* of 8 November 1877, in Clemenceau's hand. Cf. also J. Adam (Juliette Lamber), *Souvenirs*, VII, *Après l'Abandon de la Revanche* (1910), p. 85, and Scheurer-Kestner, *Journal*, Bib. Nat., NAF, 12708, pp. 49–53. The most detailed modern study of these events is F. Pisani-Ferry, *Le Coup d'Etat Manqué du 16 Mai 1877* (1965).

did much to ensure that the President was unable to play the important role envisaged by the constitution. Never again did a President of the Third Republic use his power to dissolve the Chamber before its full term had expired; as a result of the events of 1877 the Third Republic had taken a long step towards a 'Régime d'Assemblée', instead of one with a balance of power between the legislature and a strong executive power.[14]

3 CHALLENGER FROM THE LEFT

In 1879 Clemenceau began to strike out for the leadership of the Extreme Left, at first attacking Ferry with Gambetta's encouragement, but then moving on to attack Gambetta as well. His second speech in favour of amnesty for those who had taken part in the Commune, on 21 February 1879, saw the beginning of this ambitious campaign. This issue marked out the Radicals from the Opportunists, and the more Gambetta tried to play it down, the more Clemenceau and his associates stressed it. He attracted much more support in the Chamber on this question than on other issues.[15] It was popular too in his own constituency, a stronghold of the Commune. He also took up the campaign for the validation of Blanqui's election. The old revolutionary had been elected while ineligible because of his imprisonment. Blanqui endorsed Clemenceau's programme.[16] This was surprising, for Clemenceau explicitly opposed both collectivist Socialism and the recourse to violence, two basic elements of Blanquism. The majority of the Blanquists ignored the advice of their leader, and remained the focus of opposition to Clemenceau's brand of Radicalism.

Following these preliminary skirmishes on 12 May 1879 Clemenceau broke with the main body of republicans by launching an attack on Ferry's proposals regarding education and the Church, on the grounds that they were not far-reaching enough. Ferry was seeking to limit the role of the Catholic teaching Orders in French education. Clemenceau argued that Ferry's proposals were unnecessary, as the existing law, if enforced, made membership of these unauthorized Orders illegal. This was so, according to some interpretations, but the Orders concerned had enjoyed fifty years of toleration. They had been tacitly authorized, in that their place in education, both State and private, had been recog-

---

[14] See below, pp. 70-1, and Appendix II, pp. 414-5.
[15] Annales de la Chambre des Députés, 21 February 1879, pp. 178-85, J. T. Joughin, op. cit., I, p. 496, J. Kayser, Les grandes batailles du radicalisme (1962), p. 106.
[16] A. Zévaès, Clemenceau (1949), p. 47, quotes Blanqui's letter. Clemenceau's demand for the validation of Blanqui's election was made in the Chamber on 27 May 1879, Annales de la Chambre des Députés, pp. 215-17, and on 3 June 1879, pp. 62-73. Cf. J. T. Joughin, op. cit., I, pp. 253-6, and pp. 309-10.

nized, notably by the Falloux Law of 1850. Ferry greatly resented Clemenceau's attack, writing to Scheurer-Kestner that it was ridiculous to think that the teaching Orders could be simply expelled from the country without any legislation.[17] Clemenceau argued that it would be enough to abolish the special privileges given to the Church by Napoleon's Concordat and then allow it the normal freedom enjoyed by any association of private citizens. If liberty of association were granted to all, the Church could simply be placed under the common law. Not many anti-clericals were ever prepared to take such a risk. Most thought the Church potentially so powerful that it would be wise for the government to retain special powers to control its activities. Clemenceau did not, however, give the religious question a very prominent place at this time. There was little reason to attack the moderates on this, as a major legislative programme was carried through between 1880 and 1885, the 'lois laïques', which established a national education system, freed from religious influence. Although the Catholic Church continued to be linked to the State by the Concordat, and salaries of the clergy were paid by the government, it would have been difficult for Clemenceau to launch a major attack on the government for its failure to be anti-clerical at a time when Catholic opinion was almost hysterical about the persecution of the Church.

Clemenceau hoped to divide the republicans clearly into a conservative republican party on one hand, and a radical, reformist republican party on the other. In his speech at Bordeaux, during the election campaign of 1885, he stated that the two distinct elements among the republicans, honestly divided on questions of principle, were the Radical group and the conservative group led by Ribot. In between was what he called the party of equivocation, that is, the Opportunists. They declared that they were not conservatives, yet refused to implement any of the reforms of the traditional republican programme. He hoped to force some of the Opportunists to move to the left, and join his genuinely reforming Radical republican party, while the remainder linked up with the avowedly conservative republicans. He was not afraid to admit that he was dividing the republican party. A clear-cut division would allow the electorate to choose between two policies; there was no other way to conduct a genuinely democratic election, and to obtain a governmental majority determined to act. Only if there were two republican lists could the country pronounce its verdict without condemning the Republic itself.

---

[17] Scheurer-Kestner, Journal, Bib. Nat., NAF, 12708, pp. 459–61. Ferry's letter was printed in Lettres de Jules Ferry, 1846–1893 (1914), pp. 274–6. On the anti-clerical laws, see L. Capéran, Histoire Contemporaine de la laïcité française, 3 vols (1957–61), and E. M. Acomb, The French Laic Laws, 1879–1889 (New York, 1941).

The monarchist faction will only be eliminated when, by the alternating rule of the two republican parties, one conservative and one reformist, the mistakes of one section of the republican party no longer harm the Republic itself. . . . M. Ribot, by expounding the programme of the conservative republicans, has greatly aided the formation of a reformist party, and thus has performed a great service to the whole republican party.[18]

Clemenceau's campaign had three aspects. First he established a newspaper, La Justice, to act as his mouthpiece. Then he sought to establish a party organization for his Radical section of the republican party. Thirdly, he developed in a powerful series of speeches in Parliament, his own constituency, and throughout the country, the Radical programme he wished to see enacted.

The first issue of La Justice appeared on 16 January 1880. A large number of daily newspapers were published in Paris, but the great majority had only tiny circulations. This was especially true of those papers linked to a particular political figure or tendency. Even Gambetta's paper, the République Française, which had enjoyed great success for a few years, was now in difficulties.[19] The really successful newspapers with a large circulation were not the organ of one political tendency or individual. Clemenceau aimed to create his own mouthpiece, a Radical newspaper with a large circulation, not a semi-private news-sheet. This was an extremely ambitious and expensive undertaking, and it is surprising that he managed to keep it going until after the collapse of his career in 1893. At first he hoped that it would provide him with a regular income, as the articles of incorporation provided him with a salary of 30,000 francs a year as political director. The editor, his fellow Radical deputy Camille Pelletan, was to get 20,000 francs.[20] These were high sums (£1,200 and £800 respectively) and it is unlikely that the paper ever made enough profits to cover that sort of expense. The initial capital, a sum of 300,000 francs, was provided by Clemenceau's father, and probably accounted for the greater part of his inheritance.

Clemenceau wrote very little in La Justice: only after 1893 did he become a journalist. He confined himself to brief signed statements, usually in response to some attack. His speeches, of course, whether in

[18] G. Clemenceau, Discours prononcé à Bordeaux, 19 juillet 1885 (1885), p. 19.
[19] P. Sorlin, Waldeck Rousseau (1966), p. 314.
[20] Scheurer-Kestner, Journal, Bib. Nat., NAF, 12708, pp. 481–2. Scheurer-Kestner refused to contribute to the financing of the paper, but he drew up the articles of association. He was highly indignant when La Justice began to attack Gambetta, on 27 June 1880: 'From that moment it seemed to have been created with the sole aim of destroying the political influence of Gambetta.' Clemenceau's son stated that his grandfather financed La Justice: Michael Clemenceau et al., Il nous quitta il y a vingts ans (n.d. but 1949); available at Musée Clemenceau.

the Chamber or elsewhere, were reported in detail, often verbatim : and the most important were issued as small yellow-backed pamphlets distributed by the paper at fifteen centimes each, in an attempt to reach a mass public. He exercised close control, reading all the important editorials. They were the main feature of a *'journal d'opinion'* which was not intended to provide detailed news coverage. On most days, after attending the Chamber if Parliament was sitting, he went in the evening to the editorial offices to receive visitors while he supervised the composition of the paper. Besides political acquaintances, he was often visited by personal friends such as the artists Manet, Raffaeli and Carrière, receiving them in his private office, a large and well-furnished room embellished with an Egyptian mummy and a life-size replica of the Venus de Milo.[21]

There was friction between Clemenceau and his editor Pelletan, due partly to the close supervision Clemenceau exercised over the paper, reducing Pelletan's editorial prerogatives. They were also very different personalities. Clemenceau did not touch alcohol, while Pelletan was a great drinker of absinthe. Clemenceau dressed elegantly and was fastidious about his personal appearance. He made a fetish of physical fitness and was an expert horseman and fencer; when he could, he liked to get out into the country, taking long walks in the woods around Paris and making longer trips to the Vendée, which he visited for the opening of *'la chasse'* without fail. Pelletan was a city-dweller, no sportsman, and notorious for the lack of care of his clothes and person. This ill-assorted pair managed to work in harness for thirteen years, and to produce a newspaper that attained a high level of serious discussion of politics, art and literature. The staff included many able men, and the atmosphere was a happy one, providing in itself a liberal education. Clemenceau had wide interests in science, literature and art as well as in politics, while Pelletan had been a pupil of the *Ecole des Chartes*, and had written a thesis on the *Chansons de geste*. Gustave Geffroy, who became a prominent art critic, extended Clemenceau's acquaintance with an appreciation of the *avant garde* in French painting.

The paper was not, however, a financial success. One reason was that its intellectual level was far too high for its political position. Rochefort was much more successful at providing vulgar and sensational journalism which appealed to the majority of the lower-class voters who supported Radical politics. Clemenceau was offering a serious paper which bored them, while the educated middle classes to whom it might have appealed were mainly hostile to its political position. Most newspapers of this sort made losses, and as advertising revenue was negligible, were financed by individuals or interest groups in return for support of various

[21] C. Martel, 'Souvenirs de la Justice', *La Grande Revue* (1909), pp. 726–39.

kinds. Where the paper was controlled by a prominent politician, as was *La Justice*, serious ethical problems must have arisen. Favours could come either in its columns or behind the scenes in the political arena. The French Parliamentary system, in which individual deputies exercised considerable influence, not only in public debate and voting, but even more effectively in the secret discussions of the commissions, provided many opportunities for discreet action of this sort. There is no evidence that Clemenceau permitted anything that could be called corrupt, but such evidence would be hard to find. However, there were rumours that *La Justice* was losing money, and that it was backed by Cornelius Herz, the most corrupt of all the numerous individuals operating in this underworld on the fringes of business, politics and journalism. Herz bought shares in *La Justice* which Clemenceau later bought back, but Herz lost 200,000 francs in the process.[22] It is hard to believe that this was a genuine commercial transaction, although Clemenceau vigorously denied that he had repaid Herz either by facilitating his progress in the Legion of Honour, or by using his political position to advance any of Herz's many money-making schemes. There are obscurities in this relationship that will probably never be explained. Clemenceau seems to have been genuinely taken in by Herz, at least between 1881 and 1885: he even went so far as to draw up a will appointing Herz the guardian of his children. As he said, Herz was a complete scoundrel, but you could not tell that by looking at him.[23] Clemenceau claimed that Herz had bought shares in *La Justice* because he thought it would be profitable, but no one believed this; nor was it true, as he implied, that the relationship ended when Herz sold back the shares in 1885. This association with Herz was to end Clemenceau's first political career in 1893.

The characteristic features of the Parliamentary system of the Third Republic – weak, unstable governments depending on shifting coalitions of deputies who were not disciplined by membership of organized political parties – began to emerge in these years. Whereas in Britain at this time the emergence of organized political parties produced a new Parliamentary system, in France the power of the individual deputy,

[22] A. Dansette, *Les affaires de Panama*, p. 174. P. Sorlin, *Waldeck-Rousseau*, p. 186, states that *La Justice* was at first relatively successful, having a circulation of 10,000 in 1881. But there is evidence that it quite soon became a heavy financial liability. Cf. Engel's letter to Paul Lafargue, 18 January 1885, Engels-Lafargue *Correspondance*, I, p. 260; Arch. Pref. Police BA 89, 22 July 1884: 'Clemenceau is not without anxiety for the future of *La Justice*. Although this paper has seen its circulation increase considerably during the last two years (and it is now between 12 and 13,000) its editorial expenses are high, and its administration gets worse and worse. Clemenceau has up to now been fortunate enough to have a financial backer, who has already put up almost 300,000 francs, but he now refuses to provide any further funds; Clemenceau's own fortune, which is already compromised, cannot provide for the needs of his newspaper.'
[23] J. Martet, *Le Silence de M. Clemenceau*, pp. 212–13.

unrestrained by party discipline, remained. As a result France developed what has been called the *Régime d'Assemblée*, in which the members of Parliament exercised power that their colleagues at Westminster had known only for a brief period between the two Reform Acts. There are deep historical and sociological reasons for the failure of organized political parties to develop in France but the personalities involved and the details of the political battle in these first formative years of the Third Republic certainly played an important part in this situation. Clemenceau's tactics were of considerable importance for the development of the Third Republic. His role was in some ways paradoxical. For although he has been justifiably blamed for contributing so much to the tradition of weak cabinets, dependent on vacillating majorities in the Chamber, he saw clearly the need for the creation of an organized two-party system and thought that he was working towards that end.

At Bordeaux in the summer of 1885 he clearly outlined the essential role of organized political parties in a democratic system of government. He envisaged the development of 'permanent associations, open to all, formed in the commune, the canton and the department, having their own financial resources, achieving through speeches, newspapers and pamphlets, the continuous education of the electorate, organizing and controlling activity. Such associations exist in Belgium, in America and in England. . . .'[24] But his own attempts to develop an organized French Radical republican party had no success. The first of these was called the *Alliance Socialiste Republicaine*, which flourished for about three years in his own constituency, but never spread far beyond its boundaries. The second, the *Ligue Revisionniste*, set up in 1883 to press for revision of the constitution, had even less success.[25]

Equipped with a daily newspaper, prominent in Parliament and public meetings throughout the country, and organizer of various political committees and associations, Clemenceau was ready to make his challenge to the ruling faction in the republican party. In the years between 1880 and 1885 he made this challenge, in the columns of his paper, in crowded and tumultuous public meetings, and in debate after debate. He made over thirty major speeches in the Chamber, in addition to outside speeches, in great contrast to the period afterwards; from 1885 to 1889 he made only four important speeches in the Chamber, and none outside. The contrast is due to the fact that until the 1885

---

[24] G. Clemenceau, *Discours prononcé à Bordeaux, 19 juillet 1885*, p. 4.
[25] The Alliance Socialiste Républicaine has appeared in historical accounts as one of many ephemeral Socialist groups which came and went in these years. Virtually all secondary accounts are based on a few remarks by B. Malon in *La Revue Socialiste*, 25 (1887), p. 56, and ignore Clemenceau's predominant role in the organisation; this is brought out clearly, and in great detail, by the daily reports of the Prefect of Police (BA 89–93) for these years, which pay great attention to the activities of the Alliance Socialiste Républicaine.

elections the conservative republicans had a clear majority in the Chamber, and there was no chance of Clemenceau being called on to form a cabinet. His tactics were aimed at the next elections. Just as the 1881 elections saw the victory of Gambetta's group and the relative defeat of those further to the right, Clemenceau expected that the 1885 elections would provide the opportunity for the Radicals to become the dominant group in the republican party.

He was regarded as dictatorial and arrogant by most politicians. He wanted to be leader in a way that few important men were prepared to accept. His supporters were mainly very young men, like Pichon, Millerand, Laisant and Laguerre, who made their entry into politics as his lieutenants. Most of them, except for the faithful Pichon, broke away sooner or later, leaving Clemenceau isolated. He was feared, but not liked, among political circles, although he had many friends outside politics. In these years he established his reputation as the leading orator and debater of the day, the speaker who could dominate any audience, whether it consisted of a hostile Parliament, or a great popular meeting such as those of the Cirque Fernando which heard his comptes-rendus du mandat. His style was simple, direct, and above all aggressive. He nearly always spoke without detailed notes, and was one of the few genuine masters of debate in the Chamber. Himself a frequent interrupter of others' speeches, if interrupted he made a point of singling out the culprit by name, and challenging him to establish his point. In both procedures he usually managed to make his adversary look foolish. Pelletan, in a brief biography published in a series entitled 'contemporary celebrities', in 1883, gives a remarkable description of his style, and of its impact:

In debate, he is unlike anyone else. He makes no attempt at rhetoric, except for a sharp phrase from time to time or a cutting word. He does not bother with the balanced period or a harmonious style – just unvarnished dialectic. M. Clemenceau's words are like cold, sharp, well-tempered steel and his speeches resemble fencing-matches in which his direct lunges pierce his adversaries.

The energy of his countenance is well-known, like his luxuriant moustaches and close-cropped hair, his impressive fore-head, dark eyes, and strongly marked black brows, all indicating his character. His movements betray a nervous tension, mastered by an iron will and ever watchful self-control. His clear, lively, decisive voice makes his utterances all the more impressive. Many orators have something of the actor about them: the atmosphere of the rostrum invites them to use theatrical gestures and tones; but M. Clemenceau has nothing of this. On the rostrum you have the man himself, at the highest pitch of intensity when in action but just as natural as in ordinary life. He is entirely committed to the cause he is defending and nothing in his speech suggests a pretentious or self-conscious arrangement of his arguments. They are indeed arranged, but his eloquence often conceals this. It is rather as if he pauses from time to time for breath in the course of an attack. . . .

The effect of this sort of eloquence on a Parliamentary assembly cannot be called seductive. The majority in any such assembly consists of quiet men who do not like to be disturbed. But the orator's implacable logic and concentrated energy inspire the respect of his hearers and even convince them. They cannot help being influenced by the directness of his language which makes a frontal attack on every obstacle. . . . It is a difficult task to confront almost the entire assembly from the rostrum, pursuing a reasoned argument and maintaining one's self-control before a hostile audience of five hundred, in spite of their constant murmurs of dissent and their occasional outbursts, when one has only a handful of supporters lost in the crowd. It is not from his triumphant speeches that a man's calibre can be judged, but when his convictions are strong enough to allow him to clash with predominant opinion without flinching and he is capable of asserting his views in such a powerful way as to counter the hostility of the great majority.[26]

4 FIRST ROUND: TUNIS AND EGYPT, 1881–1882

In the spring and summer of 1881 Clemenceau made a major effort in preparation for the general elections. He made several important speeches in the Chamber, joining in the debates of February and March on the laws for establishing freedom of the press and freedom to hold public meetings.[27] On 23 May 1881 he expressed reservations about the treaty of Bardo, although he did not oppose it outright, which would have been difficult in view of the apparent success at virtually no cost of an operation giving France control of Tunis. But he pointed out the diplomatic implications. France had lost a friendship cemented on the field of battle (Italy) and gained a new and dangerous friend (Germany).[28]

On 31 May he made a major speech in the Chamber in support of

---

[26] C. Pelletan, *Georges Clemenceau*, pp. 5–7; for a summary of Clemenceau's ideas, J. A. Scott, *Republican Ideas and the Liberal Tradition in France* (1957), pp. 126–56. In a sample of six weeks' debates, Clemenceau appeared as the second most frequent interrupter, A. Prost and C. Rosening, 'La Chambre des députés 1881–1885, Analyse factorielle des scrutins', *Revue Française de Science Politique*, 21 (1971), p. 24.

[27] *Annales de la Chambre des Députés*, 1 February, 14 February and 31 March 1881.

[28] *See below*, pp. 76–7, for full discussion.

constitutional revision tabled by the Radical deputy Barodet. His main theme was an attack on the Senate as a negation of republican and democratic principles. So far the Senate had rejected or emasculated every reform proposed by the Chamber, while it had agreed to its dissolution by MacMahon. He ended with a justification of his democratic faith in the unrestricted exercise of national sovereignty through a single chamber representative assembly, and declared that this was the only way France could find political stability. The old monarchy had sought a safeguard in Divine Right, the constitutional monarchy in the balancing of separate powers, the Empire in brute force. They had all been swept away by violent revolutions, in spite of their artificial barriers. The only solution was to trust to the uncontrolled exercise of the popular will. Clemenceau argued that this would not lead to chimerical projects and too rapid change as most people feared. Universal suffrage, he said, was an intensely conservative force, not given to dangerous experiments. In spite of appearances, France, although sometimes daring in conception, was imbued with tradition and routine when it came to practical application. Complete democracy would not produce anarchy but at last give France political stability. The bill was, of course, rejected, although ninety-one republicans voted for it, many more than the normal Radical vote, as many of Gambetta's supporters were committed to constitutional change.[29]

August was devoted to electioneering; Clemenceau was busy, standing in three constituencies, in both parts of the 18th district of Paris and also at Arles in the far south. The main theme of his campaign speeches was the need for revision of the constitution, and an attack on clericalism, but he was drawn into arguments about Socialism with doctrinaire hecklers. He was able to point out that the practical part of the Collectivist Socialist programme was exactly the same as his, while their other supposed point of difference, that the workers should be represented by workers and not by bourgeois politicians, came oddly from a party led by Dr Brousse, whose social status was exactly the same as Clemenceau's: both were doctors of medicine. The voting showed that the Collectivist Socialists were a mere handful; his opponent in one of the Montmartre districts, Dereure, the man who had been his assistant at the *mairie* in 1870–1, and who had joined the Commune, got a derisory 468 votes against Clemenceau's 11,426.[30]

Clemenceau's election manifesto began with an attack on Ferry and his policy of systematic adjournment and compromise. There followed seventeen articles, making up the programme, beginning with a call

<hr>

[29] *Annales de la Chambre des Députés*, 31 May 1881, pp. 230–7.
[30] Clemenceau's speeches are reported in detail in *La Justice*: see, especially, 14–15 August, 22 August, 23 August, giving the results of the first ballot.

for 'constitutional revision, suppression of the Senate, and of the President of the Republic, ratification of the constitution by the people'. Six out of seventeen articles were concerned with political reform. Following the first article, there were demands for full individual liberty, freedom of the press, of meeting and association, election of magistrates, abolition of the death penalty, shorter Parliaments, *'assimilation du mandat politique au mandat civil'*, administrative decentralization and communal autonomy. Further articles demanded the Separation of Church and State, free, compulsory and secular education, divorce, and progressive taxes on income or capital, and on inheritances. Turning to social reform the programme asked for legal limitations of hours of work and prohibition of children's work in mines and factories, the recognition of trade unions and various measures to improve the position of the worker against the employer, and revision of the contracts by which the state had ceded public property to railway, mining and canal companies. Thus, as well as the intransigent demand for the establishment of a fully democratic political system, a considerable amount of attention was paid to the social question. As in a previous speech at Marseilles in October 1880, there was a close resemblance between Clemenceau's proposals and the so-called minimum progamme of the Collectivist Socialists. The last article, making obeisance to extreme republican democratic theory, said: 'the present programme will be accepted and signed by the candidate. He promises to give a report on his mandate at least once per session.' This was followed by Clemenceau's reply, which expressed his claim to represent the true republican tradition betrayed by Gambetta and Ferry. Gambetta had represented the neighbouring working-class area of Belleville since 1869, when his 'Belleville programme' had achieved fame as the summary of republican demands. Since then he had evolved towards a much more conservative position, and in this campaign he met furious opposition which prevented him from speaking. He managed to win re-election in one of the two Belleville constituencies, but only by a narrow margin; like Clemenceau he stood in both areas into which his constituency had been divided. Referring to Gambetta's betrayal of his old ideas, Clemenceau ended his manifesto:

What is your programme, but the reforms which the republican party has always advocated against the monarchical principle, still so vigorous in our institutions, in order to prepare the grand social transformation which will crown the Revolution? I accept this programme, because it is that of the entire republican democracy. It is the flag which you placed in the heights of Belleville and Montmartre in 1869, defying the triumphant Empire. The country was at first amazed at such daring, but in the hour of peril it was to that flag that it rallied. Citizens, in Montmartre, that flag still flies where you planted it; you will not allow it to be taken down. Long live the democratic and social Republic![31]

In contrast to Gambetta's poor showing, Clemenceau was elected with large majorities in both constituencies, and at Arles. At Arles he stood down for Granet, his Opportunist opponent who agreed to adopt Clemenceau's programme; this opened his association with Granet, who proved to be a doubtful character. In one of the Paris constituencies he stood down for his old friend J. A. Lafont, who was elected with his endorsement. Clemenceau's success was part of a general Radical victory in Paris and in the Rhône valley. Twenty-three out of thirty-two candidates supported by *La Justice* in the Seine department were elected. Throughout France the paper claimed that sixty-two of its candidates had been elected, while only two sitting Radicals were defeated.

As soon as Parliament reassembled Clemenceau launched an attack on Ferry for his conquest of Tunis. This began the four-year duel between Ferry and Clemenceau on the question of colonial expansion. One of the main questions in French politics between 1881 and 1885 concerned the acquisition of what was to become a colonial empire, second only in territorial extent to that of Britain. The reasons for this sudden expansion, in which France led the way, but in which she was soon followed by other European powers, have been much debated by historians. The older school, which ascribed colonialism to economic causes, has been discredited by recent studies. The prime motive was political; Professor Ganiage has thoroughly documented the reasons for the sudden reversal of policy that took France first into Tunis and then into Indo-China.[32] It was a deliberate move to reassert France's political role. Overshadowing everything was the defeat of 1870 and the loss of Alsace-Lorraine to Germany. The obvious imbalance of power between France and Germany made any attempt at *revanche* impossible; indeed France, still diplomatically isolated, was afraid that Germany would attack again. The only way, then, for France to play an active role in the world was to expand outside Europe, across the Mediterranean, or even further afield.

The danger of inaction was that Italy might well take over Tunis. exposing the eastern frontier of Algeria. The arguments against an active policy were, however, of weight. It might alienate Italy, as indeed happened, leading to the Triple Alliance; it might make France depend

---

[31] J. Kayser, op. cit., pp. 326–9.
[32] *See* J. Ganiage, *Les origines du protectorat français en Tunisie, 1861–1881* (1959) and *L'expansion coloniale de la France sous la 3ᵉ République 1871–1914* (1968); H. Brunschvig, *Mythes et Réalités de l'Impérialisme Colonial Français 1871–1914.*

on Bismarck's goodwill, another danger which also materialized to some extent, and it was certain to prove a domestic political liability. On 31 March it was announced in Paris that a nomad tribe, the Kroumirs, had crossed the frontier from Tunis into French Algeria on a marauding expedition. A punitive expedition was despatched, but the vague powers given to its commander included authority to conclude a treaty with the Bey of Tunis. On this narrow basis the Treaty of Bardo was concluded, providing for over seventy years of French rule under the legal façade of protectorate.

The original pretext for the expedition was patently false, and satirical opponents in Paris said that the government would pay a reward to anyone who could actually find a Kroumir. Instead it made straight for the capital, which was occupied without serious resistance, and imposed the Treaty of Bardo on the helpless Bey on 12 May 1881. Thus Parliament was presented with a *fait accompli*, and the treaty was ratified on 23 May 1881 by a vote of 430 to 1.[33] The dissentient was not Clemenceau but another Radical, although Clemenceau's speech posed several awkward questions. In fact he abstained, after a speech in which his main grounds of criticism were not the actual occupation, but the fact that there had been no Parliamentary authorization. Only after the elections did *La Justice* begin a sustained attack on Ferry's policy in Tunis.

The opportunity was provided when a rebellion of the war-like desert tribes occurred, and a larger army had to be sent to fight a serious campaign. This alerted French opinion to the dangers of colonial expeditions in a way impossible in May when complete control of Tunis seemed to have been achieved without effort. Disappointed speculators provided the newspapers and politicians of the Extreme Left with information which enabled them to launch an attack on their more successful rivals. At the end of September the theme of sinister financial manipulations first began to be voiced in *L'Intransigeant* and *Le Petit Parisien*, soon to be taken up by *La Justice*, and in Clemenceau's violent attack on Ferry in the Chamber on 8 November.

Ferry was in a difficult position, for there was no doubt that some individuals had profited by the seizure of Tunis, although this financial speculation was not the motive of the French government's action.[34] Ferry could not admit the real political and diplomatic motives behind the expedition, and economic considerations had been put forward as the official justification in the diplomatic Yellow Book: to confine an explanation to the Kroumirs would have been absurd, so French interests in the Enfida affair, involving speculation in land as well as in matters

---

[33] *Annales de la Chambre des Députés*, and J. Ganiage, op. cit., pp. 132, 673–4.
[34] J. Ganiage, op. cit., pp. 640–58, 675–6 and 694–8.

of railway concessions and submarine telegraph cables, were brought forward. Ferry's defence of his policy was clumsy and inadequate. His position was weak because of the electoral triumph of Gambetta's faction among the Opportunists over Ferry's more conservative supporters. Everyone was awaiting the formation of a Gambetta government, and it was obvious that Ferry's cabinet could not last long. The debate ended in inextricable confusion. The Extreme Left and Right joined to attack the Government, an attack of which Clemenceau's speech was the most effective part. The Opportunists, divided between supporters of Ferry and of Gambetta, were unable to produce a majority for any resolution, either for or against Ferry. No fewer than twenty-three resolutions were defeated in hours of confused debate. Finally Gambetta saved the day by proposing a resolution which neither condemned nor supported Ferry, but simply declared that the Chamber approved 'the integral execution of the treaty made by the French nation', which was carried 355 to 68 with 124 abstentions. Ferry resigned immediately, and Gambetta replaced him as prime minister.[35]

The Radicals remained in opposition during Gambetta's ministry, and by voting with the Right and part of the Centre, brought it down on 26 January 1882. The issue on which Gambetta fell was constitutional revision. He proposed to replace the life senators by elected senators, and to change from single-member to multi-member constituencies for the Chamber of Deputies. This was a traditional republican demand, on the grounds that small constituencies in rural areas allowed undue influence to local notables, while large multi-member constituencies would replace personalities by ideas in the political battle. However, the commission which reported on this bill, of which Clemenceau was a member, produced a hostile report; Gambetta made it a question of confidence, but the Chamber still voted against him; the 'grande ministère' fell after six weeks. This turned out to be virtually the end of Gambetta's political career, as he died on the last day of 1882.[36] The Radicals justified their opposition by saying that they wanted a much more far-reaching revision and thus were not prepared to vote for small changes, but the real reason was hostility to Gambetta; many felt that multi-member constituencies would place too much power in his hands as party leader. Thus as long as Gambetta remained alive, very little was heard of further proposals for constitutional revision. After Gambetta's death. Clemenceau returned to advocacy of multi-member constituencies. He argued that it would lead to the development of organized, disciplined, political parties. Modern political science would seem to support this

---

[35] *Annales de la Chambre des Députés*, 8–9 November 1881, pp. 149–84.
[36] L. Andrieux, *A travers la République* (1926), pp. 295–6; A. Scheurer-Kestner, *Journal*, Bib. Nat., NAF, 12708, p. 329.

view, but the system of multi-member constituencies was not given time to prove itself in France. Adopted for the 1885 elections, the Boulangist scare led to its abandonment before those of 1889, and France reverted to single-member constituencies, with a double ballot.[37]

Gambetta was only in office a short time, but during those few weeks he set in motion the train of events that led to the British occupation of Egypt. Early in 1882 he proposed joint Anglo-French action in Egypt. Preoccupied by other questions, Gladstone's government was extremely reluctant to get involved,[38] but as opposition to the Tunisian expedition had shown, there was considerable anxiety in France about military commitments overseas, and this was one factor in the vote that led to the fall of Gambetta's cabinet on 27 January 1882. Henceforth French policy was in the hands of the vacillating Freycinet; the British cabinet were equally uncertain and divided on the course to follow, and the two governments produced a compromise policy – a show of naval force in Alexandria harbour – that merely exacerbated Egyptian nationalism, leading to riots on 12 June 1882 in which sixty Europeans were killed. This convinced the British government that firm action was required, but Freycinet ordered the French fleet to withdraw, leaving the British alone to bombard Alexandria. The British government then decided on military occupation of Egypt, if possible with French participation, although Gladstone declared that the British would act alone if necessary. Freycinet asked the Chamber for a vote authorizing the credits required, insisting on the limited and temporary nature of the expedition.[39]

Clemenceau's brilliant speech dominated the debate. He began by opposing the idea of the inequality of human races, claiming that it was ridiculous when the idea of immutability of species had been banished from biological science by Darwin. He argued that European civilization could transform backward societies through peaceful economic and cultural penetration, without political and military intervention. He claimed that the genuine Egyptian nationalist party was represented not by military adventurers like Arabi, whose seizure of power had sparked off the Anglo-French intervention, but by men such as Cherif Pasha and Nubar Pasha, who, far from wishing to expel Europeans, welcomed them provided they came not as conquerors but to bring Egypt the benefit of European ideas and European economic

[37] P. Campbell, *French Electoral Systems and elections 1789–1957* (1958), pp. 70–80 and 34–7; M. Duverger, *Political Parties: their organisation and activity in the modern state* (1954), pp. 228–45, and see Appendix III below.
[38] J. Gallagher and R. Robinson, *Africa and the Victorians* (1961), p. 120.
[39] J. Ganiage, *L'expansion Coloniale*, pp. 94–101; cf. also, for general accounts of the Egyptian crisis, J. Gallagher and R. Robinson, op. cit., pp. 89–121, and P. J. V. Rolo, *Entente Cordiale, the origins and negotiation of the Anglo-French agreements of 8 April 1904* (1969), pp. 37–49.

enterprise. According to Scheurer-Kestner, Clemenceau's whole speech was dictated to him by Nubar Pasha. This would partly account for the extremely inaccurate views about the nature of Egyptian nationalism which he propounded. For Nubar Pasha was an Armenian Christian, who had been educated in France, and was completely Europeanized, not even speaking Arabic. Cherif Pasha was also a moderate, ousted by Arabi in February 1882. The difficulty of the Egyptian situation was that men such as Nubar Pasha and Cherif Pasha could not maintain themselves in power without direct European military intervention.[40]

Clemenceau's most telling arguments, however, were not concerned with the Egyptian situation but with the diplomatic balance in Europe. He argued that military intervention would not be temporary; it would last for a long time, and a joint occupation would inevitably produce conflict with England.

Indeed, the unilateral British occupation poisoned Anglo-French relations for twenty years. His final peroration was a simple appeal for eternal vigilance in Europe: France could not afford to allow her attention to be diverted from the blue line of the Vosges:

Europe is covered with soldiers: everybody is expectant, all the powers are keeping their hands free, let France remain uncommitted.

The battle of Tel-el-Kabir was to place Egypt under British control with virtually no casualties; and the tension produced between Britain and France remained for the next twenty years one of the most telling constraints on French policy. Abstention had certainly not given France more freedom of action. But it would be unfair to place responsibility for these developments on Clemenceau. The overwhelming rejection of an active policy in Egypt shows that this was the decision of the great majority of Opportunists, not just of the Radical faction. The vote of credits demanded by the government was rejected by 416 votes to 75, and the Freycinet cabinet fell – a third scalp to add to Clemenceau's collection. There was, however, no question of the Radicals being invited to join the government. The insignificant Duclerc formed a new cabinet, a coalition of the Left Centre (*Centre Gauche*), the most conservative republican group, and second-rank Opportunists. Parliamentary politics entered a quiescent period until the end of 1882.

---

[40] Clemenceau's speech is in *Annales de la Chambre des Députés*, 29 July 1882, pp. 1184–9. A. Scheurer-Kestner, *Journal*, Bib. Nat., NAF, 12708, pp. 385–6. On Nubar Pasha *see* Lord Cromer, *Modern Egypt*, I, p. 70, and II, pp. 336–9.

4

CLEMENCEAU
VERSUS FERRY

I CLEMENCEAU VERSUS FERRY, 1883–1885

In February 1883 Ferry became prime minister for the second time, forming a ministry that was to last for more than two years. Gambetta's death had simplified the political situation, as the Opportunists were no longer divided between supporters of Ferry and of Gambetta. A few of Gambetta's followers moved left to join the Radicals, while the great majority decided to support Ferry. Ferry's theme was that 'the peril is on the Left', implying that the monarchists no longer posed a serious threat, and that it was time for a realignment of French politics on new issues. *The Times* wrote that the central issue in French politics was now the conflict between the governmental republicans, led by Ferry, and the Radical opposition, led by Clemenceau.[41] From 1883 to 1885 there was a duel between Ferry and Clemenceau, the recognized leaders of the two wings of the republican party, centering on three issues: constitutional reform, the social question, and colonial policy.

Clemenceau made a long speech on constitutional reform on 6 March and others on the election of magistrates covering much the same ground on 22–3 January and 2 June.[42] His basic point was that the democratic principle should be applied to the judiciary as well as to the legislature. There was general agreement among republicans that those magistrates closely associated with political trials under the Empire and at the time

---

[41] *The Times*, 24 February 1883. There was, however, only an incipient tendency to polarization. A recent analysis using computers and factor analysis has found that there was little disciplined voting except among a small group around Clemenceau, A. Prost and C. Rosening, op. cit., p. 16.

[42] *Annales de la Chambre des Députés*, 6 March, pp. 565–80, 22–23 January, pp. 117–40, 2 June, pp. 548–53.

of the *Ordre Moral* (1873-8) should be purged; the principle of election, laid down at the Revolution, was part of traditional republican doctrine. He said that it was a great error to think that universal suffrage would support dangerous and frequent innovation. It was in reality profoundly conservative, and a fully democratic system was the only way for France to achieve political stability.

> Instead of wasting time seeking to limit popular sovereignty by means of institutions that have been condemned by experience, it is time we realized that there is nothing more conservative, in the true sense of the term, than popular sovereignty itself.[43]

At the same time Clemenceau took a prominent part in the formation of the *Ligue Républicaine pour la révision des lois constitutionnelles*, designed to put pressure on Parliament from the outside. Scheurer-Kestner wrote of this:

> It was a League composed of all the *déclassés*, malcontents, fishers in troubled waters, Bonapartists, clericals, monarchists, Caesarians in France, with Clemenceau at their head. But it misfired; the country was not interested. . . . My poor friend Clemenceau was beginning to lose touch with political reality.[44]

The Radical Parliamentary group decided on the creation of the League on 7 March 1883. Its first manifesto was published in *La Justice* on 22 March 1883; its president was Laurent-Pichat, an old friend of Clemenceau from his student days, and its secretaries his lieutenants, Pelletan, Laisant and Laguerre. (The two last became principal associates of Boulanger.) It claimed the support of five senators, sixty-five deputies, twenty-one Paris newspapers and fifty-eight provincial newspapers. Revision required a majority of both houses of Parliament sitting together; as the main item of the Radical programme was the abolition of the Senate, the Senate was not likely to embark on the process. Although revision could not begin without a favourable vote from each house, once the National Assembly met it was sovereign; the senators would be outnumbered and would have no veto. The Senate only agreed to a meeting of the National Assembly, as the joint session of the two houses was called, when they had a firm promise from the government and its supporters that revision would be limited to an agreed set of proposals. In law nothing could stop a majority of the National Assembly legislating as it saw fit, but the majority were bound by their word of honour to limit themselves to the agreed programme. The National Assembly

---

[43] *Annales de la Chambre des Députés*, 6 March 1883. p. 568.
[44] A. Scheurer-Kestner, *Journal*, Bib. Nat., NAF, 12709, p. 32. Arch. Pref. Police BA 92, 24 March 1883 et seq.; J. Kayser, op. cit., p. 126.

eventually met in August 1884, and in spite of opposition from the Radicals and the Right carried out the agreed programme.

Clemenceau argued that the agreement was void; nothing could limit its sovereignty. He declared that the problems of social and political reform were inextricably linked. Only by abolishing the Senate and establishing a democratic constitution could France provide the political framework for legislation to improve the lot of the lower classes; and only by dealing with the social problem could France achieve political stability.[45]

His arguments had no effect on the majority. The agreed programme was carried out, and new legislation on the composition of the Senate was passed in the autumn of 1884. The upshot was a very minor change. No more life senators were to be elected, and as the existing ones died, their seats were to be given to the more populous departments; other changes in the senatorial electoral colleges went a small way towards redressing the balance away from the smallest communes to the larger ones. But this did not alter the predominance of rural and small-town France in the choosing of senators. The Senate was to the end of the Third Republic the instrument by which the rural areas exercised a veto over the whole political machine. This came to be a veto exercised in the interests of moderate Republicanism and then of Radicalism. By that time Clemenceau himself was a senator for one of the most sparsely populated and economically backward departments. Revision of the constitution was still prominent in his election manifesto of 1885, but in his campaign speeches was far outweighed by attacks on colonial policy. The failure of the *Ligue pour la Révision* convinced Clemenceau that there was little public interest in questions of constitutional law.

Clemenceau's second main theme was the social question. The collapse of the *Union Générale* bank in 1882 led to a financial crash which ushered in a long period of depression. Although economic historians are no longer certain about the 'great depression' of the 1880s as a world phenomenon, these were certainly bad years for France. The phylloxera disease in the vineyards, and the fall in grain prices, produced an agricultural depression. France did not have the rapid industrial development that mitigated the agricultural crisis in Germany. Up to this time the Republic had been fortunate, for economic prosperity had accompanied its first years. Now it had to face hard times, which partly accounts for the large anti-governmental vote in 1885 and later for much of the popular support for Boulanger. The most distinctive of Clemenceau's political ideas was his linking of political and social questions ever since 1876. When he talked about constitutional reform he said that it was required so that social legislation could be passed, and when he talked

[45] *Annales de l'Assemblée Nationale*, 13 August 1884, pp. 82–9.

of the social question he declared that its solution was a prerequisite for long-term political stability. The catastrophe of the Commune, when political conflict and social discontent had fused into a class war of the most ferocious kind, was always present in his thinking. Again and again he returned to the theme that political and social questions were linked, that the task of his generation was to safeguard the political programme of the French Revolution by working out its implications in terms of social reform and economic progress. This was the burden of his speeches of 1876 and 1879, demanding a full amnesty for those who had been condemned for their part in the Commune. As he said on 9 March 1882: 'at the bottom of all our revolutions, there is a social evil, as well as a political evil, and the republican reformation must be both a political and a social reformation.'[46]

In view of his reputation after 1906 as the enemy of Socialism it is hard to realize that at this time, when definitions were much less clear-cut, Clemenceau was regarded, and regarded himself, as an advocate of Socialism. Clemenceau first achieved notoriety by his demands for social reform in a speech at the Cirque Fernando on 11 April 1880, but in his speech at Marseilles on 28 October 1880 he made his most determined bid to occupy ground claimed by the revolutionary Socialists. Mostly it was devoted to the political programme of Radicalism, the need to establish freedom of the press, freedom to hold public meetings and form associations, to destroy the Napoleonic administrative system, and that other strait-jacket Napoleon had fixed on the country, the Concordat with the Catholic Church. But at the end he turned to the social question, remarking that as political questions came to be settled and the Republic came to be accepted by all, 'questions of social reform will supersede political questions'. In these closing phrases he welcomed the development of workers' associations, and Socialist congresses; saying that as they develop they will come to represent more exactly the opinions of the whole body of workers, and their solutions will become clearer and more practical.

At the moment the existence of so many different Socialist sects shows that so far no great idea has developed which can rally the support of the masses.[47]

---

[46] *Annales de la Chambre des Députés*, 9 March 1882, p. 325. P. Sorlin, *Waldeck Rousseau*, p. 490, includes Clemenceau along with Ferry and Floquet as the generation of republicans, formed under the Empire, who thought only of political problems, ignoring economic and social questions. This is quite wrong as far as Clemenceau is concerned. On the economic depression *see* the thesis of J. Néré, *La crise industrielle de 1882 et le mouvement Boulangiste* (Sorbonne, 1959). On Clemenceau's ideas, *see* M. Sorre, 'Clemenceau: notes sur l'empiricisme radical', *Cahiers de la République*, I (1956), pp. 43–9, and J. A. Scott, op. cit.

[47] *Discours prononcé par M. Clemenceau à Marseille le 28 octobre 1880* (1880), pp. 27–8.

Nevertheless, he went on, agreement can be reached on many important points. He listed them as *éducation intégrale*, the replacement of indirect taxes by a progressive income tax and a tax on inheritance, the encouragement of tradesmen's and workers' cooperatives, and of facilities for provision of credit and insurance for the working class. There followed a section which was taken textually from the Marxist Guesde's minimum programme, including limitation of hours of work, prohibition of child labour, and the running of railways, mines and canals by their workers.[48] All these items could be found on earlier Radical Socialist platforms, notably Louis Blanc's, but their combination, and the textual quotation from Guesde's programme, produced a remarkable effect. Respectable republicans regarded Clemenceau as having moved far to the left. At that time Marx and Engels congratulated themselves on having found a new recruit. Marx wrote to Sorge on 5 November 1880:

> My son-in-law is a journalist on *La Justice*. He has worked to such effect that Clemenceau, who previously opposed Socialism, and advocated an American type of democratic republic, has, in his Marseilles speech, not only adopted our general line, but taken over parts of our minimum programme word for word.[49]

The son-in-law referred to was Charles Longuet, who had known Clemenceau when editor of a student review to which Clemenceau contributed nearly twenty years earlier. In May 1880 Clemenceau had gone to London where Longuet introduced him to the leading figures of the Socialist movement, including Marx and Professor Beesly.[50] Longuet occupied a prominent place on *La Justice*, frequently writing leading articles. In August 1880, when Clemenceau went away on holiday, he left Longuet in charge.[51] For several years Longuet and Clemenceau continued to work together. But Marx was soon disillusioned if he thought that Longuet was going to convert Clemenceau to Marxist Socialism; it was the other way round, and Longuet was one of those who hoped, with Clemenceau, to build a bridge between moderate Socialism and Radicalism.

Marx's idea that he had 'hidden strings which directed all the leaders of French Socialism from Benoit Malon and Guesde to Clemenceau', was never more than the dream of an old conspirator who compensated for the dreary reality of failure with grandoise visions of an international

---

[48] Ibid., pp. 30–1. The text of the Guesdist minimum programme is printed in M. Prélot, *L'évolution politique du socialisme français* (1938), pp. 92–4. Cf. A. Zévaès, *Notes et Souvenirs d'un militant* (1913), pp. 235–75.
[49] Marx to Sorge, 5 November 1880; Marx-Engels, *Werke*, 34 (Berlin, 1966), pp. 476–7; also Engels-Lafargue, *Correspondance*, I, p. 314.
[50] *Le Prolétaire*, 22 May and 12 June 1880; J. T. Joughin, op. cit., I, p. 396.
[51] Arch. Pref. Police, BA 89, 26 August 1880.

network dictating the political future of all Europe from his suburban villa in North London.[52] We know no more of Marx's views on Clemenceau, although it is possible that the two men met for a second time when Marx was staying in Paris immediately before his death in 1883. After Marx's death Engels continued to maintain an extensive correspondence with Socialist leaders in different European countries. Clemenceau figures frequently in this correspondence and on several occasions Engels attempted to persuade French Marxists to moderate their hostility towards him. Engels no longer expected Clemenceau to evolve towards Socialism and pointed out his basic doctrinal deficiencies in such points as the class struggle, and the abolition of private property. But as a tactical move Engels advised Guesde and the French Marxists to work for a Clemenceau government, although without much success. He saw this as an essential stage for France before going on to Socialism. Thus the sooner Clemenceau came to power the better. Then, declared Engels, his Radical-Socialism would be exposed as empty words and useless panaceas and his working-class support would melt away: in the well-known phrase, he was to be supported by the Marxists as 'the rope supports the hanged man'.[53]

Clemenceau's insistence on social reform marked him out as being on the extreme left of the republican party, and produced much of the exaggerated fear and hatred he inspired. His declaration that if social reform were denied the inevitable result would be a renewed explosion of class warfare, was misinterpreted by his conservative opponents as though he had made himself an advocate of such class warfare. There was a significant exchange between Clemenceau and Ferry during the debate on the social question in January 1884, when Clemenceau said: 'the next election will perhaps be fought on the social question. People will not be saying, "Let us make a Revolution and cut off the heads of the bourgeois", but they will be saying, "There is abominable social and economic injustice, some are too rich, and some too poor".' This produced 'exclamations and disturbances in different parts of the chamber', and Ferry interjected: 'No one has ever used such language in the Chamber before.' Clemenceau had to insist that, contrary to Ferry's misunderstanding, he was not supporting such talk, but saying that they must carry out social reform so that revolutionary violence could be avoided. He went on:

---

[52] Marx to Sorge, 5 November 1880; Marx-Engels, Werke, 34, p. 477. Already, by 30 September 1882, Marx admitted that Clemenceau had moved away from the Socialists again, Marx-Engels, Werke, 35, p. 100.

[53] See, for instance, Engels to Becker, 2 April 1885, Marx-Engels, Werke, 36, pp. 292–3. 'Before long Clemenceau will come to power, and then the workers will see how empty his promises are', Engels to Lafargue, 8 August 1885, Marx-Engels, Werke, 36, p. 353. 'Clemenceau will be in the next government: he is the last man the bourgeoisie has'.

We must decide in what way the State can intervene, without harming individual initiative, but by fostering and helping it. . . . We must find out if we can put an end to the period of revolution, or whether we are to continue having a social war every twenty years. . . . It is easy to say 'Such language has never been heard at the rostrum.' You remain shut up in your ministry, without ever looking out of the window. But we must have the courage to face up to the problem, and not shut our eyes to it. The social problem will emerge one way or another, either legally or illegally, as the masses gain understanding of their rights, and the State will be obliged to intervene.[54]

That Clemenceau rejected the dogmas of Collectivism, and was opposed by the Socialist sects, does not mean that his support for Socialism was spurious. The Guesdist, Broussist and Blanquist sects had some small support among the working-class districts of Paris; only after 1885 did they begin to build up serious electoral strength even there, while in the rest of France their influence was infinitesimal. Many who were later leading figures in French Socialism – Lucien Herr, Jean Jaurès and Léon Blum – were greatly influenced by Clemenceau's ideas in these years. Jaurès gave an extremely sympathetic picture of Clemenceau's position at that time:

For him the Revolution was a living force which had stimulated countless aspirations, a driving force that would go on growing in fervour until all human powers had developed to translate into reality its scheme of justice. While Ferry wanted to freeze it, he wished it to keep all the fluidity of a flame. What successive forms would be taken by human society under the influence of the continuing fire of the Revolution? No one could tell in detail, for the future was not determined. But it was certain that revolutionary democracy had not yet reached its full development. . . . Let the bonds be broken, the Church, the Senate, ignorance, bourgeois timidity; let the rational energy and political force of the people develop, protected against oppression and economic exploitation by the laws. . . . Then the people would be master of its own destiny. He was not afraid of Socialism, even if its advocates were utopian and supporters of violent revolution. In their own way they provided a driving force for reform, and roused a slumbering society that had to feel threatened to escape from its own egoism. Clemenceau was imbued with the revolutionary and republican tradition that had often in the past brought together bourgeois democrats and communists in the same fight for liberty and justice.[55]

[54] *Annales de la Chambre des Députés*, 31 January 1884, p. 289.
[55] J. Jaurès, 'Le Socialisme et le radicalisme en 1885', *Discours Parlementaires*, I, p. 40.

For Clemenceau the first priority was to achieve basic democratic reforms. But beyond that, and to be pursued at the same time by the radical wing of the republican party, were the social and economic reforms to improve the lot of the poor. The State should intervene by enacting laws protecting the worker against dangerous conditions, limiting hours of work, prohibiting child labour, to protect strikers and give legal recognition to trade unions, to revise the agreements by which public property had been ceded to the railway, mining and canal companies, to favour the development of insurance, and to provide credit.

Although Clemenceau had already made social and economic reform a key part of his programme, the growing economic difficulties from 1882 gave a new urgency and relevance to this aspect. He made an important speech in defence of the striking miners of the Gard in March 1882, and in 1883 and 1884 his campaign for constitutional revision was pursued in conjunction with a concerted pressure for social and economic reform. He made major speeches on 19 March and 19 June 1883 on the need for legal recognition of trade unions and government action to protect strikers and trade unionists against persecution by their employers. It was only in 1884 that trade unions were legalized in France. Clemenceau's marathon speech of 31 January 1884 developed his ideas on the social question to the fullest extent. He asked for the setting up of a great committee of inquiry, fulfilling the role of the great English Royal Commissions. This would not be like an ordinary commission of the French Chamber, deliberating behind closed doors on a precise piece of legislation; it would take evidence from the general public, from individuals and from workers' and employers' organizations, and offer a profound analysis of the crisis and the remedies offered. Ferry opposed the setting up of this commission, but Clemenceau's speech won over enough of the centre to ensure the Chamber's endorsement of the proposal by a small majority. On 19 February Clemenceau arrived in London for a few days' visit, during which he wanted to study the procedure of the British Royal Commissions, and to find out about British ways of dealing with the economic and social crisis. His friend Maxse, who is described by the police report as an ardent democrat and socialist, introduced him to various important political circles. He found time to visit a few factories but spent most of his time in high society and in the London clubs; he addressed the Cobden Club and the Cosmopolitan Club on French politics, but had no contact with the working-class movement.[56]

The *Commission chargée de faire une enquête sur la situation des ouvriers de l'industrie et de l'agriculture en France* had Clemenceau as one of its most prominent members, although the majority were con-

[56] Arch. Pref. Police BA 93, 19 February 1884.

servative-republican deputies unsympathetic to his ideas. Nevertheless he was chosen as one of those who drew up the plan of work, and designed a questionnaire to be submitted to witnesses. He was especially prominent in the Commission's involvement with the strike of the Anzin miners.[57] Clemenceau and Germaine Casse spent from 7–13 October in the mining area, interviewing representatives of the mining company, and workers who had been dismissed. The company refused to allow workers to meet the delegation, much to Clemenceau's annoyance. The two deputies produced a substantial report concluding that the Company had to face a difficult situation because of increased competition and falling prices, and had sought to deal with it by reorganizing the work so that fewer men were required. This had precipitated the strike, but it had been prolonged because the company had seized the opportunity to destroy the miners' unions by dismissing all the union leaders. Clemenceau declared that this high-handed action was in defiance of the new law legalizing trade unions: he asked Parliament to alter the terms of the laws governing mining concessions, which dated from the first Empire, so as to allow the government to intervene to defend the workers' right to form trade unions.[58]

This recommendation, along with all the other proposals discussed by the Commission, produced no practical results. The conservative-republican majority had no intention of embarking on major social experiments. The Commission held forty-nine sittings, and heard four hundred witnesses, both workers and employers; their evidence was summarized in its report, but no remedies were proposed. Probably no practical conclusion could have been expected to emerge from such an imprecise and impressionistic investigation. In any case the climate of opinion was totally opposed to government action. Scheurer-Kestner records in his memoirs, as an example of the highest form of political lunacy, the suggestion that the government should take action to prevent unemployment.[59] Even the Radicals had no proposals to offer. Their programme was one of social reform, not one of economic management. No one thought that the trade cycle could be eliminated by government action. The Radical programme was for measures to alleviate distress.

More important than either constitutional revision or the social question was the question of colonial expansion. Clemenceau made this

[57] For Clemenceau's work on this committee *see Procès-verbaux de la Commission chargée de faire une enquête sur la situation des ouvriers de l'industrie et de l'agriculture en France* (1884), pp. 6–7, 141–50 and 240. Clemenceau's own report on behalf of the sub-committee investigating the Anzin miners' strike is printed in *Impressions Parlementaires*, 3ᵉ Législature, Vol. 40, No. 2695, pp. 1–90; this is followed by minutes of the sub-committee's hearings.
[58] *Impressions Parlementaires*, pp. 86–7.
[59] A. Scheurer-Kestner, *Journal*, Bib. Nat., NAF, 12710, pp. 397–8.

the centre of his attacks on Ferry, and Ferry seemed more and more to welcome battle on this ground, in spite of his original assessment of colonial expeditions as a political liability. Success at little cost in Tunis must have changed his ideas on this point. In the end, however, in spite of the fact that the great majority of Frenchmen for the next sixty years regarded the colonial empire acquired by Ferry as one of the major achievements of their nation, it ruined his own political career. In one of the great injustices of politics, a momentary setback allowed Clemenceau to bring Ferry down, a blow from which his political career never really recovered. Clemenceau made nine major speeches in the Chamber on colonial questions between 1883 and 1885, as well as making it the theme of his extra-Parliamentary speeches; colonial expansion frequently figured in the columns of La Justice. There were good tactical reasons for this. The colonial question was the one major issue on which the opposition of Extreme Left and Right could unite.[60] On other questions, such as political and social reform, the equivocation involved in their joint onslaught on the government was obvious. But the passion with which Clemenceau pursued Ferry on this issue, and the fact that even forty years later when asked if he regretted his opposition, he was unable to admit it, suggests that he was certainly able to convince himself that he had deeper reasons for his opposition to Ferry's colonial policy than mere political tactics.

His arguments did not vary much over the two years, and all his speeches developed the following themes: he pointed out the financial burden involved, and refuted the claim that colonies could be an economic asset: free trade, and reliance on individual initiative unfettered by the heavy taxation that would result from colonial wars was the way to prosperity; existing French colonies had not proved to be of great economic advantage. Secondly, he turned to the military burden; in spite of all denials, colonial wars would weaken the military strength of France. It was not that he wanted to follow an aggressive policy in Europe, but France must be ready to defend herself if she were attacked. Thirdly, the diplomatic implications were that France would move away from Britain, with whom she would be brought into conflict by colonial expansion, and find herself diplomatically dependent on Germany – than which nothing could be more repugnant to French honour. On 27 November 1884, at the time of the Franco-German rapprochement at the Berlin conference, he said: 'Bismarck is a dangerous enemy, but even more dangerous perhaps as a friend: he showed us Tunis, placing us in conflict with England, and is now negotiating with us over the Congo.'[61] Clemenceau's main reason for opposing Ferry's colonial policy

[60] J. Jaurès, op. cit., pp. 12–14.
[61] Annales de la Chambre des Députés, 27 November 1884, p. 529.

was his fear that France would either be forced to accept a humiliating dependence on Germany or find herself helpless and isolated in the face of a new German attack. This is suggested by all that we know of his non-public statements on colonial questions. During the confidential discussions of the Parliamentary committee set up to examine the demand for further appropriations for Tonking in October 1884, Clemenceau pressed Ferry to give an account of the general diplomatic situation, suggesting that German support for French claims in Africa was being paid for by concessions in Europe, and fearing that German intervention in Belgium was a possible danger.[62] Further evidence that this was his overriding fear comes from the book of Bertha Szeps, the daughter of his Austrian friend Moritz Szeps, an acquaintance that Clemenceau cultivated as he provided access to the Archduke Rudolph, heir to the Austrian throne; one of Clemenceau's long-term plans in these years was that France could overturn German predominance by assembling Austria, Russia, and France in an anti-German alliance. In February 1885 Clemenceau wrote urgently to Szeps, asking for a meeting. They met in Zürich on 11 March 1885, when Clemenceau told Szeps, for the benefit of the Austrian Crown Prince:

> France is now strong and confident, and whoever attacks her must expect a vigorous defence. And I have good reason to believe that there are people who want to attack us. The French government has received alarming news from Courcel [French ambassador in Berlin]. Bismarck plans to use the present Socialist disorders in Belgium as a pretext for mobilizing German troops on the Belgium border. . . . Such a concentration of troops may easily result in some incident which calls for armed intervention.[63]

This fear of Bismarck's activities provides some justification for the ferocity with which Clemenceau attacked Ferry in the two debates on Tonkin on 28 and 30 March 1885. It seems that he genuinely believed that Ferry was leading France into a major war with China which would remove several hundred thousand troops to the other side of the world at the very moment when Bismarck was getting ready to bring off another diplomatic *coup* on France's own doorstep.

Clemenceau's campaign against Ferry's colonial policy was waged mainly over French conquest of Tonkin, the area now known as North Vietnam. Expansion into Tonkin from Cochin China, in French hands since 1863, brought the French into conflict with China, and desultory warfare continued throughout 1884. At first the Radical attack

---

[62] Archives Nationales C3318, 24 October 1884.
[63] B. Szeps, *My Life and History* (1938), p. 94. Szeps's interviews with Clemenceau were on 1 May 1880, pp. 17–21, 14 November 1883, pp. 77–81, 11 March 1885, pp. 94–7.

on Ferry's colonial policy had little success, in spite of the fact that they could say that France was at war although war had not been declared. In the autumn of 1883, only 185 deputies, half of them from the Right, voted against the government on this issue. Similarly only about 60 votes from the Left were cast against Ferry's policy on 27 November 1884 and 14 January 1885.[64] A naval blockade convinced the Chinese government that they could not hope to resist the French, and peace negotiations began on 10 January 1885. By the middle of March only minor formalities remained to be accomplished before the ratification of the treaty which gave France all her demands. But Ferry was pledged to secrecy, and could not reveal anything about the negotiations. On 27 March a telegram arrived in Paris announcing a slight reverse for the French forces operating on the southern frontier of China. Although there was nothing alarming in this news, a Radical deputy closely connected with Clemenceau, Granet, interpellated, and a major debate ensued on 28 March, in the course of which Clemenceau launched yet another attack on Ferry's colonial policy. He made his main theme the electoral dangers to be incurred by supporters of the government. The effect of this consideration can be seen in the voting of the *ordre du jour pur et simple*,[65] demanded by Ferry, by a majority of only fifty, much less than the normal governmental vote.[66]

Worse was to come. Ferry had insisted on the strength of the French military positions, and declared that there was no need for further reinforcements. The next day a telegram arrived, and was published in the evening papers, which gave the impression, totally unwarranted, of a disastrous defeat for the French. General Négrier, the field commander, had been seriously wounded, it stated, and Lang-Son had been abandoned; the commander-in-chief ended ominously, 'Whatever happens, I hope to be able to defend the Delta, and ask for urgent reinforcements'. In fact this panic was completely unnecessary. Négrier had been wounded in a minor skirmish after which the Chinese had also withdrawn. Ferry thought that the military defeat was only a minor

[64] J. Kayser, op. cit., p. 130. Cf. D. R. Watson, 'The French and Indo-China', *History Today*, 20 August 1970, pp. 534–42.
[65] An important element of French Parliamentary procedure was the discussion of interpellations (questions) followed by a vote on the resolution that 'the Chamber passes to the order of the day'. Such a resolution could either be *motivé* (qualified) by some such phrase as 'approving the government's handling of the situation' or 'condemning the government's inadequate measures', or else it could be *pur et simple* (unqualified). A government which was unsure of its majority, and if circumstances warranted it, would accept the voting of an unqualified resolution : if it wished to ask the Chamber to affirm its confidence, it could demand the voting of a favourable resolution, or the rejection of a critical one. It was on such debates, after interpellations, that the fate of cabinets depended, much more than on the progress of legislation. *See above*, p. 78, for discussion of the interpellation that led to the fall of Ferry's cabinet in 1881.
[66] *See* J. Ganiage, *L'expansion Coloniale*, pp. 120–39. C. A. Julien, 'Jules Ferry', *Les Politiques d'Expansion Impérialiste* (1949), pp. 11–72.

one that would not seriously compromise the French positions, but he could not be sure. As he told Hanotaux, who advised him to reveal the virtual completion of the negotiations: 'I will be told once again that I am a liar: and China might revert to her delaying tactics.' So he had no response to make to the members of his majority when they told him that they could no longer support the government. They even wanted the cabinet to resign without meeting Parliament.

Thus when Ferry went to the Chamber on the afternoon of 30 March he knew that he would be defeated. Perhaps he thought that when the successful outcome of the negotiations was revealed, the attack would rebound to the disadvantage of its authors. This would explain his fixed ironical smile during Clemenceau's diatribe. Ferry scarcely made a speech, but in the briefest of declarations asked for a symbolic vote in favour of further appropriations in order to demonstrate French determination to vindicate national honour. Afterwards, another vote could decide whether or not the present cabinet should remain in office. As soon as Ferry finished speaking, Clemenceau and the right-wing deputy Delafosse made a dash for the steps by which orators mounted to the tribune, each struggling to be the first to speak. The President of the Chamber ruled that Clemenceau, who had made a more skilful use of Parliamentary procedure, had priority.

Clemenceau moved in for the kill, ending his four-year duel with Ferry by a *coup de grâce* from which Ferry's political career never recovered. More than anything else this day gave Clemenceau his reputation as a ferocious speaker, who treated the Chamber like a duelling ground. He was nicknamed 'the Tiger' much later, but on this day he achieved the reputation that made it seem so appropriate. Zévaès says that no mere reading of the text of the debate can give a true impression of the effect of the speech. He continues:

> Clemenceau, unnaturally pale in the weak light coming through the skylights above his head, a light which accentuated the strong features of his face into a ferocious *rictus*, seemed ready to bring down his outstretched accusing hand on the shoulder of his victims. The crowded Chamber shuddered, while outside an enormous crowd raised angry shouts. Every word was like the crack of a whip, and was heard either in dramatic silence, or with a roar of applause.[67]

He began:

> Gentlemen, I do not stand here to reply to the prime minister. At this moment, no further debate can take place between his ministry and a republican member of this Chamber. All debate is finished between

[67] A. Zévaès, *Clemenceau*, p. 65.

us: we cannot, we will not discuss the interests of our country with you. They are not ministers I have in front of me, but criminals in the dock.

At this insult a few of the government's supporters objected but their protests were covered by the roars of approval from the Right and the Extreme Left. Ferry sat on his bench a few feet in front of the orator, his face set in an ironical smile. In the midst of the tumult the Catholic leader de Mun shouted out: 'They are not laughing in Tonkin, Mr Prime Minister: the country must know that you are laughing.' When the President had again restored some sort of calm, Clemenceau continued:

They are accused of high treason, and if France retains any traces of justice the hand of the law will not be long in descending upon them. Now, gentlemen, having set aside from this debate the position of the ministry, let us turn to examine the interest of the country. . . .

He went on to argue that they must, of course, send reinforcements:

When a Frenchman, even a single one, holds up the national flag in the face of the foreigner, the representatives of the nation cannot be sparing of men or money.

But, he continued, they could not give their confidence to this government, nor could they decide what ought to be done about the expedition in Tonkin until they had before them a responsible ministry with a prime minister on whose word they could rely. The danger was that France would be drawn into a full-scale war with China. The situation was very grave, and they could not commit France to a policy that would thereafter have to be maintained, whatever the cost, without having the necessary information on which to base a decision. He concluded, addressing the government's supporters in the centre,

When we are told the truth, we will be ready to take the necessary decision, and we will be proud to associate ourselves with you to defend together the highest interest of our country.[68]

Thus he skilfully obtained the maximum political advantage over Ferry, without committing himself to abandon Tonkin. The government was defeated by 306 to 149. The majority was made up of 86 members of the Right and 220 republicans, while 47 other republicans abstained. The moderate republicans, Ferry's majority, had broken into fragments. Ferry and his ministers left the Chamber but the debate continued, as the Right and the Radicals persisted in their demand that the ministry be put on trial for high treason. This proposal was, however,

[68] *Annales de la Chambre des Députés*, 30 March 1885, pp. 804–5. *See also* J. Ferry, *Discours et Opinions*, ed. P. Robiquet (1893–8), V, pp. 511–7.

rejected by 287 to 152. Ferry, braving the hostile crowd, left the Parliament building on foot. Hanotaux recalls seeing his top hat bobbing above the other heads as he pushed his way through the mob that was yelling 'down with Ferry, into the river with him'.[69]

On 4 April 1885, even before a new government could be formed, the draft peace terms were signed: they became the second treaty of Tien-Tsin on 9 June. The new cabinet was headed by Brisson, who was acceptable to all factions; it was a coalition of lukewarm Radicals and Opportunists, a caretaker government to hold the stage until the elections. On colonial matters, however, it continued Ferry's policy in Tonkin and Madagascar. Clemenceau's only important speech in the Chamber came on 30 July, in reply to a long speech by Ferry in which the latter for the first time attempted a general justification of his colonial policy.

A large part of Ferry's speech on 28 July was devoted to economic arguments. Tariff barriers were being re-erected everywhere, he said, and the only way for France to escape from her economic crisis was to win colonies which would provide outlets for exports of goods and of capital, outlets which were becoming restricted at home. He made it clear, however, in his peroration, pronounced with great intensity of feeling, that the real motive behind his colonial policy was a political one. He concluded:

> You cannot hold up before France an ideal that would be suitable for Belgium or Switzerland: France cannot merely be free; she must be great, exercising over the destinies of Europe all the influence which is rightly hers, and carrying it all over the world. . . . The alternative is a policy of abdication which will lead in the long run to decadence. Other countries which three centuries ago played a great role in the world, have now descended to the third or the fourth rank.[70]

He denied that colonial expansion was unpopular with the electorate: if the majority were not ashamed of what it had done, if it went boldly out and declared that it had willed a France that was great in all spheres, the electorate would support it.

Clemenceau began by attacking Ferry for waiting until he had fallen from power before expounding his colonial policy. The correct course would have been to expound his philosophy first, instead of surreptitiously embarking on colonial conquests without Parliamentary authorization. He then refuted Ferry's economic arguments relying on traditional economic liberalism; the expense of acquiring and governing

---

[69] G. Hanotaux, *Mon Temps*, II, pp. 404–5. Arch. Préf. Police, BA 94, 30 March and 2 April 1885. J. Ferry, op. cit., V, p. 517.
[70] J. Ferry, op. cit., V, pp. 172–220.

colonies was far greater than any possible commercial gains; the way to prosperity was to cut taxation and give free rein to individual initiative. But he did not spend long on this and turned to an attack on the basis of Ferry's political case. This was, he said, no more than a glorification of war, of the doctrine that 'Might is Right'. Since 1789 republican opinion in France had been seeking to eliminate violence from the world and to replace it by justice; no doubt such aims were far from accomplishment, but this was the first time that a French government had openly declared its policy to be one of aggressive war, and not peace. He challenged Ferry's idea that only by external aggrandizement could France avoid apathy and decadence. They had tasks enough at home – the reorganization of the army, the social question, political reform designed to see whether France could at last organize a government that combined freedom and stability. The republicans must go before the electorate as the party of peace, not as the party of war, and must therefore repudiate Ferry.[71]

2 THE 1885 ELECTIONS

The republicans went into the election campaign in extremely dispersed order. There was neither a united moderate faction behind Ferry, nor a united Radical group behind Clemenceau, in spite of the hopes that the return to *scrutin de liste* would produce a stronger party organization. The elections of October 1885 were the culminating point of the campaign Clemenceau had begun in 1879. The election campaign opened with his attack on Ferry at the end of March, and continued through the spring and summer. Although no properly organized political parties existed, there was an amazing multiplication of electoral committees of every possible title and nuance. The change of the electoral system from single-member constituencies to departments with the number of deputies varying according to population meant that the different local committees had to unite to present a common list and a common programme. This was especially difficult in the case of Paris, which became one immense constituency with thirty-nine seats. Attempts to bring together different Radical committees in Paris had begun as early as March, and continued through the summer. In the end, however, they were not successful, and at least four important Radical committees presented competing lists to the voters of the capital. Many names, of course, figured on more than one list, but with different associates. As the programmes and, even more, the titles of the different committees were vague and open to all sorts of equivocal interpretation (even the most moderate republicans tended to seek the electoral advantage of

[71] *Annales de la Chambre des Députés*, 30 July 1885, pp. 1076–86.

the word Radical), the election took place in an atmosphere of extreme confusion, and lent itself to demagoguery of the worst sort.

On 19 June Clemenceau invited the deputies of the Left to a meeting at the rooms of the Grand Orient de France, the masonic headquarters, where they drew up an electoral platform, known during the campaign as the programme of the rue Cadet. This was a deliberate attempt to provide a focus around which the widest possible spectrum of left-wing republicans could gather. It declared that its signatories 'did not seek to impose a uniform formula on the legitimate diversity of republican opinions, nor to substitute themselves for the committees and the electors who would make their own electoral agreements. . . . But they sought to lay down the minimum number of points that would allow for more than merely temporary agreement between men of different nuances.' The six points were all expressed in studiously vague terms.

1. Condemnation of the policy of adventures and conquests.
2. Constitutional reform: absolute sovereignty of universal suffrage.
3. Financial reform: balanced budget: income tax: reduction of expenses, and revision of the agreements (i.e. between the government and the railway companies).
4. Separation of Church and State.
5. Reduction of military service: suppression of exemption for seminarists, and of one year service.
6. Laws for the protection and emancipation of Labour.[72]

But Clemenceau was outflanked on the left in Paris not only by four different Collectivist-Socialist lists (none of them of any real electoral importance) but also by a more demagogic Radical-Socialist list, organized by Maujan and Rochefort.[73] They replied to Clemenceau's rue Cadet programme with one issued in the name of the *Comité Central des Groupes Républicains Radicaux-Socialistes de la Seine*, claiming to represent seventy-six Radical committees of the capital. Clemenceau replied by setting up his own *Comité Départemental Radical-Socialiste*, which

[72] J. Kayser, op. cit., pp. 136–7. Kayser prints extracts from the manifesto of the rue Cadet, op. cit., pp. 332–3. The fact that the Comité operated from the masonic headquarters does not prove that it was a masonic organization, although the sympathy and connections between freemasonry and republicanism, especially radical republicanism, are well known. The building at the Grand Orient was hired out to groups which had need of accommodation. Clemenceau himself was not a freemason. H. Coston, *La République du Grand Orient* (1964), p. 146.

[73] Maujan and Rochefort subsequently took very different roads. Maujan became a machine politician, important behind the scenes in the Radical party, and Clemenceau's principal agent in the party during his first ministry: Rochefort, whose career as a demagogic journalist extended from the Empire to the twentieth century, supported Boulanger and then the Nationalist movement at the time of the Dreyfus Affair, ending on the extreme Right. Kayser prints the programme of Clemenceau's Comité Departmental, op. cit., pp. 334–5. The rival programme of Maujan's Comité Central can be found in *La Justice*, 1 July 1885.

soon won back the allegiance of twenty of the committees that had joined Maujan, and whose programme was published on 13 September. This contained many of the same demands as Maujan's programme, but was phrased more cautiously. Various futile attempts were made to bring together the Clemenceau and Maujan committees. Attempts to get the Radical newspapers of the capital to agree to support one or other committee also failed. In the end each newspaper drew up its own list of candidates, or endorsed one or other of the competing lists.

Clemenceau did not confine his activities to Paris. On 19 July he made one of his most important campaign speeches at Bordeaux, and he was active in stirring up Radical committees and candidates throughout the country. At the beginning of August he left for another speaking tour, in the Rhône valley. On 12 September he arrived in the department of the Var, in the far south, where he was a candidate as well as in Paris. He campaigned there for a week, returning gradually to Paris, making speeches at Dôle and Dijon.[74]

The results of the first ballot, on 4 October, were an immense shock for the republicans.[75] The Right had 176 deputies, against less than 100 before the elections, while the republicans had only 127. Even in Paris only four republicans were elected, the only candidates to receive more than half the votes cast. This republican defeat was partly the result of a swing in votes; the Right recovered its voting strength of 1877, instead of the much reduced level of 1881, when abstention had been very high. But it was much more the result of the disunity of the republicans. The economic depression and hostility to colonial wars, which had everywhere been the most popular theme of anti-governmental candidates, meant that half of all the deputies in the last Chamber were defeated; those who had been most clearly the supporters of the Ferry government suffered the most.

Clemenceau, who had taken a leading part in ensuring that Radical lists should be presented wherever possible, now changed to the other tack, and joined in the urgent negotiations which reunited the republicans for the second ballot. The dangers of presenting rival republican lists had been discounted by the Radicals before the first ballot because they had assumed that the monarchist vote would decline even below its level in 1881. The surprising resurgence of the Right altered all their calculations, and the Radicals who had been latterly attacking Ferry's supporters were now forced into joint lists with them. In twenty-one departments it was agreed that the republican list which had won most votes at the first ballot should stand as the only republican list at the

<hr>

[74] *La Justice*, July, August and September 1885, reports on Clemenceau's movements and prints extracts from many of his speeches.
[75] For the results after the second ballot, *see* diagram, Appendix IV, p. 422.

second ballot. This was to the benefit of eleven Opportunist lists, nine Radical lists, and one 'Modéré' list. In eight other departments new lists combining Radicals and Opportunists were put forward. At the second ballot the single republican list in every case won virtually every vote cast for all the republican lists at the first ballot.[76]

Clemenceau, elected both in the Seine and in the Var, chose the latter constituency, which was to remain his political home for the rest of his career. Defeated as a deputy there in 1893, he returned as one of its senators in 1902, a position he retained until his retirement in 1920. His political evolution was no doubt encouraged by this move. The Var was a very different constituency from the Seine, consisting of foothills along the Mediterranean coast, behind Toulon. The coast in this area had not yet developed as a watering place, and the naval base and harbour at Toulon provided the only non-agricultural element. The great majority of the electors were peasants in an area of poor soil, hardly touched by the railways and badly served by roads. Many of the mountain villages could only be reached by mule track. Yet, such is the diversity of France, their political opinions were far removed from those of the similarly backward and remote regions of Clemenceau's birthplace in the Vendée. The Var was as strongly republican and anti-clerical as the Vendée was royalist and Catholic. The area had been one of the centres of the rising against Louis Napoleon's *coup d'état* in 1851, and the repression that had followed left bitter memories. The voting in 1881 of pensions to the victims of Bonapartism, strongly supported by Clemenceau, produced many claimants here. In the very last years of the Third Republic there were still recipients of these pensions, descendants of the 'victims of 1851', in the Var.[77]

But if the Var was solidly anti-Bonapartist and anti-clerical, Clemenceau was not at first to be troubled with Socialist rivals there. As his own political creed evolved, it came to chime in perfectly with the political atmosphere of the Var, where radicalism meant defence of the great ideals of 1789, sturdy peasant individualism against the bureaucracy of the central government, and against big business. It has often been said that in the twentieth century the Radicals were the true conservatives of France, the natural political expression of a peasant society with its roots deep in the past, unchanging politically as it was economically. Like all generalizations this is not completely true, but the radicalism

[76] J. Kayser, op. cit., pp. 142–3. Guesde, showing his usual lack of tactical sense, having rejected Clemenceau's overtures before the first ballot, tried to get him to agree to a joint Radical-Socialist and Collectivist-Socialist list for the second ballot instead of a Radical-Opportunist union. As Jaurès pointed out, although this might have worked in favour of the Left in Paris, it would have been disastrous in the rest of the country, and have produced the electoral victory of the Right: J. Jaurès, op. cit., pp. 83–4.
[77] F. Varenne, *Georges Mandel, Mon Patron* (1947), pp. 68–9.

of the Var fitted it perfectly, and as Clemenceau grew older his political position came to be more and more suited to this very traditional part of France. The change is already evident when his programme for the 1889 elections is compared with that of 1885. The proposals for social reform have been reduced to a few brief and extremely vague aspirations, while one of the few precise proposals is to increase the tariff protections of agriculture. Indeed, even in 1885, when campaigning in the Var, his programme was very different from the one he had endorsed in the Seine. His main theme in the Var was opposition to the central government, the need for decentralization, to demolish the Napoleonic administrative system that had made possible the *coup d'état* of 1851.[78]

[78] Extracts from Clemenceau's 1889 manifesto are printed in J. Kayser, op. cit., p. 337. His speech at Draguignan on 13 September 1885 is printed in *La Justice*, 17 September 1885.

5

BOULANGISM

I CLEMENCEAU HOPES FOR OFFICE, 1885–1887

In the Parliament of 1881–5 Clemenceau had represented intransigent opposition. As the Opportunists had a clear majority over both Radicals and Right combined, he had little chance of being brought into the government. His position was very different in the Parliament of 1885–9. Although the elections had proved a bitter disappointment, he seemed to have a strong tactical position in that the Opportunists no longer had a majority over all other groups. They had to form coalitions in which the Radicals could expect to wield considerable influence. Clemenceau could be expected to be the major beneficiary of this situation, and he was able to exercise much influence in these years, although he was not himself asked to join a cabinet. There is a noticeable difference in his political activities after 1885. Between 1881 and 1885 Clemenceau won his reputation as an orator with no fewer than twenty-seven major speeches in the Chamber, as well as many speeches to public meetings. His 'comptes-rendus du mandat' to his Montmartre electors at the Cirque Fernando were major events, and he made speaking tours through the provinces. He was especially active in the months immediately before the 1885 elections, but he addressed public meetings in some of the great provincial cities on several other occasions. After 1885 all this ceased: in the new Parliament his interventions were few and brief, and outside speeches ceased altogether. He was now seeking a place in the government. No longer was he the most extreme of Radical politicians. He saw the importance in politics of commanding the middle ground. Systematic opposition for its own sake was never part of Clemenceau's scheme of things. He was in politics to achieve practical results, not for the sake of sterile assertions of principle.

But the reputation for extremism Clemenceau and his circle had gained before 1885, coupled with personal antipathy, excluded him from power. An Opportunist journalist, Joseph Reinach, formerly Gambetta's secretary and now editor of the newspaper *La République Française*, wrote a pamphlet entitled *Le Ministère Clemenceau*, to demonstrate that a Clemenceau government would collapse after a few weeks of incoherent and demagogic reforming projects. Ferry was even more extreme in his denunciations, writing to Reinach on 8 September 1886 that a Clemenceau ministry 'pourrait tourner au coup de force, Boulanger aidant'.[79] The President of the Republic, Grévy, who had five years earlier been on good terms with Clemenceau, was now determined to keep him out at all costs, as a dangerous and reckless extremist.[80]

The new Chamber was divided into three almost equal parts – the Right, the moderate republicans, and the Radicals – a very different situation from that of the previous Parliament in which, normally, the moderate republicans had enjoyed a clear majority over Radicals and Right together. The new Parliament seemed to offer Clemenceau an opportunity to play a dominant role in coalitions of moderate republicans and Radicals. But it was much less than he had hoped for. Before the elections he had expected a new Chamber roughly half Radical and half moderate republican, with the Right reduced to a small remnant. This would have allowed a political realignment in which the republicans split clearly into a progressive and conservative group, the French equivalent of the British two-party system. The revival of the Right ruined this tactic, and it became steadily clearer that the moderate republicans still held the strongest card in the pack. They could either form coalition cabinets with some of the Radicals, or govern against the Radicals with the tacit support of the Right, as did Rouvier. The other factor was that the Radicals were in no sense an organized disciplined party which accepted the leadership of Clemenceau or of anyone else. Many of them had adopted the Radical label purely for its electoral benefits, and were easily persuaded to join coalition governments whose policies bore no relation to the Radical electoral platforms. The idea that *scrutin de liste* would produce a politics of ideas and programmes rather than of personalities was certainly not borne out by the behaviour of those elected in 1885. Thus the 1885–9 Chamber was almost completely barren of reforming legislation. The Opportunist cabinets of 1880–5 had achieved much more. They had legislated for freedom of the press and of public meetings, and provided a legal status for trade

---

[79] Quoted by J. Kayser, op. cit., pp. 155–6 n. The phrase is omitted from the published version of Ferry's letters, *Lettres de Jules Ferry* (1914), pp. 426–9.

[80] B. Lavergne's memoirs frequently report Grévy's criticisms of the Radicals: on 29 November 1885 Grévy declared, 'A Clemenceau ministry is not possible'. B. Lavergne, *Les Deux Présidences de Jules Grévy* (1966), p. 331.

unions. They had carried out major reform of the education system, and laid the foundations of a great colonial empire, and had carried a minor change in the constitution in a democratic direction. This was only a small part of the full republican programme, but these five years saw the achievement of a more consistent programme of reform than the Third Republic was ever to see again, while the Chamber of 1885–9 remains notorious only for its massive corruption in the Panama Canal scheme.

After the elections the Brisson cabinet remained in office. The most important political question was Tonkin. When the question of further credits came before the Chamber, Radicals and Right combined to elect a committee that was overwhelmingly hostile.[81] Pelletan was made *rapporteur*, and delivered a report that condemned Brisson's claim that he could break Ferry's colonial policy without abandoning Indo-China: there was no alternative between withdrawal and a heavy French commitment in the Far East. In the debate Clemenceau made his last onslaught on the policy of colonial expansion, arguing that it diverted attention from domestic problems:

You want to found an empire in Indo-China, we want to found the Republic at home; you have been adventurous abroad but timid at home; our policy is to be bold in domestic politics, proud but prudent in foreign policy.[82]

When the vote was taken, however, the government scraped home by six votes. All the Right except one voted against, but the Radicals divided, 94 against, 46 for the government and 3 abstaining. In spite of this victory, which ensured that the French remained in Tonkin, Brisson considered that such a small majority was a sign of no confidence and resigned. This was the object that Clemenceau had sought. Jaurès remembered that when he asked him a few months later whether he would have withdrawn from Tonking if he had come to power, Clemenceau replied, 'No, certainly not'. In view of this it is interesting to speculate whether Clemenceau's influence played a part in the careful balancing of the votes, enough Radicals voting against the government to persuade Brisson to resign, while not defeating the vote of credits.[83]

[81] It was not Clemenceau, but Rochefort, the exponent of demagogic Radical extremism, who acted as the link between Extreme Left and Right in the *bureaux* that elected the Commission, thus ensuring that the majority of the Commission were hostile to the government. A. Scheurer-Kestner, *Journal*, Bib. Nat., NAF, 12709, pp. 194–5.
[82] *Annales de la Chambre des Députés*, 24 December 1885, p. 426.
[83] A. Schmieder, 'La Chambre de 1885–9 et les Affaires du Tonkin', *Revue Française d'Histoire d'Outre-Mer* (1966), LIII, p. 175. J. Jaurès, op. cit., p. 22. J. Ferry to A. Scheurer-Kestner, 22 October 1885: 'We must support Brisson, and give him strength to resist Clemenceau. The first battle will be over Tonkin; Brisson, not to mention Freycinet on whom we can count absolutely, is formally

The fall of the Brisson government in December 1885 seemed to mark another step to power for Clemenceau. However, it was only to be one of a long chain of disappointments. Just as he had earlier offered to support Brisson provided that he rejected Ferry's supporters, and had been spurned, Clemenceau was to offer his support in turn to Freycinet, Goblet and Floquet, and always to be disappointed.[84] However, the Freycinet government of 1886 was one in which Clemenceau's protégés were prominent. Freycinet appointed Boulanger to the ministry of war to please the Radicals, especially Clemenceau.[85] He wanted Boulanger as minister of war because the general had achieved a reputation as a good republican and democrat, in spite of earlier contacts with the Orleanist prince, the Duc d'Aumâle. Boulanger was seen as ready to press on with reform in a democratic sense of the law governing conscription and recruitment: until then the sons of the middle class had been to a large extent able to escape the burdens of military service, as also had intending priests. The latter point – 'les curés sac au dos' – was especially popular with the Radicals. This was the extreme example of the sort of influence that a prominent deputy like Clemenceau would exercise even when not in office. The distribution of governmental patronage was an essential part of the political life of the Third Republic. The formation of coalition governments which needed his support meant that Clemenceau was now entitled to a share in this patronage, which he was not slow to demand.[86] Granet was another of Clemenceau's protégés, with a reputation that money stuck to his fingers more than most.

committed against a policy of national humiliation. I do not think he will yield, and I do not know whether Clemenceau himself will go to extremes, for he is only aiming at being the power behind the scenes.' A. Scheurer-Kestner, *Journal*, Bib. Nat., NAF, 12709, p. 190. The last phrase is omitted in the published version, J. Ferry, *Lettres*, p. 386.

[84] B. Lavergne reported to Grévy on 16 December 1885 a recent conversation with Clemenceau: 'I said to him: "you cannot be a minister at the moment, but you will not try to prevent any government from working?" He replied, "No, I will support any government, provided that it is active." He would give me no further explanations. It is certain that, even if he cannot be a minister, no cabinet could withstand his opposition.' B. Lavergne, op. cit., p. 338.

[85] Although Freycinet's account of his choice of Boulanger does not mention Clemenceau, Freycinet, *Souvenirs* (1914), II, p. 329-32, but cf. A. Dansette, *Le Boulangisme* (1946), p. 31 n.: 'At the time the belief that Clemenceau was responsible was unanimous. Clemenceau admitted afterwards in several conversations that he had invented Boulanger.' Cf. A. Scheurer-Kestner, *Journal*, Bib. Nat., NAF, 12709, p. 201: 'The entry of General Boulanger in the Freycinet ministry was intended to protect it from Clemenceau's attacks, and even to ensure his support. Clemenceau knew perfectly well that the general he had imposed was a man quite without intellectual value. Was he equally well aware of his protégé's lack of moral sense?' We do not know: but from my knowledge of Clemenceau's character I think that he believed that he could count on the honour of that third-rate trooper. In any case Boulanger's presence in the cabinet seemed to give great satisfaction to Clemenceau. "I also have generals among my supporters, like Gambetta," he seemed to be thinking.'

[86] J. Ferry to J. Reinach, 20 June 1886: 'The Radicals seek, wherever they are masters, to purge the first batch of republican officials so as to substitute their own protégés' (J. Kayser, op. cit., p. 152).

He had entered politics in 1881 as a deputy for Arles. Standing as an Opportunist he had been beaten by Clemenceau, but Clemenceau agreed to choose his Paris constituency, leaving the field clear for Granet at Arles, provided the latter adopted Clemenceau's programme. From that time onwards Granet figured as a Radical, and an associate of Clemenceau at least until 1886. Afterwards he deserted his patron, and became an intimate of Grévy. On 27 November 1885 Clemenceau discussed with Lavergne the possibility of a Radical-Opportunist coalition led by Freycinet. He insisted that Granet should be in the cabinet, and dismissed the idea that his financial speculations debarred him. True enough, Granet emerged in the Freycinet cabinet as minister for posts and telegraphs, and almost persuaded the government to grant a valuable concession for the construction and operation of telephones to Clemenceau's friend Cornelius Herz. Clemenceau protested, when this emerged in 1892, that he personally had voted against the scheme in the Parliamentary committee, but this hardly removes all taint. Clemenceau's influence had brought Granet into office, where he had sought to use his position in the interests of Clemenceau's financial backer, Herz.[87] A sign of Clemenceau's readiness to abandon extreme positions came in the debate over the disturbances during the strike at Décazeville in February 1886. Traditionally, the Radicals had been on the side of the strikers, and had condemned the government's too ready recourse to troops when a strike occurred. They argued that even if, in theory, troops were only sent to maintain law and order, this in fact put the State behind the employers, especially if troops were sent to preserve 'freedom to work', that is, to allow the use of blackleg labour to break the strike. In this case, law and order had been seriously endangered, and one of the mine-engineers, Watrin, had been murdered by the strikers. Although the main body of the Radicals still wished to condemn the government's policy towards labour, they were not ready to condone violence. In the group meeting of the Extreme Left, Clemenceau replied to the Socialist Basly, who had defended the murderers, that, whatever the crimes of the employers, 'private citizens are not allowed to take justice into their own hands'. This incident led to a breach between Radicals and Socialists and the setting up of the first Parliamentary group of Socialists. Engels, who had previously sought to persuade the French Marxists to support Clemenceau, rejoiced in the separation, seeing it as the first stage of the replacement of the Radicals as representatives of most working-class voters.[88]

[87] A. Dansette, op. cit., pp. 31–2 n.: 'Clemenceau, Granet, Boulanger, Chabert, the family circle!'; B. Lavergne, op. cit., p. 327.
[88] J. Kayser, op. cit., pp. 152–3. For Clemenceau's exchange with Basly, see La Justice, 5 February 1886. Engels-Lafargue, Correspondance, I, p. 340. A. Zévaès, La grève de Décazeville (1938).

About this time Scheurer-Kestner, who had previously written in his memoirs that it was impossible to conceive of Clemenceau in any role but opposition, commented that his tactical skill in disengaging from the extremists showed that he could have been capable of becoming a 'chef de parti gouvernemental', if he had not, as Scheurer-Kestner saw it, been led astray by Pelletan.[89] As the year went on it became clearer that the Freycinet government was not going to bring in Radical measures, and Clemenceau's support for it began to weaken. The government was criticized in the columns of La Justice and on 3 December 1886 it fell, the Radicals having defected in a symbolic vote refusing credits for the sous-préfectures. Their abolition was part of the Radical programme of demolition of the Napoleonic administrative strait-jacket. Goblet formed a new government, another Radical-Moderate coalition, which hardly differed from the old one : nine out of twelve members of the new cabinet had been in the old one, including Boulanger. Nevertheless, the new cabinet was treated with respect, and Clemenceau offered his support once again in spite of the complete banality of Goblet's programme.[90] On 30 March Clemenceau complained that Radical support for Goblet had brought no concessions. Instead Goblet even sought the support of the Right. Clemenceau declared that 'the day you win the confidence of the Right, you will lose ours. The day you prove that you deserve our confidence by carrying a single one of the reforms of the programme of the Left, you will be supported by the entire republican party, and you will be able to lead it to the attack against the Right. There can be no compromise between them and us, neither on political matters nor on the social question.'[91]

A few weeks later the Radicals voted against the government and brought it down on 8 May. This was welcomed by the conservative republicans, who had decided that Goblet and Boulanger were far too dangerous a combination to remain in office. Boulanger's reckless manœuvrings, with the support of Goblet, during the Schnaebele incident of April 1887, convinced those who knew what had really happened that he had almost precipitated a disastrous war with Germany. Schnaebele was a French customs official who had organized a network of spies in the lost provinces. He was decoyed over the border and then arrested by the Germans. Bismarck only wanted a display of brinkmanship to scare the French and soon released him. Ironically, in the eyes of the public, Boulanger emerged from the Schnaebele incident as a hero, the first French minister who had dared to stand up to Bismarck since 1870. This was the moment of take-off for Boulanger; within

[89] A. Scheurer-Kestner, Journal, Bib. Nat., NAF, 12709, pp. 204–5.
[90] Clemenceau's speech on 14 December 1886, Annales de la Chambre des Députés, pp. 743–7.
[91] Annales de la Chambre des Députés, 30 March 1887, p. 389.

two years he was to have the chance of overthrowing the Republic. For the moment the conservative republicans' determination to exclude him produced the longest ministerial crisis the Republic had yet seen. Although Clemenceau was already critical of Boulanger in private, he still supported him politically, and snubbed the general who eventually agreed to replace him.[92] This prevented any agreement on a new Radical-Moderate coalition, and eventually Rouvier formed an almost entirely Moderate cabinet, relying on the tacit support of the Right to make up the voting power lost by the defection of the Radicals. This was an unprecedented step: ever since 1877 the frontier between Republicans and Right had been absolute, and Clemenceau launched a bitter attack on the Rouvier government for seeking the support of the Right.

The Rouvier government was not destined to last long, for it was caught up in the scandal caused by the revelation that Wilson, son-in-law of the President, had been selling decorations and places in the Legion of Honour. Once again it was Clemenceau who brought down the government. His interpellation on 19 November 1887, with discreet references to this scandal, led to Rouvier's defeat, contrary to the general belief that the government would win easily.[93] There followed a prolonged crisis, as all political leaders refused to form a government unless the President resigned. Oblivious of his humiliations, Grévy persisted in his attempts to remain, and all possible candidates, including, for the first time, Clemenceau himself, were summoned to the Elysée and asked to form a government. All refused.[94] At last Grévy agreed to resign and Clemenceau awoke to the realization that the most likely successor would be his old enemy Ferry. He had hoped that either Freycinet or Floquet would be elected: either could be expected to ask him to form a government, while Ferry obviously would not. So there took place on the nights of 28 and 29 November 1887 a series of meetings between Radical deputies and journalists and Boulanger, meetings referred to as 'les nuits historiques' by those who took part in them. They appear now more like a comic opera than anything to be dignified by such a pretentious title, and it is hard to imagine how anyone could have taken them seriously. The essence of the plot was to find a formula to allow the formation of a Radical government, led by Floquet or Freycinet and including Clemenceau and Boulanger, a government that would allow Grévy to remain in office long enough for the plotters to agree on a

[92] A. Dansette, op. cit., p. 101, quoting Ludovic Halévy's unpublished diary. B. Lavergne, op. cit., p. 439.
[93] Annales de la Chambre des Députés, 19 November 1887, p. 261; cf. A. Dansette, L'Affaire Wilson et la chute du Président Grévy (1936), pp. 124–6. B. Lavergne, op. cit., p. 467: 'To everyone's surprise, including Clemenceau, the ministry was defeated by a coalition of Extreme Left and Right.'
[94] A. Dansette, op. cit., pp. 135–9; J. Martet, Le Tigre, p. 35; B. Lavergne, op. cit., p. 469.

substitute candidate who would keep out Ferry. A whole series of mid-night meetings took place, involving secret rendezvous between Clemenceau and Boulanger and nocturnal visits to Freycinet and Floquet. Andrieux was got out of bed in the small hours, summoned by a complete stranger, to join in the plotting; distrustful of his companion, he slipped a pistol in his pocket before allowing himself to be driven off to join the others at Marguerite Durand's flat, where they had all dined. Mlle Durand, a famous actress of the Comédie Française, was married to Laguerre, one of Clemenceau's protégés in the 1881–5 Parliament, who was permanently to ruin his political career by deeply involving himself in Boulangism. Clemenceau drew back when it became clear that Laguerre, Déroulède, Naquet and Rochefort, all Radicals who were to become Boulangists, were no longer thinking in terms of constitutional cabinet-making, but of a *coup d'état*. This did not stop him remaining in touch with Rochefort, through whom two days later he arranged a demonstration to put pressure on the members of the National Assembly not to elect Ferry. But he had no intention of allowing himself to be dragged into any military *coup*, and the definite breach between Clemenceau and Boulanger came when the general said that the army would not defend the government against a *coup d'état*. Clemenceau stared hard at him, and left the room, saying to Mlle Durand as she escorted him to the dining-room, 'Just think that a French general is listening to our proposals'. To complete the comic-opera element, on this very night Boulanger contacted the Right, leading them to believe that he would restore the monarchy, at the same time as he was plotting with the Radicals for a *coup d'état* supposed to lead to a democratic, plebiscitary republic. The intermediary between Boulanger and the Royalists was Le Hérissé, who had been not merely Catholic and Royalist, but even a *blanc d'Espagne;*[95] offered the chance of a seat in Parliament, he suddenly became a Radical republican and anti-clerical: now, two years later, he was prepared to put Boulanger in touch with the Royalists.[96] This political underworld could hardly be called sinister: it was merely comic. Ferry called Boulanger a 'music-hall version of St Arnaud', referring to the general who had managed Louis Napoleon's *coup* in 1851. Clemenceau certainly did his reputation no good by his association with them, in spite of the fact that he drew back in time. Already in December 1886 Lavergne had noted in his diary that Clemenceau was getting a reputation for lack of seriousness:

[95] The name given to those Legitimists who refused to accept the claim to the throne of the Orleanist Comte de Paris on the death of the Comte de Chambord in 1883: instead they supported the claims of a Spanish Pretender, descended from Louis XIV.
[96] On these intrigues, A. Dansette, *L'Affaire Wilson*, pp. 176–222, and *Le Boulangisme*, pp. 106–20.

His constant attendance at the Opéra, along with Laguerre and Granet, and his insistence on talking politics there, have led to him being seen as empty-headed.[97]

This feeling was multiplied by the rumours that went round political circles about his involvement in the intrigues of 29 and 30 November 1887. Grévy resigned, having waited till the first day of December to draw the new month's salary, and on 3 December the deputies and senators met to elect a new President. Although Ferry came slightly ahead of Freycinet on the first ballot at the preliminary meeting of republicans, the Radicals were able to veto his candidature. Instead they agreed to vote for Sadi Carnot, who was elected. Clemenceau argued for Carnot as a compromise candidate, saying, 'He is not much good and is also a complete reactionary, but his name is that of a great republican, and in any case there is no one better, so vote for him'. Having won a reputation for wit, witty remarks were fathered on him; this was transformed into the brutal 'Vote for the stupidest!'[98] Not surprisingly, Carnot never asked Clemenceau to form a ministry, and was just as hostile to him as Ferry could have been – yet another Pyrrhic victory for Clemenceau. But to all appearances Clemenceau's influence was at its peak. In April 1888 he tied with Méline in the election of the president of the Chamber of Deputies, although Méline took the office, being the older man.

2 BOULANGISM, 1888–1889

These personal intrigues were rudely interrupted by the development of Boulangism. Clemenceau was personally affected because it was well known that Boulanger's political career had begun under Clemenceau's patronage, and that the two men had remained in close contact down to the end of 1887. At the end of February Boulanger's name was written into the ballot in seven different by-elections, as a 'patriotic protest'. This led to his being placed on the inactive list, thus freeing him from the formal obligation not to take part in politics. On 16 March 1888 Boulanger openly entered politics, with the formation of the Republican Committee of National Protest with the former Radical, Naquet, as its President. Boulanger's political career during the next twelve months was meteoric. The best summing up of Boulangism is that it was 'the syndicate of the discontented'.[99] Carefully vague about his positive

[97] B. Lavergne, op. cit., p. 395.
[98] A. Dansette, L'Affaire Wilson, p. 229, quoting H. Rochefort, Aventures de ma Vie (1897), V, p. 108.
[99] On the Boulangist movement, see A. Dansette, Le Boulangisme, J. Néré, Le Boulangisme et la presse (1964), and F. H. Seager, The Boulanger Affair (Ithaca, 1969).

policy, it was only clear that Boulanger was against the existing Parliamentary republic. Although many suspected that he was being financed by Royalists, this was only proved after the collapse of the movement. Boulangism dealt a blow to working-class urban Radicalism, especially that of Paris, from which it never fully recovered. The receding tide of Boulangism left many of the constituencies which had been firmly Radical in the hands of Socialists; Radicalism began to appear more as a rural, and, above all, a southern affair. The general's technique was to stand in every by-election, and then resign to stand again, thus demonstrating massive support in many different parts of the country. The electoral system allowed full scope to this technique. In by-elections the whole department had to vote for one vacancy, producing massive polls in heavily populated areas such as the Nord and the Seine, giving Boulanger's success the air of a national plebiscite.

For a long time the Radicals insisted that the way to beat Boulanger was to press ahead with constitutional revision, in their programme long before it had been confiscated by Boulanger. Clemenceau spoke in the Chamber on 20 and 30 March and on 4 June 1888 defending this case. Support for Boulangism, he said, resulted from the fact that the Republic had not carried out its reforming programme, either in the political or the social and economic field. His speech of 4 June, in answer to Boulanger's halting speech in favour of a plebiscitary republic, was an eloquent defence of Parliamentary government, and of the vital role of party conflict in genuinely democratic politics.

> You have mocked Parliament: you find it strange that 580 men are here to discuss the most sublime ideas produced in the course of human history, and that they are unable, at one stroke, to resolve all the political and social problems that have been posed for mankind. . . . These debates that astonish you do honour to us all. They prove our ardour in the defence of the ideas that we believe to be just and fertile. . . . Yes, honour to the country where there is debate, shame on the country which is silent. . . . For our part, we Republicans, we accept the Republic, we accept liberty of speech here and elsewhere, with all its advantages and its dangers. . . .[100]

Although Clemenceau still demanded revision of the constitution, one can sense in this speech the evolution of his ideas about the constitution of the Third Republic. He can already be eloquent in its defence, in spite of all its defects. Revision was the policy of the Floquet government, in power from April 1888 to February 1889, putting before the Chamber a new constitution modelled on that of the U.S.A. But there

---

[100] Clemenceau's speeches are in *Annales de la Chambre des Députés*, 20 March 1888, pp. 761–5, 30 March 1888, p. 923, 4 June 1888, pp. 455–6.

was an air of unreality and half-heartedness about these proposals, which were most unlikely to be approved by the Senate. It had been obvious in 1884 that revision of the constitution bored the electorate. It was the absence of social and economic reform, and the impact of the economic depression, that provided the left-wing votes for the Boulangist coalition.

Social and economic reform was a major element in the programme of the *Société des Droits de l'Homme*, in whose setting up on 23 May 1888 Clemenceau was prominent. Its other leading members were the Possibilist Socialist Joffrin, Clemenceau's rival in Montmartre seven years before, and the Opportunist Ranc, symbolizing the common struggle of all elements in the republican party against Boulangism. But it soon became little more than a Radical organization, Joffrin resigning in August after being attacked by the Socialists for this 'class collaboration'. Ranc was always a maverick, and did not command great influence among the Opportunists, who were unsympathetic to the proposals about social and economic reform. Many Radicals also refused to support the society, and Boulanger welcomed it because, he said, far from uniting the republicans against him, it only emphasized their divisions. At the end of 1888 the society collapsed, hopelessly divided over the question of whether the electoral system should be changed to return to single-member constituencies.[101]

The Boulangist movement meant that Radicals and conservative republicans had to overcome their differences. While the Radical Floquet remained prime minister it seemed that this could mean union on a policy which included at least some Radical demands. But the continuing success of Boulanger, culminating in the triumph of his election for the Seine constituency, completely discredited Floquet.[102] On 14 February 1889, the government's proposals for constitutional revision were rejected, and Floquet resigned. He was succeeded by a moderate government, in which the dominant figure was the minister of the interior, the unscrupulous Constans. Up to this time Constans seems to have been considering joining Boulanger; the fact that he chose the other side shows which way the wind was blowing. The policy of trying to outbid Boulanger by offering reforms was abandoned. Instead, by making symbolic concessions on religious matters, the new government sought to win back conservative voters, while all the power of the State was mobilized against the Boulangist movement. Déroulède,

[101] *Le Temps*, 25 May 1888, prints the manifesto. E. Chichet, *Feuilles Volantes: quarante ans de journalisme* (1935), p. 31, states that Lissagaray, the former Communard and historian of the Commune, drew up the manifesto. Cf. F. H. Seager, op. cit., pp. 159–62.

[102] J. Kayser, op. cit., pp. 169–70. D. R. Watson, 'The Nationalist Movement in Paris', *The Right in France*, ed. D. Shapiro (St Antony's Papers, XIII) (1962), p. 83; cf. F. M. Seager, op. cit., pp. 192–203, and A. Dansette, op. cit., pp. 234–43.

Laguerre and Laisant were tried on the charge of leading a secret society, the *Ligue des Patriotes*. This was ridiculous, as the Ligue was not secret at all, and had begun as a semi-governmental organization; they could only be fined for running an unauthorized society. Constans's real aim was to frighten Boulanger into believing that he would also be arrested, and in this he was successful. On 1 April the general fled across the frontier to Belgium. Only then did Constans proceed against Boulanger, setting up the Senate as a High Court to try him on charges of plotting against the State.[103] In spite of the complete absence of evidence, he was found guilty by what was obviously not a judicial but a political procedure.

The Radicals had played a subordinate role in all this, being divided in all the votes which allowed Constans to use such strong-arm tactics. Clemenceau had opposed most of these moves, as threatening the rule of law and the liberty of the subject. It may also have occurred to him that he was closely involved in some of Boulanger's pathetic plotting. He had also opposed the return to single-member constituencies, voted just before the fall of Floquet's government, which was to prove one of the most effective anti-Boulangist devices.[104] He voted for it in the Chamber out of party loyalty, but had opposed it in the *Société des Droits de l'Homme*, and in republican discussions. On the other hand the law to forbid candidates standing in more than one constituency (the general was planning to stand in more than a hundred constituencies in the general election) was introduced by Clemenceau.[105] This was to be the most successful anti-Boulangist device of all, for it forced the general's supporters to improvise a party organization, and to reach agreement on candidatures, something which proved very difficult. But the contrast between the rising tide of Boulangism while the Radicals were in power, and its obvious difficulties as soon as the Moderates had taken over, made for a great reduction in Clemenceau's prestige. Most Radicals, even with misgivings about Constans's measures, were only too relieved to find that they were successful.

Any hopes Clemenceau might have retained of leading a great Radical reforming party were shattered by the 1889 elections.[106] Return to single-member constituencies at a time when there were no national party organizations meant that only personalities and local issues counted, apart from the basic division between supporters and opponents of the Republic. In some ways the election of 1889 looked as though it were only a moderate defeat for the Radicals, although it was clear that even numerically they had suffered. But the real significance is in the

[103] F. H. Seager, op. cit., pp. 213–22; A. Dansette, op. cit., pp. 266–80.
[104] J. Kayser, op. cit., p. 170. *See* Appendix III below.
[105] F. H. Seager, op. cit., pp. 227 and 231.
[106] *See* diagram, Appendix IV, p. 422.

fact that the distinction between Radicals and Moderates was now only a nominal one, much more so than in 1885, when *scrutin de liste* had compelled some degree of organization and agreement on programmes. This had not had much effect in the Parliament of 1885–9, and was one reason for the success of Boulangism; as the Radicals joined the government without carrying any of their reforms, their role as an opposition was left vacant. But Clemenceau's theory was that in the long run *scrutin de liste* would lead to a more clear-cut political battle, in which reforming programmes could be forced through. Boulangism, the return to single-member constituencies, and the results of the 1889 elections put an end to these hopes. The relapse from the excitements of Boulangism meant that France settled into a period of profound conservatism. Most of the Radical programme of the 1880s was abandoned. Some elements, notably the attack on the Church, were to be revived after the Dreyfus Affair had led to the rebirth of Radicalism, but many parts, especially the constitutional proposals, were abandoned for good. The characteristic form of French Parliamentarism became definitely established, and was to remain basically unchanged down to 1940. From now on the Radicals were its strongest supporters. Analysis of the candidate's electoral platforms shows a remarkable decline in demands for reform. The Separation of Church and State, demanded by 80 per cent of those elected in 1885, was now only sought by 31 per cent, while the proportion of those demanding a progressive income tax fell from 78 per cent to 20 per cent. The anodyne programme which Clemenceau put before his electors in the Var in 1889, in which one of the few concrete proposals was for protective tariffs on agricultural produce, is a very different document from the far-reaching blueprint of democratic reform which he had endorsed in 1885.[107]

[107] J. Kayser, op. cit., pp. 180–1 and 337.

Part three

DEFEAT AND RESURGENCE

1889-1906

6

PANAMA

I 'THE REVOLUTION IS A BLOC', 1889-1892

Radical influence was greatly reduced after the elections of 1889. Although the conservative republicans (the term Opportunist had now gone out of use) did not have a majority over Right and Radicals combined, they were not very far from it. They only had to detach a few Radical deputies to build a majority.[1] The demarcation line between the conservative republicans and the moderate Radicals was now so thin as to be indiscernible. The period 1889 to 1896 was one of great cabinet instability, and one in which important political issues seemed to be completely ignored in Parliamentary manœuvrings. A few of the old republican demands were still brought forward by intransigent Radicals like Clemenceau and Pelletan, but the fire had gone out of them: even the demand for Separation of Church and State appeared to be brought forward almost as a matter of form. The French Parliament was settling into one of its most quiescent periods. The tide of Radicalism had ebbed, and with it Clemenceau's influence. It is also possible that he had personal reasons for accepting a less prominent position. It has been suggested that a growing sense of his vulnerability to attack, as a result of the gradual development of the Panama scandal, influenced him. It seems more likely that growing financial difficulties, in addition to the unhopeful political situation, forced him to be less ambitious. Another factor was the break-up of his marriage. It was many years since his relationship with his American wife had been happy, and she remains completely absent from accounts of his private life. The only witness, and

[1] J. Reinach to J. Ferry, 14 November 1889, Bib. Nat., NAF, 24877, fol. 346. 'I assure you that this Chamber, without being excellent, is not as bad as you seem to think. Clemenceau counts for less than before, and he realizes it.'

not a reliable one, is Clemenceau's grandson, who has told us that, tired of her husband's neglect and notorious infidelities, she at last took a lover. At this, her husband seized the chance to divorce her as the guilty party, and, once this was granted, had her expelled from the country.[2] After some time in America, where she no longer had any family or friends, she returned to France where she lived in obscurity till her death in 1923. The cold ruthlessness with which this manœuvre is supposed to have been accomplished does not tally with the account in Scheurer-Kestner's memoirs of a visit from Clemenceau at Easter 1892. He was very surprised when Clemenceau asked to see him, as they had not been in contact for fifteen years. Clemenceau wanted to talk, not about politics, but about his marriage and divorce. Scheurer-Kestner remarks cryptically, 'I told myself after listening to his recital of this drama that one must never rely on rumour in matters of quarrels between husband and wife.' He tells us no more of what his friend had to say, but it is clear from this incident that Clemenceau was emotionally disturbed by the breakdown of his marriage, and not the cold calculator of his grandson's account.[3] It seems clear from Scheurer-Kestner's remarks that, even before the political catastrophe of 1893, Clemenceau was very depressed, found himself increasingly isolated in political circles, and felt that his political career had failed.

His Parliamentary activity for months after the 1889 elections was on a very reduced scale. He spoke on 3 March 1890 in defence of the liberty of the press, and on 12 May 1890 defending workers against employers who persecuted them for joining trade unions; he briefly intervened on 27 November 1890 in the debate about the budget for the colonies, saying that he now accepted the French colonial empire in Indo-China. It was too late to withdraw, but 'since we are colonizers, let us colonize; let us send out colonial settlers, make capital investments and build up commerce; all we have so far is an army of officials'.[4] Neither of these interventions had much political significance. Nor did another speech of 29 January 1891 have much influence on the immediate political situation, although it is of interest for the light it throws on his own political ideas. This speech was occasioned by a trivial incident, the decision by the government to suspend performances at the Comédie Française of a play by Sardou, entitled *Thermidor*. This play, which presented a hostile picture of Robespierre and the Terror, had produced a disturbance as demonstrators and counter-demonstrators fought in the theatre. The government justified its suspension in terms of the need to preserve public order, but orators from both Left and

[2] Gatineau-Clemenceau, *Des Pattes du tigre aux griffes du destin* (1961), pp. 27–8.
[3] A. Scheurer-Kestner, *Journal*, Bib. Nat., NAF, 12710, p. 207.
[4] *Annales de la Chambre des Députés*, 3 March 1890, pp. 538–9, 12 May 1890, pp. 73–5, 27 November 1890, pp. 719–20.

Right insisted on turning the debate into one about the Revolution. As on other occasions in these years, Clemenceau's intervention was quite unpremeditated. In spite of this lack of preparation, Clemenceau, in the course of his speech, coined one of his most striking phrases – 'La Révolution Française est un bloc dont on ne peut rien distraire, parce que la vérité historique ne le pernet pas'.[5] He used *Le Bloc* as the title of his weekly paper in 1901.

Joseph Reinach, an important political figure, nephew and son-in-law of the Jacques de Reinach who was to be the central figure of the Panama scandal, had attacked the government for suspending performances of the play. Clemenceau insisted that he was not, as his opponents claimed, saying that terror was morally good : 'I weep for the innocent victims, as much as you do,' but terror, that is the use of force, is an essential part of political action. He went on to ask why a trivial incident had caused such a stir. It was because

> the Revolution is not finished, it is still continuing, we are actors in
> it, the same men are still in conflict with the same enemies. The
> struggle will go on, until the final day of victory, and until that day
> we will not allow you to throw mud at the Revolution.[6]

These arguments in defence of Robespierre and the Terror were remarkably similar to those with which he had made his first essays in student journalism, thirty years before. Twenty years later, transposed to the international scene, where for him France represented liberty and progress while Germany stood for tyranny and reaction, they were the same arguments with which he confronted pacifists and would-be appeasers whether French or Anglo-Saxon. He did not become a cynical practitioner of Realpolitik, but clung firmly to his Jacobin view, that liberty and equality must be defended by the sword. This was obviously true of relations between states : it was also true in French internal politics. He was not itching to return to the guillotine as a political instrument. But, he argued, the *coup d'état* of 1851 and the threatened *coup* of Boulanger, showed that in France, a liberal, democratic system had to be defended against opponents who did not share its values. This was what Robespierre had been doing at the time of the Revolution.

[5] 'Whether we like it or not, whether it pleases us or shocks us, the French Revolution is a *bloc* (Exclamations on the Right, applause on the Left: an interrupter "—an indivisible *bloc*") . . . a *bloc* from which nothing can be separated, because historical truth does not permit it.' *Annales de la Chambre des Députés*, 29 January 1891, p. 193.
[6] *Annales de la Chambre des Députés*, 29 January 1891, p. 194. For his anticipation of this theme in *Le Travail, see above*, p. 23. He had also anticipated the image of a block, in his speech of 25 May 1884 at the Cirque Fernando, where he said of the conservative republicans: 'They have not understood that everything is linked together in the republican programme, which has emerged as a *bloc* from the French Revolution.' *Discours prononcé au Cirque Fernando, 25 Mai 1884*, p. 3.

The idea of the continuing presence of the Revolution, of the battle between the Revolution and reaction, was acquired from his father, and occurs again and again in his speeches. In 1891 it was especially relevant because of signs of a *rapprochement* between the Catholics and the conservative republicans. Only in 1892 did the Pope issue his Encyclical calling on French Catholics to rally to the republic, but already in November 1890 Cardinal Lavigerie had signalled the Vatican's changed policy, and important figures on the republican side were advocating the 'Esprit Nouveau', a new spirit of sympathy for the Church. This was the attempt, known as the *Ralliement*, to carry out a fundamental realignment in French politics.[7] It meant the attempt to establish a large conservative party in which Catholic monarchists joined together with conservative republicans. Clemenceau insisted that this could only come about if the Catholics genuinely accepted the Republic, not if they were merely seeking a Trojan horse to bring them within the walls of the city. He hoped that if the realignment took place the bulk of the republican party would reject it, thus becoming a genuinely left-wing, progressive, reforming party. Hence his insistence on the continuing presence of the Revolution, the continuing battle between revolution and reaction. By attacking Robespierre, and by joining with the *Ralliés*, the conservative republicans revealed that they were traitors to the true republican cause.

He took up a similar position in several other speeches in 1891. One of the most famous was made on 8 May in the debate over the tragic incident in the little town of Fourmies where a workers' procession on 1 May had been met with a fusillade which killed several people, including bystanders, some of whom were children. This speech was carefully prepared, and brought forward in general terms a theory of the rise of the Fourth Estate, the working class, which was throughout the whole world demanding improved economic conditions and genuine political power. He denied that he was seeking to divide the republican party, but implored the government to adhere to what he claimed was a tacit agreement made at the beginning of the session. This was that the republicans would put aside their political disagreements, and unite behind a programme of social reform. He admitted that he was as guilty as anyone in the past for letting political conflicts have priority over the pressing need to do something about the grave crisis posed for the workers; but he wished to make amends, and to carry out his part of the bargain. He even appealed, beyond the conservative republicans, to the monarchist Right, by paying tribute to de Mun's generous reaction

[7] On the *Ralliement*, see A. Sedgwick, *The Ralliement in French Politics 1890–1898* (Cambridge, Mass., 1965). A. Dansette, *Histoire Religieuse de la France Contemporaine* (1951), II, pp. 125–79.

to the sight of the executed *Communards*, which had led him to be the chief spokesman for social reform. He asked the prime minister to look beyond the Parliamentary horizon, where tactical considerations ruled supreme, to take account of the great wave bearing the demands of the Fourth Estate:

> Leave this debilitating Parliamentary environment, and look through the window at this peaceable hard-working people of ours, which only asks to be given conditions of order and peace that will allow it to work towards a more just régime. The choice which faces France is between meeting this advancing wave with violence, or with open arms. If you choose to meet it with violence, you will leave our children a legacy of civil war, a legacy of which no one can foresee the frightening consequences. . . . Think of the misfortunes that may fall on this country from within or from without. We must create a social situation which will allow every son of France to reply to the supreme call when his country is threatened. . . . Minister, I call on you to have pity on the Republic, to have pity on France; let us give an amnesty, let us forget. Let us have justice, let us have appeasement, let us forget.[8]

If Clemenceau had really hoped to win general support for social reform, he certainly did not succeed. Only the left-wing Radicals were prepared to applaud him, and the immediate political effect was not great. It was simply not true that the majority of the republican party could abandon political disagreements to embark on a policy of social reform: this was precisely the question that divided them most. Clemenceau was well aware of this, and was not looking for an immediate effect. Indeed the whole tone of this speech, with its discussion of the rise of the Fourth Estate, its care for the legacy of social strife that would be left to 'our children' if a policy of repression were followed, and its insistence on long-run international dangers at a time when the international scene was unusually calm, was in many ways like the articles on the social question that Clemenceau was to write after his expulsion from active politics in 1893. He could have no hope of producing immediate political results but was developing themes governed by a long historical perspective. Two further speeches, of 30 October and 19 November 1891, were similar in character. He again discussed the long-term implications of the rise in the economic and political aspirations of the workers, and stressed that the international situation demanded that France maintained harmony among its citizens, who might one day be called upon to defend their fatherland.[9]

[8] *Annales de la Chambre des Députés*, 8 May 1891, pp. 135–7.
[9] *Annales de la Chambre des Députés*, 31 October 1891, p. 174, and 19 November 1891, pp. 428–32.

In more practical terms, his opening to the Left was demonstrated by his being chosen as their representative, along with Pelletan and Millerand, by the workers of Carmaux in an arbitration of a dispute between them and their employers. The arbitration led to nothing, and the political leaders of the Socialist sects were as determined as ever to have nothing to do with Clemenceau. His reduced prominence in practical politics is suggested by the fact that it was not Clemenceau, but Pelletan, who took the initiative in 1892 in seeking to organize a Parliamentary group of Radical-Socialists.[10] Pelletan, who since 1880 had acted as Clemenceau's loyal disciple, began to take a more independent role, and when Clemenceau was attacked bitterly in 1893 he did little to help him. From that time there was a breach between them, and although Pelletan was a prominent Radical leader down to 1914, he was not asked to join Clemenceau's government.

In July 1891 Clemenceau attempted to take the initiative in bringing about a diplomatic *rapprochement* between France and Britain. Through his friend Maxse he arranged an interview with Joseph Chamberlain, saying that 'important members of the French government knew of his visit and would be informed of all that had passed'. Chamberlain recorded that Clemenceau 'expressed his regret that France was in a position of comparative isolation. He did not believe in any alliance with Russia, and desired closer relations with England. . . . He did not desire or anticipate war with Germany, but wished that France might be in a position to negotiate with some chance of success instead of remaining isolated without even moral support from any other power.' His precise proposals were for a settlement of points at issue between France and Britain in Egypt and Newfoundland, followed by a pledge of British neutrality in any war between France, Germany and Italy, in return for a French promise to respect the neutrality of Italy. He was certainly not authorized by the French government to make these proposals. Chamberlain, although not in office, was, as a leader of the Liberal Unionists, in close contact with the government, and passed Clemenceau's ideas on to the prime minister, Lord Salisbury, who showed no interest whatsoever: 'as long as France was afraid of Germany she could do nothing to injure us. Newfoundland was a small question, and as to Egypt we were in possession and time was on our side.'[11] There the matter rested. It is of interest not as an important diplomatic incident, but as revealing the long continuance of Clemenceau's desire for an Anglo-French entente against Germany.

---

[10] J. Kayser, op. cit., pp. 194–5.
[11] J. Chamberlain, *A Political Memoir 1880–1892*, ed. C. H. D. Howard (1953), pp. 295–7. At this time Salisbury's policy has been described as 'a tightrope act between his commitments to Italy and his desire to avoid antagonizing the French', C. J. Lowe, *Salisbury and the Mediterranean 1886–1896* (1965), p. 84.

2 THE PANAMA SCANDAL, 1892–1893

Clemenceau's first political career was brought to an end by the immense scandal which broke out in the autumn of 1892, known to history as the Panama Affair. Ferdinand de Lesseps, the French engineer who had built the Suez Canal, was determined to crown his career by building another canal through the isthmus of Panama. In 1879 the Panama Canal Company was formed, and at first proved a great success with the investing public. But as the difficulties of the work became revealed, the need to raise more capital brought the company into increasing trouble.[12] From the first the company had sought favourable publicity by giving special favours to journalists, and unusually good commission to bankers and other financial intermediaries. From 1885, when the company sought government permission to issue lottery bonds, this escalated into a vast machinery of corruption which did not produce results, as the public refused to subscribe enough capital, and in the end produced a situation in which little of the money that was raised found its way across the Atlantic to finance the digging operations. In all, about thirteen million francs were paid out to journalists and to newspaper owners, and another ten million to various financial intermediaries and politicians.[13] No doubt the company would have failed anyway; de Lesseps had grossly underestimated the difficulties and the expense, and the company's attempts to raise more money through its lottery scheme were reckless if not actually fraudulent. But the step that magnified the disaster and its political repercussions was the company's promise to pay Clemenceau's associate Cornelius Herz ten million francs if he could get Parliament to vote the law allowing it to raise money through its lottery bond scheme. Herz was probably trading on his relationship with Clemenceau, who seemed to be the coming man at the time, but he was unable to deliver the goods, and various governments refused authorization in 1887.[14] However, the company kept on trying, using its banker Jacques de Reinach, who had many connections among republican circles, both Opportunist and Radical. Herz and Reinach had been associated in various business ventures since 1879. After several refusals, on 8 June 1888 Parliament finally passed the bill allowing the Company to issue its lottery bonds. This had been accomplished by the bribery of a very considerable number of deputies; a list of 104 was talked of at one time, although this was later reduced to 26. Floquet and Rouvier admitted that, as prime ministers, they had taken money from the company, not for their personal use, but for 'the

[12] On the Panama scandals, *see* A. Dansette, *Les Affaires de Panama* (1934), and J. Bouvier, *Les deux scandales de Panama* (1964).
[13] J. Bouvier, op. cit., p. 116.
[14] Ibid., pp. 94–5.

defence of the republic'. Before the bill was voted Reinach told Cottu, the manager of the company, that Floquet needed 750,000 francs for the struggle against Boulanger. This was during the election campaign in the Nord, where the Boulangists were spending money on a vast scale. Cottu demanded to see Floquet, but Reinach brought Clemenceau instead. At the interview the money was not mentioned by Cottu, but he paid up, and the bill was duly voted.[15] Baïhaut, the minister of public works, admitted that he had taken a large sum for his own use, and was the only politician to find himself in prison as a result of the various judicial investigations. But although the others were acquitted, several had received large bribes. Although Clemenceau did vote for the lottery bill, there was no suggestion that he had been bribed. It was his close relationship with Herz, the most unpleasant figure of the whole affair, that was to bring him down.

For Herz had been in a position to extort money from Reinach since at least June 1887. The judicial investigations have left several letters between Herz and Reinach, which show him from that time adopting a threatening tone which rapidly turns to outright blackmail. As soon as the lottery bill was voted, Herz demanded his ten million francs from the company, although he had had nothing to do with the intrigues that had led to its voting. Establishing himself in Germany, where he presumably felt safer than in Paris, he telegraphed to one of the officials of the Panama company on 10 July 1888:

> Your friend [Reinach] is trying to trick me. He must pay up, or he will be exposed, and his friends with him. I will ruin everything rather than be robbed of a centime. Take care, for you have little time left.[16]

Two days later Clemenceau visited Freycinet, the minister of war, and asked him to persuade the company to give the necessary money to Reinach so that he could pay Herz. Again, in September, Clemenceau and Floquet, the prime minister, went to see de Lesseps and persuaded him to release more money for Herz. Thus prominent politicians were prepared to demean themselves to act as the agents of this unscrupulous adventurer who had arrived in France, penniless, ten years before.

But the end was near for the company: the lottery loan was much undersubscribed, and by 4 February 1889 the company was in liquidation. Silence descended while the accountants and the lawyers worked their way through the books. Not until May 1891 did they see their way clearly enough through the tangle of documents to suggest criminal proceedings, and for another fifteen months the public was to remain

[15] A. Dansette, op. cit., pp. 85–8; J. Bouvier, op. cit., pp. 192–3.
[16] Printed in J. Bouvier, op. cit., p. 134.

ignorant of the fraud and corruption uncovered. But too many people in the inner circles of politics, finance and the press knew too much; the scandal could not be buried. On 6 September 1892, the anti-semitic paper *La Libre Parole* began to publish a series of remarkably well-informed articles entitled 'Les dessous de Panama'. The campaign was designed by the former Boulangists to revenge themselves on the republicans who had defeated them in the 1889 election. Other people joined in with more revelations. Reinach was foolish enough to think that he could buy immunity for himself by providing more information. In November the *Libre Parole* began a new series of articles, with even better information, derived from Reinach himself. The intermediary between Reinach and its editor Drumont was Andrieux, acting in conjunction with Clemenceau.[17] Clemenceau's plan was to use the scandal to reopen his attack on the Opportunists, who were the principal recipients of bribes. He was taking a great risk in view of his own association with Herz. In return for his information the *Libre Parole* stopped attacking Reinach, but on 18 November the Bonapartist paper *La Cocarde* attacked the Radical leader Floquet, prime minister in 1888, and now president of the Chamber. The next day saw dramatic developments. Clemenceau's account, published in *La Justice* on 14 December 1892, is as follows:

> At four o'clock M. Rouvier approached me at the Chamber and said that he had sought me at my house an hour before. He told me that Reinach was panic-striken, and that he had told Rouvier that the attacks of certain newspapers must be stopped at all costs: it was a question of life or death for him. The only way, he said, was for Rouvier to come with him to plead with Herz. Rouvier said to me that, in view of Reinach's state, he was ready to do him this service, but that he wanted a witness, and asked me to be a witness. I agreed. At seven o'clock I arrived at Herz's house, where Reinach and Rouvier arrived at almost the same time. The conversation did not last ten minutes, for from the first Herz said that he was not in a position to do what was asked of him. Reinach heard this almost without a word, and asked me to come with him to see Constans who might have some influence on the people who were attacking him. I agreed. Constans was astonished and declared vigorously that he had no influence, direct or indirect on the people who were attacking Reinach. After five minutes we left. In the street as we parted, Reinach said to me 'I am lost'. I was not to see him again.[18]

Next morning Reinach was dead. The official verdict was cerebral congestion, but everyone realized that he had poisoned himself. Clemen-

[17] A. Dansette, op. cit., p. 156.
[18] *La Justice*, 14 December 1892.

ceau's account, and Rouvier's which is equally bald, are merely white-washing. It was not just as friendly witnesses Reinach wanted them to accompany him on his visits to Herz and Constans, but it is unlikely that we will ever know what went on at these interviews. Clemenceau implied that his relationship with Herz had ceased in 1885, or at the latest 1887: in fact Rochefort had met Clemenceau and Herz in London in 1892, and declared that Herz was still, at that time, financing *La Justice*.[19] What was Reinach hoping to achieve by these interviews, and what were Rouvier, and especially Clemenceau, working for? Rouvier, who was one of the principal suspects, had the same interest as Reinach in stopping the revelations, but Clemenceau at that point seems to have been pressing for more. As soon as the news of Reinach's suicide emerged, Herz left for London; he was to spend the last five years of his life in Bournemouth, resisting extradition on grounds of ill-health and managing to win sympathy as a victim of French political justice.[20] In the first days of December 1892 Andrieux visited Herz in England, and acquired more information about the corruption of deputies. Another source had produced the stubs of twenty-six cheques, with indications of the payee which in all but one case were decipherable. Andrieux obtained documents from Herz which confirmed this list, and also claimed that he had proof of many more names, 104 in all. He produced his evidence in small doses, to obtain the maximum effect, and obviously revelled in the panic which he was causing. This was, without doubt, the most exciting moment of Andrieux's long political career. To what extent he was acting as the accomplice of Clemenceau is obscure, although Judet claimed that this was so. He says that Andrieux came to see him with proposals from Clemenceau to fan the flames of the scandal by revealing everything about the Opportunists, but sparing the Radicals. The advantage of this was that the Radicals, knowing Clemenceau had information

[19] According to a statement of Rochefort, published in the newspaper *L'Eclair*, 29 December 1892. Clemenceau, when interrogated by the committee of enquiry into the Panama scandal about his relations with Herz, was able to point to a statement published in *La Justice*, 4 December 1886, at a time when there had been allegations of corruption in connection with Herz's attempts to get concessions for the development of the telephone system and electricity supply. The statement read: 'M. Herz is not a financial backer of *La Justice*. He was a shareholder from 26 February 1883 to 15 April 1885. M. Clemenceau gave him on 26 February 1883 half of the issued shares in return for money advanced by him between 31 March 1881 and 16 June 1883. On 15 April 1885 M. Clemenceau bought back the shares from M. Herz. M. Clemenceau has never recommended M. Herz to any minister, nor to anybody for any favour. In the telephone affair M. Clemenceau's vote in the committee of the budget was cast against the concession project.' This statement, naturally, left out more than it revealed. In particular Clemenceau was forced to admit to the Panama enquiry that Herz had lost 200,000 francs by his transactions in the shares of *La Justice*, which put a rather different complexion on the affair from that given by the bald statement published in 1886. For details of the relationship between Herz and Clemenceau, *see* the file on Herz in the Archives de la Préfecture de Police, BA 1119.
[20] *See* the article by E. J. Reed in *Fortnightly Review*, January 1897.

on them, would be in his power. This highly coloured version was used by Barrès in his fictionalized account of the affair, in *Leurs Figures*, and thus gained almost universal currency, but Judet is a very unreliable witness.[21]

On 20 December 1892 the scandal finally exploded in the Chamber. On that day the Parliamentary immunity of five deputies, including Rouvier, formerly prime minister and now minister of finance, was lifted, so that they could be tried on charges of receiving bribes. Rouvier was to remain in the background for many years, although the courts found that there was no case to answer. Floquet died soon after, his career ruined. But until almost the end of the debate it looked as though Clemenceau was going to emerge unscathed. Then a Boulangist deputy, Déroulède, made his vitriolic attack on Clemenceau. Who, he asked, had launched Herz on his meteoric career, and had given him the support he needed to move on equal terms with ministers and editors?

> This devoted friend, you all know who it is, his name is on all your lips, but no one dares to say it, for he has three things you fear, his sword, his pistol and his tongue. I defy all three, and name him, M. Clemenceau.[22]

Déroulède went on to state that Herz was a foreign agent, and that it was for the sake of his foreign employer that Clemenceau had overthrown so many ministries, and worked so hard to disorganize Parliament and the country. This would explain why Herz paid him, although *La Justice* had never supported Herz's financial operations. Clemenceau rose to reply:

> It is easy to make these accusations, but how can the victim reply. I cannot bring forward documents to prove that the motive of my action was concern for my country's interests. You have a right to disagree with my policy, but no right to issue such odious calumnies. You know that it is an abominable lie: we will settle that elsewhere. . . . I admit that my paper was financed by Herz, and by many other people, but I never supported his financial schemes, nor recommended him for decorations. What other charges have I to meet? I can find none, except the charge of betraying my country which I never thought would be made by my worst enemy. To this charge I can only reply, M. Déroulède, you lie.[23]

As Clemenceau sat down he was applauded on the far left and congratulated by his friends, but the result of this debate was as disastrous

[21] E. Judet, *Le Véritable Clemenceau*, pp. 159–72. Andrieux's memoirs, *A travers la République* (1926), omit this period.
[22] *Annales de la Chambre des Députés*, 20 December 1892, p. 780.
[23] Ibid., p. 781.

for him as for Rouvier. He had touched pitch and was defiled, however imprecise the charges and however ludicrous the idea that he had been bribed by Herz to disorganize French political life in the interests of a foreign power.

Such charges were already circulating in Paris. In May 1892 Dilke had written to Joseph Chamberlain :

> A Frenchman was here yesterday who told me an extraordinary cock and bull which is apparently believed in Paris where they will believe anything, and which I told him was a lie. . . . It is to the effect that Clemenceau's paper *La Justice* which is said to be losing money, is financed from England on behalf of Germany and England by Rosebery and you.[24]

Another Boulangist deputy, Millevoye, attempted to substantiate these charges by producing the 'Norton' letters. Norton was an employee of the British embassy in Paris, who offered documents to Millevoye which, he claimed, proved that the British government was bribing French politicians, notably Clemenceau. When Millevoye was goaded into reading out some of these documents in the Chamber on 22 June 1893 they were so obviously ridiculous that he was laughed out of court. In spite of this he persisted in his claim that the Norton letters were genuine, in a libel case settled in Clemenceau's favour on 5 August.[25] The judicial investigations in to the affairs of the Panama company continued without involving Clemenceau. But if in the eyes of the law Clemenceau had no case to answer, his political position was a different matter. In February a highly organized campaign against his re-election got under way, led by his enemy Judet, now editor of *Le Petit Journal*, a mass-circulation Paris newspaper. A local newspaper, *L'Anti-Clémenciste*, was created, and a *Ligue des Candidatures Locales*, whose purpose was to split the vote by inspiring as many different candidates to stand as possible. They would then stand down in favour of the best placed, and, it was hoped, unite all their voters against Clemenceau at the second ballot. This tactic was successful. At the first ballot on 20 August Clemenceau headed the poll, but was short of an absolute majority. At the second ballot his opponent Jourdan, a conservative republican and a complete nonentity, beat him by 9,482 to 8,609. He was defeated because the Socialist candidate stood down in favour of Jourdan, and, in spite of an appeal from Jaurès to vote for Clemenceau, the Socialist voters were not prepared to follow this advice. The traditional left-wing vote of the remote mountain villages remained loyal to Clemenceau;

[24] C. Dilke to J. Chamberlain, 11 May 1892, Chamberlain Papers, University of Birmingham, JC5/24/236.
[25] *Annales de la Chambre des Députés*, 22 June 1893, pp. 726–32. The court case was reported in *La Justice*, 7 August 1893.

the more conservative voters of the richer areas naturally voted for the conservative candidate, but it was the additional support of the Socialist voters that tipped the balance away from the normal Radical victory.[26]

Clemenceau opened the campaign on 8 August in the little town of Salernes, with a speech which has been called his greatest piece of oratory. By concentrating attention on the ridiculous charges that he had been acting as the paid agent of foreign powers, he managed to avoid explaining anything about the precise nature of his relationship with Herz. Nor, in spite of a great show of frankness, in which he exposed such details of his private accounts as the fact that he had not yet paid for the furniture of his modest flat, did he offer any satisfactory explanation of his sources of income. It was the secret of the financing of *La Justice* that required an explanation. It was not given.

> For more than thirty years I have fought on behalf of the Republic. In 1862, as a student, I went to prison for the sake of the Republic. Since then I have fought in the eyes of all, against monarchists, clericals, and reactionaries of all sorts in all disguises. . . . I have asked for nothing from my party. I have supported many applications for places, but never for my own relations, who are not in public employ. . . . It is true that I have overthrown ministries. Many people have reproached me with this. But what they omit, is that the *modérés* have, beneath all the superficial charges, left the same men in power, and followed the same vacillating policies. . . . By a ridiculous contradiction I am accused at the same time of systematic opposition, and of forming a secret government. . . . I have never refused to take power, because it has never been offered to me. . . . It is precisely because I have been prepared to sacrifice so many private interests to the public interest, that I have collected so much ill-will. . . .

Turning to the charge that he had collected millions of francs in bribes, he declared:

> I paid the debts of my youth with a loan from a Nantes lawyer, which is still outstanding. Where are the millions? My daughter was married without a dowry. Where are the millions?
>
> I have been in my present home for six years and the furniture and decoration are still not paid for. Where are the millions? To such degrading confessions are disinterested servants of the Republic forced. Let the shame be on those who have made such humiliation necessary.

[26] Y. Malartic, 'Comment Clemenceau fut battu aux élections législatives à Draguignan en 1893', *Provence Historique*, XII (1962), pp. 112–38; F. Varenne, 'La défaite de G. Clemenceau à Draguignan en 1893', *Revue Politique et Parlementaire*, CCXV (1955), pp. 255–9.

He ended with an attack on the policy of conservative concentration that made up the *Ralliement*:

> Although I declared in 1885 that the Republic would only be definitely established when the republican party divided into the two universal tendencies, one half for conservation, and one half for change, this situation must come about naturally, not as a transparent device by which the monarchists seek to insert themselves so as to attack the Republic from within. Meanwhile, we must prepare for the great struggle between the forces of progress and reaction; on the one side, led by the Church, all the passions, interests, and forces of the past, on the other the democratic masses of town and country. Let us prepare for that struggle by retempering the republican party in the living waters of the Revolution, and by maintaining its unity against the common enemy.[27]

This was one of the few speeches that Clemenceau was able to deliver; paid bands, recruited by his enemies from the riff-raff of the towns, invaded the little villages, chanting 'Aoh Yes' and 'Cornelius Herz', and breaking up his meetings. The walls were placarded with a caricature showing Clemenceau, pounds sterling pouring out of his pockets, dancing his joy at the betrayal of Marianne to John Bull. He was ill, and suffering from the late-summer heat of Provence; on several occasions his carriage was stoned. Nevertheless he persisted with the campaign, speaking in public when able, and defending himself and his ideas at private meetings with village mayors and other local notables. The day after the result was declared, refusing the prefects' suggestion that he should leave discreetly at night, he walked to the train in the early afternoon, braving the hostile crowd. Perhaps he remembered an even more menacing crowd in the steep streets of Montmartre over twenty years before, when only his personal aura had preserved him. No wonder he regarded Ibsen's *Enemy of the People* as one of the greatest masterpieces of modern literature.

3 ASSESSMENT OF CLEMENCEAU'S CAREER DOWN TO 1893

Clemenceau was to be out of Parliament for nine years until he began virtually a new political career in very different circumstances. His activities from 1870 to 1893 call for a separate assessment. At the time, the verdict had to be failure. After spectacular beginnings his career had

---

[27] *Discours de M. Clemenceau à Salernes (Var) le 8 aôut 1893* (1936). For further development of his views on the political situation *see* his contribution to E. Démolins, *La Nécessité d'un programme social et d'un nouveau classement des partis, suivie d'une réponse à M.M. Barrès, Clemenceau, de Kerohaut, Millerand, Rouanet* (1895).

run into the sands. This was the opinion of Jaurès, Scheurer-Kestner, and many others. It was that of Clemenceau himself, and was why he made a clean break in 1893 and sought to begin again as a man of letters and social philosopher. He still wished to influence the political development of his country, but he thought that he could do so more effectively through journalism than in Parliament.

Was his failure due to his own faults and mistakes, or was it the result of the system in which he had to operate? Jaurès and Scheurer-Kestner, although both were sympathetic to him, mount a formidable indictment against him. There is some justice in their views. Clemenceau had many faults, which were more apparent than his good qualities at this time. On the other hand, with the passing of time, it is easier now to see the elements in the political structure of France which made his task impossible. He tried to be the leader of a dynamic, reforming, republican party which would remould the political institutions of France and transform French society in a democratic sense. But the Third Republic set in the mould in which it had been cast in 1875, and became politically, socially, and economically, one of the most conservative and slowly changing nations in Europe. There were some dynamic features in the France of these years. But overall the non-dynamic features in politics, economy and society stand out, although cultural and intellectual life would be a different matter. As Philip Williams put it, writing of the situation in 1940:

> The country was ending a century of decline: her birth rate had touched bottom, her industry, coddled by protection and riddled by class war, lagged far behind her rivals; her standard of living was low, her social legislation backward. . . .[28]

The roots of this decline go far back, but in the years between 1880 and 1890 the forces making for stagnation got the upper hand. This view of the nature of the Third Republic is expressed in a more formal way by Stanley Hoffman in his concept of the 'stalemate society', which he dates to the period 1878–1934.[29] This model helps to explain Clemenceau's failure. The 'stalemate society' was the brick wall against which he was throwing himself in these years. Seen in this perspective his failure was inherent in the situation. Even if his faults of character and mistakes of tactics made matters worse, there was never any possibility of success. Hoffman's model has three main features. First, an economy in which the industrial revolution stopped half-way. Some sectors of the economy were modern and dynamic, but large areas, notably agriculture and distribution, remained archaic. Secondly, a social system

[28] P. Williams and M. Harrison, *De Gaulle's Republic* (1960), p. 3.
[29] S. Hoffman, 'Paradoxes of the French political community', *In Search of France* (Harvard, 1963), pp. 1–117.

in which, although there was some degree of mobility, class barriers remained difficult to cross; and, added to this, a socio-cultural tradition reinforced by the educational system, in which the values of a pre-industrial society retained their prestige. Thirdly, a political system so full of checks to action that it resembled a motor car with good brakes but no accelerator. The different elements in this model of the stagnant society interacted. The political system was static, partly because of its institutions, but also because of the economic and social structure, and the intellectual and historical traditions which prevented the growth of organized political parties. Yet the institutions themselves were important, notably the stranglehold of the Senate with its massive over-representation of rural areas, and the absence of a strong President to head the executive. The negative type of government which emerged had, in turn, a deep effect on the economic and social basis. Four generations of generous-sounding political programmes did little to make French society more egalitarian, or to provide much social security for the mass of the population. On the other hand a rapid rise in the standard of living was prevented by all sorts of misguided government intervention, beginning with the protective tariffs adopted from the 1880s onwards. The system was circular and self-reinforcing; it had by 1940 led France into a complete *impasse* from which she was only rescued by the impact of the Second World War.

The relevance of this analysis to Clemenceau's failure is that he was the one important political figure to seek to overturn this emerging synthesis in the 1880s. He was not aware of the economic problems, but he was clearly opposed to the existing *status quo* in the political and social fields. The deep-rooted nature of the social and historical forces of the stalemate society make his failure not surprising. But having placed due weight on these structural factors, it is as well to turn to the more personal interpretations of Clemenceau's failure. Tactical mistakes, and certain aspects of his character, also played a part, and his own actions may well have been counter-productive. The political institutions of the Third Republic were in their formative period when Clemenceau made his bid for power, and both Jaurès and Scheurer-Kestner thought that he contributed not a little to their unsatisfactory development. They make essentially the same charge, that Clemenceau not only divided the republican party, but did so in a way that transmitted to the conflicts among the republicans all the intensity of hatred seen in the earlier battles between republicans and monarchists.[30] They also claim that Clemenceau's tactics did a great deal to acclimatize in France the political instability, the governmental weakness in the face

[30] *See* J. Jaurès, op. cit., pp. 21–7, and A. Scheurer-Kestner, *Journal*, Bib. Nat., NAF, 12708, pp. 507–10.

of the Chamber of Deputies, that became the curse of the Third Republic. It would not be fair to Clemenceau to accept this accusation *in toto*. Similar causes produce similar results, and Parliamentary systems of government without well-organized political parties have always produced the political instability of which the French Third Republic was only one example. But Clemenceau's tactics certainly played a part in this development. He was the great 'overthrower of cabinets', and his tactics and debating skills helped accustom the Chamber to weak cabinets, always at the mercy of an unexpected adverse vote. Jaurès also points out that Clemenceau did a great deal to develop a feature that became normal in French political life, and was to prove most unfortunate. This was the practice of a coalition of extremes against the centre, coalitions which could agree on nothing beyond opposition. Again, this was inherent in the political situation, and has often occurred in other countries, most notably perhaps in the combined assault on the Weimar Republic by Nazis and Communists. But Clemenceau seized on and developed all the possibilities of the situation in his attack on Ferry. Jaurès wrote that the division among the republicans would not have mattered if the Right had been able only to cooperate with those closest to them, that is, with the most conservative republicans. In the end this could have produced a political realignment in which a conservative party faced a progressive Radical republican party. This was exactly the development envisaged by Clemenceau. But the tactics he adopted in his attack on the Opportunists worked in the opposite direction. For he forged the coalition of extremes which Jaurès denounced as the prime cause of political instability and demagogic confusion, by exploiting to the utmost three equivocal issues, namely Ferry's personality and his methods of government, constitutional revision, and the colonial question. In the short run they were immensely successful, but the Right benefited at least as much as the Radicals in the 1885 elections, while Boulangism, in which Left and Right extremes united to attack the republican régime, was the logical conclusion of Clemenceau's policy.

Scheurer-Kestner's criticism is similar to that of Jaurès. He complained that Clemenceau failed to distinguish between opposition to the Empire and to fellow republicans. As a result, he introduced among republicans the same intensity of hatred and passion that had been justified only against the Empire. He thought that Clemenceau had harmed the cause of reform.

The Separation of Church and State, reforn. of taxation, administrative decentralization, freedom of association, revision of the constitution in a democratic sense, all that has been denied us by the permanent opposition of a very intelligent man. . . . He frightened not only the moderates in Parliament, but also the majority of the electors, already cowardly and timid enough, without there being any need to add to the causes of their absurd fears.[31]

He found an excuse for Clemenceau's intransigence. He thought that Clemenceau saw his own role as one of perpetual opposition, and that he demanded the maximum so that others less extreme could win smaller reforms. Scheurer-Kestner regretted this, thinking that his mental faculties would have been better employed in office, but accepted it as a legitimate role. Jaurès had a better understanding of Clemenceau's aims and ambitions. He was aiming to exercise power – using every possible device to overthrow the Opportunists. He could not hope to win power in the 1881–5 Chamber. Scheurer-Kestner is correct in that. But he was looking to the next elections and beyond, to a time when he hoped he would impose his own terms, and come to power to carry out a genuine reforming programme. Jaurès argued that 'the capital mistake of Clemenceau's life' was that, after the great disillusion of the 1885 elections, he did not change his policy. If only, Jaurès says, he had stopped opposing the government on the colonial question, he could have become an important element in a reforming coalition cabinet, and spared France twenty years of political sterility.[32] But he did, in fact, attempt to play such a role and failed. He was much less intransigent after the 1885 elections, and was hoping to be asked to join a cabinet. But the violence of his earlier attacks on the Opportunists had brought him too many enemies.

There were, perhaps, other reasons. Clemenceau's personality was, doubtless, a factor in his failure to win power. He was not called 'the Tiger' for nothing, and although he was given this nickname twenty years later, it was already appropriate to the impression he created in the 1880s.[33] His personality was combative through and through. His physical courage could not be doubted, he was an expert duellist with pistol and sword. He was equally aggressive intellectually, and could not bear to give way in an argument. He had a keen logical mind, and although one may feel that the basis of his political creed was confused at this period – he only broke through to a coherent philosophy at the time of the Dreyfus Affair – he had an extraordinary facility in debate. In private conversation, and in debate in Parliament, he was able time and again to make his opponents look foolish. Naturally they did not like it. When Déroulède accused Clemenceau of complicity in the Panama scandal in 1892, he began by saying that he owed his previous immunity

[31] Scheurer-Kestner, op. cit., p. 509.
[32] Jaurès, op. cit., p. 21.
[33] 'Qui a le premier appelé Clemenceau "Le Tigre" ', L'Intermediare des Chercheurs et Curieux, LXXXII, col. 89, 10–30 September 1920; XCII, col. 955, 20–30 December 1929; XCIII, col. 295, 10 April 1930, and col. 946, 15 December 1930.

to the fear that he inspired – fear of his sword, fear of his pistol, fear of his tongue.

Thus Clemenceau was the very opposite of the type of personality most likely to succeed in the political life of the Third Republic. Mild and relatively colourless figures such as Freycinet, who was nick-named the little white mouse, Brisson or Floquet, were in office much more than strong personalities like Gambetta, Ferry and Clemenceau. Gambetta's long-awaited cabinet proved to be a brief fiasco, and it remains an open question whether or not he would have been able to re-establish his position if he had lived. Ferry stands out as the single politician of strong personality who had long periods in office. Resent-ment against his firm leadership played a part in his fall in 1885, and he was never again to hold office. This defeat helped to alter the political framework that had made Ferry's strong government possible. The evolution of the Opportunists into a properly organized and disciplined political party was halted, but Clemenceau was unable to develop a disciplined Radical party as an alternative. Instead politics became a struggle for office in which personalities counted far more than principles. In such a system the men most likely to win power courted popularity among their fellow Parliamentarians, and avoided committing them-selves categorically to policies. A prime minister who sought even to be *primus inter pares* was not wanted; he had to be, rather, an innocuous chairman, not seeking to impose his views on his ministerial colleagues, just as the cabinet itself did not seek to impose its leadership on the Chamber. In these years the *Régime d'Assemblée* evolved its conven-tions which favoured politicians of a very different stamp from Gam-betta, Ferry and Clemenceau.

Clemenceau was too arrogant, too assured of his own ability, of his intellectual superiority, and of his political judgement. To many others, although they might concede his brilliance in debate, his judgement seemed shaky. His friend Scheurer-Kestner was amazed at the absence of any element of self-doubt in Clemenceau's attacks on Ferry, and remarked that he seemed to lack any sense that if he were mistaken he might be doing severe and lasting damage to his country. Joseph Reinach's pamphlet, *Le Ministère Clemenceau*, displays a similar read-ing of his character. Reinach imagines Clemenceau in office, and shows him rapidly becoming a sadder and wiser man. Scheurer-Kestner and Reinach saw Clemenceau's heart as ruling his head, and thought that he was sound at heart, although mistaken, but Ferry had an abiding hatred of him long before the events of 1885. He saw him as an unscrupulous and self-interested demagogue, prepared to dally with the revolutionaries in the pursuit of his ambitions. Clemenceau's position on the extreme left of the legal political scene was easily misinterpreted; throughout the years 1880 to 1893 the conservative minded were hardly able to distinguish him from the outright revolutionary Socialists. When this advanced political position was compared with the ostentatious extravagance of his private life, his frequent presence at the Opera and the Theatre, his riding in the *Bois*, his associations with well-known *demi-mondaines*, he could appear as a cynical demagogue.

There was a widespread feeling that his associates were unscrupulous adventurers who had enriched themselves with remarkable speed. This was not altogether without justification. Clemenceau was probably never a good judge of men; certainly not at this time of his life. Cornelius Herz was the most notorious example. Clemenceau said later that 'Herz was a scoundrel, but unfortunately you could not tell that by looking at him'.[34] Many people thought that you could, or, at least, by looking at him and learning a little about his activities. Many of Clemenceau's other associates were to prove to be among the least scrupulous of an unscrupulous generation of politicians. Granet, Laisant, Laguerre, Andrieux were all suspect in one way or another. A high proportion of Clemenceau's political associates were to join the Boulangist movement. Others, such as Pichon, Millerand, Périn and Pelletan remained above suspicion, but the general impression of those around Clemenceau was not reassuring. Adventurers of all types, whose origins were often obscure, and whose way of life did not accord with bourgeois conventions, seemed to surround him. No doubt much of this impression was unjustified social prejudice. The failure of his own marriage and his notoriously irregular private life did not help. All things considered, it is not surprising that Clemenceau had become a political outsider by 1893. Too arrogant and too ambitious at the beginning, he had been unable to find a place for himself within the charmed circle of what was later to be called 'la république des camarades'.

This might seem to be the picture of an extremely unpleasant fellow. Such an impression would be false. Clemenceau had great qualities, as well as great defects, and there can be no doubt that he was a man of considerable charm. If he was not popular among politicians, he had many friends outside political circles. It was at this time that he developed through the art critic Gustave Geffroy, who wrote for *La Justice*, contacts among artistic circles. Claude Monet, perhaps the greatest of the Impressionists, was an intimate friend for the rest of his life; other artists who became his friends included Manet, Carrière and Raffaeli. He was also the friend of writers like Francisque Sarcey, Mirbeau, Anatole France, Alphonse Daudet. He was still a guest at some literary salons, notably that of Madame de Caillavet, and a friend of the rich businessman Menard-Dorian. Some of his closest friends were

[34] J. Martet, *Le Silence de M. Clemenceau*, p. 212–13.

foreigners. The best friend of his life, he once said, was the Englishman Maxse, editor of the *National Review*. He often crossed the Channel to stay with him, or gave Maxse and his family hospitality in France. After his death in 1900, Clemenceau remained a close friend of his daughter, who became first Lady Edward Cecil and then Viscountess Milner. This relationship, which went back to Miss Maxse's childhood, seems to have been like that of a favourite niece. A similar relationship was established with the Austrian journalist Moritz Szeps, editor of the *Neues Wiener Tagesblatt*, whose daughters became close friends of the Clemenceau family, one marrying his brother Paul. Another foreign friend was the Danish literary critic Georges Brandes. The two men used to meet every summer at Carlsbad, and remained friends until a spectacular public quarrel in 1915, because Brandes refused to support the Allied cause against Germany.[35]

These friendships among literary and artistic circles suggest something of Clemenceau's many-sidedness. Another aspect of his personality is revealed by his love of the countryside, especially that of the Vendée. He returned there every autumn for the hunting season and spent long days in the open air. He got on well with the local peasantry and developed a deep knowledge of their way of life and their mentality which he used to effect in his creative writing. He often claimed, and with some justice, that he knew more of the life and feelings of the ordinary people than did the Socialist intellectuals who claimed to speak on their behalf. In spite of his educated upper-class background, he retained the common touch that many politicians lacked. In appropriate circumstances his language could be earthy, Rabelaisian even, although no one could be more exquisitely polite when required, especially towards the opposite sex. Clemenceau should not be called a bourgeois. He despised the bourgeoisie for their narrow-minded materialism, their prudery, their caution. His traditions were those of an educated and cultivated gentleman, traditions of the land-owning and professional classes going back to the *ancien régime*: like them, he knew, and wanted to know, nothing of the world of commerce and industry. But he struck a chord in the France of the small towns, and the countryside, and long before he came to be the living embodiment of France's will to survive in 1917 and 1918, this resonance had been summed up in the words 'son caractère bien français'.

[35] Viscountess Milner, *My Picture Gallery 1886–1901* (1951); B. Szeps-Zuckerhandl, *My Life and History* (1938); B. Zuckerkandl-Szeps, *Clemenceau tel que je l'ai connu* (Alger, 1944); P. Kruger, *Correspondance de Georg Brandes* (Copenhagen, 1952), I. At the time of Maxse's death, he wrote to Brandes: 'One of my best friends has just died in England. . . . It leaves a great emptiness in my life.' Clemenceau to Brandes, 8 July 1900, *Correspondance de Brandes*, I, p. 302. In 1922 he said that Maxse had been his closest friend, *Lettres à une amie*, p. 143.

7

THE DREYFUS AFFAIR

I A NEW START, 1893–1898

In 1893, at the age of fifty-two, Clemenceau faced failure on all sides. His political career was ruined, not only by his own electoral defeat, but by the bankruptcy of Radicalism. Perhaps because he realized this, he did not seek to return to the Chamber by finding another constituency. His marriage had been dissolved, his children were growing up, his two daughters marrying and leaving home. His financial difficulties became acute. Not only did he lose his Parliamentary salary, but creditors who had previously been content to wait now began to press for payment. At this time he moved into the four-roomed apartment in the rue Franklin which was to be his home for the rest of his life. When more prosperous times returned he was able to afford a small house in the country, in the Vexin, near that of his friend the painter Claude Monet, but for several years the small flat in the rue Franklin was his only house. It looked like the modest home of a minor official, the impression of humble domesticity being strengthened by the fact that he kept hens in the tiny garden.[36] A cook-housekeeper and a man-servant formed his domestic establishment – a considerable contrast to his former lavish way of living. No longer was he the elegant man about town, frequenter of the Opera, and of fashionable parties. Instead he lived in a modest style, and developed friendships among artistic and literary circles. Instead of the Opera, he frequented *avant-garde* theatres such as the *Théatre Libre* of Antoine and *Oeuvre* of Lugné-Poe.[37]

[36] A. Maurel, 'Souvenirs intimes sur Clemenceau', *Revue de France* (1929), VI, pp. 706–38. *See* the description of Clemenceau's study by Drieu la Rochelle, as an introduction to his interview with him printed in *Revue Hebdomadaire* (1923), pp. 1–16. The flat is now the Musée Clemenceau, and has been preserved exactly as it was on the day of his death.

[37] S. I. Applebaum, *Clemenceau as thinker and writer* (New York, 1948), pp. 65–6.

Clemenceau began in 1893 to make a new career as a man of letters. In the next thirteen years he produced an enormous volume of journalism, as well as a novel and a play. At first he did not find writing easy, and his tortured style reveals the effort he had to make. Much of his output is now almost unreadable, and only with his espousal of the cause of Dreyfus did he find a literary style that equalled his oratory – direct and cogent in argument. One motive in his decision to take up journalism was financial. But he also saw journalism as a way of continuing political activity. Looking back on these years, he said in 1906:

> What a mistake it would be to think that political action is confined to Parliament and cabinet. Writers made the Revolution. He who has something to say is an invaluable force. The idea will find its way, in whatever form it is expressed.[38]

Already in the Chamber, as power receded from his grasp, he had adopted the stance of a semi-academic commentator. His speech on the social question of 1891 was one of several occasions on which he asked for the suspension of political controversy, while all men of goodwill united to find a solution. He was now able to develop this idea in writing, and, freed from the constraints of practical politics, attempt to develop a long-term analysis of the social problem and its solution. He also wrote on many other topics, developing the anti-Catholic 'scientist' metaphysic learned in his youth.

Beginning with an article in *La Justice* of 3 October 1893, entitled 'En Avant', he wrote almost daily for his paper until it ceased publication in October 1897. Although his pen was not able to save *La Justice*, whose circulation continued to decline, he achieved enough of a reputation to be hired by other papers. In August 1894 he began to write four articles a month for the famous Radical paper of Toulouse, *La Dépêche*. From July 1895 to January 1897 he wrote three or four times a month for *Le Journal*, and followed this with six months as a contributor to the *Echo de Paris*, desperately seeking journalistic assignments to provide him with sufficient income. *La Justice* made only losses, and in his effort to continue its publication he incurred debts which burdened him for many years. Louis Leblois paid off some of them for him in 1905.[39]

[38] Speech at Draguignan, 14 October 1906, printed in *Journal Officiel*, 15 October 1906.
[39] G. Wormser, op. cit., pp. 514–6, gives details of his journalistic work in this period. Only a very small proportion of his total output was collected and published in book form. The great majority of it can only be found in the files of the newspapers where it first appeared. P. Desachy, *Louis Leblois, un grand figure de l'affaire Dreyfus* (1934), p. 179. According to A. Maurel, 'Souvenirs intimes sur Clemenceau', *Revue de France* (1929), VI, p. 731, it was only in 1911 that he finished paying the debts incurred by *La Justice*.

Most of his articles do not make very interesting reading today. The genre, discursive comment on life and ideas, sometimes vaguely attached to a current news item, is now outmoded. He rarely commented in detail on political questions of the day, but provided little *vignettes*, character portraits of anonymous individuals, or descriptions of incidents of daily life. Some, especially those based on his knowledge of country life in the Vendée, or on his experiences as a doctor among the poorest inhabitants of Montmartre, or those recounting Jewish life in central Europe seen while on holiday trips to Carlsbad, are readable enough. Less satisfactory are the theoretical essays on social and philosophical problems. Some articles were collected and published in book form at intervals, beginning with *La Mêlée Sociale* (1895) and *Le Grand Pan* (1896). *Au Pied du Sinaï*, sketches of Jewish life, followed in 1898, with illustrations by Toulouse-Lautrec. *Au Fil des Jours* was published in 1900. *Figures de Vendée* and *Aux Embuscades de la Vie* in 1903. The most pretentious of these publications are the first two, *La Mêlée Sociale* and *Le Grand Pan*, in which theoretical articles are interspersed among character sketches and descriptive pieces, to which the later collections are confined. The first two books are prefaced by long introductions in which he seeks to provide some unity of theme. These introductions are among the worst things he ever wrote, appalling examples of 'fine writing' in an elaborate, tortured style. The introduction to *La Mêlée Sociale* attempts to link together the subsequent essays by working out his social philosophy. This amounts to a version of *Solidarisme*, the doctrine analysed in a more satisfactory way by another Radical leader, Léon Bourgeois.[40] Clemenceau's speeches over fifteen years had often advocated social solidarity as the key to the social problem. Reduced to essentials, the doctrine, which sought a middle way between laissez-faire capitalism and collectivist Socialism, is, no doubt, a perfectly sensible one. It pointed out the road taken by all advanced democratic states in the twentieth century. But at an abstract level it was in danger of being both platitudinous and vague. Bourgeois's discussion does not avoid this, and Clemenceau's effort in *La Mêlée Sociale* certainly does not. Not content with the fairly practical proposals he had made in his Parliamentary speeches, he sought to provide a cosmological setting for his theory of social evolution. He begins with a reference to Darwin and the struggle for life. There follows a description of the evolutionary process, of Nature 'red in tooth and claw' gradually evolving higher forms through the elimination of the unfit. In human society, the 'social struggle' eliminates

---

[40] L. Bourgeois, *Solidarité* (1896), cf. J. E. S. Hayward, 'Solidarity, the social history of an idea in Nineteenth Century France', *International Review of Social History*, 4 (1959), pp. 261–84, and 'The official social philosophy of the Third Republic: Léon Bourgeois and Solidarism', *International Review of Social History*, 6 (1961), pp. 19–48.

the unfit and leads to the development of more advanced types of human being, and more advanced social and political systems. But, not happy with a 'Social Darwinism', which ruthlessly accepts individual suffering, he set against this aggressive, competitive drive, an opposite impulse – altruism. 'From the eternal conflict of these two sentiments mankind will fulfil its destiny,' he says. He is, however, unable to resolve the contradiction in his thought. Does progress occur because of the ruthless elimination of the unfit, or through the development of altruistic sentiments which mitigate the struggle and protect the weak? He envelops the issue in a cloud of almost untranslatable rhetoric:

> Seen from this height, the social *mêlée* can be judged with a serenity, which, far from excluding a passion for justice, almost imposes it, if I may put it that way. . . . Let us fight the sophists who seek to translate into modern terms the ancient barbarism of 'Each for himself'. Let us preach peace because everywhere there is conflict, let us preach justice because injustice surrounds us, charity [*bonté*] because hatred is unchained.[41]

His practical conclusion from this vision of cosmic evolution was a rejection of economic liberalism, of which he certainly had little understanding. His favourite target was the journalist Yves Guyot, but his idea of the system seems to have been derived more from Herbert Spencer than the writings of economists. In his perspective the modern industrial system appeared as part of the ruthless forces of oppression against which the altruistic impulse had to struggle: 'Slavery, serfdom, the *free labour* of the wage earner, are all based on the defeat and exploitation of the weak by the stronger.' Mankind is no longer killed outright, but worn out gradually by long days of work without adequate recompense, and by frequent accidents. 'The old selection through force has been replaced by a selection based on fraud and deceit.'[42] His background in rural peasant France probably accounts to some extent for his hostility to modern industry, and his failure to see its benefits in the form of increased production which alone could lead to a better standard of living for the workers. His theory justified State intervention as an extension of individual acts of charity, the altruistic alternative to the eternal competitive struggle. At the same time he frequently said that private, individual charity must continue. For that alone gave the moral benefits of altruism. It is strange to find him so obsessed with personal charity, a virtue apparently more in keeping with the religious

---

[41] G. Clemenceau, *La Mêlée Sociale*, pp. xli–xlii.

[42] Ibid., pp. xv–xvii. In 1869 he had written in the introduction to his proposed book on *La Femme*: 'The old society rushes, all sails set, towards the reef, while on the shore industrialism unleashes egotistical passions and animal appetites, ready to plunder the wreck.' J. Martet, *M. Clemenceau peint par lui-même*, p. 258.

approach to the social question. However unsatisfactory this social philosophy seems now, it had considerable impact at the time. Lucien Herr, Jean Jaurès and Léon Blum were all influenced by Clemenceau's ideas before passing on to more rigorous systems of Collectivist Socialism in the Marxist tradition. At a humbler level F. Varenne provides evidence of his impact on a young man with Socialist inclinations: 'in 1896, at the age of twenty, I was introduced to the burning pages of La Mêlée Sociale and Le Grand Pan in which we found our common aspirations magnificently expressed.'[43]

Le Grand Pan, a collection of articles on cosmology, religion and literary subjects, is even harder to swallow today, especially its preface. Barrès, in a very critical review, offers a perceptive verdict on Clemenceau's strength and weakness as a writer:

> Clemenceau lacks nothing for success as a writer, but the fact that he has nothing to say. . . . A writer must communicate in his phrases, the rhythm of his thoughts, the throbbing of his own vital energy. Clemenceau has this energy, this rhythm, and he has shown it in Parliament.

This sincerity is lacking in Clemenceau's journalism:

> What audacity to entitle pieces of daily journalism, without any unity of theme, Le Grand Pan. . . . Clemenceau lacks the modesty of a true intellectual. . . . He ventures on every field, art, philosophy, scholarship, science; without deep meditation on his subjects he asserts his superficial ideas in an authoritative tone. . . . In any case is Clemenceau seeking anything from literature but a way of dissipating his surplus energy?[44]

Of course Barrès was unsympathetic to the ideas in Le Grand Pan, and his harsh judgements should be contrasted with the more favourable comments of Léon Blum, and even, surprisingly, of Charles Maurras. Maurras thought that the preface to La Mêlée Sociale had evocative power, and pointed out that it revealed the opposition between Clemenceau's optimistic temperament and his pessimistic ideology.[45]

> Read the preface and try to forget the meaning of each sentence: retain only the rhythm, the colour, the music of his phrases: you

---

[43] F. Varenne, Georges Mandel, Mon Patron (1947), p. 15; C. Andler, Vie de Lucien Herr (1932), pp. 27 and 95; G. Ziebura, Léon Blum, theorie und praxis einer Sozialistichen Politik (Berlin 1963), translated as Léon Blum et le parti Socialiste, I, 1872–1934 (1967), pp. 30–5.

[44] M. Barrès, 'Clemenceau', reprinted in L'Action Francaise, V, 1 September 1901, pp. 365–70. Léon Blum, however, gave Le Grand Pan a favourable review in La Revue Blanche, June 1896, reprinted in L'Oeuvre de Léon Blum (1954), I, pp. 21–4.

[45] C. Maurras, 'L'utilité de définer', Barbarie et Poésie (1925), reprinted from Revue Encyclopédique, 15 May 1895.

will find a personality that is essentially optimistic, confident and sure of itself. Re-open your eyes, do not listen any more to the sound, but pay attention to the ideas, and you will gain an impression of the blackest pessimism.

Other literary productions were the novel *Les Plus Forts*, published first as a serial in the magazine *L'Illustration*, and then in book form in 1898, and his play *Le Voile du Bonheur*, performed in 1901. On 30 October 1894 Clemenceau told Edmond de Goncourt that he wished to write a play and a novel if he could find the time.[46] He did manage to find the time, and both were completed in the next few years. Blum gave the novel an enthusiastic review, but nobody else admired it very much.[47] As a novel it is now quite unreadable. Clemenceau took all the worst features from the contemporary 'realist' novels of Zola and the Goncourts. He could neither devise a satisfactory plot, nor delineate character. As one modern study puts it:

> The uncurbed violence of the characters, the long tirades delivered at passion heat, the unrelieved profligacy of the villains, the moralizing of the hero, tend to become irritating.[48]

However, the novel is of biographical interest for what it reveals, perhaps unconsciously, about Clemenceau himself. Its hero, Henri de Puymaufray, bears him a strong resemblance. He is the one character in the book with any reality: the others are pasteboard figures. Puymaufray is an elderly impoverished aristocrat living alone, except for an aged family servant, in a tumble-down manor house in Poitou, the neighbouring province to Clemenceau's Vendée. The description of this house is based on the Clemenceau family home, the Château de l'Aubraie, and the most successful parts of the novel are the descriptions of rural life, with the old aristocrat mingling on friendly terms with the local peasantry. When the scene of the novel moves to high society in Paris, it carries no conviction. Puymaufray is the mouthpiece for Clemenceau's ideas, and many pages are devoted to their exposition.[49] The world is the scene of the battle between 'the strong' and 'the weak', tempered by the feeling of social solidarity that leads the good and noble to devote themselves to helping the less fortunate. This is worked into the

[46] E. and J. Goncourt, *Journal*, ed. définitive de l'Academie Goncourt (1935–6), IX, p. 199.
[47] *La Revue Blanche*, 15 August 1898, reprinted in *L'Oeuvre de Léon Blum*, I, pp. 52–5. Blum wrote that 'in reading *Les Plus Forts* one found more than a dramatic story; one had the rarer and higher pleasure of 'finding a man', a man who is deep, energetic, confident, without illusions and whose unshakeable faith in the future is mingled with a sensibility that has known disillusion and sadness'.
[48] S. I. Applebaum, op. cit., p. 94.
[49] Ibid., pp. 97–8. Montperrier, another character in the novel, a politician portrayed in a very unfavourable light, was supposed to be modelled on Deschanel. See G. Brandes, 'Clemenceau', *Contemporary Review*, LXXXIV (1903), p. 663.

plot as a struggle for the soul of Claude Harlé, the natural daughter of Puymaufray but legally the child of a ruthless businessman, Dominique Harlé, cast as principal villain. Twenty years before, Puymaufray had fallen in love with Harlé's wife and fathered the child. Shortly afterwards Mme Harlé died, and Harlé brought up the child, ignorant of the fact that he was not her real father. This conflict between the legal and natural parent was a commonplace of the literature of the time, but one suspects references to Clemenceau's own experiences in Puymaufray's lifelong devotion to the memory of the woman he had loved, but had been unable to marry. His retirement from the world, after an energetic youth in which he had engaged to the full in its joys and struggles, his return to the quiet and resigned pleasures of country life and philosophy, also bears some relation to Clemenceau's withdrawal from active politics, and his attempt to devote himself to the world of ideas and literature. The novel ends with Claude supporting Harlé's demand that the army fire on striking workers. Puymaufray, horrified at her siding with the strong against the weak, in spite of all his attempts to mould her character, breaks off relations with her, and at last tells Harlé that he is the girl's real father. Saying, 'I have wasted my life', he returns to his old manor house. But there is hope for the future. The novel ends with a conversation between Puymaufray and the worker who led the strike, who tells him that he is going to Paris to help organize the workers: 'They will not always be the strongest: those who are now the weak will avenge you.' To which Puymaufray replies:

> I am already revenged. What do human defeats matter, which prepare for the future triumphs of charity. The bodies of dead soldiers are needed to fill up the ditch for the victorious assault. Out of wasted lives is made, in suffering, the genius of living humanity.[50]

A little later Clemenceau tried his hand at a play. This was *Le Voile du Bonheur*, which had twelve performances in 1901, with incidental music by Fauré. In 1911 it was turned into an opera, with music by Pons, and performed at the Opéra Comique. Faguet gave it a favourable review, but most other critics found it feeble.[51] The plot concerns a blind Chinaman who recovers his sight and discovers how all those whom he had trusted had been tricking him. Eventually, disillusioned, he decides that he would rather be blind. The moral is that 'humankind

---

[50] G. Clemenceau, *Les Plus Forts* (1898), p. 400. This was a favourite sentiment of Clemenceau's. He frequently declared that activity was justified not by success or failure but by the motives of the doer. He was fond of quoting Kipling's poem 'If' as a guide to life, but said that it ought to end 'if you do all this, knowing that it is useless, but that it still must be done then you will be a man'. A. Maurel, 'Souvenirs intimes sur Clemenceau', *Revue de France* (1929), VI, p. 723.
[51] S. I. Applebaum, op. cit., p. 85.

cannot bear very much reality', but Clemenceau was unable to give expression to his rather trite idea in a form satisfactory for stage performance. The art of writing dramatic dialogue could not be easily acquired at the age of fifty-five. Clemenceau was disappointed by his lack of success as an imaginative writer. As late as 1902 he was still hoping that royalties from his novel and his play would solve his financial problems. The publisher Stock told him that he should abandon any such hopes.[52]

2. THE DREYFUS AFFAIR, 1898–1902

Barrès's remark that all Clemenceau needed for success as a writer was something to say, was justified by the transformation of his literary style in the press campaign for the revision of the Dreyfus trial. In the immense series of articles which he published on the Dreyfus Affair the vulgar rhetoric and laboured elegance of his early articles were left behind. In simple, direct, often brutal language, he hammered home his charges, with formidable logic and debating skill. He saw, and did much to create, the historical significance of the Affair. As Reinach put it:

> Like an artist, he saw the Affair as a splendid drama. The child of the Encyclopedists, he envisaged a great battle against the forces of the Middle Ages. . . . In his articles he made you feel the pitiless force of eternal truths.[53]

It was the Dreyfus Affair that allowed Clemenceau to remake his political career. Dreyfus, a Jewish officer of Alsatian origin, had been condemned as a spy in 1894, after a secret trial which created little public stir.[54] Most of those who were later to espouse his case, including Clemenceau himself, had demanded stiffer penalties in 1894. Clemenceau had the courage to reprint, as the first article republished in his collection of articles on the Affair, *L'Iniquité*, his savage attack of 1894. For nearly three years only Dreyfus's own family and one or two of their closest associates contested the verdict. The first proclamation in print of doubts about the case was Lazare's pamphlet of November 1896. Clemenceau's old friend, Scheurer-Kestner, a vice-president of the Senate, began working behind the scenes for revision in the summer of 1897. Only in November 1897 did Dreyfus's brother denounce Esterhazy as the real spy, and

[52] P. V. Stock, *Memorandum d'un éditeur* (1936), II, p. 40.
[53] J. Reinach, *Histoire de l'Affaire Dreyfus*, 2nd ed. (1929), II, p. 639, and III, p. 124.
[54] The best accounts of the Dreyfus Affair are to be found in G. Chapman. *The Dreyfus Affair, a Reassessment* (1955, new ed., *The Dreyfus Trials*, 1972); D. Johnson, *France and the Dreyfus Affair* (1966); L. Capéran, *L'Anticléricalisme et l'Affaire Dreyfus* (1948); M. Thomas, *L'Affaire sans Dreyfus* (1961).

author of the *bordereau* on which Dreyfus had been condemned, and the case become a public quarrel. In October 1897 Clemenceau ceased to control *La Justice*, and publication, and Clemenceau agreed to join a new paper, *L'Aurore*. Another contributor was to be Bernard Lazare, the journalist who had supported the cause of Dreyfus. Clemenceau insisted that, if he were to join Lazare as a writer for the newspaper, Lazare should not continue his campaign for Dreyfus in its columns.[55] But he very soon changed his mind. A few days after the first issue on 19 October 1897, Clemenceau met his old friend Ranc, who was surprised to hear of this stipulation. He said that Dreyfus was innocent, and that Scheurer-Kestner could prove it. Accordingly, Clemenceau went to see Scheurer-Kestner.[56] The latter, bound by his promises of secrecy, was unable to reveal his evidence. Nevertheless, Scheurer-Kestner was able to convince Clemenceau that Dreyfus's case ought to be investigated, and on 1 November Clemenceau's first article on the case appeared in *L'Aurore*. It was not long before Clemenceau was fully convinced, not only of the grave irregularities of the trial but also of Dreyfus's innocence. He soon seized on the significance of the case, as the latest act in the great drama being played out in France – the eternal conflict between progress and reaction, between the ideals of the Revolution and the forces of the past, symbolized in the unholy alliance of Church and Army. Partly because of Clemenceau's journalism the Dreyfus Affair was transformed from an attempt to right a grave injustice done to one individual into a great battle which divided France into two camps. The biggest single step along this road was taken with the publication in *L'Aurore* of Zola's open letter to the President of the Republic, under the arresting title, given to it by Clemenceau, of *J'Accuse*.[57]

The political effect of the Affair was to end the union of the centres that had eroded his political position in the 1890s and to reforge the

[55] *Le Procès Zola devant la cour d'assises de la Seine et la cour de cassation, 7–23 Février, 31 Mars–2 Avril 1898, Compte Rendu sténographique* (1898), II, p. 415. *L'Aurore* was financed at this time by a Belgian group, *see* E. Vaughan, *Souvenirs sans Regrets* (n.d.), pp. 32–51.

[56] A. Scheurer-Kestner, *Journal*, Bib. Nat., NAF, 12711, p. 315. Clemenceau wrote to Scheurer-Kestner, asking for a meeting, on 30 October 1897; the latter gives this account of their talk : 'I told Clemenceau how I had come to my opinion by examining the handwriting of the *bordereau*, and for other reasons of which I could only tell him in part, because of my promises. However, I showed him Esterhazy's handwriting, without giving his name. Clemenceau left, not convinced, but disturbed, and from that day began the admirable campaign in *L'Aurore* which has been so useful to us.'

[57] Clemenceau to Reinach, 19 June 1902, Bib. Nat., NAF, 13534, fol. 21 : 'It was I who gave the title 'J'accuse' to Zola's letter.' Zola's second letter, published in *L'Aurore*, 22 January 1898, was more moderate in tone, and was approved by Scheurer-Kestner. When he praised it, Clemenceau told him that he had written it himself. Zola had only changed a few words, before allowing it to be printed under his own name. A. Scheurer-Kestner, *Journal*, Bib. Nat., NAF, 12711, pp. 478–80. Zola's letter can be found conveniently in E. Zola, *J'Accuse ou la vérité en marche*, *L'Affaire Dreyfus* (1965).

republican *bloc* for which he had argued so long. Because a large section of the republicans refused to support the Dreyfusard campaign, the final effect was a Radical triumph : the dominant element in the republican coalition after the formation of the Waldeck-Rousseau government in 1899, and still more so after the elections of 1902, was the Radical element. The clear-cut division between radical and conservative republicans, leaving the radicals in the majority, which Clemenceau had been looking for since the 1880s, had come at last. In view of the powerful good done to Clemenceau's political position, his disinterestedness in espousing Dreyfus's case has been questioned. Arthur Meyer claims that in the autumn of 1897, when he asked Clemenceau if he thought Dreyfus innocent, he replied that he did not know, but that the case would be an admirable weapon in the political battle. Certainly it would be naïve to talk of the noble sacrifice he made in taking up Dreyfus's case.[58] He had nothing to lose, and everything to gain. But to see in Clemenceau's Dreyfusism nothing but cynical self-interest would be even more mistaken. Although it did bring him great political advantage this was not obvious at the end of 1897. The Affair had not then entered the political arena, and down to the second trial in 1899 the Radicals were as strongly anti-Dreyfusard as anyone. Clemenceau saw the battle as being against *all* political parties, and his sarcasm was vented on all alike. Only after the formation of the Waldeck-Rousseau government of republican defence were the lines of battle firmly drawn, republicans on one side, the Right, Catholics and their supporters on the other. Their persistence in opposing the Dreyfusard campaign ruined the position of the Right, and put an end to the realignment of parties attempted in the *Ralliement*. Clemenceau was certainly sincere in his commitment to the Dreyfus case, and in his view of what it symbolized. This sincerity gives his articles on the Affair great power. The admiration of Péguy, with his mystical-religious approach to the Dreyfus case, is clear evidence that Clemenceau's sincerity shone through. Péguy regarded Clemenceau as one of the few politicians who had not allowed 'la politique' to drive out 'la mystique'.[59] He thought that this was both cause and result of his position, half in and half out of the regular mill of politics. He wrote of Clemenceau in 1904 :

His political situation has almost always surpassed his political rank, and his political action has surpassed his official situation. . . . Politics

[58] A. Meyer, *Ce que mes veux ont vu* (1911), p. 137, S. I. Applebaum reveals his lack of insight into the political situation when he writes, op. cit., p. 82 : 'He must surely have realized that by identifying himself with the Dreyfusards he was jeopardizing his chances of ever returning to political office.'
[59] C. Péguy, 'Tout commence en mystique et finit en politique', *Notre Jeunesse* (1933), p. 27, reprinted from *Cahiers de la Quinzaine*, 17 July 1910.

make up the thread of his daily life, of his articles and speeches; but, suddenly, like the spontaneous and impulsive person he is, a person with solid loves and hates, hates which are called rancours by his opponents, he will make some gesture which overturns his own policy. . . . It is these sudden gestures that retain for him the constant, obstinate, faithful friendship of his old friends and admirers; for even at his age, after having lived so long, and undergone so many political vicissitudes, he still retains something which Jaurès has lost already, that is friends and admirers. . . . Even today he can inspire friendship and admiration among many quite young people, even among Socialists who prefer his native astringent Radicalism to the empty rhetoric of scholastic Socialism. They know his faults; but like his *verve prime-sautière*, his wit *à la* Voltaire, *à la* Diderot. . . For he is not merely a representative of the last generation, he goes far back in the traditions of the French mind. He is a philosopher, only in the Eighteenth Century sense; but, in that sense, he is exactly what was then called a *philosophe*. He is just enough aware of scientific and philosophic thought, without having studied it in depth, just well enough informed and just ignorant enough to give *exposés* of it. In the eyes of his friends and admirers he is not quite a spoiled child, but something more amusing, a spoiled father, or an old uncle who has his bad moments, but who, in his good moments, charms everyone. The ordinary activities of his Parliamentary and political life would condemn Clemenceau; what saves him and wins him the sympathy of others, are his moments of forgetfulness, the extravagances, when the natural and true part of him come to the top : it is his japes, his jokes, his clowning, his teasing, his caprices and his asides. His chronic irreverence has greatly harmed his Parliamentary career : but it has kept him the respect of honest men.[60]

Clemenceau wrote an enormous number of articles on the Dreyfus Affair. For long periods he wrote such an article every day, and from January 1898 to the end of 1899 he hardly touched another subject. It is amazing that he did not exhaust it, but on the contrary he found his feet as a writer at this time.[61] Vague generalities about the social question and aimless descriptive writing were replaced by an aggressive

[60] Péguy's article was published in *Cahiers de la Quinzaine*, 15 March 1904, reprinted in *Choix de Péguy* (1952), pp. 30-4. It is interesting that Péguy's assessment of Clemenceau's character, stressing his impetuosity, his unexpectedness, and his sincerity, so strongly resembles that which Scheurer-Kestner had made of the Clemenceau of twenty years earlier.

[61] The majority, although not all, of Clemenceau's articles on the Affair were collected and published in book form : *L'Iniquité* (1899), *Vers la Reparation* (1899); *Contre la Justice* (1900); *Des Juges* (1901); *Justice Militaire* (1901); *Injustice Militaire* (1902); *La Honte* (1903).

campaign, in which day after day he explored *minutiae* of the case, while never losing sight of its general significance.[62]

Clemenceau also took part in the legal proceedings that followed Zola's open letter. Zola was tried for libel; he had intended to use the trial as a platform to campaign for the reopening of Dreyfus's trial. Although not a lawyer, Clemenceau was allowed to join the Lawyers, Labori and his own younger brother, who defended Zola and the manager of *L'Aurore*. He made a powerful speech insisting that Zola and the other Dreyfusards were not attacking the army in seeking justice for Dreyfus. On the contrary they were the true defenders of the army, they were the true patriots.

> There was nothing more absurd than the accusation that they were insulting the army. They honoured the army by requiring it to respect the law. . . . For the last twenty-five years France has been engaged in a double enterprise, which seems contradictory to some. We were defeated . . . and we sought first to rebuild the military might of France. That is necessary, because unless we are first of all our own masters, there can be no civil law, no right or justice. And then we had a second idea, the idea of freeing ourselves from all despotisms, personal and oligarchic, and of founding in our country a democratic society, based on liberty and equality. Then the question arose of whether these two ends were contradictory. The principle of civil society is right, liberty, justice: the principle of military society is discipline, orders, obedience. . . . But soldiers have no function except that of defending the principle of civil society. If, absorbed by the idea of national defence, civil society abandoned itself to military servitude, then we might still have some soil to defend, but we would have abandoned everything which had up to now given France her glory and renown in the world, ideas of liberty and justice.[63]

Zola was condemned, and the Dreyfusards had to continue their struggle in the press with very little support in Parliament. The deputies were extremely reluctant to commit themselves just before the election of April 1898. Clemenceau had been asked to stand again in his old constituency in the Var, but he refused.[64]

Clemenceau's contempt for all the members of Parliament reached

---

[62] Clemenceau popularized the term 'intellectual' at this juncture, entitling the manifesto published in *L'Aurore*, 14 January 1898, 'the manifesto of the intellectuals'. The word had been used by the anti-Dreyfusards, as a contemptuous designation of the numerous scholars and scientists who had joined the campaign for Dreyfus's re-trial. Cf. A. Scheurer-Kestner, *Journal*, Bib. Nat., NAF, 12711, p. 191. It has been stated that Clemenceau coined the term (for example, by L. Capéran, op. cit., p. 77), but when questioned by Reinach on the point, he denied it, Clemenceau to J. Reinach, 19 June 1902, Bib. Nat., NAF, 13534, fol. 21.

[63] *Le Procès Zola*, II, p. 417.

[64] L. Capéran, op. cit., p. 117; A. Zévaès, *Clemenceau*, p. 175.

new heights when the Chamber, by a unanimous vote, in July 1898, gave to a speech of the new minister of war based on the forged evidence against Dreyfus, the honour of *affichage*: it was to be printed and posted up in a public place in every commune of France. As Clemenceau pointed out, even if the documents were genuine, they only proved the illegality of the trial: they showed that Dreyfus had been condemned on evidence not shown to the defence.[65] In fact the documents were ridiculous and clumsy forgeries. A few weeks later this was proved, and their author, Major Henry, committed suicide. Still the government, led by the old republican and freemason Henri Brisson, refused to take action. Clemenceau commented savagely, on 22 September 1898: 'Is he more stupid than cowardly, or more cowardly than stupid? Both.'[66] Even more bitter was his article a few months later, commenting on the death of the President of the Republic, who had been notoriously hostile to the Dreyfusard campaign:

> Félix Faure has just died. That does not make one man the fewer in France. But there is a good position vacant, and claimants will not be lacking. . . . There will be an auction for the right to succeed to his throne, to continue the abominable work. The day dawns for Dupuy and for Freycinet. . . . For my part, I vote for Loubet.[67]

Loubet was elected, but the revision of Dreyfus's case seemed to make no better progress. The middle-of-the-road governments, first Brisson and now Dupuy, who refused to take up a position, still had the support of a majority of the Chamber.

The turning-point came in June 1899 when the President of the Republic, making his customary formal appearance at the summer race meeting, was assaulted by an aristocratic race-goer, expressing his contempt for the Republic. The President was to make another visit a week later, and the Dreyfusards seized on this to make a vast counter-demonstration. Clemenceau was there. Along with the other journalists of *L'Aurore* he lunched with the manager Vaughan, before going across the Bois de Boulogne to the Auteuil race-course. Too impatient to wait for the carriage, Clemenceau set off on foot in spite of the great heat, with his hat on the side of his head, and his cane carried in his usual fashion upside down resting on his shoulder with the knob in his pocket.[68] Several thousand republicans were there, in contrast to the normal crowd of race-goers in which the anti-republican rich predominated, and the meeting turned into a great demonstration of republicanism.

---

[65] *See* his articles reprinted in *Vers la Réparation*, pp. 124 and 128: cf. L. Capéran, op. cit., p. 178.

[66] 'Plus bête que lâche, ou plus lâche que bête, Les deux', *Vers la Réparation*, p. 216.

[67] *L'Aurore*, 17 February 1899, quoted by L. Capéran, op. cit., p. 222.

[68] E. Vaughan, *Souvenirs sans regrets* (1902), p. 264.

This led to scuffles with the police, and when this was made the subject of a Parliamentary question the government fell.

After several days of negotiations the new cabinet was formed by Waldeck-Rousseau, whose career had begun as a very young minister of the interior in Gambetta's cabinet, but who had not played an important political role since 1885. That he stepped forward at this point again emphasizes how reluctant the Radicals were to commit themselves to the Dreyfusard line. Those in the Opportunist tradition, conservative but anti-clerical republicans, like Waldeck-Rousseau, were prepared to take the political action necessary to settle the Affair. Clemenceau commented, 'The Radical party refuses to take the post of danger and of honour: it is the final error',[69] and a little later:

> I hope that republicans of all shades of opinion, will have now realized the connection between the Dreyfus Affair, and the ideas for which the Republic stands. In the face of the threats of the Monarchy and the Church, it is time for the republican party to get a grip of itself, and give the Republic a government.[70]

Some Radicals even refused at first to vote for the Waldeck-Rousseau government. Radical support only came gradually as the cabinet began to emphasize its anti-clericalism.[71] In September Dreyfus was tried by another court-martial at Rennes, and again found guilty, but with extenuating circumstances. It was hard to imagine what these could be if Dreyfus really were guilty of betraying his country. But for two years the case had been presented in terms of a conflict between the honour of the army and Dreyfus, so that it was impossible for a group of relatively junior army officers to acquit him. By implication this would condemn their superiors who had fought to prevent the reopening of the case.

Dreyfus's defenders now had to make the difficult choice between advising him to lodge an appeal against the new condemnation, a course which bristled with legal difficulties, or accepting a pardon from the President of the Republic, which would free the victim at the cost of formally admitting his guilt. Joseph Reinach and Millerand argued that a Presidential pardon issued immediately after the verdict at Rennes would have the psychological impact of an acquittal. The military judges would be disavowed by the supreme authority in the State, and

[69] La Dépêche, 25 June 1899, quoted by L. Capéran, op. cit., p. 286. Clemenceau was among those consulted by President Loubet about the ministerial crisis: he recommended Waldeck-Rousseau, cf. his statement in L'Aurore, 13 August 1904.
[70] La Dépêche, 11 July 1899, quoted by L. Capéran, op. cit., p. 277.
[71] L. Capéran, op. cit., p. 295; J. Kayser, op. cit., pp. 285–6. P. Sorlin, Waldeck-Rousseau, p. 400 n. and p. 403, states that Waldeck-Rousseau had formal promises of unanimous Radical support even before he formed his ministry, but this is not correct.

a way found out of a situation which was juridically almost impossible.[72] The government favoured this course, as the speediest way of ending the agitation and conflict caused by the Affair. Clemenceau, however, regarded this as sacrificing honour to expediency. He had not fought, he said, out of pity for a particular human being, but for the general principle of justice in the conduct of the affairs of the State. His attitude was precisely the opposite of that of the government. Clemenceau deliberately sought to prolong the Affair and use it as a political catalyst. He wrote in a private letter on 3 September 1899: 'I believe that the good fathers [i.e., the religious orders] can be put on the carpet. . . . The poisoning of France by these people is a monstrous thing. . . .'[73] That is to say, he saw that the Affair could be used against political Catholicism; he was one of the principal agents in the creation of the myth of a military-clerical conspiracy against the Republic. The succeeding six years were to reveal the value of this tactic, with the violent campaigns of anti-clericalism that accompanied the rise of a new Radicalism. The dissolution of the religious orders and their expulsion from France, the closing down of a large number of the schools they had provided, and the Separation of Church and State, were all to flow from the political capital made by Clemenceau and his fellow Radicals and anti-clericals out of the activities of Catholics on the anti-Dreyfus side. One large part of the republican political programme of Clemenceau's youth was to be realized after thirty years – the turning of his country into a secular State in which the Catholic Church no longer had the privileged position given to it by the Napoleonic Concordat. The forging of a left-wing republican *bloc*, determined to force reforms, and possessing the Parliamentary majority, was at last achieved, while, on the other side, as he had prematurely forecast in 1885, the conservative republicans joined with the remnants of the monarchist Right. There were, however, differences between what Clemenceau had hoped for twenty years before, and what was now achieved. Then he had included measures against the Church, but placed most emphasis on social reform. Now only anti-clericalism cemented the *bloc*, and when the anti-clerical programme was accomplished, it began to divide again into its constituent parts during Clemenceau's first government.

Clemenceau was extremely bitter about the decision to accept the Presidential pardon, and, with it, an amnesty for all offences connected with the Affair. This meant, as he complained to his young English friend, Lady Cecil, in a letter of 10 December 1899, that 'General Mer-

---

[72] J. Reinach, *Histoire de l'affaire Dreyfus*, V, p. 546.
[73] Clemenceau to d'Aunay, quoted by G. Wormser, op. cit., p. 198 n. 2. The abbé L. Capéran claims that only the anti-clerical propaganda of Zola, Clemenceau and Reinach created the impression that the Catholic Church was opposed to justice for Dreyfus (op. cit., p. 87).

cier and his criminal gang cannot be brought to justice'.[74] The decision rested with Mathieu Dreyfus. His brother, completely shattered in mind and body by his ordeals, accepted his decisions. At long discussions on 10 and 11 September 1899 Clemenceau argued against accepting a Presidential pardon.[75] He does not emerge well from these discussions. As Reinach points out, he wished to sacrifice Dreyfus in order to have a better case with which to move public opinion. He was treating a man of flesh and blood as a pawn on the chess board, or a character in a great tragic drama.[76] In reality Dreyfus would not sacrifice one jot of his honour by accepting a pardon, as no unbiased person could accept the Rennes verdict as reasonable. Nor would the political campaign against the anti-Dreyfusards and the Church lose any of its effectiveness because Dreyfus was released. Precisely because the Affair had reopened a deep fissure in French society, going back to 1789 and beyond, it took on dimensions far greater than the righting of a particular individual's wrongs have ever done at any other time or place. Dreyfus himself could fade into the background, while the Affair dominated the political life of France.

After a long argument in Millerand's office, in which the principal protagonists were Reinach and Clemenceau, all except the latter agreed that Dreyfus ought to accept a pardon. Clemenceau then turned to Mathieu Dreyfus and said: 'Well, you have the majority.' But he refused to advise his brother to ask for a pardon unless Clemenceau agreed. Eventually Clemenceau said: 'If I were the brother, I would accept.'[77] A few days later President Loubet issued the pardon and Dreyfus's martyrdom came to an end. But from this time Clemenceau cut off his contacts with the Dreyfus family and refused to join in a discussion with his former associates in 1903 about the chances of a legal reopening of the case.

His journalistic campaign against the forces of reaction that had, in his eyes, seized on the Dreyfus case as part of a scheme to overthrow the Republic, continued unabated, a notable element in the great argument about the place of the Church that was to dominate French politics

[74] Clemenceau to Lady Cecil, quoted by G. Wormser, op. cit., p. 189.

[75] J. Reinach, op. cit., V, pp. 545–7 and 552–3; A. Dreyfus, Souvenirs et Correspondance (1936), pp. 258 and 326; P. V. Stock, op. cit., III, pp. 156–7. His bitterness about this decision can be seen from his letter to J. Reinach, 9 July 1902: 'Alfred Dreyfus, in signing the withdrawal of his appeal in order to be pardoned killed the Affair. I can do nothing about it, nor can you.' Reinach papers, Bib. Nat., NAF, 13534 fol. 23.

[76] J. Reinach, op. cit., V, pp. 556–7.

[77] Ibid., p. 558. Clemenceau gave a brief account of his part in this deliberation in a letter to Havet, 10 September 1909, Bib. Nat., NAF 24492, fol. 168: 'I found a meeting of seven or eight people all in favour of a pardon except for Jaurès. I spoke energetically against the pardon, and the result of my eloquence was that Jaurès changed sides. Then Mathieu said that if I were going to attack his brother, he would refuse the pardon (he had already explained to us that his brother had tubercules in the lungs). I replied that I was not one to take up heroic stances at the expense of others and I left. I omit the details and give you the substance.'

for the next six years. Supporters and opponents of Waldeck-Rousseau's government of republican defence continued the struggle in the press and on the hustings. The lines which divided them, however, were not exactly those which had divided Dreyfusards and anti-Dreyfusards in the heroic period of the Affair between November 1897 and September 1899. Many Radicals who had been hostile to Dreyfus now climbed on to the bandwagon. In December 1899 Clemenceau left *L'Aurore* after a quarrel sparked off by an article by another contributor, Urbain Gohier. Gohier was an unbalanced character, who had made hysterical attacks on the army, to the disgust of Dreyfusards like Reinach and Clemenceau, who always insisted that they were not attacking the army or advocating anti-patriotism. In spite of this Clemenceau had defended Gohier on the grounds of the right to free speech. He was justifiably annoyed when Gohier wrote in *L'Aurore* that he alone had fought the Dreyfus case on general grounds, and not from a purely personal angle. Financial questions were also involved. The paper was not prospering, and salaries had been reduced. Clemenceau had refused to accept a cut and had been continued at the old rate. Nevertheless he took this opportunity to leave what may have looked like a sinking ship.[78]

His occasional articles in *La Dépêche* continued, but no Parisian daily offered him an opening. Instead, a year later, on 27 January 1901, appeared the first number of *Le Bloc*, a weekly sheet written entirely by Clemenceau.[79] At first it had twenty pages of text, later reduced to fifteen. Rather more than a third of this was taken up by the leading article; the rest consisted of shorter articles and notes, commenting on political topics of the week, and on artistic and literary subjects. Priced fairly high, *Le Bloc* was aimed at a small élite of politicians, journalists and intellectuals, and in spite of a small circulation had considerable influence. *Le Bloc* continued for a little more than a year. In March 1902 Clemenceau left Paris to take part in the election campaign, and found that he could not continue to produce his newspaper. He promised his subscribers to resume publication as soon as possible, but he never did. Péguy, as an admirer of Clemenceau, took over the unsold copies, which, no doubt, formed part of the great pile of unsaleable literature that littered his shop, and was used as furniture by his visitors.[80] In June 1903 Clemenceau began to write again for *L'Aurore* and a little later took over as editor, when the ownership passed to Louis Leblois. Under

---

[78] U. Gohier, *La Vraie Figure de Clemenceau* (1932), pp. 33–5; E. Vaughan, op. cit., pp. 277–92; Clemenceau to Nadar, 22 December 1899, Bib. Nat., NAF, 24265, fol. 2191; and Clemenceau to Brandes, 5 January 1900, *Correspondance de Brandes*, I, p. 299.

[79] C. Lévy, 'Un journal de Clemenceau, Le Bloc', *Revue d'Histoire Moderne et Contemporaine* (1963), pp. 105–20.

[80] See Péguy's statement published in *Les Cahiers de la Quinzaine*, 5 pp. 125 and 157.

Clemenceau's control *L'Aurore* continued to lose money, but Leblois, a rich man with an immense admiration for Clemenceau, was prepared to subsidise it, until he abandoned journalism on entering the government in 1906.[81] Clemenceau's journalism never had much success with the general public, though it appealed to a certain political and intellectual circle. Both his attempts to edit and write for a popular daily newspaper – *La Justice* from 1893 to 1897, and *L'Aurore* from 1903 to 1906 – were failures from a financial point of view. It was in *Le Bloc* and *L'Homme Libre*, papers with a small circulation but considerable influence among political circles, that Clemenceau was most successful as a journalist, with the exception of his great series of articles on the Dreyfus Affair.

3 SENATOR, 1902–1906

In February 1902 one of the life senators chosen in 1875 died. His seat was added to those chosen in the normal way by the departments, and it was the turn of the Var to get an additional senator. It provided a perfect opportunity for Clemenceau to resume his Parliamentary career, without having to oust a rival, although he was at first reluctant to stand. His attacks on the Senate as an undemocratic institution were notorious. True, it was nearly twenty years before that he had been most vehement, but he had never publicly changed his creed, and as late as 1896 had written articles condemning the Senate.[82] He also seems to have thought that he would be able to exercise more influence through journalism than by rejoining Parliament. During the Affair he had condemned politicians of all parties, and he was by now quite isolated from Parliamentary politics. In *Le Bloc* he frequently criticized the Waldeck-Rousseau government. In 1901 the Radicals formed an organized party, *Le Parti Républicain Radical et Radical-Socialiste*, but Clemenceau had no contact with those who founded the party, although several, notably Pelletan, had been his political companions.[83] However, he allowed himself to be persuaded by his private secretary Winter and his publisher Stock; after a brief campaign among the political notables, mayors and departmental councillors, he had an easy victory in April 1902.[84] This campaign was very different from the hurly burly of 1893, and now he had a secure base for the rest of his career. A feature of political life

---

[81] P. Desachy, *Louis Leblois, un grand figure de l'affaire Dreyfus* (1934), pp. 180–1.
[82] His most recent attacks on the Senate had been in *La Justice* on 27 February and 30 April 1896. Cf. D. S. Newhall, *Clemenceau 1902–1906, an old beginner* (unpublished thesis, Harvard, 1963), p. 53.
[83] J. Kayser, op. cit., pp. 304–5, quoting Clemenceau's critical articles of 9 and 16 June 1901, from *Le Bloc*.
[84] P. V. Stock, op. cit., II, p. 40; F. Varenne, *Georges Mandel*, pp. 17–19; details of the election can be found in D. S. Newhall, op. cit., pp. 56–63.

under the Third Republic was that although there was a high casualty rate among deputies, senators were rarely refused re-election.

Clemenceau at once took up his place as one of the leading political figures in the country. At this period personal authority in Parliament and in political circles, not formal position in an organized party, was what mattered. This was particularly true of the Radicals, notoriously an electoral federation, short of men with qualities of leadership. Hence, Clemenceau's peculiar position; in a sense the original and most authentic Radical, and supported by the Radical group in Parliament, and yet not really one of them, not taking part in Radical Congresses, not a member of the executive committee of the party. Never more than a freelance supporter of the Radical government of 1902–5, he contributed to its fall, and yet was called on to form the government that held office for most of the Parliament that followed the great Radical victory in the 1906 elections. Clemenceau's return to Parliament coincided with a new era in French politics. As soon as the Chamber reassembled after the April elections, the prime minister, Waldeck-Rousseau, last of the Opportunists and disciple of Gambetta, resigned. He was succeeded by Combes, who formed a predominantly Radical government, and proceeded to transform Waldeck-Rousseau's cautious and moderate policy into an anti-clerical onslaught. Clemenceau, although not close to Combes, agreed with this programme, and stepped into a prominent place with his first speech in the Senate on 30 October 1902,[85] supporting Combes's decision to close a large number of Catholic schools. The law on Associations, passed under the Waldeck-Rousseau government in 1901, had distinguished between authorized and non-authorized religious Orders. But it had been vague as to whether schools which were subsidiary establishments of authorized religious Orders were themselves authorized, if in existence at the date of promulgation. Waldeck-Rousseau had assured the Church that they were, and that Orders need not apply for authorization for every separate school. Now that the time for application had expired, Combes declared that this assurance had no legal validity, and that as authorization had not been sought, the schools would be closed forthwith. To appreciate the passion behind the republican onslaught on the religious Orders, and their schools, it must be remembered that the Dreyfus Affair was seen by them as an attempt by the Catholic Church to overthrow the Republic. The strength of Catholic, anti-republican feeling among army officers and in the highest ranks of other State institutions was considered a great danger to the Republic. Education was at the centre of their preoccupations, because

---

[85] *Annales du Sénat*, 30 October 1902, pp. 69–77. For discussion of this speech, *see* L. Capéran, *L'Invasion Laïque* (1935), pp. 44–54; D. S. Newhall, op. cit., pp. 114–116.

of exaggerated fear about the degree to which Catholic schools dominated recruitment of army officers and other high-ranking government officials. There was also the general idea that the existence of almost equal numbers of pupils in the State and in the Catholic school systems had led to the bitter and deep division in the country revealed by the Dreyfus Affair. Some republicans sought to end this division by establishing a State monopoly of education, and all agreed that some measures must be taken to control Catholic schools.

Clemenceau's speech did not go into complicated legal details. What he talked about was liberty. In this, and another major speech of 17 November 1903 on a related question, he outlined the basic justification of the anti-clerical programme. He sought to rebut the charge that the Republicans were aiming to persecute and oppress the Catholics. The basis of his argument might well have been the remark attributed to the Catholic journalist Louis Veuillot that 'when you are in power we will demand liberty for ourselves according to your principles, when we are in power we will refuse liberty to you according to our principles'. As Clemenceau saw it, the republicans had a delicate task to accomplish, in that they sought to establish a truly liberal régime in a society where a large group of citizens owed allegiance to an avowedly anti-liberal organization – the Church. He distinguished between the Catholic religion, which, he said, it would be futile to attack, for political power could never win over the individual conscience, and the Catholic Church as an institution. His recipe was to end the legal privileges which the Church enjoyed, notably its financing by the State according to Napoleon's Concordat, and the privileges of the religious Orders. Only then would there be free competition between the ideals of the Church and of the Republic. One of his points was to oppose those on his own side demanding a State monopoly of education. If he had to choose between the Republic and liberty, he would choose liberty. But the choice would never have to be made, for the essence of the Republic was liberty, just as the essence of Catholicism was tyranny and oppression. He painted a great fresco of the history of Catholic intolerance, and then of the contemporary world, showing how countries dominated by Catholicism – Ireland, Austria, Bavaria, Spain – were stagnating, while those free of the Roman yoke, even Russia, were progressing in liberalism and democracy. France found herself in an intermediate position,

conquered but still upright. . . . We are the sons of the Revolution. . . . We have taken up the quarrel of our kings for independence from the Pope, and have extended it magnificently for the sake of justice and liberty. The superiority of our cause is that it will be able to accomplish through fallible liberty, what you could not accomplish through infallible authority. . . . We offer you not the peace of Rome, not the peace of domination for some and slavery for others, but the peace of France, the peace of emancipated consciences, the peace of equal rights, which offers to all men, without caste or class privilege, all the fullness of life.

In a second major speech in November he again stressed that if he had to choose between the Republic and liberty, he would choose liberty.[86] This time he was clearly on a divergent path from the republican majority, although not different from the government itself, and he declared that he was not worried to find himself adding his vote to the Right in the cause of liberty. The speech was against the Thézard amendment to a bill prepared by the minister of public instruction, Chaumié. In its original form the bill had forbidden members of non-authorized religious Orders to teach, but had in other respects confirmed the general right of individuals and corporate bodies to run schools. But it emerged from the Senate's committee with the Thézard amendment, which transformed it into a bill to establish the *monopole scolaire*, demanded by the 1903 Radical party Congress. The amendment declared that all educational institutions had to be authorized by a decree. With the ominous precedent of the law on Associations where such authorization had been refused to nearly all religious Orders, this clause was seen simply as a way of banning Catholic schools. Clemenceau's speech was a massive indictment, and was regarded at the time as playing a major part in assuring its rejection by the Senate. It was powerfully argued and gave the best expression he had ever found to his basic political creed. Many of the ideas were those that he had outlined in his youth, given a more mature form. His emphasis was on the individual, against the encroachments of the State, whereas in the 1880s, although he had never abandoned his creed of liberal individualism, he had stressed the need for State action to allow the individual to develop.

His opening words laid down his position :

I reject the omnipotence of the secular State, because I see it as a tyranny : others reject it because it is not *their* tyranny. . . . We made the French Revolution. Our fathers thought that it was to free themselves. Not at all, it seems it was only to change masters. . . . We have guillotined the King, long live the State-King. . . . We have dethroned the Pope : long live the State-Pope. . . . I know the State. It has a long history, full of murder and blood. . . . The State is by its nature implacable : it has no soul, no entrails, it is deaf to pity. . . . Because I am the enemy of the Emperor and the Pope, I am the enemy of the

[86] *Annales du Sénat*, 17 November 1903, pp. 127–36. Cf. L. Capéran, op. cit., pp. 106–9, A. Dansette, *Histoire religieuse*, II, pp. 300–16; D. S. Newhall, op. cit., pp. 126–37.

omnipotent State, the sovereign master of humanity. Do you think that I have renounced that ancient vision of a divine Providence, holding the keys of heaven and hell, that I have renounced the gospel of sweetness and charity preached on the Mount, in order to worship the State, that monster dripping with human blood, responsible for all the oppression under which humankind suffered, and is still suffering? I cannot do it.

Lintilhac, the Radical spokesman for the *monopole scolaire*, interjected that this was a far-fetched view of the consequences of a modest proposal about the school system, but Clemenceau replied that worship of the Moloch-State was the logical consequence of the steps that advocates of *monopole scolaire* wished to take. 'It is not for you and me to lay down what the State will be in the future.' He wished to remain true to the republican programme by which the State's authority was only justified in so far as it protected the rights of individuals. To betray this concept was to cut at the root of the republican ideal. Turning to more practical objections, he asked what would be the creed inculcated by the State when it had a monopoly of education; would it depend on the shifting majorities in Parliament? In Austria the State had such a monopoly; the Liberals had welcomed it when they were in a majority, but had found that it was turned against them when the Catholics gained control. His own proposal was that the Church be deprived of its privileged position, by ending the Concordat.[87] In itself this would weaken the Church because when bishops and parish priests were no longer paid by the State, Catholic charity would have to be devoted to their support, instead of being diverted to the religious Orders. He also argued that religious Orders should be dissolved, and their members banned from teaching on the grounds that their vows of poverty, obedience and chastity were repugnant to the basic ideals of a free society.

And so, having ensured the defeat of the Thézard amendment, Clemenceau spoke again on 20 November 1903, in answer to Waldeck-Rousseau, who accused the government of deforming the spirit of his law on Associations which had never been intended to ban all religious Orders.[88] Clemenceau, with brutal sarcasm, said that if Waldeck-Rousseau did not like the way his law was being applied, he had only himself to blame for resigning without having been defeated. The new government had a majority in Parliament, and this was what mattered, not the former prime minister's personal interpretation of his legislation. With Clemenceau's support the Senate adopted a new amendment, proposed by Del-

---

[87] This was basically the case which he had argued in the 1880s. *See above*, p. 67.
[88] *Annales du Sénat*, 20 November 1903, pp. 169–70.

pech, which guaranteed the principle of educational freedom but excluded all Catholic priests, not merely members of non-authorized Orders, as in the original bill. Clemenceau worked behind the scenes to get this compromise accepted, persuading Chaumié not to resign.[89] The attitude of the Catholics was that Clemenceau's defence of liberty in principle did nothing to prevent their persecution, as in practice he was prepared to strain logic to the utmost to justify anti-Catholic measures. This particular bill never became law, as it was superseded by another that became the law of 7 July 1904, banning all members of religious Orders from teaching. Clemenceau was president of the Senate Committee that reported favourably on this bill, and did all he could to push it through speedily, although he did not speak again on the subject in public session.[90] In spite of the Catholic protests that they were being subjected to the worst persecution since the time of Julian the Apostate, there was a good deal of unreality about these measures. Existing religious Orders could be dissolved, and their property seized, but in a free society it was impossible to stop people voluntarily living together as a religious community, and the Orders gradually crept back. Nor were the religious Orders ever in practice excluded from the schools. Ten years were allowed for the implementation of the law, and it was suspended with the outbreak of war in 1914.

Clemenceau's speeches of October 1902 and November 1903 have an interest that transcends the petty details of Combes's campaign against the Church. They are extremely important for an understanding of his political creed, which here found its most profound expression. It was the liberal creed, in which political authority is justified only in so far as it restricts itself to guaranteeing the rights of the individual, limiting them when they conflict with those of other members of society. If it goes beyond that, the State becomes oppressive and tyrannical. From our vantage-point Clemenceau appears remarkably prescient, denouncing the twentieth-century totalitarian state, by his exposition of the logical consequences of a tendency which then seemed only a relatively minor infringement of liberal principles. However, his denunciation of the Church as just as tyrannical and oppressive as the State might become, seems too extreme. In 1903, did he really need such strong language to denounce the Church as an enemy to liberty? And was it consistent with his liberal principles to dissolve the religious Orders, and to ban their members from teaching? His attempt to justify these anti-clerical measures strains logic, although such arguments were common to all republicans, and had even been used by Waldeck-Rousseau himself.

[89] E. Combes, *Mon Ministère, Mémoires 1902–1905* (1956), p. 143. Cf. L. Capéran, op. cit., pp. 101–14, and D. S. Newhall, op. cit., pp. 139–44.
[90] L. Capéran, op. cit., pp. 131–3.

Clemenceau remained to the end of his life marked by the atmosphere of his youth, when the Catholic Church had been the supreme opponent of liberalism, at the theoretical level in the Papal Syllabus of Errors, and at the practical level in its support for the Second Empire in France. When asked in 1927 whether he regarded the Catholic Church or Bolshevism as the greatest threat to liberty, he replied without hesitation that it was the Church.

The year 1904 saw the anti-clerical campaign move from the attack on religious Orders and Catholic schools to the measure that would make France a secular State, the denunciation of Napoleon's Concordat with the Papacy, and the Separation of Church and State. After thirty years, this item of the republican programme was at last to be realized. An interesting feature of the preparation of the Separation Law is the extent to which it was done without the intervention of the government. Combes had his own, quite different, scheme, presented to Parliament on 10 November 1904, and never discussed. It was quite unworkable, envisaging a closely-supervised Church whose unsalaried priests would be more strictly controlled by the government than the salaried priests under the existing system. Clemenceau said that it was 'a system that could only have been conceived in the addled brains of an old *curé*'.[91] In the course of 1904 Clemenceau became increasingly critical of the Combes government. In March 1904 he supported Combes against Millerand's interpellation which argued that social reform measures had been neglected because of Combes's obsession with religion, but in the summer his newspaper articles became increasingly critical of the governments' conduct of relations with the Vatican, and of its inertia about the Separation Bill.[92] In November 1904 the government lost its last shreds of moral authority when the minister of war, General André, was forced to resign after it had been revealed that he had used a network of informers, organized by the freemasons, to spy on army officers, to find out if they attended Mass. Promotion was only to go to those who demonstrated their republicanism by not attending. Clemenceau attacked such methods as Jesuitical. In January 1905 he launched a bitter attack on the government in the columns of *L'Aurore*, and along with other attacks this proved sufficient to ensure Combes's resignation.[93] His majority had gradually disappeared, as the Socialists had withdrawn their support in obedience to the decision of the international Socialist

[91] A. Dansette, op. cit., II, p. 340.
[92] D. S. Newhall, op. cit., pp. 217–9. He wrote in *L'Aurore*, 11 July 1904: 'I have too freely criticized the policy of the cabinet to say that it has not committed any errors. It is, nevertheless, true that no policy since the French Revolution has done more to create a state and a society free of all clerical influence.'
[93] On the André affair and the widespread disgust with Combes, *see* A. Dansette, op. cit., II, p. 343. Clemenceau's article of 10 January 1905 is quoted by D. S. Newhall, op. cit., pp. 231–2.

congress at Amsterdam, and as various deputies of the Centre defected in protest at Combes's petty methods. The new government, formed by Rouvier, and much more moderate, was not to Clemenceau's liking, but at least it did not interfere with the progress of the Separation Bill.

The bill was mainly the work of Briand, who dominated its drafting in the Chamber committee. Clemenceau regarded it as too favourable to the Catholic Church, and during the summer of 1905 fought a vigorous press campaign against it.[94] His objection was to Article 4, which provided for the setting up of *associations cultuelles*, which would take over the buildings and moveable property, and be legally responsible for church affairs. It had been objected to in the original draft that even a group of militant atheists or freemasons might set themselves up as an *association cultuelle* and obtain possession of a church. To meet this objection Briand had got the committee to recommend a new formula which provided that the associations must be in accordance with the rules of the religious body concerned ('les règles générales du culte'). To Clemenceau, and to other extreme anti-clericals, this was to place the associations under the control of the bishop and the Pope. It was to give Catholic principles of hierachy and obedience the support of French law, which was repugnant to republican legality. He had used the same strained argument to justify the attack on the religious Orders. On 23 November he spoke in the Senate for two-and-a-half hours on the subject of Article 4, although only to make his own position clear. He did not wish to press his opposition to a vote, as this would only be playing the game of the Right. In order to get the Separation voted before the end of the Parliamentary session he was prepared to vote for the bill as it stood. But, he declared, the question would have to be taken up again after the elections. In the event the point remained academic, for the Pope refused to allow the French Catholics to set up the *associations cultuelles*. When the question was taken up again, with Clemenceau as prime minister, it was not to strengthen the anti-Catholic side of the law, but to find an even more flexible formula to provide a legal basis for the continuation of Catholic worship in spite of Papal determination not to cooperate in any way. He ended :

> What should be the relationship between French law and Roman prerogative? We come from opposite points of the horizon. The Church represents a free system that has been turned into a system of domination, the temporal State is a despotism that is evolving towards liberty. We have come to the crossroads. Let us separate. Your destiny is to

---

[94] D. S. Newhall, op. cit., pp. 260–5; L. Capéran, op. cit., pp. 356–7 and p. 367. J. Reinach complained that 'Clemenceau is once again playing into the hands of the reactionaries', J. Reinach to Marquise Arconati-Visconti (n.d.), Bibliothèque Victor Cousin, Arconati-Visconti Papers, 291, fol. 7011.

go towards ever more authoritarianism, repression, unity, constraint and damnation. Our destiny is to evolve towards more liberty. Your ideal was realized in Russian Orthodoxy, where religious and political power were together incarnate in the person of the absolute ruler, and you have seen what the result was: both collapsed together at one blow. . . . We do not know to what destiny we will lead the nations of the world, but we know that we struggle for an ideal so high, that our defeat, if it were conceivable, would be preferable to your victory.[95]

Clemenceau's hostility to the Catholic Church was so great that it blinded him to the real religious forces that still found their expression in the multitude of different vehicles within Catholicism. Although he could pay generous tribute to the noble ideals once expressed by Christianity, he could only see them as having existed in the remote past. Now the world, as Auguste Comte had said, had passed on from its religious stage, and all that was left in Catholicism was 'a political power on which a thin veneer of faith was varnished. Politics, which was once a minor supplement to religious action, has now become the most important part of the activity of the Church.' He could not imagine the renewal of French Catholicism after the Separation, but could regard it as only a relic of the past, fighting a forlorn rearguard action against the progress of science and reason.

Clemenceau's skirmishing against the Rouvier government and its implementation of the Separation Law continued in 1906. The question now was a provision, which no one had thought contentious when the bill was drafted, that inventories should be made of Church property, to safeguard it from fraudulent dilapidation or theft. As the State officials began to enter the churches to take the inventories, in several areas riots began which were at once exploited by the Right as yet more evidence of the government's persecution of Catholics. The government showed signs of suspending the inventories, for which it was strongly criticized by Clemenceau in L'Aurore.[96] According to Ribot, it was largely because of Clemenceau that the government decided not to abandon the inventories. At this it lost support on the other side, as a certain number of deputies in the centre decided to vote against the government. They miscalculated, for instead of being succeeded by another moderate, Rouvier was followed by the Sarrien government, with Clemenceau as minister of the interior. At last, at the age of sixty-four, after more than thirty years in politics, Clemenceau was in office.

[95] Annales du Sénat, 23 November 1905, pp. 281–92.
[96] L'Aurore, 6 March 1906. Ribot's statement about Clemenceau's influence was made during the debate of 7 March which led to the fall of the Rouvier government, D. S. Newhall, op. cit., pp. 454–5.

Part four

THE FIRST MINISTRY

1906-1909

8

MINISTER OF THE INTERIOR

On 14 March 1906 Clemenceau, 'an old beginner', as he called himself, became a minister for the first time. At last he had the opportunity to show whether he could do better than the other politicians whom he had so often, and so contemptuously, criticized. For three years and four months, an unusually long period for the Third Republic, he was to have a major responsibility for the decisions of the government. As minister of the interior under Sarrien he was hardly less influential than as prime minister from October 1906 to 1909. Clemenceau came close to dominating an entire Parliament, an unusual thing in French political life. This stability was a considerable achievement, although two other long-lived cabinets, those of Waldeck-Rousseau and of Combes, occurred in this same period. However, Clemenceau's first period in office produced much more than mere stability. His first ministry has often been criticized as barren, and he has been accused of betraying the reforming ideals he advocated in opposition to become one of the most reactionary prime ministers of the Republic. Such charges were levied by Jaurès and the Socialists at the time, and have become current coin in most historical accounts. But a serious attempt at comparison shows, without falling into apologetics, that Clemenceau demonstrated much statesmanship. As a critic he had rarely offered profound analysis, and had achieved his effect by hammering home simple arguments. But in these three years he was to show real achievements, given the limitations of the French Parliamentary system. There was no one subject in which he made himself the acknowledged expert, and he was not regarded as one of the technically competent men in Parliament. He had never been important on the vital budget committee. No doubt he was handicapped to some extent by his education in medicine. Parliament was full of lawyers who had the necessary grounding to shine in technical details of financial management and in the drafting of legislation. But the wide-ranging nature of his political interest was primarily responsible. He had always offered a general view of the political situation of his country, and of the direction in which it ought to be guided, rather than a precise solution to a particular problem. Now he was to attempt to impress his vision on the malleable clay of history. As prime minister he provided a guiding vision, a general sense of purpose, a positive leadership comparatively rare in French politics. Ferry had offered such leadership from 1883 to 1885, and so had Waldeck-Rousseau from 1899 to 1902, and Combes from 1902 to 1905. But the two latter had a precise goal: the defence of the Republic against clerical reaction. Clemenceau had the more difficult task of using the political energy generated in the battle against the Church to carry out the programme he had advocated since 1870, the transformation of France into a genuinely liberal, democratic and egalitarian society. Of course he did not succeed *in toto*, and, as he said himself, to talk of total success was to mistake the possibilities of political action in the real world. Politicians must be satisfied with even a limited degree of progress: something had to be left for the next generation.[1] It has been said that such limited aspirations were in absolute contradiction to the hopes of immediate and complete transformation of society which he had expressed in opposition to the conservative republicans twenty years before. But even then he had really offered a moderate and limited programme, and his arguments with Guesde in the 1880s had already prepared him for the debate with the more sophisticated Marxism of Jaurès. He once said that political action was like a team of strong men straining at a capstan to haul along a butterfly.[2] In his oratorical duels with Jaurès, he expressed this point of view with great force, to ridicule Jaurès's commitment to the revolutionary mythology of a total transformation of society.

It is true that Clemenceau presided over the disintegration of the coalition of forces created by the Dreyfus Affair, which had carried through the dissolution of the religious Orders and the Separation of Church and State. But it would be absurd to regard this as in any way the result of personal betrayal by Clemenceau. It merely reflected the fact that the 'Left', the majority, this is, that supported Waldeck-Rousseau and Combes, and voted for the Separation of Church and State, was agreed on that programme, but on nothing else. When it came to social

[1] *Annales de la Chambre des Députés*, 19 June 1906, p. 206: 'I have one argument to bring against his theory [Jaurès's Socialist Collectivism], an *a priori* argument, but one which I think not without value: it is that it is an absolute, it totally suppresses human suffering. That is a great deal. With his organization, the evolution of man, the evolution of human society will come to a halt. I cannot accept a system which has no place for the indefinite evolution of the human spirit. . . .'
[2] A. Scheurer-Kestner, *Souvenirs de Jeunesse*, p. 11.

and economic reform, the Left encompassed widely divergent positions. The question was whether Clemenceau would lead a left-inclined coalition of Radicals and Socialists, or seek a majority slightly further to the right, centred on Radicals and *Républicains de Gauche*, as the more conservative republicans were called, somewhat paradoxically.[3] Jaurès hoped that Clemenceau might choose the former, but he chose the second course. It is easy to see why. The strength of the various factions in Parliament was such that there was no majority for a coalition of the Left, committed to drastic social and economic change. If Clemenceau had heeded Jaurès, his government would soon have been defeated. But he believed, and his period in office demonstrated, that there was a majority for more moderate reforming policies. The remarkable feature of the first Clemenceau government is not that it saw the breaking-up of the *Bloc des Gauches*, but that it demonstrated that it was possible to put through some measures of social and economic reform, in spite of all the difficulties created by French Parliamentary procedure, and by the existence of intransigent opposition on the Left. In reply to Jaurès's charges that his ministry had failed to carry out its promises, Clemenceau could point to the nationalization of the western railway, the voting of the income tax bill by the Chamber, although not by the Senate, and perhaps less justifiably to the progress made on the bill for old age pensions, finally passed under Briand in April 1910. These were not inconsiderable achievements in the circumstances. Clemenceau aimed at the creation of a realistic, moderately reforming majority, and had some success. Other cabinets that followed, seeking to use the same formula – those of Monis, Caillaux and Doumergue – were short-lived and barren. The first Briand government, which appeared to be a direct continuation of Clemenceau's, based on the same majority, and committed to the same programme, in fact meant the moving of the centre of gravity to the right, and the tacit abandonment of the income tax bill.[4]

Nor was Clemenceau's achievement limited to Parliamentary politics. One of the most difficult elements in the situation was the rapid growth of a trade union movement committed to the doctrines of revolutionary syndicalism. There is no space here for a full discussion of these doctrines, but their main elements, accepted by the Amiens Congress of the *Confédération Générale du Travail* (C.G.T.) in October 1906, were that the trade union movement should be independent of all political parties, even the Socialists, that it should work by 'direct action' for the revolu-

---

[3] This was the title of the main group of conservative republicans in the Chamber of Deputies: their party affiliation was the Alliance Démocratique. *See* Appendix IV, p. 420.
[4] J. P. Marichy, *La Deuxième Chambre dans La Vie Politique Français depuis 1875* (1969) pp. 590–1, gives a useful schematic picture of the different majorities; and *see below*, Appendices IV and V.

tion, and that the workers owed no loyalty to the bourgeois state.[5] The consequence of these doctrines was that strikes were seen not merely as ways of winning better wages and conditions of work, but as a fundamental challenge to the existing state and social order; any strike might, if conditions were favourable, turn into a general strike in which the whole proletariat would take part, and this in turn merge into the revolution. Another result was that the C.G.T. sought to organize anti-patriotic and anti-militarist movements, and defended violent action on the part of strikers as the necessary reply to the oppression of State, employer and bourgeoisie. Jaurès certainly did not agree with these extremist doctrines, but was determined not to be cut off from the trade union movement, and thus found himself defending the position of the C.G.T., and attacking Clemenceau's government for being unnecessarily provocative. Jaurès's view has been accepted in many accounts, but Clemenceau often had a better case than his critics, from any point of view but that of someone committed to the doctrines of revolutionary syndicalism. When the wave of extremism which seemed to be carrying away the trade union movement between 1905 and 1908 began to recede, it owed more to Clemenceau's handling of the situation than to the fact that his fall reduced the temperature; the turning-point came in the autumn of 1908. The years 1906–9 have often been presented as a period in which an unusual amount of blood was shed in domestic political disturbances, because Clemenceau was in some unspecified way 'a man of blood', following a policy that was either Machiavellian in its cunning duplicity, or clumsily incoherent, first encouraging radical movements and demonstrations, and then repressing them with unnecessary brutality. There is possibly some truth in this latter judgement when applied to the strike movement of March and April 1906, but afterwards his touch was more delicate, and he successfully followed a middle road between weakness and brutality.

2 MINISTER OF THE INTERIOR

The Sarrien cabinet, formed only a few weeks before the general elections, was a caretaker government presided over by a colourless politician. It included widely divergent strands of republicanism; Poincaré and Etienne came from the Centre, Bourgeois and Clemenceau from the Radical wing, and Briand from the Socialist group, although his appoint-

---

[5] F. F. Ridley, *Revolutionary Syndicalism in France* (1970) gives an account of the theories; a more perceptive analysis of their place in French trade unionism, and their very limited hold over the working class as a whole, is to be found in P. F. Stearns, *Revolutionary Syndicalism and French Labour: a cause without rebels* (Rutgers, 1971). Cf. also H. Dubief, *Le Syndicalisme Révolutionnaire* (1969).

ment led to his exclusion from the S.F.I.O., and started him on the road that was to lead very quickly from the extreme left to the extreme centre. Anti-clerical Radicals of the Combes-Pelletan type were conspicuous by their absence, but otherwise the Sarrien cabinet was a complete cross-section of republicanism. Clemenceau's portfolio resulted perhaps from the recent election of Fallières as President of the Republic. He had supported Fallières's candidacy, and it was said that in return he was to be brought into the government. An alternative version is that Briand insisted on including Clemenceau on the grounds that he could be a dangerous critic if left out.[6] This referred to the application of the law on Separation of Church and State, which Clemenceau had criticized as yielding too much to the Catholic Church. In spite of their disagreement on this question, the two men had recently become associated in a short-lived venture to join together moderate Socialists and Radicals who wanted social reform. This was an organization founded by the young Paul-Boncour, called the *Comité de la Démocratie Sociale*, which Clemenceau joined on 11 February 1906; its other members included Briand, Viviani and Millerand from the Socialist side and Doumergue, Buisson, Jeanneney and Sarraut from the Radicals.[7] Another sign that Clemenceau was seeking to unite the moderate Left, bringing together those Socialists who refused to accept the tenets and discipline of the unified party, with Radicals who wanted social reform, was his part in setting up a new group in the Senate, the *Groupe Radicale-Socialiste*. It had fifty-three members, all but eleven of whom remained members of the *Gauche Démocratique*, as did Clemenceau.[8] The manifesto of the new group, emphasizing its socialism, was published in *L'Aurore* of 26 January 1906. The *Comité de la Démocratie Sociale* also declared its support for reformist Socialism, for the development of trade unions and the nationalization of certain monopolies, while strongly condemning the Marxism and anti-patriotism of the S.F.I.O. Clemenceau had already engaged in a debate with Jaurès in the columns of their respective newspapers, *L'Aurore* and *L'Humanité*, in August and September 1905, on patriotism and Socialist internationalism.[9]

[6] R. Wallier, ed. *Le Vingtième Siècle Politique, Année* 1906, pp. 3 and 22; G. Suarez, *Briand, Sa Vie, Son Oeuvre avec son journal et de Nombreux Documents Inédits* (1938–52), II, pp. 82–7; and D. Newhall, *Clemenceau 1902–1906*, pp. 460–7. One of the most famous apocryphal witticisms attributed to Clemenceau is that he is said to have acquired the prominent post of minister of the interior by replying 'Je prends l'Intérior', when the mild Sarrien, at one of the meetings before the composition of the cabinet was fixed, asked 'what will you have?', referring to the refreshments. However ridiculous it would be to take this seriously, it does express the domination which Clemenceau clearly exercised over Sarrien.

[7] G. Suarez, op. cit., II, p. 77; D. Newhall, op. cit., p. 447.

[8] For the group system in the French Parliament, and its ambiguous relation with the political parties, *see* Appendix IV, pp. 417–21.

[9] Jaurès's articles have been reprinted in his *Oeuvres Complètes* (Paris, 1931), II, pp. 271–96. Clemenceau's can only be found in the files of *L'Aurore*.

The new government was faced with critical decisions in three fields: the religious question, foreign affairs, and that of social unrest. On the first question, the taking of inventories of Church furnishings, which had caused the fall of the Rouvier cabinet, the Sarrien government at once decided, at Briand's suggestion, to suspend inventories until they could be taken without disturbing public order. Although Clemenceau had attacked the Rouvier cabinet for showing signs of weakness about the inventories, he accepted this about-turn, and defended the government's decision in the Senate on 30 March, saying that the counting of candles could not be allowed to jeopardize human life.[10] In foreign affairs the new government took over at the most critical moment of the negotiation of the Convention of Algeçiras, and Clemenceau played a prominent part in stiffening French resolve. His intervention was much more than would normally have been expected of a minister of the interior, and showed that he was from the first one of the dominant personalities in the Sarrien cabinet.[11] Finally, on the social question, the immediate crisis resulted from the terrible catastrophe at Courrières near Lens, in the northern coalfield, on 10 March, when an explosion destroyed the main shaft and killed over a thousand miners. Rescue operations proved to be impossible, and only a handful of men escaped after several days of entombment. The disaster led to a strike affecting the whole northern coalfield, which lasted until 7 May. It began as a spontaneous outburst of resentment against the terrible impersonal forces, natural and social, that governed the lives of the miners. This was rationalized first into a protest against the mining companies and their engineers, whose callous negligence, it was claimed, had allowed the explosion to take place, and who had then refused to carry out rescue operations.[12] But the strike soon turned into a demand for increased wages. The situation was complicated because the strike erupted spontaneously, without being organized by the strong and old-established miners' union, controlled by the Socialist deputy Basly, a moderate who had worked with Clemenceau in 1884. A small group, led by Broutchoux, advocating revolutionary syndicalism and affiliation to the c.g.t., sought to exploit the situation so as to gain control of the miners, and win them over to extremist doctrines. Their attempt was unsuccessful, but it prolonged the strike for several weeks until the miners accepted the advice of their old leaders, and went back to work with a handsome increase in wages.

[10] Clemenceau's articles opposing the suspension of the inventories are in *L'Aurore* of 6 March and *La Dépêche* of 11 March.
[11] *See below*, pp. 215–18.
[12] A committee of enquiry found that these charges were unfounded, and that all normal safety precautions had been taken.

Clemenceau seized the opportunity of demonstrating a change in the government's attitude by issuing a circular to the prefects, ordering them not to call in the army unless absolutely necessary, and by visiting the scene of the disaster, and speaking to the strikers.[13] After visiting Basly's union on 19 March, he went on to a meeting organized by the Broutchoux group. General opinion was that this was a mistake, as it gave official recognition to the extremists, and reduced the authority of the moderate 'old union'. But Clemenceau argued that, at the moment, the extremists had the strikers' support, and if he wished to meet them he had to go to the Broutchoux group's meeting. However, his intervention was not a success. The audience was unable to appreciate the subtleties of his argument about the balance to be struck between the right to strike and the rights of those who wished to continue working. But they gathered from his speech that in some vague way things had changed, that troops would not be used, and that the strikers had the moral support of the government.[14] The result was that the strike rapidly became one of the most violent yet seen in France, and troops had to be sent in the next day. Workers who did not want to strike were beaten up and their houses pillaged. A young lieutenant was killed by a stone, and only the occupation of the entire area by 20,000 troops (one for every two strikers) restored order. Clemenceau claimed that there was no contradiction between this action and his promises. He had only rejected the preventive introduction of troops into the scene of a strike, and when confronted with such violence the government had no alternative but to mobilize the army. Nevertheless, his action was a great step along the road to his new reputation as 'le premier flic de France', the defender of the social order. 'I am accused of being prejudiced in favour of order,' he said, 'and I willingly admit it.'[15] Without law and order, without the protection by the State of the rights of every individual, it was a mockery to talk of fighting for greater social justice. But he was led here into head-on conflict with the ideals of the labour movement. While his liberal principles dictated that a man who wished to work had the right to do so, and to be protected, it was an equally firm tenet of the trade unionist that strikers were entitled to use any

[13] A copy of the instructions issued by the Prefect of the Department of the Nord about the use of troops is to be found in the records of the departmental committee set up to revise the regulations governing the use of the army in strikes. Archives Nationales, F⁷ 12913, *Procès-Verbaux de la Sous-commission, Requisition de la Force Armée*, Séance du 22 February 1907, Annexe. Clemenceau described his intervention in his speech, *Annales de la Chambre des Députés*, 18 June 1906, pp. 191–2.

[14] Cf. Steeg's judgement on Clemenceau: 'He was unable to realize that his own clarity of mind, which showed him the precise line of demarcation between what was possible and that which could not be allowed, was not shared by the inexperienced and easily swayed mass of ordinary people.' *Bulletin du Parti Radical*, 199, 7 August 1909.

[15] *Annales de la Chambre des Députés*, 18 June 1906, p. 199.

means to prevent strike-breaking.[16] With poorly organized unions, un-recognized by the employers who on many occasions had recourse to 'yellow' labour to replace strikers, this was an understandable attitude. A month later he made a second visit to Lens, to mediate between the mining companies and the union leadership. This intervention was equally unsuccessful and the strike did not end until 7 May.[17]

Clemenceau came into office just in time to confront the most am-bitious operation yet attempted by the c.g.t., the so-called general strike of 1 May 1906. It had been decided at the c.g.t. Congress of 1904 to proclaim 1 May 1906 the day of a great demonstration in favour of an eight-hour day. The original proposal was that workers of all trades would simply down tools after eight hours, but this had escalated into wilder projects. Some talked of an indefinite general strike that would merge into a mass revolutionary movement. The great majority who went on strike did so, however, in pursuit of definite objectives: reduced hours or increased wages, or both. 1 May saw not so much an isolated gesture in favour of the eight-hour day, and certainly not an abortive revolution, but an abnormally large number of strikes in different trades, which took the c.g.t. strike call as a starting signal. If the movement was far less successful than the c.g.t. leaders had hoped, or the bour-geoisie had feared, it was nevertheless the most widespread strike move-ment France knew before 1914. The relative success of the strike-call demonstrated that membership figures were not the only criterion of the hold of the c.g.t. over the working class. It had an audience that, in suitable circumstances, went far beyond its actual membership. The 1 May movement produced a massive wave of industrial unrest. In the whole year there were 1,309 strikes, involving 438,466 strikers and pro-ducing a loss of 9,438,594 days' work. The number of days lost was almost double that of any other year before 1919. The Ministère du Travail estimated that out of this total, 48 per cent of the strikers and

---

[16] In his speech in the Chamber on 19 June he attacked Jaurès for saying that strikers had a right to prevent other workers replacing them. Clemenceau declared that the right of the individual to work, if he chose, was the basis of any social organization; 'La concurrence vitale' was an eternal phenomenon that could only be attenuated, not suppressed. The worker who went on strike was seeking to improve his standard of living, but the worker who wished to replace him might be struggling for life for himself and his family. *Annales de la Chambre des Députés*, 9 June 1906, p. 204.

[17] Ministère du Travail, *Statistique des Grèves* (1906), pp. 752–4, Procès-Verbaux de l'Entretien du 27 Avril 1906, refer to Clemenceau's mediation on 19 April. Cf. also *Bulletin de l'Office du Travail*, April 1906, p. 326. M. Borgeaud, *Le Salaire des Ouvriers des Mines de Charbon en France depuis 1900* (1938), p. 74, and table on pp. 66–7, shows that the strike came at the end of a four-year period of falling prices and downward pressure on wages, and at the beginning of an upturn which lasted, with a brief interruption in 1909–10, until the war. This economic con-juncture explains both the bitterness of the miners, and the readiness with which, in the changed circumstances, the companies granted a substantial increase in wages.

37 per cent of the days lost was due to strikes associated with the 1 May movement; if the miners' strike is added to this, the proportion comes to 68 per cent of the strikers and 72 per cent of the days lost. When considering Clemenceau's reputation as the minister who presided over, and, it is charged, was responsible for, a bad period in French labour relations, it must be remembered that this is only true if attention is concentrated on 1906; in that year the figures were affected by those strikes which occurred within a few weeks of his taking office and for reasons which had nothing to do with his policies. His period as prime minister did not have an especially bad record for strikes, although there were some spectacular incidents. The average number of strikes, strikers, and days lost for 1907–9 is about the same as the average for the whole period 1900–13, and considerably lower than that for 1910–11. 1910–11, when the conciliatory Briand was in power, were the worst years for industrial unrest, with the exception of spring 1906. Clearly the most important factor in the fluctuation of strikes was not governmental action but the trade cycle.[18]

Such economic considerations were far removed from the panic which spread in France, especially among the middle classes in Paris, before 1 May 1906. As the C.G.T. leaders were advocating a general strike as the first step in a mass revolutionary movement, this was perhaps not unreasonable. Clemenceau was determined to crush disorder that might redound to the advantage of the Right in the forthcoming elections. He had to show that a Radical minister of the interior could preserve law and order. He interviewed Griffuelhes, the Secretary of the C.G.T., telling him: 'You are on one side of the barricades: I am on the other: it is for each of us to assume his own responsibilities.'[19] He soon showed how he saw his responsibilities, by arresting Griffuelhes, several other

[18] Figures taken from the annual publication of the Ministère du Travail, *Statistique des Grèves*. A convenient recapitulation is given in C. W. Pipkin, *Social Politics and Modern Democracies* (New York, 1931), II, pp. 116–7. The period from 1903 to 1913 was one of remarkable economic expansion in France, interrupted only by a relatively minor depression in 1907–8. There was downward pressure on prices and wages until 1905, followed by a period in which both began to rise. During the Clemenceau government wages rose faster than prices, with the result that 1909 saw real wages for male workers in Paris reach their highest point before the outbreak of the First World War. After that rising prices eroded purchasing power in spite of the workers' efforts to push up their money wages. These circumstances explain the figures for strikes in this period, except for the special circumstances of 1906. Clemenceau was fortunate in missing both the bitter battles which occurred when the downturn of the trade cycle forced employers to seek to reduce money wages, and the often shorter, but still widespread, conflicts which occurred in the upturn, as workers sought to improve their wages to compensate for rising prices and because they saw that profits had increased. The depression of 1907–8 was not severe enough to provoke the bitter conflicts of, for instance, 1902. J. Singer-Keral, *Le Coût de la Vie à Paris* (1961), tables on pp. 130 and 539; J. Marczewski, 'Le Produit Physique de l'Economie Française de 1789 à 1913', *Cahiers de l'Institut de Science Economique Appliquée*, 163, July 1965, pp. vii–cliv; and E. M. Phelps-Brown, *A Century of Pay* (1968), pp. 432–3.

[19] J. Julliard, *Clemenceau, Briseur de Grèves* (1965), p. 23.

C.G.T. militants, and a few minor figures on the lunatic fringe of the Right. Piou, the Catholic politician, states that he wanted to arrest more prominent right-wing leaders but that Sarrien refused.[20] The excuse for the arrests was the claim that a police search of the homes of C.G.T. militants involved in the miners' strike had produced documents showing that there was a plot to overthrow the Republic involving the monarchist Right and the Extreme Left. The arrests provided a graphic illustration of Clemenceau's main theme in an important election speech at Lyon on 3 May, the unholy alliance of the two extremes of Left and Right against the democratic, reforming Republic. A little while after the elections everyone was released and no more was heard of the plot. This affair was one of the principal accusations levied against Clemenceau by Jaurès, in various oratorical battles of the next three years, and it certainly did much to give Clemenceau his reputation for Machiavellianism.

3 THE ELECTIONS AND THE NEW CHAMBER

Whether because of Clemenceau's precautions, or because there had never been any danger, 1 May came and went without a revolution, and the country proceeded on 6 and 20 May to vote for the new Chamber. Clemenceau played a much more prominent part in the election campaign than did Sarrien. In his speech at Lyon he defended his record against the attack from Right and Left. He concentrated on defending his actions to maintain order in the mining areas. He did not regret his visit to the scene, and would do it again if necessary. Both the right to strike and liberty to work had to be defended, and the government had used the minimum amount of force necessary to restore order. The Right accused him of being too weak, while Jaurès's newspaper trumpeted its attacks on the odious repression when the only victims were among the troops, not the strikers. He declared that the bad habits of centuries could not be wiped out in a day, and legitimate strike action, without violation of the rights of persons and property, would only come when people had been educated in the practice of democracy. The Socialists hindered this by defending the extremists. In the elections the Socialist campaign threatened to split the vote, thus allowing the victory of reactionary candidates; but he hoped that republican discipline at the second ballot would prevent too many surprises of that kind.[21]

[20] J. Piou, D'Une Guerre à l'Autre 1871–1914 (1932), p. 225; P. Monatte, Trois Scissions Syndicales (1957), pp. 119–21.
[21] The speech was printed verbatim in the Journal Officiel for 5 May 1906, Jaurès's views on the political situation just before the elections are given in this letter; despite mutual attacks at the hustings, he envisaged Socialist-Radical cooperation at the second ballot and in the new Chamber: 'I am sure that the results will be good. Allowing for various gains and losses, the majority of the Left will be

After the second ballot on 20 May, it was clear that there had been no victory for reaction. The 1906 elections were one of the greatest victories of the Left in the history of the Third Republic. Clemenceau could also congratulate himself that the Socialist representation remained fairly small. The s.f.i.o. had fifty-four deputies, while the twenty Independent Socialists were to prove only a special variety of republican, not really on the left of the Radicals. But the republican triumph masked certain ambiguities which help to explain Clemenceau's evolution. The total number of deputies was 591, and the theoretical majority needed in a full house without abstentions was therefore 296. The distribution among different political tendencies can be schematized in this way:

LEFT		RIGHT	
Unified Socialists (S.F.I.O.)	54	Progressists	67
Independent Socialists	20	(Conservative Republicans)	
Radical-Socialists	134	Nationalists	30
Radicals	117	Reactionaries and *Action*	
Républicains de Gauche		*Libérale Populaire*	78
(Moderate Republicans)	91		
Total	416	Total	175

[22]

This classification adequately represents the political battle in the country during the election campaign. It had been a straightforward contest between Right and Left as they had emerged from the Dreyfus Affair and the subsequent conflict over the Church. The Right consisted of those who had opposed the Separation of Church and State, that is the old monarchists plus three new elements, the Nationalists, the Catholic party (the *Action Libérale Populaire*), and the Progressists, those republicans who had refused to join Waldeck-Rousseau in his swing to the

returned strengthened and toughened by the battle. . . . Immediately after 6 May, whatever my own fortune, I will return to Paris to work for republican and *laïque* unity at the second ballot. I think that the new Parliament will at last begin to deal with the social question, and work effectively for the well-being of our working people for whom so much needs to be done.' Jaurès to Marquise Arconati-Visconti, 1906 (n.d. but late April), Bibliothèque Victor Cousin, Arconati-Visconti Papers, 279, fol. 3985. The Marquise Arconati-Visconti was the daughter of A. Peyrat, a republican of the heroic period; extremely wealthy as a result of her marriage, she ran a political salon, and was the friend over many years of republican political leaders of widely differing opinions, varying from the extremely conservative to the Socialist Jaurès.

[22] The figures used here are those given by A. Soulier, *L'Instabilité Ministérielle sous La Troisième République, 1871–1938* (1939), p. 102. They agree with those quoted by G. Bonnefous, *Histoire Politique de la Troisième République* (1956), I, p. 19, from the official returns of the Ministry of the Interior, except that the latter left six seats unaccounted for. Cf. also J. P. Charnay, *Les Scrutins Politiques en France de 1815 à 1902* (1904), p. 105. For a detailed analysis of the voting, *see* P. G. La Chesnais, 'Statistique Electorale', *Revue de Paris*, June 1906, pp. 867–93.

Left, and who wished, instead, to continue the policy of allying with the Right to defend the Church as a bulwark of social order. The Left consisted of those who supported the Separation of Church and State, with all that this implied about the future of French society, a coalition that went all the way from extremely cautious and moderate men, such as Poincaré, to fanatical atheists. It included the conservative republicans of the *Alliance Démocratique* party, the Radicals and Radical Socialists, the Independent Socialists, and Unified Socialists of the Second International.[23]

But now that the religious question had passed from the front of the political stage, the majority that had passed the Separation Law was divided on questions of social and economic reform. This division went down the middle of the Radical party; it was represented in its name, *Le Parti Républicain Radical et Radical-Socialiste*, and in the careful distinction made in the election results between Radicals and Radical-Socialists. The division in reality did not exactly coincide with that between those who called themselves Radicals and those who called themselves Radical-Socialists, but the distinction existed, and was of crucial importance. It resulted directly from the fact that some Radicals had been elected at the second ballot with the support of Socialist votes, while others had needed votes that had gone at the first ballot to more conservative republicans. Thus the typical Radical was, as the old joke had it, a man with his heart on the Left and his wallet on the Right. From 1906 to the fall of the Third Republic the Radicals became the centre of gravity of political France, balancing between Left and Right; in the end they became the true Conservative party, the party that wished to defend the *status quo*. This became more obvious in the inter-war period, and before the war the Radicals appeared to be more of a reforming than a conservative party, but the Radical majority would only support moderate, limited and cautious reform.

It was possible to calculate that the new Chamber provided a majority of the Left, consisting of Socialists, Independent Socialists, Radical-Socialists and Radicals together making up 325 deputies: this could have been a majority of the *Bloc des Gauches*. But such a calculation was not realistic. Only the religious question would unite these groups; on any question of social reform the Radicals would split. A more realistic calculation was that, if the unified Socialists abstained, the Radicals and Independent Socialists made up a small majority over all other parties.[24]

[23] *See* Appendix IV for further details of the political organizations, and diagrams of the strength of different political tendencies in the Chamber.

[24] For the attitude of the Socialists towards the government, *see* the detailed study of the various votes in J. J. Fiechter, *Le Socialisme français; de l'affaire Dreyfus à la grande guerre* (Geneva, 1965), pp. 132–42. C. Seignobos, *L'Evolution de La Troisième République 1875–1914*, Vol. 8 of E. Lavisse, *Histoire de France Contemporaine* (1921), p. 248.

But such a majority would have been too small to be workable under the French system, and the situation did not develop that way. Although the unified Socialists abstained on the first vote when the Chamber expressed its confidence in the new government, on nearly every crucial vote thereafter they joined the opposition. In that case the government needed the support of the *Républicains de Gauche*, the anti-clerical but socially conservative republicans. In order to win their support, it had to follow politics repugnant not only to the S.F.I.O., but to the left wing of the Radical party itself. Thus the normal governmental majority moved towards the centre of the Chamber. Time and again, the government's majority consisted of *Républicains de Gauche* and the majority of the Radicals, against an opposition consisting of the left-wing dissident Radicals, the Socialists and the Right. But this was still a majority of the moderate Left and the Centre, not the sort of majority on which Briand and Poincaré came to rely, centred even further to the Right. Clemenceau could claim that he had presided over a reforming government which did push through legislation on social and economic questions, and which did resist demands from the Right for even more brutal repression of working-class agitation.[25] Nevertheless he ended his ministry not only regarded as the scourge of the working class by trade unions and Socialists but also condemned by many in the Radical party. The executive committee of the party disavowed his government in May 1909, and by the end of the year he had resigned from the party.

The keynote of the new Parliament was set in abstract terms by the oratorical duel between Jaurès and Clemenceau which occupied the Chamber for most of the first part of June.[26] In this lengthy debate Clemenceau replied to Jaurès's accusation that he had deliberately broken with the Socialists, instead of keeping his promise to build a majority of the Left that would vote for reforms. He in turn accused Jaurès of breaking up the *Bloc des Gauches* in response to the decisions of the German-dominated International Socialist Congress at Amsterdam in 1904. Jaurès, after arguing there in favour of continuing the policy of cooperation with bourgeois reforms, inaugurated when Millerand entered the Waldeck-Rousseau government, had ended by accepting the decision of the International, ratified by the 1905 French Socialist Congress which united the diverse families of French Socialism. This was the price he had to pay to set up a unified party that included the doctrinaire

[25] Cf. the acute analysis by de Lanessan in an article in the newspaper *Le Siècle*, 17 July 1906, quoted by F. Buisson, in *La Politique Radicale*, pp. 109–16.: 'The axis of the majority is not, as was proclaimed after the election, in the Radical Socialists, but in the Radicals, that is at the heart of the representatives of the *petite bourgeoisie*.'

[26] *Annales de la Chambre des Députés*; Jaurès's speech, 12 June 1906, pp. 128–32, 14 June 1906, pp. 142–7: Clemenceau, 18–19 June, pp. 189–200, 204–12: Jaurès's reply, 19 June, pp. 212–21.

Marxists led by Guesde. Socialists would no longer participate in bourgeois governments. A gulf of mutual incomprehension opened between
the two men, when Clemenceau expressed his contempt for a political
leader who could thus carry out an about-turn in response to the
decisions of his followers, instead of fighting on to defend his original
point of view. Jaurès, in reply, argued that, for him, the important thing
was to maintain the unity of the representatives of the proletariat, even
if this meant sacrificing, for a time, his personal beliefs. Jaurès wished
to work from within the Marxist orthodoxy imposed on the unified
party, so as to continue the policy of cooperation with the bourgeois
Radicals to achieve a programme of social reform. The Socialists, he
said, would still vote for reforming legislation if it were presented to
them. In the June debates, in spite of bitter attacks on Clemenceau for
his handling of the strikes, Jaurès still gave him the benefit of the doubt;
he thought that he was personally committed to reforms, but that they
would be sabotaged by the rest of the cabinet. Thus, in October, when
Clemenceau formed his own government (leaning to the Left), and presented a declaration of policy, which, although it in many ways repeated
that offered by Sarrien, did so in more vigorous language and with
crucial additions, the Socialists abstained, instead of voting against it
as they had against Sarrien.

In the often repeated dispute between Clemenceau and Jaurès about
which was responsible for breaking up the Socialist-Radical alliance,
there was a case to be made on either side. A strict interpretation of
the bare facts favoured Clemenceau; the Socialists had unilaterally
decided at the time of their unification to abandon the policy of participation in bourgeois governments. But Jaurès intended, nevertheless,
to continue support for reforming governments. His charge against
Clemenceau was that by his brutal repression of the strikes, and his
arrest of the C.G.T. leaders, he had made it much more difficult for him
to offer Socialist support to a Radical government. Clemenceau argued
that it was Jaurès who made cooperation impossible by condoning the
violence and extremism of the C.G.T. What would you have done, he
asked him, if you had been the minister of the interior, and had been
confronted with this challenge to public order.[27] No government could
permit such activities on the part of a tiny majority who were far from
representing the majority of the French proletariat. In any case Jaurès's
position was unrealistic. If the unified Socialists would not vote to save
a Radical government from defeat, it had to find its majority elsewhere.
He then challenged Jaurès to explain how his programme differed from
that of the Radicals. What, precisely, did this much-vaunted 'Collectivism' amount to? A modern commentator has written that today one

[27] *Annales de la Chambre des Députés*, 18 June 1906, p. 198.

is struck by the superficial and artificial character of the arguments used on both sides.[28] This seems unfair to Clemenceau, although it is certainly true of Jaurès, who, in spite of taking several hours over his explanation, revealed that he could not explain how the collectivist system would work.[29] Clemenceau's arguments were more precise and cogent than his disquisitions of the 1880s on reform of the social and economic system. He had challenged Jaurès to define Collectivism and he had been unable to do so. In what way, then, did the Socialists differ from the Radicals, except in their refusal to accept the responsibilities of office? 'You ask me,' he said, 'for my programme: why, you have taken it from me, it is in your pocket!'[30] And he quoted Bernstein, the German theorist of revisionist Marxism, to support his own view that what mattered was immediate and pragmatic reform, not the production of blueprints for a total transformation of the social and economic system that could only be the work of many generations.[31]

At the end of this debate the government had a majority of 517 to 41. Only the unified Socialists supported Jaurès. But a few days later a vote on a practical question gave a much clearer indication of the strength of the potential left-wing opposition. This was the vote of 11 July when, at the government's request, the Chamber rejected a demand for an amnesty in favour of postal workers dismissed for taking part in a strike. On this occasion the vote was 326 to 164; the minority included many Independent Socialists and Radicals as well as the members of the S.F.I.O. This was the first appearance of an issue that was to recur throughout the ministry, and on which the most bitter and close-fought battles between the government and opposition were to take place. After his summer holiday at Carlsbad and a visit to Berlin for the museums, when he refused to meet the German Chancellor Bulow, Clemenceau spent the last days of September and the beginning of October on a speaking tour of his native province, the Vendée, and of his Parliamentary home, the Var. He made several speeches in the little towns of these remote country areas, which were reported in the press and received much attention. Sarrien remained in the background, and Clemenceau was more and more appearing as the leader of the ministry. In the Vendée his speeches were nostalgic evocations of his youth, and

---

[28] F. Goguel, *La Politique des Partis sous la Troisième République* (Paris, 3rd ed., 1958), p. 130. He notes, however, that one contemporary, Barrès, found them profound.

[29] See the parody of Jaurès's oratory by P. Reboux and C. Muller, *A la Manière de . . .*, ed. livre de poche (1964), pp. 147–50.

[30] *Annales de la Chambre des Députés*, 19 June 1906, p. 205.

[31] Buré, at the time a young journalist who had collaborated with Clemenceau at *L'Aurore*, states that Clemenceau was hoping to win over as many non-doctrinaire Socialists as possible; in order to convince them he got Buré to look up references in Bernstein, the German reformist Socialist. Buré's recollections were printed in the newspaper *L'Ordre*, 14 August 1938.

lyrical expressions of his love for the countryside of his native province and for its peasant inhabitants, with their courage, their energy, and endurance, derived from their unceasing struggle with 'la terre rebelle de notre bocage'. 'I cannot claim,' he said, 'all their finer qualities, but I cannot deny that I owe to certain features of their character, their instinctively independent spirit, their critical faculties, their headstrong obstinacy and pugnacity, some of the best enmities that I have incurred on my journey through life.'[32] He also dealt with political themes. The transition was an easy one, through references to the terrible civil war between Revolution and Counter-Revolution, still vivid in the memories of old people he had known in his youth. Now the warfare was in the minds, but it still continued, between clerical reaction and the Republic. In the Var he did not attempt to inflame anti-clerical passion further, but stressed the practical problems of government:

> For an honest man, when he enters the government, the time of criticism and of pure idealism is behind him. His first duty is to set limits to his aims. Henceforth he has to take account of circumstances. He does not cease to march towards his ideal, but in order to achieve those parts of his programme that are immediately applicable, he must compromise with the customs and the habits created by the very system he wants to change. Everyone can always be seen as both a reactionary and a revolutionary, depending on the point of view. Anyone who does not accept this fact at once excludes himself from the government. It is well known that the art of government lies in the mixture of reform and conservation, and that excessive caution is just as bad as too much rashness.[33]

He thought it necessary to defend the Senate, in view of the fact that his earlier attacks on it were one of the best-known features of his past programme. Now he argued, exactly as the Senate's defenders had argued against him twenty years before, that there must be provision for reflection, for reconsideration. Otherwise there would be no guarantee that 'majorities, even well-intentioned, might not be carried away by the political struggle to commit reckless acts of which the consequences would for ever weigh on the destiny of our country'. The Senate, however unsatisfactory, provided for this reconsideration, and, he went on, 'the more we advance in social reforms, the more we need a careful study of new laws in a domain where a mistake could have the most serious consequences'.

[32] 'The difficult soil of our *bocage*.' The speech at La Roche-sur-Yon, on 30 September, is printed *verbatim* in the *Journal Officiel* of 1 October 1906.
[33] Speech at Draguignan, on 14 October, printed in *Journal Officiel*, 15 October 1906.

9

CLEMENCEAU AS PREMIER

I THE CLEMENCEAU CABINET

A few days after this speech, before Parliament reassembled, Sarrien resigned, giving ill-health as his reason. There was hardly a ministerial crisis, and after a brief delay Clemenceau formed the new cabinet. Six ministers remained in office, but the political composition of the new government was quite different. Whereas the Sarrien cabinet had consisted of five moderate republicans, five Radicals and one Socialist, the new cabinet had only two ministers from groups to the right of the Radicals, against seven Radicals, two independent Socialists, and one non-political member, General Picquart. The other notable feature was the absence of other prominent figures. Briand was as yet only at the beginning of his career, and Caillaux was the only other strong personality in the cabinet. With Picquart at the war ministry, and his friend and protégé Pichon at the foreign ministry, it was obvious that Clemenceau wished to retain control of foreign policy.[34]

A swing to the Left was noticeable in the government's declaration of policy, the most radical manifesto produced by any incoming government before the Popular Front of 1936. Several items were taken from the Sarrien government's declaration, but others were added, and the

[34] The British ambassador, Sir Francis Bertie, wrote on 4 November 1906, disputing the view that the cabinet would not survive for long. He went on: 'Clemenceau has selected as colleagues those on whom he can rely to carry out his own views. He is quite capable of being his own Minister of Foreign Affairs, and also superintending the War Department. His management of the strikes showed that he is full of resource, and since he took in hand the Church inventories question it has ceased to be a burning issue. As to M. Pichon I understand that he entirely concurs in Clemenceau's views, and is a capable man with common sense, and not impulsive.' Bertie to Mallet, 4 November 1906, Public Record Office, FO/800/164. *See below*, Appendix I, for the full composition of the cabinet.

whole welded together into a reform manifesto of an altogether more vigorous and determined character. A quite different impression was created by the new cabinet's strong commitment to the introduction of income tax, compared with the cautious pronouncements of the Sarrien declaration. Taken from Sarrien's declaration were proposals to reform military promotion procedures and military justice, laws to implement the Separation of Church and State and the abrogation of the Falloux Law, proposals to strengthen the legal position of trade unions and to provide a *statut des fonctionnaires* to regularize the position of civil servants in various ways. New proposals included the development of regional institutions and 'l'élargissement du mode de scrutin', a bill for safeguarding individual rights, the nationalization of the Western railway and a renegotiation of the concessions governing coal-mining, the transformation of the Office du Travail into a full Ministry of Labour, and a whole series of social reforms, the ten-hour day, the *Contrat Collectif du Travail*, old age pensions and accident insurance for agricultural workers.[35] Clemenceau ended his short speech by admitting that this was, no doubt, too vast a programme, especially as the Chamber and not the government controlled the allocation of Parliamentary time, but he wanted to mark out the route so that 'everyone can assume his proper responsibility in the eyes of the country, our judge'.

For the first few months the ministry had a quiet time, and was in no danger of defeat. At the beginning of the session Parliamentary salaries were raised to 15,000 francs. Of no great importance in itself, the speed with which this measure passed through all stages of the legislative process provided good ammunition for critics. While bills for old age pensions and income tax had been debated for years, and had often been lost in interminable committees, this measure went through almost without a debate and was promulgated in a few days. The rejection of an order of the day demanding modification of the Separation Law on 13 November, by 431 to 120, showed that on religious questions the great majority of the Chamber supported the government.[36] Briand was free to follow his policy of seeking to end the conflict by elaborating a workable *de facto* settlement, in spite of Papal refusal to allow French Catholics to cooperate with the government. This necessitated several laws to regularize the position of the Church. The Separation Law had provided that religious groups should set up *associations cultuelles* to be their legal representatives and to hold property. As the Pope refused to allow

[35] Clemenceau presented this declaration of policy to the Chamber on 5 November 1906. On 20 November 1906 he defended his government's policy in the Senate against an interpellation from the Right. He had read the declaration of the Sarrien government to the Senate on 12 June. *Annales de la Chambre des Députés*, 5 November 1906, pp. 5–6. *Annales du Sénat*, 12 June 1906, pp. 822–3, 20 November 1906, pp. 124–7.
[36] A. Dansette, *Histoire religieuse*, II, pp. 350–72.

Catholics to set up these associations, a new formula had to be found to leave parish churches at the disposal of Catholics. Clemenceau accepted all these steps to smooth down the religious conflict, in spite of the fact that he had previously opposed even the *associations cultuelles* scheme as too favourable to Catholics.[37] He did something to satisfy the anti-clericals by the expulsion, on 11 December, of Monsignor Montagnini, the Papal nuncio. The papers seized at his residence were used to illustrate the government's charges that the Pope exercised a theocratic dictatorship over French Catholics, and that Papal policy was dominated by political considerations.[38] On 30 January Clemenceau allowed his exasperation with the Church, and his love of a joke, to lead him publicly to condemn Briand's work on the religious question. Obviously referring to Briand's drafting of the original Separation Law, and to his own criticism of it, he said:

I have been given the task of applying a law which provided for everything except that which actually happened. M. Allard said yesterday that our position is incoherent. Yes, it certainly is. It was not I who got into this position; I was put in it: I am in it, I will stay in it.[39]

Prolonged laughter greeted this sally, but, unnoticed by the prime minister, who continued his speech, Briand rose from his seat and left the Chamber; he obviously meant to offer his resignation. When Clemenceau sat down, Jaurès rose to speak, praising Briand's work, and asking the Chamber not to let itself be carried away by personal incidents. Clemenceau, having been informed of Briand's annoyance, ostentatiously applauded, and rose again to apologize; he then went out to find Briand, and they returned arm-in-arm to show that all was forgiven. Jaurès's anxiety to make the peace is significant. He did not want Briand's resig-

---

[37] The British ambassador reported in December 1906 that the government had decided to prosecute priests who conducted services without making the declaration; this was part of the campaign of bluff designed to force the Church into a more reasonable attitude; cf. A. Dansette op. cit., II, pp. 365–7; a law of 2 January 1907 required an annual declaration by the parish priest to legalize the services, but when the Pope ordered the clergy, in the encyclical *Une fois encore*, not to make the declaration, the government repealed the requirement by the law of 28 March 1907. In the last resort Briand was determined not to persecute the Church, and Clemenceau agreed with him on this, even if they disagreed on occasions about tactics. Bertie to Grey, 11 December 1906, Public Record Office, FO/800/164.

[38] *Annales de la Chambre des Députés*, 11 December 1906, pp. 965–7, for Clemenceau's defence of this action.

[39] Ibid., 30 January 1907, p. 355. Bertie to Grey, 31 January 1907: 'I had some conversation with Pichon about the incident in the Chamber. He told me that Clemenceau's irritability and *nervosité*, which had caused him to make his extraordinarily regrettable speech, had damaged the government a good deal. . . .' On this incident *see also* the police report of 19 February 1907, Archives de la Préfecture de Police, BA 130.

nation to bring down the government, as he had not yet given up hope of reforms from the Clemenceau cabinet.

On 11 March Jaurès attacked Clemenceau for seeking to use troops to work the electricity station when the Paris electricity supply workers went on strike. The cabinet was not in danger. By the time the debate took place, the strike had already ended, and the troops had not been used. The employers did not want them, either because they were afraid of damage to the machinery or because they did not wish to poison relations with the workers. The order of the day of confidence in the government was carried by 398 to 86.[40] On this issue only a small number of left-wing Radicals joined the Socialists in opposing the government, in spite of the weak case Clemenceau presented. This was the normal pattern of votes when it was a question of conflict between the government and a group of manual workers. The government's majority was only seriously threatened when the conflict involved white-collar workers, public employees such as teachers and postmen. Then a much larger section of the Radicals voted with the Socialists against the government. The first of these crises came a few weeks later in the debate occasioned by the government's measures against trade unionism among civil servants.

Given the Napoleonic, authoritarian traditions of the French state it was inevitable that the development of trade unionism would produce difficulties. In more recent times trade unionism has been far stronger among public employees than in any other sector of the French economy. But, before 1914, it was not accepted that civil servants could form trade unions at all. From 1900 onwards associations of officials in various branches of government service, but especially among the postmen and the primary school teachers, had developed. Successive governments had vacillated in their attitude, on some occasions trying to suppress them, and on others tolerating them. In 1905, when an attempt to ban them brought strong opposition, the Rouvier cabinet, although not yielding the principle, had abandoned its proposed measures against the officials who had joined the various associations. The Sarrien Government decided to bring in comprehensive legislation, the much-talked-of

---

[40] *Annales de la Chambre des Députés*, 11 March 1907, pp. 776–9. This incident saw the beginning of the campaign of intrigue against the cabinet waged by a group of Radicals led by Berteaux which continued throughout its duration. These intrigues were reported on in detail by police informers, and can be followed in the archives of the Préfecture de Police, BA 959, Dossier Berteaux, and BA 130, 'Renseignements sur les différents groupes de la Chambre, 1906–1910'. There can be no doubt that the chief motive of this opposition, which only rarely was openly avowed, was personal, and resulted from the intriguers' exclusion from office. It had already been reported on 8 November 1906 that a group which included Doumer, Berteaux and Pelletan, prominent among the cabinet's Radical opponents, was furious at being excluded from the cabinet. Archives de la Préfecture de Police, BA 130.

statut des fonctionnaires.[41] Meanwhile it adopted a compromise policy tolerating existing associations, but forbidding the formation of new ones. The postal strike of March 1906 was caused partly by dissatisfaction with this compromise. The situation was complicated by the fact that some associations sought recognition only under the 1901 law on associations, while others called themselves *syndicats* and sought the privileges conferred on trade unions by the law of 1884. These were not really very great, but the name *syndicat* produced strong emotional reactions and a great deal of energy was devoted to the question of whether civil servants could only form associations or could also, if they wanted, form *syndicats*. Even more emotionally-charged was the question of affiliation to the C.G.T., with its doctrines of revolutionary syndicalism, violence and anti-patriotism. To the great majority of the bourgeoisie and of the Chamber, it was anathema that civil servants should be allowed to join an organization dedicated to the overthrow of the State and social order. Only a tiny minority of civil servants wished to join unions affiliated to the C.G.T., but the majority were disturbed about the vagueness of the government's attitude. It was not even clear that they would be allowed to continue to join peaceful associations concerned only with limited professional ends. Other officials, who had not joined any association, were concerned about their lack of rights, their low and fixed salaries at a time of rising prices, about arbitrary promotion and displacement as a result of political influence. This last complaint affected all ranks from those at the top who saw well-connected young men take the best positions, down to the lowliest teacher or postman, who saw promotion go to colleagues who had been able to get a deputy to intercede for them. And so, although there was little positive demand to join the few unions that affiliated to the C.G.T., there was widespread concern about what the government's attacks on them might mean for the whole body of public employees.

A group of primary school teachers from Paris and Lyon lit the fuse by declaring that their union was going to join the C.G.T. On 22 February 1907 Clemenceau met their delegation, and told them that he could not allow them to join an organization dedicated to the overthrow of the social order. However, the fact that he met the delegation conferred some sort of recognition on it. In spite of its theoretical objections the government seemed prepared to tolerate teachers' unions, but wanted

---

[41] The interest which this topic aroused at the time can be gauged by the extensive literature it provoked. Among the more notable books were J. Paul-Boncour, *Les Syndicats de Fonctionnaires* (1906), M. Leroy, *Les Transformations de la Puissance Publique, Les Syndicats de Fonctionnaires* (1907). Some of the many articles on the subject are listed in the latter book, p. 238. As well as polemical journalism for and against, much of this literature treated the subject in a very abstract way, talking of an entirely new social and political order that was supposed to be emerging.

to forbid affiliation with the C.G.T. On 11 March the government laid before the Chamber the text of its proposed law on the *statut des fonctionnaires*. As this appeared to limit severely their right to join unions, and thus to take away what had been tolerated since 1905, it inflamed the opposition. The *Fédération des Syndicat des Instituteurs* issued an open letter to the prime minister asking him in an insolent tone to justify his ban on their joining the C.G.T. This was followed by another open letter from the *Comité Central du Droit Syndical des Salariés de L'Etat*, which grouped together the militant groups of teachers, postal workers and various other categories of officials. Also militant in tone, it opposed the government's bill and demanded full trade union rights for officials.[42] The government ignored this manifesto, but replied to the teachers' letter in the press on 6 April. The prime minister listed the advantages civil servants had over employees in private industry, such as security of employment, guaranteed wages and pensions. In return they must accept that they had no place in either the C.G.T. or the *Bourses du Travail*, as doctrines were preached there that must be vigorously condemned by any teacher of the nation's young. The unions replied with another manifesto, asserting their determination to join the C.G.T., and the cabinet decided that disciplinary action would be taken against officials who had signed it, unless they recanted. Many did, claiming that they had signed under pressure or by mistake, but the secretary of the teachers' union, Nègre, and five postal workers, were brought before their appropriate disciplinary bodies. They recommended dismissal for the postmen, but not for Nègre. The Prefect of the Seine dismissed him, however, along with the postmen. These first steps had already begun to produce political repercussions, not only among the Socialists, but also in the Radical party. The executive committee of the Radical party sent a delegation to the prime minister on 25 April to ask him to avoid conflict with the unions. Clemenceau assured them that he wished to march in step with the Radical party, and had no objection to civil servants forming associations; he could not allow them, however, to join the C.G.T. For the moment the executive committee accepted these assurances.[43]

The government had to cope, however, not only with pressures from the Left, but with demands by its more conservative supporters that much stronger action be taken. The demands of the teachers and postmen were only one element in the situation, and as 1 May approached

[42] M. Ferré, *Histoire du Mouvement Syndicaliste Révolutionnaire chez les Instituteurs des Origines à 1922* (1955), pp. 106–9 and 190–3; F. Bernard et al., *Le Syndicalisme dans l'Enseignement, Documents de l'Institut d'Etudes Politiques de Grenoble* (n.d.), pp. 88–97; G. Frischmann, *Histoire de la Fédération C.G.T. des P.T.T.* (1967), pp. 135–9. Full text of the various manifestos and Clemenceau's reply in R. Walher, *Le Vingtième Siècle Politique, Année 1907*, pp. 159–62.
[43] *Bulletin du Parti Radical*, 122–3–4, 20 April, 27 April and 4 May 1907.

the leaders of the C.G.T. were again talking of their annual demonstration, although 1907 was a relatively quiet year for strikes of industrial workers. Some members of the government, and a large number of deputies, wanted the C.G.T. to be banned altogether. For a while it even appeared that the prime minister supported this demand, and the cabinet decided to consult its legal advisers on the question of whether the C.G.T. could be dissolved under existing law. They advised that it could, but Clemenceau argued that political realities made this inadvisable. On 4 May a press communiqué was issued denying that the government was envisaging the dissolution of the C.G.T., but proclaiming its firm resolve to punish those who preached crime and anti-patriotism, and that absolute respect for the law would be demanded from all State servants.[44] On 7 May Parliament reassembled after the Easter recess, and there began a week of debate about general policy, centering on the linked questions of the C.G.T. and of the right of officials to form trade unions. Day after day, crowded houses and packed public galleries listened to the debate: the fate of the government was clearly at stake. It was one of those dramatic Parliamentary crises that gave such a theatrical tone to the political life of the Third Republic, and, as usual in such crises, the debate was not about any legislative proposal, but about the vote of an order of the day, which would either support or condemn the government.[45] There was once again a seven-hour speech from Jaurès, this time aimed more at Briand than Clemenceau. For Briand, much more than Clemenceau, could be faced with the charge of hypocritical reversal of his previous position. Down to 1906 he had been a member of the Socialist party, and a few years earlier had even spoken at a Socialist Congress in favour of violent revolution and the general strike. Now his words were to be quoted against him, as the minister responsible for dismissing civil servants who had done no more than advocate the same course. This confrontation between Briand and Jaurès, which turned into a bitter personal attack, finally broke the bridges between Radicals and Socialists. From now on Jaurès and the

[44] R. Wallier, op. cit., pp. 172-4, and F. Buisson, La Politique Radicale, pp. 103-5. The British ambassador, reporting the rumours current at the time, wrote: 'According to a member of the French cabinet Clemenceau spoke with great decision at the Council yesterday on the question of the Socialist agitation, and apparently he is determined to close the C.G.T. if there is any disturbance.' Bertie to Grey, 30 April 1907, Public Record Office, FO/800/164. This report cannot be very accurate. Whatever Clemenceau did say at the council of ministers about the C.G.T., Buisson's interpretation, that this was merely a tactical move, and that he had no intention of actually dissolving the C.G.T., is almost certainly the correct one. Reinach recalled that 'when Delcassé and I asked Clemenceau to dissolve the C.G.T., he replied that it was a bogey to scare children'. J. Reinach to the Marquise Arconati-Visconti, Bibliothèque Victor Cousin, Arconati-Visconti Papers, 291, fol. 7129.

[45] For vivid descriptions of the highly-charged atmosphere, see G. Suarez, Briand, II, pp. 169-93, and R. de Jouvenal, La République des Camarades (1910), p. 89.

s.f.i.o. were firmly opposed to the government. Quite a large number of Radicals supported Jaurès on this question, and it was clear that there would be many defectors to the Left. As a result, there was a real danger that the government would either be swung over to the right, and would, after all, be forced to dissolve the c.g.t., or that it would fall.

Clemenceau and Briand between them demonstrated their skill in tactics, and also their good sense on the basic question of whether or not to dissolve the c.g.t., in avoiding being pushed into this hard-line policy, yet still retaining their majority. In many accounts this crisis is seen as a confrontation with the Left, but they were also facing pressure from the Right for a tougher policy. On 13 May, after days of argument, the *Délégation des Gauches*, which grouped the government's supporters in Parliament, voted a resolution proposed by Delcassé inviting the government to dissolve the c.g.t. Next day, Clemenceau attended the meeting of the *Délégation*, and persuaded them to reverse this decision.[46] Then, in the Chamber, he repeated his arguments against any attack on the c.g.t., affirming before a hostile audience the legitimacy and the value of a strong trade union movement. However misguided the present leaders of the c.g.t. were, it was impossible to attack them without appearing to attack the proletariat, and its aspirations for a better, more just, society. He would not be responsible for such a policy. As Buisson, a Left-wing Radical who had criticized the government's attitude towards civil servants' trade unions, put it:

> Only his personal authority prevented the Republican majority from following the path down which M. Ribot was urging it. At that moment M. Clemenceau saved the honour of the Republican party. The merit which is his can only be measured by those who saw at close quarters the strength of the current which he resisted. . . .[47]

Having explained why he would not proceed against the c.g.t., Clemenceau widened the debate, raising again the question of relations between Socialists and Radicals, and pointing to the reforming legislation which the government was supporting. In order to get these reforms voted, especially by the Senate, law and order must be maintained. If the government fell, the Chamber would be faced with choosing between outright repression or weakness that would in the end lead to anarchy. The present government offered a policy that combined the repression of disorder with reform and conciliation.

[46] Wallier, op. cit., pp. 224–4; cf. Bertie's report: 'In the delegation of the left Sarrien declined to support the resolution which Delcassé suggested because it might bring about the fall of the government.' Bertie to Grey, 19 May 1907, Public Record Office, FO/800/164.
[47] Buisson, op. cit., p. 107. For Clemenceau's speech, *see Annales de la Chambre des Députés*, 14 May 1907, pp. 121–30.

We will not, as has been suggested, move our majority to the Right. We stay where we are. We are Radicals. We are, if you do not want me to say Radical-Socialists, *des Radicaux-socialisants*. Our majorities up to now have been too large; we do not want conservative support, we want the firm and committed support of a majority that agrees with our policy, and is determined on action. I do not object to the opposition of Ribot and Jaurès, which, from their opposed points of view, is sincere, and in accordance with their principles. But there is a group of Radicals, who supported the ministry of Combes, and who will not now give us the tolerance and support that they gave to him. I see their criticisms in the press, but I can never get them to voice them here. Well, I have had enough, I will not be strangled by the mutes of the seraglio. . . . If you have charges to bring, why meet behind closed doors, in some hole or corner to waylay us, to prepare a ministerial crisis. Speak out, the rostrum is here. *Messieurs les radicaux, je vous attends.*[48]

There his speech ended, producing consternation in the Radical benches. Maujan, one of the government's firmest supporters in the Radical party machine, asked unsuccessfully that the rest of the debate be postponed to the next day. Then another deputy rose to point out the contradiction between Clemenceau's speech and Briand's, which had suggested a much tougher line against the C.G.T. Briand rose again to deny that there was any difference between him and Clemenceau, and skilfully diverted the debate by attacking the Socialists. He delicately but clearly hinted that recruits, from whatever quarter, would be welcomed, and would be sure to feel the gratitude of the government. As for the question at issue, the line of policy to be adopted towards the C.G.T., he disposed of it with phrases as vague as they were sonorous. Maujan provided the resolution that was voted by the satisfactory majority of 323 to 205; it stated merely that the Chamber 'approved the declarations of the government', leaving in obscurity just what these declarations were. The majority was made up of the great bulk of the republican party, Radicals and *Républicains de Gauche*, and some Progressists, in spite of Clemenceau's rejection of conservative support. In the minority were 92 members of the Right, 26 Progressists, 19 left-wing Radicals, 11 Independent Socialists and the full complement of 52 Unified Socialists. The government had found its majority of the Left Centre, and with its support was to endure for the next two years. There was a fair margin of safety, and although future occasions were to see narrower victories as a larger number of Radicals defected, the majority really survived to the end of the Parliament. In spite of the appearance of incoherence,

[48] *Annales de la Chambre des Députés*, 14 May 1907, p. 130.

this was one of the most stable periods in the Parliamentary history of the Third Republic. After a little more than a year in office Clemenceau had won a strong political position not only in Parliament, but also among the general public. A report from a police informer stressed his wide popularity, and gives a valuable analysis of its basis:

> In the last few days there have been rumours in political circles that the prime minister is thinking of resigning, and that, in any case, the ministry is very likely to fall after the recess. I have already told you by word of mouth of M. Clemenceau's popularity with the general public, and how his 'French' character has brought him the sympathy of all. . . . Everywhere, on all sides, and I do not mean in reactionary circles, I hear protests against the provocations of the c.g.t. The arrest of the anti-militarists produced a certain relaxation, but the people are expecting more. . . . The rumours of the prime minister's resignation are therefore causing much regret; people know that with him they have at the head of the government 'un homme à poigne' who is determined to maintain order in the streets; they are worried about his possible successor, and it is quite certain that if the present or future cabinet turns more to the Left, the Republic will have against it not only the reactionaries and the conservative bourgeois, but also 'tout le commerce républicain'. . . . In any case it is quite certain that if M. Clemenceau gives up his post, his resignation will have the most unfortunate impact on the general public, already too disposed to alarm and to see the future in red.[49]

It is significant that Clemenceau, almost from the moment he assumed office, achieved this reputation of being a strong man, 'un homme à poigne', who would suppress disorder. In fact, he combined conciliation and repression; but, while other politicians advertised their conciliatory measures and hid the repressive ones, Clemenceau did the reverse. Hence his nickname, 'the Tiger'. This served him well at the time, but has harmed his historical reputation.[50]

2 THE REVOLT OF THE WINEGROWERS

Attention was soon diverted from the problems of the civil servants by a dramatic series of events in the Midi, stemming from the collapse of the price of its low-quality wine. The fall in prices was primarily due to increased production, resulting from the replanting after the phylloxera epidemic, but the situation was aggravated by such practices as increasing the alcoholic content of the wine by adding sugar, or simply water-

---

[49] Archives Nationales, F⁷ 13950, dossier 2, 29 April 1907.
[50] Cf. A. Kriegel, *Aux origines du communisme français* (1964), I, pp. 193–4.

ing it down. The growers, reluctant to limit their production, insisted that the crisis was caused by 'fraud', but the root cause was over-production. The organization of the industry, with a multitude of tiny growers dependent on a network of middlemen, complicated the situation. After three years of disastrously low prices, by 1907 the economic distress in the four departments heavily dependent on this low quality wine – the Aude, Gard, Hérault and Pyrénées-Orientales – was very great.[51] This situation posed the worst threat to public order the government had to face, involving riots in which five lives were lost, and the mutiny of the 17th Infantry Regiment. This was the natural result of using a locally recruited regiment, whose soldiers sympathized with the grievances of the demonstrators, shared by all classes of society in the area. In Paris both Left and Right fitted these events into their ideological framework. The c.g.t. took up the cause of the winegrowers, and included the government's repressions of the riots among its propaganda about the brutality of this 'government of murderers'. On the other side, fears of the bourgeoisie about the disintegration of society increased. For the first time, there was tangible evidence that French troops might refuse to obey orders if asked to repress civil disturbance. The events in the Midi really had more in common with peasant risings of the pre-revolutionary period than with the struggle of proletariat against capital in the modern world.

The crisis was largely due to the charismatic appeal of Marcellin Albert, known as 'the Redeemer', who addressed a series of monster meetings in the towns of the area.[52] He had been an actor in a company that toured the small towns of the region, but had settled down as a small winegrower and owner of a bar in the village of Argeliers. Personally affected by the collapse of prices, he had made several attempts to organize protests. After a delegation which he had led to meet a Parliamentary committee of enquiry on 11 March 1907 had achieved some notoriety, he was able to spark off the massive protest movement organized by a network of *Comités de Défense Viticole*. He was somewhat naïve, and other men, notably Ferroul, Socialist mayor of Narbonne, used him for their own ends. But it was Albert who had the histrionic ability to attract vast crowds to protest meetings. At first they were peaceful, but from the middle of June they turned into serious riots, and energetic measures had to be used to restore order. One of the

[51] C. K. Warner, *The Winegrowers of France and the Government since 1875* (New York, 1960), p. 48, gives tables of average prices for wine. Against an average for 1890–9 of sixteen francs per hectolitre, the price fell in 1904–6 to only six francs.
[52] For a detailed account by a contemporary journalist, *see* M. Leblond, *La Crise du Midi* (1907), and for a modern version, F. Napo, *1907: La révolte des vignerons* (Toulouse, 1971). The crisis and the government's reaction to it can be followed in detail in a large collection of official documents preserved in the Archives Nationales, F⁷ 12920 and F⁷ 12794.

strangest incidents in the whole affair occurred on 23 June, when Albert, in hiding from the police, arrived at the ministry of the interior, a shabby little man carrying his suitcase, and asked to see Clemenceau. Having been conducted into his presence, and scolded by 'the Tiger' for the disastrous results of his movement, Albert burst into tears, saying that he had not meant any harm, and had had no intention of encouraging violence and riots. Clemenceau told him to return to his village, and, before giving himself up to the police, to persuade his friends to call off their agitation, and to trust the government, which was doing all it could to resolve the economic crisis. He asked if Albert had enough money for the return journey, and, as he had not, gave him a small sum.[53] All this was recounted by Albert when he arrived back, undermining his hold over the movement, which collapsed as rapidly as it had grown. On 29 June a new, stricter law controlling the 'fraudulent' practices was promulgated, and the government ordered the prefects and local tax collectors to be lenient to those who genuinely could not pay. But rich growers who had ostentatiously joined in the concerted refusal to pay taxes were to be prosecuted vigorously.[54] Better prices were received in the autumn for the 1907 harvest, an average of nine francs per hectolitre against six francs for the two previous years, an improvement maintained until the outbreak of war. There was a general rise in the price of wine from all regions, but much more marked for the Midi.[55]

The government had to meet interpellations on the riots and their suppression, couched in the usual terms, by extreme Left and Right.[56] Clemenceau defended his actions by producing documents to show that the government had throughout been determined to use the minimum amount of repression. It was ridiculous to accuse him of encouraging the protest movement because he had not sought to suppress it in May when it was still non-violent. Those who attacked him now on those grounds would have been the first to accuse him of tyranny had he done so. Once again, he said, he was being attacked by a combination of Socialists and reactionaries. The men who organized the protest movement, and who had deliberately turned it into violent paths, were well known to be either reactionary or Socialist politicians. Albert and other non-political figures were a façade. The same political combination seized on the pretext to attack the government with the support of some Radicals: 'behind these recriminations are personal questions, nothing more'. As for the government's treatment of the mutineers, he

[53] Clemenceau described the interview in his speech of 28 June, *Annales de la Chambre des Députés*, 28 June, p. 831.

[54] Archives Nationales, F⁷ 12974, fol. 456, from the prefect of the Aude department to the minister of the interior, 16 August 1907.

[55] C. K. Warner, op. cit., p. 20.

[56] *Annales de la Chambre des Députés*, 20 June 1907, pp. 686–9; 21 June 1907, pp. 705–24; 28 June 1907, pp. 823–36.

pointed out that once again he was being attacked by some for being too lenient, and by others for being too harsh. The government had not promised that if the mutineers returned to barracks they would not be individually punished. But because they had been led to believe that such a promise had been given, they would be treated in that way. There were to be no individual courts-martial, but they would be sent to serve the remainder of their period, only a few months, in the south of Tunisia. One casualty of this mutiny was the bill on reform of military justice, promised in the ministerial declaration. The government announced that it wished to postpone discussion of the bill, and no more was heard of it. During this debate Clemenceau was not in good form, complaining of the lateness of the hour and the difficulty he had in speaking in the face of constant interruption. His speech turned into a series of interchanges with the interrupters, and he allowed himself to be diverted from his theme for long periods. Nevertheless, the government survived without difficulty, supported by its usual majority of the Left Centre, securing a vote of confidence by 327 to 223 on 21 June. About 60 votes had changed since the debate of 18 June when confidence was voted by 389 to 153.[57]

Having survived this debate the government was safe until autumn, as Parliament was soon to adjourn for the summer holidays. There were no more political crises until March 1908. Clemenceau was free to take his summer visit to Carlsbad, troubled only by events in Morocco, with their possible international repercussions. On the whole, however, the international scene was calm in 1907, and the government could not have been worried about an immediate German threat, as it allowed Parliament to pass the law of 28 May 1907, providing for the premature release of the class of 1903. As a result of the 1905 law reducing the period of military service to two years, it seemed unfair that those conscripted under the old law should only be released at the same time as their juniors who had served a year less. The effect of premature release, however, was to leave the manpower of the French army at an unusually low level in the autumn and winter of 1907, until the new recruits were trained. When Parliament reassembled in the autumn it pursued its legislative work, passing several laws of minor importance, concerning military reforms, and the disposition of Church property. A committee of inquiry into the state of the navy, appointed after the disastrous explosion which sunk the battleship *Iéna* in March 1907, was pursuing its researches. The troubles of the navy were to

[57] J. Reinach commented on this occasion: 'Clemenceau lied again yesterday . . . but it was not the lie that saved him; it was the uncertainty of the political future, Millerand suspect to many, Sarrien too weak, Poincaré too neutral, Combes absent.' J. Reinach to Marquise Arconati-Visconti, Bibliothèque Victor Cousin, Arconati-Visconti Papers, 291, fol. 7256.

turn into a long fuse that in the end brought down the government, but there was no sign of that in 1907. The Chamber discussed Moroccan affairs on several occasions in November 1907, and in January and February 1908 Jaurès spoke frequently, attacking the government for following an adventurous policy, likely to bring conflict with Germany, on behalf of sinister economic interests. Diplomatic documents now show that he was wide of the mark in these charges.[58] Although on this, as on other issues, a small number of left-wing Radicals voted with the opposition, the government always had a large and secure majority. In the first months of 1908 the Chamber devoted the biggest part of its time to discussion of the income tax law. Although Clemenceau did not speak in these debates, leaving defence of the government's proposals to Caillaux, he obviously gave them his support. On several occasions the government used its authority by making the vote of certain clauses of the bill a question of confidence. As a result, in spite of the obvious reluctance of many deputies, even of many who were nominally supporters of the government and of the principle of an income tax, the bill made slow but steady progress through the cumbrous Parliamentary machine. On 9 March the government won a crucial victory with the rejection of the Villebois-Mareuil amendment giving special treatment to agricultural profits. As Pelletan said, under the guise of sparing the poor peasants, this would in fact have benefited the rich, the large landowners.[59] This vote illustrated a peculiar feature of Parliamentary procedure, known as rectification of voting: deputies who were absent could allow a colleague to cast their vote for them. They could later change their vote if they wished to claim that their proxy had cast it in a different sense from that which they desired. These rectifications would be published in the definitive record of the session in the *Journal Officiel*. Nevertheless, the voting figures proclaimed during the session were the ones with legal standing, even if a large number of rectifications meant that the majority was in fact reversed. This is precisely what happened to the Villebois-Mareuil amendment. It was rejected by 271 to 240, the figures proclaimed during the session, but after rectification the majority would have been in favour. Thus, a substantial number of deputies were able to have it both ways. They could tell their constituents that they had voted for the amendment, but their votes had been counted the other way, thus helping to defeat it.

On the question of the government's treatment of civil servants, a full-

---

[58] For full discussion of the Moroccan question, *see below*, pp. 226–34.

[59] G. Bonnefous, *Histoire Politique de la Troisième République* (1956), I, pp. 98–100. The impact of the proposed taxation of agricultural profits was reduced by several amendments voted in the autumn of 1908. On the details of the income tax proposals, and their progress through Parliament, *see* E. Pelleray, *L'Oeuvre financière du Parlement, 1906–10* (1910).

scale attack was again launched in March 1908 by Berteaux, principal spokesman for the Radicals opposed to the government. No doubt personal questions played a major part in this attack, although there were genuine grounds of principle on which some Radicals opposed the government's policy. One group was anxious about the government's policy in Morocco. Another centre of opposition was in the Combes-Pelletan group of doctrinaire anti-clericals. While Pelletan, Clemenceau's lieutenant of thirty years before, was probably too discredited to be a serious candidate for office, Combes was still a prominent and highly respected member of the Radical party. On the whole, however, he did not himself take part in the intrigues against the cabinet, which seemed to owe most to Doumer and above all to Berteaux. Another group, in which Buisson was a prominent member, wanted a more left-inclined policy, especially on the rights of teachers and other officials to form trade unions. It is interesting that a police informer reported a rumour that Clemenceau had had the intention of bringing Berteaux into the government, as minister of war, but had changed his mind.[60] This was on 12 March, and the next day Berteaux launched his attack. Two days earlier, the Chamber had accepted a Socialist amendment to a bill restoring commissions in the Army reserve to those dismissed for their Dreyfusism. The amendment calling for reinstatement of officials who had been dismissed a year earlier, was carried against the government. On 13 March Berteaux took this up and made it into a challenge to the government by proposing a resolution: 'The Chamber, maintaining Tuesday's vote and rejecting any addition, passes to the order of the day.' Clemenceau rose to oppose, saying:

> If you wish to hand over the government of the Republic to an anonymous organization of irresponsible officials, which will be able to put pressure on the government and which will remove it from the control of the Chamber, we are not the republicans who will preside over that disorganisation.[61]

The Chamber thereupon reversed its previous vote, in spite of Berteaux's protest at the humiliation which Clemenceau forced on his majority in this way. The government had a comfortable majority of 352 to 130,

<hr>

[60] Archives Nationales, F⁷ 13950, dossier 2, fol. 37. This would appear to be connected with an incident in which one of Clemenceau's assistants, Georges Mandel, at that time a very junior member of his entourage, but who was to rise to prominence as *chef de cabinet* in 1917–19, challenged Berteaux to a duel. *See* J. Sherwood, *Georges Mandel and the Third Republic* (Stanford, 1970), p. 10. *See* also the police reports of 7 and 8 March 1908, Archives of the Préfecture of Police, BA 959.

[61] *Annales de la Chambre des Députés*, 13 March 1908, pp. 736–7. *See* the police reports on Berteaux's activities at this time, 21, 22 January, 15, 22 and 25 February 1908, Archives of the Préfecture of Police, BA 959. These reports connect the intrigues against the cabinet with opposition to the income tax bill.

but 55 Radicals this time voted with the opposition, considerably more than in the previous year. The police reports for the next three months are full of accounts of the intrigues of the 'Combists', the dissident Radicals led by Combes, Pelletan and Berteaux. However, although the informers frequently reported that these intrigues would bring the government down, in fact it retained secure majorities, both after debates on interpellations, and for its legislative proposals.[62]

A major debate occurred on 6 April, dominated by another clash between Jaurès and Clemenceau. Replying to Jaurès's charges that the government had become reactionary, Clemenceau defended its legislative record.[63] If the major reforms had not yet been passed into law, they had nevertheless made real progress, at the cost of an immense amount of work, in open session, in the committees and in negotiations with the Senate. As far as the income tax law was concerned it was quite untrue that Caillaux had been abandoned by his colleagues. There had been differences of opinion, but they had been discussed at long meetings of the cabinet, which had ended with agreement on a common policy; the government had then met the Chamber, had made this policy a question of confidence, and had been successful in getting it approved. On the question of the nationalization of the Western railway, on pensions for the railwaymen, on old age pensions, the government was in the process of negotiating with the Senate, and it was to be hoped that they would soon be able to report that satisfactory solutions had been found. More progress would have been made with reform legislation if Parliament did not waste so much time discussing interpellations. He returned again to his theme that it was Jaurès who had broken up the *bloc*. He went on to say that had the 1906 election not been more favourable to the Republicans than they had any right to expect, he would have had to shift his majority to the Centre. As the elections were so good, he had not needed to do so, and he had already told Jaurès where his majority was. Now that the municipal elections were at hand, the Socialists were seeking to disown advocacy of violent revolution and anti-patriotism, and to rebuild the coalition with the Radicals. In opposition to this tactic, Clemenceau asserted, the great majority of the Radical party would remain loyal to the government. He did, however, make a significant overture to the Centre, in contrast to his position a year earlier when he had declared that he did not want their votes, saying of the Progressists that 'although their programme is very different from ours, I do not claim the right to excommunicate them from the republican party'. At the end of this debate the government had a large

[62] Archives Nationales, F⁷ 13950, dossier 2: for example, fols 38 of 21 March 1908, and 67 of 24 June 1908.
[63] *Annales de la Chambre des Députés*, 6 April 1908, pp. 1094–101.

majority of 319 to 86.[64] Legislation passed in the summer of 1908 did much to justify Clemenceau's claim that he had the support of a realistic, reforming majority. After another hard-fought debate, the income tax bill passed a crucial stage on 25 May when the application of income tax to the *Rentes*, the interest payment on the French government debt which had been proclaimed for ever free of all taxes in the revolutionary period, was carried by 349 to 120. The law for the nationalization of the Western railway was finally promulgated on 13 July. Passed by the Chamber in December 1906, it had been strongly criticized in the Senate. On 24 March 1908 the Senate finance committee had advised in favour of rejection. The government pressed hard for the bill, and after a speech by Clemenceau on 25 June the motion for rejection was defeated by 128 to 125. After amending the bill so that the required financial measures had to be provided by another law, instead of by decree, the Senate then returned the bill to the Chamber. The two Chamber committees concerned agreed to the Senate's amendment, and this was approved by the Chamber on 11 July 1908. So at least one of the major reforms proposed in the government's initial declaration had passed through all stages of its enactment.[65]

---

[64] J. Reinach thought that Jaurès's attacks in fact strengthened the cabinet, in the sense that fear of a more left-wing combination kept some moderates loyal to the government, in spite of their repugnance for its reforming legislation. He wrote: 'Clemenceau may well remain in office: he has on his side the general lack of foresight and energy, and also the Unified Socialists who could not do more for him if he were paying them.' J. Reinach to the Marquise Arconati-Visconti, n.d., Bibliothèque Victor Cousin, Arconati-Visconti Papers, 291, fol. 7175, cf. also fol. 7146. A police report on a meeting of the Progressist group on 30 March 1908 stated that Brindeau, the president of the group, had declared that their votes were becoming more and more indispensable to the cabinet, and that the prime minister had instructed the prefects to include them among those who received the favours of the administration. Archives of the Préfecture of Police, BA 130, 31 March 1908.

[65] Archives Nationales, F⁷ 13950, dossier 2, fol. 51 of 20 June 1908: 'It seems that the *Rachat de l'Ouest* will be voted in the Senate by at least 10 votes. Thus Poincaré's opposition has been overcome. The latter, as a result of his well-known evolutions, does not inspire much confidence as a future prime minister. The opposition in the Chamber wants the Senate to overthrow the government, and those in the Senate would like to see the blow struck in the Palais Bourbon. As a result the general opinion, even among the opposition, is that the government will last for a long time still: it is even added that it might preside over the election of 1910.' The minutes of the Chamber committee are to be found in the Archives Nationales, C 7353, those of the Senate committee in the Archives of the Senate, Commission des Chemins de Fer, 1907, Rachat.

10

CLEMENCEAU
AS STRIKE-BREAKER

I THE DRAVEIL STRIKE

Simultaneously the government had to face another conflict with the trade union movement. This resulted from the serious incidents at Draveil on 1 June when two workers were killed by the police, and at Villeneuve-St Georges on 30 July when a violent demonstration ended with four killed and over fifty wounded. Draveil was a village on the banks of the Seine, close to the small town of Villeneuve-St Georges, a few miles outside Paris, where gravel pits were worked. The incidents arose from a strike of the workers in the pits which began on 3 May.[66] As usual there were violent conflicts between the strikers and blackleg workers, and in the course of one such disturbance two workers were shot dead by the police on 1 June. In contrast to the 1907 riots in the Midi, and the trouble during the mining strike of 1906, it appears that on this occasion the police had acted in a quite unjustified way. Their claim that they were shooting in self-defence was without foundation. Nevertheless, in the Chamber on 11 June, Clemenceau defended the police action, accepting their version of events, and launching into an attack on the C.G.T. Obviously he had decided on a showdown. As he had pointed out on more than one occasion, in order to keep a majority for moderate reforming legislation it was necessary for the government to demonstrate that it was able to maintain public order. This he proceeded to do, as a necessary counterpart to persuading the reluctant Senate to support the government's legislative measures. Instead of condemning the police action, or even disengaging his responsibility until the judicial investigation had established all the circumstances, Clemen-

---

[66] For a detailed analysis of these events, *see* J. Julliard, *Clemenceau, Briseur de Grèves* (1965).

ceau deliberately covered the police with his authority, and turned the debate into an attack on the revolutionaries of the C.G.T. and those who supported them in Parliament, demanding that the Chamber 'pronounce whether it is with us in our policy of maintaining law and order, and is for reform and against revolution'. The Chamber did so, by 407 to 59; only the unified Socialists and a handful of others opposed, although the left-wing Radicals had been critical of the government in their paper *Le Rappel*.[67]

The shootings led to the strike becoming much more violent, and the local leaders lost control to agitators from Paris, notably Ricordeau from the anarchist-controlled building workers' union, the *Fédération du Bâtiment*. He sabotaged a settlement reached between the local union leader and the employers. The shootings had led the C.G.T., and especially the *Fédération du Bâtiment*, to pronounce the magic formula of a general strike. Although the leaders were reluctant to fix a date, foreseeing a fiasco, they found themselves the prisoners of their violent talk. They were hoping a conciliatory speech by Clemenceau would allow them to retreat without losing face, but he had no intention of letting them escape in this way, as his combative tone on 11 June showed. Nevertheless, the C.G.T. leaders refused to proclaim a general strike, and even the more militant *Fédération du Bâtiment* voted for strike action in principle, without fixing a date. This was to place the initiative in the hands of the government; if another clash occurred, trapped by their categorical declaration, they would have no alternative but to proclaim their strike, however unpromising the circumstances.[68] This clash was to occur on 30 July, as a result of a violent demonstration or riot at Villeneuve-St Georges in which four demonstrators were killed, and a large number on both sides wounded. This demonstration had been called by the *Fédération du Bâtiment* in protest at the arrest on 27 July of Ricordeau, the extremist leader of the Paris navvies who had involved himself in the Draveil affair, and Métivier, the secretary of the union of the gingerbread-bakers, who had also volunteered his services.

In view of the fact that their arrest set off a train of events which proved to be disastrous for the C.G.T., suspicions arose quite soon among the militants that Ricordeau and Métivier were *agents-provocateurs*, in the pay of the government. In the case of Ricordeau nothing was ever proven, but in 1911 the left-wing paper *La Guerre Sociale* revealed, with documentary evidence, that Métivier was a police spy, paid by the government from May 1908. Moreover, on 20 May he had had a private interview with Clemenceau himself. It was truly remarkable that the

[67] J. Julliard, op. cit., pp. 57–8; *Annales de la Chambre des Députés*, 11 June 1908, pp. 292–8.
[68] J. Julliard, op. cit., p. 70.

prime minister should concern himself with such petty affairs, if Métivier were merely an informer. There could be no doubt that Métivier had deliberately sought arrest on 27 July, and that his arrest had virtually forced the *Fédération du Bâtiment* to call their demonstration, and that the violent clash that resulted allowed the government to arrest the leaders of the C.G.T.[69]

Whereas, at the time of the first shooting on 1 June, opinion was divided, and many condemned the police action and the government's support of the police, there was support for the government's action on 30 July, except from the Extreme Left, and those among the Radicals, notably Pelletan, who were most hostile to Clemenceau. There was good reason for this; the 4,000 demonstrators had mostly arrived from Paris, and had not been the original strikers. The majority were armed with sticks, and no small number with firearms. Public opinion was fully behind the government in its determination to crush such dangerous movements, and the way seemed once again open for the banning of the C.G.T. The events also demonstrated that the extremists had little support. The general strike called for 3 August was a complete fiasco; only a few building workers in Paris came out. Next day the Draveil workers, distrusting the violent support offered them, went back to work on terms the employers had offered long before. These events proved a turning-point in the history of the French trade union movement. Although the phraseology of revolutionary syndicalism was retained for many years more, it was no longer taken so seriously either by adherents or opponents. The revolutionary vitality that had seemed between 1905 and 1908 to be building up to a crescendo, was revealed to be empty rhetoric, not a serious challenge to the authority of the state. From this moment the C.G.T. began to evolve towards a reformist position. The leaders who were arrested at this time – Griffuelhes, Pouget and Yvetot – never recovered their old authority, although they were released after a few months without having to face any charges. The commitment of the C.G.T. to violent revolution began to diminish from August 1908.

Clemenceau has often been criticized for his handling of the Draveil strike, and his arrest of the C.G.T. leadship. J. Julliard sees this provocative policy as designed to justify the banning of the C.G.T. He claims that Clemenceau was only restrained from carrying this out by Briand and

[69] Ibid., pp. 150–61. The question of whether Clemenceau deliberately provoked the demonstration of 30 July by telling Métivier to get himself arrested is debated between Julliard and some members of the Société des Amis de Clemenceau in the *Bulletin Annuel de la Société des Amis de G. Clemenceau*, New Series, 2 (1965), pp. 6–10 and 16–19. R. Brécy, *Le Mouvement Syndical en France, 1871–1921, Essai Bibliographique* (1963), p. 68, misses the point when he quotes Péricat to the effect that Métivier had no influence on events, and was not at the meeting at which the demonstration was decided upon. He was not at the meeting because he had been arrested, and the demonstration was in protest at his arrest.

Viviani, who advocated a more conciliatory policy, which was successful in that from the autumn of 1908 the C.G.T. leadership became more moderate. But he produces no evidence for his view that Clemenceau wished to ban the C.G.T., and the year before he had clearly opposed any such policy. J. Reinach, a conservatively inclined republican, had no doubt that Clemenceau was opposed to the dissolution of the C.G.T. He attacked Clemenceau for refusing to dissolve the C.G.T. in May 1907, and wrote in August 1908:

> The cabinet may have failed within a week of the reopening of the session. It is certain that the dissolution of the C.G.T. will be demanded, and that Clemenceau will oppose it. What will the Radicals do? What will the Radical-Socialists do? If they vote for a resolution calling on the cabinet to bring the C.G.T. before the courts, Clemenceau will fall. I agree that the dissolution of the C.G.T., perfectly and incontestably legal, is not a panacea, and that there are other causes of the present lamentable state of affairs. Another government may be able to live with the C.G.T., or neutralize it, or even improve it. But it cannot be denied that with Clemenceau on one side and Griffuelhes or his successors on the other, we will have the beginning of the social war.[70]

Clemenceau again outlined his view of the situation in a speech at Bandol in the Var, in October 1908, explaining that to ban the C.G.T. would be quite pointless, and would only make martyrs.

> There is no mystery about the fact that the C.G.T. has been diverted from defence of professional interests by revolutionary anarchists who have up to now been able to exercise a reign of terror over the principal Socialist leaders. To remedy this state of affairs, some conservatives demand the suppression of the C.G.T., which represents 2,000 trade unions, with 200,000 members, out of a total of 13,000 unions with 850,000 members. I have said in Parliament that, even granting such a measure to be legal, I would refuse to put it into effect, because nothing could stop the C.G.T. reconstituting itself the next day with a halo of 'persecution'. That it is for the moment in the hands of disturbers of the public peace is undesirable. But it is no less clear that the great majority of the members are hostile to violent methods, and that their wishes are at the moment falsified by a voting system designed expressly to give power to a minority. Instead of attacking these first attempts at working-class organization, it seems to us more political, and in a word, more republican, to

[70] J. Reinach to the Marquise Arconati-Visconti (n.d. but August 1908), Bibliothèque Victor Cousin, Arconati-Visconti Papers, 291, fol. 7132.

allow the majority to re-establish its own authority, by virtue of a normal voting system that would return to limbo this tiny minority of unrepresentative dictators. We have recently seen the printers' union refuse to follow the orders of the c.g.t., and the powerful miners' union, which does not seem disposed to accept the anarchist programme, has at last forced its entry into the c.g.t. It is not likely that its 60,000 members will allow themselves to be deprived of influence in the councils of the c.g.t. in proportion to their numbers. . . . When the unions have policed their own organization, and on their own initiative repaired the mistakes inevitable in the early days, profiting from their own experience, will that not be a happier result, and one more profitable to democracy, than if, by a brutal and pointless intervention, we had reawakened the distrust of some, discouraged the goodwill of others, and held back the education of all, by permitting the evil councillors to present themselves as martyrs.[71]

Clemenceau's criticism of the voting system of the c.g.t., which gave equal weight to each Federation, whether it represented a handful of members or several thousands, was only too justified. He was too optimistic in foreseeing an early change. Nevertheless he was correct in his assessment that the violent anarchists did not represent the majority opinion among the members of the c.g.t., and that the organization was developing in a reformist direction. He did not wish to weaken the trade union movement, but to see it develop as a moderate realistic institution, when it would be a factor of political stability and help to improve the economic and social conditions of the proletariat. For this evolution to take place the government had to demonstrate that violence did not pay, and this was achieved by the severe repression of the militants. There was no contradiction between Clemenceau's policy and Viviani's conciliatory speech of 23 October, in which he declared that the government was still completely opposed to the banning of the c.g.t.[72] Firmness and conciliation were both essential parts of the government's strategy, outlined by Clemenceau in May 1907, and applied then and in 1908. The success of this strategy is to be seen not in the immediate reactions of the trade union movement, but in its undeniable evolution away from revolutionary extremism over the next few years. Clemenceau had certainly shown himself capable of Machiavellian tactics in order to achieve this end. Whether or not Métivier was ordered by the government to get himself arrested on 27 July, Clemenceau's tactics

[71] Printed in the *Journal Officiel*, 10 October 1908, p. 6941.
[72] Viviani was more categorical than Clemenceau in declaring that the government would have legal justification for dissolving the c.g.t. because of its antimilitarist propaganda. *See* G. Bonnefous, op. cit., I, p. 109.

were clearly designed to force a confrontation on an unwilling C.G.T. Another example of his cynicism was his use of Métivier's extremely violent language in order to defend the government's action in arresting the militants, when well aware that Métivier was being paid by the police.[73]

The government's Parliamentary position now seemed very secure, and the unfavourable report of the commission of enquiry into the navy was dealt with by the resignation of the minister, Thomson, without posing any threat to the government. Although domestic politics were quiet, the autumn and winter of 1908–9 was a busy period for foreign affairs. The Casablanca deserters affair led to moments of real tension between France and Germany, while the Bosnian crisis cast a shadow over the international situation.[74] But these events produced little impact on the domestic scene, except to reinforce support for the government, especially as the Franco-German agreement on Morocco of February 1909 removed for a time the principal grievance of Jaurès and other critics.[75] In the autumn of 1908 the laws providing the financial measures required for the nationalization of the Western railway passed both houses, and went into force. After seemingly endless discussion the income tax bill was at last approved by the Chamber on 9 March 1909, and sent up to the Senate, from whose deliberations it was never to emerge.[76] There remains some doubt about the attitude of Clemenceau and some other members of the cabinet to the income tax bill. It was said at the time, and has often been repeated, that Clemenceau was personally indifferent or hostile to the bill. For instance, Bertie reported that

Clemenceau is dissatisfied with Barthou on account of his handling of the railway question, and with Caillaux because his scheme for an income tax has made the ministry very unpopular. He would like to shed both, but fears that Briand would in such case leave the ministry and upset him. To my enquiry as to the probability of the Senate accepting the income tax bill, Pichon replied that it would be discussed and rediscussed for ever so long. It is evident that he does not like the bill.

[73] In the debate about an amnesty for the Draveil affair on 11 February 1909. Again, during the debate of 12 July 1909, he quoted Métivier, as part of his attack on the Socialists, to prove that the Extreme Left was prepared to ally with the Right to overthrow the Republic. *Annales de la Chambre des Députés*, 11 February 1909, p. 428, and 12 July 1909, p. 1231.
[74] *See below,* pp. 229 and 232–3.
[75] Police report of 6 November 1908, at the time of diplomatic tension between France and Germany; 'Public opinion has never demonstrated such unanimous support of the government. . . . Newspapers of all opinions agree in encouraging the government not to abandon any of our rights, in Morocco or elsewhere.' Archives of the Préfecture of Police, BA 130.
[76] Bertie to Grey, 25 June 1908, Public Record Office, FO/800/164.

A police report, however, cast doubt on the rumours circulating about Clemenceau's opposition to the income tax bill, stating that they were spread by Berteaux as part of his intrigues against the cabinet; if he could create the impression that a vote against the income tax bill was not really a vote hostile to the government, he would have more chance of bringing the government down.[77]

A modern authority has repeated this contemporary polemic, stating that Clemenceau was Caillaux's chief obstacle in his campaign for an income tax bill. He has the ingenious theory that 'he was sure of keeping his majority on the left so long as the income tax bill was in suspense'. This Machiavellian interpretation seems to reveal some misunderstanding of the working of the French Parliamentary system. The Socialists could, and did, vote for the income tax bill, while being bitter opponents of the government; the fate of the government was in the balance much more often through interpellations leading to the vote of an *ordre du jour* than through the progress of legislation.[78]

2 PARLIAMENTARY CRISES, MARCH–JULY 1909

The spring of 1909 brought the usual assault on the government from its left-wing critics. The Radicals were more and more divided into 'Clémencistes' and 'Anti-Clémencistes', and, if the majority of Radical deputies and senators continued to support the government, the feeling among party militants outside Parliament was more hostile. The party congress at Dijon in October 1908 had opposed a complete break with the Socialists, although it had declared that Radicals were determined to fight both Reaction and Anti-militarism; it had, however, called for the reconstitution of the *Bloc des Gauches*, bringing the Socialists into the governmental majority.[79] The senatorial elections of 3 January 1909 provided an illustration of the conflict among the Radicals.

In Clemenceau's department, the Var, there were two Radical lists. Clemenceau's two colleagues, Méric and Sigallas, had quarrelled with him. Relying on strong local connections, and Socialist support, they sought election on a separate list. However, Clemenceau's list, in which he was joined by Louis Martin, the deputy for Toulon, and Reymonenc, a worker in the naval dockyard there, standing as an independent

---

[77] Archives of the Préfecture of Police, BA 959, 22 February 1908: but cf. police report of 3 June 1909 that Clemenceau was considering the replacement of Caillaux, who was to be tempted by a lucrative post at the head of the Banque de Paris et des Pays Bas, by 'a finance minister who was less intransigent, and disposed to allow the income tax bill to be shelved'. Archives Nationales, F⁷ 13950, fol. 90.

[78] R. Binion, *Defeated Leaders, the political fate of Caillaux, Jouvenel and Tardieu* (New York, 1960), p. 29.

[79] G. Bonnefous, op. cit., I, p. 109.

Socialist, had a large majority.[80] But many Radicals were worried about the prospects for the next general election; they needed Socialist support at the second ballot. The situation was all the more dangerous because of the possibility of a second ballot alliance between the Socialists and the Right. The two extremes had found a common cause in the campaign for proportional representation, and were threatening to unite on this issue; if they could persuade their voters to follow this tactic, many Radicals would be in a very exposed position. The issue which did most to bring the dissident Radicals and the Socialists together was the question of the rights of state employees to form unions and to take strike action. On 11 February the government had had a large majority for the rejection of an amendment extending an amnesty for those imprisoned as a result of the Draveil affair to certain other categories of prisoners. To limit the impact of the amnesty, Clemenceau insisted that there could be no question of an amnesty for anti-patriots, or for dismissed civil servants. The promised law laying down a *statut des fonctionnaires*, which would include their right to form associations, which was not in practice now being challenged by the government, was making slow progress through the Parliamentary machine. The Chamber Committee had taken the government's text and transformed it into something much more elaborate, with clauses about promotion procedure and disciplinary machinery. Pressed by the committee to bring the bill forward, Clemenceau declared that it would first have to be discussed by the various ministries concerned; the government obviously wanted to bury it.

Meanwhile the problem was being posed in a less theoretical way by the deterioration of relations between Simyan, the under-secretary for posts and telegraphs, and the postal workers. Conflict began at a meeting of 18 January between Simyan and the union leaders of the *Association Générale des Agents des Postes* about a change in promotion procedure. It rapidly became centred on Simyan himself, who was greeted with hostile demonstrations whenever he visited any postal establishment. After several postal workers had been arrested as a result of one of these *fracas*, on 12 March the Paris postal and telephone workers went on strike. The government, which felt that Simyan had been very clumsy in his handling of the situation, did its best to be conciliatory. On 21 and 22 March Clemenceau and Barthou, the minister responsible, had two interviews with the strike leaders, who demanded Simyan's resignation, and no disciplinary action against the strikers.[81]

---

[80] F. Varenne, *Georges Mandel, Mon Patron* (1947), pp. 23–4. According to a police report of 12 January 1909, the senatorial elections demonstrated the government's popularity in the country, and thus weakened the opposition, Archives of the Préfecture of Police, BA 130.

[81] G. Bonnefous, op. cit., I, pp. 125–6; G. Frischmann, op. cit., pp. 148–55.

Without being precise, the ministers declared that the government's attitude would be one of understanding if the strikers returned to work. On 22 March, Clemenceau repeated this assurance in the Chamber, and although he declared that there could be no question of the resignation of an under-secretary at the dictates of subordinates, he let it appear that a solution might be found by the transformation of Simyan's position into a technical post, occupied by a permanent official. These declarations produced a storm of protest at governmental weakness in the conservative press, but the strikers returned to work. They also issued a poster declaring that they had won all their demands, and that the postal workers no longer recognized Simyan's authority. This produced another debate in the Chamber in which Charles Benoist expounded the situation in theoretical terms as the opening of a great conflict between two opposed conceptions of the social order, the Syndicalist against the Parliamentary. Ignoring such wide issues, Clemenceau merely restated the government's position. There was no question of Simyan's resignation under pressure, but the government would do everything it could to satisfy the legitimate demands of the postal workers.[82]

As in 1907, this conciliatory attitude seemed to encourage the agitation. The movement among the postal workers for affiliation with the C.G.T., and renewed proposals for a common organization of all state employees, developed with great energy. Clemenceau and Simyan were pilloried at public meetings, and in posters, in the most insulting terms. The government responded by taking disciplinary measures against seven postal workers, and by making enquiries about the agitation.[83] On 11 May L'Humanité published a circular from the minister in which he asked local supervisors to report on the political activities of their subordinates. This produced a storm of protest from the Ligue des Droits de l'Homme, the Socialist party and the left-wing Radicals. It also produced another strike, which, like the first, was best supported in Paris, although it spread spasmodically to the provinces. The executive committee of the Radical party, at its meeting of 12 May, formally condemned the government, Pelletan remarking that it was more oppressive than the Empire

---

[82] Annales de la Chambre des Députés, 22 March 1909, pp. 979–80, 26 March 1909, pp. 1059–60. An example of the indignation at the government's weakness among conservative republicans is this letter: 'I have taken a formal decision to make a great effort at the reopening of the session not only to overthrow this nefarious cabinet, but to change the whole political atmosphere, which is becoming unbreathable. We are descending into complete anarchy. It is not a question of reaction. We must have an intelligent and methodical programme of social reforms, authority must be restored, and not merely by means of boutades, acts must conform to words, instead of jibbing with every wind.' He ended by calling Clemenceau 'a cardboard Guizot'. J. Reinach to the Marquise Arconati-Visconti, Bibliothèque Victor Cousin, Arconati-Visconti Papers, 291, fol. 7179.

[83] Archives Nationales, F⁷ 12918, contains many of the reports on the agitation.

had been.[84] 13 May saw a stormy debate in the Chamber during which the Socialist deputies sang the *Internationale*. In spite of the vote in the executive committee of the Radical party, the government won a vote of confidence by 365 to 159, with the majority of the Radical deputies supporting it. This divergence resulted from the fact that the executive committee included party militants who were not members of Parliament, and was normally to the left of the majority of Parliamentary Radicals; the latter refused to be bound by its decisions.[85] The strike soon petered out, in spite of another abortive call for a general strike from the C.G.T.: by 21 May all the strikers were back at work.

Another conflict between the government and the left came on 14 June when the Radical deputy Berteaux proposed a resolution inviting the Senate to accept the text of a law on pensions for railwaymen which had been voted by the Chamber. The government opposed this on grounds of constitutional propriety, and also because it had reservations on the substance of the law. Rejection of Berteaux's resolution was made a question of confidence in the government. Even this pressure only produced a majority for the government of 63, reduced to 26 after the rectification of votes. A substantial number of deputies on this, as on other occasions, used this means of demonstrating their loyalty to the government, and at the same time of reaping the electoral benefits of supporting the pension scheme. The Senate, in fact, approved the bill with minor modifications, and returned it to the Chamber, where it was approved on 21 June.[86] There followed a long debate on the general political situation, arising from a large number of interpellations, which occupied most of the time of the Chamber from 18 June to 15 July. Towards the end of this debate, after many of the most famous orators of the day had spoken – and this period has been called the second golden age of French Parliamentary eloquence – Clemenceau rose to reply for the government. His speech on 12 July was one of the finest of his career, and it turned out virtually to be a fitting end to his first period in office. At the beginning he had to face frequent interruptions from the Right and the Socialists, but he gradually dominated his audience, and towards the end was almost uninterrupted as he defended the record of the ministry, and, in accents of passionate sincerity, his whole life and political creed. He began with a few remarks addressed to the Right, but soon turned to his principal target, Jaurès. His task was to rally the

[84] G. Frischmann, op. cit., pp. 158–62, and *Bulletin du Parti Radical*, 188, 22 May 1909.

[85] *Annales de la Chambre des Députés*, 13 May 1909, pp. 55–6. D. Bardonnet, *L'Evolution du Structure du Parti Radical* (1960), pp. 93–5. C. Fabius de Champville, *Le Comité Executif du Parti Républicain Radical et Radical Socialiste de 1897 à 1907* (1908).

[86] G. Bonnefous, op. cit., I, p. 129. *See also* police report of 15 June 1909, Archives of the Préfecture of Police, BA 959.

majority against the seduction of the Socialist embrace, which, as the elections approached, seemed more and more attractive to many Radicals. He attacked the Socialists for seeking the support of the Right against republicans at several recent elections, and then met the charge, which had been levelled at him throughout the ministry, of violent repression. He said that he was accused of being violent, but it was Jaurès who condoned violence. Theoretically he condemned it, but whenever a violent act occurred he justified it, and put all the blame on the government. He really complained not about the brutality of the repression, but about any repression at all. For his part Clemenceau insisted that he had never resorted to repression without doing everything possible to conciliate; this was true in the Pas de Calais, in the Midi, and in the recent postal strike, which provided a good example of the tactics of his critics. When he tried to conciliate, the strikers proclaimed that the government had capitulated; when he repressed he was called brutal and savage; when he mixed conciliation with repression he was told that he was incoherent. He then turned to the Socialist complaint that the government had not carried out any of its promised reforms. On the contrary, the law on the weekly day of rest had been enforced in spite of its difficulties; the income tax law had been voted by the Chamber, and the nationalization of the Western Railway had been carried through. He told the Chamber that his friends in the Senate had asked him not to make this a question of confidence, for they wished to oppose it without overthrowing the government. He had told them that they wanted to keep him because they thought that he made a good gendarme, but he had replied that he would only act as gendarme if allowed to put through reforms; the question of confidence had been put and the bill passed. The law on old age pensions had been discussed in committee, and the necessary financial arrangements had been provided for it in the budget of 1910: it would be voted before the end of the session. As for decentralization, they had set up a committee which had produced a valuable report; the related question of a change in the electoral law, in his opinion, must wait for changes in the administrative system. In parenthesis he cast some cold water on proportional representation without saying that he was completely opposed to it; but it needed much more study and the existing system seemed to be working well. He then returned to the attack on Jaurès, who had first supported the Combes government, then, in response to a decision of the German dominated Socialist International, had turned to opposition. He could offer a list of some of Jaurès's inconsistencies. He was for reform and at the same time for revolution; he was the forger of Socialist unity, but his party contained the most divergent opinions; he defended *la patrie*, yet opposed the expulsion from the party of Hervé, the antipatriot; he voted for social reforms, but refused to vote the budget to pay for them; he preached universal peace and provoked civil war; he liked to prophesy, and the distinguishing mark of his prose was that all the verbs were in the future tense, and yet when asked to define his programme he could not do it. It was a magnificent polemic with Clemenceau's biting wit at its best. He ended with a defence of his political beliefs, and his whole career, which carried conviction in that it was both modest and proud, and had great sincerity.

> For a long time, I was accused not of incoherence, but of too much logic. Then, when I came at last into office, when I found myself alone in that great office at the Place Beauveau [the ministry of the interior] and read all the savage attacks on the republican party, I confess that I doubted whether I would be able to accomplish anything. It was my own past faults that came to my aid. I remembered that I had waged violent campaigns against the men in power and that perhaps I had been unjust. I do not cry *mea culpa*; what I have done, I have done, and I accept responsibility for it. But perhaps I showed a certain injustice towards men whose ideas I did not share, but whose characters I can respect. And so, I resolved to do what my intelligence told me was right, that I would take no account of the views of my friends if their arguments did not convince me, and that I would not yield to the interest of party. This is my incoherence. I have been inadequate, I admit, but my intentions have been to serve the Republic, liberty, justice, and the cause of the poor, which is defended so badly by you [the Socialists]. . . .

Turning to his own supporters he went on :

> Gentlemen, you can appear before the people of France, who are not all to be found at Jaurès's meetings, and you can point to the work you have done; I tell you now that the people cannot disavow you, unless it disavow the finest part of its glorious history.[87]

At the end of the debate, on 15 July, confidence in the government was voted by 331 to 147. The government seemed more secure than ever, as one attack after another had been beaten off. The police informers, who in 1907 and 1908 had frequently reported intrigues and forecast the fall of the cabinet, were now reporting that the government's majority was secure and that it would certainly survive until the elections.[88] Only five days later, however, on 20 July, the cabinet

[87] *Annales de la Chambre des Députés*, 12 July 1909, pp. 1228–45.
[88] Archives Nationales, F⁷ 13950, dossier 2, fol. 90, 3 June 1909; cf. also reports of 7 and 18 July 1909: 'The sessions is closing without the smallest cloud on the political horizon. After having replied to 189 interpellations, and having fought off the most rude assaults, M. Clemenceau can leave for Carlsbad safe in the

was to fall, as a result of Clemenceau's imprudent language in a debate on the report of the committee of enquiry into the state of the navy. This committee had been set up, at the instigation of Delcassé, to enquire into discrepancies revealed by the budget in the costs of building and equipping warships. Its report was very critical of the ministry, but there seemed no reason to believe that the report posed any danger for the government, which had already survived a more important enquiry into naval affairs by jettisoning the minister in October 1908. It was known that the government had accepted a resolution which called on it 'to give the necessary sanction to the results of the enquiry'. Delcassé, however, had proposed a critical resolution, and rose to deliver a carefully prepared speech in which he placed responsibility for the disastrous state of the navy squarely on Clemenceau's shoulders.[89] Not only was he responsible as prime minister for nearly three years, during which, according to Delcassé, the state of the navy had deteriorated immensely, but he had been president of a senate committee which had enquired into the navy in 1905. This committee had whitewashed Pelletan's administration, whose enormous mistakes, according to Delcassé, lay at the root of the subsequent trouble. Whether Pelletan's administration of the navy was quite as black as it has been painted may be doubted. He was attacked for a policy of naval building that concentrated on light cruisers and submarines instead of battleships. Given France's position, this was a sensible policy, but Pelletan's period in office became a byword for political interference and inefficiency.[90] However, the normal majority would have supported the government against Delcassé, if Clemenceau had not allowed his pugnacity, and his personal hatred for Delcassé, to carry him away into a most imprudent reply. Defending himself against the charge that, as president of the enquiry of 1904 he had ignored the deplorable state of the navy, he asserted that Delcassé's responsibility had been much greater:

---

assurance given by the successive votes of confidence which his majority has given him.' Archives of the Préfecture of Police, BA 130.

[89] Delcassé had long been seeking to use this enquiry into naval affairs against Clemenceau, cf. Bertie to Grey, 4 April 1909, Public Record Office, FO/800/164. A police report of 8 December 1908 had stated that Delcassé was even then hoping to use the various naval scandals to overturn the cabinet (Archives of the Préfecture of Police, BA 130); while a report of 24 March 1909 states that the decision to set up a special committee of enquiry, taken at that time, was connected with conservative opposition to Clemenceau because of his handling of the postal strike (Archives of the Préfecture of Police, BA 130).

[90] S. R. Williamson, *The Politics of Grand Strategy* (Cambridge, Mass., 1969), p. 26. For Delcassé's role in the committee of enquiry into the navy, *see* S. R. Williamson, op. cit., p. 230. The minutes of the senatorial committee presided over by Clemenceau are in the Archives of the Senate, Commission de la Marine, 1905: those of the two Chamber enquiries are in the Archives Nationales, C 7387–7391, 'Enquête sur la catastrophe de l'Iéna', C 7395–7397, 'Enquête sur la Marine'.

You were a minister, you led us to the brink of war, without making any military preparations [Disturbances]. You well know, everyone knows, that when the ministers of war and of the navy were asked if we were ready, they replied that we were not [Noises].[91]

What Clemenceau said was only too true, but it could not be said in public, and his intemperate words produced a wave of sympathy for Delcassé, which led to the rejection of the resolution expressing confidence in the government by 212 to 196; 62 Radicals had voted against the government, and 123 for it. It has been said that another reason for the fall of the cabinet was the absence of 176 deputies, a large number of them normal government supporters, to attend a peace congress in Scandinavia; a recent change in the regulations, due to the increasing scandal of rectified votes, had made it impossible for their votes to be cast by proxy.[92] But they had gone because the government seemed to be in no danger, although the debate on the report of the committee on the navy was foreseen; it was not the report, but Clemenceau's attack on Delcassé, that caused the fall of the government. Professor Bruun has speculated that Clemenceau deliberately organized his own fall by arguing that obscure ramifications of diplomatic and financial intrigue involving the affairs of Crete and Greece are at the origin of this strange move. There is not the least suggestion of any such need for Clemenceau suddenly to disappear in accounts of these events.[93] Another possibility would be the financial scandal known as the Rochette affair in which Clemenceau's enemies sought to involve him after his fall. But Clemenceau had nothing whatsoever to hide in connection with this affair; in any case, it is difficult to see what he could have hoped to

---

[91] *Annales de la Chambre des Députés*, 20 July 1909, p. 1527.
[92] G. Bonnefous, op. cit., I, p. 138.
[93] G. Bruun, *Clemenceau* (1942), pp. 101–3; E. Driault and M. Lhériter, *Histoire Diplomatique de la Grèce de 1801 à nos Jours* (1925–6), IV, p. 572; R. Poidevin, *Les Relations Economiques et Financiers entre la France et l'Allemagne de 1898 à 1914* (1969), pp. 562–6. The source of Bruun's story is to be found in various rumours that were circulating in the press at the end of 1909, which are conveniently summarized in *The Times* of 10 November 1909. It reproduces a despatch from the Athens correspondent of the *Neue Freie Presse* of Vienna, stating that Clemenceau had promised King George of Greece that he would press for the reunion of Crete with Greece, and had then withdrawn when it appeared that this initiative could mean a Turkish boycott of French trade. 'The effect of this was to bury M. Clemenceau's proposal and indeed to bring about the fall of the ministry for which the navy debate, according to this account, must have been a mere pretext. *Le Temps* has submitted the foregoing statements to Clemenceau. . . . When M. Clemenceau read the statement regarding the cause of his fall, his only reply was to shrug his shoulders and laugh.' Bertie to Grey, 29 January 1909, Public Record Office, FO/800/164, mentioned a divergence of views between Clemenceau and Pichon on the Cretan question, but there would seem to be no foundation here for the idea that there was any connection between this and the fall of the ministry.

gain by falling from power.[94] Bruun's view completely ignores the long battle which the government had just fought, against the interpellators, culminating in Clemenceau's powerful speech of 12 July, in which he had exerted all his tactical skill and oratory in order to retain a majority and remain in office. The explanation is much simpler. Clemenceau had quarrelled with Delcassé over ten years before, on a personal matter, and their mutual antipathy had not ceased to grow from that time.[95] In view of their fundamental agreement about the danger Germany posed to their country, this was another example, one of many in Clemenceau's career, of personal hostility blinding him to their common purpose; his attitude to Ferry and Poincaré was similar. Given this personal hatred, Delcassé's attack infuriated Clemenceau, and brought out that element in his character that made him respond without weighing the effect of his words. He sincerely believed what he said, and it was a fair answer to Delcassé's accusation, but its effect was the opposite of what he intended. He had the best of the verbal exchange, but Delcassé won the sympathy of the Chamber.

[94] *See* L. Lépine, *Mes Souvenirs* (1929), pp. 253–64, and Clemenceau's declaration to the committee of enquiry into the Rochette affair, Archives Nationales, C 7451. G. Suarez, *Briand*, II, pp. 344–5.

[95] He asked Delcassé, when he became foreign minister in 1898 to appoint the Comte d'Aunay to an ambassadorial post. The count and his wife were among Clemenceau's most intimate friends, and he had been dismissed as ambassador in Copenhagen in 1893, probably because of his connection with Clemenceau, Delcassé refused. *See* D. Newhall op. cit., pp. 292–4.

11

FOREIGN POLICY

I THE ALGEÇIRAS CONFERENCE, 1906

Clemenceau's involvement in foreign affairs from the time he entered the Sarrien government until the fall of his own cabinet must now be considered. The formation of the Sarrien government came at a time of considerable international tension. Rouvier fell on 7 March 1906; the Sarrien cabinet took over the conduct of affairs on 14 March when the conference of Algeçiras had reached a critical point. What was at stake was the new diplomatic alignment created during Delcassé's tenure of the foreign ministry. The previous three years had seen important changes in the European diplomatic scene, beginning with the Anglo-Japanese alliance of 1902. As France had been the ally of Russia since 1893 the deterioration of relations between Russia and Japan might have signalled a renewed period of tension between Britain and France, but in fact the opposite occurred. The two countries concluded the Entente Cordiale of 8 April 1904.[96] This was in no way an alliance, but a settling of old grievances which had embittered Anglo-French relations for many years. In practical terms it meant that France accepted British control of Egypt, while Britain agreed not to interfere in various French spheres of interest : the most important of these areas turned out to be Morocco, not because of the intrinsic value of that barren land, but because Germany chose this issue on which to challenge the Anglo-French entente. A year after its signature the German Emperor made a ceremonial visit to Tangier and made effusive declarations of support for Morocco. Germany did not want Morocco for itself but sought to demonstrate to France that

[96] See P. J. V. Rolo, *Entente Cordiale* (1969); C. Andrew, *Theophile Delcassé and the making of the Entente Cordiale* (1968); and N. Rich, *Friedrich von Holstein, Politics and Diplomacy in the era of Bismarck and William II* (1965), II, pp. 678–745.

the entente was useless, and that she could only win Morocco by coming to terms with Germany.

The first result of the German initiative was Delcassé's resignation. He thought that France ought to call Germany's bluff, but Rouvier and the rest of the cabinet realized the danger of such a policy, given the relative military strength of the two countries. France was virtually without an ally. In 1904 Russia had been decisively defeated by Japan and was in the throes of revolution. For the moment at least the Franco-Russian alliance had ceased to be of any value. Precisely for this reason Germany thought that the time was ripe for a show of strength that would remove the danger of encirclement and a war on two fronts. Overtures were made to Russia, producing the abortive treaty of Björko signed by the Kaiser and the Tsar in July 1905 but promptly repudiated by the Russians. At the same time Germany hoped that France could be forced by diplomatic pressure to abandon her fundamental hostility. The resignation of Delcassé gave them grounds for hope, and was followed by French agreement to the German proposal of an international conference at Algeçiras to determine the future of Morocco. But before long the attempt to appease Germany was abandoned, and the conference became a trial of strength between France, supported by Britain and Russia, and Germany. As Delcassé had hoped, and against the intentions of Lansdowne, the British foreign secretary who had concluded the agreement, the entente became an anti-German combination. War still seemed a remote possibility in 1906, but the diplomatic alignment of 1914 first appeared in Algeçiras.

The Kaiser's landing at Tangier, and the German insistence on an international conference to decide the future of Morocco, were designed to demonstrate to the French that their entente with England would prove a broken reed. Instead the conference turned into a forum in which not France but Germany was diplomatically isolated, supported only by Austria. Germany's military predominance, at a time when morale in the French army was at its nadir as a result of the repercussions of the Dreyfus Affair, and when Russia was in chaos after her defeat by Japan, was complete. But her clumsy attempt to translate this into a diplomatic victory over France was to be completely defeated. The French devoted just as much attention to putting pressure on England and Russia as they did to Germany, for their allies were ready for a compromise settlement as soon as the Germans yielded. They thought that France was taking unnecessary risks and poisoning the atmosphere for minimal gains. The main dispute was whether the French, helped by the Spanish, should control the police in Casablanca, as well as in the other Moroccan ports. The fact that the French extracted the maximum concession from Germany owes much to the work of the professional diplomats, but they needed the authorization and support of the new cabinet. Clemenceau, though not foreign minister, played a part in stiffening the new cabinet, and also in convincing England and Russia that they had to support France. Already, on 10 March, Grey, the British foreign secretary, had advised the French to accept the first German compromise proposals, saying that 'the Germans have, in effect, climbed down'. The British desire for a compromise was transmitted to the new government in an exaggerated form.[97] On 15 March Clemenceau called on the British ambassador in Paris, Sir Francis Bertie, and told him 'that, at the Cabinet Council on the 14th instant doubts had been raised about the fidelity of England to France. She had been suspected of making some arrangement with Germany behind France's back. . . . Clemenceau, had, he asserted, been the only one at first to combat the supposition.'[98] These tactics had the desired effect. Grey, although he was indignant about the French suspicions, and thought that France was 'unreasonable and did not know how to take her advantage when she had it', decided that he must support them; 'as the French take Casablanca so seriously we must take it so, too'.[99] On 16 March Bertie called on Bourgeois, Clemenceau and Etienne, the minister of war, and assured them of full British support.[100]

Clemenceau was also a prominent figure in discussions with the Russians. His presence in the cabinet was not welcome to the Russians, as he had frequently criticized the Tsarist autocracy, and had welcomed the 1905 revolution in his newspaper articles. Before the new government was formed, the Russian ambassador had warned President Fallières against Clemenceau. Whether because of Clemenceau's appointment, or whether because, like the British government, the Russians thought that the first German offers should be received in a compromising spirit, on 13 March the Russian representative at Algéçiras was told to advise the French to be more conciliatory. Quick action was required. On 15 March the Russian ambassador was received by Sarrien and Clemenceau.[101] Clemenceau assured the ambassador that the new cabinet was anxious to remain on good terms with Russia. In particular, in spite of his recent articles denouncing the raising of loans in Paris by the Russian government, no obstacles would be placed in the way of further loans, which the Russian government desperately needed to rebuild the army, and also to free itself from dependence on taxes voted by the Duma, the

[97] C. Monger, The End of Isolation (1963), p. 277.
[98] E. Grey, Twenty-five Years (1925), I, pp. 188–9. Cf. also British Documents on the Origins of the War, 1898–1914, ed. G. P. Gooch and H. Temperley (1927 seq.), hereafter referred to as BD, III, p. 356, Bertie to Grey, 15 March 1906.
[99] C. Monger, op cit., p. 278.
[100] BD, III, 358, Bertie to Grey, 16 March 1906.
[101] P. Renouvin, 'Finance et Politique: l'Emprunt russe d'Avril 1906 en France', Schweizer Beitrage zur Allgemeinen Geschichte, 18–19 (1960–1), pp. 507–15.

newly created Parliament. This had been precisely the argument used by Clemenceau, in his article in *L'Aurore* of 30 January, to oppose the granting of a loan which could be used to crush the infant Russian liberal movement.[102] Now he allowed international politics to override his liberal sympathies. On 19 March the Russians gave full diplomatic support at Algeçiras, and, with the British also supporting the obstinate French, the conference proceeded smoothly to its final conclusion. The Germans climbed down completely, agreeing to French and Spanish control of the police in all the Moroccan ports, with only token supervision by a Swiss inspector. More important than details of the settlement in Morocco was that the German intention to demonstrate to the French that the entente with England was worthless had been completely defeated. Only after another confrontation with Germany five years later was France able to turn Morocco into a protectorate. But the Algeçiras agreement guaranteed her a predominant influence there. Subsequent diplomatic activity did not call in question French predominance but rather the price that she would be required to pay to Germany before she was allowed to complete the conquest of Morocco. The importance of the Moroccan question in the growing conflict between France and Germany that eventually erupted in 1914 was more that it acted as a symbol of their mutual trust or hostility than its intrinsic value to either.

The Russians collected their part of the bargain on 31 March when the French cabinet agreed to negotiate about a new loan, authorized on 19 April after Clemenceau met Kokovtsov, the Russian finance minister. Clemenceau told him that the Tsar ought to make the liberal Milyukov prime minister.[103] But this was not a sign of serious opposition, and the loan went through. Within a month the Russian fear that Clemenceau's entry into the cabinet might weaken the alliance had been laid to rest. Instead it had been strengthened through the mutual obligations assumed. The shadow of Björko had been removed, as had any fears that the Anglo-French entente meant France moving away from

[102] *L'Aurore*, 30 January 1906.

[103] V. M. Kokovtsov, *Out of my Past* (Stanford, 1935), p. 116, G. Wormser, op. cit., p. 262, misinterprets this incident and states erroneously that Kokovtsov was the Russian ambassador in Paris. He also quotes Caillaux, *Mes Mémoires* (1942), I, p. 269, to the effect that Clemenceau did not value the Russian alliance very highly. This does not seem likely to be a correct view. While Clemenceau was, with good reason, doubtful about Russian military capacity in the immediate future, the Franco-Russian alliance was the keystone of the French diplomatic system and he was careful not to endanger it. As Nekloudof put it in his despatch of 14 December 1910: 'M. Clemenceau, who in his newspaper covered official Russia with mud as long as he was in opposition, as soon as he took office as minister of the interior, told the Russian ambassador that as a member of the government he could only have sympathy and confidence in Russia and its government.' R. Marchand, *Un Livre Noir, Diplomatie d'avant guerre d'après les documents des archives russes* (1922–34), I, p. 15.

Russia. Instead, England and Russia were to bury their differences in the Anglo-Russian entente of 1907. Professor Bruun states that the Franco-Russian alliance was strengthened by a new military convention more favourable to France. This is not correct. As Russian mobilization, provided for by Article 2 of the military convention, could not take place because of the disorganization of the Russian army, the French also reduced their commitments, cancelling the clauses of 1900–1 that provided for French mobilization against England.[104]

After the first critical days of the Sarrien ministry Clemenceau probably played little part in the conduct of foreign policy until he came to form his own government at the end of October 1906.[105] In the new cabinet he remained at the ministry of the interior while Stéphen Pichon replaced Bourgeois as foreign minister. This was a clear sign that Clemenceau intended to exercise a close control over foreign policy. Pichon had been a friend and political associate of Clemenceau for over twenty years. One of the group of young men around Clemenceau in the 1880s, Pichon had been the only one who had not broken with him. After losing his seat in the Chamber in 1893, he entered the diplomatic service, and since that time had been out of politics. After various routine postings he emerged as the French envoy at Peking during the Boxer rising, and then became resident at Tunis. Pichon, it is clear, was by this time more of a professional diplomat than a politician, and he did not have an independent political position.[106] He remained at the foreign ministry until March 1911: for a period in 1912–13 he was said to have separated rather from Clemenceau, but by 1915 they had resumed their collaboration, and he returned to office with him in 1917. There can be no doubt that he accepted Clemenceau's overall control of foreign policy.[107]

Neither the minister for war nor the minister for the navy were men likely to take an independent line. Indeed, Clemenceau's whole cabinet included few men of strong personality, or who had the political stature to challenge his leadership. Briand and Caillaux are the exceptions, but

[104] G. Bruun, op. cit., p. 93. Bruun's statement is based on G. P. Gooch, *Recent Revelations of European Diplomacy*, 2nd edn (New York, 1967), p. 166, and on *Les Alliés contre la Russie* (1926), a propagandist collection issued under the auspices of the Soviet government. A sounder interpretation is to be found in P. Renouvin, 'Les engagements de l'alliance franco-russe: leur évolution de 1891 à 1914', *Revue d'Histoire de la Guerre Mondiale* (1934), p. 305. The text of the military convention is given in *Documents Diplomatiques Français, 1871–1914* (1929 seq.), 2ᵉ Serie, *1900–1911*, hereafter referred to as DDF 2, X, 119, annexe; but it was never ratified by the Russian government.

[105] But he complained to the British ambassador about Bourgeois's indecisiveness. Bertie to Grey, 11 October 1906, Public Record Office, FO/800/164.

[106] He had, however, been elected to the Senate in January 1906. For a man who was foreign minister for nearly seven years Pichon is a very obscure figure; there is no biography, except for a few pages by G. Normandy in a collection of essays and speeches in S. Pichon, *Dans la Bataille* (1908).

[107] *See* D. R. Watson, 'The making of French foreign policy under the first Clemenceau government, 1906–9', *English Historical Review*, LXXXVI, 1971, pp. 774–82.

seem to have played little part in the conduct of foreign affairs. The minister of war was Picquart, Clemenceau's most idiosyncratic appointment. He was neither an important figure in the military world nor a politician. But Clemenceau had always regarded him as the true hero of the Dreyfus Affair. Dreyfus had been an innocent victim, involved against his will, but Picquart had deliberately sacrificed himself, in order to right the wrong done to Dreyfus. Clemenceau resolved to make full recompense by placing him at the head of the military hierarchy that had behaved so abominably towards him. It was a characteristic gesture, but not a wise one. It did not help to restore morale amongst the highest ranks of the army, where it was seen as one more example of the vicious interference of politicians in their private professional field. Nor did Picquart, however noble his role in the Dreyfus Affair, have the qualities to occupy the position of minister of war. Before long Clemenceau came to regret his choice, saying to Lyautey, 'It's you I should have made minister of war, instead of that . . . Picquart.'[108]

2 FRANCE, RUSSIA, GERMANY AND BRITAIN

The overriding problem for French foreign policy was relations with Germany. Clemenceau thought that in the long run war between France and Germany was inevitable, not because France had any intention, after all these years, of seeking revenge for the defeat of 1870, but because, as he put it in his speech of 10 February 1912, 'The difficulty between us and Germany is this: that Germany believes that the logic of her victory means domination, while we do not believe that the logic of our defeat is serfdom [vassalité]'.[109] This same thought was expressed time and again over the years. On 9 January 1906 he wrote in a private letter to his Danish friend, the literary critic G. Brandes: 'No, my friend, Germany will not declare war on us [at this moment]. But in my opinion the European situation is such that a great armed conflict is inevitable at some time which I cannot foresee, and our duty

---

[108] *Les Carnets de Georges Louis*, I, pp. 8–9, 7 March, 1908. Picquart, as a major in the counter-intelligence branch at the War Office, had made the crucial revelations that led to proof of Dreyfus's innocence, and he had persisted in his stand in the face of all the pressures brought to bear by his superior officers. Like Clemenceau himself he was always rather separate from the main body of the Dreyfusards, and he seems to have remained in contact with Clemenceau. At one point Picquart came to Joseph Reinach as an emissary from Clemenceau, asking for money to finance a newspaper. J. Reinach to the Marquise Arconati-Visconti, Bibliothèque Victor Cousin, Arconati-Visconti Papers, 291, fol. 7105. His appointment as minister of war stunned political circles, and enraged the Right. On the general feeling that Picquart was unable to live up to the noble reputation he had acquired during the Affair, see D. Johnson, *France and the Dreyfus Affair* (1966), p. 210.
[109] *Annales du Sénat*, 10 February 1912, p. 279, extracts reprinted in G. Clemenceau, *La France devant l'Allemagne* (1916), pp. 23–4.

is to prepare for the worst.'[110] He remarked to the French diplomat Georges Louis, on 28 July 1908: 'I think war is inevitable. We must do nothing to provoke it, but we must be ready for it; helped by Russia and England, doubtless by Spain also and perhaps by Italy as well, we may be able to win. In any case it will be a life and death affair: if we are beaten we will be crushed.'[111] The impulsiveness of the Kaiser, and the consequent aberrations of German diplomacy, were what he feared, rather than a deliberate and coolly-calculated German attack. He told Grey on 28 April 1908: 'The German Emperor was the most incalculable factor in Europe: he was impulsive, he was sensitive as to his own prestige, and he had at his disposal enormous forces. . . . Germany was always making blunders, going first on one tack and then on the other.'[112]

In spite of this distrust of Germany it would be wrong to think that Clemenceau's policy was one of provocation and hostility. E. M. Carroll's statement that 'Clemenceau was giving a definitely anti-German direction to French policy that was in accord only with the chauvinist section of public opinion',[113] is not borne out by the documentary record. G. Michon, in his biography of Clemenceau and in his book on the Franco-Russian alliance, has likewise castigated Clemenceau for his anti-German policies. Michon was one of the left-wing revisionists who reacted violently against the war-time propaganda theme of exclusive German war-guilt, seeking to attribute the heaviest blame to the French and Russian governments. Resentments from the period of the second Clemenceau government are responsible for this inaccurate interpretation of Clemenceau's policy in the very different circumstances of 1906–9. More cautiously, E. Weber has written that 'Clemenceau's public speeches during his period of office were the most chauvinistic a prime minister has yet made'.[114] It is hard to see the justification even for this statement. Clemenceau made relatively few public speeches on foreign affairs while in office. Weber refers to a speech in the Vendée

---

[110] P. Kruger, *Correspondance de Georg Brandes* (Copenhagen, 1952), I, p. 305.

[111] *Les Carnets de Georges Louis* (1926), I, p. 21. The British ambassador reported similar sentiments on numerous occasions. On 17 April 1907 Bertie reported that 'The French government are anything but bellicose. They are terribly afraid lest Germany should place France in a position in which war would become unavoidable.' On 25 December 1907, Bertie wrote to Grey: 'Clemenceau said to him he would never do the slightest thing which could be considered as a step towards war with Germany, for he well knew the existence of France could be at stake.' Public Record Office, Bertie papers, FO/800/164.

[112] E. Grey, *Twenty-five Years*, II, 290–1, Appendix C, Memorandum of conversation between Sir Edward Grey and M. Clemenceau, 28 April 1908, and cf. his remarks to King Edward VII on 26 August 1908, DDF 2, XI, 434, Clemenceau to Pichon, 29 August 1908.

[113] E. M. Carroll, *French Public Opinion and Foreign Affairs, 1870–1914* (1931), pp. 225–6; G. Michon, *Clemenceau*, pp. 130–2; G. Michon, *L'Alliance Franco-Russe, 1891–1917* (1927), pp. 139–49.

[114] E. Weber, *The Nationalist Revival in France, 1905–1914* (Los Angeles, 1959), p. 86.

early in 1906, and to one at the unveiling of the Scheurer-Kestner monument in February 1908. In the latter he dwelt on the contribution of Alsace in all fields of French activity, and declared, 'What a blow it would be to our self-esteem and to our esteem in the eyes of others, if we do not dare give full expression to the feelings which well up in our hearts when we remember the two hundred years of life in common'.[115] But it would be unfair to see this as a chauvinistic, or provocative, speech, and Clemenceau stated that he had been congratulated on it by the German ambassador.[116]

Clemenceau's public statements on relations with Germany were firm rather than chauvinistic, and the policy of his government of seeking good relations with Germany had considerable success. While he was in office, Franco-German relations were better than either before or after. In spite of the continuing difficulties of the Moroccan situation, France and Germany did not quarrel over Morocco while Clemenceau was in power. Instead they made the agreement of February 1909. It was Rouvier and Caillaux, both eager to improve relations with Germany, who were in power in 1905 and in 1911 respectively, when France and Germany came close to war over Morocco. Clemenceau had good reasons for postponing the inevitable conflict with Germany for as long as possible. When he came to power the military balance was completely on the side of Germany. Russia would take years to recover from her defeat at the hands of Japan, while Britain had as yet done almost nothing to turn herself into a serious military power, capable of effective intervention on the Continent. As the general assumption was that the war would be a brief struggle in which the decisive battles would occur in the first few months, effective British help required both a firm British commitment to land an army on the Continent, and also the creation of an expeditionary force large enough to be of use. Clemenceau thought that at least half a million men were needed. Attempts to get a British military commitment, and to make the Russian promises worth more than the paper they were written on, were two of Clemenceau's major concerns. Until this could be achieved it was vital to remain on reasonable terms with Germany, provided that this could be done with dignity. Another important consideration was the need for French public opinion to be united if war came. He had to cope with strong pacifist and anti-militarist feelings, which were by no means confined to the Socialists. A large section of his own Radical party shared them. It was essential that, if war came, it should be seen to be the result of intolerable German provocation. French public

[115] Full text in *Scheurer-Kestner*, 1908 (B.N. LN 27 53761). Extracts printed in G. Clemenceau, *La France devant l'Allemagne*, p. 4.
[116] E. Grey, *Twenty-five Years*, II, p. 291, Appendix C, memorandum of interview between Sir Edward Grey and M. Clemenceau, 28 April 1908.

opinion would not understand a war which resulted from some obscure issue in Morocco or in the Balkans, unless it were made abundantly clear that France's vital interests were at stake. For these reasons Clemenceau was extremely cautious in authorizing French penetration of Morocco, and even more sparing in the support he was prepared to measure out to Russia during the Bosnian crisis.[117]

The most important development in the diplomatic scene in the first months after the formation of the Clemenceau government was the negotiation of the Anglo-Russian entente of 31 August 1907. While this was welcome to Clemenceau there was little scope for any active French involvement in the talks between Britain and Russia.[118] In no sense at all was Britain adhering to the Franco-Russian alliance, which remained completely independent of the ententes. The negotiations were concerned with the delimitation of British and Russian interests in areas where they might conflict, mainly Persia, Afghanistan and Tibet, and French involvement in the negotiations went no further than general expressions of approval, addressed particularly to the Russians.[119]

A more active part was played by French diplomacy in various attempts to strengthen the Anglo-French entente, so as to virtually turn it into a military alliance. Clemenceau was particularly concerned about the lack of a large British army ready to intervene on the Continent. The Anglo-French military conversations of January 1906 were not regarded as adequate by the French, and Clemenceau made several attempts to improve on them. To his consternation he found that the tendency of the British government was rather to reduce and reinterpret the commitment which the French thought they already had. The first of several incidents occurred soon after Clemenceau formed his government. Asked point-blank by a senator of the Right 'Is there or is there not a military agreement between France and England?', Clemenceau replied that such questions should not be asked. This much annoyed some people in the British Foreign Office who thought that he could have issued a straight *démenti*, although Grey said that, if questioned in

[117] *See below*, pp. 232–3.
[118] Clemenceau had written newspaper articles advocating a French-Russian-English entente in 1905. N. Rich, op. cit., II, p. 714.
[119] One of the first acts of the foreign minister when the Clemenceau government was formed was to see Izvolsky, and to press for the conclusion of an Anglo-Russian entente. DDF 2, X, 244; note, in Pichon's own hand, of his conversation with Izvolsky of 27 October 1906: 'I said that if, as I thought, the Entente Cordiale of the Paris government with that of London could help in the accomplishment of this task, we were at the disposition of our allies. I stressed our keen desire to see this aim achieved, as it was so necessary for the consolidation of the forces of peace.' E. M. Carroll, op. cit., p. 222, states: 'French diplomacy aided at every turn the development of the Anglo-Russian *rapprochement* of August 1907.' But the documents to which he refers amount to no more than general expressions of approval. G. Monger, op. cit., pp. 281–93, and cf. R. P. Churchill, *The Anglo-Russian Convention of 1907* (Cedar Rapids, 1939), passim.

the House of Commons, he was prepared 'to avoid a public denial'. In fact the incident passed unnoticed by the English critics of Grey's secret diplomacy.[120]

More serious was the brush between Clemenceau and the British prime minister Campbell-Bannerman, when the latter visited Paris in April 1907. Clemenceau tried to raise the question of a larger British army for use on the Continent. He was much taken aback by Campbell-Bannerman's reply that 'He did not think English opinion would allow of British troops being employed on the Continent'. Clemenceau at once asked through Bertie, the ambassador in Paris, if Campbell-Bannerman was aware of the Anglo-French military conversations. Grey replied that he was, and that Clemenceau had misunderstood the import of the British prime minister's remarks; he had not meant that under no circumstances would Britain send an army to the Continent.[121] The French were soon to get even better reassurances of British support. On 16 May 1907, the 1904 agreement on Morocco was strengthened by the exchange of identical British and French notes with Spain, declaring the common desire of the two powers to maintain the *status quo* 'in the Mediterranean and in that part of the Atlantic that washes the shores of Europe and Africa'. This was a much wider commitment than the original entente, and tied Britain and France together in a way that was little short of an alliance. Cambon reported that, when he asked Grey, 'In a word, if Germany seeks a quarrel with us, can we count on you?' Grey replied 'Yes'.[122] But Clemenceau's preoccupation remained that of the disproportion between the strength of France's diplomatic position and the weakness of the military force of the entente powers. With Russia's military strength still an unknown quantity, there was a great danger that in the Anglo-French combination France would play the part of the hostage, unless Britain could be persuaded to match her military preparations to her diplomatic commitments. The year 1908 saw several attempts by Clemenceau to bring this home to the British government. In London for the funeral of Campbell-Bannerman, he had a meeting with Grey on 28 April 1908, in which Grey noted :

He dwelt with great emphasis upon the certainty that we should have to intervene on the Continent of Europe against any power which

---

[120] *Annales du Sénat*, 20 November 1906, p. 125. Cf. S. R. Williamson, op. cit., p. 101.

[121] S. R. Williamson, op. cit., p. 102, and R. B. Jones, 'Anglo-French negotiations 1907, a memorandum by Sir Alfred Milner', *Bulletin of the Institute of Historical Research*, 31 (1958), pp. 224–7. Cf. Mallet to Bertie, 13 April 1907 : 'I trust Sir Edward's explanation will smooth Clemenceau down. It is very stupid of him to raise this question again now *à propos* of nothing, and with Campbell-Bannerman of all people. His Majesty's government will never give a categorical assurance of assistance but they went very far last year.'

[122] DDF2, XI, 17, Cambon to Pichon, 8 June 1907; Monger, op. cit., p. 322.

attained a position of domination there just as we had to do in the time of Napoleon. He said we ought to be prepared for this. He realized that conscription might not be suitable for us. . . . But he thought it might be possible for us to adopt something like the Swiss system, which would put us in a position to intervene on the Continent if need be.[123]

When Grey said that Britain must concentrate on naval armament, and that 'Russia ought to be looked to as a great counterpoise to Germany on land', Clemenceau replied: 'it was very desirable that Russia should become such a counterpoise. But at present she had no efficient Government and no money, and for an indefinite period she would continue to be weak.' Clemenceau followed this conversation by getting Tardieu to write a series of articles in Le Temps, pointing out that France was endangered by Anglo-German hostility, and demanding a stronger British army.[124] Then, while on his summer visit to the Austrian spa of Carlsbad, he reverted to this theme in conversation with the British journalist Wickham Steed, and with King Edward VII, who invited Clemenceau and Izvolsky, the Russian foreign minister, to lunch at Marienbad. Clemenceau stressed that he feared Anglo-German tension as the most likely cause of war. In that case France would be the victim:

Germany will seek in France an indemnity for the losses likely to be suffered at sea at the hands of England. What can England do to help us? Destroy the German fleet? That would make a nice hole in the water. . . . One hundred thousand men in Belgium would not be much good, but 250,000 or 500,000 would change the course of the war. As it is England could not send even 100,000 without the greatest difficulty. Your territorial army is a play-thing. I am convinced that our position will be one of extreme danger until England has a national army worthy of the name.

Steed writes that 'he spoke with all the force and velocity of an express train. For nearly two hours he let himself go. He censured the British public, the British government, Sir Edward Grey and British statesmanship in general with astonishing vigour. I defended England to the best of my ability and tried to give him as good as he sent. The hotter the fight the more Clemenceau seemed to enjoy it, and we parted on the best of terms'.[125] Clemenceau's arguments very much annoyed Asquith, the

---

[123] Grey, op. cit., pp. 290–1.
[124] Clemenceau told Wickham Steed that he inspired Tardieu's articles, Wickham Steed, Through Thirty Years (1924), I, p. 287. Cf. Williamson, op. cit., p. 102.
[125] Wickham Steed, op. cit., I, pp. 284–7. Steed's notes were given to the King before he had his own talk with Clemenceau, and the King told him that Clemenceau had virtually repeated his diatribe at their meeting on 26 August. Goschen's

new British prime minister, who wrote to Grey that 'while the French Premier railed against the ignorance of British public men, his own was great if he thought the British were going to keep a standing army of half or three quarters of a million men ready to meet the Germans in Belgium'.[126]

Clemenceau was not optimistic about achieving a change of British policy, and French attempts to get definite military commitments from Russia were equally fruitless. As Williamson puts it:

> Each time the French pressed for offensive action the Russians evaded or gave the vaguest promises, while displaying their customary cupidity with regard to French loans for railway construction. By 1909 all that had been secured by the French were Russian promises to accelerate mobilization. Thus, in spite of the long-time military conventions with Russia, French military planners could not count with certainty on Russian help if war came. Above all Paris could not be confident of Russian offensive action which might compel the Germans to reduce their forces in the west.[127]

3 THE FRANCO-GERMAN AGREEMENT ON MOROCCO

It is not then surprising that French policy in Morocco, where the likelihood of a Franco-German conflict was greatest, was cautious, and that in December 1908 the French seized on the chance to reach agreement with Germany. The Algeçiras agreement had produced a situation in which the French government was bound to equivocate. France had been granted a preponderant influence there, symbolized by her virtual control of the police in the Moroccan ports, but she was limited by her engagements, particularly by the vague stipulations about economic participation, which could at any moment be used by the German government if it wished to cause trouble. France could not turn Morocco into a protectorate, and yet a purely negative policy was ruled out because of the increasing disorder in the country. The Sultan's authority, which had never been complete, was increasingly challenged; by the end of 1907 civil war had broken out, and by July 1908 the Sultan

---

report of his conversation (BD, VI, 100) is on the same lines. Clemenceau's version, in a despatch to Pichon on 29 August 1908, is printed in DDF 2, X, 434.

[126] Asquith to Grey, 7 September 1908, quoted by S. R. Williamson, op. cit., p. 103. Steed had included in his note of Clemenceau's remarks the sentence 'Some of your public men are appallingly ignorant', and this had been underlined in red by the King. It is illuminated by Clemenceau's letter to Pichon on 21 August 1908 (Pichon Papers, Institut de France, MSS 4396, fol. 165), in which he says that Lloyd George's ignorance of the political state of the peoples of Europe and America is phenomenal. 'He had had five minutes' conversation with him here, and could give unbelievable examples of it.'

[127] Williamson, op. cit., p. 120, referring to DDF 2, XI, 116 and 455.

Abd-el-Aziz had been defeated by Moulay Hafid. To some extent this was a reaction to the dependence of Abd-el-Aziz on the French. Domestic politics also limited the freedom of action of the French government. On the one hand there was a small, but vocal and influential, group centering on Etienne, with his *Comité de L'Afrique Française*, involved with economic interest-groups in Algeria, demanding the annexation of Morocco under one guise or another. On the other hand Jaurès made opposition to further French advance in Morocco one of the central planks in his political platform. This was not so much because of opposition to colonialism as such, but because he saw Franco-German conflict in Morocco as the greatest danger to European peace. The opposition of the Socialists was not serious, but a section of the Radicals shared their misgivings, and the government had to tread cautiously to avoid losing their support, which would have brought it down.[128] As Clemenceau said in the Chamber on 24 February 1908:

> I am faced with two contradictory criticisms. M. Jaurès says 'Evacuate Morocco'. M. Etienne, together with a great number of his friends, and of our colleagues of the Centre and on that side of the House [the Right], says 'Send more troops to Morocco'.[129]

The policy of the government was between these two extremes. It would not withdraw from Morocco, because, contrary to Jaurès's view, that would greatly increase the danger of a European conflict; for if France was not there to protect the European settlers, other powers would intervene. On the other hand, France would not do more than necessary to restore order in the ports. The most that Clemenceau authorized was military occupation of an area around Casablanca sufficient to protect the town from further attack by rebel tribes. He declared, 'We will not go to Fez, we will not go to Marrakesh'. When reproached by advocates of a forward policy with having said this, Clemenceau is reported to have said, 'Well, yes, we will go to Fez, but we cannot say so'.[130]

The question for the French government was the likely reaction of Germany to a French attempt to go beyond the provisions of the Algeçiras agreement and establish a protectorate over Morocco. Clearly this

[128] Comte de St Aulaire, *Confession d'un vieux diplomate* (1954), p. 188: 'The ministry is the prisoner of the majority, which on the Moroccan question is dominated by the Socialist party. For a brief account of the French penetration of Morocco, *see* J. Ganiage, *L'Expansion Coloniale de la France, 1871–1914* (1968), pp. 243–73.
[129] *Annales de la Chambre des Députés*, 24 February 1908, pp. 545–6. However, C. M. Andrew and A. S. Kanya-Forstner have stated that Etienne's colonial pressure group was much weaker between 1906 and 1910 than either earlier or later: it had been completely split by domestic political questions: *see* 'The French colonial party: its composition, aims and influence, 1885–1914', *The Historical Journal*, XIV (1971), pp. 99–128, especially pp. 120–22.
[130] *Les Carnets de Georges Louis*, I, p. 9, 7 March 1908, reporting gossip from Denys Cochin and de Voguë.

could only be done by agreement with Germany, but the price Germany wanted was not clear. On many occasions it seemed that she was asking France to break with England and Russia, and turn to Germany. Such a solution would have made France virtually a German satellite. No French statesman could consider such a policy. But if Germany were prepared to settle for less there need be no obstacle to Franco-German agreement on Morocco, and negotiations continued intermittently from 1907 down to the final agreement of November 1911, by which France got Morocco in return for the concession to Germany of some worthless territory in central Africa. In March 1907 French troops moved across the frontier from Algeria after a French doctor had been murdered in Marrakesh. On 30 July nine Europeans were murdered in Casablanca, leading to further French intervention. Clemenceau was paying his summer visit to Carlsbad, and for once we have some evidence about his relations with Pichon, and his private views on Moroccan policy.[131] He was concerned lest Pichon be carried away by the pressures for large-scale military intervention, and was determined to keep the military on a short rein. He wrote to Pichon on 10 August 1907 :

> I have never doubted that you wished to limit yourself to observation of the Algeçiras agreement, but I feared, I admit it, the suggestions of our 'Africans', and, above all, the *entraînement* of the military leaders. That is why I was unwilling to give the admiral and the general forces of such a size that they might be tempted to undertake an operation that went beyond the limits laid down. . . . As for Germany, I continue to be wary of her 'Well Done!' For if we give the least pretext, and if Bulow can pretend to believe that we have gone beyond the Algeçiras agreement, we will have a sudden about-turn, in which they seek revenge. . . .[132]

The need for close control of the military is shown by the eagerness with which St Aulaire, the junior diplomat on the spot and a naval officer, seized the chance to commit French forces as soon as they heard of the Casablanca incident. St Aulaire was worried about the government's weakness, which he attributed to Clemenceau's opposition to colonial expeditions, and wanted to face them with a *fait accompli*.[133] In fact the Germans accepted the limited French occupation that followed, although negotiations on various economic matters were allowed to lapse. Through the winter of 1907–8 cautious French military

[131] D. R. Watson, op. cit., pp. 776–7.
[132] Clemenceau to Pichon, 10 April 1907, Pichon Papers, Institut de France, MSS 4396, fol. 162; and again on 16 August 1907, MSS 4396, fol. 163: 'My only fear is that you place too much trust in Germany who might, in my view, at any moment turn against us.'
[133] St Aulaire, op. cit., p. 180.

intervention continued, while the Sultan found himself increasingly threatened by the rebellion of Moulay Hafid. Finally, on 19 August 1908, with Clemenceau again at Carlsbad, the Sultan Abd-el-Aziz was defeated and fled to the French lines. Clemenceau's telegrams to Pichon about the unfortunate Sultan showed again the close supervision he gave to Moroccan affairs.[134]

On 25 September an incident at Casablanca led to the worst moments of tension between France and Germany during Clemenceau's government. This was the result of the arrest by the French of some Germans who had deserted from the Foreign Legion, whom the German consul was trying to smuggle on to a boat. The French demanded an apology for the actions of the German consul, while the Germans thought that the French ought to apologize for the rough treatment given the consul. This trivial affair has often been exaggerated: Clemenceau is supposed to have replied to the German ambassador, who said that unless France apologized he would be forced to leave Paris, 'What time does your train go?' Clemenceau denied this, saying that such brutal insults were not his style, and that he was on friendly terms with Radolin, the German ambassador. The published documents do not mention any personal interview. The affair was carried on through regular diplomatic channels.[135] The incident never had great significance, except to strengthen those on the German side who argued that the policy of pinpricks in Morocco was futile and dangerous; thus it was a catalyst of Franco-German rapprochement. But the main motive for seeking a settlement in Morocco, on both sides, was the crisis caused by the Austrian annexation of Bosnia on 7 October 1908. The diplomatic repercussions of the Bosnian annexation went on gathering force through the winter, reaching their most acute point in March 1909, and both French and German governments wished to mend relations because of the dangerous situation in the Balkans.

The initiative came from the German side, beginning at a subordinate level with talks between Lancken, a German diplomat in Paris, and Tardieu, who combined a post at the Quai d'Orsay with that of leader writer on Le Temps; Caillaux, the minister of finance, joined in on 13 December.[136] The decisive step came on 6 January 1909 when the Germans proposed a Franco-German agreement on Morocco. Pichon responded eagerly, on 9 January 1909, insisting that talks on Morocco

<hr />

[134] Pichon Papers, MSS 4396, fol. 164.
[135] G. Suarez, Clemenceau, II, pp. 121-2; J. Martet, M. Clemenceau peint par lui-même (1929), pp. 77-80; DDF 2, XI, 521, Cambon to Pichon, 2 November 1908; DDF 2, XI, 528, Pichon to Cambon, 3 November 1908.
[136] A. Mendelsohn-Bartholdy, et al., ed., Die Grosse Politik der Europäischen Kabinette (Berlin, 1922-6), hereafter cited as GP, XXIV, 8471, Lancken to Bulow, 14 December 1908; cf. E. W. Edwards, 'The Franco-German agreement on Morocco, 1909', English Historical Review, 78 (1963), pp. 483-513.

should be seen as a continuation of the negotiations begun in 1907, so that a settlement 'would have no apparent link with events in the East'. However, the link was there; on the same day the German ambassador reported to his government that Pichon had told him that France would remain neutral if war broke out over Bosnia.[137] The agreement was signed on 9 February 1909: the Germans recognized the special political interests of France in Morocco, and promised not to hinder them; in return the French promised the Germans equality of treatment for commercial and industrial interests there. The terms were more or less those Germany had rejected in 1907.[138]

The significance of the agreement was more in its implications for the European diplomatic system than its impact on Morocco. It was seen as part of a general Franco-German rapprochement, and was followed over the next twelve months by various other proposals, such as the opening of the Paris bourse to German shares, and French participation in the financing of the Baghdad railway. These proposals, like so many other schemes for economic cooperation between France and Germany in those years, were vetoed by the French government and came to nothing as political tension mounted again.[139] But at the time the agreement could be seen by the alarmist Nicolson, British ambassador to Russia, as the beginning of the collapse of the Anglo-French-Russian understanding. He wrote to Grey on 24 March 1909:

> The Franco-German agreement was the first step and France is a quarter of the way towards a fuller understanding with Germany. . . . The Franco-Russian alliance has not borne the test, and the Anglo-Russian entente is not sufficiently strong or sufficiently deep-rooted to have any appreciable influence. The hegemony of the Central Powers will be established in Europe, and England will be isolated.[140]

Grey was not as disturbed as Nicolson, and his initial reaction to news of the agreement was favourable, but its implications for future French policy made him rather uneasy. The French attitude in the Bosnian

---

[137] DDF 2, XI, 596, Cambon to Pichon, 6 January 1909; DDF 2, XI, 604, Pichon to Cambon, 9 January 1909; GP, XXIV, 8481, Radolin to Bulow, 9 January 1909. Cf. M. B. Cooper, 'British policy in the Balkans, 1908-9', *The Historical Journal*, VII (1964), pp. 258-79, especially p. 278, where Hardinge is quoted as saying on 26 January 1909 that while Britain had loyally supported Russia, the French were 'coquetting with Austria in the hope of obtaining a free hand from Germany in Morocco'.

[138] Text of the declaration is in DDF 2, XI, 642. For a detailed study of the intermittent negotiations between France and Germany about Morocco, *see* R. Poidevin, *Les relations économiques et financières entre la France et l'Allemagne de 1898 à 1914*, pp. 439-47, 458-66. The entire period of the Clemenceau government is included in the section of Poidevin's book entitled 'Vers un rapprochement économique et financier franco-allemand? 1906-1910'.

[139] Poidevin, op. cit., pp. 469-510.

[140] BD, V, 764, Nicolson to Grey, 24 March 1909.

crisis, together with the agreement, revealed them to be unreliable partners.

Why did the French government make the agreement? According to Caillaux's memoirs,[141] there had been since 1907 a conflict between Pichon, who wished to improve relations with Germany, and Clemenceau, whose policy was much more anti-German. Caillaux states that the February 1909 agreement was negotiated by Pichon behind Clemenceau's back, and then presented to him, with the support of the majority in the cabinet, and he was forced to agree. This interpretation is not plausible. It runs counter to everything known about the personal authority Clemenceau exercised in the cabinet, and in particular his relationship with Pichon. Among the few letters of Clemenceau available to scholars there are two groups from Clemenceau to Pichon, written during his summer visits to Carlsbad in August 1907 and August 1908.[142] These letters show clearly that Clemenceau exercised very close supervision over foreign policy, and especially over Moroccan affairs. It is unlikely that Pichon attempted to follow an independent line on such an important matter, and impossible to believe that he imposed it on a reluctant Clemenceau.[143]

It has to be explained, then, why Clemenceau authorized the agreement. One reason was that it was useful ammunition in internal politics, helping to ward off Jaurès's attacks. Bertie reported that 'the Franco-German agreement on Morocco has gained Clemenceau great credit in the press and public estimation'.[144] But his main motives were to be found in the international situation. The British government learnt at

[141] J. Caillaux, *Mes Mémoires*, I, p. 277, and Poidevin, op. cit., p. 461. Caillaux's views were naturally affected by the treatment meted out to him during the war, and his picture of Clemenceau is extremely unreliable. He has a fantastic theory that Clemenceau followed a secret personal policy with regard to England, and that for some mysterious reason he was under the control of that 'redoubtable and almost autonomous' English institution, the Intelligence Service. He hints that this all-knowing organization had compromising documents on Clemenceau dating from the time of his relationship with Cornelius Herz. Caillaux, op. cit., I, pp. 290–4. This far-fetched nonsense should be enough to discount Caillaux's evidence about Clemenceau's conduct of foreign policy, but it does not appear to have done so. D. R. Watson, op cit., pp. 781–2.

[142] Pichon Papers, MSS 4396, fols 160–73. Lancken reported that Pichon had told him that for the moment he must wait for the French reaction to developments in Morocco, while one of Pichon's entourage had said that decisions about Morocco were reserved for Clemenceau alone. Lancken to Bulow, 26 August 1908, GP, XXIV, 8411.

[143] The British ambassador more than once had reported rumours of slight disagreement between Pichon and Clemenceau, but he concluded that Clemenceau always imposed his will on the foreign minister: 'There is gossip of acid cabinet conversations between Clemenceau and Pichon, but it is not of sufficient importance for me to trouble Grey with it. However much Pichon may resent and kick in Cabinet against Clemenceau's criticisms of the Quai d'Orsay organization he will always in the end submit when the whip is cracked in earnest.' Bertie to Charlie (Lascelles), 26 December 1907, Public Record Office, FO/800/164, and cf. Bertie to Grey, 3 January 1909, Public Record Office, FO/800/164.

[144] Bertie to Grey, 18 February 1909, Public Record Office, FO/800/164.

the beginning of February 1909 that Clemenceau was very annoyed with them, when Bertie forwarded a report from *The Times'* correspondent, Saunders, of a talk with Clemenceau,

> whom he had found in a state of considerable nervous irritation. The Prime Minister began by complaining bitterly of the action of His Majesty's Government in regard to financial matters in Turkey. . . . M. Clemenceau then exclaimed that he had been much astonished at a proposal . . . that the Germans should be allowed a share in a railway loan in China. 'There is a cleft in the entente,' said M. Clemenceau at the conclusion of the interview, 'and care must be taken that it does not widen.'[145]

According to Professor Bruun, Clemenceau was annoyed at the British refusal to countenance a scheme for the annexation of Crete by Greece, part of a wider plan for winning Greece away from Germany.[146] But it is not likely that these minor elements of friction governed Clemenceau's decisions, although he may well have worked himself up into a state of righteous indignation about them, when he had decided to make the agreement with Germany. His main consideration was doubtless the exposed position in which France found herself, as a result of the weakness and unreliability of Russia and the British refusal to create a serious army that could be used at the outbreak of a Continental war. The Bosnian crisis had underlined the dangers of the situation, and Clemenceau had no intention of getting involved in a war with Germany over Bosnia in order to rescue Izvolsky from a situation which he had brought on himself by attempting to do a deal with Austria.

The provinces of Bosnia-Herzegovina (now part of Yugoslavia) were, down to 1908, legally under the sovereignty of the Ottoman Empire, although they had been garrisoned and administered by Austria since 1878. In September 1908 Izvolsky and Aehrenthal, the Austrian foreign minister, made the 'Buchlau bargain' by which Austria was to proclaim its sovereignty over the provinces, while, in return, the Russians gained the freedom to move their warships through the Straits from the Black Sea to the Mediterranean. This had been forbidden by various international treaties. Austria went ahead at once, proclaiming the annexation on 5 October 1908, but Izvolsky found that Britain and France could not support his claim to the opening of the Straits. Thus an arrangement that had been intended to improve relations between Austria and Russia turned into a humiliation for Russia and a diplomatic victory for the Austro-German alliance. France's failure to support Russia was a

---

[145] BD, VII, 148, Bertie to Grey, 1 February 1909.
[146] G. Bruun, op. cit., pp. 101–2.

major factor in this outcome, and was directly connected with the Moroccan agreement.[147]

When Germany renewed her offers of an agreement on Morocco, it is not surprising that Clemenceau was ready to talk. The change of policy came more from the German side than the French, who for the last two years had been open to a bargain by which Germany got economic rights in Morocco in return for the abandonment of political claims there. The difficulty had been that the Germans had demanded more. In a sense there was even now a *quid pro quo* in that France was conciliatory over Bosnia. It has been said that the agreement was 'an error of judgement' that might well have done serious damage to France's relations with her allies.[148] However, British policy does not seem to have been greatly affected by the agreement, and when Germany again provoked a crisis over Morocco in 1911, France got full British support. In the Agadir crisis Russia was lukewarm to say the least, repaying France for her indifference at the time of the Bosnian crisis. The agreement was only a tactical move, and it certainly did not mean that France had moved over to the German camp. On 13 September 1908, Clemenceau had told Bertie that Germany's

> policy was to endeavour to separate France and England, and to take every opportunity of being disagreeable to both those countries and hampering their action, so as to impress on each that nothing could be done without the consent of Germany, and to prevail on one or the other to come to an understanding with her apart from the other.

He was aware of the trap, and did not intend to fall into it.[149] He had no intention of presiding over a *renversement des alliances* that would leave France the satellite of Germany. The Bosnian crisis ended peacefully in March 1909 when the Russian government accepted the annexation, although it was a major factor in the deterioration of relations between Russia and the Austro-German alliance that was to continue down to the outbreak of war in 1914. No further major diplomatic incident occurred before the fall of the Clemenceau cabinet in July 1909, as a result of his clumsy handling of Delcassé's attack on his government's record in naval affairs.[150]

Clemenceau exercised a preponderant influence over foreign policy decisions and was very far from pursuing an adventurous and aggressive policy. He was extremely cautious, and, although he remained con-

---

[147] 'The French attitude at the time of the Bosnian crisis was decidedly reserved'. B. E. Schmitt, *The Coming of the War* (New York, 1930), I, p. 43; cf. also B. E. Schmitt, *The Annexation of Bosnia* (1937), and A. J. P. Taylor, *The Struggle for Mastery in Europe, 1848–1918* (1954), pp. 450–6.
[148] Edwards, op. cit., p. 513.
[149] BD, VII, 104, Bertie to Grey, 13 September 1908.
[150] *See above*, pp. 212–14.

vinced that war with Germany would come some day, he was determined to do nothing to give the German government an excuse for attack, provided that this did not conflict with French honour and prestige, and with the maintenance of good relations with Russia, and, even more, with England.

Part five

OPPOSITION
1909-1917

12

IN OPPOSITION
BEFORE THE WAR

1 LECTURES ON DEMOCRACY

Immediately after his resignation, Clemenceau wrote the following letter:

> I am full of joy at the deliverance. No more people to see. No more demands. Nothing but freedom. An empty ante-room. . . . I slept last night from eleven to seven without interruption. It is a long time since that last happened.[1]

No doubt a man of sixty-seven, in imperfect health, would feel this physical relief at the moment of shedding the burdens of office. But it would be foolish to take this letter as an expression of his deepest feelings. He had got immense satisfaction from the exercise of power, and he remained a candidate for office. In the short term, however, the wisest thing was to remove himself from the political scene. Briand, recommended by Clemenceau as his successor, retained many of the members of the last cabinet, and there was no marked difference between the political complexion of the new cabinet and that which had fallen. Clemenceau could hardly oppose the new cabinet, and did not feel like supporting it. For the next two and a half years he remained in the background, making no public speeches and writing no articles. A police report states that he was involved in a plan to establish a newspaper in August 1911, but nothing came of it for almost two years.[2]

Only in the autumn of 1911 did he become politically active again. In the meantime he took long holidays at Carlsbad and other spas, and

[1] G. Wormser, op. cit., p. 213.
[2] Archives Nationales, F⁷ 13950, dossier 2, fol. 99, 11 August 1911.

spent much time at his country cottage, close to the rural retreat of his friend, the painter Claude Monet. He talked of a trip to Egypt, but did not achieve this ambition; instead he spent the summer of 1910 on a lecture tour in South America. He sailed on 29 June, and returned on 27 October 1910. He lectured on democracy, and this provides an opportunity to examine the evolution of his political ideas.[3]

In contrast to his earlier criticism of the constitution of the Third Republic, Clemenceau now defends it. He does not think it perfect, but his criticisms are of points of detail, and he defends all its main institutions. This is not necessarily inconsistent. He said, sensibly enough, that a constitution is not good or bad in itself, but depending on the way it is applied, and the conventions that grow up around it. The constitution of 1875 had produced a political system very different from that envisaged by its designers. They had thought that it would provide a strong and fully independent executive power. Precisely on this ground it had been attacked by Radicals like Clemenceau who advocated a *Régime d'Assemblée*, modelled on the Convention of 1792–3. However, the independence of the executive soon diminished, and the Third Republic developed into a form of *Régime d'Assemblée*.[4] Clemenceau's mistake was to think that such a system would provide strong government. It only did so in time of crisis, as in 1792–3, or again in 1917–18 Under normal conditions it provided a very weak form of government, under which it was difficult to put through a positive programme, as Clemenceau had discovered when in office. He saw the problem now, but his solution can hardly be called satisfactory.

The greater part of his lectures was devoted not to discussion of such technical details, but to a great fresco covering political life from prehistoric times, through ancient Babylon and India, to Greece and Rome. After speaking for an hour and forty-five minutes he had only got to Rome. Then a quick dash through medieval history brought him to the American and French Revolutions at the end of his first lecture.[5] The second lecture was mainly devoted to the French Revolution, which, he said, had revealed the fallacy of eighteenth-century optimism: 'if the people is always just and good, how could it accept being crushed by tyrants . . . to believe, without reserve, in the sovereignty of the people

[3] The two sources for Clemenceau's ideas at this time are M. Ségard, *Sur la Démocratie, Neuf Conférences par G. Clemenceau* (1930), and L. Abensour, 'Un grand projet de Clemenceau', *La Grande Revue* (1930), pp. 529–50. Ségard was a young doctor who accompanied Clemenceau on his trip, acting in a medical and a secretarial capacity. He kept some of Clemenceau's notes which he used to produce his version of the lectures. Abensour was a journalist who was engaged as a research assistant by Clemenceau on his return to Paris, when he planned to work up his lectures into a seven-volume work on the history and philosophy of democratic government.
[4] *See below*, Appendix II.
[5] M. Ségard, op. cit., p. 28.

is to lay oneself open to great disillusionment.'[6] The third reflected on British and French experience of Parliamentary democracy in the nineteenth century, and marked his abandonment of his youthful ideas about direct democracy:

> At one stage of my life, when I was closer to theory than to reality, I had faith in the Single Chamber, the direct representation of popular feeling. I thought that the people was always sensible. I have changed my mind. Events have taught me that the people must be given time to reflect; the time for reflection is provided by the Senate.[7]

His view now was that

> the essential thing for a democratic government, the one thing that can make it a reality, not a façade, is the formation of its ruling élite.[8]

He declared, therefore, that political parties were essential for the proper working of a democratic government But despite his clear analysis of the difference between democratic governments in America, Britain and France, Clemenceau seems to have been unable to see clearly the nature of the problem and its possible solution. For in discussing the faults of the French system he complained that 'there was more concern to vote for or against a ministry, than to vote well prepared laws'. He does not seem to have realized that the essential element of the strong Parliamentary government he desired was precisely that deputies did vote for or against a ministry in a disciplined fashion, relinquishing their right to judge each issue on its merits. He was critical of the French system, saying, 'the Parliamentary régime has not achieved what was expected of it, because it has been at the mercy of chance majorities'.[9] He said that there was need of reform to increase the power of Parliament to control the executive, and at the same time diminish its tendency to substitute itself for the executive. But he offered no practical way of doing this.

A strong current of opinion in France advocated proportional representation as one way of achieving these ends. Strangely enough, in view of the modern view that proportional representation leads to fragmentation of parties and weak government, its advocates in France at that time saw it as a way of strengthening the executive, as well as providing for a better and juster representation of the opinions of the electorate. But Clemenceau was one of the leaders of the opposition to proportional representation.

[6] Ibid., pp. 42–3.
[7] Ibid., pp. 64–5.
[8] L. Abensour, op. cit., p. 540.
[9] M. Ségard, op. cit., pp. 159–60.

2 AGADIR AND THE FALL OF CAILLAUX

For nearly a year after his return from South America he took little part in politics, although he was consulted by Caillaux about the formation of his ministry in June 1911. Caillaux says that Clemenceau advised him to take de Selves as foreign minister.[10] This was to be an appointment with unfortunate consequences. Totally without experience of diplomacy, the new foreign minister was not competent to deal with the highly dangerous situation resulting from the German decision to send a gunboat to Agadir on 1 July 1911. De Selves wanted to reply by sending a French warship. Both Caillaux and the naval minister, Delcassé, were horrified and vetoed this rash move.[11] Caillaux put no trust in de Selves after this, being suspicious of the dominant influence exercised over him by anti-German permanent officials at the Quai d'Orsay. He decided to take negotiations with Germany into his own hands, and conducted them partly through unofficial channels. Caillaux's negotiations were remarkably successful, and the Agadir crisis proved to be the biggest blunder of German diplomacy before 1914. Once again the German government had not clearly formulated what it hoped to gain by this dramatic gesture, this 'thumping the table', as Kiderlen-Wächter, the German foreign minister, himself described it. The background to the despatch of the *Panther* to Agadir was the French march on Fez, prelude to their conquest of Morocco, seen by the Germans as another provocation. They were breaking the Algeçiras settlement, and straining the 1909 agreement by turning political influence into outright conquest, while refusing to give Germany the promised economic concessions. In reality Caillaux was ready to give Germany concessions in return for a free hand in Morocco. He was the foremost advocate of a policy of cooperation with Germany. But the spectacular publicity of the *Panther* incident made it more difficult for him to make concessions without appearing to be buying Morocco at the price of accepting German hegemony. The original German demand for the whole of the French Congo in compensation was whittled down to a bargain by which Germany got extensive but worthless territory in the Congo, which the French had scarcely developed or even controlled. In return, by the treaty of 4 November 1911, France at last got a free hand to conquer Morocco, and to turn it into a protectorate.[12]

[10] J. Caillaux, *Agadir, ma politique extérieure* (1919), p. 106. F. Varenne, op. cit., p. 46, states that Clemenceau at first welcomed the formation of Caillaux's cabinet.
[11] J. Caillaux, op. cit., pp. 107–8.
[12] C. M. Andrew and A. S. Kanya-Forstner, 'The French colonial party, 1885–1914', *The Historical Journal*, XIV, 1971, pp. 123–6; J. Ganiage, *L'expansion coloniale de la France sous la Troisième République, 1871–1914*, pp. 268–72; L. C. F. Turner, *Origins of the First World War* (1970), pp. 12–19; I. Barlow, *The Agadir Crisis* (1940).

This was certainly not a bad bargain for France, but it led to the fall of Caillaux's government, and instead of improving Franco-German relations, led to their deterioration. French opinion was convinced that they had to stand up to German bullying, and there began a remarkable revival of French self-confidence. A. J. P. Taylor has gone so far as to say that 'French history reached its most dramatic and unexpected turning-point since the Revolution'.[13] Far from Caillaux getting credit for having stood up to German demands, he was to suffer the undeserved and vaguely formulated charge that he had sacrificed French interests by his unofficial negotiations. Rumours of sinister financial interests, evolving from the extremely complicated N'Goko-Sangha affair, gave an added dimension to the scandal. Clemenceau skilfully manœuvred the charges so as to bring about the fall of Caillaux. It was known in political circles that he was going to attack Caillaux as soon as the treaty was signed on 4 November 1911.[14] His chance came on 9 January 1912 at the meeting of the Senate committee appointed to report on the ratification of the treaty. Pichon opened the proceedings by asking about various Franco-German financial arrangements, implying that the national interest had been sacrificed to private profit. Caillaux denied this, and went on to state, on his word of honour, that there had been no unofficial negotiations. This was very foolish, for they were well known. Clemenceau seized his opportunity and asked de Selves whether he would confirm that there had been no unofficial negotiations. The embarrassed foreign minister replied:

> I have a regard for the truth, and also for the correct attitude commanded by my function; I ask to be allowed not to reply to that question.

After Clemenceau's reply, Caillaux interjected – 'I maintain my declaration' – to which Clemenceau retorted that he had not asked the prime minister, but the minister of foreign affairs. De Selves said, 'You have not understood me', to which Clemenceau replied, 'I have. The prime minister made such a definite statement that I felt obliged to put my question. I do not wish to pursue this conversation. But I could not hear such declarations without protesting.'[15] At this point the chairman adjourned the meeting, Caillaux asked Clemenceau to accompany him

[13] A. J. P. Taylor, 'The secret of the Third Republic', *From Napoleon to Stalin* (1950), p. 104.
[14] Archives Nationales, F⁷ 13950, 2, fol. 100, 20 November 1911, and fol. 101, 21 November 1911. On the N'Goko-Sangha affair, *see* R. Poidevin, op. cit., pp. 481–7, 621–3; a French company, which had been given a concession in part of the French Congo, was seeking to use the political situation to gain excessive financial compensation.
[15] Archives of the Senate, Commission de la Convention Franco-Allemande, 1911–12, Séance du 9 Janvier 1912.

and de Selves into a private room where they had a bitter exchange of views ending with de Selves's resignation.

Until Caillaux's unfortunate assertion, there had been no question of an immediate ministerial crisis, although there was already wide-spread disquiet about Caillaux's diplomacy. The British ambassador had reported on 8 December 1911 that 'Pichon does not think Caillaux's ministry will live long. This is the general opinion, and the word has gone round to declare that Caillaux is not mad enough to be locked up, but sufficiently so to be set aside as a public danger in matters political'.[16] Quite apart from distrust of Caillaux's methods, there was the fear that by moving too close to Germany he would break up the entente with Britain. Bertie reported to Grey on 22 January 1912 that Poincaré had said to him :

> He was convinced that Caillaux in reality was a sincere advocate of the Entente, but he was rash and impulsive, and did not measure his words. If he had gone any length in advances to Germany to the detriment of the Entente with England, his ministry would have broken up and it was the suspicion in the public and the Chambers that his proceedings had been dangerous to the cordiality of the Entente which caused his position to be so damaged that he had to resign.[17]

The general opinion was that the ministry would survive until the treaty had been ratified, and that its fall would be engineered shortly after-wards.[18] Even now Caillaux did not realize the true position, and thought that he could carry on, replacing de Selves by Delcassé as foreign minister. He asked Poincaré to replace Delcassé at the ministry of the navy. But Poincaré refused and so did two other candidates, and Delcassé's friends persuaded him to change his mind. Caillaux was forced to resign and Poincaré formed the new cabinet. According to a police informer, Clemenceau was at the centre of the intrigues that had made it im-possible for Caillaux to continue. Not only did he wish to oust Caillaux, but he was determined to keep his old enemy Delcassé out of the foreign office, even at the price of support for Poincaré whom he disliked only slightly less than Delcassé.[19]

Thus the Poincaré government was formed, a step that has been presented as a decisive stage in a 'national revival'. The treaty with Germany was ratified. But the tone of French policy became quite

[16] Bertie to Grey, 8 December 1911, Public Record Office, FO/800/164.
[17] Bertie to Grey, 22 January 1912, Public Record Office, FO/800/164.
[18] Bertie to Tyrrell, 1 January 1912, Public Record Office, FO/800/164, reporting Clemenceau's views.
[19] R. Poincaré, *Au Service de la France*, I, pp. 10–12, and Archives Nationales, F⁷ 13950, 2, fol. 102, 12 January 1912.

different, and much less conciliatory to Germany. In the public debate of 10 February Clemenceau opposed ratification of the treaty, in a powerful speech, although not one of his best. He was in great pain while delivering it. His health was poor, and shortly afterwards he was to undergo an operation for the removal of the prostate. He began by declaring that if he thought that the treaty would produce peace, he would support it, in spite of his reservations. But it needed two to be conciliatory, and there was no sign of a conciliatory attitude from Germany. He agreed that the century-long struggle between France and Germany must be ended. But that could only come about when there came a victor who could rise above his victory, and remain moderate at the moment of victory. Napoleon had not been such a man, nor had the German rulers in 1870. He said:

> we want peace, because we need it to rebuild our country. But if war is imposed on us, we will be ready. The difficulty between Germany, and us is this: Germany believes that domination is the logical result of her victory, but we do not believe that the logical result of our defeat is serfdom. . . .[20]

This speech, and his criticism of the agreement with Germany, marked another stage in Clemenceau's evolution towards the Right. Most of the Radicals accepted the treaty, and were opposed to the more chauvinistic tone that appeared under Poincaré. Only eleven other Radicals joined Clemenceau in voting against the treaty in the Senate, where it was ratified by 212 votes to 42: the majority of the opposition came from the Right. In the next two years Clemenceau's vigorous support of the law extending the term of military service from two to three years accentuated his conflict with the majority of the Radical party.

3 ELECTORAL REFORM AND THE 'THREE YEAR LAW'

On the other main political issue of the time, Clemenceau was fully in agreement with the majority of the Radical party. This was opposition to the proposal, supported by the Right and the Socialists, to introduce proportional representation. There were good reasons for this alignment. As several statistical studies had shown, the existing double ballot system gave the Right and the Socialists fewer deputies than their share of the vote indicated, while the Radicals were over-represented. The double

---

[20] Annales du Sénat, 10 February 1912, pp. 272–81, extracts printed in G. Clemenceau, *La France devant l'Allemagne* (1916), pp. 7–24.

ballot system, offering the possibility of making second ballot electoral alliances either with Socialist or with more conservative candidates, as local conditions warranted, was the essential element of the Radical predominance in Parliament. Nevertheless, on this, as on every question, the Radicals were divided. After long and complicated debates, the Chamber eventually voted in favour of a system of proportional representation on 10 July 1912. The next day, Combes and Clemenceau, burying their mutual antipathy, established a committee for the defence of universal suffrage, with thirty senators and thirty deputies, almost all Radical-Socialists, as members, and Clemenceau issued to the press a powerfully argued attack on proportional representation. Minority opinions were, he said, represented over the country as a whole, in a reasonably equable fashion, under the existing system. But proportional representation would swing the balance of power from the republican parties, which were disorganized, to the Right, which had a national organization in the Catholic Church. Far from providing for stronger government, he argued that proportional representation would make governmental action even more difficult:

> In this country where the anti-constitutional parties have retained all their leadership, a majority for action, already so difficult to form, will be placed in check by the increasing activity of opposing minorities. We will see the formation of a stalemate majority, without political views, without authority, without courage, which will demand nothing from the government, balanced in inertia, but vacillating schemes and half-hearted proposals producing endless abortive projects.[21]

Poincaré's government presided over the voting of the proportional representation bill by the Chamber – yet another reason for Clemenceau's dislike of him. He gave free rein to this feeling when Poincaré emerged as the leading contender in the Presidential election in January 1913. Mainly in the hope of keeping Poincaré out, the idea of a preliminary election among republican deputies and senators to decide on a candidate was revived. This gave the Radical nonentity Pams a small lead over Poincaré. As the Right would vote for Poincaré against Pams this meant he would be elected unless bluffed into withdrawing. A delegation of republicans went to Poincaré, and, with Clemenceau as spokesman, sought to persuade him not to stand. Angrily protesting that his republican credentials were just as good as Pams's, he refused. Two days later the National Assembly elected Poincaré by 483 votes to 296 for Pams. Clemenceau made no secret of his anger at Poincaré's betrayal of 'republican discipline', and Charles Benoist is reported to have said

[21] The manifesto was printed in *L'Annuaire du Parlement*, 1911–12, X, pp. 229–36.

that he would never forget the ferocious expression on Clemenceau's face immediately after the election. 'Well, it's over now,' said Benoist; 'No, it has just begun,' said Clemenceau.[22]

Clemenceau's intense dislike of Poincaré came from a mixture of personal antipathy and political disagreement. It has been said that their conflict had its origin in a family quarrel involving one of Clemenceau's daughters.[23] Whether or not this is true, their personalities were so different that they could hardly have hoped to remain on good terms. Poincaré was stiff, formal, rather humourless, and extremely respectable. Clemenceau was the opposite in every respect. Poincaré resented Clemenceau's arrogant assumption of intellectual superiority, and disliked his biting wit. Clemenceau regarded Poincaré as pedantic and stupid.

There were also political reasons for their rivalry. Poincaré's rise in these years represented a political realignment that shifted the fulcrum of politics a little to the right. Clemenceau, although forced to accept because of the international situation, was strongly opposed to this tendency on most domestic issues. But his hatred for Poincaré, like his vendetta against Delcassé, shows his worst side, and did him much harm. His bad temper suggested a lack of balance and judgement, as well as producing strong reactions from the victims. His historical reputation must also take account of these personal quarrels. Delcassé and Poincaré were leading figures in the reassertion of France's place on the international scene in these years, something which Clemenceau supported wholeheartedly. Yet he did all he could to oppose them, without weighing the consequences that would have resulted if he had been successful. Jaurès had pointed out the same lack of judgement in his attacks on Ferry. In all three cases he took relatively minor disagreements, and acted as if they involved fundamental questions of principle. In spite of the fact that Poincaré was magnanimous enough to bring him back into office in 1917, his judgement of Poincaré remained extremely hostile to the end.

He was soon to have opportunity for revenge. The committee for the defence of universal suffrage had been doing good work among the senators, and the report of the senate committee on the proportional representation bill was hostile. On 18 March the new prime minister, Briand, came to the Senate to defend the proportional representation bill. After an eloquent speech by Clemenceau, arguing that the simple principle of majority rule had brought political stability to France since the Revolution, and should not be put at risk by the chimerical arithmetic of the proportionalists, the Senate rejected proportional representation,

[22] R. Poincaré, op. cit., III, pp. 51–63; G. Wright, *Raymond Poincaré and the French presidency* (1942), pp. 43–50. G. Bonnefous, op. cit., I, p. 321, recounts Benoist's recollections.
[23] G. Gatineau-Clemenceau, op. cit., p. 29.

bringing down the government.[24] By this time Clemenceau's political position was as prominent as it had ever been, in spite of his breach with the organized Radical party in 1909. Although some argued that it was unconstitutional for the Senate to overthrow the government on the question of proportional representation, which had the support of a substantial majority of the Chamber, Briand had no hesitation in resigning. No more was to be heard of proportional representation until a bastard form of it was enacted by the Clemenceau government at the end of the war.

On 5 May 1913 Clemenceau's political position was strengthened by the appearance of the first number of his daily paper *L'Homme Libre*. This was not a mass-circulation paper, but it was a professionally produced organ, with a staff of able journalists, not an amateur weekly sheet like *Le Bloc*. The editor was a young graduate of the Ecole Normale, François Albert, and the talented team of journalists included Roland Dorgelès, later a successful novelist, Emile Buré, and Georges Mandel. It is not known how Clemenceau solved the financial problems involved in setting up a newspaper. *L'Homme Libre* was unlikely to have been very profitable before the outbreak of war, when its circulation improved as a result of the popularity of Clemenceau's belligerent leading articles. There are several reports in the police files about Clemenceau's financial combinations, including one that talks of the possibility of an English group backing him, but they seem to be only ill-informed gossip. Caillaux stated that Alphonse Lenoir, whose son was tried as a German agent and executed during the second Clemenceau ministry, was his backer. But Lenoir would have been an agent, not a principal.[25] The paper at once attained an important position among the political élite as Clemenceau's mouthpiece, and he contributed a long leading article almost every day until November 1917. Clemenceau's leader was followed by scraps of political gossip, and other essays on literary and political topics. There was quite a large sports section, and the usual reporting of *faits divers*, but not very much hard political news. Apart from opposition to Poincaré and to the electoral reformers, the main themes of Clemenceau's editorials in *L'Homme Libre* were support for the 'three year law', extending the period of military service, and articles on foreign affairs calling for a firm stand against Germany.

On 7 August the 'three year law' was passed by the Senate without difficulty, in contrast to the Chamber, where it had met violent opposition from Socialists and left-wing Radicals. As a practical measure of military

[24] *Annales du Sénat*, 18 March 1913, pp. 363–6.
[25] Archives of the Préfecture of Police, BA 1176, report of 8 February 1910, stating that Clemenceau was about to buy control of the newspaper *La France*. Archives Nationales, F^7 13950, 2, fol. 113, report of 18 November 1912, on his financial problems. J. Caillaux, *Mes Prisons* (1920), p. 276.

reorganization its importance was not very great, but as a symbol of the new French determination to withstand German pressure it was very important.[26] Its passing showed that the Chamber had moved to the right. Clemenceau was hostile to this in general, but he was not prepared to attack the Barthou government until the three year law had been voted.[27]

By autumn, however, he began to campaign against the Barthou government, in the columns of his newspaper, and in the antechambers of the Senate. He was very sarcastic about the attempt of Barthou, Briand and Millerand to patch up an electoral alliance which they baptized the *Fédération des Gauches*, to combat the Radical organization. One of the main issues in the 1914 election campaign was the 'three year law', and the victory of the Left in the elections might seem to have threatened it. In spite of this danger Clemenceau was a firm supporter of the Left in this electoral campaign, although he thought the Radicals had made too many concessions to the Socialists. But, campaign rhetoric notwithstanding, the law was not repealed. After the elections, Viviani, a Republican-Socialist, was asked to form a government more in keeping with the political complexion of the new Chamber. Although other reforms were promised, the 'three year law' was to remain. Throughout the spring and early summer of 1914 the main theme of Clemenceau's articles was France's need to remain vigilant in the face of the threat of German aggression. On occasions, as in the famous article 'Vouloir ou mourir' of May 1913, he gave vent to his emotions, expressing his deep patriotic sentiment. In other articles he presented the case for military preparations. The continuing oppression of Alsace-Lorraine demonstrated that the German Empire rested on brute force. In such circumstances it was ridiculous for Socialists and other pacifists to produce schemes of arbitration that would remove the necessity for war. Even more dangerous was Jaurès's plan for replacing the French army by a citizen militia, when the German military machine was being tuned to an ever higher pitch of preparedness. He wrote:

> When I am told that we should live in peace with our neighbours, I agree . . . but let us not forget that it needs two to make peace. . . . The great mistake of the revolutionary Socialists is to think themselves superior to the rest of mankind because they are not prepared to bend their ideology before the irreducible realities of human nature.[28]

[26] On the political battle over the three year law, *see* the detailed account, very hostile to the law, of G. Michon, *La préparation à la guerre, la loi de trois ans 1910–1914* (1935), also D. B. Ralston, *The Army of the Republic* (1967), p. 363.
[27] Archives Nationales, F⁷ 13950, 2, fol. 117, 30 July 1913.
[28] *L'Homme Libre*, 4 June 1914, reprinted in *La France devant L'Allemagne* (1916), pp. 56–7. This book includes a useful selection of Clemenceau's articles for the period 5 May 1913 to 14 May 1916.

The outbreak of war was soon to justify his forebodings. Although he thought war likely, he had no particular feeling of crisis in the summer of 1914. In his article of 6 July 1914 he noted the assassination of the archduke at Sarajevo as another example of sparks that might one day set Europe ablaze, but without placing any particular significance on it. Only on 2 August was his daily article couched in the sombre terms appropriate to the supreme crisis. France and her allies had now to choose between war and German domination:

> The hour of grave resolutions has come: it is a question, for France, of life or death. . . . There, on the other side of the Rhine, is a strong and great nation that has the right to live, but not to crush all independent life in Europe. . . . Russia has the choice of suicide or resistance. Our case is no different. If Russia, standing alone, is beaten, it will only be a matter of time before France is despatched: then England's turn will come.[29]

[29] *La France devant l'Allemagne*, pp. 80–4.

13

OPPOSITION IN WARTIME

I OPPOSITION IN WARTIME: AGAINST VIVIANI AND
BRIAND, 1914–1917

Although Clemenceau stands in history as the leader of his country in
the First World War he was only in office from 16 November 1917, for
its last twelve months. For more than three years his contribution to
the war effort was as an unflagging critic of a succession of cabinets,
most of them headed by prime ministers he cordially despised – Viviani,
Briand, Ribot, Painlevé. After the first German thrust was halted at the
Marne in September 1914, the two armies settled down to face each
other in their trenches across the plains of northern France. Strategy
was reduced to the hopeless quest of a decisive breakthrough; endless
slaughter for no commensurate strategic gains came to be dignified with
the title of a war of attrition.

Hopes that the Russian front might provide a decision were vain.
The Allies' attempts to use the mobility conferred by their command
of the sea led to nothing but failure at the Dardanelles and at Salonika.
Debate raged at the time, and has continued since, as to whether these
defeats were inevitable, or whether they resulted from the fact that the
military command, obsessed by the western front, refused to divert
sufficient resources to make success possible. Even the bribing of Italy
to join the Allies, at the cost of promises resulting in endless difficulties
at the peace settlement, turned out to be almost as much a liability as
an asset. Germany and Austria were able, for four years, to hold off
their ring of enemies, maintaining a stalemate on the western front,
grinding down Russia so that she collapsed in revolution in February
1917, and winning decisive victories over Italy and in the Balkans.

Clemenceau agreed with the military leaders on the all-importance

of the western front, and was a consistent critic of attempts to follow
alternative strategies. He attacked the Salonika expedition in 1915, and,
when in office, resisted Lloyd George's attempts to divert resources to
the Middle East. But he was a violent critic of the way the fighting was
actually managed on the western front, claiming that the methods of
the high command were destroying French resources, both human and
material, to no purpose. It is not clear, however, that he could offer
any well-thought-out alternative to the tactics of Joffre and the high
command. But if his criticism was technically inadequate and vague, it
won for him the reputation that was to make him the final and inevitable claimant to office at the end of 1917. Clemenceau's second government, covering the desperate struggles of the last twelve months of the
war, has come to be seen as one of the occasions when France has been
saved from the inadequacy of her political system by the appeal to a
saviour, able to stand above the ordinary battles of politics, and to incarnate in his own personality the national will to survive, to provide a
living embodiment of the highest common factor among the diversity
of political tendencies. A large part of the aura that surrounds him came
because of his success as prime minister, his refusal to panic in the
darkest days, and his association with the final victory; *Père-la-Victoire*,
he came to be familiarly called. But his image, as the embodiment of
the national determination to fight on, was acquired in the first three
years of the war, when he was one of the government's severest critics.[30]
Paradoxically this brought him into contact with the Left, the only
other critics of the government. In spite of the fact that the Left had
won the elections of May 1914, the whole of the Right rallied to the
support of the left-wing Viviani cabinet in the 'sacred union' of August
1914. When the 'sacred union' was challenged, it was from the Left, and
throughout the war the Right and Right Centre remained loyal supporters of whatever government was in power. Thus, when those who
had governed France during the first three years of the war became discredited, Clemenceau stood out as the one political figure who had
challenged them by demanding more vigorous conduct of the war, not
from a left-wing position based on illusory hopes of a compromise
peace. Clemenceau was asked to join the government on 2 August 1914
as minister of justice, together with Briand and Delcassé. He declared
that he would only accept office as prime minister or minister of war:
if he could not have those posts, he wanted to go as prefect to the
department of the Nord. In the end neither Clemenceau nor Briand nor

---

[30] In his article of 3 August 1914 Clemenceau already expressed the sentiment
that was to inspire him and through him to inspire France to continue the struggle
in the worst days of the war: he wrote 'one is only defeated when one recog-
nizes that one is defeated'. *La France devant l'Allemagne*, p. 88.

Delcassé joined the ministry at this time, and only minor changes were made in it.[31]

In his daily editorials for L'Homme Libre, soon renamed L'Homme Enchaîné, he brought before the public his criticism of the government and the military leadership. His pungent articles on the conduct of the war brought his newspaper many readers, and its circulation, estimated at over 100,000, became much more healthy than before the war. This was a relatively high figure for a newspaper of opinion and is comparable with such well-known rivals as Le Figaro. Like everybody else, Clemenceau had virtually no information during the first few weeks of the war, and could only print rhetorical exhortations. But by September 1914 his bitter attacks on the authorities began. His article of 28 September, attacking the inadequacy of the medical services, after he had been horrified at the sight of a train full of uncared-for wounded soldiers, led to the banning of his paper by the government when he refused to make cuts demanded by the censor. It was after this incident that he renamed his paper L'Homme Enchaîné.[32] From this time his articles remained predominantly critical of the government. The lack of medical services was a frequent theme, as was the inadequate supply of munitions. If allowed, he was also prepared to criticize the general conduct of the war. As Caillaux and Malvy pointed out, in their post-war polemics, he was frequently quoted by La Gazette des Ardennes, the German-controlled newspaper published in occupied territory.[33] His articles were frequently censored, but he evaded this to some extent by printing the censored passages and sending them by post to his subscribers, and to senators, deputies and other people in political circles.[34]

His criticism, however, was often too vehement and too hysterical to be effective. It lent colour to Poincaré's charge that he was impetuous and lacked judgement. Poincaré, having asked Clemenceau to meet him on 27 August 1914, found himself subject to a hysterical attack, accused of appointing a cabinet of incompetents who were leading France to disorder and defeat. Poincaré says:

[31] This incident was recounted by Briand at a luncheon on 24 August 1914 at which J. Reinach was present. He made detailed notes of Briand's remarks, on which the above account is based; I am grateful to Mme P. Goujon for making these notes available to me. Poincaré's memoirs mention the offer to Briand and Delcassé but say nothing of Clemenceau, although he describes an interview with him on 6 August, in which, he says, Clemenceau offered a truce in their quarrel. R. Poincaré, op. cit., V, p. 20.
[32] G. Gatineau-Clemenceau, Des Pattes du Tigre aux griffes du destin (1961), pp. 150–2; M. Berger and P. Allard, Les Secrets de la censure pendant la guerre (1932), pp. 69–72.
[33] J. Caillaux, Mes Prisons, pp. 279–96.
[34] M. Berger and P. Allard, op. cit., p. 72. The censored passages can be read in the copies of L'Homme Enchaîné at the Musée Clemenceau, which preserve the original version as well as the censored one.

He spoke with the hatred and violent incoherence of a man who had completely lost control of himself and with the fury of a disillusioned patriot who thought that he alone could bring victory.

He added that Clemenceau could not sleep and was living on drugs.[35] Clemenceau's articles insisted, day after day, on the need to expel the German invader from French territory. No doubt everyone agreed on this; but the difficulty was how to achieve it. His relentless attacks on the stupidity and incompetence of all those in authority only encouraged those who saw him as totally obsessed by unwarranted confidence in his own abilities and lacking in understanding of the difficulties faced by the government. As he went a good deal further in private conversation than he could in print, and as these opinions were rapidly circulated around the political élite, the number of influential people with reason to dislike the thought of a Clemenceau ministry was considerable. Apart from anything else, his attitude towards Poincaré seemed to rule him out as a potential prime minister. Poincaré, as President, had the task of inviting potential prime ministers to form a cabinet, and Clemenceau's refusal to heal his old feud made him ineligible for office. It seemed for a long time that a Clemenceau government would lead at once to the resignation of Poincaré, an event that could not be lightly envisaged in wartime.[36] Apart from personal considerations, the hysterical element in Clemenceau's views about the conduct of the war did not encourage belief in the soundness of his judgement. One of his schemes was to ship Japanese troops to fight on the western front. He had the naïve idea that the Japanese government would be willing to send its army to Europe, if only the British asked them to do so.[37] Another topic he developed in articles, and then published as a book, was the superiority of the Russian to the French political and administrative arrangements for carrying on the war.[38] Again, this did not suggest sound judgement to anyone with knowledge of the developing chaos in Russia. Poincaré's memoirs frequently mention Clemenceau's emotional attacks, and reveal Poincaré's distrust of his judgement; the President also complained about his indiscreet revelations. On more than one occasion, Poincaré recorded that Clemenceau burst into tears at meetings of the Army committee. The hearing of the prime minister and the

[35] R. Poincaré, op. cit., V, pp. 189–91. Cf. G. Gatineau-Clemenceau, op. cit., p. 147, for Clemenceau's fury at the news of the French defeats and the German invasion.

[36] Bertie to Grey, 27 December 1914, Public Record Office, FO/800/164, reports Clemenceau's contempt for Viviani and Poincaré, although a police report denied that he would seek Poincaré's resignation, Archives Nationales, F⁷ 13950, fol. 149, 10 December 1915.

[37] In fact the British government did attempt to persuade the Japanese to intervene in the European fighting. See V. H. Rothwell, 'The British government and the Japanese military assistance 1914–1918', History, LVI, 1971, pp. 35–45.

[38] G. Clemenceau, La Leçon de la Russie (1915).

minister of war by the Army committee on 11 May 1915 provides an example of Clemenceau's highly emotional attitude; he ended his speech thus, apparently in tears

> I hoped for a word of salvation, the cry of a will that sought achievement! I thought there would be a hand held out to me, and a voice that would say – 'The pact is sworn, I know from now on neither friend nor enemy. We are one willpower, and we can march together.' . . . Well, I did not hear that word: I only heard a defence of the past. Thus I have only one thing to say to you: I have lost hope.[39]

Nevertheless Clemenceau's criticism was by no means without a sympathetic audience. As the months went by and the bloody stalemate on the western front remained, the feeling that had prevailed in 1914 that the conduct of the war must be left to the government and to Joffre's general staff, began to evaporate. As Clemenceau put it in one of his most famous witticisms, 'War is too serious a business to be left to the generals'. Parliament, which had suspended its sittings a few days after the outbreak of war, met again, and demands arose for the resumption of normal Parliamentary methods of control over governmental activity. Clemenceau argued in articles of 31 December 1914 and 6 January 1915 that censorship of the press made it all the more important that Parliament resume its normal role. But wartime conditions made this impossible. Too much had to be left as military secrets for normal Parliamentary procedures to operate. Wartime conditions meant that the government could call on an unprecedented fund of loyalty when it asked for a vote of confidence. Only once was a government defeated during the war – Painlevé's, leading to the formation of the Clemenceau government. Still, after January 1915 some ordinary features of political life were re-established. If military secrecy prevented serious discussion of many major problems in public session, the traditional confrontation of ministers with leading deputies and senators in the Parliamentary committees became even more important than in peacetime. There, also, information had to be withheld, but more could be given than in public session. Grilling of ministers by the committees was supplemented between June 1916 and October 1917 by several secret sessions (*Comités Secrets*) of both Chamber and Senate. This meant that proceedings were not printed in the *Journal Officiel*, although it was obvious that nothing like complete secrecy would be observed by every single deputy and

---

[39] Archives of the Senate, Commission de l'Armée, Auditions des Ministres, 11 May 1915. For Poincaré's comments, *see*, for example, R. Poincaré, op. cit., VI, pp. 184, 200; VII, pp. 163–4, 172, 224 and 331; for Clemenceau's tears at the meeting of 11 May 1915, Poincaré, op. cit., VI, p. 204.

senator. Discretion was still needed, but remarkable revelations were made in the course of these secret sittings.

Clemenceau was the most formidable of the government's critics on the two most important Parliamentary committees – the Senate committees for foreign affairs and for the Army. The Senate committees had much more prestige and influence than their counterparts of the Chamber.[40] It epitomizes the ambiguous nature of wartime politics that, although the Senate never failed to give every government a large majority in votes of confidence, Clemenceau and other persistent critics were always re-elected to the standing committees, which reaffirmed their support by maintaining him as President. He was elected to the Army committee on 29 January 1915, at the same time becoming one of its vice-presidents: he at once assumed a dominant position in the committee, and led it into serious conflict with the government. He was elected to the foreign affairs committee on 4 February,[41] became president of both committees on 4 November, and remained president until he formed his own cabinet two years later. In these key positions Clemenceau obtained a good deal of confidential information, which he did not hesitate to use in his newspaper whenever the censor allowed, and was able to bring steadily increasing pressure to bear on the government's conduct of the war. Loucheur's diary reveals the trepidation with which Albert Thomas, the minister for munitions, went to face a grilling by Clemenceau's committee.[42] Already, in May 1915, the Senate committee for the army adopted a very hostile attitude towards Joffre, the commander-in-chief. After the presentation of a critical report by Jeanneney, Clemenceau, carried away by anger, went so far as to declare, on 29 May 1915:

> When I thought that the government was guilty only of negligence and 'laisser-aller', I did not despair of the final result. But today has been a revelation to me: there has been treason somewhere, and I will not collaborate with treason.[43]

[40] Mermeix, *Au sein des commissions, Fragments d'Histoire 1914–1919* (1924), VII, pp. 250–1.

[41] Clemenceau's role in the Army Committee can be followed in detail from the records preserved in the archives of the Senate. They consist of the minutes of the ordinary meetings of the committee, altogether twenty-three books covering the period 19 December 1914 to 29 December 1919, the separate minutes of meetings attended by members of the government, *Auditions des Ministres*, available except for the period May 1916 to January 1917, which are missing, and the various reports adopted by the committee. The records of the Foreign Affairs committee are much less complete: all that was available to me was the series *Auditions des Ministres*. These sources were used by G. Monnerville, *Clemenceau* (1968), pp. 401–33.

[42] L. Loucheur, *Carnets Secrets 1908–1932* (Brussels, 1962), pp. 31–2.

[43] Archives of the Senate, Procès-Verbaux de la Commission de l'Armée, II, p. 36, 29 May 1915.

In 1915, partly under the influence of Clemenceau, with Doumer the most persistent of the government's critics, the Senate army committee became increasingly hostile to Joffre, and the government which protected him. Viviani, Millerand and Thomas, respectively prime minister, minister of war and minister of munitions, were frequently heard by the committee and increasingly forced on to the defensive. Clemenceau launched an especially bitter attack on 31 July[44] and took up the same theme, in an article of 11 August, refused publication by the censor, opposing the government's claim that it could refuse to give information to the committee. Clemenceau argued, making no allowance for the need to adapt Parliamentary government to wartime conditions:

> No minister has the right to say to the representatives of the nation 'This is in the domain of the high command'. For the domain of the high command is that of the government, and therefore of the Parliament. . . .[45]

Throughout the autumn Clemenceau's attacks continued in the press and Senate committees. Besides criticizing the detailed management of the war, particularly with respect to medical services and munitions, he attacked the general strategic plans of the government. He was very hostile to the Salonika expedition, claiming that it only diverted attention from the vital western front. He wrote on 26 December 1915:

> Is it so difficult to understand that with the French front in the position it is, the conquest of France is the vital concern of the war, which can end only with a German victory in France, or a French victory in Germany?[46]

The British ambassador reported:

Clemenceau is very apprehensive that owing to the persistence of the French government in continuing the Salonika folly there will be a deficiency of French and British men for the French front. A successful offensive from Salonika would be impossible, and there are now held there by about 30,000 Germans an Anglo-French force of 220,000.[47]

The Viviani government fell on October 1915 and was replaced by a Briand government with General Gallieni (succeeded by General Roques) as minister of war. But Joffre remained as commander-in-chief, and little more information about the war was provided for Parliamentary critics. Briand's government, which included influential politicians from

[44] Archives of the Senate, Commission de l'Armée, Auditions des Ministres, 31 July 1915.
[45] Quoted by G. Monnerville, op. cit., p. 417.
[46] L'Homme Enchaîné, 26 December 1915; cf. G. H. Cassar, The French and the Dardanelles (1971), pp. 204–5.
[47] Bertie to Foreign Office, 18 April 1916, Public Record Office, FO/800/164.

nearly every tendency – Freycinet, Combes, Bourgeois, Cochin, Malvy, Ribot, Painlevé, Méline and Doumergue – seemed unbeatable. Briand asked Clemenceau to join the government, but he refused, saying that he would never enter a cabinet of which he was not the head.[48] Clemenceau's attacks continued, but seemed to be making little impact on majority opinion.[49] Right-wing opinion, later to rally to Clemenceau with great vigour, at this time regarded him as a wrecker, just as dangerous as critics on the Extreme Left. In January 1916 Maurras, in *L'Action Fran-çaise*, demanded 'l'enchaînement définitif de l'homme prétendu enchaîné'. Certainly Clemenceau's articles at this time leant themselves to the charge of defeatism, however much he himself took the blackest news as an argument for carrying on the struggle with even more tenacity. On 3 March 1916 the headline of *L'Homme Enchaîné* was 'La Prise de Verdun'. If it had been true, this would, of course, have been a devastating blow to French morale. The issue was banned by the censor, and the paper suspended from the 5 to 13 March, as punishment for persistent infringement of the censorship regulations.[50] Clemenceau's dislike of Briand sharpened into real hatred as a result of these activities of the censor, which he regarded as a personal attack by the prime minister. As the French armies were bled almost to exhaustion in the struggle for Verdun, the pressure for secret sessions of the two houses of Parliament, in which the government could be forced to answer questions about the conduct of the war, built up. The government eventually agreed and the first secret sessions were held from 16 to 22 June in the Chamber, and from 4 to 9 July in the Senate.

Before the Chamber secret sessions Clemenceau had great hopes that they would lead to the fall of Briand, and to the formation of a new cabinet of which he would be a member. Bertie wrote to Grey on 5 June 1916:

> There is a fresh set against Joffre and the ministry which supports him. The combination is stated to be Clemenceau, Barthou, Doumer, Barthou to be prime minister and the war department in dispute between Clemenceau and Doumer. Castelnau to replace Joffre.[51]

After meeting Clemenceau, Bertie wrote on 8 June that 'the leaders of the movement against Briand are confident of upsetting his ministry'. But next day, after a talk with Pichon, he reported that the latter was

---

[48] R. Poincaré, op. cit., VII, pp. 203–4.
[49] Archives Nationales, F⁷ 13950, 2, fol. 156, 25 January 1916, and fol. 157, 26 January 1916.
[50] M. Berger and P. Allard, op. cit., pp. 52–3; R. Poincaré, op. cit., VIII, pp. 97–9.
[51] Bertie to Grey, 5 June 1916, Public Record Office, FO/800/164. In fact, Clemenceau did not like Castelnau, see Archives Nationales, F⁷ 13950, 2, fol. 142, 11 October 1915. For Clemenceau's close relations with Foch, see G. Gatineau-Clemenceau, op. cit., pp. 153–4.

not so confident as Clemenceau had been; nor did he think that Barthou would be able to form a government.[52] Pichon's judgement on the political situation proved to be more accurate than that of his patron, for the government won a vote of confidence in the Chamber by 444 votes to 80. In the Senate on 9 July, only 6 votes were cast against the government; those of Clemenceau, Pichon and four others. Unfortunately there are no proper records of the Senate debates. The minutes of the secret sessions of the Chamber were printed after the war in the *Journal Officiel*, but those of the Senate were not published at that time. They remained in the archives in the form of the original shorthand notes, and after the expiry of fifty years large portions of them proved to be unreadable.[53] The surviving records do not include Clemenceau's main speech. We are told that it lasted four hours, and that it was one of his weakest performances. He was not in good health, and is reported to have faltered and found it difficult to express himself. Briand, at his most suave and polite, pointed out that Clemenceau's intemperate articles had been a comfort to the enemy.[54] Earlier in the debate, Clemenceau had exchanged bitter words with Malvy, minister of the interior, about defeatist propaganda among the workers. The feud with Malvy twelve months later was to place Clemenceau in a commanding political position.

In spite of this defeat Clemenceau's attacks on the government and on the army leaders continued unabated in the army committee and, as far as the censor allowed, in the press. His influence in the committee did not seem to have diminished in any way. As the stalemate on the western front continued, and French casualties mounted from terrifying to unbelievable numbers, Parliamentary opposition grew. Not many were prepared to break the sacred union by voting against the government, but the sense of unease was spreading to wider circles. As the government insisted on linking its lot with that of the army command, criticism of Joffre was also criticism of the government. A further series of secret sessions in the Chamber from 28 November to 7 December 1916 ended with a vote of confidence carried by 344 to 160. Briand regarded this increase in opposition as a defeat, realizing that the discontent affected far wider circles than those prepared to vote against the government. He decided to reconstruct his ministry, and to sack Joffre.

[52] Bertie to Grey, 8 and 9 June 1916, Public Record Office, FO/800/164.
[53] The decipherable parts of the records of the secret sessions of the Senate have been published in the *Journal Officiel, Débats Parlementaires, Sénat, numéro spécial*, 29 September 1968.
[54] *Journal Officiel, Débats Parlementaires, Sénat*, 29 September 1968, pp. 709–24. Cf. G. Monnerville, op. cit., pp. 443–50; G. Suarez, *Briand*, III, pp. 342–8; Mermeix, *Joffre, Fragments d'Histoire 1914–1919* (1920), p. 177; A. Zévaès, *Clemenceau*, p. 233; J. Martet, *Le Tigre*, pp. 205–7, on Clemenceau's poor health: he suffered badly from diabetes at that time.

Even after this, many observers regarded the cabinet as precariously based. The British ambassador noted,

> The ministry is very sick. The combination against it is very strong, viz. Clemenceau, Pichon, Doumer, Humbert, Painlevé, Klotz, and a host of disappointed office seekers, viz. Franklin-Bouillon, Tardieu, etc.[55]

With the prestigious Lyautey as minister of war, and having replaced Joffre as supreme commander by the comparatively junior Nivelle, Briand met his critics in four days of secret sittings in the Senate. Clemenceau, still in poor health, made another long speech on 23 December, the last day of the secret session. Unfortunately the defective records do not give the major part. He began by declaring 'after two years of war France had arrived at an alarming degree of disorder, economic, diplomatic and military'. He proposed to deal with these areas in turn, but we only have the minutes of his opening remarks about the economic situation in which he listed munitions factories unable to operate because of shortage of coal.[56] Briand made an effective reply, which Clemenceau frequently interrupted, turning the session into a personal duel. The opposition increased from 6 in July to 56 in the vote at the end of this debate, against 191 for the government. Briand carried on for another three months, although his government was weak. The British ambassador reported on 21 February 1917 that

> Briand, though not popular in the Chamber, and though his conduct of affairs is much criticized there, manages to keep himself in office, partly by his Parliamentary skill and his persuasive eloquence, and owing to the non-existence of a suitable successor, and no combination of parties constituting a majority in the Chamber being able to agree on the choice of substitute. Clemenceau, who not very long since was thought of, has from his continual but unreasoning attacks in his newspaper on M. Briand and the authorities generally, and his recent defeat in the Senate, rendered himself impossible. Poincaré made advances to him for a reconciliation but was unsuccessful.[57]

Only a month later, however, Briand resigned after his minister of war, General Lyautey, had walked out of the Chamber in a fit of temper.

2. THE MUTINIES AND THE ATTACK ON MALVY, APRIL–AUGUST 1917

Ribot, an eighty-year-old conservative republican, formed the new government. He was popular with the Left, as he had supported the

[55] Bertie to Charlie (Lascelles), 18 December 1916, Public Record Office, FO/800/164.
[56] *Journal Officiel*, 29 September 1968, pp. 757–9. Cf. G. Monnerville, op. cit., pp. 480–9.
[57] Bertie to Foreign Office, 21 February 1917, Public Record Office, FO/800/164.

income tax law, and the Left held key posts in the new cabinet; Malvy, a left-wing Radical, and the Socialist Albert Thomas remained, while the Republican Socialist Painlevé became minister of war. The new cabinet was soon faced with the most dangerous situation of the entire war. American entry into the war in April 1917 brought prospects of reinforcement in the long term, but no appreciable military help could be expected for at least twelve months. On the other hand, the outbreak of the Russian Revolution in March, although at first greeted by nearly everyone in France, including Clemenceau, with joy, as something that would revitalize their ally, was soon found to have produced the opposite effect.[58] Before long, revelations about the secret diplomatic agreements made between the Allies were to come out of Russia, providing fuel for those who sought to prove the imperialistic war aims of both sides. Socialist support for the war was seriously affected, in a way that eventually led to a complete split in the Socialist party. Even more serious in the short term was the devastating effect on Allied shipping of the first few weeks of the German unrestricted submarine warfare campaign. Fear that this would soon bring the Allied war effort to a halt intensified the Allied leaders' desire to believe that the new commander, Nivelle, could succeed where Joffre had failed, and achieve a sudden and decisive break in the German lines.

However, Nivelle's great offensive, at Chemin des Dames, opening on 16 April, proved to be disastrous. Its results were little worse than those of earlier offensives and losses no greater, but the hopes and expectations which Nivelle's grandiose optimism had aroused meant that failure was far more serious than in the previous year's dogged battles around Verdun. The nerve of the French army cracked. The offensive was abandoned on 29 April, and from that moment sporadic outbreaks of mutinous incidents began. The crisis reached its height in the second half of May, and began to decline in June, but the complete restoration of discipline was not achieved until long after that.[59] Pétain, who had replaced Nivelle as commander-in-chief on 15 May, dealt with the mutinies by a combination of concessions and firmness, and by abandoning the tactical and strategic doctrines that had produced the crisis. He was already convinced of the futility of these frontal attacks by the infantry, before the outbreak of the mutinies. It was a long time before the armies were completely restored to their normal condition. Pétain dated the end of the crisis to October 1917, and the historian of the mutinies has stated

---

[58] *L'Homme Enchaîné*, 18–21 March 1917, shows Clemenceau's initial enthusiasm for the Russian revolution, but from 24 March onwards he begins to realize the danger that the revolution would bring the peace party to power in Russia.
[59] All previous accounts of the mutinies have now been superseded by the study, based on the archives of the ministry of war, of G. Pedroncini, *Les Mutineries de 1917* (1967).

that only in January 1918 did the number of disciplinary incidents return to a normal level.[60] At the height of the crisis in May and June the situation was very serious indeed, although fortunately the Germans got no inkling of it. Even the British were not informed of its full gravity. It has often been said that because the troops actually in the front line never took part, there was no danger of a military collapse. But the extent of mutinies among troops withdrawn from the line was such that the French army, for several weeks, ceased to exist as a real fighting force, and if the Germans had attacked powerfully the situation would have been grave.

The mutinies produced a political crisis starting with the secret sessions of June and July 1917 and continuing through the autumn, bringing down first Ribot, then the weak Painlevé cabinet, and eventually bringing Clemenceau to power. Although the general public only heard rumours of the mutinies, some information was bound to reach political circles. Many deputies and senators had close links with military leaders, and Clemenceau was not alone in making frequent visits to the front. No statement about the mutinies could, of course, be made in public sessions, and even in secret sessions most speakers were discreet. But in the Parliamentary committees the debates in secret sessions of June and July they were referred to in disguised form on several occasions. Other factors combined to build up the political tension. There was renewed pressure from the Socialists to be allowed to take part in an international Socialist meeting at Stockholm, with German delegates attending, in the hope of opening the way to a negotiated peace. At home there was much labour unrest, with several strikes and violent demonstrations. Since the outbreak of war there had been very few strikes, but the rapid rise in prices, especially of food prices because of shortages caused by the German attacks on Allied shipping, produced economic motives for them.[61] To some extent these were mingled with political protest and the desire to see an end to the war. With the Russian example in everyone's mind, either as a beacon or a dreadful warning, the situation was grave.

These elements were combined in the attack on the government in which Clemenceau played a prominent part. Apparently eclipsed in the first months of 1917, his star was now visibly rising. Poincaré noted that, at the cabinet meeting of 3 July, Albert Thomas, the Socialist minister of munitions, said they must choose between a policy of union with the working class and Clemenceau's policy. Viviani declared that if Clemenceau came to power, he would produce widespread labour

---

[60] G. Pedroncini, op. cit., p. 60, and *Les Mutineries des Armées françaises* (1968).
[61] A. Kriegel, op. cit., I, pp. 157–67. A. Fontaine, *French Industry during the war* (1926), Appendix XII, for statistics of strikes.

unrest, as he had done in 1907, and then be unable to control it.[62] Poincaré dismissed this as an attack of nerves, but such considerations deterred him from calling on Clemenceau until the last possible moment. Ironically, once Clemenceau was in office, Poincaré was full of complaints of his weakness towards trade union leaders, and his desire to conciliate rather than repress working-class protest. But it was becoming clear that Clemenceau was the real contender for power if the existing group should fail.

The link between the mutinies, the industrial unrest, and the diplomatic situation was provided in its most extreme form by the fanatics of the Action Française, who claimed that Malvy, minister of the interior, was a traitor in German pay. They said that he had deliberately provoked the mutinies by sending agents to spread defeatist propaganda among the troops. Clemenceau's attacks avoided such paranoia, but he also regarded Malvy as the root of the trouble.[63] Without claiming that he was literally in German pay, he argued that his weak attitude towards defeatist agitation behind the lines had allowed a dangerous situation to develop, causing the strikes, and then infecting the troops. This was the argument of the military leadership. They could not accept that their own mistakes had caused the mutinies. Pedroncini writes that the mutinies were essentially a military crisis, unconnected with industrial unrest and the movement for immediate peace.[64] The infantry had been pressed beyond the limits of human endurance, and then harassed, after the offensive, by pernickety observance of traditional military routine. But the military leaders sincerely believed that the mutinies could only be explained by contamination from the ferment of political agitation behind the lines. This was the interpretation adopted by Clemenceau in his attacks on Malvy.

Clemenceau had long mistrusted Malvy, and in the secret session of July 1916 had already complained about his lax control of anti-patriotic propaganda. He was not alone in this mistrust, and at the time of the formation of Briand's government there had been an attempt to remove Malvy from the ministry of the interior. He had refused, however, to accept any other portfolio, and the Radical-Socialist group of the Chamber had insisted that he should remain.[65] He had held that post in successive governments, from before the outbreak of war, till Clemenceau forced his resignation in August 1917. The Army committee's investigation into the failure of the April offensive soon turned into an

---

[62] R. Poincaré, op. cit., IX, pp. 184–5.
[63] In L'Homme Enchaîné of 6 October 1917 Clemenceau criticized Daudet's accusation that Malvy was a traitor, saying that to bring such charges without any proof reminded him of the Norton affair.
[64] G. Pedroncini, Les Mutineries des Armées françaises, p. 310.
[65] R. Poincaré, op. cit., VII, pp. 205–10.

attack on Malvy. On 11 June Painlevé, minister of war, appeared before the Army committee and asked it to postpone an interpellation on the April offensive. Clemenceau insisted that Painlevé give them all the information he had on the mutinies, so that they could judge for themselves the real gravity of the situation. Painlevé was not able to deal with the serious questions raised. Another meeting was fixed for 16 June at which Painlevé was joined by Ribot, the prime minister, and by Malvy. This session turned into a severe cross-examination of Malvy, on the charge of allowing pacifist agitation behind the lines. Bérenger said :

> The mutineers who had been shot were only the limbs; the brain was behind the lines, where it had been allowed to develop ever since December 1914; at this moment in every munitions factory there was a centre of pacifist propaganda.[66]

The three ministers disputed this view of the origins of the mutinies, minimizing the importance of the pacifist agitation, and stating that the real cause lay in weariness after three years of war, and in the failure of the military leadership to pay enough regard to morale.

A sub-committee for national security was set up, which attempted to investigate the charges against Malvy. He refused to cooperate, however, and their researches met with little success. But Clemenceau and the army committee were well supplied with documents by their contacts among the army command.[67] Relations between the army leaders and the government were now very bad; and those between the government and the Army committee were deteriorating rapidly. Ribot and Painlevé came before the committee again on 25 June. In a long intervention Clemenceau sought to separate Ribot from his minister of the interior, denying that he was hostile to the cabinet as a whole. They did not seek, he said, access to police documents to attack the ministry : they wanted to cooperate with it in this grave crisis, and sought only to demonstrate to the prime minister that he had been misled by his colleague. It was vitally important to maintain morale; if they could hold on for a year the Americans would come, and victory would be certain; but there was a grave danger that, if things were allowed to continue as they had, France would fall into the abyss. He had a letter from General Nivelle : it was a devastating document, a terrible accusation against anarchist propaganda. Bérenger knew of a similar document produced by General Pétain. Ribot replied that if they listened to every-

---

[66] Archives of the Senate, Commission de l'Armée, Auditions des Ministres, 16 June 1917.

[67] Archives of the Senate, Procès-Verbaux de la Commission de l'Armée, XVII, sessions of 11, 16, 20, 22, 28 June, and 3, 17 July, 1917; Auditions des Ministres, 11, 16, 25 June 1917. Cf. G. Monnerville, op. cit., pp. 426–33.

thing the generals said, there would be neither freedom of the press, nor of anything else.[68] In the end a compromise was reached about the communication of the documents demanded by the Committee, but this proved to be unsatisfactory in practice.

It was decided that Bérenger and Clemenceau should speak on behalf of the committee on the question of pacifist agitation in the full session of the Senate. From 10 July Clemenceau's articles in *L'Homme Enchaîné* had been nearly all directed against Malvy and his refusal to take strong measures against the pacifist propaganda.[69] The army committee was also investigating the failure of the April offensive; Bérenger's report, submitted to the full Senate in the secret session of 19–21 July, took the form of a defence of Nivelle, and blamed the government for calling off the offensive.

In the end Malvy's position was made impossible by the slowness with which he pursued investigations into the *Bonnet Rouge* affair. Here there was real evidence of traitors in the pay of Germany. The *Bonnet Rouge* was a left-wing paper with a tiny circulation, financially supported by Caillaux before the war. For some time during the war it had received subsidies authorized by Malvy, and had then gone into the pay of Germany. It could not publish anything without the censor's approval, but within those limits it had become notorious for its defeatism. Suspicions were confirmed when Duval, one of the staff of *Bonnet Rouge*, was found returning from Switzerland on 15 May with a cheque for a large sum. Nevertheless, not until 7 July did the government decide to institute a serious investigation, and only on 15 July was the *Bonnet Rouge* suspended. On 4 August, with Viviani temporarily replacing Malvy at the head of the ministry of the interior, its editor, an extremely suspicious character known as Vigo or Almereyda, a notorious pre-war anarchist, was arrested. Malvy was guilty of nothing more than laxity and negligence in this affair, but at the time there was some reason to fear graver charges. The atmosphere of intrigue and suspicion was compounded on 20 August, when Almereyda was found dead in prison. No doubt he committed suicide, as he had good reason to do in the circumstances, but many thought that he had been liquidated because he knew too much about men in high places.

Before matters had reached this pitch, on 22 July, after the Senate had completed its secret sessions on the April offensive and the subsequent crisis, Clemenceau in public session launched his devastating attack on Malvy. His long speech was published the next day in *L'Homme*

[68] Archives of the Senate, Commission de l'Armée, Auditions des Ministres, 25 June 1917.
[69] *L'Homme Enchaîné*, 10, 12, 15, 16, 17, 18 July.

Enchaîné, and then as a pamphlet entitled *L'Antipatriotisme devant le Sénat*.[70] Clemenceau argued that the negligence, if it were no more than that, revealed in Malvy's refusal to pursue Almereyda and other defeatists, had been the primary cause of the mutinies. It was difficult, as he could not refer in open session to the mutinies, but he managed to make his point obvious to all who knew what had happened. Indeed he came very near to referring openly to the mutinies. As he could not dwell on them, much of his speech was concerned with Malvy's refusal, as minister of the interior at the outbreak of war, to implement the arrest of those named on *Carnet B*, the famous list of anti-war agitators who were supposed to be taken into custody at the outbreak of hostilities. He also spent much time on Malvy's indulgence to various foreigners, with the implication that they were spies; most of these cases were of no importance, and one, the Marguliès-Rosenberg affair, could even have been counter-productive. In this quarrel between two foreign business-men, whose financial combinations dating from before the war crossed the frontiers between the Allies and the central powers, Clemenceau could be accused of supporting one alien financier against another who had a better claim to be regarded as a loyal supporter of France. Poin-caré thought so, noting on 27 August that, although Clemenceau was demanding light on all the scandals, he was himself compromised by his advocacy of Rosenberg, whose lawyer was his brother Albert.[71]

But such considerations did not detract from the impact of his diatribe against Malvy, especially when the arrest and suicide of Almereyda revealed something solid behind his charges. Malvy denied that there was any evidence of defeatist propaganda being a cause of 'a certain lassitude' among the soldiers, and claimed that his refusal to arrest those listed on *Carnet B* had been proved right by the cooperation of working-class organizations in the war effort. He wished, he said, to continue this policy of conciliation and cooperation.[72] Although the government won a vote of confidence, its position was now very weak. His attack on Malvy had for the first time brought Clemenceau the support of the extreme Right, journalists such as Daudet, Maurras and Barrès, and the

---

[70] It can now be found most conveniently in G. Clemenceau, *Discours de Guerre* (1934), pp. 64–135. For Malvy's side of the case *see* L. J. Malvy, *Mon Crime* (1921), *passim*. J. Martet, *Le Tigre*, pp. 210–26, gives a vivid description of the debate, of the dramatic effect produced by Clemenceau's speech, and the very poor showing made by Malvy, who was no orator.

[71] Poincaré, op. cit., IX, p. 258: cf. also Paul Meunier, *Clemenceau et Rosenberg* (1921), although this polemic by a left-wing Radical, editor of the newspaper *La Vérité*, who regarded his arrest in 1919 as being due to Clemenceau's personal inter-vention, has to be treated with caution. Cf. also Bernain de Ravisi, *Sous la Dicta-ture de Clemenceau: un forfait judiciaire* (1926).

[72] Annales de la Chambre des Députés, 22 July 1917, reprinted in G. Clemenceau, op. cit., pp. 136–48.

sections of opinion for which they spoke.[73] The British ambassador reported that

> Logically Clemenceau ought to be asked to form a ministry, but Poincaré will probably send for Painlevé, who will not succeed, and this will strengthen Clemenceau.[74]

Poincaré would have liked Clemenceau to join the Ribot government, but neither of them would consider that. On 31 August, discredited by the Almereyda affair, Malvy resigned, and this, together with their resentment at the government's refusal to allow them to take part in the proposed international Socialist congress, led to the withdrawal of Socialist support. The government was too weak to continue, and a few days later Ribot gave in his resignation. Painlevé was asked to form a cabinet, and invited Clemenceau to join him, but he refused.[75]

3 AGAINST A COMPROMISE PEACE, SEPTEMBER–
NOVEMBER 1917

Painlevé formed his weak and short-lived cabinet on 13 September. It coincided with the disastrous period that saw the Italian defeat at Caporetto and the Bolshevik revolution in Russia. At home allegations of treason in high places multiplied; three more cases emerged, involving the obscure deputy Turmel, and the more conspicuous figures of Humbert, senator and owner of the popular newspaper *Le Journal* and Bolo Pasha, whose acquaintances included the President of the Republic. Behind them, the accusation went, was bigger game still, Malvy and Caillaux, and perhaps also Briand. For the most serious question posed in 1917 was whether France should continue the war, or seek to make peace on the best terms she could get from a victorious Germany. Caillaux was the advocate of negotiations, although not in a position to play any effective role, having been virtually excluded from power and influence since 1914.[76] Painlevé had also sought to open negotiations with Germany through Sophie Clemenceau, wife of Clemenceau's younger brother Paul, who was of Austrian birth. Finally, Briand, who was no longer in office, had been approached in June 1917 by an emissary of

---

[73] *See*, for example, L. Daudet's article, reprinted in *Flammes*, p. 193. For Daudet's criticism of Clemenceau down to this time, see E. Weber, *L'Action Française* (1964), p. 130. However, when Clemenceau came to power it was reported that Daudet was less enthusiastic in his support than Maurras, Archives Nationales, F⁷ 13950, 2, fol. 174, 18 November 1917.

[74] Bertie to Balfour, 25 August 1917, Lloyd George Papers, F/51/4/32.

[75] R. Poincaré, op. cit., IX, p. 275–83; Bertie to Balfour, 10 and 12 September 1917, Lloyd George Papers, F/51/4/36 and 37.

[76] Bertie to Harding, 17 September 1917, reported that Klotz and Peret 'laughed at the possibility of Caillaux coming to the front politically', Lloyd George Papers, F/51/4/38.

Lancken, a German diplomat now head of the political section of the German government in Belgium.[77] The government decided to reject the German approach but Briand did not give up hope that he would be able to pursue the negotiations. Clemenceau knew that Briand, whom he described later as '*le chef d'orchestre* of defeatism', was the only man with the political stature and influence to take France into negotiations for a separate peace with Germany.[78] He was determined to nip any such schemes in the bud by bringing Briand's discreet contacts with the German emissaries into the open. Ribot, a leading figure in Painlevé's Cabinet, provided the opportunity, by some remarks in the Chamber and by a fuller account which he gave to Clemenceau privately. Bertie reported on 11 October 1917:

> I asked Clemenceau what sort of terms agents claiming to speak for Germany are offering to France. Clemenceau said that Ribot gave him his word of honour that no specific terms have been mentioned. . . . Clemenceau added that even if Germany offered Alsace-Lorraine, the left bank of the Rhine *and* Holland, it would not be accepted as it would embroil France with England and the two countries must remain united.[79]

Clemenceau used these confidences to force the question into the open by an article in *L'Homme Enchaîné* of 15 October. He wrote:

> May I ask M. Ribot, our minister of foreign affairs, why, after having revealed at the rostrum the secret of a German machination aimed at a separate peace to be bought at the price of Alsace-Lorraine, and after having told us that he had heard of this through a 'high political personage', he thought proper, after a sharp exchange with an eminent deputy, to cut this important part of his speech out of the *Journal Officiel*?

This led to a Socialist interpellation, discussed in secret session the next day. Ribot declared that the offer supposed to have been made to Briand, that Germany would return Alsace-Lorraine to France, could not possibly be genuine. In any case, even if that were offered, France could

---

[77] On these secret negotiations there is some information in Mermeix, *Les Négociations secrètes et les quatre armistices, Fragments d'Histoire, 1914–1919*, V, pp. 106–14, and in G. Pedroncini, *Les Négociations secrètes pendant la grande guerre* (1969), which is based on archive material, but is very brief; cf. C. J. Lowe and M. L. Dockrill, *The Mirage of Power*, II, p. 262. A thorough study of the question has not yet been produced. For the intervention of Sophie Clemenceau, referred to under her maiden name of Szeps, see G. Pedroncini, op. cit., p. 69.

[78] See Briand's explanation of his intentions to the Senate Foreign Affairs Committee, Archives of the Senate, Commission des Affaires Etrangères, Auditions de Ministres, 14 November 1917. G. Clemenceau, *Grandeurs et Misères d'une Victoire* (1930), p. 315.

[79] Bertie to Balfour, 11 October 1917, Lloyd George Papers, F/51/4/44.

not make a separate peace without her Allies. Briand confirmed Ribot's account and declared that there could be no question of his lending himself to negotiations that would consecrate a German victory. He had laid down as *minima* the restoration of Alsace-Lorraine, the evacuation of all occupied territories, and no separate peace. All that remained was to explain how he could imagine that Germany would be interested in such terms.[80] He continued to declare that Germany had been prepared to offer generous terms. Haig's diary records a conversation with Lord Esher on 3 November 1917 in which he said that in a recent conversation with Briand

> the latter gave him details of the offer of peace made to him by Germany in September. It was a *bona fide* offer and Germany conceded all the Allies wanted as regards Belgium, Alsace-Lorraine etc. . . .[81]

At the end of the debate the government won a vote of confidence by 313 to 0, with the Socialists abstaining to mark their belief that peace negotiations should have been pursued. Now that the German archives have been explored, it is clear that there was not the least foundation for Briand's optimism.

An essential part of the case of those who attack Clemenceau for his supposed role in preventing a compromise peace in 1917 is that there was a real possibility of making peace on terms acceptable to a substantial part of the French public. But no such compromise peace was possible.[82] Michon's biography, which from this period becomes a sustained invective against Clemenceau, is based on the illusion that the Socialist ideal of 'a peace without annexations and indemnities' was on offer, and was spurned by the war profiteers and economic imperialists, using Clemenceau as their tool. Bruun, maintaining judicious detachment, wrote: 'Whether a better, a less vindictive, a more equal peace could have been negotiated in 1917 is a question which now can never be resolved.'[83] However, the German government would only have accepted a peace that consecrated their victories; they were only prepared to

---

[80] *Journal Officiel*, 2 April 1933, reprints the record of this secret session. A convenient summary can be found in G. Bonnefous, *Histoire Politique de la Troisième République*, II, pp. 318–37. Cf. G. Pedroncini, *Les Négociations secrètes*, pp. 69–73.

[81] R. Blake, *The Private Papers of Douglas Haig, 1914–1919* (1952), pp. 262–3, and R. Poincaré, op. cit., IX, p. 409, 11 December 1917: 'Briand continued to spread the rumour that we were offered Alsace-Lorraine.'

[82] The source material on German policy has been presented in A. Scherer and J. Grunewald, *L'Allemagne et les problèmes de la paix au cours de la première guerre mondiale* (1962–6), two volumes so far published, for the period down to December 1917. Discussion in F. Fischer, *Germany's Aims in the First World War* (1967), pp. 405–50; P. Renouvin, *La Crise Européenne* (1969), pp. 488–506; H. W. Gatzke, *Germany's Drive to the West* (1950), pp. 219–51; G. Pedroncini, *Les Négociations secrètes*, pp. 21–9.

[83] G. Michon, *Clemenceau*, pp. 172–8; G. Bruun, *Clemenceau*, p. 128.

offer insignificant frontier rectifications in Alsace-Lorraine, in return for great additions to territory elsewhere. As Poincaré realized, Briand and Painlevé were victims of an illusion if they thought it likely that Germany would offer acceptable terms when the collapse of Russia had brought complete victory once more within her grasp.[84]

As Painlevé faltered from one crisis to another, making a deplorable impression of weakness in Parliament, more and more people were convinced that Clemenceau would soon be asked to form a government. On 18 October Poincaré had already told Painlevé and Barthou that he was contemplating asking Clemenceau to form a government. Barthou said that he himself could form a government and that he was on much better terms than Clemenceau with the Socialists, but Poincaré told him that if he became prime minister, Clemenceau would attack him, and bring him down. He continued that unless the party leaders and the Presidents of the Assemblies gave him different advice, he thought that

> Clemenceau is indicated by public opinion because he wished to see things through to the end with regard to the war and the judicial affairs and that, in these circumstances, I did not have the right to exclude him simply because of his attitude towards me.[85]

Demands for a thorough investigation of the scandals continued, in the press and in the Chamber, and on 13 November the Painlevé government found itself in a minority, the only wartime government to be actually defeated. It was only a procedural matter, but the authority of the cabinet was completely gone, and Painlevé took his resignation to the President. His cabinet was a left-wing combination, and had been weakened throughout its short existence by the Socialist refusal to support it with their votes. The Right and Centre, in spite of their tendency during the war to support any government for patriotic reasons, had had enough of Painlevé, and so, deserted on both sides, he fell. Albert Thomas now hoped that he might be asked to form the new cabinet with large Socialist participation, but this was not realistic.[86] Those Socialists who, on hearing the result of the vote, shouted out 'Down with Clemenceau', had a better appreciation of the situation. The Sacred Union was ended, and the Socialist party adopted a position of clear-

[84] R. Poincaré, op. cit., IX, p. 291.
[85] Ibid., p. 321. On the weakness of the Painlevé cabinet, see ibid., pp. 310–47, and the letters of the British ambassador, Bertie, to Balfour, 11, 15, 20, 24, and 26 October 1917, Lloyd George Papers, F/51/4/44, 48, 49, 50, 52. On 11 October 1917 Bertie wrote to Balfour, after a talk with Clemenceau, who said that Painlevé would soon fall: 'Clemenceau did not say that he expects to have to form a ministry on the fall of Painlevé but I think that such is his expectation.'
[86] B. W. Shaper, Albert Thomas, Trente Ans de Réformisme Social (Assen, 1959), pp. 167–72; C. Andler, Vie de Lucien Herr (1932), pp. 243–5; H. Wickham Steed, Through Thirty Years (1924), II, pp. 157–9; Archives Nationales, F⁷ 13950, 2, fol. 173.

cut opposition to the new cabinet. General opinion was that a Clemenceau government would be short-lived; his chances of being supported for a long period by the predominantly left-wing Chamber did not seem good. The British ambassador reported to Lloyd George on 14 November 1917 that it might even come to a military *coup*:

> Thomas and his particular friends in the Socialist party are determined to wreck any ministry in which they do not have a representative, unless they can exercise a predominant influence in such a cabinet. . . . They have vetoed a Clemenceau ministry, and a portion of the Radical Socialist party would be strongly opposed to such a ministry. There is, however, in the middle classes and the people generally, a strong feeling in his favour. . . . He might soon be outvoted in the Chamber, but I believe that in such event he might be capable of bringing a *Corps d'Armée* to Paris to maintain order, and that the people generally would welcome the momentary suppression of the violent Socialists.[87]

Next day Poincaré called in Clemenceau. He noted:

> The Tiger arrives; he is fatter, and his deafness has increased. His intelligence is intact. But what about his health, and his will-power. I fear that one or the other may have changed for the worse, and I feel more and more the risk of this adventure. But this *diable d'homme* has all patriots on his side, and if I do not call on him his legendary strength would make any alternative cabinet weak.[88]

Their conversation was friendly, and Clemenceau's reasonableness seems to have reassured Poincaré. Indeed he felt that he was not resolute enough about the scandals; 'he spoke sympathetically of Malvy, and even of Caillaux with great moderation'. Clemenceau told Poincaré that he thought Pétain, in spite of his pessimism and other faults, the best military leader. Poincaré consulted several leading politicians before recalling Clemenceau and definitely asking him to form a cabinet. One of those consulted was Loucheur, whose diary recounts his interview with Poincaré. The President told him that

> people were trying to frighten him about a Clemenceau ministry, threatening a general strike. I told him that I did not think that things would go that length. He told me of his conversation with Clemenceau. Clemenceau said to him: 'I hear that you have said that I am impulsive.' 'Yes,' said the President, 'and credulous as well.' He told me that he counted on me to quench the Tiger's ardour.[89]

---

[87] Bertie to Lloyd George, 14 November 1917, Lloyd George Papers, F/51/4/55.
[88] R. Poincaré, op. cit, IX, pp. 367–8.
[89] L. Loucheur, *Carnets Secrets* (Brussels, 1962), p. 48.

Most thought Clemenceau the best choice, although Steeg and Franklin-Bouillon thought that he would come into head-on conflict with the working class. Franklin-Bouillon even talked of civil war. Clemenceau said that he would form his cabinet 'without taking account of political affiliations. He would not court the Socialists.'[90] However, he sent his assistant, Mandel, to negotiate with the Socialists through Laval. In spite of Laval's attempts to persuade his party to allow him to join the Clemenceau government, they refused.[91] When the cabinet was formed, it proved to take account of groups to some extent. Nail at the ministry of justice, and Lafferre, at that of education, were invited, as Clemenceau told Poincaré, to please the Radical party. 'With Lafferre,' he added, 'they cannot accuse me of not being far enough to the left'; Lafferre was a prominent freemason, and in that way a gilt-edged anti-clerical.[92] But the important ministries, responsible for the conduct of the war, were distributed according to Clemenceau's personal decision without much account of their holders' political support. Clemenceau took the ministry of war and brought his faithful lieutenant Pichon back to the foreign ministry, much to the annoyance of Barthou, who had hoped to remain there. Jeanneney, Clemenceau's trusted colleague on the Senate committees, headed a prime-ministerial secretariat, a new departure in French administration. Loucheur and Claveille, both from outside Parliament, had the important posts of minister of munitions and of public works and transport respectively.[93] Except for these technicians, the cabinet was almost entirely Radical, but did not include many leading members of the Radical groups.[94] Although no member of the Right was in the cabinet, it received enthusiastic support from that direction. The press generally was favourable to the new ministry. *L'Opinion*, of 24 November 1917, commented that 'at least he will not have M. Clemenceau against him'. The article continued;

It would be unjust not to recognize that M. Clemenceau has taken up a heavy burden, and that the country expects from him what can be expected of a Saviour – a little more than is possible – because it feels that he is in fact capable of pushing back the limits of what is possible.[95]

[90] R. Poincaré, op. cit., pp. 370–1.
[91] G. Warner, *Pierre Laval and the Eclipse of France* (1968), pp. 13–14; J. M. Sherwood, *Georges Mandel and the Third Republic* (1970), p. 25.
[92] R. Poincaré, op. cit., IX, pp. 373–4.
[93] For full details of cabinet membership, *see below*, Appendix I.
[94] A. Aulard, E. Bouvier and A. Ganeau, *Histoire Politique de la Grande Guerre* (1924), p. 288: 'except for its head the cabinet included no one of the first rank'. Abel Ferry, who refused the post of under-secretary at the ministry of war, with responsibility for manpower, called it a cabinet of 'obedient underlings'; *Carnets Secrets, 1914–1918* (1957), p. 209.
[95] I owe this reference to M. Albert Krebs.

In spite of the hostility of some leading Radicals, the Radical-Socialist parliamentary group, meeting jointly with the executive committee of the Radical party, voted by 59 to 26 to allow their members to join the new cabinet.[96] Even the Socialists were not completely hostile in the vote of confidence for the new cabinet, with 64 Socialists voting against and 25 abstaining; later, two Socialists were allowed to take office as 'commissioners' without being expelled from the party.

On 20 November, the new cabinet met the Chamber of Deputies, and Clemenceau pronounced the ministerial declaration. It was brief, but eloquent, expressing his conviction that France, *champ-clos des idéals*, was fighting, along with all civilized nations, against 'modern forms of ancient barbarism'. He evoked, in a few words, a picture of the entire nation united in this great struggle,

> workers in the factories, women, old men and children bent at the toil of tilling the fields, they were all also soldiers for France.

He continued,

> Mistakes have been made; do not think of them except to rectify them. Alas, there have also been crimes, crimes against France which call for a prompt punishment. We promise you, we promise the country, that justice will be done according to the law. . . . Weakness would be complicity. We will avoid weakness, as we will avoid violence. All the guilty before courts-martial. The soldier in the court-room, united with the soldier in battle. No more pacifist campaigns, no more German intrigues. Neither treason, nor semi-treason : the war. Nothing but the war. Our armies will not be caught between fire from two sides. Justice will be done. The country will know that it is defended.[97]

In these staccato phrases, not even composed into grammatical sentences, he achieved extraordinary rhetorical effect. The style exactly expressed the thought, eschewing any superfluity of words, as his programme avoided anything beyond the need to continue the terrible struggle. The contrast between the determination and authority of this speech, and the vacillations of Painlevé, was extreme. Even though the trials of Malvy and Caillaux were to show that no prominent politicians had been compromised by contact with the Germans, the psychological importance of Clemenceau's leadership was very great. It did not matter that, once in office, he began to minimize the importance of the scandals,

[96] G. Bonnefous, op. cit., II, p. 345.
[97] *Annales de la Chambre des Députés*, 20 November 1917, reprinted in G. Clemenceau, *Discours de Guerre*, pp. 157–82. According to Martet, who heard him read the declaration, it lost some of its effect, as he read it badly : but when he spoke impromptu, replying to questions, he transmitted the full impression of his determination. J. Martet, *Le Silence de M. Clemenceau*, pp. 223–5.

in contrast to his newspaper articles of October and November. The atmosphere was quite different from that of 1917: even when the Germans broke through on the western front in April and May 1918 there was no weakening of French morale. Under Clemenceau's leadership France was determined to fight on.

Part six

PERE-LA-VICTOIRE

1917-1918

14

SECOND MINISTRY:
DOMESTIC POLITICS

I PÈRE-LA-VICTOIRE

Clemenceau formed his second ministry on 16 November 1917, almost precisely one year before the armistice that ended the war with Germany. He was seventy-six years old, but this year saw the supreme moments of his life, and placed him in the pantheon of French national heroes. Clemenceau's incarnation of France's will to survive through these last terrible months was expressed in a new nickname, Père-La-Victoire. Impossible to translate, it expresses the feelings of respect, confidence and affection which he inspired. Père so-and-so is the sort of nickname given in French villages to an old man, probably a prosperous peasant or craftsman, who is regarded by his fellow villagers with friendly respect. It is an appellation that suggests how Clemenceau had completely outstepped limits of social class, of educational and cultural distinctions, and of sectarian politics. It suggests his 'common touch'. His speeches might use classical allusions – in his inaugural speech he talked of the day when he might have to answer for his mistakes at 'the tribunal of Aeacus, Rhadamanthos and Minos' – but he managed also to talk in a direct and earthy way that everybody could understand. More than anything, his frequent visits to the front line gained him general respect. The *poilus*, the infantry soldiers of the trenches, gave him the new nickname, expressing a different facet of his character from that which had earned him the sobriquet of 'the Tiger'.

His first concern was the preservation of national unity: he sought to prevent a gulf opening between the soldiers fighting at the front and the civilians who still enjoyed the comfort and security of peacetime life, and to prevent political disputes leading to too bitter a conflict between the different classes of society. In the long run it might be said that he failed. In these years the seeds were sown that led to the creation of a mass Communist party, expressing a gulf between the classes, and based largely on the emotional drive produced by revulsion from the war. At the time he was successful in inspiring his fellow citizens to continue the terrible struggle. There were, of course, exceptions. The left-inclined majority of the Chamber only accepted his rule reluctantly and the majority of the Socialist group went into outright opposition. But Clemenceau was sure that their following in the country as a whole amounted to very little, and declared that it was this general support that forced the deputies to vote for his continuance in office.

Some historical accounts have continued to express the rancour of contemporary opponents and have presented Clemenceau as a 'dictator' forcing a reluctant populace to fight on against its will through the use of harsh repressive measures. This is not a tenable view. As Professor Renouvin has pointed out, Clemenceau's unique success in making the French Parliamentary system provide a strong and effective form of war government was only possible because he had the support of public opinion. He concluded :

> previous cabinets had appeared more conscientious than energetic, and the public welcomed a programme showing a determination to rule. . . . A wave of confidence, springing from the very soul of the country, cleared the way for the government, and swept aside the whims of the Parliamentary opposition and the hesitations of critical minds. . . . It was these profound sentiments of the nation's collective soul, sentiments so foreign to all French habits, that supported the 'war government' and render it intelligible.[1]

To some it seemed that France was taking the first steps down the slippery path that had brought Russia to collapse. Abel Ferry wrote in his diary shortly after the formation of Clemenceau's cabinet :

> Clemenceau's contribution is that by the judicial prosecutions he has prevented the almost physical fatigue of the body politic going to the head, as it did in Russia.[2]

Many were looking for the French Kerensky, and the French Lenin. In reality, it was not likely that without Clemenceau the outcome would have been a repetition of Russian events; it would rather have been some

---

[1] P. Renouvin, *The Forms of War Government in France* (1927), pp. 154–7. Professor Renouvin has substantiated this early judgement by a recent article based on newly released archive material, 'L'opinion publique et la guerre en 1917', *Revue d'histoire moderne et contemporaine*, XV, 1968, pp. 16–17. Further confirmation can be found in the police reports, Archives Nationales, F⁷ 13950, 2, fols 174, 177, 179, 180, 183, of 18 November to 22 December 1917.
[2] A. Ferry, *Carnets Secrets 1914–1918* (1957), p. 230.

form of nationalist or military take-over. Bolshevik ruthlessness and fanaticism did not exist on the French Left, and the national mood, which still demanded continuation of the war, was far removed from that of Russia. Clemenceau's contribution was not that he prevented France from following the Russian example, but that he gave strong government while maintaining republican legality.[3]

Discussion of Clemenceau's relations with the other members of his government is hampered by the fact that the French cabinet did not keep formal minutes. Moreover the cabinet, as a collectively responsible body, did not play the same part in the political process in France as in England. In a *Régime d'Assemblée*, with cabinets formed of ministers owing allegiance to several different political groups, the idea of collective cabinet responsibility was weaker. In any case Clemenceau overshadowed the others. Although the cabinet contained able men, some of the most important, like Loucheur, were technicians brought in by the war. They accepted Clemenceau's domination, and allowed him the monopoly of important decision-making. This is clearly shown by Poincaré's memoirs. He complains repeatedly about the absence of proper discussion in the cabinet. For example, he reported that Pams, the minister of the interior, complained that:

> he served Clemenceau with fidelity and devotion, but that he had to be completely docile, or else there would be a breach between them. Clemenceau, he told me, lives a solitary life, lunches and dines alone, rises early, and goes to bed early, and besides the work of his own ministry, in that solitude he ruminates about questions of persons, and seems to amuse himself by settling them with an extraordinary passion.[4]

Another who accepted Clemenceau's lead was Pichon, the foreign minister. Poincaré remarks on Pichon's subordination on several occasions. On 5 March 1918 he wrote:

> Cabinet meeting. Following their deliberate habit, neither Clemenceau nor Pichon mentioned anything, nor did they have any proposals. . . . This method has grave disadvantages. Clemenceau, very impulsive, and absorbed by other cases, having a poor knowledge of many of the important questions, and not knowing the files at all, comes to quick and shallow decisions, as he has done all his life. Pichon, who trembles before him, does not dare to utter any opinion. Decisions

---

[3] P. Renouvin, op. cit., p. 155: 'Authority, but within the framework of the constitution, was the peculiar feature of this régime. . . . M. Clemenceau did not swerve from the path marked out by the political constitution of the country: but he was in a position to impose his will on Parliament.'
[4] R. Poincaré, op. cit., X, pp. 358–9; cf. also ibid., p. 10.

are really taken by Clemenceau alone without the government being consulted.[5]

Clemenceau's domination of Pichon is confirmed by evidence from the British side. The British ambassador wrote:

Clemenceau is the only man in the government; whether it be Pichon, Leygues, or anybody else who speaks to you, it is Clemenceau alone who can give a definite answer on any subject.[6]

There was little discussion of problems by the cabinet as a whole. Each minister ran his own department, and conferred when necessary with the prime minister. In many ways as important as cabinet ministers were Clemenceau's *chefs de cabinet*, General Mordacq and Georges Mandel, for military and civil affairs respectively. Mandel's two assistants were Jean Martet and Georges Wormser. Mandel had overall supervision and took charge of important or delicate questions, and seemed almost to have the role of minister of the interior, leaving only routine work to Pams. In particular he carried out a thorough purge of prefects and *sous-préfets*, installing new and loyal men throughout the country.[7] Mandel was also responsible for the press censorship. This private secretariat worked in a large room next to Clemenceau's office at the ministry of war.

Clemenceau did not live in an official residence but stayed in his own modest apartment in the rue Franklin. He rose between five and six in the morning, and gave some time to reading the current files. At 7.30 a.m. his physical training instructor arrived for his exercises, wrestling and massage. At 8.45 a.m. he arrived at the ministry of war, and at 9.30 a.m. received Pichon, Mordacq and General Alby, liaison officer with the Army command, followed by Mandel, who reported on the day's newspapers and on internal affairs. What remained of the morning was devoted to a cabinet meeting, a meeting of the *Comité de Guerre*, or such other committee as might be necessary. At noon he returned to the ministry to meet his *chefs de cabinet*, and the under-secretary Jeanneney. He then went home for lunch, returning at 2 p.m. to receive

---

[5] Ibid., pp. 67–8.

[6] Derby to Balfour, 24 May 1918, Lloyd George Papers, F/52/1/35. On 12 October 1918, Derby complained: 'I wish he [Clemenceau] did not go to the front so much, as when he is away the government really does not exist.' Derby to Balfour, Lloyd George Papers, F/52/2/39; cf. Bertie to Lloyd George, 15 November 1917, and Bertie to Balfour, 18 November 1917, Lloyd George Papers, F/51/4/57 and 59. Derby to Balfour, n.d. but c. 10 October 1918, Lloyd George Papers, F/52/2/38. Lord Derby replaced Lord Bertie as British ambassador in Paris in April 1918.

[7] B. Favreau, *Georges Mandel*, pp. 75–8; J. Sherwood, *Georges Mandel*, pp. 24–7; M. Berger and P. Allard, op. cit., pp. 244–5 and 273–8 for Mandel's control of the censorship. A highly-coloured picture of Mandel and Clemenceau at work is given by General E. Spears, *Assignment to Catastrophe* (1954), I, pp. 57–9. Hankey's diary records Spears making similar remarks about Clemenceau's 'reign of terror' at the time. Cf. S. Roskill, *Hankey, Man of Secrets* (1970), I, p. 535.

visitors. At 3 p.m. he would go to the Chamber or the Senate if necessary, or perhaps attend a meeting of a Parliamentary committee. As soon as he could get away, he returned to the ministry, usually about 5.30 p.m., to sign papers and despatch current business. When the day's work was over, the circle of intimate political associates would form in his office for a little gossip or more serious discussion. This circle consisted of Mordacq, Jeanneney, who brought the gossip of the Senate, Ignace, under-secretary for military justice, who did the same for the Chamber, Raux, the prefect of police who could report on what was being said by the general public, and Mandel. Mordacq adds that after the end of the war Tardieu, who had been away in America, Cambon, Piétri, and Dutasta joined the group. No cabinet minister was a member of this intimate circle. By 8.30 p.m. they retired, and Clemenceau then received a few old personal friends, mainly journalists and members of his family, especially his brother Albert, sometimes his grandchildren. At 9 p.m. he returned to the rue Franklin for supper and bed. He never accepted invitations, or had any other social life. As he told Mordacq, for a man of his age to do any useful work he had to concentrate his physical and mental energy on the task in hand. He relied on the devoted cooperation of this group to translate his ideas into effective action.[8]

Whether Clemenceau's authority over his colleagues could justly be called 'dictatorial', is a moot point. The British ambassador, on 9 December 1917, was already reporting such complaints:

I hear that some of Clemenceau's colleagues complain that he is dictatorial and will not listen to their representations. The Tiger did not invite the individuals to be members of his cabinet in order to hear what they might have to say, but to carry out his views. It is practically a one man ministry.[9]

It was a willingly accepted dictatorship, and there was no cabinet revolt against Clemenceau. There are only a few rumours of some members of the cabinet making contacts in view of a possible fall from power during the crises of March and early June 1918. Such rumours were endemic in French politics, and did not amount to serious intrigues against Clemenceau, although he was very angry at such conduct.[10]

At no time did the government come anywhere near defeat in the Chamber. During the war the weakest position was the vote of 18 January 1918 of 368 to 155. After the two most dramatic debates – that of 8 March in which the Socialists launched a bitter attack on Clemen-

---

[8] General J. J. H. Mordacq, *Le Ministère Clemenceau, Journal d'un Témoin* (1930–1), I, pp. 26–32.
[9] Bertie to Lloyd George, 9 December 1917, Lloyd George Papers, F/51/4/64.
[10] J. J. H. Mordacq, op. cit., I, pp. 49 and 281; Derby reported on 17 June 1918 that there had been talk of resignation by some ministers, Lloyd George Papers, F/52/2/5.

ceau for his 'provocation of the working class', and that of 4 June after the great German advance in Champagne – the voting was 368 to 115 and 377 to 110 respectively. After the war the government's majorities declined somewhat. But there was never any question of the Chamber overthrowing the cabinet. The fact that the Clemenceau government was condemned by the Socialist party, and the sacred union formally abandoned, was an element of Parliamentary strength, not of weakness. Whereas earlier governments had sought to conciliate the Socialists, there was now no need for such tenderness. There was a clear-cut confrontation between supporters and opponents, and the opposition was revealed to be only a small part of the Chamber, consisting of the Socialists, some of the Republican-Socialists, and a certain number of left-wing Radicals. A British observer noted in June 1918:

> After 6 months the government's majority has, so to speak, crystallized. Each successive vote shows results practically identical with the one before it. The Opposition comprises the Socialist party, plus about 20 Radicals of Socialist tendencies who are on terms of more or less personal friendship with Caillaux. The opposition can number in all 110 or 120 votes.[11]

To what did Clemenceau owe his support in the Chamber? It is generally agreed, to quote the same report,

> that, generally speaking, the Clemenceau ministry was imposed on the Chamber by the country in opposition to the private and personal wishes of many members of the Chamber.

Clemenceau himself said as much to Martet:

> In addressing the Parliament, it was really always the country as a whole that I spoke to. My speeches passed over the heads of deputies and senators, and always pointed out that, outvoted or not, in the last resort, it was the country that would judge, both them and me.[12]

The same British report stresses this in its account of the strengthening of Clemenceau's overall position after the debate of 4 June. Clemenceau had found it difficult to speak because of interruptions and

> it was generally thought that apart from the actual voting, Clemenceau had not had his usual success. At the time it appeared as if the

[11] Reports on the political situation in France, May 1918 (but written after the debate of 4 June) by Captain Arthur Capel, Milner Papers, 117, fols 135–8. According to J. J. H. Mordacq, op. cit., I, p. 308, Capel was 'an intimate friend of Clemenceau'.
[12] Ibid. Cf. also, Foreign Office political intelligence department, memorandum of 22 August 1918, Public Record Office, CAB 24/62, Cabinet Paper GT 5557: Clemenceau 'was never the choice of Parliament but of the country as a whole'; J. Martet, M. Clemenceau peint par lui-même, pp. 215–6.

day's proceedings had in some degree diminished the government's prestige, but this impression had to be revised. It was found that the country showed extreme resentment of the Parliamentary habits which can prevent a prime minister who is popular and respected from getting a fair hearing in a serious crisis. Forty-eight hours after the debate it was generally recognized that the government's position was as solid as ever while the opposition on the other hand was so placed as to make it impossible for it at once to embark again on a manœuvre so universally condemned.[13]

Clemenceau's speeches in Parliament gave the whole nation a renewed feeling of self-confidence through the darkest days of the war and are a remarkable phenomenon. Without any of the modern methods of communication, this old man, speaking in the closed circle of the Chamber of Deputies (he rarely spoke outside Parliament during the war), was able to generate a national mood that transformed the political situation.

It is not surprising that Clemenceau had such a hold over cabinet and Parliament after the tide of battle turned in August 1918. But it is remarkable that his position was so strong during the first seven months of his ministry, when the military position often seemed very dangerous. There were attacks in Parliament after the German victories in March and June 1918, but his majority remained solid.

The most salient point about the military situation is that during the first seven months of Clemenceau's ministry Germany came closer to victory than at any time after the first weeks of the war.[14] From the autumn of 1914 the position had been one of stalemate; the central powers had sizeable gains on all fronts, but the military power of the Allies remained unbroken. As they refused to give up the fight, and as neither side was able to break the deadlock on the western front, there followed three years of terrible battles of attrition. Amateur strategists, of whom the most important were Churchill and Lloyd George, sought to find a way round through the Balkans. But the professional military planners of both Britain and France alike were convinced that the German army had to be beaten in France. German use of European railways gave her a mobility that could not be matched by Allied shipping. Thus to seek decisive victory from any of the sideshows was a chimera, on which the Allies could only waste their resources.

The main reason for Allied hopes of final victory was that their command of the sea allowed them to impose a blockade depriving Germany

[13] Milner Papers, 117, fols 135–8.
[14] For succinct accounts of the military operations *see* C. Falls, *The First World War* (1960), J. E. Edmonds, *A Short History of World War I* (1951), B. Pitt, *1918 The Last Act* (1962), P. Renouvin, *La Crise Européenne et la Grande Guerre* (new edition, 1969).

of essential raw materials. In the end, they hoped that a war of attrition would lead to German defeat for this reason. Conversely, the Germans hoped to use the U-boat to cut off the British Isles from food and supplies from overseas. After long hesitation, in the spring of 1917 Germany embarked on unrestricted submarine warfare as the only way of weakening the enemy's military potential before the blockade strangled her. At first the German decision seemed to have been correct, as merchant shipping was decimated around the shores of Britain and France. But the adoption of the convoy system reduced shipping losses to tolerable amounts, and the wheels of British and French industry continued to turn. Instead of being a trump card in the German hand, the U-boat campaign, which brought the United States into the war, turned the scales to the Allied side. In the long run, with American help, the Allies had much more reason to hope for a decisive victory.

In the interim the situation was dangerous indeed. American intervention at once eased the financial problems of the Allies, but did little else for over a year. American armies had to be raised, trained, equipped, and shipped to Europe – all formidable problems. But the summer of 1917 saw the final collapse of the Russian military effort. Ironically, if only Germany had waited, she could have got most of her essential supplies from the east, without taking the fatal decision to unleash her submarines against neutral merchant ships. Germany was only able to make a separate peace with Russia in March 1918, but with the collapse of the Kerensky offensive in the summer of 1917 it was obvious that there would be no further danger from that quarter. German troops were transferred from the eastern to the western front in increasing numbers, a process accelerated after the second revolution, the Bolshevik *coup* of November.

Germany was no longer fighting on two major fronts, and could concentrate her strength for an all-out blow in the west. Ludendorff, who controlled German strategy, had a gambler's mentality, and played for the highest stakes – total victory over Britain and France before American intervention could turn the balance of forces on the western front back to the Allied side. For the first time he could count on superior manpower there. For their part the Allies had no reasonable course but to await the German attack. There were some on the Allied side who hankered after another offensive. It has been argued that Lloyd George deliberately refused Haig, British commander-in-chief, the reserves he would need to launch a new offensive, in order to prevent a repetition of the terrible losses in the autumn battles at Ypres and Passchendaele. In the event the Allies did await the German onslaught, without taking the offensive themselves.

To provide a framework for Clemenceau's actions it is necessary only to outline the main military events. Soon after he took office the British fought the battle of Cambrai, using tanks in large numbers for the first time. It was mismanaged and produced no decisive result. Afterwards there was little action on the western front until the devastating German attack on the Somme of 21 March 1918. This almost separated the British and French armies, which would have been disastrous. But the attack was held, as were further German assaults in April, after which the battle died down for a while. On 27 May another German onslaught broke through the French line at Chemin des Dames, and the Germans were able to advance over forty miles, bringing them back to the Marne, where they had not been since 1914. But these great tactical victories could not be transformed into the decisive strategic victory the Germans needed. The British and French armies remained in being, reserves were moved up, and the line re-established. Ludendorff was unable to achieve the complete destruction of his enemies' powers of resistance, unlike Hitler in May 1940. The result of these great advances was only to leave the Germans with bulging salients to hold which needed more men than their previous line had done. A further attack, on 15 July, although it began with more German gains, proved to be the turning-point. The Allies counter-attacked, and met increasing success. 8 August 1918 was the 'black day' of the German army, after which it was clear that the initiative had passed to the Allies. The Germans retreated fighting, and still appeared a formidable enemy. The Allies were still thinking of victory only after a campaign in 1919, but morale was beginning to go on the German side. Allied success in the Balkans proved to be the last straw, and by the end of September Ludendorff's nerve had cracked. He began to seek ways in which an armistice could be granted. With strange naïvety he thought that the Allies would grant terms that would allow him to re-establish his position and then renew the fight. But once the process of seeking terms began, it rapidly led to his own removal from power, and to a disintegration of authority in Germany that placed her at the mercy of the Allies.

2 DOMESTIC POLITICS

Clemenceau's own role can now be examined: first his part in the maintenance of morale and his control of the domestic political situation, and then his part in the formulation of strategy and policy, and in the control of the armies.

Although at a technical level the re-establishment of discipline among the troops had already been largely achieved before he came to power, in the last resort the morale of the troops depended on the morale of the nation.[15] There was truth in the idea of corruption of the army by the atmosphere behind the lines, if not in the precise sense of the military leaders and the political Right. The war had become a struggle in which a vital element was the mobilization of the energies of the whole nation. Contrary to pre-1914 expectations, the democratic countries, France and England, proved able to summon the last ounce of national strength for the final struggle. In spite of years of defeat and discouragement, they were able to hold out, while the authoritarian societies, Russia and Germany, collapsed. As Clemenceau put it, allegedly quoting a Japanese proverb, 'victory goes to the combatant who continues for a quarter of an hour longer than his enemy'.[16]

The Left in Parliament argued that Clemenceau's high-handed methods would be dangerous because they would produce an outburst of opposition from trade union and working-class spokesmen outside Parliament. One of the reasons for Poincaré's hesitation in asking Clemenceau to form a government had been his fear that he would divide the nation by harsh repression of 'defeatism' and working-class agitation. Clemenceau denied that these self-proclaimed leaders of the working class represented the majority of the proletariat. They were mainly not of working-class origin, but déclassés, failed members of the bourgeoisie. He reminisced ten years later:

> These individuals make a noise if they are allowed to: when you say 'Enough' they shut up. . . . I never had any trouble with those characters. When Malvy told us in the Senate 'Don't touch those people! It may mean revolution,' he was fooling us. I did not even have to fight them. They melted away like shadows. Poincaré and Foch gave me much more trouble than the anarchists.[17]

There was no widespread opposition to the new government among the working class. Whereas 1917 had seen 696 strikes, involving 293,810 strikers and producing 1,481,621 days lost, in 1918 there were only 499 strikes, involving 176,187 strikers and producing 979,632 days lost.[18] Mme Kriegel, in the most detailed study of the working-class movement in these years, has stated that 'the movement of 1918 cannot be compared in depth with that of the spring of 1917', and she analyses at length the reasons for its failure to develop. Her main points are the

---

[15] As Clemenceau said to a Chamber committee, 'The state of mind of the army, that of the civilians, and total military activity, are all linked together . . .', Journal Officiel Documents Parlementaires, Chambre des Députés, annexe au procès-verbal du 18 décembre 1917, Document 4088, minutes of session of 16 December 1917, on the lifting of Caillaux's immunity.
[16] Discours de Guerre, p. 210.
[17] J. Martet, M. Clemenceau peint par lui-même, pp. 13–14.
[18] M. R. Clark, History of the French Labor Movement 1910–1928 (University of California, 1930), p. 53.

efficiency of the government measures to contain the strikes, the difficulty of passing from a strike begun for economic reasons to a political
movement, and the fact that the French working class believed in the
need to defend their country.[19]

One reason for the reduction in the number of strikes in 1918 was
that employers were readier to grant wage increases, and were encouraged
by the government to do so. As a result the inflationary process began
to accelerate in France. Clemenceau had little understanding of financial
matters, and, in any case, his priorities were abundantly clear.[20] He was
not the man to let financial considerations stand in the way of all-out
prosecution of the war effort. Thus, from the beginning of 1918, the
gap between the amount raised in taxation and in long-term funded
debt, and the amounts expended, widened enormously through the use
of short-term credit instruments. The implications of this were disguised,
as inter-Allied control measures ensured a relative stability of the franc
on the foreign exchanges. But when these controls were removed at the
end of the war, the franc began its slide that ended only with stabiliza-
tion, in 1926, at one-fifth of its 1914 dollar value. It is ironical that
Clemenceau, by now the hero of the French bourgeois and *rentier*
classes, was in this way one of their grave-diggers. It would not have
disturbed him, for from the beginning to the end of his life he remained
contemptuous of the bourgeoisie, their caution, selfishness, and
materialistic system of values.

Clemenceau's policy was well calculated to ensure that he did not
enter into sharp conflict with the working class. Soon after taking office
he met union leaders and told them that if they confined their demands
to improvement of wages and working conditions he would do everything he could to help them. He even went so far as to say that he
would not interfere with pacifist propaganda within their own groups
and private meetings. He had every sympathy with the internationalist
ideal, but it was not the moment to allow such talk in public.[21] At one
point the C.G.T. leader Jouhaux was asked to join the government.[22]

[19] A. Kriegel, *Aux origines du communisme français*, I, pp. 214–5.
[20] The way to stop inflation, he said, was to arrest a few big businessmen, J.
Martet, *M. Clemenceau peint par lui-même*, p. 88. The price index showed only a
fairly moderate increase from 283 to 343, between the last quarter of 1917 and the
last quarter of 1918 (1914=100), but the increase in the money supply prepared the
later price inflation. *See* the tables in G. Bonnefous, op. cit., II, pp. 457–9. The
documents preserved in the Dossier du Président du Conseil, II, 5, in the archives
of the ministry of war, Fonds Clemenceau, contain a note from A. Tardieu of 24
June 1918 pointing out the danger of relying on paper money and *Bons du Trésor*.
[21] Bertie to Balfour, 10 February 1918: 'I have never seen in M. Clemenceau, in
the thirteen years that I have known him, any distrust of the working classes.'
Lloyd George Papers, F/52/1/11. Clemenceau's own account of his talk with the
union leaders was given to the Chamber Army committee on 12 December 1917,
Archives Nationales, C 7499.
[22] B. Georges and D. Tintant, *Léon Jouhaux, Cinquante ans de syndicalisme* (1962),
pp. 193–5.

The difference between Clemenceau and earlier governments was, according to Mme Kriegel, that while they had publicised their conciliatory measures and kept the repression secret, he publicised his limited repression and kept the conciliation secret.[23] Poincaré made the same point:

> Now that he is in power he does exactly the opposite of what he demanded when he was in opposition. He gives complete liberty to Merrheim, and to *La Vérité*.[24]

Clemenceau and Mandel had frequent meetings with trade union leaders, and Clemenceau got on well with them. He told Poincaré, on 18 May, that Merrheim was a very good fellow, intelligent and subtle. Clemenceau and Merrheim came to a tacit understanding about the measures taken against the militants who had tried to turn the May strikes into a demonstration against the war. Clemenceau reported it to Poincaré in these terms:

> I told Renaudel and Merrheim that the young conscripts would all have to go [to the front]: they accepted this. The sanctions imposed on the agitators, whether they had been arrested or sent to the front, would be maintained. I said that I could not yield, and that I could not promise clemency, but that I was not an ogre, and that I would see what could be done when the strike ended. They sought to ask me about war aims. I replied 'No'. That is not a working-class or a trade union question.[25]

Clemenceau's aim was to ensure that trade union leadership confined itself to the defence of the economic interests of the working class, so ensuring that strikes were not given a political overtone incompatible with the maintenance of wartime morale. He was successful. Such attempts, on the part of a few militants, in May 1918, were easily suppressed. Clemenceau was able to arrest the extremists without producing a sympathetic reaction among the strikers.[26]

Poincaré also complained that Clemenceau's actions belied his words when it came to the investigation of treason charges. Minor figures were

---

[23] A. Kriegel, op. cit., I, pp. 193–4.

[24] R. Poincaré, op. cit., X, pp. 56, 171, 14 May 1918: 'Clemenceau, who previously said that he would be very firm, this morning expounded to the cabinet the dangers of a tough line and the advantages of a conciliatory attitude.' Merrheim, leader of the metal workers union, was prominent in the protest movement against the war; Renaudel was a Socialist leader in Parliament; *La Vérité* an opposition newspaper. Cf. A. Kriegel, op. cit., I, p. 219, and B. Georges and D. Tintant, op. cit., p. 194.

[25] R. Poincaré, op. cit., X, p. 178.

[26] A. Kriegel, op. cit., I, pp. 215–19. For an analysis of Merrheim's position, and of his relations with Clemenceau, ibid., pp. 223–30.

brought to trial, and several, including Duval, Bolo and Lenoir were executed. But all these cases had been under investigation before Clemenceau came to power, and although Mordacq states that Clemenceau had Ignace, under-secretary for military justice, frequently report about the investigations, there is no evidence that the change of government made much difference.[27] No important new cases were discovered. Nor was rapid progress made, as the public had expected, in the investigations concerning Malvy and Caillaux. Clemenceau's attitude to these two cases differed. He did not concern himself much with Malvy, thus showing that he did not take seriously the accusations of treachery levied against him by the extreme Right. It was Malvy himself, who, on 18 November, asked the Chamber to appoint a committee to decide whether or not he had a case to answer. At the time this seemed a good way of avoiding the danger of trial by court martial, which was, he thought, the fate Clemenceau had prepared for him. The device backfired, however. For although the majority of the committee were friendly to Malvy, they did not feel that public opinion would be satisfied without a proper trial. They had, therefore, to recommend that he be tried, according to a rarely used provision of the Constitution, by the Senate, sitting as a High Court. In August 1918, when Malvy at last faced his judges, it turned out that there was not the least evidence of treachery. At the last moment, however, when it was clear that Malvy must be acquitted on that charge, it was proposed and carried that he should be found guilty of improper conduct ('forfaiture').[28] In spite of the defence lawyers' protests that this meant that he was being judged on a charge for which he had not been defended, he was condemned to five years' exile.

Clemenceau was, however, much more concerned with the investigations into Caillaux's activities. He said to Poincaré on 21 November:

Callaux is a bandit. I do not yet know whether he will be brought before the High Court or a Court Martial. But justice will be done.[29]

On 11 December he asked the Chamber to suspend Caillaux's parliamentary immunity, and a few days later spoke before the committee set up to report on this issue. The news that Clemenceau had asked for the

[27] J. J. H. Mordacq, op. cit., I, p. 49.
[28] On the legal difficulties involved in Malvy's trial, see P. Renouvin, The Forms of War Government, pp. 114–19. Clemenceau did not regard these legal objections as serious, for he recommended the French procedure as a model when the arrangements for the proposed trial of the German Kaiser were discussed by the Allies. Minutes of the inter-allied conference of 2 December 1918 (IC 98), Public Record Office, CAB 28/5.
[29] R. Poincaré, op. cit., IX, p. 382. On 11 October 1917 he had said to the British ambassador that 'Caillaux's complicity with Bolo and enemy agents will be proved and he will, Clemenceau who is an optimist hopes, be shot'. Bertie to Balfour, 11 October 1917, Lloyd George Papers, F/51/4/44.

suspension of Caillaux's parliamentary immunity produced a sensation among political circles. A report of 12 December 1917 states:

> There was no real surprise but a feeling of seriousness, of anxious reflection. It was felt that the comedy was turning into a drama, perhaps a tragedy. Everywhere one heard 'No, not really? The Tiger has gone hunting then?' . . . And one heard people say 'Has he really got proof? A gesture like this can't be attempted without having all the cards in one's hand. . . . And what if he loses the trick? Or even if he does not win it completely? What a blow for him and for us! . . . It cannot be denied that Caillaux is very unpopular and that Clemenceau has become definitely popular. . . . The general public is undoubtedly in favour of the accusation. . . .[30]

On 22 December the Chamber agreed, and investigation into Caillaux's affairs began. He was arrested on 22 January 1918, but was only brought to trial in March 1920.

The long delay could be interpreted in two ways. It could be said that Clemenceau allowed the trial to be postponed so that Caillaux would not be tried in the hysterical wartime atmosphere, or, on the other hand, that he did not wish the trial to proceed because of the extreme fragility of the evidence against Caillaux. The latter was removed from the political scene by his imprisonment, while the excuse that judicial investigations were proceeding could be used to avoid answering embarassing questions. Bertie, the British ambassador, who frequently saw Clemenceau and was on very good terms with him, reported that Clemenceau was sure he had good evidence against Caillaux. Pichon told him that

> he does not consider it possible that Caillaux can be entirely acquitted. This confirms me in the belief which I have already expressed to you that Clemenceau has some damaging evidence which is not disclosed in the indictment against Caillaux by the Governor of Paris. Pichon said that in the *most* improbable event of Caillaux being entirely acquitted, Clemenceau and all his cabinet will fall, and there will be Socialist chaos, and perhaps Soviets, for there is nobody fit to take Clemenceau's place, to sweep out the interior uncleanness and to face the enemy. . . .[31]

---

[30] Archives Nationales, F⁷ 13950, 2, fol. 177. The minutes of the sessions of the committee appointed to report on the suspension of Caillaux's immunity are in Archives Nationales, C 7705: they were printed in the report, *Journal Officiel, Documents Parlementaires, Chambre des Députés, annexe au procès verbal du 18 Decembre 1917, Document 4088.*

[31] Bertie to Lloyd George, 6 January 1918, Lloyd George Papers, F/52/1/2. Cf. also, Bertie to Lloyd George, 4 December 1917, 7, 10, 12 and 17 January 1918, 11 and 12 February 1918, Lloyd George Papers, F/51/4/62, and F/52/1/4, 5, 6, 7, 11 and 13.

However, as weeks went by, and no public announcements were made, interest in Caillaux's case died down. There are no more reports that the fate of the government hung on proving Caillaux's guilt. The fate of Caillaux ceased to be of great interest, as the political tension of 1917, which had made the treason charges so important, diminished. The verdict on Caillaux was as illogical as that on Malvy. He was found guilty of treason, but with extenuating circumstances, and condemned to three years' imprisonment, five years of banishment from all large cities, and ten years' loss of civic rights. As he had already served twenty-seven months in prison he was released immediately, and retired to his country house at Mamers.[32]

The new government reaped the psychological advantage of having initiated proceedings against these prominent men. At the same time the trial and condemnation of the lesser figures, Bolo and Duval, were given great publicity, and created the impression that the new government was acting vigorously to repress German espionage as promised. Leymarie, Malvy's *chef de cabinet*, was sentenced to two years' imprisonment for having returned to Duval the cheque which had been seized by the French customs on his return from meeting the German agent in Switzerland.

8 March 1918 saw the most violent confrontation between Clemenceau and the Socialists, in a debate arising out of an interpellation on the Bolo treason trial. Renaudel, leader of the Majority Socialists, accused the prime minister of favouring anti-republican campaigns in Parliament and the press against the previous governments. Clemenceau launched an all-out attack on the Socialists, finishing with a demand for an end to their equivocation on whether they would vote the war budget. Clemenceau accused the Socialists of attacking him on principle, irrespective of what he did.

A great misfortune occurred at the birth of my cabinet. I was blackballed by M. Renaudel and his friends, before they knew what I would do or say. They decided, in the light of their fine system of dogma, that I was a danger to the working class and to the defence of the nation. Gentlemen, the working class is not your property. The hands of M. Renaudel and M. Albert Thomas are no more calloused than mine. I am sorry for their sakes, but they are bourgeois, just as I am. . . .

He asked his opponents why they attacked him if they accepted the continuation of the war. If they wanted peace, he replied in fierce staccato,

so do I, but it is not by bleating of peace that we can silence Prussian militarism. A moment ago M. Constant complained of my silence

[32] G. Bonnefous, op. cit., III, pp. 116–17.

about foreign policy. My foreign policy and my domestic policy are
all one. Internal policy, I wage war; foreign policy, I still wage war;
I still wage war. Russia betrays us; I continue the war: unfortunate
Rumania is forced to capitulate; I continue the war, and I will continue it down to the last quarter of an hour.[33]

The Socialists were divided into several factions over their attitude to
the war, division which played a great part in the subsequent split
between Socialists and Communists. Three Socialists had even been
allowed to join the government as 'commissioners' without expulsion
from the party, in spite of violent attacks from other Socialists. A
British report thought that much of the Socialist opposition was purely
formal:

> About forty, led by Varenne, vote against the government while at
> the same time in private conversation they express their confidence
> in it. It is only the Socialist Centre led by Renaudel and Sembat who
> appear to be absolutely irreconcilable, even the Minority Socialists
> who follow M. Longuet adopt, generally speaking, an attitude of
> reserve, and distinguish sharply between their public attitude and
> their personal convictions.[34]

A month later, immediately after the dramatic events of the end of
March when a German breakthrough seemed imminent, the Czernin
incident threatened Clemenceau's prestige among political circles. A
press agency announced on 4 April that the Austrian foreign minister,
Count Czernin, had declared that just before the opening of the current
offensive, the French government had asked Austria on what basis peace
negotiations could begin. Informed of this, Clemenceau simply declared
that 'Count Czernin lied'. Public opinon enjoyed this brusque retort,
and the sight of the destroyer of ministries taking another scalp, this
time in Vienna, when Czernin was forced to resign.[35] The Austrian
government had for nearly twelve months been seeking a way of bringing the war to an end, and had been involved in secret unofficial talks
with Britain, France and the United States. All had proved fruitless, and
Czernin hoped to win a point at home, weaken French morale, and
perhaps also sow dissention among the Allies, by revealing the Armand-
Revertera talks of February 1918. The initiative for the resumption of the

---

[33] Annales de la Chambre des Députés, 8 March 1918; G. Clemenceau, *Discours de
Guerre*, pp. 201–22.
[34] Milner Papers, 117, fols 135–8. On Socialist divisions at this time, *see* D. Ligou,
Histoire du Socialisme en France, 1871–1961 (1962), pp. 298–301, G. Ziebura, *Léon
Blum*, pp. 139–43, and A. Kriegel, *Aux origines du Communisme française 1914–
1920*, I, pp. 204–33.
[35] Report from British military mission to the French government, Milner Papers,
117, fols 139–45.

talks had come from the French side, but Czernin's statement that France had approached Austria with the offer of a separate peace was a travesty of the truth. It allowed Clemenceau to expose both Czernin and the Emperor as liars and double-dealers, by the publication of the earlier approach from the Austrian side through Prince Sixte de Bourbon.[36] It could, however, be argued that it was unwise of Clemenceau to uncover the Emperor in this way, in that it put an end to any Austrian attempts to withdraw from the war, and tied her firmly to Germany to the bitter end. Clemenceau's action was criticized along these lines at the time. A police report of 20 April 1918 stated that:

> The opponents of the cabinet continue to say that Clemenceau was wrong to uncover the Emperor of Austria, whom he has turned into an irreconcilable enemy of France,[37]

thus preventing further talks with Austria through the mediation of Spain. Ribot wrote in his diary on 24 April 1918:

> The idea is spreading that there could have been a separate peace. It does not stand up to examination. But the public does not have enough information to make a reasoned judgement, and for that reason the publication of the letter was dangerous.[38]

In fact, as Ribot said, a separate peace with Austria was now impossible. It was important for French morale that Clemenceau should make it clear that France was in no way the suppliant. This is what he did by his actions, however undiplomatic, and he was able to defend himself with success before the foreign affairs committees of the Chamber and Senate.[39] He expressed his position to the Senate committee on 19 April in terms that are worth quoting for the light they throw on his general view of the situation. He began by denying that his brusque retort was

[36] The public exchanges between the French and Austrian governments are reprinted in G. Clemenceau, *Discours de Guerre*, pp. 222–35. Cf. G. Pedroncini, *Les Négociations secrètes*, pp. 73–8, Mermeix, *Les Négociations secrètes*, pp. 159–79, and C. J. Lowe and M. L. Dockrill, op. cit., II, pp. 265–74.

[37] Archives Nationales, F⁷ 13950, 2, fol. 193. Cf. report from the British embassy, 20 April 1918, 'Clemenceau had a rough time at the secret session of the joint Army-Foreign Affairs Committee of the Senate . . .', Lloyd George Papers, F/52/1/25, and a similar view in Derby to Balfour, 24 May 1918, Lloyd George Papers, F/52/1/35.

[38] A. Ribot, *Journal et Correspondances inédites* (1936), p. 247, cf. V. H. Rothwell, *British War Aims and Peace Diplomacy 1914–1918* (1971), p. 170.

[39] Minutes of all these meetings are available, except for those of the 17 April session of the Chamber External Affairs committee, which were kept by the president, Franklin-Bouillon, and not returned to the file. The Chamber committees are to be found in the Archives Nationales, C 7491, Procès-Verbaux de la Commission de l'Armée. The Senate committee's minutes are at the Archives of the Senate, Commission des Affaires Etrangères, Auditions des Ministres. For the Senate, only the minutes of sessions with ministers present are available; the subsequent discussion and voting are not.

another example of his impulsiveness. Those who made that accusation could not distinguish between thoughtless impulsiveness and premeditated determination. As for the idea that France had anything to gain by courting Austria, it may have been true in the past, but it was chimerical now.

> . . . Do we need Austria? Whether I am right or wrong, I will say frankly that I expect nothing from Austria. Although many people have had the illusion of a half-peace over the last three or four years, events have shown very clearly that we are not going to have a half-peace: we must either conquer or be conquered. . . . If we conquer I do not say that we need act savagely towards Austria, but if we are conquered we can expect nothing from her, and I assure you that the authority that she will then have with William II will be the same as she has to-day, that is none. What are our war-aims? A principal one is national self-determination. I do not say that even as victors we will work the miracle of freeing all the peoples of the world. . . . But Austria is the school of oppression, *par excellence*. You cannot court Austria and keep your promises to the Czechs, the Poles, the Italians, the Yugoslavs, and the Rumanians.[40]

He used the same arguments to the Chamber committee on 3 May, stressing that there was no possibility of separating Austria from Germany. Czernin's aim had been to weaken French morale and her attachment to her allies. It was of vital importance that this aim should not be achieved.

> I could not allow it to be thought that at the time I summed up my policy in the words 'I wage war', I was lying, and that I was asking Count Czernin for peace. That would have been a blow to the moral, psychological and sentimental strength of my country.[41]

[40] Archives of the Senate, Commission des Affaires Etrangères, Auditions des Ministres, 19 April 1918.
[41] Archives Nationales, C 7491, minutes of 3 May and 8 May 1918. Cf. Poincaré, op. cit., X, pp. 157–8 and 163–4.

15

MILITARY STRATEGY

I FOCH BECOMES SUPREME ALLIED COMMANDER

Clemenceau's firm hand in the area of policy and strategy was an important factor in the re-establishment of national self-confidence. He put a stop to the secret sessions of Parliament which had been threatening the authority of the government. Criticism had now to be made either by interpellation in public session, or in the Parliamentary committees.

Although Pétain, the commander-in-chief on the western front, had won great authority by his re-establishment of morale after the mutinies, he did not seek the independence from political control that Joffre had enjoyed in the first two years of the war. Foch's position as chief-of-staff provided an alternative source of military advice for the civilian authorities.[42] Clemenceau was not in the unhappy position of Lloyd George, who thought that Haig and Robertson (the British equivalents, respectively, of Pétain and Foch) were linked in a sort of tacit conspiracy that prevented any consideration of alternative military policies by the government. Foch and Pétain were totally dissimilar in their temperaments and their views on strategy. Pétain was cautious, perhaps over-cautious, and determined to reduce casualties to the minimum, while Foch had a much more aggressive spirit. This allowed Clemenceau to retain ultimate authority in his own hands.[43] To help him exercise it,

[42] G. Pedroncini, *Le Haut-Commandement et la conduite de la guerre Mai 1917–Novembre 1918* (Sorbonne thesis, 1971) is the indispensable source on this question. The *soutenance de thèse* of 22 May 1971, reported in *Le Monde*, 9 June 1971, gives some indication of Pedroncini's views on the relations between Foch, Pétain and Clemenceau.

[43] He said so to the Senate Army committee on 14 December 1917: 'Foch is a man who exactly counterbalances Pétain's faculties, both good and bad. They fit together because they are not alike; as they give out different notes they allow one to make a reasoned judgement.' Archives of the Senate, Commission de l'Armée, Auditions des Ministres.

he had the services of General Mordacq, as *chef de cabinet militaire*; he was rarely separated from him for more than a few hours between November 1917 and the armistice.

He did insist on changes in Pétain's staff, whom he thought shared too much of their chief's caution, but never tried to remove Pétain himself.[44] There were good reasons for this. To the rank and file of the French army, Pétain stood as guarantee that they would not again be sacrificed in useless and unprepared offensives. Although Clemenceau was sarcastic about Lloyd George's idea that Pétain had some magic method of avoiding casualties, he agreed with the commander-in-chief on overall strategy. He had told Sir Henry Wilson in July 1917 that he was glad that Pétain was in command, for the only possible strategy was to conserve Allied manpower until the Americans arrived in force.[45] No casualties should be incurred by pointless offensives, as they did not have enough troops to exploit a breakthrough. Clemenceau developed these views before the Chamber Army committee on 12 December, and before the Senate Army committee on 14 December.

> We cannot afford to make a single further mistake, or to run any more risks. We will still lose men in remaining on the defensive, but fewer than if we took the offensive, and we would not risk total defeat.

He went on to say that it was even possible that the Germans would make peace overtures, knowing the Americans were coming.

> I believe that the Germans will make their greatest effort since the beginning of the war, greater than at Verdun. There is no doubt of it. . . . But, if we hold them, the Germans might not wait any longer before offering peace terms which might be acceptable to us.[46]

Did he really believe that a compromise peace could be made before American strength had been brought to bear, or was this merely to satisfy the advocates of a compromise peace on the committee? It is significant that he said nothing of this to the Senate committee two days later, but was even more pessimistic about the immediate military

---

[44] Clemenceau only made changes in the command structure when Foch became Allied commander-in-chief in April 1918. At that point the *Etat-Major* was reorganized, and placed under General Alby. J. J. H. Mordacq, op. cit., I, pp. 46–7.

[45] C. E. Callwell, *Field Marshall Sir Henry Wilson* (1927), I, p. 364. He said the same thing at the Army committee of the Senate, on 25 June 1917: 'America arrives. The programme is to hold on for a year. In a year we will have a million Americans at the front.' Archives of the Senate, Commission de l'Armée, Auditions des Ministres. Clemenceau's reply to Lloyd George's query about Pétain's 'casualty-saving system' was transmitted by Bertie to Balfour, 13 December 1917, Lloyd George Papers, F/51/4/68.

[46] Archives Nationales, C 7499, Commission de l'Armée de la Chambre des Députés, 12 December 1917.

prospects, although still confident of final victory.[47] He complained that, in spite of all his efforts, the British refused to strengthen their forces in France. Lloyd George had promised to extend the British line, but had been unable to impose his will on Haig. And yet, at the same time, the the British were maintaining 400,000 men in Palestine in order to carry out Lloyd George's private scheme of conquering the holy places. He grew indignant at their poor military contribution, and said that he intended to get America to put pressure on Britain to change her policy.[48]

Just before Clemenceau came to power, machinery for Allied cooperation had been set up in the form of the Supreme War Council. This consisted of arrangements for regular monthly meetings of the political leaders of Britain, France and Italy (plus an American observer), and a permanent body of military experts, installed at Versailles. The latter were to draw up general directives on overall strategy, which would be discussed by the politicians. Clemenceau was not enthusiastic about these arrangements, but was soon persuaded that there had been a firm commitment by the French government. He would have preferred a more definite machine for coordinating military policy, without the arrangements for political meetings.[49] The main attraction of the scheme for Lloyd George was that it by-passed the Chief of the Imperial General Staff, Robertson, whom he distrusted, but could not yet remove. From the French point of view the new arrangements did not have the same importance.

The strategic problems with which Clemenceau had to deal were threefold. The first was to secure implementation of the British promise to take over more of the front in France. The second was the question posed by Lloyd George of the relative importance of the western and eastern fronts. The third was the strategy to be adopted on the western

[47] Speaking to the External Affairs committee of the Chamber on 19 December 1917, he said that 'the German interest is to make a peace in 1918, while ours is to make peace in 1919 when we will have an indisputable victory. . . . If we speak of peace today it would be disastrous, unless we are offered terms in keeping with our dignity.' Archives Nationales, Commission des Affaires Extérieures de la Chambre des Députés, C 7490, 19 December 1917.

[48] Archives of the Senate, Commission de l'Armée, Auditions des Ministres, 14 December 1917.

[49] Callwell, op. cit., II, p. 32. Bertie to Lloyd George, 9 December 1917, Lloyd George Papers, F/51/4/64. Clemenceau was very sarcastic about the arrangements in his speeches to the Army committees of the Chamber and the Senate. He said that, whereas at an earlier date the British would have accepted subordination to the French command they now had an inflated idea of their military capabilities, while the failure of the French offensive of 16 April 1917 had reduced their respect for their allies. Archives Nationales, C 7499, 12 December 1917, and Archives of the Senate, Commission de l'Armée, Auditions des Ministres, 14 December 1917. Cf. also C. Seymour, *The Intimate Papers of Colonel House* (1926–8), III, pp. 262–8, D. F. Trask, *The United States in the Supreme War Council, American War Aims and Inter-Allied Strategy 1917–1918* (1961), pp. 20–52, S. Roskill, op. cit., I, p. 465, J. C. King, *Generals and Politicians* (1951), pp. 198–200, M. P. A. Hankey, *The Supreme Command 1914–1918* (1961), II, p. 731.

front; was it to be purely defensive, or was it to have an offensive element, as Foch advocated? The questions were interconnected, which contributed to the unfortunate combination of decisions.

Clemenceau gave first priority to extending the British share of the front line in France, the best way of ensuring that Lloyd George was prevented from diverting British resources to other theatres of war. As he told the Chamber Army committee, the French could not organize defence in depth unless their line were shortened: they held 630 kilometres, the British 160, although much of the French part of the line was not likely to be attacked, and was only lightly defended.[50] Even in Champagne, where the Germans were poised for attack, the French could give ground in a way impossible for the British, who would have lost vital coalfields and communications, and even run the risk of being pushed back to the sea. Nevertheless, the French had a strong case when they argued that the British were in a position to take over more of the line, and agreement had been reached on this before Clemenceau came to power. Clemenceau pushed very hard for its implementation. He was obsessed by the looming manpower shortage which threatened to reduce the effectives of the French armies, and felt that Britain was not bearing a military burden comparable to that endured by France. Even now, he argued, conscription was not imposed on Ireland, and numerous exemptions were granted. In addition, Britain was dispersing her resources by retaining men at home, and by pursuing ambitious campaigns in the Middle East, while France could not find another man anywhere. Lloyd George was not unsympathetic to the demand for the extension of the British front. He thought that it would force Haig to abandon any idea of further offensives. He was haunted by thoughts of the useless slaughter of Passchendaele.[51] In fact, the British line was extended forty miles, to Barisis, in January, in accord with the earlier agreement. Clemenceau also won acceptance at the end of January for a further extension of the British line, but this was not put into effect before the great German attack put everything back into the melting pot.

On the second question of an eastern as opposed to western strategy, Clemenceau was adamantly opposed to Lloyd George's strategic conceptions, and firmly wedded to the professional soldier's view that the Germans had to be beaten on the western front. Concentration on the western front was even more vital now that the Germans had numerical

---

[50] Archives Nationales, C 7499, 12 December 1917. Clemenceau's remarks on this occasion, and those which he made before the External Affairs committee on 19 December 1917 (Archives Nationales, C 7490), are very illuminating for his views on strategy. On 19 December 1917 he said that the great danger was that the Germans would separate the British and French armies: it was essential that there should be perfect liaison between them, but it was difficult to achieve in practice.

[51] J. Terraine, D. Haig, The Educated Soldier (1963), pp. 390–2; M. P. A. Hankey, op. cit., II, pp. 752–5.

superiority there. The British representatives on the Versailles board put forward Joint Note 12, which reflected Lloyd George's views about the advantages of an offensive against Turkey. Weygand, the French representative, insisted on the addition of an 'annexure', which presented Foch's plan for a vigorous counter-offensive on the western front, and was in complete contradiction with the ideas outlined in Joint Note 12 itself, and also with the views of Haig and Pétain.[52] The latter regarded both proposals as equally unrealistic, as they knew they would need every man they had, merely to resist the expected German attack on the western front.

The third issue was bound up with the proposal to create a general reserve from among the troops in France. This was an essential part of Foch's scheme for reacting to the German threat by a strong counter-offensive. Clemenceau told the Parliamentary committees in December that the creation of this strategic reserve was essential, and he continued to work for it. He had to accept, however, that the British refusal to concentrate on the western front meant that it had to be postponed. As for the immediate situation, he generally accepted Pétain's views, although, as he told the Army committees in February, he had criticized some of Pétain's decisions about the creation of defensive systems involving three or four lines of trenches.[53]

All these questions were debated at the Supreme War Council at Versailles from 30 January to 2 February.[54] After long discussion of the manpower question, there followed a debate on grand strategy, based on Joint Note 12. Clemenceau began by stating that maintenance of the number of troops in France was a necessary condition and that previous discussion had revealed that this could not be achieved; the proposals for a Turkish offensive therefore automatically lapsed. Lloyd George objected to this dismissal of his favourite scheme, claiming that they had always over-insured on the western front. It had been abundantly shown that neither side could break through there, and that the

---

[52] Joint Note 12 is printed in *History of the Great War based on Official Documents, Military Operations, France and Belgium, 1918, Appendices* (1935), as Appendix 9, pp. 37–42, with the Annexure as Appendix 10. pp. 43–4. L. Amery states that he drafted Joint Note 12, *My Political Life* (1953–5), I, p. 136. The best account of these deliberations is provided by the official histories, *Military Operations France and Belgium* (1918), I, pp. 57–90, and *Les Armées Françaises dans la Grande Guerre*, VI, i, pp. 42–91.

[53] Archives Nationales, C 7499, Commission de l'Armée de la Chambre des Députés, 15 February 1918. Archives of the Senate, Commission de l'Armée, Auditions des Ministres, 20 February 1918. Cf. J. J. H. Mordacq, op. cit., I, pp. 139–42. S. Ryan, *Pétain the Soldier* (1963), p. 152, and R. Griffiths, *Marshal Pétain* (1970), p. 156, give an exaggerated account, derived from J. de Pierrefeu, *G.Q.G. Secteur 1* (1920), II, p. 111, of the degree to which Clemenceau was in conflict with Pétain.

[54] The minutes of these meetings are at the Public Record Office, CAB 28/3, IC 38–IC 44. Cf. also, Callwell op. cit., II, p. 55, D. F. Trask, op. cit., pp. 53–9, Maréchal F. Foch, *Mémoires* (1931), II, pp. xlvii–liii, M. Weygand, *Mémoires* (1952–6), I, pp. 450–9, P. Guinn, *British Strategy and Politics, 1914–1918* (1965), pp. 284–90.

only way to victory was to defeat Germany's weaker partners. Clemenceau completely disagreed:

> The security of the western front overrode all other considerations The treason of Russia (he used the word deliberately) had exposed the Allies to the greatest danger they had yet met. His plan was to hold out this year, 1918, till the American assistance came in full force; after that America would win the war. He protested against embarking on this eastern adventure when so dreadful a danger was imminent near to Paris.[55]

Lloyd George protested that with the present balance of forces the Allies were taking fewer risks than the Germans had done in previous years; did Clemenceau actually propose that we abandon Jerusalem, Baghdad and Salonika, for the sake of the relatively small additions this would make to their effectives in France? Discussion continued for a long time, and eventually at the next session a compromise formula (of the type known in French domestic politics as *nègre-blanc*) was agreed. This stated:

> The Supreme War Council accepts Joint Note 12 of the military representatives on the plan of campaign, the British government having made it clear that in utilizing in the most effective fashion the forces already at its disposal in the eastern theatre, it had no intention of diverting forces from the western front.[56]

Clemenceau then asked Robertson if he had anything to say. To Lloyd George's intense annoyance he obliged by declaring that he thought a Turkish offensive would be very dangerous.

Debate then moved to Foch's plan for a counter-offensive. Pétain stated that no offensive could be contemplated unless more troops were provided, and that there must be some overriding authority to organize the attack. Clemenceau said that they could not again dismiss the question of effectives, and that the Supreme War Council would provide the necessary coordination. Then the creation of a general reserve was discussed. The soldiers were unenthusiastic, and proposed that if a reserve were created it should be under the control of the chiefs-of-staff of each ally. Clemenceau argued in favour of a general reserve and said that

> in the conditions proposed by Cadorna and Pétain, he did not understand of what the Inter-Allied reserve would consist. Each general

---

[55] Public Record Office, CAB 28/3, IC 40. Clemenceau told the Army Committee of the Chamber on 27 March 1918 that 'Lloyd George had said that my speech was "dramatic". It was not my speech that was dramatic but the situation to which it alluded. I said to Milner the other day "now Mr Lloyd George has his drama under his nose".' Archives Nationales, C 7500.
[56] Public Record Office, CAB 28/3, IC 41.

would have a reserve of his own. In this scheme he did not see how the great army of reserves, which he wanted, was to be created. . . .[57]

Eventually, on 2 February, it was agreed to create a reserve army smaller than the forty divisions at first suggested, and to place it under the control of the permanent military representatives at Versailles, now renamed the Executive War Board, with Foch as chairman. Clemenceau raised the question of a further extension of the British line in France, and it was agreed that the British front should be extended to the river Ailette. Pétain, however, told Haig that he would not seek implementation of this and in fact the British line was never extended beyond Barisis.[58]

The upshot was that Lloyd George's plan for a Turkish campaign had not really been endorsed, and that Foch had been given some scope to influence strategic decisions on the western front. But this was soon to be rendered void. Lloyd George, in his memoirs, argues that Clemenceau was hostile to Foch, and that as a result he at once began to help Haig and Pétain to sabotage the decisions reached at these meetings.[59] This is a travesty of the facts. He states that Clemenceau was hostile to Foch because of the latter's Catholicism. This is obviously not true. Clemenceau had shown, years before, when he appointed Foch as the head of the *Ecole Supérieure de Guerre*, that he would not let such considerations override his respect for Foch as a soldier. Still less would he do so at this critical moment. In fact, Clemenceau was eager to have Foch in control of a strategic *masse de manœuvre*, a reserve army of realistic dimensions. This is not to say that he supported Foch against Pétain in all his conceptions. He was convinced of the basic correctness of Pétain's defensive attitude, and fully aware of the desperate shortage of fighting troops on the western front, something Foch tended to ignore in his grandiose visions of a developing counter-offensive.[60] Milner pro-

[57] Public Record Office, CAB 28s, IC 42.
[58] Public Record Office, CAB 28/3, IC 43.
[59] D. Lloyd George, *War Memoirs* (1938), II, p. 1716–7. J. C. King, op. cit., p. 205, following Lloyd George and the very unreliable P. E. Wright, *At the Supreme War Council* (1921), gives a very inadequate account of Clemenceau's role at this time. On Wright, *see* S. Roskill, op. cit., I, p. 491.
[60] Clemenceau told the Parliamentary committees that he thought that Pétain was too defensive, and Foch perhaps too optimistic, 'but in any case he puts heart in everybody'. His statement to the Senate committee about the reserve army illuminates his view of this question. He told them that its organization would require three months, that is, that it would be ready for the counter-offensive when the Germans had weakened themselves in the expected attacks. Archives Nationales, Commission de l'Armée de la Chambre des Députés, C 7499, 15 February 1918, Archives of the Senate, Commission de l'Armée, Auditions des Ministres, 20 February 1918. For further evidence of Clemenceau's view of Foch, *see* his remarks to the Parliamentary committee quoted above, p. 293 n., E. E. Herbillon, *Du général en chef au gouvernement, souvenirs d'un officier de liaison* (1930), J. J. H. Mordacq, op. cit., I, pp. 186–7, and A. Tardieu, *La Paix* (1921), p. 43, reporting a conversation of 20 December 1917. Clemenceau stated in *Grandeurs et Misères d'une Victoire* (1930), p. 19, that there was never any question of anyone but Foch for the post of Allied commander-in-chief.

bably characterized Clemenceau's attitude very well, in a letter of February 1921,

> It is not quite fair to Clemenceau to say that he was ever 'personally hostile' to Foch, or supported Pétain against him. The hostility between Foch and Clemenceau was of much later growth. When I went to France in March, Clemenceau was, I think, much divided in mind between Pétain and Foch, but he was certainly leaning to the opinion that Pétain, a splendid man in his way, was not taking a broad view of the situation.[61]

Lloyd George's account is an elaborate smokescreen to hide the fact that he was himself mainly responsible for the failure to create a general reserve. He had to bow before Haig's refusal to assign it any troops, because this was the price Haig exacted for acquiescing in the sacking of Robertson. Lloyd George could not face losing both his commander-in-chief and his chief-of-staff at the same time, and his first priority was to replace Robertson by Sir Henry Wilson as C.I.G.S. This occurred on 16 February, and from this time the plan for a general reserve under the control of Foch and the Versailles committee ran into the sands.[62]

On 22 February Clemenceau told Poincaré that difficulties had arisen between Foch and Pétain, but that if a crisis came he (Clemenceau) would be there to arrange things.[63] Poincaré was not comforted by this prospect of Clemenceau in supreme command. On the same day Haig's and Pétain's staff met to finalise their arrangements for mutual support when the inevitable German attack came, ignoring Foch and his committee altogether. Two days later Clemenceau paid a visit to Haig's H.Q., and learnt that he had refused to hand over any divisions. Haig's diary notes that Clemenceau's reaction to this news was as follows:

> My statement indicated his line of action. He would arrange to '*écarter*' [set aside] Foch gradually. He personally looked upon a close agreement between Pétain and myself as the surest guarantee of success.[64]

It is not likely, however, that this was Clemenceau's real view of the situation. On 27 February he told Mordacq that he wanted Foch as supreme commander, but that the British would not agree.[65]

The arrangements made by Haig and Pétain were confirmed at the

[61] Milner Papers, 146.
[62] P. Guinn, op. cit., p. 297.
[63] R. Poincaré, op. cit., X, p. 58.
[64] R. Blake, op. cit., p. 288.
[65] J. J. H. Mordacq, op. cit., I, pp. 185–7.

next meeting of the Supreme War Council in London (14–16 March) over the prolonged and violent protests of Foch. Most of these protests are not noted in the minutes, but Haig's diary states that

> in reply to Lloyd George's question if anyone had anything further to say, General Foch asked leave to speak. He stated that he 'objected to the whole resolution'. This led to a wordy altercation between Clemenceau and him, which finally ended by C. waving his hand and shouting 'silence'. Clemenceau then thoroughly sat on Foch![66]

A week later the Germans made their expected attack, at dawn on 21 March.[67] It was more successful than even the most pessimistic on the Allied side had feared. The most dangerous feature of the situation was that the Germans were on the verge of capturing Amiens, which would have paralysed vital communications. It was easy to envisage that the Germans would be able to separate the British and French armies. If that happened they could deal in turn with the two separate and much weaker enemy forces. The German breakthrough at once revealed the inadequacy of the arrangements for mutual support made by Haig and Pétain. While Haig wanted Pétain to move all his reserves over to the left to fill up the breach opening between British and French, Pétain was afraid that this attack was only a feint, a prelude to another German attack on the French front much further to the east. Pétain thought that the breach had been opened by the British retreating west and north, so that they could fall back on the channel ports, instead of maintaining contact with the French armies by retreating southwards. The defeat was so great that information was very slow to filter back to Haig, and on 22 March he was still not unduly disturbed. But on the 23rd he visited 5th Army H.Q. and realized the gravity of the situation: that afternoon he met Pétain and appealed for large-scale French support.[68]

By this time rumours of a grave defeat had reached London and Paris. In Paris Clemenceau told Poincaré of the serious situation, and said that he had paid a visit to the Chamber, where he had walked up and down the antechambers 'with a smile on my face' to restore confidence.[69] His own confidence was to be severely tested that evening by a visit to Pétain's H.Q. at Compiègne, during which the commander-in-chief prophesied defeat. Clemenceau said to Mordacq, on their return

[66] R. Blake, op. cit., p. 293; cf. S. Roskill, op. cit., p. 509, C. E. Callwell, op. cit., II, p. 71. The official minutes of the meetings are available at the Public Record Office, CAB 28/3 IC 47–IC 50.
[67] Accounts of the fighting are to be found in *Military Operations, France and Belgium, 1918*, I, pp. 170–544, and *Les Armées Françaises dans la Grande Guerre*, VI, I, pp. 231–327.
[68] J. Terraine, op. cit., pp. 419–21.
[69] R. Poincaré, op. cit., X, p. 81.

journey, 'After an interview like that, you need an iron-bound spirit to retain your confidence'.[70] It is significant for Pétain's actions at this time that he was already pessimistic about Allied chances, even before the German attack. At least a police report of 20 March stated that rumours coming from the G.O.G. had it that

> while Clemenceau counts on the army to finish the war, Pétain is convinced that the war can only be ended by negotiations in the near future: he would rather have a diplomatic than a military offensive.[71]

Next day Clemenceau again met Pétain at Compiègne. He learnt that there was a gap between the British and French into which the Germans were advancing.[72]

Haig was now highly alarmed at Pétain's decisions; his diary records, after a meeting with Pétain on the night of 24 March:

> I gathered that he had recently attended a Cabinet meeting in Paris, and that his orders from his Government are to 'cover Paris at all costs'. On the other hand, to keep in touch with the British Army is no longer the basic principle of French strategy.[73]

On learning this he telegraphed Sir Henry Wilson, asking him to come over to France with Milner, 'to arrange that Foch, or some other determined general who would fight, be given supreme control of operations in France'.[74]

Early in the morning of the 25th, Mordacq found Clemenceau 'very calm and confident, master of himself, but naturally a little anxious'. He told Mordacq that this time he was determined to achieve unity of command.[75] At 10 a.m. he met Milner, already despatched to France before Haig's telegram arrived. They both went, together with Loucheur and Poincaré, to meet Pétain and Haig at Compiègne. Milner states that Clemenceau told him that 'it was necessary at all costs to maintain the connection between the British and French armies, and that both Haig and Pétain must at once throw in their reserves to stop the breach'. He added that 'it would be necessary to bring pressure to bear upon Pétain

---

[70] J. J. H. Mordacq, op. cit., I, p. 228.

[71] Archives Nationales, F⁷ 13950, 2, fol. 192.

[72] R. Poincaré, op. cit., X, pp. 84–6; J. J. H. Mordacq, op. cit., I, pp. 232–6.

[73] R. Blake, op. cit., p. 297. Pétain's orders, on the evening of 24 March, which so alarmed Haig, are printed in Les Armées Françaises dans la Grande Guerre, VI, 1, pp. 287–8, and in Military Operations France and Belgium, 1918, I, pp. 448–50.

[74] Pétain had not attended a cabinet meeting but had been in frequent contact with Clemenceau. G. Pedroncini assumes that Clemenceau approved of Pétain's decisions, but produces no evidence for this, op. cit., p. 1197.

[75] J. J. H. Mordacq, op. cit., I, p. 236.

to do more in that direction'.[76] The meeting took place in the late afternoon, but without Haig and Wilson, who had not been informed in time. Without them, no decision could be taken.

The decisive meeting took place the next morning, 26 March, at the town hall of the little town of Doullens, north of Amiens, within earshot of the battle. Once again the politicians drove out from Paris to meet the military commanders. Clemenceau arrived early, and talked with Pétain before the official meeting commenced. The latter's pessimism convinced Clemenceau that it was essential to bring Foch in. Clemenceau said to Poincaré, who arrived a little later:

> Can you imagine what he said to me, something which I would not repeat to anyone except you? It is this: 'the Germans will defeat the English in open country, after which they will defeat us'. Should a general talk, or even think, like that?[77]

The meeting began at noon, with Poincaré in the chair. Haig and Pétain outlined their plans, Pétain's pessimism again producing a bad effect on everyone. His exposé was followed by a moment of silence, after which Clemenceau took Milner into the window bay, and whispered to him. Milner then spoke to Haig, asking him if he would accept Foch's control, while at the same time Clemenceau spoke to Pétain. Haig gladly agreed, and then Clemenceau wrote out a draft stating that

> General Foch is charged by the British and French governments with the coordination of the action of the British and French armies in front of Amiens.

Haig at once pointed out that Foch could achieve nothing unless he had authority over all operations on the western front, and the draft was altered to this effect, and the words 'Allied armies' substituted for 'French and British armies'.[78] As Clemenceau told the Army committee

[76] Public Record Office, CAB 28/3, IC 53. Memorandum by Lord Milner on his visit to France, conference at Doullens, 26 March 1918. Milner's account has long been known from the excerpts published in the New Statesman, 23 April 1921. Other accounts now available are L. Loucheur, Carnets Secrets, ed. J. de Launay (Brussels, 1962), pp. 50–61, of which excerpts were published in L'Illustration, 24 March 1928, and Clemenceau's long report to the Army committee of the Chamber on 27 March, Archives Nationales, C 7500, as well as the older accounts of R. Poincaré, op. cit., X, pp. 86–90, and J. J. H. Mordacq, op. cit., I, pp. 236–46, who also gave a more detailed account in Le Commandement Unique (1929).
[77] R. Poincaré, op. cit., p. 88. G. Pedroncini argues that Pétain has been unjustly treated with respect to his conduct at this time. But he ignores the psychological aspect; Pétain's pessimistic attitude had created a very bad impression on all involved, and this alone ruled him out as commander-in-chief. G. Pedroncini, op. cit., pp. 1171–266. A brief résumé of Pedroncini's position is provided in the report of his soutenance de thèse, Le Monde, 9 June 1971.
[78] Public Record Office, CAB/23, IC 53; another version in the Milner Papers, 146. Cf. J. J. H. Mordacq, op. cit., I, p. 245.

of the Chamber the next day, as soon as the paper was signed, Haig and Pétain appeared relieved of immense anxiety :

> They acted like a dog shaking itself when it comes out of the water. They both gave a sigh of relief. . . . General Pétain had had the feeling that something was lacking in the support he was receiving, and Marshal Haig had felt the same. Now there was a man between them responsible for this outside support, and who could distribute it to right and left in the common interest and without quarrelling with them.[79]

Foch at once set off to visit the army commanders, and ordered Fayolle, now given command of the group of reserve armies being brought into action, to remain in contact with the British at all costs.[80] Foch's appointment could not, of course, miraculously provide immediate material assistance. It took time to bring up reserves, but the effect on the morale of the commanders was immense. The German attack was already faltering, and on 5 April the first stage of the battle came to an end. Clemenceau remained very active, making almost daily visits to the front, and to the H.Q.s of Foch, Haig and Pétain. In between he sought to re-establish confidence in Paris by visiting the Chamber, informally, and by addressing the committees.[81]

2 CONDUCT OF THE WAR, APRIL–JULY 1918

Another inter-Allied meeting was held at Beauvais on 3 April.[82] On this occasion Foch's powers were enlarged, so that he could order offensive action, and American acceptance of his position was secured. A few days later he was given the official title of 'commander-in-chief of the Allied

[79] Archives Nationales, Commission de l'Armée de la Chambre des Députés, C 7500, 27 March 1918.

[80] *Military Operations, France and Belgium* (1918), II, pp. 6–8 and *Les Armées Françaises dans la Grande Guerre*, VI, 1, *Annexes* 2, Annexe 764, p. 280, and Annexe 791, p. 306. An amusing sidelight on the question of whether it was Foch or Pétain who saved the situation is provided by Fayolle's diary entry for 30 March 1918 : 'Foch is there at Beauvais ready to say if we succeed "I won the battle". Pétain, on his side, if the plan fails, will say "It was not my fault". The truth is that Foch conceived a plan, Pétain provided the means of executing it, and that I am the one who actually has to conduct the battle.' General Fayolle, *Carnets Secrets de la Grande Guerre*, ed. H. Contamine (1964), p. 266.

[81] On 28 March Clemenceau visited Foch's H.Q.; on 29 March he went to the front at Montdidier and to Pétain's H.Q. On 30 March, he made a long tour in the company of Winston Churchill, to Foch's H.Q., then to meet Haig, then to the front, and then to Pétain's H.Q. On 1 April he again visited Foch and Haig, and went to the front line, where he was under shellfire, and nearly killed. J. J. H. Mordacq, op. cit., I, pp. 247–64. He spoke to the Chamber committee of the Army on 27 March and 5 April, and to the Senate committee on 23 March and 5 April.

[82] Public Record Office, CAB/28/3, IC 55 and 55A. Cf. also J. J. Pershing *My Experiences in the World War* (1931), pp. 329–36. Clemenceau reported on the Beauvais meeting to both Senate and Chamber Army committees on 5 April; Archives of the Senate, Commission de l'Armée, Auditions des Ministres, and Archives Nationales, C 7500.

armies in France.' But it would be a mistake to regard Foch as really exercising the powers of a genuine commander-in-chief, whatever his title. British, American and French armies were still, in the last resort, under the command of their respective governments, and provision had been made for their commanders to appeal against Foch's orders if they thought the security of their armies was being threatened. More important was the practical matter that Foch did not have the staff to exercise an effective detailed command, and he was never in a position to issue proper executive orders. His orders were general exhortations, usually of the variety – 'never yield an inch of ground', or 'all-out attack on all fronts'. In June Sir Henry Wilson became very sarcastic about Foch's orders not to yield an inch. which were followed by the precipitate French retreat from the Chemin des Dames to Château-Thierry. Wilson wrote to Lloyd George on 21 June 1918:

> Foch has as his principal, I might almost say, only, Staff Officer, Weygand. . . . Being away from French GHQ and our GHQ he was not fully informed as to the position of affairs, the state of the railways . . . and a thousand other things which only a large staff of trained men can deal with. As a consequence orders were often issued which it was quite impossible, impracticable or inadvisable to carry out.[83]

Foch remained an inspirer and coordinator, rather than a commander. This was an important role, but as Liddell Hart put it,

> in the actual conduct of the battle it is more difficult to put one's finger on any point where Foch had a definite effect, either in accelerating the arrival of reinforcements, or in parrying enemy thrusts. . . . Foch's instructions were drawn up in broad outline, comprehensive yet insubstantial. They were exhortations, rather than specific directions.[84]

Thus Clemenceau still had a role to play in coordinating the Allied military effort. It could not be left entirely to Foch. The first German attack was broken off on 5 April, but on 9 April another onslaught commenced on the British line further to the north. Already, on 8 April, Haig had appealed to the cabinet against Foch's refusal to move adequate reserves to the north. At the worst of the German attack Haig felt that he was being left in the lurch by Foch. In response to his appeals, the British cabinet decided to send Milner across the channel

[83] Lloyd George Papers, F/47/7/28; C. E. Callwell, op. cit., II, p. 105. Cf. the discussion of 17 June 1918, recorded in the 'X' series of cabinet minutes: Public Record Office, CAB 23/17 (x14); on these informal discussions between Lloyd George, Milner, Wilson, Hankey and Amery, see S. Roskill, op. cit., p. 533; Lloyd George decided to press Clemenceau for the formation of a genuinely inter-allied staff, under Foch, but nothing came of this.
[84] B. H. Liddell Hart, Foch, the Man of Orleans (1931), p. 289; cf. J. Terraine, op. cit., p. 426. G. Pedroncini argues, op. cit., pp. 1267–8 and 1406–90 that Foch's role was to make mistakes from which Pétain rescued the allies.

again. On 15 April he met Clemenceau and Foch at Beauvais.[85] In spite of Milner's arguments, Foch, with Clemenceau's support, refused to allow his reserves to be dissipated by using them before the Germans had made a decisive breach in the British line. He thought, correctly, that Ludendorff was holding back the bulk of his strength for an attack on the French much farther south.

Towards the end of April the German attacks died away. The next meeting of the Supreme War Council was held at Abbeville on 1–2 May.[86] Among much else the situation on the western front was discussed, and it was agreed that, if the Germans were able to break the British line, Haig should order a retreat southwards, so as to remain in contact with the French, even at the risk of losing the Channel ports. It was agreed that, in the last resort, it was essential to keep the two armies together. Another subject of discussion was the employment of the American troops. Clemenceau was not at his most tactful in these debates, and he had a violent dispute with Milner, the new British minister of war, over an agreement with Pershing, the American commander-in-chief, by which six American divisions were to go to the British sector. In the end it was agreed that the American troops disembarked in May and June should go to the British sector in view of Haig's desperate need for immediate reinforcement, but that arrivals from July onwards should be disposed according to Allied agreement to be reached at a later date. In his report to the Parliamentary committees, Clemenceau was very critical of the British high command. He told them that, after a taste of fighting with the British, the Americans would soon be clamouring to be incorporated in the French sector. But, whatever the fighting troops may have thought, Pershing was determined to form a separate American army as soon as possible.

Lloyd George agreed at this meeting to allow a French military planner, Colonel Roure, to visit London to advise the British on manpower mobilization. In other words he was to check whether the British argument, that they could not utilize a higher proportion of their manpower without jeopardizing essential parts of the economic war-effort, was justified. Others on the British side were highly indignant at Lloyd George's concession; Derby called Clemenceau's demand 'a great piece of impudence',[87] and Milner asked sarcastically : 'Did Clemenceau intend

---

[85] J. J. H. Mordacq, op. cit., I, pp. 300–4. This informal meeting is not minuted in the IC series. Cf. J. Terraine, op. cit., pp. 431–2, and *Les Armées Françaises dans la Grande Guerre*, VI, 1, pp. 455–8.

[86] Public Record Office, CAB 28/3. IC 56–9. Clemenceau reported on the Abbeville discussions to the Army committee of the Chamber on 7 May, and to the Army committee of the Senate on 8 May, Archives Nationales, C 7500, and Archives of the Senate, Commission de l'Armée, Auditions des Ministres. Cf. also J. J. Pershing, op. cit., pp. 372–87. G. Pedroncini, op. cit., p. 1306, J. J. H. Mordacq, op. cit., II, pp. 3–8, S. Roskill, op. cit., p. 536 and D. F. Trask, op. cit., pp. 85–9.

[87] Derby to Balfour, 1 May 1918, Lloyd George Papers, F/52/1/31.

to organize the British army?' Perhaps Lloyd George agreed to Clemenceau's proposal, as part of his quarrel with the military experts, on the question of manpower, which culminated in the famous Maurice debate of 9 May 1918. At any rate, he gave Clemenceau to understand that he sympathized with his case.[88] Clemenceau wrote to Lloyd George on 16 May, and returned to the charge at the meeting of the Supreme War Council of 1–3 June 1918, at which Foch presented a memorandum showing that the French were making a much greater effort than the British: 'At the moment of decisive effort on the part of the enemy, the strength of the British army is decreasing day by day. It even decreases more rapidly than that of the American army increases.'[89] Clemenceau put the strongest pressure on Lloyd George to increase British effectives in France. He said

> The French had lost two million men in this war, nevertheless, they intended to maintain 100 divisions, even if they had to fill them up with niggers.

Lloyd George replied that

> he thought we could keep up our divisions if we incorporated niggers.

Clemenceau said

> he did not mind how we did it. The French had Moroccans and Czechs, and would have Ethiopians if they could get them. If you took 1,000 Frenchmen between the ages of 19 and 41, you will find that 662 were in fighting units, whereas in Britain it was 487.[90]

The upshot was that Lloyd George agreed to another visit from Colonel Roure, with increased powers to investigate British methods of recruitment. Clemenceau told the Army committee of the Chamber on 3 June 1918 that these powers would allow him to overcome the resistance of the British high command, 'unless good faith has been altogether banished from human transactions'. On 19 June he was again telling the Army committee of the Chamber that the British had accepted

[88] According to Clemenceau's report to the Army committee of the Chamber, on 3 June 1918, Archives Nationales, C 7500.

[89] Clemenceau's letter to Lloyd George is reproduced in *Grandeurs et Misères d'une Victoire*, pp. 80–4. Foch's memorandum is printed as an appendix to the minutes of the Supreme War Council of 1 June 1918, Public Record Office, CAB 28/3, IC 63B. A copy of a letter of 20 May 1918 from Clemenceau to Milner on the same theme, is in the Archives of the Ministry of War, Fonds Clemenceau, carton 59.

[90] Public Record Office, CAB 28/3, IC 63B, minutes of meeting of 1 June 1918. The reference to Ethiopians was not hyperbole: the French government had for some time been trying to arrange for the use of Ethiopian mercenary troops, and Clemenceau had bitterly commented on the objections raised by the Italians and the British.

all Colonel Roure's recommendations.[91] In fact the British reaction was very different. Lloyd George spoke indignantly in the cabinet about Clemenceau's attempt to force the British to increase their effectives in France. He claimed that Foch was using his powers as commander-in-chief to achieve this end. He said:

The French were intending to get the whole of the American army into their sector. He was convinced that this was part of the political game which Foch was playing at Clemenceau's instigation. The object of it was, by depriving us of the support of the American troops, to force us to keep up our present total of 59 divisions, regardless of the effect upon our industries and national life generally. It was intolerable that the French should attempt to put the screw on us in that way and he was determined that if this continued, he would ask the authority of the cabinet to refuse the French any ships for the conveyance of American troops to France.[92]

On the same day Clemenceau told the Army committee of the Chamber that the British had not, after all, followed Roure's suggestions, and that he found their latest proposals unacceptable; what they amounted to was that the British and French should demobilize, and let the Americans finish the war.[93] He told the committee that he would continue to argue with Lloyd George, 'going to the absolute edge of rupture, for he could not accept a breach at any price'. His letter to Lloyd George of 17 August shows that he was disturbed lest relative military strength at the end of the war might have a decisive effect on the peace terms. If Britain and France did not maintain their military strength, America would be able to act as arbitrator:

No one appreciates more than I the value of American assistance. But our old Europe, which engaged in war without counting on that help, cannot consider the possibility of 'passing the hand' to its transAtlantic ally for the completion of the military task which will found a new Europe.[94]

[91] Archives Nationales, C 7500. Clemenceau said on 3 June that as soon as Lloyd George made his offer, he got him to confirm it in writing: this is presumably the sheet of notepaper, headed Conseil Supérieur de Guerre, in the Fonds Clemenceau at the ministry of war, Dossier President du Conseil, II, 13 bis, on which is scrawled in pencil: 'If an officer nominated by the Prés. du Conseil can come at once and show us where and how to find more men I will instruct Sir Auckland Geddes and the War Office to communicate to him every list in our possession. No one will be more grateful than ourselves if he can help us to improve our position as far as manpower is concerned.'
[92] Public Record Office, CAB 23/17, X20 of 12 July, and X25 of 26 July, 1918.
[93] Archives Nationales, C 7500.
[94] Clemenceau to Lloyd George, 17 August 1918, Lloyd George Papers, F/50/3/15. Lloyd George's reply of 31 August 1918, F/50/3/17, and Clemenceau's reply, n.d., F/50/3/18. Cf. also Derby to Balfour, 27 August 1918, Lloyd George Papers, F/52/2/29, reporting a conversation with Clemenceau about the manpower question.

Lloyd George refused to enter into these considerations, and replied that 'the reserves of the Allied army are in America'; the best way to utilize Allied manpower, he said, was for British and French industry to continue working at full stretch to provide munitions for their own armies and for the Americans. These discussions, based on the premise that the war would only end in 1919, were brought to an end by the German demand for an armistice in October 1918.

Although the argument about British manpower continued almost to the end, tension between the British and French governments was greatest in the crisis days of May and June, especially in the period that followed the second German breakthrough of 27 May. Although this rapid advance had a shattering effect on morale in Paris, for geographical reasons it was not as dangerous as the earlier German successes against the British line. Again Clemenceau was to be seen in the corridors of the Chamber of Deputies, seeking to restore confidence by appearing confident himself. But many politicians thought that his ministry was about to fall.[95] In these dramatic days he was in his element, rushing to and fro between Paris and as near to the front line as he could get, then on to Foch's and Pétain's H.Q.s, and then back to Paris.[96] His sheer physical vitality was not the least remarkable feature of this performance.

He had to interrupt these excursions for the meeting of the Supreme War Council at Versailles from 1–3 June, at which British and French recriminations reached a new peak of bitterness.[97] The French were convinced that British failure to reinforce their armies in France was the cause of the repeated Allied defeats. Clemenceau and Foch went to the limit in their pressure upon the British in increase their strength. For their part the British felt that Foch was too much a French general to act as a genuine Allied commander, and feared that he gave more consideration to French than to British interests.[98] They were at odds about policy in Russia, and there was also disagreement between Britain and Italy about naval command in the Mediterranean.[99]

Although no word of this was breathed to the French, the British

---

[95] Cf. Derby to Balfour, 17 June 1918, Lloyd George Papers, F/52/2/5.
[96] J. J. H. Mordacq, op. cit., II, pp. 42–84, for the diary of Clemenceau's activities between 28 May and 16 June; he visited the front or the various military H.Q.s on 28, 29, 30, 31 May, and 5, 6, 8, 15 and 16 June.
[97] Minutes of these meetings are available at the Public Record Office, CAB 28/3, IC 63B–68.
[98] Complaints about Foch's decisions recur frequently in the secret discussions of Lloyd George and his military advisers: they culminated in the cabinet decision of 11 July 1918 that 'the prime minister should write to Clemenceau informing him that Foch was an *Allied* not merely a French Commander-in-Chief, and that he must make his dispositions from that point of view, not merely from the point of view of French interests'. Public Record Office, CAB/23/14, WC 444A.
[99] On discussions about policy in Russia, *see below*, pp. 322–4.

were at this point contemplating what action to take if the French army collapsed entirely. They had little confidence in its fighting capacity. A 'Dunkirk'-type operation to rescue the British troops in France was considered, and the wider strategic implications of a French defeat were also mooted. A letter from Milner to Lloyd George, of 9 June 1918, shows how minds were moving:

> We must be prepared for France and Italy both being beaten to their knees. In that case the Germano-Austro-Turko-Bulgar block will be master of all Europe and Northern and Central Asia up to the point at which Japan steps in to bar the way, if she does step in, and has not been choked off by the more than disastrous diplomacy of the Allies. It is clear that unless the only remaining free peoples of the world, America, this country and the Dominions, are knit together in the closest conceivable alliance, and prepared for the maximum of sacrifice, the central bloc, under the hegemony of Germany, will control not only Europe and most of Asia, but the whole world. . . . The fight will now be for southern Asia, and above all for Africa (the Palestine bridgehead is of immense importance) and success may depend on what supplies we can get from India and Australia. Last year we discussed terms of peace. If this year, we were seriously to consider the necessities of the New War it would be more to the purpose. . . . All this depends on what America will do. Is not the time approaching when we should try to find out what she *will* do in case of collapse of the Continental campaign against Germany?[100]

Clemenceau could not know of these deliberations. But British actions spoke louder than words, and Lloyd George's hankering after a strategy centred on the Middle East was no secret. Clemenceau complained that Britain was jeopardizing the Allied position in France, in order to foster these extra-European schemes. Britain might be able to survive a German victory on the western front, but France could not. Hence his desperate insistence on getting every available soldier into the trenches of France and Flanders.

Clemenceau had to turn from these inter-Allied discussions to the re-establishment of his government's authority at home. On 3 June he met the Army committee of the Chamber and explained the military situation. He admitted that mistakes had been made, and promised the fullest investigation, but was not prepared to see the sacrifice of any scapegoat generals unless negligence were proved. The middle of the

---

[100] Milner Papers, 145, Milner to Lloyd George, 9 June 1918, and the discussions of 30 May, 5 June, and 28 June 1918, Public Record Office, CAB 23/17, X6, X8, and X18. Cf. G. L. Cook, 'Sir Robert Borden, Lloyd George and British Military Policy 1917–1918', *Historical Journal*, XIV (1971), pp. 371–95.

battle was not the moment, in any case, to change commanders.[101] He reiterated these views in public debate in the Chamber the next day.[102] Only the left-wing section of the Socialists expressed open opposition, and the government received its usual majority. In his later quarrel with Foch, Clemenceau could justifiably point to the way he had covered Foch and Pétain with his own authority at this critical moment. He stated categorically that he would resign at once rather than endorse any criticisms of them. The atmosphere was very different from that fourteen months earlier, after the failure of the Nivelle offensive.

Three days later he was once more negotiating with the British. Haig had again appealed to the British cabinet against a decision of Foch.[103] Milner and Wilson, together with Haig, met Foch and Clemenceau at the ministry of war in Paris. Haig feared another major German attack, and stated that Foch must either give him more support, or authorize him to withdraw so as to shorten his line. Foch would do neither, and refused to budge, as he judged that the next German offensive would come, as it did, further to the south, against the French. Haig was also incensed that Foch had ordered the withdrawal of some French troops, previously moved into reserve behind the British lines, without informing him. Clemenceau at once ruled in favour of Haig on this point; Foch must not issue orders directly. Milner reported that Clemenceau's tactful handling did a great deal to remove the friction between Foch and Haig:

> The effect of the meeting certainly was calculated to improve relations between Foch and the British Commander-in-Chief who always seem to get on quite well together when brought face to face. At the close of the meeting Clemenceau, whose conduct of it throughout had been extraordinarily skilful and conciliatory, laid great emphasis on this point. He said that he felt that what was most wanted was that Foch and Haig should meet one another more often. I think this is quite true, but I also think that what made the result of this particular meeting so satisfactory was the presence and influence of Clemenceau himself.[104]

At the next meeting of the Supreme War Council, on 2–4 July, there was more acrimonious discussion of the British manpower question, and of American reinforcements.[105] Lloyd George was annoyed when Tardieu

[101] Archives Nationales, C 7500.
[102] Annales de la Chambre des Députés, 4 June 1918, reprinted in G. Clemenceau, *Discours de Guerre*, pp. 236–60.
[103] Public Record Office, CAB 23/17, X7 and X8 of 5 June 1918.
[104] Milner Papers, 146, report on his visit to France, 6–8 June 1918.
[105] Public Record Office, CAB 28/3, IC 69–71, cf. D. F. Trask, op. cit., pp. 95 and 132–5.

raised the question of shipping arrangements for the transport of troops and supplies from America, arguing that, as all the shipping was either British or American, the French had no right to interfere. But the biggest row came because Clemenceau had given orders for the preparation of an offensive at Salonika, without consulting his allies. Clemenceau was not able to put up much of a case. Hankey, Lloyd George's invaluable administrative assistant, who organized the Secretariat for the Supreme War Council meetings, found the incident 'the more mysterious, as Clemenceau has always been, and still professes to be, a violent opponent of the Salonika expedition.' A more fundamental clash between British and French policy was, however, avoided. Hankey's diary reveals that he foresaw a head-on confrontation between the French insistence on the primacy of the western front, and Lloyd George's increasing determination to concentrate British effort in other areas. Hankey wrote:

> Lloyd George and c.i.g.s. [Sir Henry Wilson] want to take the offensive in Palestine in the autumn, which will necessitate the withdrawal of divisions from France. Foch wants himself to undertake certain operations of a secondary character, and will protest against any withdrawal of divisions from the Western Front, as he will want to keep them for an offensive next year. The question is whether to take your fight with Clemenceau and Foch now or later. Wilson thinks it is fairer to take it now. The Prime Minister and Milner are inclined to get everything ready in Palestine, and then in the autumn insist on withdrawing them. It is a matter of tactics.[106]

Only the collapse of the Central Powers in October 1918 prevented this divergence of views leading to a major clash.

Another proposal was to allow the Versailles war board, virtually functionless since Foch had taken over as commander-in-chief on the western front, to continue with the task of long-range strategic planning. Foch opposed this idea, which was supported by Clemenceau and by the British. At one point, Hankey reports, he got very angry with Foch and Weygand, exclaiming

> 'Ils me font fou' – and relapsing into English, 'When I am fou I usually try to kill someone – a general if possible.' Whereat the old boy of 78 began to chase Wilson round the room like a schoolboy.[107]

No doubt this sort of behaviour helped to relieve the tension, and smoothed the way to an agreed solution.

[106] Hankey's diary for 3 July 1918, part quoted in M. P. A. Hankey, *Supreme Command*, II, p. 821, and part in S. Roskill, op. cit., I, p. 520.
[107] M. P. A. Hankey, op. cit., II, p. 823.

It was already clear that the western front was much more secure than it had been, and Clemenceau was now willing to consider releasing troops for use in other theatres. A few days later, on 15 July, Ludendorff made a final attack and was met by a strong Allied counterattack. According to G. Wormser, Clemenceau was personally involved in authorizing the counter-attack, which for the first time placed the Germans on the defensive on the western front.[108] From that moment the situation evolved rapidly in favour of the Allies, and Clemenceau no longer needed to play the part in military decisions that he had between March and July. Foch, Haig and Pétain could be safely left to continue hammering at the German armies, while Clemenceau concentrated on raising the morale of the French troops.

Mordacq writes that

> Clemenceau wished to make his conviction, that the initiative had now passed to the Allies, enter into the brains, the souls and the hearts of the fighting troops. To that end he undertook, from late July and throughout the month of August, those frequent trips to the front which had such a great influence on the morale of the *poilus* and their leaders.[109]

He insisted on getting as near to the front line as possible, exposing himself on many occasions to considerable danger. Mordacq complained that such actions were silly; nevertheless he could not help but admire Clemenceau for them.[110] Clemenceau's speeches had impact because they obviously came from the heart, and because his reckless visits to the front showed that he was careless of his own life, however irrational such action might seem to be. These visits had deep emotional impact on Clemenceau himself. One in particular, made just before the last German offensive, he described on 2 October 1921, at the inauguration of the war memorial in his native village Ste Hermine:

> Hidden in folds of the ground, hairy heads, powdered with the dusty soil of Champagne, emerged fantastically from invisible machine-gun emplacements. . . . They greeted us! Sometimes only with their eyes, which burned with an invincible resolution. Impenetrable blocks of heroism, they were a rear guard, whose orders were to get themselves killed to the last man without ceasing fire. Through death to victory; everyone of them had understood. The terrible silence of hearts who had abandoned all chance of surviving to the triumph for

---

[108] G. Wormser, op. cit., pp. 300–1. This is, however, expressly denied by General Mordacq, who discusses the incident in detail, J. J. H. Mordacq, op. cit., II, pp. 122–5.
[109] J. J. H. Mordacq, op. cit., II, p. 134.
[110] Ibid., p. 171.

which they offered their life. . . . And slowly we continued our return to the plain, obsessed with the vision of those blue helmets, laden with tragedy, emerging from the hillside to inspect their inspectors, and returning, like *automata*, to the bowels of the earth to await the great confrontation between all the hopes of life and the sacrifice of everything forever. . . . Those lower down had time to prepare. . . . They came to meet the visitor, vague shapes all white with the dust, who made the gesture of lining up to give the military salute while their leader stepped forward and in staccato tones shouted out, 'Ist Company, 2nd batallion, 3rd regiment, present'! And with his rough hand he offered a little bouquet of chalky flowers. . . . Ah, those frail dried-up stalks. The Vendée will see them; for I have promised that they will go to the grave with me. . . . And the old man, choking with a superhuman emotion, grasped with all his strength that iron hand, and could only stammer incoherent words and swear that that little bunch of flowers, without colour and without sap, a pledge of the most sublime self-sacrifice to an ideal, would never leave him. He who has not lived through such moments does not know what life can give.[111]

The bouquet was preserved in his study until he died, and then was placed in his coffin.

[111] G. Clemenceau, *Discours à Ste Hermine* (1921), pp. 6–7, extracts quoted in J. J. H. Mordacq, *Clemenceau Au Soir de la vie* (1933), I, pp. 174–8.

16

RUSSIAN INTERVENTION
AND VICTORY

I INTERVENTION IN RUSSIA, 1918

Clemenceau's role in Allied deliberations about the Russian question from November 1917 to the armistice must now be dealt with.[112]

Ten days before Clemenceau formed his ministry the Bolsheviks seized power in Petrograd, ousting the provisional government headed by the democratic Socialist Kerensky, who had sought to keep Russia in the war. This meant a grave crisis for the Allies. The Bolshevik slogan, 'Peace, Land, Bread', indicated that they would extricate Russia from the war, if at all possible, and there was plenty of evidence that the Bolsheviks had been financed and aided by the German government precisely with that end in view. Quite apart from the immediate military effects, the possibility that Germany would be able to build a vast empire in the east was a major danger. The strategic reasons for intervention have been obscured by the idea that it represented an attempt by capitalist governments to overthrow a Socialist régime. Modern studies have made the motives of the Allied governments abundantly clear. Clemenceau's views were no different from those of the British and French. Although he had an extreme dislike of Bolshevik economic and political ideas, and of their methods, it was because the Bolshevik revolution led to the withdrawal of Russia from the war that it incurred his detestation. He always talked of it in emotional language, calling it

---

[112] On Russian intervention, see R. H. Ullman, *Anglo-Soviet Relations 1917–1921*, Vol. I, *Intervention and the War* (1961); J. Bradley, *Allied intervention in Russia* (1968); G. A. Brinkley, *The Volunteer Army and Allied Interventions in South Russia*; D. F. Trask, op. cit., pp. 100–29; C. J. Lowe and M. C. Dockrill, op. cit., II, pp. 304–34; F. S. Northedge, *The Troubled Giant, Britain among the great powers 1916–1939* (1968), pp. 46–90; G. F. Kennan, *Soviet-American Relations 1917–1920*, Vol. 2, *The Decision to Intervene* (1958), and *Russia and the West under Lenin and Stalin* (1961).

treachery and betrayal, and refused to make any allowances for the pitiable condition to which Russia had been reduced by the war.

He was convinced that Lenin and his party were in the most direct and literal sense the paid agents of the German government. He emphatically agreed when Barthou gave this succinct description of the Bolsheviks to the Senate Foreign Affairs committee:

> That gang is in German pay and we cannot recognize them as a government. In addition most of them do not use their real names. They are mostly Jews of German origin, with German names which they have turned into Russian. My counterpart as foreign minister calls himself Trotsky, but his real name is Braunstein [sic].

Clemenceau added:

> He was prosecuted here as a spy, but was protected by certain members of Parliament.[113]

When, in December 1917, the British were toying with the idea of avoiding an open breach with the Bolsheviks by releasing Russia from her promise not to make a separate peace with Germany, he declared emphatically that 'if all the celestial powers and M. Maklakov [Russian ambassador in Paris, appointed by the provisional government] asked him to give Russia back her word, he would refuse.[114]

Even after the Armistice, his main concern was the possibility of German expansion into a power-vacuum created by the chaos in Russia, not an ideological crusade against Bolshevism as a political doctrine or a desire to protect the interests of French holders of Russian government bonds. He showed little sign of taking seriously the view that Bolshevism was a sort of contagious disease, that would spread throughout Europe if it were not eradicated. On several occasions, this view was presented by Wilson and Lloyd George as an argument for a more conciliatory attitude towards Germany. He always refused to accept it, saying that the supposed danger of Bolshevism in Germany was only a bluff, a weapon used by the old ruling class, which remained firmly in control, in order to hoodwink the Allies. His eyes remained firmly fixed on the danger from the Right, Prussian militarism, and were not to be deflected by the supposed new danger from the Left.[115] Thus, although he condemned the Bolsheviks and opposed attempts to enter into negotiations with them, on this, as on other questions, the Tiger's growls were worse than his bites. The number of French troops at any time engaged in

[113] Archives of the Senate, Commission des Affaires Etrangères, Auditions des Ministres, 12 November 1917.
[114] Quoted by Lloyd George, War Memoirs, II, p. 1543.
[115] He said that the Catholic Church was a more dangerous enemy to liberalism than Bolsheviks, J. Martet, M. Clemenceau peint par lui-même, pp. 243-4.

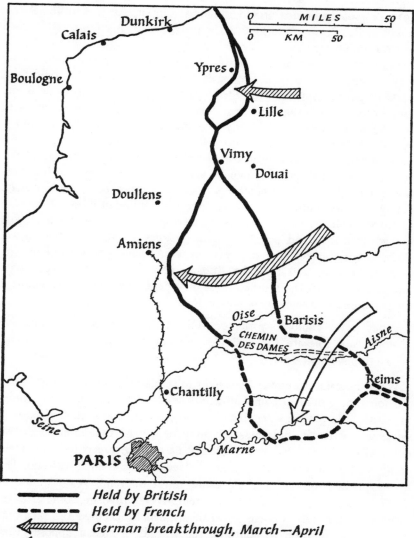

Calais
Dunkirk
Boulogne
Ypres •
•Lille
Vimy •
•Douai
Doullens •
Amiens •
Oise
•Barisis
CHEMIN
DES DAMES
Aisne
Reims •
•Chantilly
Seine
Marne
PARIS

MILES
0   50
0   KM   50

——————— Held by British
– – – – – Held by French
◀▨▨▨▨▨ German breakthrough, March—April
◀▭▭▭ German breakthrough, May—July

2. The Western Front in 1918

Russia was tiny – a few hundred at Murmansk, playing a minor part in the British-commanded force, and a limited involvement of a few regiments at Odessa from December 1918 to the beginning of April 1919. Nor could France provide financial support for the anti-Bolshevik forces in Russia on anything like the British scale; her financial position was far too precarious.

Nevertheless Clemenceau shares responsibility for the unfortunate way in which Allied policy towards Russia developed. The basic fault of that policy was that it failed either to come to terms with the Bolsheviks, or to bring sufficient force to bear against them so as to remove them. This was exactly the line he advocated throughout – verbal condemnation, and limited financial and military support for their enemies, without serious use of Allied power to oust the Bolsheviks. His unrealistic attitude is shown by the fact that he advocated intervention even before the Bolshevik *coup*. On 3 October 1917, in the Senate Foreign Affairs committee, he advocated the sending of a French mission to Russia, which was to act 'as a rallying-point for elements outside the government', and asked whether Japanese troops could be used. When Ribot objected that such actions would have a very bad effect on Russian opinion, and that the Russian government would not invite Japanese assistance, he brushed these considerations aside. He discounted the possibility of a separate peace, saying:

> What peace could they make? William [i.e. the German Emperor] would not tolerate for a single moment a Maximalist [Bolshevik] government next door.[116]

When he came to power he sought to implement his idea of a French mission that would in some miraculous way rally the 'healthy' forces in Russia. More than once Lloyd George would have liked to seek a settlement with the Bolsheviks. It may be argued that internal British political considerations would, in any case, have prevented him from doing so, but he was certainly not helped by the French attitude. The first expression of this attitude came at the Supreme War Council of 30 November 1917. The British were tentatively proposing some arrangement with the new Russian government which accepted the fact that it was in no position to continue the war. Clemenceau opposed this, saying, 'if Russia made a separate peace, she would betray us. Let us keep the moral advantage of being betrayed.' This would obviously not prevent the Bolsheviks from making peace with Germany. He advocated intervention by American and Japanese troops, to which the British

[116] Archives of the Senate, Commission des Affaires Etrangères, Auditions des Ministres, 3 October 1917.

318

were reluctant to agree. Balfour pointed out that it would be a major operation:

> The proposal was in essence an attack on Russia. This might be a legitimate proceeding, but it was a very uncomfortable one, and it was impossible to know where it might lead. He preferred to encourage the elements in Russia that were still on the side of the Allies, without the necessity of invading or attacking Russia.[117]

As President Wilson was quite unprepared to sanction an American expedition to Russia, and as the Japanese would not act without American support, the French ideas had no chance of success at this time, and Balfour's alternative policy was adopted. Britain and France began to give financial aid to various anti-Bolshevik forces in Russia. On 23 December 1917, two members of the British Cabinet, Milner and Cecil, crossed to Paris to discuss the Russian question. Cecil outlined two policies: support for the anti-Bolsheviks, or seeking 'to work with the Bolsheviks and persuade them not to supply Germany'; the British Government had not made a clear choice between them. Clemenceau also refused to choose; his ideas appeared vague and confused. He said

> . . . he would prefer to decide nothing. It was not right in a matter of this sort for us to risk everything on a gambler's last throw. We should not take decisions on which we did not know the facts. Our interest was to see that our officers did not get mixed up in a civil war in Russia. We should keep contact with the Bolsheviks as long as possible. . . . There was only one thing that mattered, that was to shut off supplies from Germany by every possible means, and the most important source of supplies to shut off was the Ukraine.[118]

When Milner asked: 'What if Trotsky were to say that we were fostering civil war, and that we must stop, or he would join hands with

---

[117] Public Record Office, CAB 28/3 IC 35, 35A and 35B. Clemenceau told the Army committee of the Chamber on 12 December that the Bolsheviks were beginning to realize that they would not be able to make an acceptable peace with Germany. Pichon said the same to the Senate Foreign Affairs committee on 10 December. Archives Nationales, C 7499, and Archives of the Senate, Commission des Affaires Etrangères, Auditions des Ministres, 10 December 1917.

[118] Public Record Office, CAB 28/3, IC 37, gives the minutes of this meeting. Cf. G. F. Kennan, *Russia and the West*, pp. 43-7, who implies that there was a greater divergence between British and French policy than appears in the minutes; R. H. Ullman, op. cit., pp. 53-5; J. Bradley, op. cit., pp. 13-14; and Z. A. B. Zeman, *A Diplomatic History of the First World War*, (1971), pp. 296-7. Zeman is not well informed about French attitudes; he implies (ibid., p. 291) that Clemenceau was never concerned about the Russian alliance, quoting the article he wrote in February 1906 condemning Tsarist oppression, an attitude he reversed on coming into office the next month, *see above*, pp. 217-18; he also quotes an extremist article by Gustave Hervé (ibid., p. 292), calling him a 'Socialist party deputy'. Hervé was never a deputy, and in 1914 had abandoned his Left-extremism for an equally extreme Right-wing position.

Germany', Clemenceau interjected that he would deny fostering civil war, which hardly met the point. Milner said that the point was to have a clear idea as to whether or not we were prepared in the last resort to quarrel with the Bolsheviks. Clemenceau replied:

> he would lengthen the spoon to the uttermost, but not let the Ukraine go.

They agreed that, although reluctant to break with the new Russian government, which had not yet made peace with Germany, they would risk this in order to support anti-Bolshevik forces in the Ukraine which, they hoped, would also be anti-German. They proceeded to divide the area concerned into a British and a French zone, an agreement since presented by Russian historians as a typical piece of imperialist brigand-age. In fact it was merely a practical device for avoiding duplication of aid, and certainly did not imply that the areas were to be added to the British and French empires. Britain took the more easterly areas, the Cossack lands, the Caucasus, Armenia, Georgia and Kurdestan, while France was to be responsible for Bessarabia, the Ukraine, and the Crimea.[119] Unfortunately, the forces they sought to help proved to be broken reeds. The Cossack leader Kaledin was defeated by the Bolsheviks in February, while the Ukrainian *Rada* came to terms with the Germans even before the Bolsheviks did.

Thus, by February 1918, the Allies returned to the policy of seeking to organize a large invading force of American and Japanese. Fantastic though it may sound, the idea was that such a force could be landed at Vladivostock, and move across Siberia in order to re-establish an eastern front that would prevent the Germans concentrating all their troops in the west.[120] This danger was the factor that governed intervention. Another major concern was to deny Germany access to Russian raw material and food supplies, enabling her to overcome the effects of the Allied blockade. It was not yet certain that Allied forces landed in Siberia, and in the Arctic, would be opposed by the Bolsheviks. In February, France and Britain were in touch with the Bolshevik leaders through unofficial channels.[121] It still seemed possible that the draconian German peace terms might be rejected and that the Bolsheviks would

---

[119] Public Record Office, CAB 28/3 IC 37.

[120] This scheme was proposed in a telegram from Balfour to Bertie, 26 January 1918, preserved in the Fonds Clemenceau, carton 59. Balfour stated that 'all the information that we have been able to collect appears to indicate that some form of foreign intervention in Russian affairs would be welcome to Russians, and would be more welcome in shape of Japanese acting as mandatories of Allies, with no thought of annexation or future control than in shape of Germans. . . .'

[121] *See* R. H. Ullman, op. cit., p. 76, J. Bradley, op. cit., p. 31, and G. F. Kennan, *Russia Leaves the War* (1956), p. 432. J. Sadoul acted as the French contact with the Bolsheviks; *see* his *Notes sur la Révolution bolchévique, Nov. 1917–Jan. 1919* (1919).

turn back to the Allies. On 29 March 1918 Pichon was still telling the External Affairs committee of the Chamber that cooperation with the Bolsheviks was not ruled out. However, at the Supreme War Council on 15 March he had said that it was obvious that the Bolsheviks would oppose intervention but 'many Russians desired intervention. . . . We need not trouble ourselves too much about Trotsky's views.'[122] But Lenin carried the day in favour of accepting peace with Germany and on 15 March 1918 the Russians ratified the treaty of Brest-Litovsk.

On the same day, the Supreme War Council met in London and discussed the Russian situation, among other things. Balfour was still reluctant to press for intervention, as he thought that it would swing non-Bolshevik opinion in Russia behind the Bolsheviks and against the Allies, but the French insisted that this was not important. Clemenceau stated that:

> We were at war with Germany, and Russia's collapse was becoming ever more complete. Siberia was a province from which the Germans could draw much in the way of supplies. We ought to try and stop Germany utilizing these resources.[123]

The Supreme War Council agreed to press President Wilson to sanction Japanese intervention in Siberia, but American agreement was not forthcoming, and without it the Japanese refused to act. The problem was that neither Britain nor France had any troops to spare for Russian intervention, nor did they want to divert American reinforcements from Europe to Russia – hence the pipedream of a Japanese intervention that would seriously influence events in European Russia. In fact the Japanese had no intention of doing more than improve their position along the Pacific coast of Russia. From this time another element in the situation began to exercise an influence on events. This was the presence in Russia of the Czech legion – former prisoners of war who had been organized to fight on the Russian side, after defecting from the Austro-Hungarian army. It had been decided to remove them by way of the trans-Siberian railway and Vladivostock, so that they could fight in France. March 1918 found them strung out along the whole length of the trans-Siberian railway. As a result of the complete disintegration of the Russian army, in many places they were by then the largest body of disciplined troops. At this point the British military planners came up with a better idea than shipping them halfway round the world. The governing factor in all Allied strategy was shortage of shipping, and the same amount of shipping would be far better employed shuttling American troops across the Atlantic. On the western front the Czechs

---

[122] Archives Nationales, C7491 and Public Record Office, CAB 28/3, IC 51.
[123] Public Record Office, CAB 28/3, IC 51.

would be a negligible factor, but in Russia they could be decisive. The plan was that they should join up with the small British detachment landed at Murmansk, in the Arctic, on 6 March to protect the huge stock of war material which had been landed there to supply the Russian armies, and which now seemed in danger of falling into German hands. There they would be trained by British officers, then they could move south, link up with the Japanese moving west from Vladivostock, and establish a new anti-German front in the Urals. All this, it was hoped, could be done by agreement with the Bolsheviks; but, if they objected, the British military planners were prepared to ignore their objections.[124]

Clemenceau did not agree with this strategy. Eager though he was to see Japanese troops in Russia, because there was no possibility of employing them on the western front, he was not prepared to give up even the small contribution to fighting strength on the western front represented by the Czechs. He was searching desperately for every few thousand men that might be added to Allied strength on the western front. So this period saw a prolonged argument between British and French on the question of whether the Czechs should be used in Russia, or shipped to the West. Clemenceau, however, was in a very weak position, as the French had no shipping, and all his arguments achieved nothing.[125]

It is ironical that Clemenceau has collected so much odium for Russian intervention when he fought hard to get the Czechs removed. For the Czechs acted as the catalyst that won President Wilson's agreement to intervention, and thus set in motion the train of Allied involvement in Russia that continued until 1920. It is strange that Clemenceau was unable to see that the Czechs could be used as a means of forcing President Wilson's hand, and getting him to agree to intervention. The Czechs became embroiled in conflict with the Bolsheviks, and within a fortnight had won control of the railway line and all the towns along it from a point west of Samara on the Volga to one west of Irkutsk.

Thus, by June, the Allied statesmen faced an entirely new situation. The Czechs provided a sizeable military force already *in situ* in Russia; they also made certain, as it had not been previously, that Allied intervention would be condemned by the Bolsheviks. The French still reiterated their demands for the evacuation of the Czechs. Pichon came over to London on 28 May to discuss Russian affairs with the British. Cecil, hinting at the use that could be made of the Czech revolt to put pressure on President Wilson said :

[124] G. F. Kennan, *Russia and the West*, pp. 49–79 and 91–104; R. H. Ullman, op. cit., pp. 128–90; J. Bradley, op. cit., pp. 65–98.
[125] G. F. Kennan, *Russia and the West*, p. 71.

The French were agreed on the need for intervention in Siberia: after failure of representations at Washington, he would like to know what the French plan was.

Pichon replied:

The only possible plan was to continue to use every effort to induce Wilson to agree to Allied action. Intervention by the Czechs would achieve nothing.[126]

Clemenceau returned to the charge (at the meetings of the Supreme War Council on 1–3 June) saying that means must be found to ship the Czechs out of Russia. When Lloyd George argued that a Japanese expedition to Siberia, in conjunction with the Czechs, would do far more to relieve German pressure on the western front, Clemenceau produced another far-fetched argument:

50,000 Czechs in France, apart from their value as a fighting force, might produce a revolution in Prague.[127]

The myopia with which Clemenceau concentrated on the western front can only be understood in the context of the fighting there over the previous two months; one German attack after another had been held, but only just, and it seemed that the war of attrition might yet produce a decision in favour of Germany. If that happened, no doubt the British Empire would survive, but France would not, except as a German satellite. The French government had to face pressure from the Parliamentary committees, where even more unrealistic views of the Russian situation prevailed. Pichon explained the failure to intervene effectively in Russia to the Senate Foreign Affairs committee, by saying that the British would only support intervention if the Bolsheviks agreed to it. Doumergue complained that the French were also in touch with the Bolsheviks, and said that hundreds of French officers were helping to organize the Red Army. Pichon admitted that there had been contact with Trotsky earlier, but said it had now ceased.[128] But French resistance was of little importance in view of their lack of control over events, and the Czech revolt was soon to produce the desired response from President Wilson. On 6 July he authorized the use of American troops in Siberia to rescue the Czechs.[129]

Wilson's plan bore little relation to the realities of the situation in

[126] Public Record Office, CAB 28/3, IC 62–3.
[127] Public Record Office, CAB 28/3, IC 66, meeting of 3 June 1918. Cf. R. H. Ullman, op. cit., pp. 202–3.
[128] Archives of the Senate. Commission des Affaires Etrangères, Auditions des Ministres, 5 June 1918.
[129] R. H. Ullman, op. cit., pp. 213–5; G. F. Kennan, Russia and the West, p. 101.

Russia, but the important thing was that his acquiescence could be used to allow very different intervention plans to go ahead. On 5 July Clemenceau virtually abandoned his attempt to get the Czechs moved to the western front, although the instructions given to General Janin, French commander of the Czechs, in August, still envisaged the eventual withdrawal of some Czechs for service in France.[130] In practice, however, he accepted the British policy of using the Czechs in Russia. No doubt he was persuaded not only by the impossibility of forcing his own ideas on to the British, but also because German pressure began to ease. But France played a very small part in Russia; as Kennan puts it :

> The French sent neither any sizeable body of armed men, nor any serious amount of actual military aid. The French contribution took the form, primarily, of several high-ranking military officers, who, it was hoped in Paris, could somehow or other continue to take command of the whole situation. This device operated mainly to confound the existing confusion, and to saddle the French government with the maximum moral responsibility for the Siberian intervention without its having made any appreciable physical contribution.[131]

2 VICTORY, AUGUST–NOVEMBER 1918

Clemenceau's activities in August and September 1918 do not have the same importance as his crucial interventions during the first seven months of the year. Military success greatly strengthened his political position. The British ambassador, who had reported rumours of threatened resignation from the cabinet in June, and had said that 'people who a month ago were enthusiastic while still saying that he is the only man for prime minister, shrug their shoulders at his methods . . .', was writing on 10 August that Clemenceau was much stronger and 'the whole tone in France is better'.[132] From this point Clemenceau's apotheosis begins, and there could be no doubt about his control of Parliament for as long as he wished to remain in office. A police report of 3 September 1918 gave a justifiably optimistic picture of the cabinet's strength :

> It is considered in well-informed political circles that the Clemenceau ministry has nothing to fear from its enemies at the moment. It is

---

[130] French embassy in London to Lloyd George, 19 August 1918, enclosing instructions for General Janin, 7 August 1918, Lloyd George Papers, F/50/3/17.
[131] G. F. Kennan, *Russia and the West*, p. 113. Pichon spoke on French policy in Russia to the External Affairs committee of the Chamber, on 6 June, 5 July, 12 July, and 2 August 1918, without saying anything very illuminating. Archives Nationales, C 7491.
[132] Derby to Balfour, 17 June, Lloyd George Papers, F/52/2/5; Derby to Balfour, 10 August, Milner Papers, 117, fols. 135–8.

likely that the interpellations already rumoured either will not be brought forward by their originators, or else discussion of them will be postponed to a distant date. In addition, it is thought that any Parliamentary debate is bound to be of advantage to the government which would find nearly 400 supporters in the Chamber.[133]

Clemenceau's two speeches, in the Chamber and Senate, for the opening of the new Parliamentary session in September, were triumphs.[134] The Senate speech, after reminding his hearers of the fifty years of German hegemony preceding the war, went on :

The most terrible balancing of accounts between peoples has begun. The account will be paid. For, after four years of glory, now comes the unexpected – for them, but not for us – reversal of fortune. . . . Yes, that day, announced more than a century ago by our national hymn has truly arrived : the sons are in the course of accomplishing the immense task begun by their fathers. . . . I hear it said that peace cannot be achieved by a military decision. That was not what the German said when he let loose the horrors of war on a peaceful Europe. It was not what he said even yesterday when his orators and leaders were sharing out people like enslaved cattle, threatening in our case, and realizing in practice in Russia, the partitions that would leave the world powerless beneath his iron law. A military decision has been willed by Germany, she has forced us to seek it. Our dead gave their blood in witness that we took up the greatest challenge ever offered to the laws of civilized humanity. Let it be then, as Germany has willed it, as Germany has made it. We seek only peace, a solid and just peace so that those to come will escape the abominations of the past. Allez donc, enfants de la patrie, go on to liberate the peoples of the world from the last furies of shameful force. Go on to spotless victory, all France, all thinking humanity is with you.[135]

Clemenceau continued to concern himself with military policy until the last days of the war, but as the German retreat continued, there was no longer the same atmosphere of crisis, and the need to intervene between Foch, Haig, Pétain and Pershing, as in the early summer. He managed, however, to have a major row with Foch, by requiring him to exert his authority over the American army. This followed critical French reports on the first major battle conducted independently by the American army. He was able to say later that while the marshal had

[133] Archives Nationales, F⁷ 13950, 2, fol. 206.
[134] Annales de la Chambre des Députés, 5 September 1918, and Annales du Sénat, 17 September 1918; G. Clemenceau, *Discours de Guerre*, pp. 271–8.
[135] G. Clemenceau, *Discours de Guerre*, pp. 276–8.

expected him to give orders to the other Allied statesmen, Foch himself had not dared to give orders to Pershing.[136]

But these questions were soon eclipsed by the German demand for an armistice on 5 October 1918. Clemenceau, unlike Poincaré and Pétain, did not hesitate for a moment about the desirability of an armistice, provided that the necessary safeguards were obtained. As he told Martet:

> At the first request for an armistice, I nearly went mad, mad with joy. It was finished. I had seen too much of the front, too many of those water-filled holes where men had lived for four years. . . . M. Poincaré could keep calm, and write me his little letters – 'You should not hamstring etc.' – all in his tiny, cramped handwriting. . . .[137]

It was a sign of Clemenceau's nervous tension at this time that Poincaré's intervention produced a violent reaction. He threatened to resign, unjustly accused Poincaré of wishing to institute 'personal rule', and wrote uncharitably of his role during the war.[138] It was some time before Mordacq and Loucheur managed to make the peace. During these days also he had one of his most violent altercations with Lloyd George.[139] Mordacq reports that, on the evening of 7 October, his conversation, far from being joyful at the news of the German plea, was unusually pessimistic.[140]

On 19 October he visited the liberated towns of northern France, Lille, Douai, and Lens, amid scenes of immense enthusiasm.[141] In the Chamber on 5 November, after reading out the terms of the armistice with Austria, he recalled, now that victory was sure, that he was the last survivor of those who had signed the protest against the treaty relinquishing Alsace-Lorraine in 1871. He paid tribute to those who had fought for France in that terrible year, to Gambetta, to Scheurer-Kestner, and to Küss, the mayor of Strasbourg. He went on to say that the problems of peace would be as great as those of war, and that they must learn to compose their quarrels, to make a reality of national solidarity. 'Let us continue to dispute about ideas, but let such disputes cease when the *patrie* is in danger.'[142] On 11 November he read out the text of the armistice

---

[136] Pétain's critical report on the American operations of 26–30 September 1918, and Clemenceau's letter to Foch, of 21 October 1918, are in the Fonds Clemenceau at the ministry of war, Dossier Président du Conseil, II, 12. Cf. also F. Foch, op. cit., II, p. 252, and G. Clemenceau, *Grandeurs et Misères d'une Victoire*, pp. 60–75.

[137] J. Martet, *Le Tigre*, p. 192. This refers to a letter from Poincaré demanding that the German request for an armistice be refused, and that the Allies march on Berlin; an armistice, said Poincaré, would 'hamstring our victorious troops'.

[138] Poincaré reproduced most of this correspondence in his memoirs, op. cit., X, pp. 377–86.

[139] *See below*, pp. 367.

[140] J. J. H. Mordacq op. cit., II, p. 261.

[141] Ibid., pp. 282–4; G. Clemenceau, *Discours de Guerre*, pp. 282–4.

[142] G. Clemenceau, *Discours de Paix* (1938), pp. 1–7.

with Germany in both the Chamber and the Senate, and followed it with a brief declaration of welcome to

Alsace-Lorraine, at last returned to France, one and indivisible, as our fathers called her,

and of

gratitude to our noble dead, who have given us this wonderful day.

He ended thus:

France, formerly the warrior of God, now the warrior of humanity, always the warrior of the ideal, will recover her place in the world, to continue her magnificent unending race in pursuit of human progress.[143]

The entire Chamber burst into the *Marseillaise*, as the ceremonial guns began to sound, and the crowds in the street shouted and cheered and joined in the national anthem. But in the evening, after the emotional tension of the day, Clemenceau was withdrawn and depressed. As he said to General Mordacq:

we have won the war: now we have to win the peace, and it may be more difficult.[144]

[143] G. Clemenceau, *Discours de Guerre*, pp. 285–7; J. J. H. Mordacq, op. cit., III, pp. 2–3.
[144] J. J. H. Mordacq, op. cit., III, p. 5; G. Wormser, op. cit., p. 341.

Part seven

THE PEACE SETTLEMENT
AND AFTER

1918-1929

17

THE VERSAILLES TREATY

I THE ARMISTICE

The sudden collapse of the enemy powers in the late summer of 1918 presented the Allies with the task of preparing armistice terms, a situation for which they had made no provision. Even in August it still seemed most likely that a campaign would be needed in 1919. Then, in quick succession, came the Bulgarian request for an armistice, and on 5 October the German and Austrian notes to President Wilson demanding an armistice on the basis of the Fourteen Points. Bulgaria was out of the war by 29 September, Turkey by 31 October, Austria-Hungary by 3 November and Germany on 11 November. Only the German armistice produced much top-level negotiation among the Allies.[1] The Allies were uncertain about how far Germany could be pushed, as her fighting capacity had by no means disappeared. At the same time they were determined not to give terms allowing the German army time to withdraw to a better defensive position from which it could resume the war. Thus their minimum terms were to ensure that the Germans would be unable to resume war, and to provide the main desiderata of the eventual peace settlement. This introduced the question of the nature of the peace terms and these negotiations between the Allies foreshadowed their conflicts about the terms to be imposed on Germany during the peace negotiations themselves. The situation was complicated by the fact that the Germans

[1] The best study of the armistice with Germany is now P. Renouvin, *L'Armistice de Rethondes* (1968). F. Maurice, *The Armistices of 1918* (1943), is a useful collection of the texts of the various armistices. Cf. also H. I. Nelson, *Land and Power, British and Allied policy on Germany's frontiers, 1916–1919* (1963), pp. 53–87, S. P. Tillmann, *Anglo-American Relations at the Paris Peace Conference of 1919* (1961), pp. 39–54, and D. R. Watson, 'The making of the treaty of Versailles', in N. Waites (ed.), *Troubled Neighbours, Franco-British Relations in the Twentieth Century* (1971).

had approached President Wilson alone, and not the Allies as a whole. For the United States was only an 'associated' co-belligerent, not bound by a formal alliance to the others. Thus it was possible for Wilson to put pressure on the others by threatening to make a separate peace. For some time it seemed that Wilson was seeking to use the fact that the Germans had approached him to dictate his own terms, but in the end the Allies were able to re-assert their influence at the price of some lip service to Wilson's vague shibboleths.

The Allied premiers were in Paris at the Supreme War Council on 5 October when the news of the German note came through.[2] They decided to ask their military advisers (the inter-Allied body sitting at Versailles) to draw up detailed proposals, embodying a scheme of which the main features were the evacuation by the enemy of all occupied territory (the Germans withdrawing behind the Rhine but without Allied advance into German territory, not even into Alsace-Lorraine) and the cessation of submarine warfare.[3] It is rather strange that Clemenceau even considered such moderate terms, and that he allowed the Supreme War Council to apply to the Versailles Committee, very much a back-water manned by second-string figures, rather than to Foch, and the other active commanders. However Foch intervened, writing on his own initiative to Clemenceau on 8 October giving his views on the terms.[4] The main difference between Foch's demands and the scheme of the Versailles Committee was that Foch demanded Allied occupation of the left bank of the Rhine, and of three bridgeheads on the other bank. The British reaction to Foch's terms was that they amounted to unconditional surrender.[5] Clemenceau supported Foch in the discussion at the Supreme War Council of 8 October, but was determined to assert control over final policy decisions, against Foch and Poincaré. The President infuriated Clemenceau by expressing his opposition to any armistice, which would, he said, hamstring the victorious advance of the Allied armies to Berlin. There followed an angry exchange of letters, in which Clemenceau threatened to resign.[6] In the end Poincaré had to withdraw completely, and accept his exclusion from the decision-making. After this rebuff Poincaré made no further attempt to influence

[2] Minutes of their discussions are available at the Public Record Office, CAB 28/5, IC 76–82.
[3] Public Record Office, CAB 28/5, IC 79 and IC 85.
[4] For the fact that Foch sent his proposals to Clemenceau without being asked, see F. Foch, op. cit., II, p. 270, and R. Blake, op. cit., p. 330. A copy of Foch's note is in the Lloyd George Papers, F/50/3/28, and it was printed in Lloyd George's *War Memoirs*, II, pp. 1955–6.
[5] The reaction of Bonar Law at the meeting of 8 October; Lloyd George said that Foch's terms 'amounted to saying "No" with a swagger'. Public Record Office, CAB 28/5, IC 80.
[6] R. Poincaré, op. cit., X, pp. 379–86; J. J. H. Mordacq, op. cit., II, pp. 262–4; L. Loucheur, *Carnets Secrets*, pp. 62–4.

Clemenceau directly, although he remained in contact with Foch, and encouraged the supreme commander's opposition to Clemenceau.

On 16 October Foch made the first of his many attempts to play a political role, asking for a Foreign Office official to help him prepare the armistice terms. He argued that he could not settle them without knowing the Government's peace proposals, and in particular their plans for the status of the Rhineland. Was it to be annexed, or turned into an autonomous neutral area? No other possibility was envisaged by Foch's letter. Clemenceau's reply was less insulting than his answer to Poincaré, but equally firm that according to the constitution the government alone had authority to deal with the questions Foch raised. Political decisions must be clearly separated from military advice.[7] Pétain was also an opponent of the armistice.[8] But only Foch and Clemenceau were involved in the armistice negotiations, on the French side, and Clemenceau insisted that Foch was only required to give military advice; decisions had to be left to the politicians. The cabinet was not, it seems, consulted. Clemenceau told the president of the Chamber External Affairs committe, who offered the collaboration of the committee, that 'the cabinet had given him and Pichon *carte blanche*, and had agreed, for the moment, not to be informed. It would therefore be difficult to communicate information to a Parliamentary committee that members of the government themselves had agreed not to have.'[9]

Meanwhile the Allied governments had persuaded President Wilson to send his representative, House, to join them in their discussions. At the next series of meetings of the Supreme War Council, from 29 October to 5 November, the precise armistice terms were worked out.[10] The starting-point was the documents presented by the various military and naval commanders, and the armistice was a formidable ultimatum which would ensure that Germany was in no position to recommence the war. It was a very different proposition from anything the Germans had hoped to receive by appealing to Wilson, but internal developments

---

[7] The text of Foch's letter is given by R. M. L'Hôpital *Foch, l'armistice et la paix* (1938), pp. 33–6. English translation in F. Maurice, op. cit., pp. 34–5.

[8] *See* the suggestions in G. Pedroncini, *Les Négociations secrètes*, pp. 99–105, and his thesis, *Le Haut Commandement, la conduite de la guerre, mai 1917–novembre 1918*, pp. 1583–7. Cf. also the account of his *soutenance de thèse*, *Le Monde*, 9 June 1971.

[9] Commission des Affaires Extérieures de la Chambre des Députés, 31 October 1918, Archives Nationales, C 7491.

[10] Minutes of these meetings are in the Public Record Office, CAB 28/5, IC 83–96. Extracts taken from Loucheur's copy of the French minutes, have been published in J. de Launay, *Secrets Diplomatiques, 1914–1918* (Brussels, 1963), pp. 83–153. Extracts from the minutes for 29 October were published by Lloyd George in *The Truth about the Peace Treaties* (1938), I, pp. 75–80, and Mermeix, *Les Négociations secrètes et les quatre armistices*, published extracts for 31 October–4 November, pp. 204–15, and pp. 226–66.

in Germany made acceptance inevitable. In the inter-Allied discusssions about the armistice Lloyd George was most opposed to President Wilson's activities. Clemenceau acted rather as a restraining influence, trying to avoid hurting Wilson's feelings.[11] Lloyd George was most adamantly opposed to the second of the Fourteen Points, the freedom of the seas. Clemenceau did support him in his stand against this, but the general impression given by the debate is that the French could not really understand why so much energy was devoted to discussion of issues more concerned with Anglo-American relations than with the German armistice. House concentrated on winning Allied acceptance of the general aspirations expressed in Wilson's Fourteen Points – open covenants, freedom of the seas, removal of trade barriers. Freedom of the seas was in effect rejected, and the other points were seen to carry no precise commitment and were therefore accepted.[12]

Meanwhile House had taken little interest in the precise clauses being drafted by the British and French. He did not support Foch's reservations about the stiff naval terms proposed by the British admiralty, or British objections to the French proposals to occupy the Rhineland. House wrote to Wilson that Clemenceau 'gave us his word of honour that France would withdraw after the peace conditions had been fulfilled.[13] Thus the terms of the French soldiers and British sailors were incorporated into the armistice, although Balfour was able to delete a clause that the German Army in the east should withdraw to the frontier of 1772, which would have had the appearance of prejudging the question of future German-Polish boundaries.[14] Nor did House object to the interpretation of Wilson's vague reference to the restoration of Belgium and the invaded French territory as providing a basis for 'Reparation' claims against Germany. Just how far this could be stretched was to be demonstrated by the final peace terms.

The crucial moment for Allied acceptance that the armistice was based on Wilson's programme came when House said that the President 'had insisted on Germany accepting all his speeches, and from these you could establish almost any point that anyone wished against Ger-

[11] Until the hard bargaining of March and April 1919, Clemenceau seems to have thought that the United States was more likely than Britain to support France's demands. House, who was on very friendly terms with Clemenceau, often gave the impression that the United States was ready to accept the French case. Clemenceau found Wilson much less satisfactory, although he did allow House to make some crucial concessions to the French. *See* C. Seymour, *The Intimate Papers of Colonel House* (1928), IV, p. 196.

[12] As Lloyd George put it, 'He had no objections to any of the other clauses. They were wide enough to allow us to place our own interpretation upon them.' Public Record Office, CAB 28/5, IC 83.

[13] Public Record Office, CAB 28/5 IC 87; cf. H. I. Nelson, op. cit., p. 82. House to Wilson, 30 October 1918, C. Seymour, op. cit., IV, p. 121.

[14] Public Record Office, CAB 28/5 IC 88. Cf. T. Komarnicki, *The Rebirth of the Polish Republic* (1957), p. 233, and H. I. Nelson, pp. 82–3.

many'.[15] The end result was that the extreme French programme, leaving Germany helpless in the face of the Allies, went through with very little modification. Lloyd George argued for more moderate terms, saying that the Germans would not accept. To this Clemenceau replied that

> the situation of the Allies *vis à vis* the enemy had never been so crushing before. The American effectives were enormous. Tomorrow the Allies would be able to march across Austria against Germany. He had little doubt that the first reply of the German government would be to refuse our terms, but as we increased our advantage they would concede them.[16]

Lloyd George reluctantly allowed himself to be overruled, although he insisted on placing his disquiet on record. As internal developments in Germany made further German resistance impossible, the French were right rather sooner than they had envisaged, and on 11 November the armistice was signed. In spite of subsequent criticism from the political Right and the army leadership, Clemenceau could feel considerable satisfaction about the strong bargaining counters he had obtained. Continued fighting would have emphasized the weakness of the French army compared with the British and the American. So there were good reasons, quite apart from humanitarian ones, for ending the war as soon as possible, even at the price of allowing the German army to march home unconquered.[17] In any case the prospect of occupying and administering large areas of Germany in the chaotic conditions of 1918–19 was a daunting one. This was envisaged when it seemed that all governmental authority might collapse in Germany, but was abandoned with relief when it emerged that the provisional republican government had asserted sufficient control to comply with the armistice terms.[18]

Over two months elapsed between the armistice and the opening of the peace conference in Paris on 12 January 1919, and nearly another

---

[15] Public Record Office, CAB 28/5, IC 83: quoted in D. Lloyd George, *The Truth about the Peace Treaties*, I, p. 80.

[16] Public Record Office, CAB 28/5, IC 87, meeting of 1 November.

[17] G. Perdoncini does not seem to agree with this view, as he writes that the November offensive desired by Pétain and Pershing would have 'definitely settled the question of German military defeat, while giving a decisive role to the French army'. *Les Négociations secrètes*, p. 104, and his thesis, pp. 1573–87.

[18] Clemenceau to Lloyd George, 9 November 1918, 10 h 30 du soir; 'Signature does not seem in doubt, but the present condition of Germany places us before the unknown. . . . The signature of a government that is not obeyed would only increase the confusion,' and Clemenceau to Lloyd George, n.d. (but probably 10 November 1918): 'It may happen that, in the absence of a regular government to negotiate with, we have to continue the war, and decide for ourselves how much German territory to occupy.' Lloyd George Papers, F/50/3/46 and 47; extracts from these communications were printed by Lloyd George in his *War Memoirs*, II, pp. 1983–4.

two before the questions vital to France were thrashed out between Clemenceau, Wilson and Lloyd George. There were several reasons for delay. As Clemenceau wrote to Lloyd George, it would be advisable to 'let the German Revolution settle down a little so that we can see what we have to deal with'.[19] They also had to await the arrival of President Wilson, whilst Lloyd George wished to hold the British elections, and there was a whole round of ceremonial visits and celebrations to be completed. Meanwhile the time could be occupied in formulating French demands, presenting them to the Allies, and sounding out British and American intentions. Various individuals and organizations were set to work drawing up French proposals. But Clemenceau was careful not to commit himself to any particular scheme. When he spoke in the Chamber on 29 December 1918, he refused to make any statement about French peace proposals, contenting himself with reminding his audience that the peace must be a compromise between all the Allies.[20]

A body of academics, the *Comité d'Etudes*, had been set to work in 1916 to provide background studies. They had, so far, formulated few conclusions, and Tardieu was told to extract a precise programme from their studies.[21] At the Quai d'Orsay, Philippe Berthelot produced a series of outline proposals, which dealt with the procedure and organization of the Peace Conference as well as with substantive French demands. Paul Cambon wrote that Clemenceau found Berthelot's memoranda absurd.[22] Nevertheless they were presented in slightly different versions to Britain and to the United States at the end of 1918, and were remarkably similar to the French proposals for which Clemenceau fought in March and April 1919. They demanded that Germany give up large areas, mainly inhabited by non-Germans; but the principle of self-determination was abandoned with respect to the Saar, and in so far as was necessary to make Poland and Czechoslovakia strong states. Three questions were essential, stated a note entitled 'Propositions for a preliminary peace with Germany'. Firstly, the military neutralization of the left bank of the Rhine, without its political separation from Germany, together with the

[19] Clemenceau to Lloyd George, n.d., Lloyd George Papers, F/50/3/56, quoted in D. Lloyd George, *The Truth about the Peace Treaties*, I, pp. 148–9.
[20] *Annales de la Chambre des Députés*, 29 December 1918, reprinted in G. Clemenceau, *Discours de Paix*, pp. 12–34.
[21] On the *Comité d'Etudes*, see C. Benoist, *Souvenirs* (1934), III, pp. 324–33. The *Comité* produced two volumes of background studies, published as *Travaux du Comité d'Etudes* (1919).
[22] P. Cambon, *Correspondance* (1940–6), III, p. 291 : 'Clemenceau finds Berthelot's schemes for the organization of the Congress absurd.' Berthelot was acting director of political affairs at Quai d'Orsay : see J. Laroche, *Au Quai d'Orsay avec Briand et Poincaré* (1957), pp. 62–3. These proposals are preserved among the Fonds Clemenceau at the Ministry of War, carton 44X; they have been printed in Department of State, *Papers Relating to the Foreign Relations of the United States, the Paris Peace Conference, 1919* (Washington, 1946), I, pp. 344 *et seq.*, hereinafter referred to as F.R.U.S., P.P.C.

return to France of the territory taken in 1815 as well as in 1871 (i.e. the Saar as well as Alsace-Lorraine); secondly, the creation of a strong anti-German and anti-Bolshevik Poland: thirdly, that the domestic political system of Germany be left to the Germans to decide, but that, nevertheless, federalist tendencies be encouraged.[23]

In so far as the Rhineland was concerned, these proposals were notably more moderate than those put forward under the signature of Foch on 27 November. This tallied with a scheme drafted by Hanotaux, and submitted to Foch at the beginning of November.[24] The essential element in the Foch memorandum was the plan to incorporate the Rhinelanders in the Allied armies. Only in this way, Foch argued, could the demographic imbalance between the western alliance and Germany be rectified. Although Foch later argued only for the creation of an 'autonomous' Rhineland state, or states, his first version was considerably more ambitious. Clemenceau certainly never accepted this proposal. The British ambassador reported Clemenceau's views in the following terms on 14 December 1918:

> He said that the Rhine was a natural boundary of Gaul and Germany and that it ought to be made the German boundary now, the territory between the Rhine and the French frontier being made into an Independent State whose neutrality should be guaranteed by the great powers. I can see that he intends to press that very strongly. Foch had put forward a suggestion that an Independent Army should be raised in those parts for its defence, but Clemenceau had vetoed that on the grounds that it was unnecessary and dangerous. He tells me however Foch looks upon it as a military necessity and will press for it at the Conference.[25]

When Clemenceau and Foch visited London at the beginning of December he was pointedly absent from the meeting at which Foch presented his plan to the British. Lloyd George stated that this was because Clemenceau thought that such ideas would be presented more per-

---

[23] F.R.U.S., P.P.C., I, p. 372. Cf. H. I. Nelson, op. cit. pp. 130–1.

[24] The text of Foch's memorandum, and those of 10 January and 31 March 1919, are conveniently found in Mermeix, Le Combat des Trois (1922), pp. 205–22. Cf. J. C. King, Foch versus Clemenceau, France and German Dismemberment 1918–1919 (1960), pp. 16–27. J. Bardoux, De Paris à Spa, la bataille diplomatique pour la paix française (1921), p. 55 claimed that he drafted Foch's document. Hanotaux's memorandum was preserved among the Klotz Papers, dossier 18, and has been commented on by H. I. Nelson op. cit., p. 114–15. Nelson treats it as if it might represent official French policy. Hanotaux, however, had no official position and was in contact only with Foch. This document, along with others drafted by Hanotaux for Foch was printed in G. Hanotaux, Le Traité de Versailles du 28 juin 1919 (1919). He states, ibid., p. xvii, that they were later forwarded to the Foreign Ministry 'à titre personnel'.

[25] Derby to Balfour, 14 December 1918, Lloyd George Papers, F/52/2/52.

suasively by Foch, with all his prestige as commander-in-chief.[26] It is more likely that Clemenceau wanted Foch to realize how unsympathetic the British were to such ideas. It would also demonstrate to Lloyd George the moderation of Clemenceau's own proposal compared with that of Foch. Also discussed was the Middle Eastern settlement, in informal private conversation between Clemenceau and Lloyd George.[27] Many of the formal meetings were devoted to plans to bring the Kaiser to trial, which had Clemenceau's enthusiastic support. Paris was agreed as the venue of the conference and other procedural matters discussed, although the arrangements later adopted did not bear much relation to those proposed. At this stage the idea was still prevalent that the work could be divided into a 'preliminary peace', laying down the main lines of the settlement, which could be agreed on quickly: only then would the full conference assemble to arrange the details and draw up the final treaty. This idea was gradually abandoned as it became obvious that agreement on general principles was unimportant, but that it was their applications in detail that mattered and required arduous negotiations between the supreme political leaders. Russia was also discussed, Clemenceau firmly opposing any suggestion that the Bolsheviks should be invited to the peace conference: the Russian part of the settlement would simply have to wait until the situation became clearer. Mordacq reports that Clemenceau returned to Paris, dissatisfied and discouraged about the prospects for the peace settlement, after these inter-Allied meetings.[28]

2 PEACE PRELIMINARIES

Clemenceau never considered that his task was done when the war ended. He was well aware that France's victory was precarious, that her position *vis à vis* Germany needed to be strengthened in every possible way by the peace settlement, and that there was bound to be conflict between the measures needed to achieve this, and the equally imperative necessity of maintaining the unity of the wartime alliance. He regarded himself, with good reason, as better fitted than anyone else to combine two aims: the achievement of French demands from

[26] D. Lloyd George, *The Truth about the Peace Treaties*, I, p. 132. Lloyd George quotes extensively from the minutes of this and the subsequent meetings, but with significant omissions, ibid., pp. 132–47. He misdates the meeting with Foch (ibid., p. 131) to 30 November instead of 1 December, and has been followed in this by many authorities, including F. S. Marston, *The Peace Conference of 1919, Organisation and Procedure* (1944), pp. 44 and 235. The full minutes are now available at the Public Record Office. CAB 28/5, IC 97–102.
[27] *See below*, pp. 368–9.
[28] Clemenceau's remarks on Russia were made at a meeting of the Imperial War Cabinet on 3 December, Public Record Office, CAB 23/42. J. J. H. Mordacq, op. cit., III, p. 29. *See below*, pp. 327–9.

Germany and the maintenance of Allied unity. He was determined to retain overall control of French policy in his own hands. In this he was remarkably successful, and for good or ill, Clemenceau bears the responsibility for the French contribution to the peace settlement of 1919.[29] Obviously one man could not hold all the threads of such a complicated settlement in his own hands. But he determined French policy on all important questions, and seems to have been remarkably free to make his own decisions. There were strict limits to the concessions he could make to his allies, set by French public opinion as well as by his own assessments of French interests. But he had a free hand in the sense that he made his own judgement of these limits. The public were not informed of the details of the treaty until Clemenceau was able to present it as a package, to be accepted or rejected *in toto*. He insisted that Parliament had no part to play in the negotiations and that its constitutional role was confined to an examination of the complete treaty after it had been accepted by the enemy. This meant, in practice, that Parliament had no means of influencing the treaty. Although much criticism of particular clauses was expressed during the examination of the treaty by the Parliamentary committees, and in the public debates in the autumn of 1919, there was no way of voting for or against individual clauses. Parliament had to ratify or reject the whole treaty.[30]

Clemenceau was perfectly correct constitutionally in insisting on the government's sole responsibility for negotiating the treaty. But charges of dictatorial ways had some foundation in that he made no attempt to bring other leading politicians into the negotiations. Briand thought that he should have been invited, but found himself completely excluded. The French delegation to the Peace Conference consisted of Clemenceau, Pichon, the foreign minister, Loucheur, minister of munitions, Klotz,

---

[29] There has been no really satisfactory study of the peace settlement as a whole since P. Birdsall, *Versailles Twenty Years After* (1941). G. Schulz *Revolution and Peace treaties 1917–1920* (1972), a translation of *Revolutionen und Friedensschlusse 1917–1920* (1967), is brief and general. Nor is A. J. Mayer, *Politics and Diplomacy of Peacemaking, Containment and Counter-Revolution at Versailles, 1918–1919* (1968), focussed on the negotiations. The story is presented from the British side in F. S. Northedge, *The Troubled Giant, Britain among the great powers 1916–1939* (1966), pp. 91–124, and in C. J. Lowe and M. C. Dockrill, *The Mirage of Power*, II, pp. 335–74. P. Miquel, *La Paix de Versailles et l'opinion publique française* (1972). is the definitive work on that topic, but it is not directly concerned with the negotiations. P. Renouvin, *Le Traité de Versailles* (1969), is only a brief introductory text book. H. Elcock, *Portrait of a Decision, the Council of Four and the Treaty of Versailles* (1972), appeared too late to be utilized by me.

[30] On 5 November 1918 he told Franklin-Bouillon, president of the Chamber External Affairs committee, that he accepted their collaboration in principle, but in practice the committee found that it was completely excluded from the negotiations. Clemenceau even refused to address the committee while the negotiations were in progress. The most that they could achieve was that he receive a delegation, which reported back to the committee on 5 February 1919. *See* the minutes of the Commission des Affaires Extérieures de la Chambre des Députés, 5 November 1918, 29 January and 5 February 1919, Archives Nationales, C 7491.

finance minister, Tardieu, the ex-Commissioner for Franco-American Cooperation, who had no ministerial post, and Jules Cambon, secretary-general of the Quai d'Orsay. The latter, a professional diplomat, seems to have been consulted mainly on technical matters. The others were Clemenceau's intimate associates, except for Klotz, who only had influence on financial questions, and they were all prepared to accept Clemenceau's leadership, regarding their role as that of technical assistants. Even Pichon, the foreign minister, accepted Clemenceau's domination, and does not seem to have played a very important part in decision-making. The full cabinet was apparently rarely consulted, although the absence of records of cabinet meetings makes it impossible to be certain. One of the most important decisions, to abandon the demand for an autonomous state in the Rhineland, was discussed informally between Clemenceau, Pichon, Tardieu and Loucheur. Only after a great deal of pressure from Poincaré did Clemenceau agree to a full cabinet discussion of the question. On 6 April Poincaré said that it was essential. He seems to have done nothing to arrange it, however, as on 16 April, Poincaré, Foch and Dubost, the president of the Senate, meeting to decide how best to oppose Clemenceau's policy, agreed that the first step would be for Poincaré to insist on its discussion by the cabinet. A special cabinet meeting, attended by Foch, was arranged for 25 April, but turned out to be a formality.[31] Clemenceau had told Poincaré on 18 April that he was sure that he would have the support of the cabinet, and so it was.

Poincaré and Foch did attempt to influence Clemenceau's decisions. Poincaré frequently wrote to him at great length, but there is no indication that Clemenceau took any notice at all of these communications.[32] Foch tried by other means to promote his own ideas, but he was firmly excluded from the vital bargaining with the Allies, and all his activities turned out to be empty gestures of protest. Although Clemenceau successfully asserted his control over policy against Foch's attempts to interfere, this was not an easy task, and he had to turn a blind eye to Foch's activities on several occasions. When the British told Clemenceau that if Foch were insubordinate he should be dismissed, he replied that in advocating such a course they revealed their ignorance of the political situation in France. The French army did not

[31] On Poincaré's activities, and his conversations with Clemenceau, see his Notes Journalières, Poincaré Papers XLIII, Bibliothèque Nationale, NAF 16034. Poincaré's diary gives no details of the cabinet meeting of 25 April: it is reported, with what degree of reliability it is impossible to say, in Mermeix, Le Combat des Trois, pp. 226–31; cf. also M. Weygand, Mémoires, II, p. 46, and P. Miquel, op. cit., p. 390. For Clemenceau's discussions with Loucheur, Tardieu and Pichon, see Loucheur, Carnets Secrets, pp. 71–2.

[32] The Musée Clemenceau has forty-nine letters from Poincaré to Clemenceau for the period of the second ministry: they cannot be consulted, but some of Poincaré's drafts are available in the Poincaré Papers, XLII and XLIII.

intervene in domestic politics between 1851 and 1958, but the possibility of such intervention remained. The prestige of the army and its leaders had never been higher than at the end of the war, while that of civilian politicians had sunk low.[33] The collaboration between Foch and Poincaré, which Clemenceau suspected at the time, can now be documented from Poincaré's diary. The two discused the action they should take when Clemenceau abandoned the plan for an autonomous Rhineland in return for the offer of the British and American treaties: this led to Foch's address to the cabinet on 25 April. On 2 May Poincaré records a long talk with Foch in which the Marshal asked him if he could not intervene, to take the negotiations out of Clemenceau's hands. Poincaré told him that it was constitutionally impossible. All he could do was to resign, and such a step would be an empty gesture; it was too late now to hope to obtain better terms from Wilson and Lloyd George.[34] Clemenceau also had to deal with attempts by General Mangin, commander of one of the occupying armies, to promote a separatist movement in the Rhineland. He found these incidents highly embarrassing, as he was trying to convince Wilson and Lloyd George that military occupation of the Rhineland would not produce political complications.[35]

The opening of the French archives for this period will probably not add much to our knowledge of the processes of decision-making. The vital decisions were made when the seventy-eight-year-old Clemenceau lay awake, with the insomnia of old age, alone with his sombre thoughts, or in the early morning when he arose to prepare his breakfast, a peasant dish from the Vendée, half porridge, half stew; fortified with this, he would spend several hours alone at his desk before his gymnastic instructor and masseur arrived for the day's physical training session. But there is a great deal of material, not on the way French claims were reached, but on their presentation to the Allies, and the negotiations by which they were developed into the final terms to be presented to the Germans. The discussions took place in two bodies. From the opening of the conference in January down to 24 March 1919, it was in the

---

[33] Clemenceau's reply to the British was made at the Council of Four on 13 June 1919, P. Mantoux, op. cit., II, p. 48. Weygand states that Foch knew very well that Clemenceau could not dismiss him, M. Weygand, op. cit., II, p. 48. Cf. P. C. F. Bankwitz, *Weygand and Civil-Military Relations in Modern France* (1968), p. 31, J. C. King, op. cit., pp. 48–72, and P. Miquel, op. cit., pp. 283–386.

[34] These talks with Foch are reported in detail in Poincaré's *Notes Journalières*, Poincaré Papers XLIII, Bibliothèque Nationale, NAF 16034, especially 15–19 April, 2 and 6 May.

[35] These incidents are discussed in J. C. King, op. cit., pp. 31–43 and pp. 73–112, but more material has now become available. Poincaré's diary records Clemenceau's complaint that 'Mangin is insupportable, as bad as Boulanger', *Notes Journalières*, 23 May, Poincaré Papers XLIII, Bibliothèque Nationale, NAF 16034. The Mangin papers in the Archives Nationales have little information about Clemenceau's relations with Mangin, but an important document the interview of Mangin and Jeanneney of 24 May 1919, was published by G. Wormser, op. cit., pp. 504–6.

Council of Ten, a continuation of the Supreme War Council, consisting of two delegates from each of the great powers—France, Britain, Italy, the United States and Japan. It met, with some degree of formality, in the foreign secretary's room at the Quai d'Orsay, with Clemenceau in the chair. The tact with which he conducted its proceedings has been described by Lansing, the American secretary of state:

> Within the council chamber his domineering manner, his brusqueness of speech, and his driving methods of conducting business disappeared. He showed patience and consideration towards his colleagues and seldom spoke until the others had expressed their views. It was only on rare occasions that he abandoned his suavity of address and allowed his emotions to affect his utterances. It was then only that one caught a glimpse of the ferocity of The Tiger.[36]

His manner when presiding over the plenary sessions of the Conference was very different. Harold Nicolson, a junior British diplomat, gave this description:

> Clemenceau rather high-handed with the smaller powers. 'Y-a-t-il d'objections? Non? – Adopté.' Like a machine gun.[37]

As assistants and experts were frequently called in, these meetings often involved quite large attendances, and the Council of Ten became unwieldly: serious breaches of secrecy occurred and slow progress was made in approaching vital parts of the settlement. This was in part due to the complex and multiple questions involved, but also to Clemenceau's deliberate delaying tactics; the French were in charge of the agenda. Barthou, a member of the delegation from the Chamber External Affairs committee that interviewed Clemenceau on the progress of the negotiations, said that, in reply to complaints about slow progress, he declared:

> My method is to deal first with the questions easiest to resolve, on which there could be immediate agreement between the allies, and to reserve what I have to ask for to the last moment. . . . In the interval, by making concessions, I will have been able to obtain support. When the moment comes to claim France's rights, I will have leverage that I might not have at this moment.[38]

---

[36] R. Lansing, *The Big Four* (1922), p. 27. Minutes were taken by Hankey's secretarial team, and have been published in F.R.U.S., P.P.C., Vols. III and IV.
[37] H. Nicolson, *Peacemaking 1919* (1964, first edition 1933), pp. 241–2.
[38] Commission des Affaires Extérieures de la Chambre des Députés, 5 February 1919, Archives Nationales, C 7491. Cf. J. J. H. Mordacq, op. cit., III, p. 118, who states that after a long conversation with Lloyd George and Balfour on 6 February 1919, Clemenceau realized that it would be very difficult to win British support for French plans for an autonomous Rhineland: he decided, therefore, to postpone it for the time being.

In any case Wilson's absence in America from 15 February to 14 March, Lloyd George's return to London from 8 February to 5 March, and Clemenceau's withdrawal from 19 February to 1 March after an assassination attempt, meant that no important decisions could be taken in that period.

Clemenceau was shot at by a young anarchist called Cottin, at 9 a.m. on 19 February, as he was being driven from his home to the peace conference. A bullet lodged between his ribs, fortunately without touching any vital organ. The doctors decided not to attempt extraction, and after ten days' rest he was able to return to work, declaring that he felt fitter than before. Observers felt that he had been weakened, and the attack was one reason for the extreme exhaustion which often affected him during the crucial sessions of March and April. However, his willpower was sufficient to carry him through, and he was able to summon up the energy to fight for the points he saw as essential. Cottin was seized by the small crowd assembled to watch Clemenceau's departure, and was at once arrested. He proved to have no accomplices and, although obviously unbalanced, was regarded as fit to plead. He was sentenced to a long term of imprisonment, which he did not serve in full, being released after a few years, much to Clemenceau's indignation.

At the beginning of March the vital questions began to be seriously discussed, in informal meetings between Clemenceau, Lloyd George and House, representing Wilson. One of vital importance took place on 14 March, as soon as Wilson returned to Paris, when Wilson and Lloyd George agreed to offer France the Anglo-American treaties of guarantee. No formal records were kept and the informal atmosphere facilitated compromise. Accordingly, the three statesmen agreed not to resume sitting in the Council of Ten, but instead to continue holding these completely informal meetings, with Orlando as Italian spokesman. From 24 March they began to hold the regular series of meetings, often several times a day, which came to be known as the Council of Four.[39] These meetings were much more intimate than those of the Council of Ten, usually taking place in Wilson's private residence, sometimes in Clemenceau's room at the ministry of war, or in Lloyd George's flat in the rue Nitot. In these discussions, to which a few advisors were sometimes invited, all important elements of the peace settlement were decided, not without arduous bargaining and, on occasion, violent disagreement.

[39] Sources for these meetings are the notes of the interpreter, P. Mantoux, Les Délibérations du Conseil des Quatre (1955), 2 vols, and Hankey's minutes from 5 April are printed in F.R.U.S., P.P.C., Vols V and VI. The Italian interpreter also published his version, L. Aldrovandi-Marescotti, Guerra Diplomatica (Milan, 1937), and Nuovi Ricordi et Frammenti di Diario (Milan, 1938).

3 THE CRUCIAL BARGAINS

The four main areas of disagreement will be discussed, in order to out-line Clemenceau's contribution to the settlement. These are the questions of the Rhineland and guarantees for France against German attack, the Saar, Germany's eastern frontier, and Reparations. Clemenceau had taken little interest in the February discussions about the disposition of the German colonies, and the setting up of the League of Nations. The French representative, Léon Bourgeois, had advocated, without success, a French version of the League which would have made it an institutionalized military alliance against Germany. There was obviously no chance of this version being accepted by President Wilson, and Clemenceau told Robert Cecil on 8 March that the French had merely sought to demonstrate that the League of Nations, as designed by the Anglo-Saxons, could not provide for their security.[40]

Nor was Clemenceau much concerned about the proposals for German disarmament, although there was a wide divergence between the original British and French positions on this. The British wanted to prohibit conscription, while Foch thought that it was a professional long-serving army that would be a danger to peace. However, Clemenceau accepted the British position, overruling Foch, although the French insisted that, as the German army was to be a volunteer professional force, it should be limited to 100,000 men, an even smaller force than originally intended.[41]

Meanwhile the French were presenting to their allies their principal demand, in Tardieu's memorandum of 25 February, which summed up the arguments already brought forward on various occasions, notably in Foch's plan of 10 January.[42] This note began by pointing out that the containment of Germany was not merely a French interest, but of concern to all the Allies, and argued that only military control of the Rhineland could provide security. Neither disarmament nor the League of Nations could be relied on. For disarmament could not be ensured and France required, not the assurance of eventual victory in a new war, but a guarantee that never again would she have to face a German invasion. Only the separation of the Rhineland from Germany could give that guarantee. A committee – Kerr for Britain, Mezes for America, and Tardieu for France – was set up to examine the French proposals. By 12 March it was deadlocked. Clemenceau was furious at what he claimed was Lloyd George's backsliding. He seemed to have got the

---

[40] Cecil to House, 8 March 1919, quoted by P. Birdsall, *Versailles Twenty Years After*, p. 132. Cf. S. P. Tillman op. cit., pp. 129–33.
[41] Cf. S. P. Tillman, op. cit., pp. 161–6.
[42] Tardieu's note is printed in A. Tardieu, *La Paix* (1920), pp. 165–87.

impression from Lloyd George's remarks in the Council of Ten, on 10 March, that the British prime minister was more favourable to the French proposals than was the case. It is clear from the minutes of the British cabinet of 4 March 1919 that Lloyd George never contemplated acceptance of the French proposals for an autonomous Rhineland state. Indeed

> he doubted whether the French government were really behind the Marshal's proposals, though they might appear to be supporting them. It was unlikely that France would accept permanently the burden of maintaining a garrison of something like 300,000 men on the Rhine.[43]

There are several indications of Clemenceau's anger at Lloyd George at this point: he had not yet realized that Wilson could be worse to deal with. Loucheur's diary of 12 March states that Clemenceau is 'angry with Lloyd George, who is no longer willing to give us the left bank of the Rhine'. House's diary notes that Clemenceau had complained to him the same day that 'Lloyd George had broken his word over the Rhineland, Syria, and the division of Reparations'.[44] On 14 March Poincaré and Clemenceau went to greet President Wilson on his return from the United States. While waiting at the station they talked about the negotiations, and Poincaré made this record of Clemenceau's remarks in his diary:

> Today Clemenceau is angry with the English, and especially with Lloyd George. 'I won't budge,' he said, 'I will act like a hedgehog, and wait until they come to talk to me. I will yield nothing. We will see if they can manage without me. Lloyd George is a trickster. He has managed to turn me into a 'Syrian'. . . . I don't like being double-crossed. Lloyd George has deceived me. He made me the finest promises, and now he breaks them. Fortunately, I think that at the moment we can count on American support. What is the worst of all, is that the day before yesterday, Lloyd George said to me, 'Well, now that we are going to disarm Germany, you no longer need the Rhine.' I said to Clemenceau: 'Does disarmament then seem to him to give the same guarantees? Does he think that, in the future, we can be sure of preventing Germany from rebuilding her army?' 'We are in complete agreement,' said Clemenceau; 'it is a point I will not yield.'[45]

[43] Public Record Office, CAB 23/15, 541A.
[44] L. Loucheur, *Carnets Secrets*, p. 71; House's diary, XV, p. 93, quoted by H. I. Nelson, op. cit., p. 220.
[45] Poincaré, *Notes Journalières*, 14 March 1919, Poincaré Papers, XLII, Bibliothèque Nationale, NAF 16033.

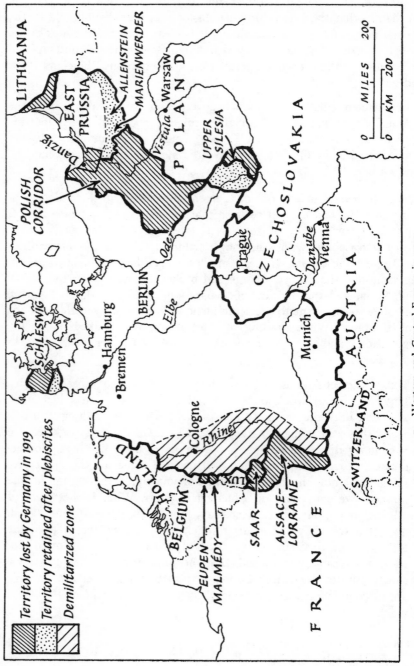

3. Western and Central Europe in 1919

LITHUANIA

EAST PRUSSIA

ALLENSTEIN

MARIENWERDER

Danzig

Vistula Warsaw

P O L A N D

Oder

UPPER SILESIA

POLISH CORRIDOR

C Z E C H O S L O V A K I A

Prague

Danube Vienna

BERLIN

Elbe

Hamburg

Bremen

SCHLESWIG

A U S T R I A

Munich

Cologne

Rhine

H O L L A N D

BELGIUM

LUX.

EUPEN MALMÉDY

SAAR

ALSACE-LORRAINE

F R A N C E

S W I T Z E R L A N D

Territory lost by Germany in 1919

Territory retained after plebiscites

Demilitarized zone

0   MILES   200

0   KM   200

Lloyd George sought to break the deadlock by offering France an Anglo-American guarantee of immediate aid against a German attack, as an alternative to the Rhineland buffer state. As soon as Wilson returned to Paris on 14 March, Lloyd George suggested this joint guarantee, and won his acceptance. The same afternoon Wilson and Lloyd George put the proposal to Clemenceau at an informal meeting. Clemenceau, in *Grandeurs et Misères d'une Victoire*, calls Lloyd George's offer 'an unprecedented historical event. What a stroke of fortune for France! The American agreement was secondary.'[46] While Clemenceau regarded the American guarantee as secondary, to Lloyd George it was of the utmost importance. In the cabinet discussion of 4 March 1919 he had stated that 'if the United States and ourselves would guarantee France against invasion, she would be satisfied. This, however, was impossible, as the President would not hear of any entangling alliances, as he put his faith in the League of Nations.'[47]

Clemenceau asked for time to consider it and discussed the proposal with Pichon, Loucheur and Tardieu over the next three days. There is no indication that he consulted his cabinet. Loucheur's account of the discussions shows that from the first Clemenceau argued for acceptance. He was, says Loucheur, much moved by Lloyd George's offer to build a Channel tunnel so that troops could be moved quickly to the aid of the French : Professor Nelson's comment on this is that 'the ebullient Welshman surely jested'. Pichon and Tardieu were hesitant, while Loucheur agreed with Clemenceau. At this point Clemenceau seems to have envisaged giving up the claim to the military occupation of the Rhineland in return for the guarantee, but it was decided, as expressed by the French reply of 17 March, to ask for the military occupation as well as the treaties of guarantee. All that the French conceded was their demand for the political separation of the Rhineland from Germany. The British and Americans refused to accept this.[48] By this time there was complete deadlock between Clemenceau on the one hand, and Wilson and Lloyd George on the other, not only on the Rhineland, but also on the Saar, on Reparations, and on Germany's eastern frontier. Clemenceau used the Reparations negotiations as a bargaining counter. On 23 March Poincaré recorded in his diary :

A few days ago Clemenceau, wishing to subordinate everything to a French success on the territorial questions, said to Loucheur 'be con-

[46] G. Clemenceau, *Grandeurs et Misères d'une Victoire*, p. 163. As this was before the meetings of the Council of Four had become formalized, there are no minutes of this meeting. Sources are Lloyd George, *The Truth About the Peace Treaties*, I, p. 403, A. Tardieu, *La Paix*, p. 195, Mermeix, *Le Combat des Trois*, p. 198. Cf. H. I. Nelson, op. cit., pp. 220-1.
[47] Public Record Office, CAB 23/15, 541A.
[48] L. Loucheur, *Carnets Secrets*, p. 71-2, H. I. Nelson, op. cit., p. 220.

ciliatory on financial questions. Study ways of giving some satisfaction to England, even on the question of priority'. . . . But in view of Lloyd George's latest attitude on territorial questions, Clemenceau told Loucheur to be more resistant.[49]

Lloyd George retreated to Fontainebleau for the week-end of 22–24 March, returning with a memorandum advocating a moderate peace as the only alternative to plunging Germany and the greater part of Europe into Bolshevism. The precise proposals made in the Fontaine-bleau memorandum included the following:

(i) the demilitarization of the Rhineland, but no occupation
(ii) the 1814 frontier for the Saar, or French right to obtain coal for 10 years
(iii) a Polish corridor to Danzig that would include the smallest possible number of Germans.

Clemenceau's reply accused Lloyd George of demanding the utmost concessions from Germany in everything that directly involved British interests, and then seeking to appease her at the expense of France. He claimed that this would not even satisfy Germany, as she was concerned above all with her overseas ambitions:

The note suggests that moderate territorial conditions should be imposed upon Germany in Europe in order not to leave a profound feeling of resentment after peace. This method might have value, if the late war had been for Germany a European war. This, however, was not the case. Before the war Germany was a great naval power whose future lay upon the water. This world power was Germany's pride: she will not console herself for having lost it. . . . If it is necessary to appease her she should be offered colonial satisfaction, naval satisfaction, or satisfaction with regard to her commercial expansion.[50]

As for the danger of Bolshevism, Clemenceau stated that Lloyd George's proposals would lead to Bolshevism in France and in the eastern European states. Lloyd George returned an even more bitter reply, which he did not expect to be taken very seriously.[51] The memorandum was

---

[49] *Notes Journalières*, 23 March 1919, Poincaré Papers XLII, Bibliothèque Nationale, NAF 16033.
[50] Lloyd George printed the main part of the memorandum, entitled 'Some considerations for the peace conference before they finally draft their terms', in *The Truth About the Peace Treaties*, I, pp. 404–16: Clemenceau's answer, and Lloyd George's reply to him, follow, pp. 416–22.
[51] Lloyd George to Wilson: 'I enclose reply I am sending to Clemenceau's paper. I thought on the whole it was better not to take it too seriously,' Wilson papers, VIII, A₁₃₁, quoted by H. I. Nelson, op. cit., p. 228. The discussion of the memorandum by the Council of Four on 27 March is reported in P. Mantoux, op. cit., pp. 42–8.

discussed by the Council of Four on 27 March, and this seems to have been the end of the matter. Negotiations continued on the various detailed questions at issue, without further reference to these exchanges. Relations were at their worst on 28 March, when Clemenceau and Wilson quarrelled violently in the Council of Four.[52] In the first two weeks of April the possibility of agreement on the main issues began to appear.

On the whole it was Wilson and Lloyd George who retreated. Clemenceau did not get all that he had asked for, but nevertheless won much more than he had been offered in March. He gave up most where the German-Polish frontier was concerned. On 3 April the Council of Four abandoned the earlier plan of giving Danzig to Poland, and agreed to set it up as a free city, with guaranteed freedom of transit for Poland. This compromise was very much Lloyd George's victory, although it is significant that a French memorandum of December 1918 had already envisaged this situation.[53] In other ways the German-Polish frontier was progressively whittled down by Lloyd George until a much less anti-German solution emerged than had originally been proposed.

But in the west Clemenceau gave up much less. He had to abandon the French claim to annex the Saar, but he was able to win the separation of the Saar from Germany for fifteen years, after which a plebiscite would be held to decide its future. This was far more than Wilson and Lloyd George had originally contemplated; they had merely thought of a temporary arrangement by which France would get the Saar coal.[54] No doubt the French interest in the Saar was primarily economic. But a temporary promise of coal deliveries was by no means satisfactory to them. They wished to provide for the permanent economic coordination of Saar coal and Lorraine iron ore, within the framework of a mercantilist war-time conception of economic life. The only real safeguard for such a scheme would have been outright annexation. The next best situation was the one eventually adopted, which as least guaranteed French economic control, and in a disguised way political control, for fifteen years. The French did not accept that the Saar was simply an economic question. Their first memorandum claimed that a substantial part of the population was French-speaking, or sympathetic

[52] On the question of the Saar, P. Mantoux, op. cit., I, pp. 63–75. Although Poincaré notes on 27 March that Clemenceau said: 'Yesterday, I was not happy, but today things went well. I have got what I wanted for the Rhine. . . .' Poincaré's comment was, 'He is a weak and vain old man, a toy in the hands of Wilson and Lloyd George.' Poincaré, *Notes Journalières*, Poincaré Papers XLII, Bibliothèque Nationale, NAF 16033. Clemenceau's remark is strange as the debate in the Council of Four on 27 March was one in which the gulf between Lloyd George and Wilson on the one hand, and Clemenceau on the other, appeared at its widest.

[53] 'Une méthode d'action en Pologne', Klotz Papers, Fol. 223, Res. 14 (1), Bibliothèque de Documentation Internationale Contemporaine, quoted by H. I. Nelson, op. cit., pp. 117–19: ibid., pp. 145–97, for discussion of the negotiations about the German-Polish frontier. Cf. also S. P. Tillman, op. cit., pp. 202–9.

[54] H. I. Nelson, op. cit., pp. 249–81, and S. P. Tillman, op. cit., pp. 184–9.

to France.[55] During their argument on the Saar Clemenceau told Wilson that if a hundred years was a long time in American history it was not long in French history, and that it was not too late to recall the events of the revolutionary period.[56] It is difficult to decide how seriously he expected these arguments to be taken. Certainly he obtained a régime that would give France the maximum opportunity to favour the growth of pro-French feeling among the population. Unlike many in France, he did not believe that German particularism was a living force in Germany proper or even in the Rhineland, but he seems to have had some illusions about the pro-French feelings of the Saar. Strangely enough Clemenceau had originally believed that the Americans would be more sympathetic than the British to French claims in the Saar. On 9 November 1918 he had told House that France and the United States, the two sister republics, were the only Allied powers of a high ethical character able to adopt an unselfish attitude. Coming down to practicalities, he said that he hoped that the United States would support the French claim to the Saar; England, he said, would oppose it, as she wished France to be dependent on her coal.[57] In fact Clemenceau was mistaken in this belief. Lloyd George accepted a French plan that was a disguised annexation, and only Wilson's obstinate resistance preserved the Saarlanders' right to a plebiscite to decide their nationality.[58]

But on the question of the military occupation of the Rhineland, Wilson gave way first. Clemenceau conceded a little by reducing his demand to an occupation of fifteen years; Wilson accepted this on 14 April. Mordacq reports that Clemenceau was very cheerful on 15 April: he told him,

In the last three days, we have worked well. All the great issues of concern to France are almost settled. Yesterday, as well as the two treaties giving us the military support of Britain and the United States in case of a German attack, I obtained the occupation of the Rhineland for fifteen years, with partial evacuation after five years. If Germany does not fulfil the treaty, there will be no evacuation either partial or definitive. At last I am no longer anxious. I have obtained almost everything I wanted.[59]

[55] The French memoranda on the Saar are printed in A. Tardieu, op. cit., pp. 279–89 and pp. 294–6. When Lloyd George said that French interest in the Saar was purely economic, Clemenceau denied it; he said, 'that depends on the sector of opinion you are thinking of: for the businessmen, yes. But the rest of France places a different importance on the Saar.' P. Mantoux, op. cit., I, p. 204.
[56] P. Mantoux, op. cit., I, p. 71.
[57] House's diary, XIV, p. 31, quoted by H. I. Nelson, op. cit., p. 134.
[58] H. I. Nelson, op. cit., p. 281.
[59] J. J. H. Mordacq, op. cit., III, pp. 220–1. Poincaré noted that Clemenceau telephoned him at 7 p.m. to say 'Well, I have the 15 years. Now I consider that the peace is made.' Poincaré, *Notes Journalières*, 15 April 1919, Poincaré Papers XLIII, Bibliothèque Nationale, NAF 16034.

On 22 April Lloyd George followed suit, albeit with great reluctance. Wilson and Lloyd George regarded their concession as being merely verbal, allowing Clemenceau to cover himself against domestic criticism. House wrote cynically:

> I have my doubts as to the Senate accepting such a treaty, but that is to be seen. Meanwhile it satisfies Clemenceau and we can get on with the real business of the Conference.

At this very time, Clemenceau told Poincaré that House had said Wilson was wrong in stating that American opinion would not accept the French claim to the Rhineland.[60]

Lloyd George insisted on a clause permitting an earlier withdrawal of the occupation force if the Germans demonstrated their good faith by making all possible efforts to fulfil the treaty. Clemenceau, on the other hand, on 30 April managed to insert a clause (Article 429) providing for an extension of the occupation beyond fifteen years if adequate guarantees for French security had not been given. This was intended to cover the danger that the American Senate would not ratify the treaty of guarantee, thus nullifying both guarantees, as the British guarantee was dependent on the Americans joining in.[61] Precisely that did occur.

Foch and Poincaré made a last effort to sabotage Clemenceau's bargain. Foch argued his case before the Council of Four on 31 March, and at a special meeting of the French cabinet on 25 April, while on 28 April Poincaré sent Clemenceau a long letter pleading for a military occupation to continue as long as Reparation payments remained due.[62] At the Cabinet meeting of 25 April only Foch spoke against the government's terms: Poincaré was silent. In defence of his policy Clemenceau re-stated his conviction that the preservation of the entente with Britain and the United States was of far greater value than an isolated France

[60] House Diary, XV, p. 105, quoted by H. I. Nelson, op. cit., p. 229, Poincaré, *Notes Journalières*, 19 March 1919, Poincaré Papers XLII, Bibliothèque Nationale, NAF 16033.

[61] On these negotiations, *see* H. I. Nelson, op. cit., pp. 240–4. L. A. R. Yates, *United States and French Security 1917–1921* (1957), p. 80, stated 'the British had determined to give France a guarantee against a German attack even if the United States did not'. This is a strange view. A much more convincing interpretation is that of Professor Nelson, who says that in Lloyd George's eyes the treaty was 'a fulcrum on which to lever Wilson and his colleagues into acceptance of a precise political and military commitment by the United States in western Europe'. H. I. Nelson, op. cit., pp. 219–20, and D. R. Watson, 'The making of the treaty of Versailles', in N. Waites (ed.), *Troubled Partnership*, pp. 77–9.

[62] Poincaré's letter was forwarded by Clemenceau to Lloyd George: it is in the Lloyd George Papers, F/51/1/20 and was printed in Lloyd George, *The Truth about the Peace Treaties*, I, pp. 427–32. Poincaré suspected that Clemenceau did not even read it, and followed it with an even longer letter to Pichon, on 3 May, in which he listed his criticisms of the treaty as a whole. This letter did not find its way into British hands. *Notes Journalières*, 2–3 May 1919, Poincaré Papers XLIII, Bibliothèque Nationale, NAF 16034.

occupying the Rhineland. Indeed, he cast doubt on the military arguments for the occupation, saying that it was a conception out of keeping with modern warfare. But he also sought to have it both ways. For he argued that he had in fact provided for an occupation that would last at least fifteen years, perhaps longer, and obtained a cast-iron British and American guarantee as well. He said to Poincaré: 'In fifteen years I will be dead, but if you do me the honour of visiting my tomb, you will be able to say that the Germans have not fulfilled all the clauses of the treaty, and that we are still on the Rhine.[63]

The fifteen-year occupation was paradoxical in that it provided a guarantee against Germany when she was weak, but removed it when she might be assumed to have recovered from the effects of the war. But the situation was not seen in those terms. It was thought that at the end of the war the presence in Germany of millions of trained soldiers offered an immediate danger. The French were well aware of the war weariness that had affected their armies in the last year of the war. And so it was thought that the danger was a short-term as well as a long-term one. At this time Foch and Poincaré were arguing for the immediate imposition of a preliminary peace, on the grounds that the demobilization of the Allied armies would soon deprive them of their assured superiority over the Germans. If France could be given security for fifteen years, by the treaty, then she could rebuild her shattered military strength, and hope to stand once again as an equal to Germany. Clemenceau saw the basic problem as psychological. Fundamental was the need to restore French vitality and national willpower. As he put it in June, when arguing against Lloyd George's attempt to reduce the period of the occupation:

> We need a barrier behind which, in the years to come, our people can work in security to rebuild its ruins. That barrier is the Rhine. I must take national feelings into account. That does not mean that I am afraid of losing office. I am quite indifferent on that point. But I will not, by giving up the occupation, do something which will break the willpower of our people.[64]

Clemenceau was criticized in France for having abandoned the tangible security of the Rhineland buffer state for the paper promise of the treaties of guarantee. These critics said that the treaties gave France nothing she did not already have. For if Germany attacked France,

---

[63] Mermeix, *Le Combat des Trois*, pp. 228–30; M. Weygand, op. cit., II, p. 46; cf. P. Miquel, op. cit., p. 390. Poincaré had noted in his diary on 6 April that Clemenceau criticized the idea of a permanent occupation of the Rhineland, saying that it would cause trouble with the local population and would necessitate three years' military service. *Notes Journalières*, Poincaré Papers, XLIII, Bibliothèque Nationale, NAF 16034.

[64] P. Mantoux, op. cit., II, p. 410. Quoted in A. Tardieu, *La Paix*, p. 219.

whether or not there was a treaty, Britain at least would be forced to come to her aid, in her own interests, just as she had in 1914. Clemenceau was aware of this. But he had never regarded the claim for a buffer state in the Rhineland as feasible or desirable. He said later to Martet:

> The policy of Foch and Poincaré was bad in principle. It was a policy no Frenchman, no republican Frenchman could accept for a moment, except in the hope of obtaining other guarantees, other advantages. We leave that sort of thing to Bismarck.[65]

In other words he had argued for the separation of the Rhineland from Germany only as a bargaining counter. And if the practical importance of the treaties of guarantee was small, their psychological importance was immense, as a tangible symbol that the wartime Allies were determined to remain united, that they would not allow the Germans to play them off against each other. In his eyes this was the essential requirement for the future, and the break-up of the alliance after he left office filled him with doubts and despair about the international situation. As he wrote in *Grandeurs et Misères d'une Victoire*,

> Never has there been such a collapse of victorious powers in the face of a defeated nation which, simply by showing a revival of energy, placed its conquerors in disarray and sudden paralysis.[66]

Clemenceau stated in his memoirs that on Reparations France was faced with common British-American opposition, and that on no question except that of the Rhineland was the gulf between the Anglo-Saxons and the French so great.[67] This is a strange comment, as the British position on Reparations fluctuated violently and at crucial moments was close to the French. Only this Anglo-French cooperation persuaded Wilson to accept Reparations clauses which departed so violently from his original conception of a just peace.[68] Nevertheless, the French were equally responsible with the British for the most disastrous part of the treaty.

There is no sign that Clemenceau ever realized the economic impossibility of the Reparations clauses.[69] It is true that Clemenceau said to Poincaré, 'Oh, Germany cannot pay what we thought', but this was in the context of Poincaré's even more inflated demands: it is clear that Clemenceau himself expected Germany to pay sums that were quite

---

[65] J. Martet, *Le Silence de M. Clemenceau*, p. 248.
[66] G. Clemenceau, *Grandeurs et Misères d'une Victoire*, p. 166.
[67] Ibid., pp. 261–2.
[68] S. P. Tillman, op. cit., 243.
[69] Poincaré, *Notes Journalières*, 27 March 1919, Poincaré Papers XLII, Bibliothèque Nationale, NAF 16033, and G. Clemenceau, *Grandeurs et Misères d'une Victoire*, pp. 261–74, on the financial mutilation of the treaty.

impractical, even if less than Poincaré wanted. The French were as insistent as the British on the need to force the Germans to admit liability for the full costs of the war. They supported the British claim that the costs of pensions would be included among the items for which Germany was asked to make reparation. In his bitter criticism of his successors for failing to exact full payment, Clemenceau shows no recognition of the impossibility of making financial transfers on such a scale. No doubt, as Keynes said, Clemenceau wanted the sum demanded in Reparation to be as large as possible, quite irrespective of the practicalities of payment, so that France would have a good excuse for interfering in German affairs, on the grounds that the treaty had been broken. The first French plan for Reparation involved an elaborate scheme for the 'Ottomanization' of Germany, a system of Allied control over the financial and economic life of the country on the model of the Commission that had controlled the financial affairs of the Ottoman Empire.[70] These plans came to nothing, but the Rhineland occupation, although not designed as security for Reparations, could obviously be so used. Nevertheless, Clemenceau really imagined that it would be possible to exact very large sums from the Germans, although not the total amount. He was notoriously incompetent in financial matters, and the advice which he got from the finance minister Klotz was not realistic.[71] Clemenceau is supposed to have said about Klotz, 'Just my luck to get hold of the only Jew who can't count.' Klotz was responsible for the reckless methods which allowed the French unfunded debt to snowball in 1919, and presided over the rapid decline of the value of the franc in the foreign exchanges. His justification for this policy of *laisser-aller* was that Germany would pay huge sums in Reparation, thus allowing the re-establishment of budgetary equilibrium and the maintenance of the value of the franc. Clemenceau must take responsibility for this disastrous financial policy.[72]

[70] French proposals for the Reparations clauses of the treaty are printed in L. L. Klotz, *De la guerre à la Paix, Souvenirs et Documents* (1924), pp. 215–49. Cf. P. M. Burnett, *Reparation at the Paris Peace Conference* (1940), I, p. 436: 'Keynes suggested that in his opinion the French demand for a big indemnity was a basis for continued occupation and ultimate acquisition of the Rhine provinces.' Keynes developed this theme, of course, in his famous pamphlet, *The Economic Consequences of the Peace* (1919). Cf. M. Barrès, *Les Grandes Problèmes du Rhin* (1930), p. 386: 'Clemenceau said to me – "Germany will not pay, and we will remain".'
[71] Clemenceau told Poincaré that he was ignoring Klotz, whose proposals were totally unrealistic; he was referring to Klotz's plan for an Allied financial combination. Poincaré, *Notes Journalières*, 27 March 1919, Poincaré Papers XLII, Bibliothèque Nationale, NAF 16033.
[72] Lloyd George, *The Truth about the Peace Treaties*, I, p. 402–3: 'M. Clemenceau did not at any stage of the discussions take any active interest in the subject of Reparations. He left that entirely to M. Loucheur.' Poincaré's diary, however, shows that Clemenceau took an interest in the Reparations clauses, in the sense, that he used them as a bargaining counter, *see above*, pp. 347–8. Poincaré, with an amazing obstinacy, refused to admit that France needed to compromise on any-

As a result of the Anglo-French stand on Reparations the Americans gave way. 5 April was the crucial day, when House deputized for Wilson who was ill; it was agreed to present Germany with a clause admitting total liability for the war, Article 231, the famous 'war-guilt' clause. Although this produced immense resentment in Germany, it was not regarded as important, except as demonstrating to British and French public opinion that the Germans had been forced to admit liability for the full costs of the war, although it was not practically possible to exact payment for them; 'this is simply a matter of drafting,' said Clemenceau.[73] At the same meeting the American attempt to establish a *de facto* limitation to Reparations, by empowering the Reparations Commission to fix Germany's capacity to pay on the basis that thirty years was the maximum period, was defeated. No time limit was to be fixed, thus opening the way to the presentation of astronomical demands.

There can be little justification for the Reparations clauses, except in terms of the demands of public opinion. Perhaps Lloyd George's position, in spite of its apparent shiftiness, was the most sensible. He admitted in private that the sums demanded in Reparations could never be collected, but agreed that public opinion would not be satisfied with anything less. The best way out of this dilemma was not to set a fixed sum in the treaty, but to leave the Reparations Commission to fix the total and methods of payment, at a time when the pressure of anti-German public opinion would not be so great.[74] Clemenceau supported this, but seems to have entertained greater illusions than Lloyd George about the sums that could be expected eventually from Germany. The most detailed study of Reparations has argued that the French made a profound mistake in their conduct of the negotiations. It argues that the French demand for an indemnity to cover the full cost of the war, and then the specious argument by which the cost of pensions was included, only led to an increase in the British share at the expense of France and Belgium. If the original formulation of the costs of restoration of damaged civilian property had been adhered to, they would have collected almost all the German payments.[75] However, Clemenceau was well aware that Britain would not help to extort Reparations from Germany, if her own share in them was tiny. Only by associating

---

thing; he told Tardieu on 23 March that 'Clemenceau gains nothing by making concessions on financial matters, in the hope of obtaining more in the matter of the Rhine. All these concessions weaken his position instead of strengthening it. Again, on 2 May, he complained to Pichon that Clemenceau dissipated his energy in quarrels with individuals, but he yielded on the basic questions. *Notes Journalières*, Poincaré Papers, XLII and XLIII, Bibliothèque National NAF 16033–4.

[73] P. Mantoux, op. cit., I, p. 152.

[74] *See* P. Birdsall, op. cit., pp. 238–63, for a brief discussion of the negotiations on Reparations.

[75] E. Weill-Raynal, *Les Réparations Allemandes et la France* (1938–46), I, p. 128.

Britain with her in the expected benefits could France hope to get British support in putting pressure on Germany. Moreover, the British government always insisted on linking Reparations with the problem of war debts. If Britain found herself excluded from the benefits of Reparations, while France was receiving large sums, this would merely have produced a tougher British attitude towards France's war debts to Britain.

On 4 May there was an especially long meeting of the French cabinet, which was presented, for the first time, with the treaty, and asked for its approval. Poincaré complained, in his diary, that the business was so arranged that real discussion was impossible. All those concerned in the negotiations were invited to give a report on their respective sections of the treaty; this involved Tardieu, Klotz, Loucheur, Clémentel, Leygues, Simon and Claveille. Clemenceau and Pichon did not speak. Poincaré noted:

> All these reports took up a great deal of time, and made any discussion impossible. That was obviously Clemenceau's object.

Clemenceau then spoke on relations with Italy, and was extremely critical of the Italian demands, much to Poincaré's annoyance. Poincaré said that Italy was closer to them than Britain and America, and their Latin sister would, if French policy continued unchanged, throw herself into the arms of Germany. Clemenceau disagreed, and declared that Italy's military value had been small. It was far more important to remain on good terms with the United States. In spite of Poincaré's criticisms, the cabinet unanimously endorsed the peace terms.[76]

On 7 May 1919 the Allied terms were presented to the German representatives at a formal session of the full Peace Conference in the great Hall of Mirrors at Versailles, where Bismarck had proclaimed the creation of the German Empire after the French defeat in 1871. Clemenceau presented the document with a brief speech. He was furious at the arrogant reply of the German spokesman, Brockdorff-Rantzau, although, as he said to Mordacq, in reality this German attitude could do nothing but good, as it would help persuade the British and Americans that his assessment of the German character had been correct.[77] The assembled statesmen then turned to drawing up the Austrian treaty, in the intervals of their discussion of the German representations. Some detailed modifications were accepted quickly and easily but the major confrontation between Clemenceau and Lloyd George occurred on 2 June,

[76] Poincaré, *Notes Journalières*, 4 May 1919, Poincaré Paper LXIII, Bibliothèque Nationale, NAF 16034. There is no space here to develop the question of Franco-Italian relations; they can be studied in R. Albrecht-Carrié, *Italy at the Paris Peace Conference* (1938), and S. I. Minerbi, *L'Italie et la Palestine 1914–1920* (1970).
[77] Clemenceau's brief speech is to be found in G. Clemenceau, *Discours de Guerre*, pp. 89–90; his remarks to Mordacq, in J. J. H. Mordacq, op. cit., III, p. 263.

after the British prime minister had drawn up, in consultation with his cabinet and Imperial War cabinet colleagues, a programme of concessions. This was put in the form of an ultimatum:

> they were not prepared to continue the war, and march on Germany or join in the reimposition of the blockade unless certain defects in the Peace Treaty were put right.

Lloyd George declared bluntly that his colleagues would not agree to the occupation of the Rhineland beyond two years. The other concessions for which he asked were a revision of the German-Polish frontier, with a plebiscite in Upper Silesia, and, in imprecise terms, a revision of the Reparations settlement.[78]

Clemenceau was obviously extremely hurt by Lloyd George's attempt to reverse previously agreed decisions, but he did not refuse to discuss the question. He showed that he was readiest to accept Lloyd George's proposals for the Polish frontier, but expressed adamant opposition to the reopening of the question of the occupation of the Rhineland. He made an eloquent plea for the preservation of unity among the victors:

> My policy, at the conference, and I hope that you realize this, is one of close union with Great Britain and America. I am aware that you have important interests far away from what concerns us most, I know something of the great American continent, and of the immense achievements of the British Empire. Because I have made the entente with England and America the basis of my policy I have been attacked from all sides as weak and inadequate. If I fall, you will be faced with even greater divergences of views than those which separate us to-day. There remains the possibility of a final disagreement between us. I do not wish even to contemplate it. Let us try to reduce these questions to a minimum, let us simply look at the facts and see what really separates us. If, after that, there remain insoluble differences between us, I do not know how we can envisage the future. I do not wish to believe that we must tell the public that we are forced to bring our negotiations to an end because we are incapable of giving a joint reply to the Germans.[79]

Although he was prepared to discuss concessions with his allies he pointed out that, in his eyes, this was the wrong way to treat the Ger-

[78] Lloyd George's report on the views of his British and Dominion colleagues to the Council of Four, 2 June 1919, F.R.U.S., P.P.C., VI, pp. 139–42.

[79] P. Mantoux op. cit., II, p. 271. Clemenceau complained to Poincaré, on 30 May 1919, about Lloyd George's desire to conciliate Germany: he said he was much more worried about Lloyd George than about Wilson, but that he was determined not to yield, certainly not on the left bank (of the Rhine). Poincaré, Notes Journalières, Poincaré Papers LXIII, Bibliothèque Nationale, NAF 16034.

mans. Concessions would only be interpreted as a sign of weakness; 'the more concessions we made, the more the Germans would demand; it was best to act firmly'.

In the inter-Allied negotiations that followed, Clemenceau was not forced to give up much. This was largely due to Wilson's attitude, which was that once the Allies had agreed on the terms they thought just, they should not alter them merely to please the Germans. The peace was harsh, but just, he told Smuts, in reply to the latter's plea for a more conciliatory attitude.[80] At this point Wilson's inflexible and dictatorial character brought him close to Clemenceau in his attitude towards Germany, and separated both from Lloyd George, who, in spite of all his fluctuating positions, never lost sight of the fact that the German attitude towards the peace terms was an important element in the situation. Once again the Poles paid the price of Allied unity. In spite of Clemenceau's plea for a strong Poland to provide a barrier against German expansion eastwards, the major concession made to the Germans as a result of Lloyd George's action was the decision to held a plebiscite in Upper Silesia. As a result, a large area which had been assigned to Poland remained part of Germany. No other important changes were made, and the clauses governing the occupation of the Rhineland remained unaltered, in spite of Lloyd George's original assertion that they were unacceptable.[81]

On 16 June the final Allied terms were submitted to the German delegation, which advised its government not to sign. The Council of Four called in Foch to hear his plans for military action in case the Germans refused the treaty, and were surprised to discover that whereas a few week earlier he had told them that a march on Berlin would be without danger or difficulty, he now produced all sorts of objections, and demanded a much more cautious approach, with the signing of separate armistices with the southern German states. The statesmen, Clemenceau in particular, were extremely annoyed at yet another attempt by Foch to mix up political and military matters; instead of providing a precise plan of military operations, he offered an elaborate political programme. He was sent away to produce a purely military plan.[82] However, this did not prove necessary as a majority of the German Parliament was eventually in favour of signing. On 22 June the new German Government offered to

---

[80] Wilson to Smuts, 16 May 1919, quoted by H. I. Nelson, op. cit., p. 325. 'Justice had shown itself overwhelmingly against Germany,' said Wilson on 3 June 1919, opposing further discussion with the Germans. F.R.U.S., P.P.C., VI, p. 159. The common factors in the personalities and outlook of Wilson and Clemenceau have been portrayed, perhaps in a rather exaggerated way, by J. B. Duroselle, in his article 'Wilson et Clemenceau', *Centenaire Woodrow Wilson* (Geneva, 1956).
[81] H. I. Nelson, op. cit., pp. 321-2.
[82] P. Mantoux, op. cit., II, pp. 430-8, 442-4, 447-50, and 458-67; F.R.U.S., P.P.C., VI, pp. 501-9, 521, 523-4, 543-51.

sign the treaty if clauses 227 to 231, concerning the trial of war criminals and war-guilt, were removed. Erzberger, who had been in touch with American and French representatives in Germany, had gained the erroneous impression that the Allies might accept this. He had been told by the French agents that the treaty would in practice be enforced leniently on this point. Clemenceau, on 11 August 1919, argued at a meeting of the Heads of Delegations for limiting the trial of war criminals 'to a few symbolic persons'.[83] Without any hesitation, Wilson, Clemenceau and Lloyd George rejected the German plea, and on 23 June the German Parliament voted for ratification. On 28 June the German representative again met the assembled Allies, in full session of the Peace Conference, at Versailles.[84]

4 DEFENCE OF THE TREATY

With the signing of the treaty the regular meetings of the Council of Four came to an end, as Wilson and Lloyd George returned home. The peace conference, however, remained in session, with the task of drawing up the other treaties, with Austria, Hungary, Bulgaria, and Turkey, and generally supervising the re-establishment of normal government throughout the areas of eastern Europe, the Balkans and Turkey where the former political authorities had largely disappeared. Supervision of these activities, previously carried out by the Councils of Ten, of Five, and of Four, was now vested in a body referred to as the Heads of Delegations. Clemenceau was frequently present at its meetings, especially in July and August. Only in the autumn did his attendance gradually decline, when he left the task of representing France to Pichon or to a permanent official. As a great deal of the work of this body was relatively unimportant it is surprising that he found it necessary to continue his attendance for so long. After September Lloyd George decided that Britain could not spare a cabinet minister for this work and appointed a permanent official, Sir Eyre Crowe, as British representative. But Clemenceau continued to be a participant in the meetings until December 1919.[85]

His other main task was to defend the German treaty in the French Parliament. Clemenceau's speeches in the Chamber on 24 and 25

---

[83] K. Epstein, *Matthias Erzberger and the Dilemma of German Democracy* (1959), p. 319; K. F. Nowak, *Versailles 1919* (French translation 1928), pp. 269–75. Clemenceau's remarks at the meeting of the Heads of Delegations are printed in *Documents on British Foreign Policy 1919–1939*, First Series, I, pp. 390–1.

[84] Clemenceau's brief remarks, and a description of the scene by J. Bainville, are published in G. Clemenceau, *Discours de Paix*, pp. 99–103. Cf. also J. J. H. Mordacq, op. cit., III, pp. 352–6.

[85] His role in this body can be followed in the minutes printed in *Documents on British Foreign Policy 1919–1939*, First Series, vols I, II.

September, and in the Senate on 11 October 1919, are important sources for an understanding of his views on the peace settlement: his last major Parliamentary speeches, they are, in a sense, his political testaments. He spoke first, briefly, in reply to Barthou, the *rapporteur* of the Chamber committee on the treaty, on 24 September. Up to this point he had sat silent on the government bench, allowing his ministers to answer criticisms of particular sections of the treaty.[86] But on 24 September Barthou demanded an answer from the prime minister himself. It had already become apparent that the United States Senate might not ratify either the Treaty of Versailles or the treaty of guarantee. Barthou complained that, in that case, France would have lost the guarantee of security for which she had agreed to surrender her claim to the Rhine frontier. Clemenceau replied, no doubt disguising his real opinions, that he was sure that the American Senate would ratify the treaties. In any case, he said, if ratification did not occur, a special clause provided France with a means of ensuring her security:

> There is an article, which I myself got adopted, which provides that in that case, we will make new arrangements concerning the Rhine. As a result, we are safeguarded in that respect, and everything has been provided for.[87]

This declaration, which implied that France had a unilateral right to prolong the occupation of the Rhineland, was highly misleading, and was not accepted by Barthou. The relevant clause stated that

> if at that date the guarantees against unprovoked aggression were not considered sufficient by the Allied and Associated governments, the evacuation of the occupying troops may be delayed to the extent regarded as necessary for the purpose of obtaining the required guarantees.[88]

Lloyd George had strenuously, and successfully, resisted the much more sweeping wording first proposed by the French, which would have given

---

[86] Clemenceau's speeches are printed in *Discours de Paix*, pp. 156–281. As well as the full report of the debates in the *Journal Officiel*, E. Beau de Lomenie, *Le débat de ratification du traité de Versailles à la Chambre des Députés et dans la presse* (1945), provides a useful summary, and commentary. The books produced by members of the various Parliamentary committees provide a convenient source for the reaction of Parliament to the treaty: they reproduce parts of the various committee reports. L. Barthou, *Le Traité de Paix* (1919); L. Bourgeois, *Le Traité de Versailles* (1919); C. Benoist, *Les nouvelles frontières d'Allemagne et les nouvelles frontières d'Europe* (1920). Barthou was the *rapporteur* of the Chamber committee, Bourgeois of the Senate committee, Benoist of a sub-committee reporting on the European political clauses of the treaty.
[87] G. Clemenceau, *Discours de Paix*, p. 159.
[88] Article 429 of the treaty, p. 330 in the text of the treaty printed in H. W. V. Temperley, *A History of the Peace Conference of Paris* (1920), III.

France alone the right to postpone evacuation. But Clemenceau and Tardieu implied that France alone did have the right, under this clause, to prolong the occupation.

Clemenceau's main speech in defence of the treaty was made the next day, 25 September. He did not discuss it in detail. Indeed he said that the great mistake of earlier speakers had been to present detailed criticism of particular sections of the treaty. He knew that it was imperfect. But the war had been fought by a coalition, and the treaty must express the lowest common denominator of the views of all the partners. It was easy to see how many details could be improved on. But the important thing was to look at the treaty as a whole, not in a carping, critical, negative spirit, but to see what could be made of it. This theme he developed with great eloquence in his peroration. He declared:

> The treaty, with all its complex clauses, will only be worth what you are worth; it will be what you make it. . . . What you are going to vote to-day is not even a beginning, it is a beginning of a beginning. The ideas it contains will grow and bear fruit. You have won the power to impose them on a defeated Germany. We are told that she will revive. All the more reason not to show her that we fear her. . . . M. Marin went to the heart of the question, when he turned to us and said in despairing tones, 'You have reduced us to a policy of vigilance.' Yes, M. Marin, do you think that one could make a treaty which would do away with the need for vigilance among the nations of Europe who only yesterday were pouring out their blood in battle? Life is a perpetual struggle in war, as in peace. . . . That struggle cannot be avoided. Yes, we must have vigilance, we must have a great deal of vigilance. I cannot say for how many years, perhaps I should say for how many centuries, the crisis which has begun will continue. Yes, this treaty will bring us burdens, troubles, miseries, difficulties, and that will continue for long years.[89]

These passages elevated the debate to the emotional level attained by his great wartime speeches. Whatever the criticism of points of detail, there could be no denying that he had drawn out the historical significance of the treaty in a way no other speaker had attempted. Over the next twenty years his insistence on the need for France to continue her wartime effort was to take on steadily more significance. The great mistake, not only of France but of all the victorious Allies, was to believe that the treaty could preserve for ever the balance of forces achieved in 1918. It was not a mistake Clemenceau made. The treaty

[89] G. Clemenceau, *Discours de Paix*, pp. 207–8 and 216–17.

was ratified by 372 votes to 53, the opposition consisting of rather more than half the Socialist deputies, of Franklin-Bouillon, a persistent Radical critic of the government from the time of its formation, and of the right-wing deputy Louis Marin, whose views Clemenceau had seized on in his speech.[90]

On 11 October Clemenceau spoke again in defence of the treaty in the Senate. Here the persistent opposition of the Chamber was absent, and ratification was voted unanimously. He made many of the same points as in his speech in the Chamber but in a less combative, and more philosophic spirit. A main theme of his speech in the Senate was to combat those who advocated splitting up Germany. He declared that to attempt to destroy national unity, which depended on feelings, by institutional devices, would be self defeating. France must therefore find a way of living alongside sixty million Germans. He ended with some general reflections on what he had, in 1891, referred to as the rise of the Fourth Estate. The bourgeoisie, he said, like the aristocracy of the *ancien régime*, had failed as a ruling class, and now it was the turn of the working class to seek to become a ruling class. This led him back to the need for national unity, and a final plea for a demographic revolution.

> The treaty does not state that France will have many children, but it is the first thing that should have been written there. For if France does not have large families, it will be in vain that you put all the finest clauses in the treaty, that you take away all the Germans guns, France will be lost because there will be no more French.[91]

It is ironical that he chose this subject for the closing remarks of his last Parliamentary speech. For the twenty years that followed saw the birth-rate fall to a phenomenally low level. There could hardly have been a more pointed indication that France was not prepared to follow the arduous road to national greatness pointed out for her by Clemenceau in these speeches. Precisely what he feared did take place. The great effort of the war had been too much. National will-power and energy had been sapped in a fundamental way, so that the continuing German challenge was not to be met by an ever-vigilant and self-confident France.

An assessment of Clemenceau's part in the peace settlement in 1919 is central to any judgement on his place in history. As he was well aware, victory in the war would be fruitless unless safeguarded by a satisfactory peace. In the light of subsequent events, the peace of Versailles can hardly be called a success. Precisely the situation its makers had sought to avoid did occur. Germany was allowed, in spite of all the restrictions

[90] G. Bonnefous, op. cit., III, p. 57.
[91] G. Clemenceau, *Discours de Paix*, p. 280.

imposed on her, to achieve a position from which she could challenge the 1919 settlement. The peace turned out to be only a truce and in 1939 the war began again, in circumstances far less favourable to the western powers. France, particularly, suffered from the breakdown of morale, of national energy and will-power, which Clemenceau had seen to be the greatest danger. To what extent, in the light of these later developments, can Clemenceau be blamed?

It is now clear that the view according to which there was a clear gradation on all issues from Clemenceau's vindictiveness, through Lloyd George's intermediate position, to Wilson's high-minded advocacy of compromise and conciliation, is not correct. The position of all three statesmen was more complicated than that, and in the last resort, all three were agreed on measures which, in German eyes, were vindictive and unacceptable.[92] Clemenceau, in order to protect his domestic position, argued for demands which he did not expect or desire to achieve; in the last resort the terms he was prepared to accept were not incompatible with those of Wilson and Lloyd George. Nevertheless, if Clemenceau alone must not bear responsibility for the harshness of the peace, he must share it with Wilson and Lloyd George; and on certain key issues he fought for and won terms that were more anti-German than the Anglo-Saxon statesmen desired. The peace Clemenceau negotiated was a Diktat, as the Germans said. It was a settlement the Germans would not willingly accept, and would therefore have to be imposed on them by the superior force of the victorious powers; it was not a peace of compromise and reconciliation.

But was anything else possible in the circumstances? The time for a compromise peace was before Germany had been defeated. Even in August 1918, those in command in Germany were only prepared to accept terms that would consecrate their victory, and provide for German hegemony in Europe. Instead they had been defeated, and had to pay the price. E. L. Woodward has said of the 'failure' of the treaty:

> I never expected a satisfactory peace settlement. Europe had been torn apart with such savagery that reconciliation must be far distant.[93]

The peace treaty did contain several items which served no real purpose, and were merely pin-pricks exciting German resentment. Such were the war-guilt clause, and the provisions for the trial of the Kaiser and of war criminals; while the Reparations clauses were an unmitigated disaster. However, it is difficult to believe that removal of these clauses

[92] Cf. D. R. Watson, 'Anglo-French relations in the making of the treaty of Versailles', in N. Waites (ed.) *Troubled Partnership*, pp. 86–8.
[93] E. L. Woodward, *Great Britain and the War of 1914–1918* (1967), pp. xxvi–xxvii.

would have so transformed opinion in Germany that the settlement would have been willingly accepted. Nor were these clauses the particular responsibility of Clemenceau. Lloyd George had sought them just as eagerly, and Wilson had not seriously objected. They were demanded by public opinion in all the victor countries, and could not be omitted for that reason. Only the Reparations clauses had practical effects, which were disastrous enough in all consequence, for it was to the economic convulsions, the inflation of 1923 and the depression of 1930, connected with the Reparations clauses, and the failure to re-establish the international financial system on a sound basis, that Hitler owed his rise to power. But the blame lies more with those in power in the ten years following the treaty than with the provisions of the treaty itself.

A more cogent criticism of Clemenceau may be that from the Right, expressed most succinctly in Bainville's phrase that the peace treaty was 'trop douce pour ce qu'elle a de dur'. In other words, it was folly to leave Germany as the most populous, and therefore potentially the most powerful, European state, economically and politically. The Right argued that security could only be obtained by splitting up Germany into several small states. Again Clemenceau could reply that such a policy was totally impossible. France's allies would not consider it, and a war won by an alliance could not produce a peace dictated by France alone. In any case, contrary to Keynes's belief, he was not a cynical practitioner of Realpolitik, envisaging an eternal prolongation of the struggle between France and Germany. He declared that the peace of Europe depended on a victor who would not behave as Napoleon and Bismarck, who in the moment of triumph claimed no more than his rightful due. He argued that this had been done in 1919, and that Germany had not been deprived of any territory rightfully hers. Bainville tells us that Clemenceau's entourage told him that the policy of breaking up Germany was totally unacceptable, for the events of the war had greatly strengthened the force of German nationalism, and an attempt to impose such a solution would produce a violent German reaction.[94] Clemenceau claimed that he was not anti-German in principle. The German nation had as much right to exist as the French, provided that they also were prepared to allow the French to exist in full independence. He did not believe, however, that the present generation of Germans would ever willingly accept peaceful co-existence.[95] Thus he had a very different estimate from Wilson and Lloyd George of the measures necessary, over the years to come, to defend the treaty against German attempts to overthrow it. The argument of Clemenceau, and of those who defend his policy, is that the disastrous evolution of international relations in

[94] J. Bainville, *Les conséquences politiques de la Paix* (1920), p. 65.
[95] J. Martet, *Le Tigre*, pp. 71–2.

the inter-war period came not from the defects of the treaty, but from the failure of the victors to remain united in defence of the settlement. From first to last this was his theme; the Allies must remain united.[96] The potential political and economic power of Germany could not be destroyed in a world based on nation states, but it could be neutralized as long as the Allies remained united, and defended the limitations they had placed on Germany's exercise of her strength.

[96] It was the theme of his farewell address to the assembled Allied statesmen on 20 January 1920, *Documents on British Foreign Policy 1919–39*, First Series, II, pp. 952–4.

18

THE MIDDLE EAST
AND RUSSIA

I THE MIDDLE EAST

Clemenceau was also involved in the drafting of the Austrian treaty, and the settlement in eastern Europe and the Middle East, although these treaties were not finalized before he left office. Only the Middle East posed problems serious enough to warrant discussion.[97] The background to Anglo-French conflict in the Middle East involves a number of complicated wartime agreements. The essence of the matter was that Britain had made contradictory promises to the French, the Italians, the Arabs, and the Zionists, in order to defeat Turkey, Germany's ally, the existing ruler of the area. As far as France was concerned the key bargain was made in May 1916 and known as the Sykes-Picot agreement. This gave the French considerable, if ill-defined, rights over a large area of territory, centred on Syria. At the time Britain saw no need to extend her own territory in the area. But the agreement soon came to seem a bad bargain in Britain, as the French contributed nothing to the defeat of Turkey, and the commitment to France conflicted with promises made to the desert Arabs. British ruling circles remained divided, not to say confused, on the question, but Lloyd George developed an obstinate concern to win tangible benefits to justify his support for military activity in the Middle East. Only with difficulty was he brought to realize, in the course of 1919, that if Britain extended her empire in the Middle East, it would bring more burdens than benefits, quite apart from the fact that quarrels over this area were endangering relations with France.

[97] On the Middle East, *see* C. J. Lowe and M. L. Dockrill, op. cit., II, pp. 208–33 and 357–64, M. S. Anderson, *The Eastern Question, 1774–1923* (1966), pp. 310–67, J. Nevakivi, *Britain, France and the Arab Middle East, 1914–1920* (1969), and H. M. Sachar, *The Emergence of the Middle East 1914–1924* (1969).

It seems strange that the most violent conflict between Clemenceau and Lloyd George, among all their hard-fought negotiations, took place on Middle Eastern affairs – questions not of the first importance, to France at least. But perhaps precisely because of this, the two men could afford to indulge their mutual hostility, by taking up extreme positions, in a way that would have been too dangerous on European questions. However, Lloyd George said, on Middle Eastern questions alone was there personal unpleasantness between him and Clemenceau. This erupted first in the Supreme War Council of 7 October, when Lloyd George objected in violent terms to the French Salonika commander's plans for a triumphal march into Constantinople, led by French troops. Lord Robert Cecil described the incident to Balfour:

> The two spat at one another like angry cats. However, ultimately it was all smoothed over, the plan stopped, and Franchet d'Esperey had his knuckles rapped – Clemenceau became relatively calm, telling me aside what a poor opinion he had of Lloyd George who had been talking *sottises* to him. They then made common cause in sneering at Wilson.[98]

This quarrel was at once followed by another. On 15 October Lloyd George wrote to Clemenceau proposing that the naval forces advancing on Constantinople be commanded by a British admiral. Clemenceau refused, in a letter of 21 October, arguing that it had been agreed that the French should exercise supreme command in the Mediterranean, and as he had already conceded Lloyd George's demand about the military command, it was unreasonable now to expect this as well.[99] But he was to be confronted with a *fait accompli*. The Turks approached the British admiral and negotiated an armistice, without consulting the French. This led to another violent confrontation between Clemenceau and Lloyd George at the Supreme War Council of 30 October – House reported that 'they bandied words like fish-wives, at least Lloyd George did'. This is borne out by the minutes:

> The British had captured three or four Turkish armies, and had incurred hundreds of thousands of casualties in the war with Turkey. The other governments had only put in a few nigger policemen to see that we did not steal the Holy Sepulchre. When it came to signing an armistice all this fuss was made.

[98] Cecil to Balfour, 7 October 1918, Public Record Office, Balfour Papers, FO/800/201.
[99] Lloyd George to Clemenceau, 15 October 1918, Lloyd George Papers, F/50/3/37, and Clemenceau to Lloyd George, 21 October 1918, Lloyd George Papers, F/52/2/43. Cf. also Derby to Lloyd George 18 October 1918, and Derby to Balfour, 23 October 1918, Lloyd George Papers, F/52/2/40 and 44.

After prolonged discussion, in which Clemenceau argued, as he always did when Lloyd George raised the point about relative contributions to the defeat of Turkey, that the war had to be seen as a whole, and that British forces in the Middle East had been deducted from her forces fighting Germany, the French finally gave way. As Pichon put it:

> in a spirit of conciliation which the French government always felt to apply in dealing with Britain, they would accept the *fait accompli*.[100]

On 8 November, the French joined the British in a declaration affirming their support for self-determination in the Middle East. They scarcely attempted to deny, however, that in their eyes self-determination was to be interpreted in a very special way that did not conflict with the Sykes-Picot agreement. Pichon made a public reference to the British promise in the Senate on 29 December 1918.[101]

Clemenceau was, however, prepared to make concessions to Lloyd George over the Middle East, no doubt with a view to obtaining his support on other matters more vital to France. At their meetings in London, on 1–3 December 1918, in a purely informal conversation, without witnesses and with no written record, Clemenceau agreed to Lloyd George's demand that the oil-bearing area of Mosul, which in 1916 had been placed in the French zone, should be transferred to the British, and that Palestine, which had been reserved for some form of international control, should also join the British sphere. Lloyd George, the only direct source for this bargain, says in his Memoirs:

> He asked me what it was I especially wanted from the French. I instantly replied that I wanted Mosul attached to Iraq, and Palestine from Dan to Beersheba under British control – without any hesitation he agreed.[102]

The French were promised a share in the oil production of Mosul. It was also implied that, with these modifications, the rest of the Sykes-Picot agreement would stand good as the joint Anglo-French position on the Middle East. Hence Clemenceau's indignation when Lloyd George sought to reduce French influence there. There is no evidence that Clemenceau was given a specific *quid pro quo* in Europe, but there can be little doubt that Lloyd George gave the impression that Britain would be more understanding to French demands in Europe if concessions were made in the Middle East. His obsession with the Middle East was

---

[100] House diary, 30 October 1918, quoted by J. Nevakivi, op. cit., p. 70. The minutes are available at the Public Record Office, CAB 28/5, IC 84. Lloyd George quoted his outburst in *War Memoirs*, II, p. 1974.
[101] J. Nevakivi, op. cit., p. 82.
[102] D. Lloyd George, *The Truth About the Peace Treaties*, II, p. 1038.

unfortunate. It betrayed a strange estimate of the relative importance of the two areas to Britain herself, and poisoned relations between him and Clemenceau when he attempted to go back on the December agreement.[103]

Little progress was made on the Middle East for several months, as the statesmen's attention was absorbed by the German treaty. But developments on the ground, with the British army in control, and various British agencies encouraging the Arabs, seemed ominous to the French. The French saw the independent Arab state, under French influence, promised by the Sykes-Picot agreement, in terms of their protectorates of Morocco and Tunisia, tightly controlled from Paris. At the same time they thought that British encouragement for Arab nationalism was designed to create an Arab state that would be under British rather than French control. Certainly there was much evidence for this view in the activities of British soldiers and officials on the spot. In February, Clemenceau and Milner talked about the Middle Eastern situation but came to no agreement.[104] Absorbed in the battle for French interests in the German treaty, Clemenceau only wished at this point to play a waiting game over the Middle East. At the meeting of the Council of Four on 20 March he left the presentation of the French case to Pichon, and then agreed in principle to Wilson's suggestion of an Inter-Allied Commission to ascertain public opinion in the areas concerned. In the end, he was to refuse to appoint the French members of this commission, which became a purely American one. But in March he saw no objection to the Commission. He told the French cabinet on 21 March that at the previous day's meeting he had made an energetic statement of French rights in Syria, 'but now that our position has been clearly defined, I am going to leave the question on one side, and concentrate on our Rhine frontier'.[105] On 13 April, during the crucial period of decisions about the western frontier of Germany, Clemenceau met the Emir Feisal, son of Husain, Sharif of Mecca, to whom the British had made their promises. In an extreme example of diplomatic euphemism, Clemenceau sent Feisal a draft letter stating that the French government

> recognizes the right of Syria to independence in the form of a federation of autonomous local communities corresponding to the traditions and wishes of their populations. France is prepared to give material and moral assistance to this emancipation of Syria.

---

[103] J. Nevakivi, op. cit., pp. 118 and 148, C. J. Lowe and M. L. Dockrill, op. cit., II, pp. 359–60.
[104] J. Nevakivi, op. cit., p. 127; D. Lloyd George, *The Truth About the Peace Treaties*, II, pp. 1046–50.
[105] Minutes of the meeting of 20 March are printed in F.R.U.S., P.P.C., V, pp. 1–12. The cabinet meeting of 21 March is recorded in Poincaré's *Notes Journalières*, Poincaré Papers XLII, Bibliothèque Nationale, NAF 16033.

This letter was to be sent officially, if Feisal made a satisfactory reply. But he did not, although continuing to seek a *modus vivendi* with the French.[106]

The most violent confrontation between Clemenceau and Lloyd George occurred at the meeting of the Council of Four on 21 May. Clemenceau accused Lloyd George of a breach of faith, on the grounds that he had first offered France a mandate for part of Anatolia, and now opposed it, and because the British were proposing to detach large areas from the French protectorate in Syria to provide for a railway line from Mesopotamia to the Mediterranean. Without really meeting Clemenceau's points Lloyd George fought all over again his wartime strategic battles, complaining that France had done nothing to help in the campaign against Turkey, and was now insisting on rights given her on the assumption that she would contribute to the Turkish campaign. To this Clemenceau replied that there had been no such promise of French support, and that if the British troops used against Turkey had been sent to France the war could have been shortened by several months.[107] But by the summer British policy-makers were coming to realize that a French Syria might be more convenient than one under the control of Arab nationalists.

In September 1919 the situation was clarified when Lloyd George at last faced realities. As on other issues, his increasing concern for the British financial situation forced him to take action, together with the urgent need to reduce British military commitments as demobilization continued. It was quite impossible to keep a large British army in Syria and on 9 September 1919 he decided on the withdrawal of British troops by November. This meant that Feisal, having been encouraged so long in the belief that the British would force the French to give him reasonable terms, was to be left alone to face the French as best he could.[108]

The meeting of the two Prime Ministers on 13 September, at which the lines of a settlement in the Middle East were agreed, was preceded by an exchange of letters on 11 September, and by a talk between Clemenceau and Lloyd George's assistant Philip Kerr on 12 September.[109] The latter's report to Lloyd George shows how Clemenceau presented his demands:

[106] J. Nevakivi, op. cit., p. 141. Clemenceau's draft letter was printed in F.R.U.S., P.P.C., V, p. 115. Robert de Caix told Wickham Steed at the end of April that Lloyd George 'had promised Clemenceau to tell the Emir Feisal that, in future he must agree with France, who would pay him his subsidy: but, apparently, Lloyd George had done nothing of the kind.' On 4 May Clemenceau complained to Steed about Lloyd George's duplicity over Syria. H. Wickham Steed, *Through Thirty Years*, II, pp. 323–4.
[107] P. Mantoux, op. cit., II, pp. 133–43, 159–64.
[108] C. J. Lowe and M. C. Dockrill, op. cit., II, p. 362.
[109] These letters are printed in *Documents on British Foreign Policy 1919–39*, First Series, IV, pp. 379–84. Cf. Nevakivi, op. cit., pp. 188–93.

He personally was not particularly concerned with the Near East. France, however, had always played a great part there, and from the economic point of view a settlement which would give France economic opportunities was essential, especially in view of their present financial condition. He further said that French public opinion expected a settlement which was consonant with France's position. He could not, he said, make any settlement which did not comply with this condition. . . . He again reverted to the supreme importance he attached to maintaining the unity between Great Britain and France. He thought it even more important than the union with America. He was very anxious that Lloyd George should help him in maintaining this unity. It was no longer a question of securing agreement between monarchs, but between peoples, and if this was to be done, the governments of both sides must actively promote understanding. . . . If unity was to be maintained, it was necessary to clear up all these outstanding questions, and in order to do this England must help France to a just settlement in accordance with her historical rights and her economic and political necessities in the Middle East.[110]

Clemenceau kept on asserting lack of interest in the Middle East. In November 1917, with reference to Syria, he had said, 'if Lloyd George could get him a protectorate, he would not refuse it, as it would please some reactionaries, but he attached no importance to it'.[111] But expressing his personal detachment was hardly helpful, as he then declared that public opinion forced him to fight for French demands in the Middle East. No doubt he was correct in this assessment, and a complete abdication of French claims in the Middle East was quite impossible for domestic political reasons.[112] His remarks to Kerr, however, show that he was not just acting as the reluctant spokesman of French colonialist opinion. Although he might continue to believe that France was far too deeply involved in European affairs to have any material reason for seeking to build an empire in the Middle East, he presented the French claims there as a test of Anglo-French relations. The primary reason for his obduracy about the implementation of the various Anglo-French bargains about the Middle East was that he was not prepared to allow France to be treated as a subordinate partner. He was very conscious that Britain had emerged from the war as the greatest military power in the world, while French military strength had been shattered. It was all the more important that France should not adopt the psychology of a defeated nation. This could be best achieved by standing up to British demands

[110] Lloyd George Papers, F/51/1/40.
[111] As noted in Hankey's diary, S. Roskill, op. cit., p. 466.
[112] The External Affairs committee of the Chamber frequently pressed the government to defend French 'rights' in the Middle East, see for example the minutes of the sessions of 3, 5, 6 and 12 December 1918, Archives Nationales, C 7491.

even while maintaining the Alliance. If France were not to appear merely as a British satellite, he could not allow Lloyd George unilaterally to change the terms of the Anglo-French bargain over the Middle East.

This policy he brought to a successful conclusion – in diplomatic terms – in the autumn of 1919. No doubt he had been wise to postpone decisions until this time. As time went on it became easier to organize a large French army to occupy Syria, although only in the spring of 1920 were enough troops made available for the conquest of Syria after the Arab revolt. By that time it was being increasingly brought home to Lloyd George that ambitious plans for British control of the Middle East would require a military backing quite out of proportion to its possible strategic advantages. British troops were withdrawn, handing over to the French in the Lebanon, the coastal zone, and to the Arabs in Damascus and the Syrian interior. But Britain made it clear to Feisal that he would have to make his own terms with the French. It was only a matter of time before the Arabs either accepted French control or had it forced on them by conquest.

Clemenceau and Feisal negotiated in October and November, finally coming to an agreement formalized in a letter to Feisal of 17 December. Syria was to be a French protectorate, or, to use the new League of Nations term, mandate. In practice this would mean the same sort of tight administrative control that France exercised in her other protectorates, something very different from what President Wilson had envisaged when he agreed to the principle of mandates.[113] The result was a revolt which forced Feisal in March 1920 to repudiate the agreement and proclaim Syrian independence, shortly before the San Remo conference agreed to the French mandate in Syria. By July the Syrian revolt was crushed and the French were firmly in control. Clemenceau had been responsible for the addition of a large new colony to the already extensive French empire. This was not a very wise move; as he was well aware, France was already overstrained.

2 RUSSIAN INTERVENTION, 1919

Clemenceau has often been presented as a chief architect of Allied intervention against the Bolsheviks, and his motives have been ascribed to his desire to defend European capitalism against this threat to its existence. In these interpretations the importance of Allied intervention is usually magnified, and its motives misunderstood. Recent studies have shown that confusion and the inability to agree on any positive policy are the reasons for the continuation of intervention after the armistice,

[113] J. Nevakivi, op. cit., pp. 197–233, and H. M. Sachar, *The Emergence of the Middle East* (1969), pp. 270–2.

and not any capitalist conspiracy against the proletarian revolution. In any case France played a small part in Russian intervention before Clemenceau's resignation.[114] On several occasions Foch pressed for a great anti-Bolshevik crusade, but Clemenceau gave even less support to this than to Foch's other scheme for the political separation of the Rhineland from Germany. Immediately after the armistice, French troops were taken from the Salonika army, and transported to the Odessa area, where they landed on 18 December, remaining until 6 April 1919. The German withdrawal would otherwise have left a vacuum into which the Bolsheviks could move. Whereas in the areas assigned to Britain by the December 1917 agreement local anti-Bolshevik forces were already for the most part in control, in the French areas such forces had been excluded by the German occupation. Perhaps the French sought, by this occupation, to keep their options open, and, had it produced easy and satisfactory results, it might have been extended.[115] But the opposite proved to be the case. Clemenceau's orders to the French commander, General Janin, on 13 December 1918, envisaged a peaceful takeover from the Germans. After supervising the German withdrawal, the small French and Greek force was to allow the anti-Bolshevik forces in the Ukraine to regroup and then to move on to the attack, but no offensive activity by the Allied troops was envisaged. In fact they at once found themselves involved in fighting in a fantastically confused situation, caught between five mutually hostile groups, the Bolsheviks, Deniken's Volunteer Army, the Ukrainian Nationalists under Petlyura, Makhno's anarchists, and the Cossacks. On finding the situation so difficult, the French troops were withdrawn on 6 April, simultaneously with the mutinies in the French fleet in the Black Sea.

This limited involvement in Russia did not mean that Clemenceau had changed his views on the need to avoid entanglements there. At the Supreme War Council meeting of 3 December, he declared that he was in complete agreement with Balfour on the subject, that is, 'to let the Russians stew in their own juice', not to invite any Russian government to take part in the peace conference, and to await developments.[116]

---

[114] For the anti-Bolshevik crusade see G. Michon, Clemenceau, pp. 209–14. For recent views see C. J. Lowe and M. L. Dockrill, op. cit., II, pp. 304–34, R. H. Ullman, Anglo-Soviet Relations 1917–1921, vol. I, Intervention and the War (1961), vol. II, Britain and the Russian Civil War (1968), J. M. Thompson, Russia, Bolshevism and the Versailles Peace (1968), and G. F. Kennan, Soviet-American Relations 1917–1920, vol. I, Russia Leaves the War (1956), vol. II, The Decision to Intervene (1958). J. Bradley, Allied Intervention in Russia 1917–1920 (1968), and 'L'intervention française en Siberie 1918–1919', Revue Historique, 234 (1965), pp. 375–88, have most material on French policy, but offer little interpretation.
[115] J. Bradley, op. cit., p. 140; R. H. Ullman, op. cit., II, pp. 47–8; J. M. Thompson, op. cit., pp. 58–9.
[116] Public Record Office, CAB 23/42, quoted by Lloyd George, The Truth About the Peace Treaties, I, p. 320. But the French version in the Fonds Clemenceau Ministry of War, carton 44X, gives a fuller account of Clemenceau's remarks.

He would not even commit himself on the question of whether Russia should be split into a number of separate states. It has been suggested that the French were thinking of encouraging the setting up of small independent states in the western borderlands of Russia, the Ukraine and the Crimea. But this would have been likely to produce conflicts with Poland, Rumania, and Czechoslovakia, who wanted some of the same territory. To concentrate on building up these successor states as an eastern counterweight to Germany, while keeping options open with regard to Russia, was a sounder policy.[117] At this time Lloyd George was pressing for some way of ending the Russian civil war through negotiation, and would very much have liked to invite the various Russian parties to meet in Paris. Clemenceau vetoed this scheme, but gave his reluctant consent to an alternative version by which the assembled statesmen issued an invitation to all the Russian parties to meet on the Turkish island of Prinkipo. Although Clemenceau gave his agreement to this invitation on 21 January 1919, with the air of a great concession to Wilson and Lloyd George, in fact it amounted to very little. The French government assured the Whites, the anti-Bolsheviks, that they need not accept, as they would go on receiving Allied support in any case; from the British side Churchill gave the same assurances. Not surprisingly, the invitation was rejected.[118] There followed the surprising interlude of Churchill's visit to Paris of 15–17 February, in which he attempted to win support for a much more vigorous anti-Bolshevik policy. As Lloyd George declared that his own ideas were quite different, Churchill got little support. Even Clemenceau did not advocate his wholehearted policy of military intervention. Clemenceau's views were remarkably inconsistent.

> He did not favour the policy of leaving Russia to her own devices, because she would rapidly fall a prey to the Germans. He favoured the policy of encirclement: the policy of setting up a barrier around Russia. The results of such a policy would be that in the end the Russians would ask the Allies to intervene.[119]

Although he refused to recognize the Bolshevik government, his policy at this time was limited support for anti-Bolshevik elements in Russia, without Allied military intervention on a serious scale.

---

[117] J. M. Thompson, op. cit., pp. 57–8, and P. S. Wandycz, *France and her eastern allies, 1919–1925* (Minneapolis, 1962), pp. 104–31.
[118] J. M. Thompson, op. cit., pp. 122–4; R. H. Ullman, op. cit., II, pp. 99–135.
[119] F.R.U.S., P.P.C., IV, p. 17. A. J. Mayer, *Politics and Diplomacy of Peacemaking, Containment and Counter-Revolution at Versailles, 1918–1919* (1968), pp. 450–62, places a different emphasis on Clemenceau's policy at this time but he does not prove that Clemenceau endorsed Foch's plans for military intervention. Discussion of this meeting in R. H. Ullman, op. cit., II, pp. 123–7, Thompson, op. cit., p. 138, G. F. Kennan, op. cit., II, pp. 128–30, C. J. Lowe and M. C. Dockrill, op. cit., II, p. 324.

Clemenceau was at this point temporarily removed from the scene. He stated that he wished to devote the day of 19 February to a consideration of the Russian situation, but as he left his house that morning he was wounded in the attempted assassination, and remained out of action for over a week: he only returned to the council chamber on 1 March. During this period, when not only Clemenceau but also Wilson and Lloyd George were absent, Foch brought forward an ambitious plan for military intervention in Russia, linked with his other scheme for imposing a rapid preliminary peace on Germany, by which she yielded what Foch regarded as the essential points of the settlement. The French government had held similar ideas at the time of the armistice, but it had soon become obvious that they were totally unrealistic. The broad lines of a settlement could not be separated from the details. It was precisely the details that led to the most arduous bargaining between the Allies. But Foch had so far refused to see the unrealistic nature of his scheme for imposing a preliminary peace.[120] He presented it to the Council of Ten on 25 February, as the first step of a vast programme. The preliminary peace would allow the Allies to transfer their military resources to the east; 'Finns, Poles, Czechs, Rumanians and Greeks as well as the Russian pro-Ally elements' could be used, under Allied 'unique command'. He declared:

if this were done, 1919 would see the end of Bolshevism, just as 1918 had seen the end of Prussianism.

The statesmen were taken aback by this grandiose scheme. Balfour pointed out that:

the proposition which he [Balfour] moved yesterday was that the Polish divisions, now in France, should be sent to Poland: a small and modest suggestion involving no particular question of principle at all. On that narrow foundation Marshal Foch had started out to build a great plan stretching from the Rhine to Vladivostock, which involved the immediate conclusion of the preliminary terms of peace with Germany.[121]

He continued that it was quite impossible for them to think of dealing with such great issues in the absence of Clemenceau, Wilson and Lloyd George. It is difficult to judge whether Foch intended his plan to be taken seriously. Certainly, after Balfour's reply, he accepted discussion

[120] In this he was supported by Poincaré, who wrote a long letter to Pichon on 4 March, demanding the rapid conclusion of a preliminary peace, which would give France her essential requirements from Germany, Poincaré Papers XLII, Bibliothèque Nationale, NAF 16033: the letter is marked as being to Clemenceau, but it is obviously to Pichon.
[121] F.R.U.S., P.P.C., IV, pp. 122–3.

of the much more limited question of the Polish troops, without further reference to his grand strategy. But he returned to the charge on 17 March, and, with a slightly revised version based on the need to dispose of the Communist régime established in Hungary, on 27 March.[122]

Clemenceau, who was present on these two subsequent occasions, gave no support to Foch. When Foch, on 27 March, presented his plan for dealing with the Hungarian Bolshevik, Bela Kun, which involved an Allied occupation of Vienna, and the formation of two Allied armies, one to be employed against the Bolsheviks in Russia, and one against the Hungarians, Clemenceau gave him no support at all.[123] Virtually his only remark was to say that he agreed entirely with President Wilson, who had objected that Foch's plan bore no relation to the much more modest scheme on which he had been asked to report as military adviser. The only decision taken at this meeting was to withdraw the French troops from Odessa. In July, Clemenceau laughed at Foch's plans, saying that they were 'more ambitious than Napoleon's march on Moscow'. He added that France had neither the men nor the money to embark on them.[124]

From March to August 1919 French policy with regard to Russia was passive. Clemenceau opposed the Hoover-Nansen plans for using famine relief as a political tool in Russia, but, as over Prinkipo, eventually agreed to join his allies in a declaration in favour of the proposal. Again, as over Prinkipo, this declaration had no practical consequences, as the scheme was quite impossible to implement. He supported the recognition of Admiral Kolchak, leader of the anti-Bolshevik forces in Siberia, at the end of May, but was not at all prominent in this. Kolchak seemed to the French to be a British protégé, and to them the intervention in Siberia was of marginal importance. One of the reasons for the victory of the Bolsheviks was that their various opponents never managed to unite. The Bolsheviks held the central areas, and were able to deal with their enemies one by one – Kolchak in Siberia, Denikin in the south, Yudenitch in the Baltic provinces. Foreign troops were only employed on the extreme periphery of the vast Russian land-mass in the Caucasus, at Archangel in the far north, and at Vladivostock on the Pacific. These were hopeless points from which to attempt military intervention.[125] Only at the end of August 1919 did French policy become

[122] Ibid., pp. 379–84.
[123] P. Mantoux, op. cit., I, pp. 51–7; cf. C. J. Lowe and M. L. Dockrill, op. cit., II, p. 306, A. J. Mayer, op. cit., pp. 597–602, J. M. Thompson, op. cit., p. 205, R. H. Ullman, op. cit., II, p. 140.
[124] *Documents on British Foreign Policy, 1919–1939*. First series, I, pp. 19–20, meeting of Heads of Delegations, 5 July 1919.
[125] On the fighting *see* D. Footman, *Civil War in Russia* (1961), G. A. Brinkley, *The Volunteer Army and Allied Intervention in South Russia 1917–1921* (Notre Dame, 1966).

more active. By then Kolchak was in full retreat, and attention turned to South Russia and Denikin. It has been claimed that Clemenceau was spurred into action by learning on 27 August that the British had helped to organize a base for Denikin, in the Crimea, part of the French zone according to the December 1917 agreement. This led to a revival of French interest in Denikin, in order to counterbalance the British.[126] But not until November 1919, when the British were on the point of abandoning Denikin, did France take any initiative. Then, a mission under General Mangin having reported that, given financial support, Denikin would transfer his loyalties from Britain to France, Clemenceau authorized a credit of thirty million francs. Very little of this money ever reached Denikin, however, and Clemenceau virtually ignored Mangin's recommendations for a large-scale French effort to support him.

Meeting Lloyd George in London on 11–13 December, Clemenceau agreed on the futility of further intervention in Russia. Lloyd George gave this report to the British cabinet of Clemenceau's views after their conversation on 11 December 1919:

> In his opinion, the Russians were Orientals, and were thoroughly enjoying themselves at the present moment with their fighting, their tortures and so on, and he had come to think that we had made a great mistake in interfering. . . . Clemenceau also stated that he did not apprehend any danger of Bolshevist infection in Germany. The German people were temperamentally lovers of order and discipline. As regards Poland, Clemenceau thought of that country not in reference to Russia, but in respect of Germany only. . . . He had never liked Denikin, probably because he regarded him as a British protégé, and Kolchak he did not like because of his past.[127]

He was more than ever concerned to build up a strong Poland as the essential barrier to German expansion eastwards. As Polish ambitions were as likely to lead to conflict with the anti-Bolshevik Russians as to war with the Bolsheviks, there was little point in attempting to intervene in Russian affairs. At the inter-Allied conference next day, Clemenceau said that intervention had failed, and it would be useless to continue:

> He would suggest making, as it were, a barbed wire entanglement round Russia, in order to prevent her from creating trouble outside it, and in order to stop Germany from entering into relations with Russia, whether of a political or military character. . . . The support

[126] J. Bradley, op. cit., pp. 159–62, cf. C. J. Lowe and M. L. Dockrill, op. cit., II, pp. 326–8.
[127] Public Record Office, CAB 23/35, 11 December 1919.

of Poland was the best way to check Germany. . . . It would be a great mistake if we did not maintain Poland in order to dam up the Russian flood and provide a check to Germany.[128]

He thought the revolutions had removed Russia as an important element in the international equilibrium for a long time to come, and a well-organized alliance of the small states of eastern Europe would be an adequate substitute. He even said that, as democratic states, they would be a more effective barrier to Germany than Russia had been.

He was, judged with hindsight, much too sanguine; of the eastern European new states, only Czechoslovakia remained democratic for very long. But whereas many accounts have presented Clemenceau as dominated by the need to combat 'revolution' and for that reason hostile to Bolshevism, the documentary record shows that he never saw things in that light. The principal purpose of the *cordon sanitaire* was not to keep the Bolshevik contagion out of Europe, but to prevent the Germans using the chaos and disintegration produced by Bolshevism to turn eastern Europe and Russia into an informal German empire. This perspective makes sense of Clemenceau's views on the Russian problem. On the face of it, to refuse to accept the Bolsheviks as the *de facto* government of Russia, or to enter into negotiations with them, and yet not to be prepared to give their opponents enough support to achieve their overthrow, was to get the worst of all worlds. But it had a certain *rationale* if Russian politics were viewed in relation to Germany. During the war the most vocal arguments for cooperation with Germany had come from the Russian conservatives: even after the armistice an agreement between the Whites and the Germans remained a possibility. After all, only in December 1919 were German troops finally removed from the Baltic states. Thus it was important to keep in touch with the Whites, and to give them enough support to ensure that, if they succeeded in ousting the Bolsheviks they came to power tied to the Allied cause, and not as German protégés. It is probable that until the autumn of 1919 Clemenceau saw this as the most likely outcome. Like most people, he underestimated the viability of the Bolshevik régime, and overestimated the strength of their opponents. But he saw no need to overstrain French strength to assist the Whites, especially in view of the possibility that they would be little more favourable to the Allied cause than were the Bolsheviks. As he said on more than one occasion, the best policy for the Russians was to let them stew in their own juice, meanwhile building up Poland to replace Russia as the eastern check on Germany.

[128] *Documents on British Foreign Policy, 1919–1939*, First Series, II, pp. 744–5. Cf. R. H. Ullman, op. cit., II, pp. 313–4, J. Bradley, op. cit., pp. 165–6, C. J. Lowe and M. L. Dockrill, op. cit., II, pp. 328–9.

Almost his last political decision was to agree with Lloyd George, in January 1920, on the opening of economic negotiations with the Bolsheviks for the resumption of trade.[129] A change of emphasis came when Millerand replaced Clemenceau as French prime minister; he supported Denikin, and encouraged the Poles to attack the Bolsheviks. On 14 January 1920 Foch presented yet another version of his anti-Bolshevik crusade. This time Millerand had to deal with it, and he gave much more countenance to Foch's ideas than Clemenceau had ever done. Only after Clemenceau's fall did French and British policy become seriously divergent. Clemenceau's contribution to Allied intervention was marginal, and furthermore, the Allied role was a marginal one in the Russian civil war. Its principal causes are to be found in internal Russian politics, rather than in Allied policy. Whatever other criticism may be levied against Clemenceau's policy towards Russia, it was certainly not an ideological crusade against Bolshevism.

[129] *Documents on British Foreign Policy, 1919–1939*, First Series, II, pp. 867–75, meeting of 14 January 1920. Cf. R. H. Ullman, op. cit., II, pp. 326–39.

19

DOMESTIC POLITICS
AND LAST YEARS

I DOMESTIC POLITICS

Clemenceau concerned himself mainly with the negotiation of the peace
settlement in 1919, but his government was responsible for domestic
policies in what proved to be a very turbulent year. One of the principal
concerns of the government was the mounting wave of social unrest.
Membership of the C.G.T. increased dramatically, reaching almost one
and a half million by July 1919. The Socialist party, which had moved
well to the left and was controlled by the wartime *minoritaires*, also
reported a membership that increased ten times between the armistice
and the end of 1919.[130] Strikes were widespread. There were many reasons
for this great increase in left-wing activity, among them revulsion against
the war and enthusiasm for the supposed achievements of the Russian
revolution. But the root cause of the groundswell of support for militancy
came from the inflationary situation. This was inherited from the war,
but the policies of the government in 1919 only exacerbated the situation. Government expenditure remained high, not only for military
reasons, but also for payment of pensions and the reconstruction of the
devastated areas of the invasion zone. Revenue covered only a small
proportion of this. The finance minister claimed that the extraordinary
expenditure would be covered by German Reparations payments, and
there was therefore no need to devise new taxes to increase revenue,
or even to make a serious attempt to increase the yield of existing taxes.

[130] A. Kriegel, op. cit., I, pp. 238–47. During the war the Socialists had divided
into a majority and a minority faction, the former continuing to support participation in the war effort, while the minority opposed it. The minority faction
steadily increased in strength, until by the end of the war it became the majority,
and won control of the main party organs. These dissentions continued until
the Tours Congress of December 1920, when they contributed to the splitting of
the party into a Socialist and a Communist party.

In the interim the deficit was covered by short-term borrowing. This policy produced a serious financial problem for the future.[131] In 1919 the full gravity of the situation was not yet realized, but the ending of the inter-Allied wartime agreements, which had artificially upheld the value of the franc on the foreign exchanges, began to drive home the rapid fall in the value of money, previously partly disguised. The cost of living, *la vie chère*, became one of the principal preoccupations of the general public, and especially of the organized industrial workers who were determined to force up their wages to keep pace with the inflationary spiral. In this aim, given the boom conditions of 1919, they were largely successful. The social unrest never became really serious. But many of the strikes were dramatic enough to give the impression of a very grave danger of social revolution, as Bolshevism seemed to be spreading from Russia into central Europe.

Clemenceau, as in 1918, was determined to avoid a head-on clash with the proletariat, as an essential part of his policy of promoting national unity. When the trade union movement brought forward the demand for the eight-hour day, the government hurriedly brought in a law thus limiting hours of work. It was passed without delay, being voted by the Chamber on 17 April, and by the Senate a week later, without a single opposition vote. The general strike of 1 May, organized to press for the eight-hour day, was pre-empted. Clemenceau claimed that he had long supported such a measure, and had intended to introduce it during his first ministry, but the political situation had not been favourable. But it was passed rapidly in order to take some steam out of the protest movement. The general strike on 1 May took place nevertheless; in Paris it took the form of a mass demonstration, which was suppressed by the police, not without serious injuries on both sides.[132] This incident, however, had no serious political effect except probably to strengthen the position of the government. As a police report of 14 April 1919 put it:

It is rumoured that certain friends and supporters of Clemenceau would not be unhappy to see bourgeois circles overcome by panic; such a state of mind could only profit the present cabinet. The more they are afraid, the more they will rejoice to have a strong man [*un homme à poigne*] at the head of the government![133]

---

[131] There is a considerable literature on these financial problems; the basic facts are provided by H. G. Moulton and C. Lewis, *The French Debt Problem* (1925), pp. 70–87 and 96–104, and H. E. Fisk, *French Public Finance in the Great War and To-Day* (1922), pp. 13–24.
[132] There is a file on the incidents of 1 May 1919, Archives Nationales, F⁷ 13273.
[133] Archives Nationales, F⁷ 13950, 2, fol. 240, 14 April 1919, and fol. 243, 22 April 1919.

Another of 22 April stated that the deputies would not overthrow Clemenceau because of their fear of a serious crisis on 1 May, while on 5 May it was reported that

> The French bourgeois is determined to defend himself against the Bolshevist wave which he sees behind the demonstration of the C.G.T. Clemenceau has never been so highly esteemed by the bourgeoisie and the reasoning public.[134]

In the debate of 6 May the government obtained more than its usual majority, and only one vote was cast against it, by a left-wing Radical. The Socialists had walked out of the debate in protest against the fact that only Pams, the minister of the interior, not Clemenceau, was there to present the government's case. The other left-wing Radicals, who were on occasion prepared to vote against the government, did not wish to seem to support revolutionary agitation. After these events it was clear that the government had a secure majority for as long as it cared to remain in office. On 16th June it was reported that Briand was resigned to remaining out of office :

> he thinks that the recent attacks on the cabinet have been clumsy and inopportune. There can be no question of overthrowing Clemenceau before the signing of the peace; no serious observer could believe that the Chamber would agree to that.[135]

After this high point the unrest died down, only to revive because of the worsening economic situation after Clemenceau had left office. A further attempt to organize a general strike on 21 July was a fiasco: its declared aim, as well as domestic economic demands, was to protest against intervention in Russia. The militants of the Extreme Left saw it as the beginning of the proletarian revolution. The moderate leadership of the C.G.T. were reluctant to support the movement, but found it difficult to avoid being dragged along with the Extreme Left.[136]

Clemenceau took care to keep in touch with the C.G.T. leadership, and met them on 28 May. The conversation took a high philosophical tone. Clemenceau declared that he was still a progressive, and welcomed the inevitable historical evolution from the rule of the bourgeoisie to that of the proletariat organized by the C.G.T.; he was to take up this theme again in his Senate speech of October. But, he said, the transition must be gradual, not based on violence, but on legal evolution. At another meeting on 18 July he promised a partial amnesty to political offenders,

---

[134] Archives Nationales, F⁷ 13950, 2, fol. 245, 5 May 1919.
[135] Ibid., fol. 248, 16 June 1919.
[136] There is a file on the general strike of 21 July 1919, Archives Nationales, F⁷ 13310.

more rapid demobilizations, and a reduction in the cost of living. But, he ended, 'if they wanted a fight the government was ready and would reply with all the power at its disposal'. Railwaymen and postal workers were told that if they went on strike they would be tried by military courts. However, a Parliamentary incident was arranged by Mandel through his contacts with the Socialist deputy Laval, which offered the C.G.T. leaders a road of retreat. Laval attacked the minister of supply, Boret, for the high cost of living. Boret found himself without support from the rest of the government, and offered his resignation, which was accepted.[137] Thus the C.G.T. could announce that they had won a victory over the government, and could call off the general strike. Once again Clemenceau had combined conciliation and repression skilfully and reduced the temperature of the social crisis. Partly as a result of this meeting, relations between the government and the trade union leadership remained reasonably good behind the scenes, although mutual denunciation continued in public.

The other main domestic political question in 1919 was the reform of the electoral system. Although before the war Clemenceau had been a vigorous opponent of schemes to introduce proportional representation, he now refused to take a position on the renewed proposals for electoral reform. He declared that electoral reform was a matter for Parliament to decide, without being influenced by the government. This was in spite of the fact that his assistant Mandel was a firm opponent, and argued that it would work against the development of strong government and a two-party system which he, like Clemenceau, wished to see.[138] In fact the electoral law adopted in 1919 was far from being a proper system of proportional representation. It provided for multi-member constituencies, usually consisting of a department, in which an electoral list that won a majority of the votes took all the seats. Only if no list got an absolute majority did proportional representation apply. This placed a high premium on drawing up a coalition list that could win a majority vote. In doing this the Left was handicapped by the intransigence of the Socialists. Desperately seeking to maintain their own party unity in the face of the challenge posed by the Bolshevik revolution, the Socialist party refused to take part in any coalition. This left the Radicals isolated as well, unless they agreed to join Centre and Centre-Right lists. In the new political atmosphere the moderate republicans, who had before 1914 usually sought electoral support to the left rather than the right, joined with the Right in drawing up many departmental lists. The result was the electoral triumph of what was

[137] A. J. Mayer, *Politics and Diplomacy of Peacemaking*, pp. 778–83 and 867–8; B. Georges and D. Tintant, *Léon Jouhaux*, I, p. 367; R. Wohl, *French Communism in the making 1914–24* (1966), p. 138; J. Sherwood, op. cit., p. 32.
[138] J. Sherwood, op. cit., pp. 36–8.

called the *Bloc National*, a coalition of Centre and Right, and the over-whelming defeat of Radicals and Socialists. The swing to the Right was partly due to a change in voting, but much more to the arbitrary work-ing of the new electoral system.[139]

That Clemenceau presided over the electoral triumph of the *Bloc National* was indeed a measure of the extent to which his political posi-tion had moved to the Right. This had not been so apparent before the election campaign. In the old Chamber, although reluctantly, the great majority of the Radicals had supported the government. The political situation had been basically the same as that during his first ministry, in which he had kept the support of the bulk of the Radicals, being opposed only by a left-wing minority of Radical-Socialists and Socialists. But the victory of the *Bloc National* under his patronage marked another stage in his evolution to the Right. His political disciples, Mandel and Tardieu, were to enter politics as members of the Right. Clemenceau had not taken much part in the election campaign. No doubt he regarded himself now as more a national figure than the leader of a partisan majority. This was the source of the difficulties in which Mandel and Tardieu found themselves when they sought to use Clemenceau's name to help them found a solid right-wing party.

He was only prepared to intervene on two occasions. One was at Strasbourg during the election campaign on 4 November 1919; the other was his decision to stand for election as President of the Republic. In his speech at Strasbourg, with Millerand at his side, Clemenceau gave his accolade to the programme and the men of the *Bloc National*. His speech was essentially an appeal for national unity, and for vigilance and effort in all spheres to safeguard the achievements of victory, a repetition of his Parliamentary speeches in defence of the peace treaty. But he also supported some specific proposals of the *Bloc National*. Although he declared that the *lois laïques* were intangible, he said that he would welcome Catholics into the Republic if they sincerely aban-doned their ties with reaction. He pointed out the need for strong government, and declared that this could be achieved not by constitu-tional reform, but by the creation of a solid governmental majority, determined to carry out its programme. The only constitutional reform he envisaged was decentralization, with provincial representative assem-blies. He had, he said, planned this during his first ministry; but his pro-posals were still shelved in the files of the administration. In even vaguer terms he spoke of the need for social reforms to encourage equality, and of the need to put an end to the conflict between Labour and Capital. The most striking point, however, was his condemnation of Bolshevism. It sought, he said, to destroy the republic and to install

[139] G. Lachapelle, *Elections Législatives du 16 Novembre 1919* (1920).

on its ruins the bloody dictatorship of anarchy. He continued that this implied the condemnation of the Socialist party as a whole, which had refused to break with its extremist elements.[140]

The disunity of the Left, the electoral system, and Clemenceau's prestige combined to bring a sweeping victory to the *Bloc National*, and to provide in the *Chambre Bleu Horizon* the most right-wing Chamber France had known since the National Assembly of 1871. Mordacq reports that Clemenceau himself was disconcerted by the extent of the swing to the Right.[141] Meeting the new Chamber, and questioned on his general policy on 23 December 1919, Clemenceau refused to enter into any commitments. As soon as the electoral cycle was completed, the government would resign; it merely intended to remain for three weeks more until the new President of the Republic was elected. On this he was given a vote of confidence by 434 to 63 votes, the opposition, as usual, consisting of the Socialists. Up to this point Clemenceau had given no indication that he would be prepared himself to stand as President. On the contrary, he had said more than once that he sought only to complete his wartime task by ensuring the ratification of the peace treaties, and that he would then be happy to retire to private life. For a man of seventy-eight, after two years of the most exhausting activity, this would seem to be a sensible decision.

Nevertheless, about 15 December, he gave in to Mandel's pressure and agreed to allow his name to be put forward for the Presidency. He thought it a foregone conclusion that he would be elected. Thus the fact that only on 15 January 1920 did he allow Mandel to state publicly that he would be prepared to serve if elected, and his later protestation that he had never been a candidate, were mere formalities.[142] Why did he decide to stand for the Presidency? The position of the President was that of a mere figurehead, and Poincaré had failed in his attempt to rebuild a strong Presidential position. But the degree of Presidential authority depended on personalities. Poincaré himself had exercised more authority before Clemenceau became prime minister. With roles reversed, and Clemenceau as President, enjoying all his prestige as the father of victory, he could hope to play a more prominent role than Poincaré had done. The President did have one important power, the right to choose the prime minister. It might have been possible for Clemenceau as President to choose a loyal supporter as prime minister, and with joint authority weld the *Bloc National* into a coherent political force. This was the plan. It appealed to ambitious men like Tardieu and

---

[140] G. Clemenceau, *Discours prononcé à Strasbourg le 4 novembre 1919* (1919).
[141] J. J. Mordacq, op. cit., IV, p. 182.
[142] G. Wormser, op. cit., pp. 392–423, discusses his decision to stand for the Presidency, and his defeat, in great detail. Cf. also J. J. H. Mordacq, op. cit., IV, pp. 218–21 and 264–92; J. Sherwood, op. cit., pp. 48–52.

Mandel, who had tied their fortunes to Clemenceau; his retirement left them in the wilderness. On the other hand there were many obstacles in the way of such a development: all constitutional conventions were against it, and Presidents who tried to exercise a serious influence on politics provoked resentment in Parliament.

He was not to be elected. Instead he was to find himself rejected in favour of the colourless Deschanel. A few months later Clemenceau got an ironical revenge when Deschanel turned out to have gone mad. Clemenceau could probably have been elected if he had fought for the post. But he wished to be chosen as a national symbol, as it were by acclaim. The decisive vote came not in the formal National Assembly, but in the preliminary meeting of the republican caucus. Clemenceau had been highly indignant when Poincaré, in 1913, had refused to accept the decision of such a caucus, and had gone on to win with the votes of the Right. This precedent was no doubt one reason why he refused to follow a similar course, although the old division between republican and non-republican deputies had virtually ceased to have meaning. The caucus had been open to all who cared to attend. It voted 408 for Deschanel and 389 for Clemenceau. As well as the normal left-wing opposition, a large proportion of the *Bloc National* were Catholics who decided not to vote for Clemenceau because of his anti-clericalism. Others, such as Briand, were personally hostile, and argued that Clemenceau as President would upset the balance of the constitution, reducing the power of Parliament. When his *chef de cabinet* brought him the news, Clemenceau at first could not believe it. But when his defeat had registered, he said: 'That's it: I do not wish to be voted for tomorrow.'[143] He remained immovable, in spite of the fact that, like Poincaré, he could very well have been elected by the full National Assembly. He explained that he did not want to be elected by a tiny minority. Only if he were chosen by virtually unanimous acclaim would he have the prestige and authority he needed to negotiate with the Allies.[144] Whether this calculation was his deepest motive may be doubted. Certainly he felt the defeat as a personal affront, and from this moment his comments on the men and affairs of his native country take on a new bitterness.

Clemenceau's entourage have claimed that the failure to elect him to the Presidency led to the failures of French diplomacy in the 1920s. They argue that he would have been able to prevent the rapid dissolution of the Versailles settlement. Clemenceau himself, on several occasions, complained about his successor's destruction of his diplomatic achievement. He argued that he would have been able both to maintain the entente with England, and perhaps even with the United States,

[143] G. Wormser, op. cit., p. 406.
[144] J. J. H. Mordacq, op. cit., IV, p. 265.

while enforcing all the provisions of the Treaty. Instead, those in power allowed relations with England to become very bad, without even maintaining French rights under the treaty. He declared:

I assure you that if I had been in power in 1920, at the time of the occupation of Frankfurt, I would never have accepted the English not being at our side, and they would have finished by coming. But, instead of being open with them, we have tried to show that we could manage without them. To be completely open would have been the only way to combat the hostile policy of Lloyd George; in the face of such an attitude on our part, he would not in the end have been supported by the English people, who have always been loyal to us.[145]

He similarly condemned Poincaré's occupation of the Ruhr in 1923, as a demonstration of the breach between French and English policy.

There seems to be a great deal of wishful thinking in these comments. They are reported in great detail by Mordacq, and have been repeated by some biographers as well-founded judgements; they lament the 'sabotage' of the treaty of Versailles that occurred after Clemenceau's retirement. But it is not at all clear how Clemenceau could have achieved the *tour de force* of combining a policy even more rigorous towards Germany than that followed by his successors, with the maintenance of the entente with England. England, under Lloyd George or under any other prime minister, was not prepared to be dragged in the wake of a French policy of chauvinistic anti-Germanism, which with regard to the exaction of Reparations was in any case not realistic. There is no reason to believe that if Clemenceau had been President, developments would have been very different. His last remarks to his cabinet colleagues, on 18 January 1920, before handing over his powers, were that he had wished to restore French self-confidence:

We must show the world the extent of our victory, and we must take up the mentality and habits of a victorious people, which once more takes its place at the head of Europe. But all that will now be placed in jeopardy. . . . It will take less time and less thought to destroy the edifice so patiently and painfully erected than it took to complete it. Poor France. The mistakes have begun already.[146]

This was to set himself an impossible task, given the military and economic strength of France relative to that of the other great powers. France could not be made the dominant partner in the Franco-British

[145] J. J. H. Mordacq, *Clemenceau au soir de la vie* (1933), I, p. 274; for his criticism of the occupation of the Ruhr, op. cit., pp. 264–7.
[146] G. Wormser, op. cit., p. 416.

entente simply through the exercise of Clemenceau's personality. He would have had to deal with Lloyd George, a man whose character and determination were just as strong as his own, and one not likely to allow France to set the pace. Clemenceau, like his successors, would have had to choose between good relations with England and the maintenance of a strict anti-German policy.

2 LAST YEARS

As soon as the Presidential election was held, Clemenceau resigned as prime minister. For well over a year after his resignation Clemenceau was removed from the political scene. The day of the Presidential election, visiting his old friend the painter Monet at his country house at Giverney, he told him that he was going to visit Egypt. He did so, only two weeks later, setting off on 2 February 1920. After a trip in which he penetrated as far as the swamps of the Nile in the Sudan, he returned to France on 21 April. He abstained from all comment on political events, and after spending part of the summer at Vichy set off for the Far East on 20 September 1920. He only returned to France on 21 March 1921, after visiting Singapore, the Dutch East Indies and British India. The rest and the long sea voyages restored his health, in spite of arduous travels by rail in India, and he returned home much fitter than when he left office.[147] In June 1921 he visited England to receive an honorary degree at Oxford, and to visit his many English friends. He first refused to meet Lloyd George, but eventually he agreed to do so. The meeting was not a success. He reproached the British prime minister with having become the enemy of France the moment the armistice was signed, to which Lloyd George replied: 'well, was not that always our traditional policy?' Although this exchange was jocular, Clemenceau, brooding over the evolution of British policy, took it with deadly seriousness. He rejoiced on hearing of Lloyd George's fall from power, saying

> As for France, it is a real enemy who disappears. Lloyd George did not hide it: at my last visit to London he cynically admitted it.[148]

There was nothing sentimental about Clemenceau's pro-English policy, in spite of his large number of English friends. Contrary to the belief of his many critics in France, he sought an entente with England only because power politics made it necessary. Piétri, a friend who accompanied him on his Indian tour, reports that he said

> He did not like the egoism of England; personally he had nothing to learn about that; he had suffered from it enough during his discussions

[147] J. J. H. Mordacq, op. cit., I, pp. 1–145.
[148] Ibid., pp. 157–9 and 256.

with Lloyd George. He knew all about it, but he said that we have no choice; whether we wish it or not, we must remember that we are in no position to quarrel with England.[149]

In autumn 1921 Clemenceau again began to think of playing a political role. He told Mordacq that he did not wish to take part himself in the political struggle, but thought he had a duty to support those who had helped him create the treaty and who were now seeking to defend it. He had decided to help Tardieu to play a more important part than he had so far been able to do. He helped him assemble financial support to set up a newspaper, *L'Echo National*, which appeared on 10 January 1922, with Clemenceau's name on its masthead, as 'founder', along with Tardieu's as political editor. He disappointed expectations, however, by not writing for the paper, and it was not successful, publication ceasing after two years. Before long Clemenceau was expressing dissatisfaction with Tardieu's policy, although not so strongly as he condemned some of his other former colleagues. Loucheur was bitterly criticized for joining Briand's cabinet. Clemenceau gradually isolated himself from all his old political associates by his tendency to regard their every action as a personal betrayal.[150]

In the autumn of 1922 he undertook a lecture tour of the United States, speaking in all the major cities of the north-east. His theme was defence of French policy, especially with regard to war-debts and Reparations, and condemnation of the American withdrawal from the alliance. It is hard to imagine what he expected to achieve. Although he was well received, and had large and enthusiastic audiences everywhere, the impact of his views on the American public was negligible. The United States was not to be diverted from its policy of isolation by the exhortations of the old French statesman.[151]

Although he still followed political developments closely, Clemenceau now resigned himself to the fact that his active political career was at an end. He only took one more initiative, again concerned with the question of the French war-debts to America. This was his open letter of 9 August 1926 to President Coolidge, protesting against the American insistence that France repay all debts contracted during and after the war. This was not, he said, simply a financial matter; it was a political question, and 'France is not for sale, even to her friends'.[152] Like his lecture tour, this political gesture had no impact on American policy.

He returned in these last years to the intellectual pursuits which had always tempted him in the intervals of his political career. He published

[149] Ibid., p. 139.
[150] Ibid., pp. 166–7 and 185–6.
[151] On his American tour, *see* J. J. H. Mordacq, op. cit., I, 224–62.
[152] Reprinted in G. Clemenceau, *Grandeurs et Misères d'une Victoire*, pp. 369–72.

two short biographies in a series entitled *Nobles Vies, Grandes Oeuvres,* one of Demosthenes, and one of his old friend Claude Monet. In addition he produced a massive two-volume work, *Au Soir de la Pensée,* of philosophical-historical-scientific speculation. Clemenceau's study of Demosthenes can be read as an allegory of his own life. The Attic orator, seeking to galvanize the cultured, refined and freedom-loving citizens of Athens to defend their city against the attacks of Philip of Macedon, is described by Clemenceau in terms that could well be applied to his own wartime role. He saw France, like the Athens of the time of Demosthenes, as the home of civilization and freedom, attacked by the brute force of German barbarism, as Athens had been attacked by the barbarians of Macedon. Clemenceau's reflections on Demosthenes's role throw some light, then, on his feelings about his own achievement. It is not without significance that in the end Demosthenes failed. Athens did not respond strongly enough to his oratory, and was defeated. Was this how Clemenceau saw the likely outcome between France and Germany? Certainly, by 1926, he was sufficiently disillusioned about the transience of the victory of 1918 to take this attitude. But, in the last analysis, he declared that Demosthenes could not be said to have failed, in spite of appearances. The important thing in human life was to have fought nobly for a noble cause, whether the immediate outcome appeared to be victory or defeat.

> Since all men are doomed to suffering, call the man happy who has struggled for a noble cause, and pity the man who, having never strived for anything beyond himself, knows only the ashes of a life vainly consumed in egotism. The annals of mankind are full of temporary defeats which in the perspective of the centuries turn into victories.[153]

Another interesting feature of Clemenceau's account is his analysis of Demosthenes's oratory. He wrote:

> An orator moves an assembly less by the actual nature of his arguments than by the total impression of himself that he gives. . . . He who seeks to convince, must first be convinced himself. It is not enough to win over the minds of the audience, if their hearts are not moved by his emotional force.[154]

This is a good description of the source of Clemenceau's own power as a speaker. He was not an eloquent orator, judged by traditional French rhetorical traditions. When he sought to achieve a highly polished style, his speeches became literary in the worst sense, full of abstractions and

[153] G. Clemenceau, *Démosthène,* pp. 118–19.
[154] G. Clemenceau, op. cit., pp. 50–1.

complicated syntax. But his great oratorical triumphs came when, speaking without much preparation, his staccato phrases came out with all the force and sincerity of his character. This was apparent from his first attacks on Ferry in the 1880s, to his *apologia pro vita sua* at Salernes in 1893, to his combative defence of the record of his first ministry, and his great wartime speeches. As he said of Demosthenes, it was not so much the argument and the style that mattered, it was the force of character behind the words, the sense that here was a man who truly revealed his deepest feelings. There was all the difference in the world between the emotional force of Clemenceau's patriotic appeals of March and September 1918, and the empty rhetoric of many other wartime politicians. It may have been that their patriotic emotions were as sincere and deep as Clemenceau's, but they were not able to project them in their oratory in the same way.

His study of Demosthenes is the most interesting of the writings of these last years. His short book on Monet, while a moving tribute to his long friendship with the great painter, is not particularly memorable as a piece of writing about art. Although Clemenceau had a life-long interest in art, and is said to have been a brilliant guide around art exhibitions, serious aesthetic analysis was beyond his scope. As for the two volumes of philosophical speculation, *Au Soir de la Pensée*, which occupied most of his time between 1923 and 1927, they are, no doubt, a remarkable achievement for a man of over eighty. They show that his intellect was functioning as well as ever, that his perseverance and energy were undiminished, as was his immense curiosity about everything in the world around him. Nevertheless, they are two volumes that must have given much more satisfaction to Clemenceau in the writing than they have ever given anyone to read. They are, indeed, virtually unreadable. There are many passages of vigorous writing in this work, but as a whole it is 'prolix, repetitive and badly organized'.[155] It attempts to give a total account of the evolution of the universe, somewhat in the manner of H. G. Wells's *History of the World*, but at greater length and covering a wider field. In addition, Clemenceau digressed into questions such as 'the phenomenon of knowledge', and into the field of religious speculation. *Au Soir de la Pensée* demonstrates the immense breadth of Clemenceau's intellectual interests and the range of his knowledge. The digressions and footnotes are often the most interesting parts of the book, rather than the over-schematic main argument.[156] Judged by professional academic standards in the many different fields on which

---

[155] S. I. Applebaum, *Clemenceau, thinker and writer* (1948), p. 172.
[156] One interesting point that Clemenceau made was to equate the Fascist and Soviet systems in an equal condemnation as 'showing to what point of intellectual disarray nations can be brought when led by popular oligarchies'. *Au Soir de la Pensée*, II, p. 438.

it touched, it was amateurish and extremely old-fashioned; many of Clemenceau's authorities were the scientists of the early nineteenth century. His basic position remained that of nineteenth-century materialism, the world-view imbibed from his father, in itself largely derived from the French materialist philosophers of the eighteenth century, and their descendants the Idéologues. Even in the field he knew best, biology and evolution, he insisted on defending Lamarckian doctrines against the Darwinian system from which modern biology descended. As the most thorough study of the work puts it:

> With an almost sentimental tenacity he clung to the mechanism of another century, and rejected the more flexible doctrines of contemporary materialists. He never wavered in his loyalty to the philosophy of the Idéologues fashioned by Diderot, Helvetius and d'Holbach. Even when he incorporated the findings of Twentieth Century scientists, he merely reinforced his beliefs from an older materialism.[157]

The last seven years of Clemenceau's life were spent in writing these books. His life was divided between Paris, where he continued to live in the modest apartment that he had first occupied in 1893, and the Vendée, where he had a simple holiday cottage on the edge of the sea at St Vincent-sur-Jard, a remote and tiny village. He took great delight in creating a garden in the sandy soil there, being especially triumphant at being able to grow roses, which everyone had told him would be impossible on such ground. He had taken this cottage in 1921, as a replacement for a country retreat nearer Paris which he had used for a few years, in the Seine valley close to the home of Monet. He came to spend most of the summers in the Vendée, looked after by his faithful servants, the cook-housekeeper Clotilde, the manservant Albert and the chauffeur Brabant. The latter drove him around the countryside, and to and from Paris, at great speed in a powerful limousine presented by an admirer during the war. Although he was isolated from the political world, he retained many friends in other walks of life, old friends of younger days like Geffroy and Monet, more recent acquaintances like General Mordacq and Nicolas Piétri. He also enjoyed, for several years, what may be called *une amitié amoureuse* with Mme Baldensperger, the wife of a Sorbonne professor, who came into contact with him while negotiating about the publication of his study of Demosthenes. This friendship produced a voluminous correspondence, which has recently been published.[158] This intimate relationship with a woman forty years his junior did a great deal to preserve his *joie de vivre* in these last years.

---

[157] S. I. Applebaum, op. cit., p. 159. J. Moreau, *Clemenceau en bloc*, 1931, argues that Clemenceau's views were not incompatible with modern scientific thinking.
[158] G. Clemenceau, *Lettres à une amie* (1968).

Until the very end, he enjoyed good health, and retained a remarkable degree of energy, both physical and mental. His last years were over-shadowed by the deaths of old friends and of his brother and sisters. The deaths of Geffroy and Monet, both life-long friends for whom he had great affection, moved him deeply. The death of his brother Albert, twenty years younger than himself, in 1927 was a bitter blow. He had always been much closer to Albert than to his other brother Paul, an engineer, who lived on to 1946, the only one of the family to survive him. His sister Sophie died in 1923, Adrienne in 1927, and Emma in 1928. Of the sisters it was Emma, only one year older than himself, with whom he had been most intimate. Clemenceau's own children had long married and produced grandchildren who were already adult. His eldest child, Madeleine, married a lawyer called Jacquemaire, and was herself a writer, publishing, among other works, a study of Mme Roland, and an autobiographical novel, *Le Pot de Basilic*. This book, which recounted her childhood, and therefore referred to the private life of her father, annoyed him intensely, and he tried to prevent its publication.[159] He did not succeed in this, but presumably he persuaded her to be more discreet than she had originally intended. The result is a rather strange work, with mysterious gaps; there is, for instance no mention of her mother at all. His son, Michel, after a difficult start in life, became a successful businessman; through his father's friendship with Basil Zaharoff he was taken into the French subsidiary of the arma-ments firm Vickers. His youngest daughter, Thérèse, made an unsatis-factory marriage with a certain Louis Gatineau, and later remarried, becoming Mme Yung. The first marriage gave Clemenceau a grandson, Georges Gatineau, who became the black sheep of the family. Together with his mother, he lived for a time with his grandfather, after the break-up of the marriage in 1906–7. His memoirs, *Des Pattes du Tigre aux Griffes du Destin*, throw an interesting, although lurid and unreli-able, light on the private life of his grandfather.[160]

The last months of Clemenceau's life were devoted to the composition of *Grandeurs et Misères d'une Victoire*. He had on several occasions declared that he would not write his memoirs, but he reacted to the publication of *Le Mémorial de Foch*. Foch had arranged for the publica-tion of this posthumous work, consisting largely of attacks on Clemenceau. He claimed that Clemenceau had opposed his elevation to the supreme command during the war, and went on to attack his policy at the time of the peace settlement. Clemenceau began his work primarily to refute Foch's charges, but it turned into a more general defence of his policy during the war and at the peacemaking, and into a diatribe

[159] G. Clemenceau, *Lettres à une amie*, pp. 282–3 and 286.
[160] G. Gatineau-Clemenceau, *Des Pattes du Tigre aux griffes du destin* (1961).

against his successors, who had allowed the treaty to be destroyed. It would not be fair to judge it as a finished product, as he only had time to produce a first draft. Before he was able to revise it he succumbed to his final illness; after two days of agony he died shortly after midnight on the night of 23–24 November 1929.

His will read:

I wish to be buried at Le Colombier, by the side of my father. My body is to be carried to the burial place without any cortège or ceremony of any kind. . . . Around the grave there is to be nothing but an iron railing, without any name, as for my father. Place in my coffin my walking stick with an iron knob, which was mine in my youth, and the little casket of goatskin in the left hand corner of my wardrobe, with inside it the little book that was placed there by the hand of my dear mother. Finally place there also the two little bunches of dried flowers which are on the mantelpiece of the room by the garden. . . .[161]

All these instructions were carried out; the procession left Paris at 2 a.m., so it was not surprising that only a small crowd watched its departure. At Le Colombier, the old farm, close to the village of Mouchamps, in the possession of the Clemenceau family from the early eighteenth century, there were only the peasants of the neighbourhood, members of the family, the few intimate friends who had accompanied the body from Paris, and a few press photographers. The grave remains unmarked, except for a bas-relief of Minerva by the sculptor Sicard which Clemenceau had had placed there. Remote, and difficult to find, it is visited rarely.

Clemenceau had always insisted on keeping his private life private. His funeral, as he wished, was in no way a State occasion. The son of the Vendée returned to his native soil, to be buried alongside his father on ground owned by his ancestors for two centuries. His death did not have a great impact in France. Naturally it produced a rash of magazine articles, and after a little delay, a number of biographies. His private secretary, Jean Martet, seized the opportunity to publish a few documents Clemenceau had given him, along with an account of several conversations with Clemenceau. But already he seemed to be a figure from a distant past, whose preoccupations had no relevance to current political problems.

[161] J. J. H. Mordacq, op. cit., II, p. 172.

Part eight

CONCLUSION

20

CONCLUSION

Clemenceau was first and foremost a political animal. But he was a many-sided man, with many different fields of interest. Politics was his profession, and his principal concern, but as a journalist he sought to be a man of letters in the widest sense, and attempted creative literature in various forms – short stories, descriptive pieces and moral essays, even a novel and a play. However unsuccessful this attempt, it is important that it was made. He also had a life-long interest in the arts, and was a close friend of the critic Gustave Geffroy and the painter Claude Monet. Many people paid tribute to his qualities as a *Cicerone* after he conducted them round special exhibitions or the permanent collections of the Louvre.[1] He never forgot his early scientific training, although during his lifetime science became a matter of professional specialization that made it quite impossible for the intelligent amateur to keep abreast of the latest research. Thus, if he seemed to some political associates to be an isolated figure, it was not because he was solitary, but because he did not devote his time entirely to politics, except in the special circumstances of the second ministry. He moved in other circles and had other interests. In his early life and middle age he moved in 'society' – not the high society of the aristocracy and *haute bourgeoisie*, which would not have accepted such a representative of republican and democratic ideas, but republican society which had its own salons, and the world of the opera, and fashionable theatres. But after his separation from his wife, and as he grew older, he moved more in intellectual, journalistic, and artistic circles, and spent his time with old and close friends. He was attractive to women, and had several

[1] B. Z. Szeps, *My Life and History*, pp. 137–40.

love affairs, this being an aspect of his life that he took care to separate from politics. But some knowledge of his private life counterbalances the tales of a domineering, harsh and ruthless personality, based on a misreading of his political behaviour; his political posture has been falsely interpreted as the reflection of a temperament which was not that which he revealed to those closest to him. The number of close friends that he managed to retain over many years was striking.[2] The idea that he quarrelled frequently with those close to him is quite wrong. Anyone who came close to him recognized the charm of his personality.

Of course he was not called 'the Tiger' for nothing, and there was a certain brusqueness in his manner. Like many witty people he could not resist making jokes at other people's expense, even cruel and un-deserved ones.[3] This aspect of Clemenceau's personality and its political effects has been greatly exaggerated by his critics. Nevertheless it existed, and has done much to give him a reputation for violence and ruthlessness that his actions belie. This image, however, was one reason for his success in 1918. The very fact that Clemenceau was in office reassured those who were calling for harsh measures against 'defeatism', while his actions were moderate. One may speculate to what extent, at this stage, Clemenceau realized the value of this reputation, and went out of his way to exaggerate it.[4] General Mordacq has said that he was really soft-hearted and sentimental, and there is plenty of evidence of this.[5] He liked to test people, particularly new acquaintances, to see if they would stand up to him in argument. He was addicted to debate, and could not resist a good argument. Wickham Steed's account of a meeting in 1909 during which Clemenceau poured out his criticisms of British policy 'at the speed of an express-train', is a good example of his conversational methods.[6] No doubt this created a bad impression on those who did not have the quickness of mind or the self-confidence to answer him. But his life-long relationships with widely differing indi-viduals show that he had a great capacity for friendship.

In politics he adopted a deliberately authoritative stance. He believed

[2] B. Bastoul, *Clemenceau vu par un passant inconnu* (1938), pp. 82–3; J. J. H. Mordacq, *Clemenceau* (1939), pp. 198–9.
[3] The question of 'who first called Clemenceau the Tiger?' gave rise to a pro-longed discussion in *L'Intermédiaire des Chercheurs et Curieux* (1930–2), but no definite answer appeared. The nickname seems to have been given around 1906–7.
[4] B. Bastoul, op. cit., p. 129, thinks that his violent and seemingly impulsive lan-guage was simultaneously 'instinctive and calculated', citing his brusque 'Count Czernin has lied' as an example.
[5] J. J. H. Mordacq *Clemenceau*, pp. 205–8. He was reduced to tears at the time of the Armistice, and on one occasion during the war at the meeting of the Senate Army committee.
[6] H. Wickham Steed, *Through Thirty Years*, I, pp. 284–7. Cf. B. Bastoul, op. cit., pp. 79–80, and G. Suarez, *Briand*, II, p. 93, who states that 'in the course of an argument Clemenceau would never yield one inch, even when he was defending furiously that which he had opposed the day before'.

that the lack of firm and definite leadership was the main reason for the cabinet instability which had vitiated the working of the Parliamentary system in France. He sought to demonstrate that a strong prime minister, relying on the support of a committed majority, could provide the continuity and authority needed. By a strange misinterpretation this has sometimes been called the expression of a 'dictatorial' temperament. In fact the fundamental achievement of his second ministry was to take France through the political crisis, to which she had been brought by weak governments, without having recourse to dictatorial methods. If Clemenceau had not still been on the field in November 1917, it is hard to see who else could have brought France through the last year of the war while still preserving the full constitutional system of Parliamentary government. He took no extraordinary powers beyond a very limited power to legislate by decree for the control of food supply, and based his authority on the support of a majority in the Chamber of Deputies. Of course, this was a very different form of Parliamentary government from that which had become normal under the Third Republic, one that bore more resemblance to the British form, in which a coherent and disciplined majority supported a cabinet which decided on policy. This was what Clemenceau meant when he told the Chamber that 'the question of confidence will always be put'.[7] Under the French system, this was not normal. The second Clemenceau ministry virtually achieved that increased authority for the executive against the legislative branch sought by advocates of various constitutional reforms over the next forty years.

Clemenceau was a complex character, as, in the last resort, every human being is complex. We all behave in different ways in different circumstances, and there is nothing in which there is so much room for disagreement as views about the character of others. In the case of a politician, the difficulty of arriving at an assessment of character is much accentuated. There is the contrast between the public image and the private personality, which may be considerable. There is the fact that an important politician in a democratic state acts by representing certain ideas and interests which he comes to embody. This distorts our view of his personality, which comes to be the vehicle for the expression of deeper forces. Clemenceau, Père-la-Victoire, the embodiment of France's will to survive as a great nation, did this more than most. In a community as deeply and bitterly divided as France was, such a role produced both exaggerated enthusiasm and exaggerated hostility. Clemenceau had more than his share of both,[8] and many views

[7] On 20 November 1917, *Discours de Guerre*, p. 161. Cf. P. Renouvin, *The Forms of War Government in France*, p. 155.
[8] J. J. H. Mordacq, *Clemenceau*, p. 76, reporting Clemenceau's speech at a banquet after the inauguration of the war memorial at the Lycée of Nantes, 28 May 1922.

of his personality are the product of strong political prejudice, both for and against. It is also true that he changed over a lifetime of eighty-eight years. One reason for the picture of Clemenceau as highly idiosyncratic is that it was based on his last years, when he had reached an age at which it is normal to indulge one's eccentricities. He appeared eccentric in details of dress, merely because he retained clothes made in fashions long outdated, after the habit of old people.

But behind all the changes of seventy years, from the republican student waging war on the Second Empire to avenge his father, to the old statesman making the peace of Versailles, basic features of his character stand out. There is his clarity of mind, revealed in his verbal felicity and debating skill, his insistence on honesty and frankness, and above all, his instinctive sense of personal human dignity, and *amour-propre*, both his own and that of others. Because he would always defend his own honour, he could respect the *amour-propre* of others when they showed that they had the courage and the will to defend it. It is important to remember that he was famed as a duellist. G. Suarez has remarked that, in spite of his democratic ideas, he remained in habit and temperament an aristocrat, or rather a 'gentleman' with all that was implied by that term under the *ancien régime*. Keynes remarked perceptively that, although Woodrow Wilson had been a university professor, he was a less cultivated man than Clemenceau – 'he had not much even of that culture of the world which marks M. Clemenceau and Mr Balfour as exquisitely cultivated gentlemen of their class and generation'. Clemenceau remarked that Lloyd George was totally lacking in general culture, and regarded this as his chief fault, seeming to imply that it was in some way bound up with his deviousness.[9] He had, it is true, the defects of his qualities, a tendency to arrogance, obstinacy, impulsiveness, and the carrying of political disagreement to the point of personal vendetta. His attitude towards Ferry, Delcassé and Poincaré showed that this remained with him throughout his life. In each case personal hatred blinded him to the fact that his opponent was carrying out an essential part of the policy that he himself advocated. Ferry, with his educational reforms, was doing more than anyone else to free France from the control of the Catholic Church; Delcassé was building the alliance system that would allow France to withstand German attempts at domination; Poincaré was playing an essential, even if symbolic, role in that resurgence of French self-confidence that backed diplomatic with military revival. These defects were apparent in the headstrong youth carried away by his passion for Hortense Kestner. They remained obvious in his onslaught on Ferry between 1880 and 1885; as Scheurer-Kestner sadly remarked, they prevented his friend

[9] G. Suarez, *Briand*, II, p. 92. J. M. Keynes, op. cit., p. 37.

from playing at that time the political role that he might have had.[10] He returned to politics after the Dreyfus Affair, in many ways a chastened man, and his first ministry represented a remarkable exercise in politics as the art of the possible. But his personal feuds with Delcassé and Poincaré show that he had not entirely changed. The three years of wartime opposition also gave reason to believe that age had merely accentuated some of his worst qualities. His criticism of the military and political leadership was often too violent to be effective, and his own proposals were highly unrealistic. But during his second ministry he showed that, in office, he could master himself. He remained impulsive and obstinate on small matters. On important political questions he was very different. By this time he was a master of political tactics. This was revealed in his negotiating ability, in his skill at steering a small group, even if composed of strong personalities with widely divergent ideas, to a compromise solution. This skill was revealed in the meetings of the Allied statesmen and military leaders in the Supreme War Council, and in the peace negotiations at the Council of Four, where his tactical skill has often not been stressed enough. That he, Wilson, and Lloyd George, were able to agree on the terms to present to Germany, was in large part due to Clemenceau's bargaining skill. He rarely adopted a completely intransigent position, but managed to safeguard what he saw as essential for France, and to steer the discussion unobtrusively towards a compromise. Patience, as well as dialectical and argumentative ability, were necessary for this.

His role in the peace negotiations was the occasion for the most influential of character-sketches of Clemenceau, painted by J. M. Keynes in a few skilful pages of his pamphlet, 'The Economic Consequences of the Peace'. Keynes's view of Clemenceau, although in some ways distorted, like all successful caricatures, achieves verisimilitude by seizing on some features of its subject that really existed. And Keynes's portrait, which was *nuancé*, has been coarsened by other writers who have used it to produce a picture of Clemenceau as a cynical practitioner of *Realpolitik*.[11] Keynes weaved a physical and psychological description of Clemenceau into an extremely convincing portrait. He described him presiding at one of the meetings of the delegates to the Peace Conference;

> . . . throned, in his grey gloves, on the brocade chair, dry in soul and empty of hope, very old and tired, but surveying the scene with a

---

[10] A. Scheurer-Kestner, *Journal*, pp. 523–4. Bibliothèque Nationale, NAF, 12711.
[11] W. L. Shirer, *The Collapse of the Third Republic* (1970), offers some of the worst examples; almost every mention of Clemenceau has 'cynical' as a sort of Homeric epithet.

cynical and almost impish air. . . . He felt about France what Pericles felt of Athens – unique value in her, nothing else mattering: but his theory of politics was Bismarck's. He had one illusion – France; and one disillusion, mankind, including Frenchmen and his colleagues not least. His principles for the peace can be expressed simply. . . . You must never negotiate with a German or conciliate him: you must dictate to him. On no other terms will he respect you, or will you prevent him from cheating you. But it is doubtful how far he thought these characteristics peculiar to Germany, or whether his candid view of some other nations was fundamentally different. His philosophy, therefore, had no place for 'sentimentality' in international relations. Nations are real things, of whom you love one and feel for the rest indifference – or hatred. The glory of the nation you love is a desirable end – but generally to be obtained at your neighbour's expense. The politics of power are inevitable, and there is nothing very new to learn about this war, or the end it was fought for; England had destroyed, as in each preceding century, a trade rival; a mighty chapter had been closed in the secular struggle between the glories of Germany and of France. . . . From the belief that essentially the old order does not change, being based on human nature which is always the same, and from a consequent scepticism of all that class of doctrine which the League of Nations stands for, the policy of France and of Clemenceau followed logically. . . . This is the policy of an old man, whose most vivid impressions and most lively imagination are of the past and not the future. He sees the issue in terms of France and Germany, not of humanity and of European civilization struggling forwards to a new order. The war has bitten into his consciousness somewhat differently from ours, and he neither expects nor hopes that we are at the threshold of a new age.[12]

This portrait mingles insight with serious mistakes about Clemenceau's position. It is true that he believed that 'the politics of power' were inevitable, and was sceptical about 'all that class of doctrine which the League of Nations stands for'. But now that we have seen what happened in the subsequent twenty years, it may well be asked which was the more realistic view, that of Keynes with his hopes for a new and more civilized age, or that of Clemenceau who thought that human nature did not suddenly change, especially in the circumstances of 1919. It was not Clemenceau who was cynical, but Keynes who was naïve. What Keynes meant, of course, was that in the particular case of the motives of those who held power in Germany, Clemenceau was much less disposed than Keynes to believe in their goodness. This was not so

[12] J. M. Keynes, op cit., pp. 28–33.

much a result of a general cynical disposition of mind, as of his assessment of the particular situation, an assessment which proved to be more accurate than that of Keynes. Nor is it true that Clemenceau's 'theory of politics' was Bismarck's. He did genuinely believe in national self-determination, not only 'as an ingenious formula for rearranging the balance of power in one's own interests'. This is not to say that he thought that it could be used as a formula to solve all the frontier problems in the world. In practice, neither Keynes, nor President Wilson, nor anyone else who actually had to deal with the problems of drawing frontiers, thought that it could so be used. But on the basic question of the continuance of a German national state, however dangerous this was to France, Clemenceau recognized that nationalism was too strong to be ignored. There is a strange contradiction at the heart of Keynes's view, which simultaneously condemns nationalism and justifies the principle of national self-determination. In contrast to the extreme French nationalists, Clemenceau did not deny the right of Germany to exist as a nation. Keynes shows no awareness of the strength in France of those who really did hold the doctrines he ascribed to Clemenceau, and how hard he had to fight to maintain his authority against them. If Keynes's view were correct, Clemenceau should have been found on ·the extreme right of French politics, instead of on the left centre. It was not true that Clemenceau saw the 'glory' of France as the end for which the war had been fought, nor that he regarded military victory as the supreme end of political action. He made his views clear on many occasions, and they were far removed from the hysterical chauvinism of Déroulède, of Maurras, Daudet and the Action Française. He did not believe that only France mattered: other nations had a right to exist, and to exercise their rightful role. He rejected France's heritage of imperialistic glory, and had just as much contempt for Napoleon I as for Napoleon III.[13]

But if he did not believe that Might was Right, he did believe that 'Covenants without the sword are but words', and that Right must be defended by Might. He had been forced to think out his position on these matters to justify his position as a defender of Dreyfus, who was not a pacifist. At that time he had said:

I hate warfare just as much as Jaurès, but I do not believe that it rests with us to decree a universal peace.

In his speech at Zola's trial he had explained that the national army, the sacrifice and discipline it demanded, were only justified to defend

[13] J. J. H. Mordacq, *Clemenceau Au Soir de la Vie*, I, p. 84. Cf. B. Bastoul, op. cit., p. 86. 'This patriotism has nothing *Cocardier* about it. . . . He knew nothing of what was then called chauvinism, and is now known as nationalism. . . . He did not believe that his people were the chosen people.'

the values of a free and civilized society.[14] He saw the fallacy in the pacifist argument: he pointed out that if communities which have reached a higher level of civilized behaviour refuse to defend themselves, then the world would be plunged back under the rule of naked force and barbarism, as those without such scruples took over. Clemenceau was a liberal, and his supreme values were individualistic. He was not a nationalist like those who saw national glory and aggrandizement as ends in themselves. He had said in 1903, with great eloquence, that his whole political philosophy was based on the rights of the individual against oppression from all quarters, including the Moloch State.[15] But there were circumstances in which the individual had to sacrifice his own life in order to preserve the nation of which he was a part, and which alone provided the framework in which he could find fulfilment as a free individual. This was his theme in countless articles before the war. He wrote in June 1914 of

> the independence and dignity of a people, without which the life of the individual, like that of the nation, can only be shameful and abject.

A little later he reflected on the military parade of 14 July,

> a spectacle of sublime grandeur, force in the service of an idea. The idea is *la patrie*, which calls on men to die so that others may live in the glorious unbroken chain of those who have been and those yet to be born. . . . The first law of nations is this: we must defend our historical heritage, by organizing a force that will oppose an invincible resistance to aggression. We are a defeated people, but a people that wants to live, not in the abdication of serfdom to the victor, but with honour in the independence of thought and action through which our ancestors made the history of France.[16]

A correct assessment of the relations between individualism and nationalism in Clemenceau's philosophy of life is essential to an understanding of his character and the significance of his historical role. In absolute terms he did not give normative value to the nation but to the individual. But it was by means of his social character that man had risen from the animal level to the level of civilization. In the modern world all other associations and communities were dependent

---

[14] *See above*, p. 149.
[15] *See above*, p. 159.
[16] Articles in *L'Homme Libre*, 25 June and 15 July 1914, reprinted in *La France Devant l'Allemagne*, pp. 67 and 77. It remained his theme from 1905 down to 1914 that France would never seek revenge by attacking Germany, but that she must be prepared to defend her independence against another German attack. An early example of his position was the article in *L'Aurore*, 19 June 1905, quoted by C. Digeon, *La Crise Allemande de la Pensée Française 1870–1914* (1959), p. 506.

on the national community. Through the nation civilization and culture were transmitted, and each generation was able to build on the shoulders of those who had gone before. In this perspective he saw the victory of France in 1918 as the victory of the ideals of the French Revolution. A perceptive analyst of Clemenceau's character and ideas has written that his ideal was in the last resort cosmopolitan, that religion of humanity propounded by Comte and Littré. But

> while remaining attached to the great principles of human solidarity, Clemenceau saw in *la patrie* the essential element of progress towards this ideal: it was national solidarity that became the lynchpin of his faith.[17]

Of course his patriotic fervour was not adopted as a result of any intellectual process, although it could be rationalized in those terms. It was an instinctive response coming from the deepest level of his personality. It found its most lyrical expression in the tribute he paid to his own birth-place and its inhabitants, the Vendée, '*la terre ingrate de notre bocage*', and the peasants who laboured to win a meagre living from its soil. The emphasis which he placed on the continuity of generations making up *la patrie* drew its emotional strength from the deep love and respect which he paid to his own parents. It is ironical that the one attempt to give a psychoanalytic interpretation of Clemenceau's character is totally vitiated by the mistaken belief that his relations with his father were bad.[18] There is abundant evidence to the contrary, both in the letters which he wrote to his friend Scheurer-Kestner in his early twenties, and in his recollections of his early life reported by Martet.

Keynes was mistaking Clemenceau's own ultimate standard of values when he wrote that:

> One could not despise Clemenceau or dislike him, but only take a different view as to the nature of civilized man, or indulge at least, a different hope.

Clemenceau himself 'indulged the hope'. Only he had a different time-scale. He believed that humanity was progressing towards a freer, more just and humane form of social organization, but progress was slow, and had to be fought for at every step. Hence his contempt for Utopian theorists like Jaurès, or President Wilson, who seemed to believe that the dark and tragic side of human history could be ended at a blow, by the signing of the Covenant, or by the proclamation of

---

[17] B. Bastoul, op. cit., p. 94.
[18] P. Lacombe, 'The enigma of Clemenceau', *The Psychoanalytic Review*, 33 (1946), pp. 165–76, and a French version in *Revue Française de Psychoanalyse* (1947).

the Socialist Revolution. Whatever he may have thought in the ardour of youth, by middle and old age he thought that moral progress towards the ideals of liberty, equality and fraternity postulated in 1789 would be an extremely long process. He also thought this could only take place within the framework of national communities, and that those who had already reached a higher level, which the French and Anglo-Saxon democracies had, compared with Germany, must be prepared to defend their social and political system by force of arms.

The hardest part of Clemenceau's life to defend to a modern audience is his role in the First World War. His articles in *L'Homme Enchaîné*, with their rabid anti-Germanism, are difficult to swallow. He went much too far in his characterization of Germany as barbaric, and believed too readily stories of German atrocities. But he was not altogether wrong in these views. It is not a question of whether Germany before 1914 should be painted entirely in black. But a German victory would have consecrated the domination of the military over Germany and over Europe.

G. F. Kennan has written of

> the staggering price paid by the Western people for their insistence on completing a military victory over Germany in 1917 and 1918. Can it conceivably have been that the end in view was worth the price? . . . I hold the First World War to have been the great catastrophe of western civilization in the present century. I think it an endless pity that it did not cease in November 1917.[19]

No doubt it is true that the First World War was the great catastrophe of Western civilization, but its consequences could not be averted in November 1917. They were unleashed long before that time. There could be no genuine compromise peace in November 1917, because the German High Command would accept nothing but a peace that confirmed their victory, with all that victory implied both for Europe and for German domestic politics. Recent historical research has confirmed Clemenceau's views about what a peace with Germany in 1917 would have involved, against the revisionist historians of the inter-war period. Kennan's view cannot be regarded as a realistic one. At the outset of the war, Germany was not very different from the fully democratic states of western Europe, but as the war went on the darker forces that were only to develop fully in the Nazi system began to emerge.

Hostile views of Clemenceau imply that he was the representative of similar chauvinistic and militaristic tendencies in France. Such views cannot be substantiated. His nationalism remained that of a nineteenth-century liberal, who saw the national community as the framework

[19] G. L. Kennan, *Russia and the West under Lenin and Stalin*, pp. 32 and 47.

for the exercise of individual liberties. His wartime ministry demonstrated that he would apply these principles in practice. For all the charges of dictatorship, a glance at the left-wing press for 1918 shows that the powers of the censor were not used to stifle criticism and opposition. In a perceptive article, R. Girardet has written that underneath the well-known transposition of nationalist sentiment from the Left of the political scene, where it was to be found in the first half of the nineteenth century, to the Right where it was most obvious in the twentieth century, there are important cross-currents and elements of continuity.[20] He mentions Barrès, who began his political career on the Left, before becoming one of the chief exponents of right-wing nationalism. Even more significant is Clemenceau, whose long political career is the personal embodiment of one strand of continuity in French nationalism. In his youth the tradition of Jacobin nationalism, as expounded by Michelet, took him naturally to the confines of the extreme left of the political scene, and to sympathy with those whose rejection of the humiliating peace was expressed in the revolt of the Commune. By the end of his life, although he had not changed his ideas, his continued adherence to this nationalist ideology had alienated him from much of the Left, and brought him the support of the extreme Right. But he did not share the whole value-system of the extreme Right. Precisely the fact that Clemenceau represented the old republican style of nationalism, linking French national survival and prestige with the triumph of the ideas of 1789, allowed him to be the symbol of national unity in 1918. Coming from the Left, and still in the centre of the political spectrum, he was the guarantee that France would remain a liberal democratic society. But France's dependence on the existence of one man to incarnate this vital element of the national heritage was to lead to the collapse of the Third Republic when it faced its next challenge in 1940.

[20] R. Girardet, 'Pour une introduction à l'histoire du nationalisme français', *Revue Française de Science Politique*, VIII (1958), pp. 505–28, especially p. 515. Cf. also R. Girardet, *Le Nationalisme Français 1870–1940* (1966), Z. Sternhel, 'Barrès et la Gauche', *Le Mouvement Social*, 75 (1971), pp. 77–130, and D. R. Watson, 'The Nationalist Movement in Paris, 1900–1906', St Antony's Papers XIII, for the transposition of Nationalism from Left to Right. A. Thibaudet, *Les Idées Politiques de la France* (1932), pp. 131–5, discusses the importance of Clemenceau as the exponent of Radical nationalism.

APPENDICES

SOURCES
and
BIBLIOGRAPHY

INDEX

Appendix I

Membership of the Clemenceau Cabinets

Prime Minister and Min. of Interior	G. Clemenceau	Senator, Radical-Socialist
Justice (After 4 January 1908 Justice and Public Worship)	J. Guyot-Dessaigne A. Briand	Deputy, Radical Deputy, Socialist
Foreign Affairs	S. Pichon	Senator, Radical
Finance	J. Caillaux	Deputy, Radical-Socialist
War	General Picquart	Non-Parliamentarian
Navy (After 22 October 1908)	G. Thomson A. Picard	Deputy, Radical-Socialist
Public Instruction, Fine Arts and Public Worship (After 4 January 1908 Public Instruction and Fine Arts)	A. Briand G. Doumergue	Deputy, Ind. Socialist Deputy, Radical-Socialist
Public Works and Posts and Telegraphs	L. Barthou	Deputy, Radical
Commerce and Industry (After 4 January 1908)	G. Doumergue J. Cruppi	Deputy, Radical-Socialist Deputy, Gauche-Radicale
Agriculture	J. Ruau	Deputy, Radical
Colonies	R. Milliès-Lacroix	Senator, Radical-Socialist
Labour	R. Viviani	Deputy, Ind. Socialist

Under-secretaries

War	H. Cheron	Deputy, Républicain de Gauche
Fine Arts and Public Worship	H. Dujardin-Beaumetz	Deputy, Radical

Under-secretaries (contd.)

Posts and Telegraphs	J. Simyan	Deputy, Radical-Socialist
Interior	A. Sarraut	Deputy, Radical-Socialist
(After 20 July 1907)	A. Maujan	Senator, Gauche-Démocratique

2 THE SECOND CLEMENCEAU MINISTRY, 16 NOVEMBER 1917– 20 JANUARY 1920

Prime Minister and Minister of War	G. Clemenceau	Senator, Radical
Justice	L. Nail	Deputy, Radical-Socialist
Foreign Affairs	S. Pichon	Senator, Radical
Interior	J. Pams	Senator, Radical
Finance	L. L. Klotz	Deputy, Radical-Socialist
Navy	G. Leygues	Deputy, Républicain de Gauche
Public Instruction and Fine Arts	L. Lafferre	Deputy, Radical-Socialist
(After 27 November 1919)	L. Berard	Deputy, Gauche Démocratique
Public Works and Transport	A. Claveille	Non-Parliamentarian
Commerce, Industry, Posts, Telegraphs and Merchant Navy	E. Clémentel	Deputy, Gauche Radicale
(After 27 November 1919, Commerce and Industry)	L. Dubois	Deputy, Progressist
Agriculture and Food	V. Boret	Deputy, Gauche Radicale
(After 20 July 1919)	J. Noulens	Deputy, Gauche Radicale
Colonies	H. Simon	Deputy, Radical-Socialist
Labour	P. Colliard	Deputy, Republican Socialist
(After 2 December 1919)	P. Jourdain	Deputy, Bloc National
Munitions (After 26 November 1919 Industrial Reconstruction)	L. Loucheur	Non-Parliamentarian
Blockade and Liberated Territories	C. Jonnart	Senator, Gauche Démocratique
(After 23 November 1917,	A. Lebrun	Deputy, Gauche Démocratique
after 6 November 1919, Liberated Territories)	A. Tardieu	Deputy, Independent

Under-secretaries

War	J. Jeanneney	Senator, Gauche Démocratique
War, Effectives and Pensions	L. Abrami	Deputy, Républicain de Gauche

War, Air Force	J. L. Dumesnil	Deputy, Radical-Socialist
War, Medical services (After 5 February 1918)	J. Godart L. Mourier	Deputy, Radical-Socialist Deputy, Radical-Socialist
War, Military justice	E. Ignace	Deputy, Union Républicaine
War, Demobilization (After 6 December 1918)	L. Deschamps	Deputy, Républicain de Gauche
Navy	J. Cels	Deputy, Gauche Radicale
Commerce and Industry	H. Lémery	Deputy, Union Républicaine
Agriculture and Food	E. Vilgrain	Non-Parliamentarian
Public Works (After 19 November 1918)	J. Cels	Deputy, Gauche Radicale
Finances, disposition of material (After 27 November 1919)	P. Morel Y. Le Troquer	Deputy, Gauche Radicale Deputy, Socialist
Posts and Telegraphs (After 27 November 1919)	L. Deschamps	Deputy, Républicain de Gauche
Interior	A. Favre	Deputy, Gauche Radicale
Finances	C. Sergent	Non-Parliamentarian

Appendix II

The Constitution of the Third Republic

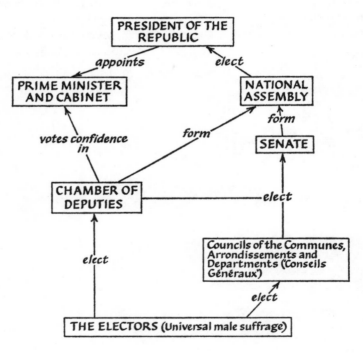

HEAD OF STATE   President of the Republic: elected for a seven-year term by the two houses of Parliament (known as the National Assembly when in joint session).

EXECUTIVE   Prime Minister and Cabinet: chosen by the President, but must have the confidence of a majority of the Chamber of Deputies.

LEGISLATIVE (i) the Senate, elected for nine-year terms by electoral colleges consisting of the deputies and members of local government councils in each department. Life senators, one-quarter of the total by the laws of 1875, were discontinued in 1884, although those already chosen remained.

(ii) the Chamber of Deputies, elected by universal male suffrage (for details of the electoral methods *see* Appendix III).

JUDICIARY Judges normally independent of the executive once appointed, although this was suspended in 1883 to allow a purge of monarchist judges. The republican demand for election of judges was never put into practice.

The constitution was drawn up by the National Assembly, elected in 1871 with its monarchist majority, so as to severely limit the democratic element, represented by the Chamber of Deputies, elected by universal male suffrage. The President and the Senate, both indirectly elected, had wide powers, and if they both agreed, the Chamber could be dissolved, and new elections held. Abuse of this power in 1877 meant that it was never again exercised. The republicans had won control of all three political institutions by 1879, but the system remained one which was only to a limited degree responsive to pressure from the voters. The Senate retained and exercised its veto over legislation, while the absence of disciplined political parties meant that the electorate was never in a position to choose between two alternative governments. The constitution did not preserve the dominance of the upper classes, the traditional 'notables', as had been intended, but provided the framework for a *Régime d'Assemblée*, in which professional politicians played a subtle game over whose combinations the influence of the voters was limited.

Appendix III

Electoral Systems

Dates of Elections	Type of Constituency	Number of Ballots
(1) 1871	Multi-Member	Single
(2) 1876, 1877, 1881, 1889, 1893, 1898, 1902, 1906, 1910, 1914, 1928, 1932, 1936	Single-Member	Double
(3) 1885	Multi-Member	Double
(4) 1919, 1924	Multi-Member	Single*

* In practice; there was provision for a second ballot but this was necessary in only one constituency in 1919; this system was a modified form of proportional representation, which worked in a complicated and arbitrary fashion.

System 2 was the normal electoral system under the Third Republic and has been restored since 1958. If no candidate won an absolute majority of votes cast at the first ballot, a second ballot was held at which a relative majority sufficed. In practice the first ballot acted as a primary election in the American style, and usually only two serious candidates stood at the second ballot.

Under the multi-member systems the department usually formed the constituency, although in 1919 and 1924 some departments were divided. The number of deputies varied according to population, and each elector could cast as many votes as there were deputies to be elected. 1871 offers the only example of a simple majority system; combined with multi-member constituencies, and the unusual political circumstances, it produced an anomalous result.

Appendix IV

The Political Parties

'Political party' is a term with two meanings. There is the modern sense of an organized institution with formal membership and official hierarchy: a political party, in this sense, in a democratic state, is an institution that links the political leaders in a representative assembly with the local party members, the 'militants', in the constituencies. On the other hand there is the older and vaguer sense in which one talks, say, of the Whig and Tory parties in seventeenth- and eighteenth-century England. They had no institutional embodiment, but were the sections into which the politically conscious elements of the nation divided. The transition from the first to the second of these senses took place in the mid-nineteenth century in Britain. In France it was long delayed, and was still not completed by the end of the Third Republic. Formed 'groups' existed in the Chamber and the Senate, but before 1900 there were no party organizations in the country, unless one counts the Socialist sects. There was a kaleidoscopic mass of local committees, usually the organ of individual deputies, and not linked to each other in any national institutions. Clemenceau's attempts between 1880 and 1885 to link up various Radical committees had not been successful. Even after the appearance of party organizations from 1900 on, the parties were weak, had little control over the deputies and senators who belonged to them, and could not command much loyalty on the part of the voters; nor did they cover the entire political spectrum, as the classical Right remained without any party organization. Clemenceau's position between 1900 and 1920 illustrates the weakness of the party organizations. He was the most prominent Radical politician in France, but he was never the leader of the Parti-Républicain Radical et Radical-Socialiste, and after 1909, not even a member of it.

This appendix lists:

(1) the main political tendencies in the period 1870–1900, and
(2) provides a list of the parties founded between 1900 and 1919, and a table relating them to the Parliamentary groups, and to the generic names of the main political tendencies: these generic names have been used in the text as far as possible.

I POLITICAL TENDENCIES, 1870–1900

(a) *The Left*
  (i) Collectivist Socialists, divided into several sects, Reformists, Blanquists, Guesdists, Allemanistes, etc., but in total of little significance in this period.

417

(ii) Radical and Radical Socialist Republicans.

(iii) Moderate Republicans, known first as Opportunists, later as Progressists, frequently simply as '*Modérés*'.

(iv) Conservative Republicans, known as the *Centre Gauche*.

(b) *The Right*

(i) *Ralliés*, i.e. monarchists who abandon their opposition to the principle of a Republic and 'rally' to the existing régime; from 1893 onwards.

(ii) Bonapartists ⎫

(iii) Orleanists ⎬ after 1885, virtually fused, and known simply as 'the Right'.

(iv) Legitimists ⎭

(c) *Boulangists*

The supporters of General Boulanger in 1889; most originated on the Left but their allegiance to the general brought them close to the Right: they cannot really be classified with either Left or Right.

2 POLITICAL PARTIES, 1900–1919, with date of foundation.

(a) *The Left*

(i) *Section Française de l'Internationale Ouvrière (S.F.I.O.) (1905)*: the Socialist party, formed by the union of the two Socialist parties, *Parti Socialiste Français*, and *Parti Socialiste de France*, led by Jaurès and Guesde, respectively, that had emerged in 1899 from the earlier sects. As its name implies it regarded its participation in the Second International as very important, and unification had resulted from pressure from the international Socialist movement at the Amsterdam Congress of 1904.

(ii) *Parti Républicain Socialiste (1911)*: the very weak organization for those Socialists not in the s.f.i.o., known usually as the Independent or Republican Socialists.

(iii) *Parti Socialiste Français (1899)*: another weak organization for Socialists who did not join the s.f.i.o.; the name was first given to the party led by Jaurès in 1899 and it survived into the inter-war period, except for 1911–1913 when it was amalgamated with the above.

(iv) *Parti Républicain Radical et Radical-Socialistes (1901)*: the organized expression of the Radical tendency that had existed from the beginning of the Third Republic, and indeed, earlier.

(v) *Alliance Démocratique (1901)*: the close relations of next below, but counted as a party of the Left because of their participation in the Dreyfusard campaign.

(b) *The Right*

(i) *Fédération Républicaine (1903)*: descended from the conservative republicans, but separated from their former colleagues by their rejection of the Dreyfusard cause and the anti-clerical campaign that followed.

(ii) *Action Libérale Populaire (1902)*: an unsuccessful attempt to organize the Right as a Catholic party. An unkind joke said that it was so-called because it was neither active nor liberal popular.

(iii) The Nationalist Leagues, *Ligue de la Patrie Française (1899)*, *Ligue des Patriotes (1882)*: they were only significant in Parliamentary politics from 1899–

1906, although an offshoot the *Ligue de l'Action Française* remained in existence, and was important outside Parliament.

(iv) The Right was always much less organized than the Left, and an important part of its representatives, avowedly or tacitly Royalist, remained unorganized even in the weak form of the political parties of this period.

N.B. Even after the formation of these political parties between 1900 and 1905, the political groups of the Senate and the Chamber of Deputies remained independent of them. The Parliamentary groups, many of which antedated the parties, would tend to be associated with one party, but the correspondence was not complete except in the case of the Socialists (s.f.i.o. type). Until 1910 many deputies and senators were members of more than one group, while some did not belong to any. In 1910 it was decided to conduct elections for membership of the Chamber committees in the groups, making it necessary for all deputies to belong to a group (hence the appearance of 'the group of deputies not belonging to any group'), and to belong to one group only. This prohibition of double membership did something to simplify the group system in the Chamber, but in the Senate the old methods continued. For further details reference can be made to the list of the Chamber groups in G. Dupeux and F. Goguel, *Sociologie Electorale, Esquisse d'un bilan et guide des recherches*, Cahiers de la Fondation Nationale des Sciences Politiques, 26 (1951). The names of the Senate groups, and more complete information on the Chamber groups, can be found in contemporary reference books, the *Année Politique*, 1875–1905, and the *Annuaire du Parlement*, 1900–1914.

	Generic Name	*Party Name*
I	THE LEFT	
	(a) Unified, or Revolutionary, or Collectivist Socialists	Section Française de l'Internationale Ouvrière
	(b) Independent or Republican Socialists	Parti Socialiste Français Parti Républicain-Socialiste
	(c) Radicals and Radical-Socialists	Parti Républicain-Radical et Radicale-Socialiste
	(d) Moderate Republicans, or Républicains de Gauche	Alliance Démocratique
II	THE RIGHT	
	(a) Conservative Republicans, or Progressists	Fédération Républicaine
	(b) Catholics or Ralliés	Action Libérale Populaire
	(c) Nationalists	Ligue des Patriotes Ligue de la Patrie Française Ligue de l'Action Française
	(d) Reactionaries or 'Classical Right'	

Main Associated Parliamentary Groups

Groupe Socialiste, 1902–1906
Groupe Socialiste Unifié, 1906–1910
Groupe du Parti Socialiste, 1910–1919

Groupe Socialiste Indépendante, 1902–1906
Groupe Socialiste Parlementaire, 1906–1910
Groupe Républicain Socialiste, 1910–1919

Groupe de la Gauche Radicale-Socialiste, 1902–1910
Groupe de la Gauche Radicale, 1902–1919
Groupe des Républicains Radicaux-Socialistes, 1910–1914
Groupe du Parti Républicain Radical et
Radicale-Socialiste, 1914–1919

Groupe de la Gauche Radicale, 1902–1919
Groupe de l'Union Républicaine Radicale et
Radicale-Socialiste, 1914–1919
Groupe de la Gauche Democratique, 1905–1919
Groupe des Républicains de Gauche, 1914–1919

Groupe des Républicains Progressistes, 1902–1914
Groupe de l'Union Démocratique, 1902–1910
Groupe de l'Union Républicaine, 1906–1914
Groupe de la Fédération Républicaine, 1914–1919

Groupe de l'Action Libérale Populaire, 1902–1919

Groupe des Républicains Nationalistes, 1902–1910

Groupe des Droites, 1910–1919
Groupe des Deputés non Inscrits aux Groupes, 1911–1919
Groupe Indépendant, 1918–1919

Political tendencies in the Chamber of Deputies

(i) 1871-1902

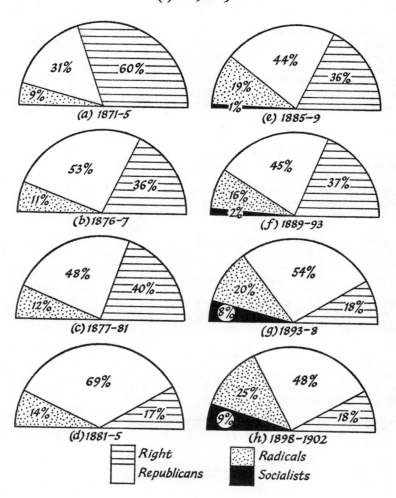

(a) 1871-5 — 31% · 9% · 60%

(b) 1876-7 — 53% · 11% · 36%

(c) 1877-81 — 48% · 12% · 40%

(d) 1881-5 — 69% · 14% · 17%

(e) 1885-9 — 44% · 19% · 1% · 36%

(f) 1889-93 — 45% · 16% · 2% · 37%

(g) 1893-8 — 54% · 20% · 8% · 18%

(h) 1898-1902 — 48% · 25% · 9% · 18%

Right
Republicans
Radicals
Socialists

(ii) 1902-1924

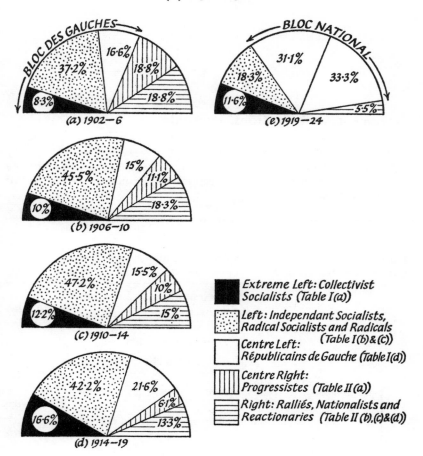

BLOC DES GAUCHES
BLOC NATIONAL

(a) 1902—6
16·6%
37·2%
18·8%
18·8%
8·3%

(e) 1919—24
31·1%
18·3%
33·3%
11·6%
5·5%

(b) 1906—10
45·5%
15%
11·1%
18·3%
10%

(c) 1910—14
47·2%
15·5%
10%
15%
12·2%

(d) 1914—19
42·2%
21·6%
6·1%
13·3%
16·6%

■ Extreme Left: Collectivist Socialists (Table I(a))

▨ Left: Independant Socialists, Radical Socialists and Radicals (Table I(b) & (c))

□ Centre Left: Républicains de Gauche (Table I(d))

▥ Centre Right: Progressistes (Table II (a))

▤ Right: Ralliés, Nationalists and Reactionaries (Table II (b),(c)&(d))

Compiled from:

J. P. CHARNAY, *Les scrutins politiques en France de 1815 à 1962*
J. P. MARICHY, *La deuxième chambre dans la vie politique française depuis 1875*
J. KAYSER, *Les grandes batailles du radicalisme*

N.B. There is a certain degree of arbitrariness in all such classifications, and this is especially marked in 1914, when Briand's Fédération des Gauches sought to cut across existing alignments.

Appendix V

Governments and Elections, 1870-1920

(i) Cabinets that lasted more than two years are indicated by block capitals.

(ii) After the republicans split into factions the term 'Republican' is used to indicate a conservative republican tendency, Opportunist, Progressist, *Républicain de gouvernement, modéré*, etc.

Name of President of the Republic	Name of Premier	Main Political Tendency of Cabinet	Dates
		Government of National Defence (Republican)	4 Sep. 1870– 19 Feb. 1871
		ELECTIONS 8 Feb. 1871	
	THIERS*	Republican/Monarchist	19 Feb. 1871– 18 May 1873
	De Broglie	Monarchist	25 May 1873– 22 May 1874
	De Cissey	Monarchist	22 May 1874– 10 March 1875
MACMAHON	Buffet	Republican/Monarchist	10 March 1875– 9 March 1876
		ELECTIONS 20 Feb. and 5 March 1876	
	Dufaure	Republican	9 March 1876– 12 Dec. 1876
	Simon	Republican	12 Dec. 1876– 17 May 1877
	De Broglie	Monarchist	17 May 1877– 23 Nov. 1877

* In this period, before the constitution of the Third Republic had been drawn up Thiers occupied the position both of head of state, i.e. President, and of prime minister.

Name of President of the Republic	Name of Premier	Main Political Tendency of Cabinet	Dates
		ELECTIONS 14 and 28 October 1876	
	Rochebouet	Non-Parliamentary	23 Nov. 1877–13 Dec. 1877
	Dufaure	Republican	13 Dec. 1877–4 Feb. 1879
	Waddington	Republican	4 Feb. 1879–28 Dec. 1879
	De Freycinet	Republican	28 Dec. 1879–23 Sep. 1880
	Ferry	Republican	23 Sep. 1880–14 Nov. 1881
		ELECTIONS 21 Aug. and 4 Sep. 1881	
	Gambetta	Republican	14 Nov. 1881–30 Jan. 1882
	De Freycinet	Republican/Radical	30 Jan. 1882–7 Aug. 1882
GRÉVY	Duclerc	Republican	7 Aug. 1882–29 Jan. 1883
	Fallières	Republican	29 Jan. 1883–21 Feb. 1883
	FERRY	Republican	21 Feb. 1883–6 April 1885
	Brisson	Republican/Radical	6 April 1885–7 Jan. 1886
		ELECTIONS 4 and 18 Oct. 1885	
	De Freycinet	Republican/Radical	7 Jan. 1886–11 Dec. 1886
	Goblet	Republican/Radical	11 Dec. 1886–30 May 1887
	Rouvier	Republican	30 May 1887–12 Dec. 1887
	Tirard	Republican	12 Dec. 1887–3 April 1888
CARNOT	Floquet	Republican/Radical	3 April 1888–22 Feb. 1889
	Tirard	Republican	22 Feb. 1889–17 March 1890

Name of President of the Republic	Name of Premier	Main Political Tendency of Cabinet	Dates
		ELECTIONS 22 Sep. and 6 Oct. 1889	
	De Freycinet	Republican/Radical	17 March 1890– 27 Feb. 1892
	Loubet	Republican/Radical	27 Feb. 1892– 6 Dec. 1892
	Ribot	Republican/Radical	6 Dec. 1892– 4 April 1893
	Dupuy	Republican	4 April 1893– 3 Dec. 1893
		ELECTIONS 20 Aug. and 3 Sep. 1893	
CASIMIR-PERIER	Casimir-Perier	Republican	3 Dec. 1893– 30 May 1894
	Dupuy	Republican	30 May 1894– 26 Jan. 1895
	Ribot	Republican	26 Jan. 1895– 1 Nov. 1895
	Bourgeois	Radical	1 Nov. 1895– 29 Apr. 1896
FAURE	MÉLINE	Republican/Rallié	29 Apr. 1896– 28 June 1898
		ELECTIONS 8 and 22 May 1898	
	Brisson	Radical/Republican	28 June 1898– 1 Nov. 1898
	Dupuy	Republican/Radical	1 Nov. 1898– 22 June 1899
	WALDECK-ROUSSEAU	Republican/Radical/Socialist	22 June 1899– 7 June 1902
LOUBET		ELECTIONS 6 and 20 May 1902	
	COMBES	Republican/Radical	7 June 1902– 23 Jan. 1905
	Rouvier	Radical/Republican	23 Jan. 1905– 14 Mar. 1906
	Sarrien	Radical/Republican	14 Mar. 1906– 25 Oct. 1906
FALLIÈRES		ELECTIONS 6 and 20 Oct. 1906	
	CLEMENCEAU	Radical/Ind. Socialist	25 Oct. 1906– 24 July 1909
	Briand	Radical/Ind. Socialist	24 July 1909– 2 Mar. 1911

Name of President of the Republic	Name of Premier	Main Political Tendency of Cabinet	Dates
FALLIÈRES		ELECTIONS 24 Apr. and 8 May 1910	
	Monis	Radical	2 Mar. 1911– 27 June 1911
	Caillaux	Radical	27 June 1911– 14 Jan. 1912
	Poincaré	Republican/Radical	14 Jan. 1912– 21 Jan. 1913
	Briand	Republican/Radical/ Ind. Socialist	21 Jan. 1913– 22 Mar. 1913
	Barthou	Republican/Radical	22 Mar. 1913– 10 Dec. 1913
	Doumergue	Radical	10 Dec. 1913– 10 June 1914
POINCARÉ		ELECTIONS 26 Apr. and 10 May 1914	
	Ribot	Republican/Radical	10 June 1914– 13 June 1914
	Viviani	Ind. Socialist/Radical	13 June 1914– 26 Aug. 1914
	Viviani	Union Sacré	26 Aug. 1914– 29 Oct. 1915
	Briand	Union Sacré	29 Oct. 1915– 20 Mar. 1917
	Ribot	Union Sacré	20 Mar. 1917– 12 Sep. 1917
	Painlevé	Union Sacré	12 Sep. 1917– 16 Nov. 1917
	CLEMENCEAU	Radical	16 Nov. 1917– 20 Jan. 1920
		ELECTIONS 16 and 30 Nov. 1919	

Appendix VI

Biographical List of the most important characters mentioned

BERTIE, Francis Leveson, first Viscount Bertie of Thame (1844–1919): a professional diplomat, British ambassador in Paris 1905–18. 'M. Clemenceau, who placed implicit trust in him, gave him on his retirement such proofs of esteem on behalf of France as a British ambassador can rarely have received' (*Dictionary of National Biography*).

BLANQUI, Louis Auguste (1805–81): a lifelong revolutionary, frequently imprisoned: he began as a member of the Carbonari, and continued their policy of secret, tightly disciplined revolutionary organizations. In 1870 he edited a newspaper, *La Patrie en Danger*, advocating social revolution and prosecution of the war to the utmost: he was arrested on 17 March 1871, and thus missed the Commune, where his followers were prominent. Blanquists remained a distinctive sect among French Socialists for twenty years after his death.

BOULANGER, Georges Ernest Jean Marie, general (1837–91): a professional soldier, promoted to general in 1880: minister of war from 7 June 1886 to 30 May 1887: became a popular hero, and on being placed on the retired list as a result of his political intrigues, led a movement aiming at constitutional revision. After spectacular electoral victories in 1888, the Boulangist movement petered out when Boulanger was frightened into exile, and his followers were left leaderless, in spite of a certain success in the 1889 elections.

BRIAND, Aristide (1862–1932): lawyer and journalist. Regarded as an extreme left-wing Socialist at the beginning of his political career, he rapidly moderated his position; he was a deputy in 1902, a minister in 1906, prime minister in 1909, and thereafter scarcely ever out of office for long periods, except from 1917–20. Regarded as a renegade by the Socialists of the s.f.i.o., he occupied a position in the Centre of the political spectrum, and was perhaps the most typical professional politician of the period. Clemenceau disliked him intensely, although Briand was a minister in his first cabinet.

CAILLAUX, Joseph (1863–1944): he began as a high civil servant, an *Inspecteur des Finances*, becoming a deputy in 1898. Originally a moderate republican, he moved leftwards, becoming the leader of the Radical party in 1913. He was minister of finance in the Waldeck-Rousseau cabinet, 1899–1902, and again in the first Clemenceau cabinet. As prime minister in 1911 he negotiated the Agadir settlement with Germany. Accused of treason because of his advocacy of a compromise peace, he was tried by the Senate, sitting as a High Court, in

428

February 1920, and condemned to loss of political rights. They were restored in 1925, but he never again played an important political role.

COMBES, Justin Louis Emile (1835–1921): he studied in Catholic seminaries, writing theses on St Thomas Aquinas and on the conflict between St Bernard and Abelard, but abandoned the Catholic religion and became a doctor. He was never a deputy, but was elected Senator in 1885. His one political concern was anti-clericalism, to which he devoted himself when prime minister from 1902 to 1905. An important leader of the Radical party.

DELCASSÉ, Théophile (1852–1923): a journalist on Gambetta's newspaper, *La République Française*, he became a deputy in 1889, under-secretary for the colonies in 1893, and foreign minister from 1898 to 1905. He played a crucial part in strengthening France's diplomatic position against Germany in these years, but fell from office as a result of German pressure. A personal quarrel poisoned his relations with Clemenceau, and Delcassé was able to revenge himself by bringing down the Clemenceau cabinet in 1909. He returned to office as minister for the navy and was again made foreign minister at the outbreak of war, but soon resigned, and no longer played an important political role.

FERRY, Jules François Camille (1832–93): a lawyer, and a leader of the Parliamentary opposition to the Second Empire. His political positon was at the centre of the Republican party, slightly to the right of that of Gambetta. He was almost continually in office from 1879 to 1885, as minister of public instruction, then as prime minister and foreign minister. In spite of his remarkable achievements in recasting the education system, providing free and compulsory primary schools and removing the influence of the Catholic Church from State schools at both primary and secondary level, and in the field of colonial policy, his career never recovered from the blows inflicted by Clemenceau in 1885, and he did not again hold office.

FLOQUET, Charles (1828–96): a lawyer, and member of the republican opposition under the Second Empire; elected a deputy for Paris in 1871, like Clemenceau he tried to mediate between the Commune and the government. He was a moderate Radical and was prime minister in 1888–9, failing to deal effectively with the Boulangist crisis. His political career was ended in 1893 as a result of his involvement in the Panama scandal. He married Hortense Kestner, with whom Clemenceau had fallen in love as a young man.

FOCH, Ferdinand, Marshal (1851–1929): a professional soldier, given command of the *Ecole Supérieure de Guerre* in 1907, advocate of recklessly aggressive military tactics. In command of a *corps* in 1914 he was given command of the 9th Army at the battle of the Marne: he was the principal French field commander in 1916, in charge of the battle of the Somme, but was passed over for the post of commander-in-chief when Nivelle replaced Joffre in December 1916. In May 1917 he was made chief of staff, but was brought back into the command structure as Supreme Allied Commander in France as a result of the Doullens conference of March 1918. After the armistice his relations with Clemenceau deteriorated as a result of Foch's clumsy attempts to influence the terms of the peace settlement.

FREYCINET, Charles Louis de Saulces de (1828–1923): an engineer he was Gambetta's aide in 1870, organizing the volunteer armies to continue the war against Prussia. Elected senator in 1876, he occupied a key position on the fringe of the Opportunist and Radical factions of the republican party, and thus was frequently prime minister between 1879 and 1892. He was not subsequently prime minister but remained an active politician, specializing in military matters, until a very advanced age, being in the cabinet during the war.

GAMBETTA, Léon (1838–82): a lawyer and a leader of the Parliamentary opposition to the Second Empire. His Belleville programme, a manifesto for the 1869 elections, was seen as a summary of Radical Republican demands, many of which Gambetta himself abandoned when he moved to a more moderate position. He was minister of the interior in the Government of National Defence, and after escaping from Paris by balloon, was the main inspirer of the policy of continuing the war. His refusal to accept the treaty of peace with Prussia separated him from the majority of the republicans, but he adopted a more moderate stance and was seen as the outstanding republican leader from 1871 to 1881. However, his long-awaited cabinet (November 1881–January 1882) proved a fiasco. He died on 31 December 1882, before it was clear whether or not he would have been able to recover his political position.

HERZ, Cornelius (1844–98): an adventurer whose early career is somewhat mysterious: he was born in France of a German father but spent his youth in the U.S.A. where he gained a medical qualification. Re-established in France from 1870, by the 1880s he was associating with leading personalities in journalism and politics. He passed for a rich man, but seemed to have few solid financial resources. He was concerned primarily with seeking profitable exploitation of recent technical inventions such as the telephone, and electricity. The Panama affair allowed him to extract huge sums through blackmail from Baron Jacques de Reinach, on whose suicide he fled to England, where he remained for the rest of his life.

JAURÈS, Jean (1859–1914): secondary school teacher and university professor, moderate republican deputy 1885–9, returned to the Chamber in 1893 as leading theorist of Socialism. He played an important part in the Dreyfus case, and cooperated with the Combes Radical government, 1902–5. At the same time he was working to achieve a unified Socialist party, and in order to achieve this end he accepted the decisions of the Amsterdam (1904) Congress of the Socialist International, imposing the principle of non-participation in 'bourgeois' cabinets. In spite of this he sought to preserve Parliamentary and reformist Socialism through a synthesis of different Socialist theories, and to preserve the unity of the S.F.I.O. in spite of its strong centrifugal tendencies. In 1904 he founded the first successful Socialist daily newspaper, L'Humanité. One of his principal political concerns came to be the attempt to organize Socialist opposition to war in France and Germany. This proved ineffective in 1914, and Jaurès himself was assassinated by a fanatic on 31 July 1914.

LONGUET, Charles Félix César (1839–1903): journalist and professor. An opponent of the Second Empire, he was imprisoned and forced to go into exile for various offences against the press censorship. He was a member of the General Council of the First Socialist International, and a member of the Commune. After the Commune he fled to London, resumed his place in the International, and married Karl Marx's daughter Jenny. Returning to France in 1880 he became a journalist on Clemenceau's paper, La Justice, and worked for a moderate reformist type of Socialism, not adhering to the rigid Marxist orthodoxy.

MACMAHON, Edmé Patrice Maurice, Comte de, Duc de Magenta (1808–93): a leading general of the Second Empire, commanding in the Crimean and Italian campaigns. Regarded as a suitable figurehead who could act as head of state until such time as a restoration of the monarchy could be achieved, he was voted personal powers for seven years when Thiers was forced to resign in 1873. Although reluctant to accept the republican victories in the elections of 1876 and 1877, he refused to carry out a *coup d'état*, eventually resigning in 1879, allowing Jules Grévy, a republican, to be elected President.

MALVY, Louis (1875–1949): Radical-Socialist deputy 1906–19 and 1924–40, minister of the interior 1914–17 and again in 1926. Accusations that as minister of the interior he had failed to hunt out traitors and defeatists were a central element in the political crisis of 1917. He was tried on these charges in August 1918, by the Senate acting as a High Court, and deprived of his political rights. They were restored in 1924, and to some extent he was able to resume his political career in the Radical party.

MILLERAND, Alexandre (1859–1943): lawyer and journalist, one of Clemenceau's assistants on *La Justice*. A Radical deputy in 1885, he became an Independent Socialist in 1889. His St Mandé speech of 1896 was seen as the charter of reformist Socialism. A minister in the Waldeck-Rousseau cabinet, 1899–1902, he introduced various social reforms, especially concerned with labour conditions. He refused to join the S.F.I.O., and moved towards the political Centre. Minister of war, 1914–15, he forbade Parliamentary investigation into the conduct of the war, giving full control to General Joffre, and the high command. In spite of his criticism of Millerand at this time, Clemenceau made him High Commissioner for the liberated territories of Alsace-Lorraine in 1919. He was a leading member of the conservative *Bloc National*, and succeeded Clemenceau as prime minister in 1920. President of the Republic 1920–24, he was regarded by the left-wing parties as so blatantly biased against them that they forced his resignation after their electoral victory in 1924, thus ending his political career.

MILNER, Alfred, Viscount (1854–1925): Liberal Unionist politician and Imperial administrator in Egypt and South Africa, 1890–1905; in 1916 he entered Lloyd George's War Cabinet and became Secretary of State for War in April 1918, after taking part in the meeting at Doullens that made Foch Supreme Allied Commander on the western front. He had been acquainted with Clemenceau before the war, and in 1921 he married the widow of Lord Edward Cecil, the former Violet Maxse, daughter of Clemenceau's closest English friend.

PELLETAN, Camille (1846–1915): trained as an archivist, he became a journalist, editor of *La Justice*, and was a Radical deputy from 1881 to 1912. Closely associated with Clemenceau until 1890, he separated from him and was prominent in the organization of the Radical party in 1901. He was minister of the navy in the Combes cabinet, 1902–5, and remained important in the Radical party, although not again holding office.

PÉTAIN, Phillipe, Marshal (1856–1951): a colonel in 1914, he was promoted to general, given command at Verdun in 1916, and made commander-in-chief in May 1917 after Nivelle's failure; his main task was to restore the morale of the armies after the mutinies of May–June 1917. In contrast to Foch and Nivelle, both advocates of offensive tactics, Pétain believed in defensive methods and sought to safeguard the human resources of the army. His reputation as a military leader led to his being made head of state with autocratic powers on the collapse of France in 1940.

PICHON, Stéphen (1857–1933): journalist, associate of Clemenceau on *La Justice*, Radical deputy 1885–93, professional diplomat 1893–1906, being French resident at Peking in 1900, and in Tunis 1901–6; senator 1906–24, foreign minister 1906–11, March–December 1913, and 1917–20.

POINCARÉ, Raymond (1860–1934): lawyer, deputy 1887–1903, senator 1903–13, President of the Republic 1913–20, senator 1920–34. A moderate republican, he held ministerial office at an early age, 1893–5, but only briefly after that until 1912. He was concerned to strengthen France's diplomatic and military resistance to Germany, and became President in the hope, which proved vain, that he would be able to strengthen the President's role, thus providing stronger government and a more effective French international presence. His relations with Clemenceau during the latter's second ministry were bad, especially after the end of the war, when Poincaré sought unsuccessfully to influence the peace settlement. After his Presidential term expired he returned to active politics, becoming prime minister 1922–24, seeking to use strong measures against Germany.

REINACH, Joseph (1856–1921): journalist and politician; he was Gambetta's *chef de cabinet* in 1881, editor of *La République Française*, deputy 1889–98 and 1906–14. He was one of the chief instigators of the campaign on behalf of Dreyfus, and wrote a detailed history of the Dreyfus Affair. He was the nephew and son-in-law of Baron Jacques de Reinach (1840–92), the financier involved in the Panama scandal. The family was of Alsatian Jewish origin.

RIBOT, Alexandre (1842–1923): a high civil servant, member of the *Conseil d'Etat*, deputy 1878–85, 1887–1909, senator 1909–23. His political tendency was Centre Gauche, the most conservative shade of republicanism; foreign minister 1890–3, he was a chief promoter of the Franco-Russian alliance of 1893; he was separated from the main body of the republicans by his opposition to the anti-clerical measures that followed the Dreyfus Affair; finance minister 1914–17, and prime minister from March to September 1917.

SCHEURER-KESTNER, Auguste (1833–99): a republican opponent of the Empire, deputy 1871, elected life-senator in 1875. A rich businessman, engaged in chemical manufacture at Thann in Alsace, he was connected by marriage with leading republican politicians, Ferry and Floquet; the political disciple of Gambetta, he edited his newspaper, *La République Française*, 1879–84. He never held cabinet office but was an influential member of the Senate, becoming its vice-president. He was the first political figure to take up the case of Dreyfus.

TARDIEU, André (1876–1945): journalist and diplomat, deputy 1914–24, 1926–36. He was High Commissioner for Franco-American Affairs in 1917, and Clemenceau's chief personal assistant during the negotiation of the peace settlement, although not holding cabinet office. He became a leading conservative politician, holding office several times between 1926 and 1932. He retired from active politics in 1934 and wrote several books advocating constitutional reform.

THIERS, Adolphe (1797–1877): a journalist and historian, he played a prominent role in the 1830 revolution and the creation of the July monarchy under Louis Philippe. Prime minister for brief periods in 1836 and 1840, he was thereafter excluded from office and leader of the dynastic opposition. Although he did not welcome the 1848 revolution, he played a leading part in the political life of the Second Republic, organizing the conservative 'party of order' and supporting Louis Napoleon's candidacy for President. On the establishment of the Second Empire he was arrested, and exiled briefly, remaining out of politics until 1863. Re-elected to Parliament he criticized the Empire from the point of view of a liberal constitutional monarchist, and opposed the declaration of war on Prussia. In February 1871 the National Assembly made him 'head of the executive power', in which capacity he ruthlessly crushed the Commune. He announced his conversion to republicanism and was forced to resign in 1873, being replaced as head of state by Marshal MacMahon. Elected deputy in 1876, he was the leader of the republican campaign in 1877 but died before the elections.

VIVIANI, René (1863–1925): lawyer and journalist, deputy 1893–1902, 1906–22. Independent Socialist, he was expelled from the S.F.I.O. on accepting office in the first Clemenceau cabinet, as minister of labour, and was a leading member of the Republican Socialist group. He was prime minister at the outbreak of the war, June 1914–October 1915 and remained as minister of justice in subsequent cabinets, October 1915–September 1917. He was a famous orator, but has few other claims to remembrance.

WALDECK-ROUSSEAU, René (1846–1904): lawyer. Opportunist deputy 1879–89, senator 1894–1904, minister of the interior in the Gambetta cabinet of 1881–2, and the Ferry cabinet of 1883–5, during which he introduced the law regularizing the legal position of trade unions (1884). He retired from active political life in 1889, returning in the crisis of 1899 to lead the cabinet that liquidated the Dreyfus Affair. His government put through the law on Associations (1901) but he was strongly opposed to the use made of this law by Combes to dissolve the religious orders.

Appendix VII

Chronological table

	General events		Clemenceau's career
1830	July Monarchy		
		1841	Birth
1848 –51	Revolution Second Republic		
1851 –70	Coup d'Etat Second Empire	1858	Begins medical studies at Nantes
		1861	Enters Paris medical school
		1862	Imprisoned
1863 –70	'liberalization' of the Empire	1865	Graduates and goes to U.S.A.
		1869	Marries and returns from U.S.A.
1870 July –71 –Jan.	Franco-Prussian War	1870	Appointed mayor of 18th arr. of Paris
1870 Sep.	Revolution: formation of Government of National Defence		
Sep. –71 –Jan.	Siege of Paris		
1871 Feb.	Election of National Assembly. Thiers becomes 'head of executive power'	1871	Feb., elected deputy for Seine department
Mar. –May	Commune of Paris		March, resigns as deputy and mediates between Commune and government
1873	Thiers resigns: MacMahon president		
1875	Constitutional laws voted		
		1876	Elected deputy for 18th arr. of Paris
1877	Seize Mai crisis		

General events		Clemenceau's career	
1879	MacMahon resigns: Republic definitely established	1880	*La Justice* begins publication
		1880 –85	Leads Radical attack on Opportunists (Gambetta and Ferry)
1881 Nov. –82 –Jan.	Conquest of Tunis Gambetta ministry		
1882 July	French withdraw from Joint Anglo-French expedition against Egypt		
Dec.	Death of Gambetta		
1883 –85	Ferry in power: conquest of Indo-China (Tonkin)		
1884	Constitutional Revision	1885	Re-elected for Seine and Var departments: opts for Var
1888 –89	Boulangist crisis		
1892	Panama Affair	1892	Attacked by Déroulède for association with Herz
1893	Franco-Russian alliance	1893	Defeated at general elections and leaves Parliament
1893 –98	Ralliement		
		1897	Loses control of *La Justice*
1898 –1901	Dreyfus Affair	1898– 1901	Campaigns for Dreyfus in *L'Aurore*
1899 –1902	Waldeck-Rousseau cabinet Delcassé becomes foreign minister	1902	Elected to Senate for Var
1901	Law on Associations (used to ban religious orders)		
1902 –05	Combes cabinet		
		1903 –06	Editor of *L'Aurore*
1904	Anglo-French entente		
1905	Delcassé resigns Separation of Church and State		
1906	Algeçiras agreement	1906	March, Minister of Interior in Sarrien cabinet

	General events		Clemenceau's career
		1906	9 Oct.–July, First Ministry
1907	Revolt of the Wine-growers		
1908	Draveil strike		
1909 Feb.	Franco-German agreement on Morocco		
Mar.	Bosnian crisis ended		
		1910	Lecture tour in South America
1911	Agadir crisis		
1912 –1913	Balkan Wars	1912	Jan., Overthrows Caillaux cabinet
1913	Poincaré President of the Republic	1913	L'Homme Libre begins publication
1914 –18	First World War		
1914	Battle of the Marne		
1915 –16	War of attrition on the western front (Somme and Verdun)	1915	President of Senate Committee for War and Foreign Affairs
1915	Gallipoli and Salonika expeditions		
1916 Dec.	Nivelle replaces Joffre as commander-in-chief		
1917 Mar.	Russian Revolution: formation of Provisional Government		
April	U.S.A. enters the war. Failure of offensive at Chemin des Dames		
May	Pétain becomes commander-in-chief: mutinies in French army		
1917 Sep.	Fall of Ribot cabinet	1917	July, attacks Malvy for 'defeatism'
Nov.	Italian defeat at Caporetto Bolsheviks seize power in Russia Fall of Painlevé cabinet	1917–20	Nov.–Jan., Second Ministry
1918 Jan.	President Wilson's 14 Points		
Mar.	Treaty of Brest-Litovsk between Russia and Germany German offensive on the western front		

General events		Clemenceau's career
	Foch made supreme Allied commander in France	
May–June	Renewed German offensive	
July	The turn of the tide: Allied offensive on western front	
Oct.	Central powers appeal for Armistices	
Nov. 11	Armistice with Germany	
1919 Jan.	Peace Conference opens	1919 Feb. 19, assassination attempt
Mar.–April	Crucial bargaining in Council of Four	
May 7	Treaty presented to Germans	
June 28	Treaty of Versailles signed	
Nov.	General elections – triumph of Bloc National	
		1920 Jan., resignation
		1929 Nov., death

Sources and Bibliography

Unpublished sources

I CLEMENCEAU'S PAPERS

There is no extensive collection of private papers and correspondence. In this Clemenceau is comparable to other French politicians, few of whom left behind anything comparable to the private papers of British statesmen. General Mordacq reports (*Clemenceau Au Soir de la Vie*, II, pp. 179–81) that in 1928 he helped Clemenceau to classify his papers. They were divided into five groups, and the following decisions were taken about their disposal;

(1) nearly all the letters that Clemenceau had received in the course of his life were burnt
(2) letters from Poincaré, 1918–19, were given to 'a safe friend'
(3) official documents were returned to the Quai d'Orsay
(4) 'certain documents which referred to some of the most agitated periods of his life' were given to Piétri, together with drafts of his speeches
(5) copies of telegrams which he sent, in 1918–19, to foreign governments, were given to 'a discreet person', who was presumably different from the one who received Poincaré's letters, and who was to give them to the French government at the end of twenty years.

Mordacq's account shows that the greater part of the papers Clemenceau had amassed were simply destroyed. In any case, he had not kept copies of his outgoing letters, so they would consist of letters received, not his own letters, which have to be sought among the papers of the recipients. It is difficult to say what happened to the documents that Mordacq says were preserved. J. Chastenet reported (*Raymond Poincaré* (1948), p. 302) that Poincaré's letters to Clemenceau were held by the *Association des Amis de Georges Mandel*: I suspect that these are the letters from Poincaré now at the Musée Clemenceau, which cannot be consulted; drafts of some of them are available in the Poincaré Papers (*see below*). The other documents listed by Mordacq seem to have disappeared without trace. The Quai d'Orsay states that it has no special Clemenceau collection; presumably the documents returned to it were reintegrated in the ordinary files; nor is there any indication of what happened to the copies of telegrams to foreign governments which were to be returned to the government after twenty years; they are not at the Archives Nationales, nor at the Quai d'Orsay as a special collection. As for the intriguing documents which Mordacq states were handed to Piétri. Piétri's executor did not reply to my letter requesting information about their whereabouts: Piétri died in 1966. However, there are other documents, not mentioned by Mordacq, which have survived.

(1) The principal collection is at the Musée Clemenceau, Clemenceau's apartment in the rue Franklin. The Musée Clemenceau has letters written by Clemenceau to the following individuals:

Comte d'Aunay
Comtesse d'Aunay
Mlle Mary d'Aunay
Albert Clemenceau
Cristal
Mlle Lambiette
Léon Martin
F. A. Maxse
L. J. Maxse
Miss Violet Maxse, later Lady Edward Cecil, then Viscountess Milner
Claude Monet
Nicolas Piétri

The Musée Clemenceau also has a considerable number of letters written to Clemenceau; with the exception of fifty letters from Poincaré, all but one written in 1918 and 1919, there is no sizeable collection of letters from any one individual, and for the most part there are only one or two letters from each. Scholars are not allowed to consult these letters: a certain number, both of the letters received and of those written by Clemenceau, have been printed, either completely, or in extracts, by G. Wormser in *La République de Clemenceau*. Three letters from J. Jaurès to Clemenceau, in the collection at the Musée Clemenceau, were published in *Bulletin de la Société des Etudes Jaurèsiennes*, 5 (1962), p. 3.

(2) J. Martet was allowed to take away certain documents, many of which he published immediately after Clemenceau's death. He states, however (*Le Silence de M. Clemenceau*, p. 269), that others remained unpublished, in particular Clemenceau's own account of his role during the Commune, of which he published only the part referring to the events of 18 March 1871. These documents are still in the possession of Mme Martet, who refused to allow me to consult them.

(3) G. Monnerville, *Clemenceau*, p. 762, refers to correspondence between Clemenceau, Barthou and Tardieu in the Collection Baldensperger, whose whereabouts he does not disclose.

(4) In the archives of the Service Historique de l'Armée at the Château de Vincennes there is a collection known as the Fonds Clemenceau. At the time of writing this collection was not open to the public, although G. Pedroncini was given permission to consult it extensively. I was allowed to see only four *cartons*, a small proportion of the total. It was opened for research in 1972, and it is now possible to confirm, as I had suspected, that it in no sense represents Clemenceau's personal papers. It consists of documents assembled by General Mordacq, as the *Chef de cabinet militaire*, mainly official documents for the period November 1917 to January 1920. It will be an essential source for detailed research on French policy during those years, but this material is of little direct interest from a biographical point of view.

II OTHER PRIVATE PAPERS CONSULTED

(1) *Bibliothèque Nationale*
   (a) Poincaré Papers, Nouvelles Acquisitions Françaises, 15992–16063
   (b) Reinach Papers, Nouvelles Acquisitions Françaises, 24874–24913
   (c) Scheurer-Kestner Papers

Journal, Nouvelles Acquisitions Françaises, 12704–12711
Correspondance, Nouvelles Acquisitions Françaises, 24409–24410
(d) Zola Papers, Nouvelles Acquisitions Françaises, 24510–24524
(e) Miscellaneous collections, Nouvelles Acquisitions Françaises, 13534, 14114, 24265, 24492

(2) *Bibliothèque Victor Cousin, at the Sorbonne*
The papers of Marquise Arconati-Visconti

(3) *Bibliothèque de Documentation Internationale Contemporaine*
Klotz Papers

(4) *Bibliothèque de l'Institut de France*
Pichon Papers, MSS 4395–4398

(5) *Archives Nationales, Papiers Privés*
Floquet Papers
Mangin Papers
Painlevé Papers

(6) *Beaverbrook Foundation, 33 St Bride Street, London*
Lloyd George Papers

(7) *Birmingham University Library*
Joseph Chamberlain Papers

(8) *Bodleian Library, Oxford*
Milner Papers

(9) *Scottish Record Office, Edinburgh*
Lothian Papers

(10) *British Museum, London*
Balfour Papers

III PUBLIC ARCHIVES

(1) *Archives Nationales, Paris*
  (a) down to 1906
  BB¹⁸ 1649, dossier 6657
  C 3318, Commission . . . crédits pour Tonkin

  (b) 1906–1914
    (i) Commissions of the Chamber of Deputies
    C 7353–4 Rachat de l'Ouest
    C 7387–91 Enquête sur la catastrophe de l'Iéna
    C 7392 Enquête viticole
    C 7395–7 Enquête sur la Marine
    C 7399 Commission de Législation Fiscale
    C 7400 Impôt sur le Revenu
    C 7450–4 Affaire Rochette

    (ii) Ministry of the Interior
    F⁷ 12794 and 12920 Crise Viticole

F⁷ 12913 Réquisition de la Force Armée
F⁷ 12914–7 Affaire Draveil
F⁷ 12918 Grève Postale
F⁷ 13950, dossier 2, Clemenceau 1906–24

(c) 1914–1920

(i) Commissions of the Chamber of Deputies
C 7490–1 Commission des Affaires Extérieures
C 7499–7501 Commission de l'Armée
C 7560–1 Commission du Budget
C 7705 Affaire Caillaux
C 7766 Affaire Malvy

(ii) Ministry of the Interior
F⁷ 12951 Notes Jean, 1919–22
F⁷ 13950 dossier 2, Clemenceau 1906–24
F⁷ 13969 Affaire Bonnet Rouge
F⁷ 13970 Affaire Malvy
F⁷ 13971 Affaire Caillaux

(2) *Archives of the Prefecture of Police, Paris*
BA 89—94 Rapports Quotidiens du Préfet, 1879–85
BA 130 Renseignements sur les groupes différents de la Chambre, 1906–10
BA 959 Dossier Berteaux
BA 1119 Dossier Herz
BA 1216 Dossier Pelletan
BA 1587 – 8 and 1614 Physionomie de Paris
BA 1639 Situation Morale

(3) *Archives of the Senate, Paris*
Procès-Verbaux de la Commission des Établissements Congréganistes 1901
Procès-Verbaux de la Commission des Demandes d'Authorisation des Congrégations, 1903
Procès-Verbaux de la Commission de la Marine, 1905
Procès-Verbaux de la Commission des Chemins de Fer, 1907, Rachat
Procès-Verbaux de la Commission de la Convention Franco-Allemande, 1911–12
Procès-Verbaux de la Commission de l'Armée, 1915–19, and Auditions des Ministres
Procès-Verbaux de la Commission des Affaires Etrangères, Auditions des Ministres, 1915–19

(4) *Public Record Office, London*
(a) Cabinet Papers
CAB 23/13–17 Cabinet minutes
CAB 28/3–6 Inter-Allied conferences
(b) Foreign Office Papers
FO 800/201 Balfour Papers
FO 800/164 to 169 Bertie Papers

N.B. The archives of the Quai d'Orsay were not open for the period of the peace settlement at the time of writing.

IV UNPUBLISHED THESES

M. Anderson, 'The Parliamentary Right in France, 1905–1919' (Oxford, 1961).
J. Q. Graham, 'The French Radical and Radical Socialist Party 1906–1914' (Ohio State, 1962).

J. Néré, 'La crise industrielle de 1882 et le mouvement Boulangiste' (Sorbonne, 1959).

D. S. Newhall, 'An old beginner, Clemenceau 1902–1906' (Harvard, 1963).

G. Pedroncini, 'Le Haut-Commandement et la conduite de la guerre, Mai 1917–Novembre 1918' (Sorbonne, 1971).

Published sources

I CLEMENCEAU'S WRITINGS

(1) Books arranged in order of composition:

De la Génération des éléments anatomiques (1865, 2nd edn 1867).

American reconstruction 1865–70, ed. F. Baldensperger (New York, 1928), an English translation of the articles Clemenceau contributed to *Le Temps* between 1865 and 1870, new edition with introduction by O. H. Olsen (New York, 1969).

La Mêlée Sociale (1895).

Le Grand Pan (1896).

Les Plus Forts, Roman Contemporain (1898), first published in *L'Illustration*, English translation 1919.

Au Pied du Sinaï (1898), illustrated by Toulouse-Lautrec, English translation 1922.

L'Iniquité (1899).

Vers la Réparation (1899).

Au Fil des Jours (1900).

Contre la Justice (1900).

Le Voile du Bonheur (1901), incidental music by Fauré, English translation privately printed 1920.

Des Juges (1901).

Justice Militaire (1901).

Injustice Militaire (1902).

La Honte (1903).

Figures de Vendée (1903).

Aux Embuscades de la Vie, dans la foi, dans l'ordre établi, dans l'amour (1903), English translation 1920.

Notes de Voyage dans l'Amérique du Sud (1911), English translation 1911.

Dans les Champs du Pouvoir (1913).

La Leçon de la Russie (1915).

La France devant l'Allemagne (1916), English translation 1919.

Demosthène (1926), English translation 1926.

Au Soir de la Pensée (1927), English translation 1929.

Claude Monet, les nymphéas (1928), English translation 1930

Grandeurs et Misères d'une Victoire (1928), English translation 1930.

He translated, but without adding any preface or material of his own,

J. S. Mill, *Auguste Comte et le Positivisme* (1868).

(2) Speeches: The only collections of Clemenceau's speeches are

Discours de Guerre (1934, new edition, 1971),

Discours de Paix (1938).

Pour la Patrie, Pages extraites des articles et discours (1934).

Many of his speeches were published separately at the time of their delivery, notably his principal speeches both in the Chamber and outside from 1880 to 1885, which were published by *La Justice*; neither the Musée Clemenceau nor the

Bibliothèque Nationale has a complete collection. Also, *L'Antipatriotisme devant le Sénat*, 22 July 1917, *Discours de Strasbourg*, 4 November 1919, *Discours à Ste Hermine*, 2 October 1921; the *Discours de Salernes*, 8 August 1893, was published by the Société des Amis de Clemenceau in 1936.

His other speeches have to be sought either in the Journal Officiel in the case of those delivered in Parliament, or in the contemporary press. The Journal Officiel also printed important speeches made by ministers outside Parliament, and his principal speeches as minister of the interior and prime minister from 1906 to 1909 can be found there: during the second ministry he made no important speeches outside Parliament except for the Strasbourg speech before the 1919 elections. I have used the annual retrospective volumes *Annales de l'Assemblée Nationale*, *Annales de la Chambre des Députés*, and *Annales du Sénat*, for his Parliamentary speeches.

(3) Reports of Clemenceau's conversations:
In the last years of his life several people made records of their conversation with Clemenceau, notably his former private secretary, Jean Martet, who published them as
M. Clemenceau peint par lui-même (1929).
Le Silence de M. Clemenceau (1929).
Le Tigre (1930).
An English version was published, entitled *Clemenceau, the events of his life as told by himself* (1930).

Martet took notes, and his record may be regarded as reasonably reliable, but the others must be treated with caution.
L. Abensour, *Dans la cage du tigre, Clemenceau intime* (1928).
R. Benjamin, *Clemenceau dans la retraite* (1930).
P. Drieu la Rochelle, 'Paroles d'outre-tombe', *Revue Hebdomadaire*, 7 December 1929.
F. Neuray, *Entretiens avec Clemenceau* (1930).
A. de Villiers, *Clemenceau parle* (1931).
W. Williams, *The Tiger of France, conversations with Clemenceau* (New York, 1949).
The books by General Mordacq, *Le Ministère Clemenceau, Journal d'un témoin*, 4 vols (1929–30), and *Clemenceau, Au Soir de la Vie*, 2 vols (1933), also contain accounts of his conversations.
Sur la Démocratie, neuf conférences par Georges Clemenceau, rapportées par M. Ségard (1930) gives the lectures delivered in South America in 1911.
G. Pierredon, *L'Esprit de Clemenceau* (1919), and L. Treich, *L'Esprit de Clemenceau* (1925), are collections of his *bons mots*, without much guarantee of authenticity.
(4) Published Letters:
G. Clemenceau, *Lettres à une amie* (1968), containing the letters written to Mme Baldensperger, in the last years of his life, is the only substantial collection of published letters, although a few scattered letters can be found, notably in the following:
L Altiéri, *Nicolas Piétri, un grand ami de Clemenceau* (1967).
G. Brandes, *Correspondance*, vol. I (Copenhagen, 1952).
A. Dreyfus, *Souvenirs et Correspondance* (1936).
H. L. Dubly, *La vie ardente de Clemenceau* (1930).
A. Zévaès, *Louise Michel* (1938).
(5) It would be quite impossible in the space available to attempt to give a complete list of Clemenceau's journalistic writings. A useful, but incomplete, list of

Clemenceau's newspaper articles is given in G. Wormser, *La République de Clemenceau*, pp. 512-18.

His principal contributions are to be found in *Le Travail*, 1861-2, 22 December 1861-22 February 1862.

Le Temps, 1866-9, anonymous reports from America.

La Justice, 1880-97, very few articles before 3 October 1893, after which virtually one article per day.

La Dépêche, 1894-1902, four articles per month from 2 August 1894.

Le Journal, 1895-7, 3 July 1895-29 January 1897, occasional articles.

L'Aurore, 1897-99, and 1903-6, an article almost every day from October 1897 to December 1899, and from June 1903 to March 1906.

Le Bloc, 1901-2, a weekly publication written entirely by Clemenceau from 27 January 1901 to 25 March 1902.

Neue Freie Presse, Vienna, 1902 – five articles

L'Homme Libre and *L'Homme Enchâiné*, March 1913-November 1917—an article almost every day.

H. P. Thieme, *Bibliographie de la Littérature Française de 1800 à 1930* (1933), I, pp. 454-6, gives some references to Clemenceau's articles in periodicals, but not in newspapers. H. Talvert and J. Place, *Bibliographie des Auteurs Modernes de Langue Française 1801-1927* (1931), III, pp. 163-73, is the most detailed bibliographical guide, but does not list articles by Clemenceau. I make no attempt to list all previous biographies, most of which are without value.

II OTHER PUBLISHED WORKS REFERRED TO

L. Abensour, 'Un grand projet de Clemenceau', *La Grande Revue* (1930).

E. M. Acomb, *The French Laic Laws 1879–1889* (New York, 1941).

J. Adam (Juliette Lamber), *Souvenirs, VII, Après l'Abandon de la Revanche* (1910).

R. Albrecht-Carrié, *Italy at the Paris Peace Conference* (1938).

L. Aldrovandi-Marescotti, *Guerra Diplomatica* (Milan, 1937), translated as *Guerre Diplomatique, 1914-1919* (1939).

——, *Nuovi Ricordi et Frammenti de Diario* (Milan, 1938).

Les Alliés contre la Russe, avant, pendant et après la guerre mondiale (1926), a translation of Kto Dolshnik, ed. A. C. Shliapnikov (Moscow, 1926).

L. S. Amery, *My political Life*, 3 vols (1953-5).

M. S. Anderson, *The Eastern Question 1774-1923* (1966).

C. Andler, *Vie de Lucien Herr* (1932).

C. M. Andrew and A. S. Kanya-Forstner, 'The French colonial party: its composition, aims and influence, 1885-1914', *The Historical Journal*, XIV (1971).

L. Andrieux, *A travers la République* (1926).

Année Politique, 1874-1905 (ed. A. Daniel).

Annuaire du Parlement, 1906-14.

Anon (in fact L. Brunschweig), *Souvenirs d'un Vieux Nantais* (Nantes, 1888).

S. I. Applebaum, *Clemenceau as Thinker and Writer* (New York, 1948).

E. Arago, *L'Hôtel de Ville de Paris au 4 Septembre, et pendant Le Siège* (1874).

Ministère de la Guerre, Etat Major de l'Armée, Section Historique, *Les Armées Françaises dans la Grande Guerre*, 56 vols (1922-35).

A. Aulard, E. Bouvier, and A. Ganeau, *Histoire Politique de la Grande Guerre* (1924).

J. Bainville, *Les conséquences politiques de la Paix* (1920).

F. Baldensperger, 'L'Initiation Américaine de Clemenceau', *Revue de Littérature Comparée*, VIII (1928).

P. C. F. Bankwitz, *Weygand and Civil-Military Relations in Modern France* (1968).

D. Bardonnet, *L'Evolution du Structure du Parti Radical* (1960).

J. Bardoux, *De Paris à Spa, la bataille diplomatique pour la paix française* (1921).

E. Baring, 1st earl of Cromer, *Modern Egypt* (1908).

I. Barlow, *The Agadir Crisis* (1940).

A. M. Barrès, 'Clemenceau', reprinted in *l'Action Française*, V (1901).

——, *Les Grandes Problèmes du Rhin* (1930).

J. L. Barthou, *Le Traité de Paix* (1919).

B. Bastoul, *Clemenceau vu par un passant inconnu* (1938).

E. Beau de Lomenie, *Le débat de ratification du traité de Versailles à la Chambre des Députés et dans la Presse* (1945).

C. Benoist, *Les nouvelles frontières d'Allemagne et les nouvelles frontières d'Europe* (1920).

——, *Souvenirs*, 3 vols (1920).

M. Berger and P. Allard, *Les secrets de la censure pendant la guerre* (1932).

F. Bernard *et al.*, *Le Syndicalisme dans l'Enseignement, Documents de l'Institut d'Etudes Politiques de Grenoble* (n.d.).

R. Binion, *Defeated Leaders, the political fate of Caillaux, Jouvenal and Tardieu* (New York, 1960).

Biographie Complète des 534 Députés, par trois journalistes (1876).

P. Birdsall, *Versailles Twenty Years After* (1941).

R. Blake, *The Private Papers of Douglas Haig, 1914–1919* (1952).

L. Blanc, *Questions d'Aujourd'hui et de Demain*, 5e. série (1884).

L. Blum, *L'Oeuvre de Léon Blum*, I (1954).

G. Bonnefous, *Histoire Politique de la Troisième République*, 7 vols (1956–67).

M. Borgeaud, *Le Salaire des Ouvriers des Mines de Charbon en France depuis 1900* (1938).

L. V. A. Bourgeois, *Solidarité* (1896).

——, *Le Traité de Versailles* (1919).

J. Bouvier, *Les deux Scandales de Panama* (1964).

F. H. Brabant, *The Beginning of the Third Republic in France* (1940).

J. Bradley, *Allied Intervention in Russia* (1968).

——,'L'intervention française en Sibérie 1918–1919', *Revue Historique* 234 (1965).

G. Brandes, 'Clemenceau', *Contemporary Review*, LXXXIV (1903).

R. Brécy, *Le Mouvement syndical en France, 1871–1921, Essai Bibliographique* (1963).

G. A. Brinkley, *The Volunteer Army and the allied intervention in South Russia* (1966).

G. Bruun, *Clemenceau* (1943).

F. E. Buisson, *La Politique Radicale* (1908).

Bulletin Annuel de la Société des Amis de G. Clemenceau.

Bulletin de l'Office du Travail (1906).

Bulletin du comité exécutif du Parti Radical (1906–9).

Bulletin de la Société de l'Histoire du Protestantisme Français (1929).

P. M. Burnett, *Reparation at the Paris Peace Conference*, 2 vols (1940).

P. Barral, *Les Fondateurs de la Troisième République* (1968).

J. M. A. Caillaux, *Agadir, ma politique extérieure* (1919).

——, *Mes Prisons* (1920).

——, *Mes Mémoires*, 3 vols (1942).

C. E. Callwell, *Field Marshal Sir Henry Wilson*, 2 vols (1927).

P. Cambon, *Correspondance*, 3 vols. (1940–6).

445

L. Capéran, *L'Anticléricalisme et l'Affaire Dreyfus 1890–9* (Toulouse, 1948).

——, *L'Invasion Laique* (1935).

——, *Histoire Contemporaine de la laïcité française*, 3 vols (1957–61).

E. M. Carroll, *French Public Opinion and Foreign Affairs, 1870–1914* (1931).

G. H. Cassar, *The French and the Dardanelles* (1971).

J. Chamberlain, *A Political Memoir, 1880–1892*, ed. C. H. D. Howard (1953).

C. Fabius de Champville, *Le Comité Exécutif du Parti Républicain Radical et Radical-Socialiste de 1897 à 1907* (1908).

G. Chapman, *The Dreyfus Case, a Reassessment* (1955), new edition, *The Dreyfus Trials* (1972).

J. P. Charnay, *Les Scrutins Politiques en France de 1815 à 1962* (1964).

J. Chastenet, *Raymond Poincaré* (1948).

P. G. le Chesnais, 'Statistique Electorale', *Revue de Paris* (1906).

E. Chichet, *Feuilles Volantes: quarante ans de journalisme* (1935).

R. P. Churchill, *The Anglo-Russian Convention of 1907* (Cedar Rapids, 1939).

J. Claretie, *Histoire de la Révolution de 1870–1871*, 2 vols (1874).

M. B. Clark, *History of the French Labour Movement 1910–1928* (University of California, 1930).

M. Clemenceau et al., *Il nous quitta il y a vingt ans* (n.d. but 1949).

M. Clemenceau-Jacquemaire, *Le pot de Basilic* (1928).

E. Combes, *Mon Ministère, Mémoires 1902–1905* (1956).

G. L. Cook, 'Sir Robert Borden, Lloyd George and British Military Policy, 1917–1918', *Historical Journal*, XIV (1971).

M. B. Cooper, 'British Policy in the Balkans, 1908–9', *The Historical Journal*, VII (1964).

H. Coston, *La République du Grand Orient* (1964).

E. Cresson, *Cent Jours du Siège à la Préfecture de Police* (1901).

F. Damé, *La Résistance, les maires, les députés de Paris, et le comité central du 18 au 26 mars* (1871).

A. Dansette, *Les Affaires de Panama* (1934).

——, *L'Affaire Wilson et la Chute du Président Grévy* (1936).

——, *Les Origines de la Commune de 1871* (1944).

——, *Le Boulangisme* (1946).

——, *Histoire Religieuse de la France Contemporaine*, 2 vols (1951).

——, *L'Attentat d'Orsini* (1964).

L. Daudet, *Flammes* (1930).

J. Dautry and L. Scheler, *Le Comité Central Républicain des Vingt Arrondissements de Paris* (1960).

E. Démolins, *La Nécessité d'un programme social et d'un nouveau classement des partis, suivie d'une réponse à MM. Barrès, Clemenceau, de Kerohaut, Millerand, Rouanet* (1895).

P. Desachy, *Louis Leblois, un grand figure de l'affaire Dreyfus* (1934).

M. Dessai, *Un Révolutionnaire Jacobin, Charles Delescluze 1809–1871* (1952).

C. Digeon, *La Crise Allemande de la Pensée Française 1870–1914* (1959).

Documents on British Foreign Policy 1919–1939, 1st series, vols I and II.

Documents Diplomatiques Français 1871–1914 (1929 et seq.), 2ᵉ sére 1900–1911.

M. Dommanget, *Les Idées Politiques et Sociales d'Auguste Blanqui* (1957).

——, *Blanqui et l'Opposition Révolutionnaire à la fin du Second Empire* (1960).

M. M. Drachkovitch, *The Revolutionary Internationals 1864–1963* (1966).

A. Dreyfus, *Souvenirs et Correspondance* (1936).

A. P. Dréo, *Gouvernement de la Défense Nationale, Procès-verbaux des Séances* (1906).

E. Dréolle, *La Journée du 4 septembre* (1871).

J. E. Driault and M. Lhéritier, *Histoire Diplomatique de la Grèce de 1801 à nos Jours*, 5 vols (1925–6).

P. Drieu la Rochelle, article in *Revue Hebdomadaire* (1923).

H. Dubief, *Le Syndicalisme Révolutionnaire* (1969).

G. Dupeux and F. Goguel, *Sociologie Electorale, Esquisse d'un bilan et guide des recherches*, Cahiers de la Fondation Nationale des Sciences Politiques, 26 (1951).

A. Duquet, *La Guerre de 1870–1871* (1888–95).

J. B. Duroselle, 'Wilson et Clemenceau', *Centenaire Woodrow Wilson* (Geneva, 1956).

G. Duveau, *Le Siège de Paris* (1939).

M. Duverger, *Political Parties* (1954), translated from *Les Partis Politiques* (1951).

L'Eclair (1892).

Les Ecoles de France, Journal littéraire et Scientifique (1864).

E. W. Edwards, 'The Franco-German agreement on Morocco, 1909', *English Historical Review*, 78 (1963).

S. Edwards, *The Paris Commune 1871* (1971).

H. Elcock, *Portrait of a Decision, the Council of Four and the Treaty of Versailles* (1972).

F. Engels and P. Lafargue, *Correspondance*, 3 vols. (1956).

Enquête Parlementaire sur l'insurrection du 18 mars 1871, 3 vols (1872).

K. D. Epstein, *Matthias Erzberger and the Dilemma of German Democracy* (1959).

P. Eudel, *Le Comité républicain de Nantes 1870–74* (Niort, 1903).

B. Favreau, *Georges Mandel, un Clémenciste en Gironde* (1969).

General M. E. Fayolle, *Cahiers secrets de la Grande Guerre*, ed. H. Contamine (1964).

M. Ferré, *Histoire du Mouvement Syndicaliste Révolutionnaire chez les Instituteurs des Origines à 1922* (1955).

A. Ferry, *Carnets Secrets 1914–1918* (1957).

J. F. C. Ferry, *Lettres de Jules Ferry 1846–1893* (1914).

——, *Discours et Opinions*, 7 vols, ed. P. Robiquet (1893–8).

J. J. Fiechter, *Le Socialisme Français; de l'affaire Dreyfus à la grande guerre* (Geneva, 1965).

F. Fischer, *Germany's aims in the First World War* (1967), translated from *Griff Nach der Weltmacht* (Dusseldorf, 1964).

H. E. Fisk, *French Public Finance in the Great War and Today* (1922).

Maréchal F. Foch, *Mémoires*, 2 vols (1931).

A. Fontaine, *French industry during the war* (1926).

W. de Fonvielle, *La Foire aux candidats, Paris électoral en juin 1871* (1871).

G. Frambourg, *Le Dr Guépin, un Philanthrope et Démocrate Nantais* (Nantes, 1964).

C. L. de S. de Freycinet, *Souvenirs*, 2 vols (1912).

G. Frischmann, *Histoire de la Fédération C.G.T. des P.T.T.* (1967).

L'abbé Gaillard, 'L'Aubraie des Clemenceau' and 'Le Catholicisme et les Clemenceau', in *Revue du Bas Poitou* (1930, 1931, 1932).

J. Gallagher and R. E. Robinson, *Africa and the Victorians* (1961).

L. M. Gambetta, *Discours et Plaidoyers Politiques*, 11 vols, ed. J. Reinach (1880–5).

J. Ganiage, *Les origines du protectorat français en Tunisie, 1880–1881* (1959).

——, *L'Expansion coloniale de la France sous la 3ᵉ République 1871–1914* (1968).

G. Gatineau-Clemenceau, *Des Pattes du Tigre aux griffes du destin* (1961).

H. W. Gatzke, *Germany's Drive to the West* (1950).

Gazette des Hôpitaux Civils et Militaires (1861, 1862, 1863).

B. Georges and D. Tintant, *Léon Jouhaux, Cinquante ans de syndicalisme*, 1 (1962).

L. Girard, *La Garde Nationale, 1814–1871* (1964).

R. Girardet, 'Pour une introduction à l'histoire du nationalisme français', *Revue Française de Science Politique*, 8 (1958).

——, *Le Nationalisme Français, 1871–1914* (1966).

F. Goguel, *La Politique des Partis sous la Troisième République* (1958).

U. Gohier, *La Vraie Figure de Clemenceau* (1932).

E. L. A. and J. A. de Goncourt, *Journal, Mémoires de la vie littéraire*, ed. définitive de l'Académie Goncourt, IX (1935–6).

G. P. Gooch and H. Temperley (eds), *British Documents on the Origins of the War, 1898–1914*, 11 vols (1927).

G. P. Gooch, *Recent Revelations of European Diplomacy* (New York, 1967).

P. F. G. de la Gorce, *Histoire du Second Empire*, 7 vols (1894–1905).

R. Gossez, 'Le 4 septembre 1870, initiative et spontanéité', *Actes du 77ᵉ Congrès des Sociétés Savantes, Section d'Histoire Moderne et Contemporaine* (1952).

J. Gouault, *Comment la France est devene républicaine* (1954).

E. Grey (Viscount Grey of Fallodon), *Twenty-five Years*, 2 vols (1925).

R. Griffiths, *Marshal Pétain* (1970).

H. Guillemin, *Les Origines de la Commune*, 3 vols (1956–1960), vol. I, *Cette curieuse guerre de 70*, vol. II, *L'Héroïque Défense de Paris 1870–1871*.

P. Guinn, *British Strategy and Politics 1914–1918* (1965).

J. E. S. Hayward, 'Solidarity, the social history of an idea in Nineteenth Century France', *International Review of Social History*, 4 (1959).

——, 'The official social philosophy of the Third Republic: Léon Bourgeois and Solidarism', *International Review of Social History*, 6, (1961).

M. P. A. (Lord) Hankey, *The Supreme Command 1914–1918*, 2 vols (1961).

——, *The Supreme control at the Paris Peace Conference, 1919* (1963).

G. A. Hanotaux, *Mon Temps*, 4 vols (1933–47).

——, *Le Traité de Versailles du 28 juin 1919* (1919).

E. E. Herbillon, *Du général en chef au gouvernement, souvenirs d'un officier de liaison*, 2 vols (1930).

S. Hoffman, 'Paradoxes of the French political community', *In Search of France* (Harvard, 1963).

M. Howard, *The Franco-Prussian War* (1960, Fontana edn, 1967).

L'Intermédiaire des Chercheurs et Curieux (1930–2).

J. Jaurès, 'Le socialisme et le radicalisme en 1885', printed as introduction to *Discours Parlementaires* (1904)

——, *Oeuvres Complètes*, 9 vols (1931–9).

F. Jayle, 'Clemenceau, sa vie professionelle', *La Presse Médicale*, 73, (1934).

E. Jéloubovskaia, *La Chute du Second Empire et la Naissance de la Troisième République en France* (Moscow, 1959).

D. Johnson, *France and the Dreyfus Affair* (1966).

R. B. Jones, 'Anglo-French Negotiations 1907, a memorandum by Sir Alfred Milner', *Bulletin of the Institute of Historical Research*, 31 (1958).

J. T. Joughin, *The Paris Commune in French Politics 1871–1880*, 2 vols (Baltimore, 1955).

R. de Jouvenal, *La République des Camarades* (1910).

E. Judet, *Le Véritable Clemenceau*, (1920).

C. A. Julien, 'Jules Ferry', *Les Politiques d'Expansion Impérialiste* (1949).

J. Julliard, *Clemenceau, Briseur de Grèves* (1965).

La Justice (1880–97).

J. Kayser, *Les Grandes Batailles du Radicalisme, 1820–1901* (1962).

G. F. Kennan, *Soviet-American Relations 1917–1920*, vol. I, *Russia leaves the war*, vol. II, *The decision to intervene* (1956–8).

——, *Russia and the West under Lenin and Stalin* (1961).

J. M. Keynes, *The Economic Consequences of the Peace* (1919).

J. C. King, *Generals and Politicians* (1951).

——, *Foch versus Clemenceau, France and German Dismemberment 1918–1919* (1960).

L. L. Klotz, *De la guerre à la Paix, Souvenirs et Documents* (1924).

V. M. Kokovtsov, *Out of my Past* (Stanford, 1935).

T. Komarnicki, *The Rebirth of the Polish Republic* (1957).

M. Kranzberg, *The Siege of Paris 1870–1871* (Ithaca, 1950).

A. Krebs, 'Le mariage de Clemenceau', *Mercure de France* (1955).

——, 'Le secret de Clemenceau', *Miroir de l'Histoire* (1958).

——, 'Le secret de Clemenceau, révélé par les souvenirs d'Auguste Scheurer-Kestner', *Bulletin de la Société Industrielle de Mulhouse* (1969).

A. Kriegel, *Aux Origines du Communisme Français*, 2 vols (1964).

P. Kruger, *Correspondance de Georg Brandes*, 4 vols (Copenhagen, 1952).

G. Lachapelle, *Elections Législatives du 16 novembre 1919* (1920).

P. Lacombe, 'L'enigme de Clemenceau', *Revue Française de Psychoanalyse* (1947).

R. Lansing, *The Big Four* (1922).

J. Laroche, *Au Quai d'Orsay avec Briand et Poincaré* (1957).

J. de Launay, *Secrets Diplomatiques, 1914–1918* (Brussels, 1963).

B. Lavergne, *Les Deux Présidences de Jules Grévy* (1966).

M. Leblond, *La Crise du Midi* (1907).

H. Lefebvre, *La Proclamation de la Commune* (1965).

A. Lefèvre, *Histoire de la Ligue d'Union Républicaine des Droits de Paris* (1881).

L. Lépine, *Mes Souvenirs* (1929).

M. Leroy, *Les Transformations de la Puissance Publique, les Syndicats de Fonctionnaires* (1907).

C. Lévy, 'Un journal de Clemenceau, le Bloc', *Revue d'histoire Moderne et Contemporaine*, x (1963).

R. M. M. L'hopital, *Foch, l'armistice et la paix* (1938).

B. H. Liddell Hart, *Foch, the Man of Orleans* (1931).

D. Ligou, *Histoire du Socialisme en France, 1871–1961* (1962).

P. O. Lissagaray, *Histoire de la Commune de 1871* (1876, ed. Maspero, 1969).

D. Lloyd George, *The Truth About the Peace Treaties*, 2 vols (1938).

——, *War Memoirs*, 2 vols (1938).

E. Lockroy, *La Commune et l'Assemblée* (1871).

C. J. Lowe, *Salisbury and the Mediterranean, 1886–1896* (1965).

C. J. Lowe and M. L. Dockrill, *The Mirage of Power*, 3 vols (1972).

L. Loubère, *Louis Blanc* (1961).

L. Loucheur, *Carnets Secrets 1908–1932* (Brussels, 1962).

G. Louis, *Les Carnets de Georges Louis*, 2 vols (1908).

F. Maillard, *Affiches, professions de foi, documents officiels, clubs, et comités pendant la Commune* (1871).

J. Maitron, *Dictionnaire Biographique du Mouvement Ouvrier Français, Première Partie 1789–1864* (1964–6).

Y. Malartic, 'Comment Clemenceau fut battu aux élections legislatives à Draguignan en 1893', *Provence Historique*, XII (1962).

L. J. Malvy, *Mon Crime* (1921).

P. E. Mantoux, *Les Délibérations du Conseil des Quatre* (1955).

E. L. G. H. de Marcère, *L'Assemblée Nationale de 1871* (1904).

R. Marchand, *Un livre noir, Diplomatie d'avant guerre d'après les documents des archives russes*, 6 vols (1922–34).

J. Marczewski, 'Le Produit Physique de l'Economie Française de 1789 à 1913', *Cahiers de l'Institut de Science Economique Appliquée*, 163 (1965).

J. P. Marichy, *La Deuxième Chambre dans la Vie Politique Française depuis 1875* (1969).

F. S. Marston, *The Peace Conference of 1919, Organisation and Procedure* (1944).

C. Martel, 'Souvenirs de la Justice', *La Grande Revue* (1909).

J. Martet, *Le Silence de M. Clemenceau* (1929).

——, *Clemenceau peint par lui-même* (1929).

——, *Le Tigre* (1930).

K. Marx and F. Engels, *Werke*, 39 vols (Berlin, 1964–8).

A. Maurel, 'Souvenirs intimes sur Clemenceau', *Revue de France* (1929).

F. Maurice, *The Armistices of 1918* (1943).

C. M. P. Maurras, 'L'utilité de définer', *Revue Encyclopédique* (1895), reprinted in *Barbarie et Poésie* (1925).

A. J. Mayer, *Politics and Diplomacy of Peacemaking, Containment and Counter-revolution at Versailles, 1918–1919* (1968).

A. Mendelssohñ-Bartholdy *et al.* (eds), *Die Grosse Politik der Europaischen Kabinette*, 40 vols (Berlin 1924–7).

Mermeix (G. E. Terrail), *Fragments d'Histoire 1914–1919* (1920–4), *Au sein des commissions, Joffre, la première crise de commandment, Les négociations secrètes et les quatre armistices, Le combat des Trois*.

P. Meunier, *Clemenceau et Rosenberg* (1921).

A. Meyer, *Ce que mes yeux ont vu* (1911).

J. Michelet, *Journal*, ed. P. Viallaneix, 2 vols (1959–62).

G. Michon, *L'Alliance Franco-Russe* (1927).

——, *Clemenceau* (1931).

——, *La préparation à la guerre, la loi de trois ans 1910–1914* (1935).

History of the Great War based on official documents, *Military Operations, France and Belgium, 1918*, compiled by J. E. Edwards (1935–).

(Viscountess) V. G. Milner, *My Picture Gallery, 1886–1901* (1951).

S. I. Minerbi, *L'Italie et la Palestine 1914–1920* (1971).

P. Miquel, *La Paix de Versailles et l'opinion publique française* (1972).

G. de Molinari, *Les Clubs Rouges pendant le Siège de Paris* (1971).

P. Monatte, *Trois Scissions Syndicales* (1957).

Le Monde (1971).

G. Monger, *The End of Isolation* (1963).

G. Monnerville, *Clemenceau* (1968).

L. Monnier, *La Révolution de 1848 en Vendée* (Fontenay, 1949).

General J. J. H. Mordacq, *Le Commandement Unique* (1929).

——, *Le Ministère Clemenceau, Journal d'un Témoin*, 4 vols (1930–1).

——, *Clemenceau au soir de la vie*, 2 vols (1933).

——, *Clemenceau* (1939).

J. Moreau, *Clemenceau en bloc* (1931).

H. G. Moulton and C. Lewis, *The French Debt Problem* (1925).

F. Napo, *1907: La révolte des vignerons* (Toulouse, 1971).

H. I. Nelson, *Land and Power, British and Allied policy on Germany's frontiers, 1916–1919* (1963).

J. Néré, *Le Boulangisme et la presse* (1964).

J. Nevakivi, *Britain, France and the Arab Middle East, 1914–1920* (1969).

New Statesman (1921).

H. G. Nicolson, *Peacemaking, 1919* (1933, new edn 1964).

F. S. Northedge, *The Troubled Giant, Britain among the great powers 1916–1939* (1968).

C. F. Nowak, *Versailles* (Berlin, 1927), French translation 1928.

L'Ordre (1938).

United States Department of State, *Papers Relating to the Foreign Relations of the United States, the Paris Peace Conference 1919*, 13 vols (Washington 1942–7).

J. Paul-Boncour, *Les Syndicats de Fonctionnaires* (1906).

——, *Entre Deux Guerres, Souvenirs sur la IIIe République*, 3 vols (1945–6).

G. Pedroncini, *Les Mutineries de 1917* (1967).

——, *Les Mutineries des Armées françaises* (1968).

——, *Les Négotiations secrètes pendant la grande guerre* (1969).

C. P. Péguy, 'Clemenceau', from *Cahiers de la Quinzaine* (1904), reprinted in *Choix de Péguy* (1952).

——, *Notre Jeunesse* (1933), reprinted from *Cahiers de la Quinzaine*.

E. Pelleray, *L'Oeuvre financière du Parlement, 1906–1910* (1910).

C. Pelletan, *Georges Clemenceau* (1883).

J. J. Pershing, *My Experiences in the World War* (1931).

E. M. Phelps-Brown, *A Century of Pay* (1968).

S. Pichon, *Dans la Bataille* (1908).

J. de Pierrefeu, *G. Q. C. Secteur I*, 2 vols (1920).

J. Piou, *D'Une Guerre à l'autre 1871–1914* (1932).

C. W. Pipkin, *Social Politics and Modern Democracies*, 2 vols (New York, 1931).

F. Pisani-Ferry, *Le coup d'Etat Manqué de 16 mai 1877* (1965).

R. Poidevin, *Les Relations Economiques et Financiers entre la France et l'Allemagne de 1898 à 1914* (1969).

R. N. L. Poincaré, *Au Service de la France*, 10 vols (1926–33).

M. Prélot, *L'Evolution Politique de Socialisme Français* (1938).

La Presse Médicale, 73 (1965).

Le Procès Zola devant la cour d'assises de la Seine et la cour de cessation, 7–23 février, 31 mars–2 avril 1898, Compte Rendu sténographique, 2 vols (1898).

Le Prolétaire (1880–2).

A. Prost and C. Rosening, 'La Chambre des députés 1881–1885', *Revue française de Science Politique*, 21 (1971).

D. B. Ralston, *The Army of the Republic* (1967).

A. Ranc, *Souvenirs, Correspondance 1831–1908* (1913).

O. (really A.) Ranc, *De Bordeaux à Versailles* (1877).

B. de Ravisi, *Sous la Dictature de Clemenceau: un forfait judiciaire* (1926).

P. Reboux (P. Amillet) and C. P. E. Muller, *A la manière de . . .* first series (1910–13 livre de poche edn. 1964).

J. Reinach, *Le Ministère Gambetta* (1884).

——, *Le Ministère Clemenceau* (1885).

——, *Histoire de l'Affaire Dreyfus*, 7 vols (1901–11).

F. Rémi, *La Marianne dans les Campagnes* (Auxerre, 1881).

P. Renouvin, *La Crise Européenne et la Grande Guerre*.

——, *The Forms of War Government in France* (1927).

——, 'Les Engagements de l'alliance franco-russe: leur évolution de 1891 à 1914', *Revue d'Histoire de la Guerre Mondiale*, 12 (1934), new edn, *La Crise Européenne et la Première Guerre Mondiale* (1969).

——, 'Finance et Politique: l'Emprunt Russe d'Avril 1906 en France', *Schweitzer Beitrage zur Allgemeinen Geschichte* (1960–1).

——, 'L'Opinion publique et la guerre en 1917', *Revue d'Histoire Moderne et Contemporaine*, XV (1968).

——, *L'Armistice de Rethondes* (1968).

——, *Le Traité de Versailles* (1969).

Le Réveil (1870).

La Revue Socialiste (1887).

A. F. J. Ribot, *Journal et Correspondances Inédites* (1936).

N. Rich, *Friedrich von Holstein, Politics and Diplomacy in the era of Bismarck and William II*, 2 vols (1965).

F. F. Ridley, *Revolutionary Syndicalism in France* (1970).

C. Rihs, *La Commune de Paris, structure et doctrines* (Geneva, 1955).

H. Rochefort (V. H. de Rochefort-Luçay), *Les Aventures de ma Vie*, 5 vols (1896–7).

P. J. V. Rolo, *Entente Cordiale, the origins and negotiation of the Anglo-French agreements of 8 April 1904* (1969).

S. Roskill, *Hankey, Man of Secrets*, 2 vols (1970–2).

A. Rossigneux, *La Vérité sur la Démission de M. Albert Gigot, préfet de police, février-mars 1879* (Vienna, 1922).

V. H. Rothwell, 'The British Government and Japanese military assistance 1914–1918', *History* (1971).

——, *British War Aims and Peace Diplomacy 1914–1918* (1971).

J. Rougerie, *Procès des Communards* (1964).

——, *Paris Libre 1871* (1971).

S. Ryan, *Pétain the Soldier* (1963).

J. Sadoul, *Notes sur la Révolution Bolchévique, Nov. 1917–Jan. 1919* (1919).

H. M. Sachar, *The Emergence of the Middle East 1914–1924* (1969).

(Comte de) St Aulaire, *Confession d'un vieux diplomate* (1954).

A. Scherer and J. Grunewald, *L'Allemagne et les problèmes de la paix au cours de la première guerre mondiale*, vols. I and II (1962–6).

A. Scheurer-Kestner, *Souvenirs de Jeunesse* (1905).

A. Schmieder, 'La Chambre de 1885–9 et les affaires du Tonkin', *Revue Française d'Histoire d'Outre-mer* (1966).

B. E. Schmitt, *The Coming of the War*, 2 vols (New York, 1930).

——, *The Annexation of Bosnia* (1937).

G. Schulz, *Revolutionen und Friedensschlusse, 1917–1920* (Munich, 1967), translated as *Revolution and Peace Treaties 1917–1920* (1972).

J. A. Scott, *Republican Ideas and the Liberal Tradition in France* (1951).

F. H. Seager, *The Boulanger Affair* (Ithaca, 1969).

A. Sedgwick, *The Ralliement in French Politics 1890–1898* (Cambridge, Mass., 1965).

M. Ségard, *Sur la Démocratie, Neuf Conférences des Clemenceau* (1930).

C. Seignobos, *L'Evolution de la 3ᵉ République*, in E. Lavisse, *Histoire de la France Contemporaine*, vol. 8 (1921).

C. Seymour, *The Intimate Papers of Colonel House*, 4 vols (1926–8).

B. W. Shaper, *Albert Thomas, Trente ans de Réformisme Social* (Assen, 1959).

J. M. Sherwood, *Georges Mandel and the Third Republic* (Stanford, 1970).

W. L. Shirer, *The Collapse of the Third Republic* (1970).

F. Simon, *La Marianne, Société secrète au Pays d'Anjou* (Angers, 1939).

J. F. Simon, *Souvenirs du Quatre Septembre* (1874).

W. M. Simon, *European Positivism in the Nineteenth Century* (Ithaca 1963).

J. Singer-Kéral, *Le Coût de la Vie à Paris* (1961).

P. Sorlin, 'Gambetta et les républicains Nantais en 1871', *Revue d'Histoire Moderne et Contemporaine* (1963).

——, *Waldeck-Rousseau* (1966).

M. Sorre, 'Clemenceau, notes sur l'empiricisme radical', *Cahiers de la République*, I (1956).

A. Soulier, *L'Instabilité Ministérielle sous la Troisième République, 1871–1938* (1939).

(General) E. L. Spears, *Assignment to Catastrophe*, 2 vols (1954).

A. B. Spitzer, *The Revolutionary Theories of Louis Auguste Blanqui* (New York, 1957).

Statistique des Grèves, Ministère de Travail (1906).

P. F. Stearns, *Revolutionary Syndicalism and French Labour: a cause without rebels* (Rutgers, 1971).

Z. Sternhel, 'Barrès et la gauche', *Le Mouvement Social*, 75, (1971).

P. V. Stock, *Mémorandum d'un éditeur*, 3 vols (1935–8).

G. Suarez, *Briand, sa vie, son oeuvre avec son journal et de nombreux documents inédits*, 6 vols (1938–52).

——, *Soixante Années d'histoire française, Clemenceau*, new edn of 'La vie orgueilleuse de Clemenceau,' 2 vols (1932).

B. Szeps (Szeps-Zuckerkand), *My Life and History* (1938).

B. Zuckerkandl-Szeps, *Clemenceau tel que je l'ai connu* (Alger, 1944).

A. P. G. A. Tardieu, *La Paix* (1921).

A. J. P. Taylor, *From Napoleon to Stalin* (1950).

——, 'La Conférence d'Algéciras', *Revue Historique*, ccviii (1952).

——, *The Struggle for Mastery in Europe 1848–1918* (1954).

J. Tchernoff (also known as I. A. Chernov), *Dans le creuset des civilisations*, 4 vols (1936–8).

——, *Le parti Républicain au coup d'Etat et sous le Second Empire* (1906).

H. W. V. Temperley, *A History of the Peace Conference of Paris*, 6 vols (1920).

Le Temps (1886–1920).

E. Tenot and A. Dubost, *Les Suspects en 1858* (1869).

J. Terraine, *D. Haig, The Educated Soldier* (1963).

A. Thibaudet, *Les Idées Politiques de la France* (1932).

M. Thomas, *L'Affaire sans Dreyfus* (1961).

J. M. Thomson, *Russia, Bolshevism and the Versailles Peace* (1966).

S. P. Tillmann, *Anglo-American Relations at the Paris Peace Conference of 1919* (1961).

D. F. Trask, *The United States in the Supreme War Council, American War Aims and inter-Allied strategy 1917–1918* (1961).

Le Travail (1862).

Travaux du Comité d'Etudes, 2 vols (1919–20).

L. C. F. Turner, *Origins of the First World War* (1970).

R. H. Ullman, *Anglo-Soviet Relations 1917–1921*, vol. I, *Intervention and the War* (1961), vol. II, *Britain and the Russian Civil War* (1968).

F. Varenne, *Georges Mandel, Mon Patron* (1947).

——, 'La Défaite de G. Clemenceau à Draguignan en 1893', *Revue Politique et Parlementaire*, ccxv (1955).

E. Vaughan, *Souvenirs sans Regrets* (1902).

La Vérité.

R. Wallier (ed.), *Le Vingtième Siècle Politique* (1906, 1907).

C. K. Warner, *The Winegrowers of France and the Government since 1875* (New York, 1960).

G. Warner, *Pierre Laval and the Eclipse of France* (1968).

D. R. Watson, 'The Nationalist Movement in Paris', *The Right in France*, ed. D. Shapiro, (St Antony's Papers XIII) (1962).

——, 'Clemenceau and Mill', *The Mill News Letter*, VI, i, (1970).

——, 'A note on Clemenceau, Comte and Positivism', *The Historical Journal*, XIV, (1971).

——, 'Pillar of the Third Republic', *History Today*, 18 (1968).

——, 'The French and Indo-China', *History Today*, 20 (1970).

——, 'The making of French Foreign Policy under the first Clemenceau government, 1906–9', *English Historical Review*, 86 (1971).

——, 'Anglo-French relations in the making of the treaty of Versailles', in N. Waites (ed.), *Troubled Partnership* (1971).

E. J. Weber, *The Nationalist Revival in France, 1905–1914* (Los Angeles, 1959).

——, *L'Action Française* (1964), translation of *Action Française* (Stanford, 1962).

E. Weill-Raynal, *Les Réparations Allemandes et la France*, 3 vols (1938–47).

M. Weygand, *Mémoires*, 3 vols (1950–7).

H. Wickham Steed, *Through Thirty Years*, 2 vols (1924).

P. M. Williams and M. Harrison, *De Gaulle's Republic* (1960).

R. L. Williams, *The French Revolution of 1870–1871* (New York, 1969).

S. R. Williamson, *The Politics of Grand Strategy* (Cambridge, Mass., 1969).

R. Wohl, *French Communism in the making, 1914–1924* (1966).

R. Wolfe, 'The Parisian Club de la Révolution of the 18th arrondissement 1870–1871', *Past and Present*, 39 (1968).

E. L. Woodward, *Great Britain and the War of 1914–1918* (1967).

G. Wormser, *La République de Clemenceau* (1961).

G. Wright, *Raymond Poincaré and the French Presidency* (1942).

P. E. Wright, *At the Supreme War Council* (1921).

L. A. R. Yates, *United States and French Security 1917–1921* (1957).

Z. A. B. Zeman, *A Diplomatic History of the First World War* (1971).

A. Zévaès (G. A. Bourson), *Notes et souvenirs d'un militant* (1913).

——, *La Grève de Decazeville* (1938).

——, *Clemenceau* (1949).

A. L. Zévaès, *Louise Michel* (1936).

G. Ziebura, *Léon Blum, Theorie und praxis einer Sozialistischen Politik* (Berlin, 1963), translated as *Léon Blum et le parti Socialiste*, I, 1872–1934 (1967).

E. E. C. A. Zola, *L'Affaire Dreyfus, La vérité en marche* (1901), new edition *J'Accuse ou la vérité en marche, l'affaire Dreyfus* (1965).

Index